"This literate and learned book is the first major commentary on Daniel of the twenty-first century. It is distinguished from previous commentaries by the extensive treatment of the history of reception, but it also provides an informed and engaging treatment of the book in its ancient historical context."

—John J. Collins, Holmes Professor of Old Testament Criticism
and Interpretation, Yale Divinity School

"Carol Newsom's work is a worthy successor to Norman Porteous's volume on Daniel, one of the great commentaries in the original Old Testament Library. Whereas Porteous wrote against the background of the biblical theology movement, Dr. Newsom writes against the background of postcolonial study and interest in reception history, and her commentary is aware of those approaches to interpretation. (It was an excellent move to get Brennan Breed to provide substantial studies of each chapter's reception history.) Traditional critical questions about history and language also get thorough and judicious consideration. Serious students of Daniel in our twenty-first-century context will profit hugely from this commentary."

—John Goldingay, David Allan Hubbard Professor of Old Testament,
Fuller Theological Seminary

"Carol Newsom's superb commentary on Daniel focuses on its central narrative—the quest to uncover the mysteries of heaven and understand the true nature of God's relationship with history and humanity. Supplementary sections by Brennan Breed outline the reception history of key themes of each chapter of Daniel from the ancient world to the present. The result is a brilliant exposition of the most enigmatic book in the Hebrew Bible that details its profound influence on Western culture and sheds new light on its meaning for readers both then and now."

—Lorenzo DiTommaso, Professor of Religion,
Concordia University Montréal

DANIEL

THE OLD TESTAMENT LIBRARY

Editorial Advisory Board

WILLIAM P. BROWN
CAROL A. NEWSOM
BRENT A. STRAWN

Carol A. Newsom
with Brennan W. Breed

Daniel
A Commentary

© 2014 Carol A. Newsom

First edition
Published by Westminster John Knox Press
Louisville, Kentucky

14 15 16 17 18 19 20 21 22 23—10 9 8 7 6 5 4 3 2 1

All rights reserved. No part of this book may be reproduced or transmitted in any form or by any means, electronic or mechanical, including photocopying, recording, or by any information storage or retrieval system, without permission in writing from the publisher. For information, address Westminster John Knox Press, 100 Witherspoon Street, Louisville, Kentucky 40202-1396. Or contact us online at www.wjkbooks.com.

Unless otherwise indicated, Scripture quotations outside the book of Daniel, with slight adaptation, are from the New Revised Standard Version of the Bible, copyright © 1989 by the Division of Christian Education of the National Council of the Churches of Christ in the U.S.A., and are used by permission. Other versions occasionally cited are listed with the Abbreviations. Daniel is translated by the author.

See pp. xv–xvi, "Acknowledgments and Credits," for other permission information.

Book design by Jennifer K. Cox

Library of Congress Cataloging-in-Publication Data
Newsom, Carol A. (Carol Ann), 1950–
  Daniel : a commentary / Carol A. Newsom, with Brennan W. Breed.—First edition.
     pages cm.—(The Old Testament library)
  Includes bibliographical references and indexes.
  ISBN 978-0-664-22080-8 (hbk : alk. paper)—ISBN 978-0-664-26016-3 (pbk : alk. paper) 1. Bible. Daniel—Commentaries. I. Breed, Brennan W. II. Title.
  BS1555.53.N49 2014
  224'.507—dc23
                                                                           2014016541

∞ The paper used in this publication meets the minimum requirements of the American National Standard for Information Sciences—Permanence of Paper for Printed Library Materials, ANSI Z39.48-1992.

Most Westminster John Knox Press books are available at special quantity discounts when purchased in bulk by corporations, organizations, and special-interest groups. For more information, please e-mail SpecialSales@wjkbooks.com.

To my students

CONTENTS

List of Figures	ix
Preface	xi
Acknowledgments and Credits	xv
Abbreviations	xvii
Bibliography	xxiii
Introduction	1
The Masoretic Book of Daniel in Literary Context	2
Texts and Versions	3
The Masoretic Text and Qumran	3
Greek Versions (LXX)	4
Non-Masoretic Danielic Compositions	5
Composition and Development of Daniel MT	6
Genres	12
The Court Tales: Setting and Social Function	12
Danielic Court Tales: Accommodationist or Resistance Literature?	15
The Apocalyptic Dream Visions: Origins, Genre, and Rhetoric	18
The Social Location of the Authors of Daniel	21
The Historical Context of Daniel 7–12	23
History of Daniel's Reception, by Brennan W. Breed	28

COMMENTARY

Daniel 1–6	Exiled Jews and Gentile Kings: Lessons in Knowledge and Power	33
1:1–4:37 (4:34)	The Education of King Nebuchadnezzar	33
1:1–21	Agency, Knowledge, and Power	35

2:1–49	Nebuchadnezzar's Dream: The End of Divine Delegation of Sovereignty	59
	Excursus 1: Origin and Development of the Four-Kingdoms Schema	80
3:1–30	The Statue of Gold: A Clash of Sovereignties	97
4:1–37 (3:31–4:34)	Hubris and Humiliation, Arrogance and Understanding	124
	Excursus 2: The Harran B Inscription and Daniel 4	130
	Excursus 3: *Prayer of Nabonidus* (4Q242)	132
5:1–6:28	The Education of Feckless Kings	158
5:1–31 (5:1–6:1)	Belshazzar and the Handwriting on the Wall: A Lesson Belatedly Learned	159
6:1–28 (2–29)	Darius and the Pit of Lions: A Lesson Gratefully Learned	186
Daniel 7–12	**The Eschatological Clash of Sovereignties**	**211**
7:1–28	Revisiting the End of Divine Delegation of Sovereignty in a New Context	212
	Excursus 4: The Divine Throne, Judgment Scenes, and Daniel 7:9–10	227
8:1–27	Ironies of Power: Breaking the Horn That Challenges Heaven	252
9:1–27	Prophecy and the Deep Structures of History	283
10:1–12:13	Using History's Deep Structures to Predict the Future	320
10:1–11:2a	Revelation and Sublime Terror	328
	Excursus 5: Michael	332
11:2b–45	History as Revelation	336
	Excursus 6: Skeleton Key to Daniel 11	338
12:1–13	Revelation of the End	360

Index of Sources Up to Reformation Times	**375**
Index of Subjects and Authors	**396**

LIST OF FIGURES

1. Manuscript page from the *Book of Jamasp*   32
2. Stone relief from the South-West Palace of Sennacherib, prisoners playing lyres   43
3. Stone panel from the Palace of Sennacherib   44
4. Sculpture of Daniel the Prophet by Antônio Francisco Lisboa ("Aleijadinho")   57
5. "Daniel's Dream Map" in *Eine Heerpredigt wider den Türken*, Martin Luther, 1542   91
6. An illuminated vellum sheet illustrating Nebuchadnezzar's dream and its interpretation   96
7. Limestone relief from the east stairway of the Apadana in Persepolis (5th c. B.C.E.)   105
8. Three youths in fiery furnace under the protection of archangel Michael (10th century)   123
9. Stele of Nabonidus   129
10. Reconstruction drawing of the Ishtar Gate in Babylon (1918)   147
11. *Nebuchadnezzar with Blue Flowers and White Dog* (1969) by Arthur Boyd   157
12. The Standard of Ur, side showing scenes of peace   167
13. *Belshazzar's Feast* (ca. 1636–38) by Rembrandt Harmensz van Rijn   169
14. *The Handwriting Upon the Wall* (1803) by James Gillray   184
15. Seal of Darius   199
16. *Daniel in the Lions' Den* (ca. 1614/16) by Peter Paul Rubens   200
17. Daniel in the Lions' Den. Two-Sided Pendant (1200 or later)   205
18. The Archangel Michael. Two-Sided Pendant (1200 or later)   206
19. Manuscript page from the Las Huelgas Beatus (1220)   250
20. A manuscript of the book of Jeremiah from Qumran (4QJer^b)   291
21. *Book of Daniel* by Clarence Larkin   319
22. *Daniel's "Seventy Weeks"* by Clarence Larkin   320

PREFACE

A commentary is frequently a project that develops over a long period of time. This one has perhaps had a longer gestation than most. At the very beginning of my academic career, having taught one of my first courses on the book of Daniel, I decided that I wanted to write a commentary on this fascinating book. When I broached this idea with a representative of the Westminster Press (as it was in those days), I was politely informed that very junior professors were generally not invited to write commentaries. While I was embarrassed at my faux pas, I continued to be interested in the book. Over the years I taught courses on Daniel, to both M.Div. and Ph.D. students, and I also had the opportunity to supervise some dissertations on the topic. When I joined the board of the Old Testament Library Commentary series and learned that it was customary for board members to write a commentary for the series, the choice for me was obvious. But other projects, already committed, prevented my turning to Daniel for some time. Eventually, however, I was able to engage once again with this intriguing book.

To write a commentary is to attempt to understand and to aid others in understanding a writing that both makes sense and eludes sense. As one engages the book of Daniel, one becomes hyperaware of this activity, for at the heart of Daniel is the hermeneutical quest itself. This focus is most evident in the dramatized scenes of interpretation—the revelatory dreams of chapters 2 and 4, the decipherment of the mysterious writing of chapter 5, the prophecy of Jeremiah in chapter 9 that turns out to be richer in meaning than Daniel suspects, and the presentation and interpretation of the symbolic and coded apocalypses of chapters 8–12. The book also dramatizes the anxiety that accompanies not only the inability to understand but also certain acts of understanding or partial understanding. One can understand the fear that attends Nebuchadnezzar's and Belshazzar's confrontation with a divine message that they sense is ominous but that they do not grasp. More perplexing is the reaction by Daniel to the angel's interpretation of his visions in chapters 7 and 8. Daniel is shaken not only by the mysterious vision he sees (7:15) but also by the angel's interpretation (7:28). Yet after the supposedly clarifying vision in chapter 8, his psychic distress is connected with his statement that he *does not* understand (8:27). Similarly, in the final vision, though the superscription indicates that Daniel understands (10:1), he himself protests that he does not (12:8). He has understood enough to grasp that he does not understand fully. And indeed, the angelic interpretations leave many aspects of the visions uninterpreted. Potential meaning seems always to exceed interpretation. But Daniel's distress also appears to be connected in part to the unshareable nature of what has been communicated to him (8:26; 12:9). The character Daniel has no interpretive community with which to engage. Finally, the angel's words in chapter 12 point to another critical aspect of the hermeneutical enterprise: its temporal dimension. What blocks Daniel's full understanding is that the words pertain to a time in the distant future (8:26). In this eschatological hermeneutics only those who exist in that critical time have access to full understanding. Only at that time is a hermeneutical community constituted by those who understand (12:10). Ironically, of course, that critical time continues to be deferred, and with it, so is full understanding. But the very delay of the eschaton, rather than deferring hermeneutical engagement, stirs it into greater activity, as the rich history of the reception of Daniel attests.

Indeed, recognizing the centrality of hermeneutics to the book of Daniel, I realized that a commentary on this book demands attention to the ways in which meaning has continued to be generated by engagement with this text. Yet this research was something that exceeded my expertise. At this juncture I asked Brennan Breed if he would write sections on the history of reception of Daniel for the commentary. I was delighted that he agreed, as this project is immeasurably enriched by his contributions.

As one can see both in the chapters of Daniel itself and in the history of reception, the hermeneutical concerns raised by Daniel are matters of the utmost importance: What is the ultimate foundation of political authority? Does history have a meaningful shape? If so, how is it discerned? Is there an intrinsic structure to the rise and fall of sovereign states? Is there a transcendent shaping of history that overrides the impulses of sovereigns who mistakenly think they act autonomously? How is the power of knowledge related to the power that political figures wield? How do acts of resistance disclose the impotence of certain kinds of power? Many of the assumptions made by the book of Daniel would not be shared by modern thinkers, and its particular resolutions may be contested. But if read with the sympathetic openness that all writings from antiquity invite, the positions articulated by the book of Daniel can be engaged as serious dialogue partners in contemporary conversations about history, power, and resistance in both religious and secular contexts.

To write a commentary is also to discover how much one is in debt to the work of others. Certainly, a number of previous commentators on the book of Daniel have become my daily conversation partners. But the engagement with Daniel has also been enriched by a wide range of scholars, not only in the field of biblical studies but also beyond it. The bibliography included in this volume

Preface

only begins to gesture to those intellectual debts. My own thinking about Daniel has been greatly enhanced by the students in my M.Div. and Ph.D. classes and in particular by the dissertations of my students Danna Fewell, Kathy Lopez, and Amy Merrill Willis. To the research assistants who supported my work, including Chris Hays and Davis Hankins, I owe particular thanks. Aubrey Buster, who has seen the manuscript to completion, has performed miracles in chasing down citations, clarifying bibliography, and otherwise retrieving the strayed sheep of the project. Particularly deep thanks is due to Anne Stewart, who not only assisted with a variety of research-related tasks but also, most importantly, searched out, located, and arranged permissions for the images used in this commentary. The Candler School of Theology has supported this project in numerous ways, including research-leave time, funding for research assistants, and a grant underwriting the cost of securing permissions for the images. The directors and editors at Westminster John Knox Press, particularly David Dobson and Bridgett Green, have been unfailingly supportive of this project, and I thank them for the opportunity to do this work. I am particularly grateful to the Old Testament Board editor, Brent Strawn, for his excellent editing of this project. And, as with all of my writing projects, the deepest expression of gratitude goes to my husband, Rex Matthews. At a moment when the software problems for producing transliterated Hebrew with a Mac seemed insoluble, Rex spent countless hours working with the very helpful Dan Braden from Westminster John Knox to resolve the issues and to get the project back on track. But it is not just for Rex's technical expertise and generosity that I thank him but also for his unflagging emotional support for a project that sometimes seemed destined for completion only at "the end of days."

ACKNOWLEDGMENTS AND CREDITS

This page constitutes a continuation of the copyright page, with the list of credits for all other art used with permission.

Figure 1. Manuscript page from the *Book of Jamasp*
© The British Library Board (add 24962, f. 11v)

Figure 2. Stone relief from the South-West Palace of Sennacherib,
prisoners playing lyres
© The Trustees of the British Museum

Figure 3. Stone panel from the Palace of Sennacherib
© The Trustees of the British Museum

Figure 4. Sculpture of Daniel the Prophet
by Antônio Francisco Lisboa ("Aleijadinho")
Photograph courtesy of Brian McMorrow

Figure 5. "Daniel's Dream Map"
Courtesy of the Richard C. Kessler Reformation Collection,
Pitts Theology Library, Candler School of Theology, Emory University

Figure 6. An illuminated vellum sheet of
Nebuchadnezzar's dream and its interpretation
Courtesy of Kestenbaum & Company Auctioneers, New York

Figure 7. Limestone relief from the east stairway of
the Apadana in Persepolis (5th c. B.C.E.)
Courtesy of the Oriental Institute of the University of Chicago

Figure 8. Three youths in fiery furnace under the protection of archangel Michael
Photograph courtesy of Brian McMorrow

Figure 9. Stele of Nabonidus
© The Trustees of the British Museum

Figure 10. Reconstruction drawing of the Ishtar Gate in Babylon. 1918.
Courtesy of bpk, Berlin/ Vorderasiatisches Museum, Staatliche Museen/
Koldewey, Robert Johann (1855–1925)/Art Resource, NY

Figure 11. *Nebuchadnezzar with Blue Flowers and White Dog* (1969)
by Arthur Boyd
Reproduced with permission of Bundanon Trust

Figure 12. The Standard of Ur
© Trustees of the British Museum

Figure 13. *Belshazzar's Feast* (ca. 1636–38) by Rembrandt Harmensz van Rijn
© National Gallery, London/ Art Resource, NY

Figure 15. Seal of Darius
© The Trustees of the British Museum

Figure 16. *Daniel in the Lions' Den* (ca. 1614/16) by Peter Paul Rubens
Courtesy National Gallery of Art, Washington

Figure 17. Daniel in the Lions' Den. Two-Sided Pendant. 1200 or later.
Serpentine, 2 ¼ x 1 $^{5}/_{16}$ x $^{9}/_{16}$ in. (5.7 x 3.4 x 1.4 cm).
Gift of Mrs. Hayford Pierce, 1987 (1987.442.4).
The Metropolitan Museum of Art, New York, NY, U.S.A.
© The Metropolitan Museum of Art. Image source: Art Resource, NY

Figure 18. The Archangel Michael. Two-Sided Pendant. 1200 or later.
Serpentine, 2 ¼ x 1 $^{5}/_{16}$ x $^{9}/_{16}$ in. (5.7 x 3.4 x 1.4 cm).
Gift of Mrs. Hayford Pierce, 1987 (1987.442.4).
The Metropolitan Museum of Art, New York, NY, U.S.A.
© The Metropolitan Museum of Art. Image source: Art Resource, NY

Figure 19. Commentary on the Apocalypse and Commentary
on the Book of Daniel, fol. 163r
Photographic credit: The Pierpoint Morgan Library, New York

Figure 20. A manuscript of the book of Jeremiah from Qumran
Photograph courtesy Israel Antiquities Authority

ABBREVIATIONS

×	times (with numbers)
AB	Anchor Bible
ABD	*Anchor Bible Dictionary.* Edited by David N. Freedman. 6 vols. New York: Doubleday, 1992
ABR	*Australian Bible Review*
ABRL	Anchor Bible Reference Library
Aeg	*Aegyptus*
AfO	*Archiv für Orientforschung*
AJN	*American Journal of Numismatics*
AJP	*American Journal of Philology*
AJSL	*American Journal of Semitic Literature*
AJSR	*Association for Jewish Studies Review*
Akk.	Akkadian
AM	*Arte medievale*
AMI	Archaeologische Mitteilungen aus Iran
ANEP	*The Ancient Near East in Pictures Relating to the Old Testament.* Edited by James B. Pritchard. Princeton: Princeton University Press, 1954
ANET	*Ancient Near Eastern Texts Relating to the Old Testament.* Edited by James B. Pritchard. 3d ed. Princeton: Princeton University Press, 1969
AnSt	*Anatolian Studies*
AOAT	Alter Orient und Altes Testament
AOS	American Oriental Series
APP	Ancient Peoples and Places
Aram.	Aramaic
ARM	Archives royales de Mari
AT	author's translation
ATSAT	Arbeiten zu Text und Sprache im Alten Testament
AUSS	*Andrews University Seminary Studies*
b.	Babylonian Talmud
BASOR	*Bulletin of the American Schools of Oriental Research*

BBC	Blackwell Bible Commentaries
BBR	*Bulletin for Biblical Research*
BDB	Francis Brown, Samuel R. Driver, and Charles A. Briggs. *A Hebrew and English Lexicon of the Old Testament.* Oxford: Clarendon, 1907
BETL	Bibliotheca ephemeridum theologicarum lovaniensium
BHS	*Biblia Hebraica Stuttgartensia.* Edited by K. Ellinger and W. Rudolf. 5th ed. Stuttgart: Deutsche Bibelgesellschaft, 1997
Bib	*Biblica*
BibInt	*Biblical Interpretation*
BIOSCS	*Bulletin of the International Organization for Septuagint and Cognate Studies*
BJS	Brown Judaic Studies
BKAT	Biblischer Kommentar, Altes Testament
BSJS	Brill's Series in Jewish Studies
BZAW	Beihefte zur Zeitschrift für die alttestamentliche Wissenschaft
c.	century
ca.	circa, approximately
CAD	*The Assyrian Dictionary.* Edited by Ignatius J. Gelb et al. Chicago: Oriental Institute of the University of Chicago, 1956–
CAL	Comprehensive Aramaic Lexicon. A database of Aramaic texts. Hebrew Union College, Jewish Institute of Religion. Cincinnati. 1986–. http://cal1.cn.huc.edu/
CBQ	*Catholic Biblical Quarterly*
CBSC	Cambridge Bible for Schools and Colleges
CCT	Companions to the Christian Tradition
CD	Cairo Genizah copy of the *Damascus Document*
cf.	*confer*, compare
CFTL	Clark's Foreign Theological Library
CJA	Christianity and Judaism in Antiquity
CL	Collection Latomus
CMD	Classica et Mediaevalia, Dissertationes
ConBNT	Coniectanea Biblica: New Testament Series
ConBOT	Coniectanea Biblica: Old Testament Series
COS	*The Context of Scripture.* Edited by William W. Hallo. 3 vols. Leiden: Brill, 1997–2003
CP	*Classical Philology*
CSMC	*Les Cahiers de St.-Michel de Cuxa*
CTU	*The Cuneiform Alphabetic Texts from Ugarit, Ras Ibn Hani, and Other Places.* Edited by M. Dietrich, O. Loretz, and J. Sanmartin. 3d, enlarged ed. of KTU. Münster: Ugarit-Verlag, 2013
d.	died

DB	Darius, Behistun Inscription
DBI	*Dictionary of Biblical Interpretation*. Edited by John H. Hayes. 2 vols. Nashville: Abingdon, 1999
DJD	Discoveries in the Judaean Desert
DSSR	*The Dead Sea Scrolls Reader*. Part 3, *Parabiblical Texts*. Edited by Donald W. Parry and Emanuel Tov. Leiden: Brill, 2005
EANEC	Explorations in Ancient Near Eastern Civilizations
EdF	Erträge der Forschung
esp.	especially
et al.	*et alii*, and others
FAT	Forschungen zum Alten Testament
FC	Fathers of the Church. Washington, DC, 1947–
fem.	feminine
fig.	figure
frg(s).	fragment(s)
FRLANT	Forschungen zur Religion und Literatur des Alten und Neuen Testaments
G	Greek versions
GKC	*Gesenius' Hebrew Grammar*. Edited by E. Kautsch. Translated by A. E. Cowley. 2d ed. Oxford, 1910
HALOT	Ludwig Koehler et al. *The Hebrew and Aramaic Lexicon of the Old Testament*. Translated by Mervyn E. J. Richardson et al. 5 vols. Leiden: Brill, 1994–2000
HAT	Handbuch zum Alten Testament
HCS	Hellenistic Culture and Society
HDR	Harvard Dissertations in Religion
Heb.	Hebrew
HeyJ	*Heythrop Journal*
HKAT	Handkommentar zum Alten Testament
HOS	Handbook of Oriental Studies
HSM	Harvard Semitic Monographs
HTS	Harvard Theological Studies
HUCA	*Hebrew Union College Annual*
HZAG	*Historia: Zeitschrift für alte Geschichte*
i.e.	*id est*, that is
IA	Islam in Africa
IBC	Interpretation: A Bible Commentary for Teaching and Preaching
IBHS	Bruce K. Waltke and Michael O'Connor. *Introduction to Biblical Hebrew Syntax*. Winnona Lake, IN: Eisenbrauns, 1990

ICC	International Critical Commentary
IEJ	Israel Exploration Journal
ILBS	Indiana Literary Biblical Series
IOS	Israel Oriental Society
ITQ	Irish Theological Quarterly
JA	Journal asiatique
JANES	Journal of the Ancient Near Eastern Society
JATS	Journal of the Adventist Theological Society
JBL	Journal of Biblical Literature
JHS	Journal of Hellenic Studies
JNES	Journal of Near Eastern Studies
JQR	Jewish Quarterly Review
JSJ	Journal for the Study of Judaism in the Persian, Hellenistic and Roman Period
JSJSup	Journal for the Study of Judaism in the Persian, Hellenistic and Roman Period: Supplement Series
JSOT	Journal for the Study of the Old Testament
JSOTSup	Journal for the Study of the Old Testament: Supplement Series
JTS	Journal of Theological Studies
KAT	Kommentar zum Alten Testament
KB	Koninklijke Bibliotheek, the Hague
KEHAT	Kurzgeffasstes exegetisches Handbuch zum Alten Testament
Kethib	"[what is] written" in the Hebrew text (consonants)
KJV	King James Version
KWKHSAT	Kurzgefasster wissenschaftlicher Kommentar zu den Heiligen Schriften des Alten Testaments
LAHR	Late Antique History and Religion
LCL	Loeb Classical Library
lit.	literally
LXX	Septuagint (OT's earliest extant Greek version = OG)
m.	Mishnah
masc.	masculine
MdB	Monde de la Bible
MRLLA	Magical and Religious Literature from Late Antiquity
MS(S)	manuscript(s)
MSup HACA	Mnemosyne Supplements: History and Archaeology of Classical Antiquity
MT	Masoretic Text of the OT
MTS	Marburger theologische Studien
MW	The Muslim World
NABRE	New American Bible, Revised Edition

Abbreviations

NIB	New Interpreter's Bible
NIV	New International Version
NJPS	New Jewish Publication Society Translation
*NPNF*²	*Nicene and Post-Nicene Fathers, Series 2*
NRSV	New Revised Standard Version
NSKAT	Neuer Stuttgarter Kommentar Altes Testament
NT	New Testament
NTT	*Norsk Teologisk Tidsskrift*
OAJ	*Oxford Art Journal*
OBO	Orbis biblicus et orientalis
OG	Old Greek (LXX of OT before its recensions = G). Translation, http://ccat.sas.upenn.edu/nets/edition/
OIS	Oriental Institute Seminars, University of Chicago
olim	formerly (so identified or numbered)
OT	Old Testament
OTG	Old Testament Guides
OTL	Old Testament Library
OTP	*Old Testament Pseudepigrapha*. Edited by J. H. Charlesworth. 2 vols. Garden City, NY: Doubleday, 1983–85
OtSt	*Oudtestamentische studiën*
PCHL	Polity Cultural History of Literature
PHC	People's History of Christianity
PRSt	*Perspectives in Religious Studies*
PSPA	Publications of the Society for Psychological Anthropology
PTA	Papyrologische Texte und Abhandlungen
Qere	"[what is to be] read" in the MT (using the Masoretic vowel points)
RB	*Revue biblique*
RCS	Reformation Commentary on Scripture
RevQ	*Revue de Qumran*
RIBLA	*Revista de interpretación bíblica latinoamericana*
S	Symmachus (a Greek translation)
SASRH	St. Andrews Studies in Reformation History
SB	Sources bibliques
SBLEJL	Society of Biblical Literature Early Judaism and Its Literature
SBLSP	Society of Biblical Literature Seminar Papers
SBLWGRW	Society of Biblical Literature Writings from the Greco-Roman World
SBS	Stuttgarter Bibelstudien
SCH	Studies in Cultural History
sg.	singular

SHBC	Smyth & Helwys Bible Commentary
SJLA	Studies in Judaism in Late Antiquity
SJSJ	Supplements to the Journal for the Study of Judaism
SMRT	Studies in Medieval and Reformation Traditions
SNTSMS	Society for New Testament Studies Monograph Series
STDJ	Studies on the Texts of the Desert of Judah
StPB	Studia post-biblica
SUNY SNES	SUNY Series in Near Eastern Studies
SVT	Supplements to Vetus Testamentum
SVTP	Studia in Veteris Testamenti Pseudepigrapha
Syr	Syriac
TAD	*Textbook of Aramaic Documents from Ancient Egypt*. Copied, edited, and translated into Hebrew and English by Bezalel Porten and Ada Yardeni. 4 vol. Jerusalem: Hebrew University, 1986–99
TCS	Texts from Cuneiform Sources
TDNT	*Theological Dictionary of the New Testament*. Edited by G. Kittel and G. Friedrich. Translated by G. Bromiley. 10 vols. Grand Rapids: Eerdmans, 1964–76
Th	Theodotion (Greek recension of OT). Translation, http://ccat.sas.upenn.edu/nets/edition/
TLB	*Theologisches Literaturblatt*
trans.	translated by, translation
TSAJ	Texte und Studien zum antiken Judentum
TSJTSA	Texts and Studies of the Jewish Theological Seminary of America
TSK	*Theologische Studien und Kritiken*
TThSt	Trierer theologische Studien
UCOP	University of Cambridge Oriental Publications
UF	*Ugarit Forschungen*
VC	*Vigiliae christianae*
Vg	Vulgate (Latin)
VT	*Vetus Testamentum*
WBC	Word Biblical Commentary
WestBC	Westminster Biblical Commentary
WMANT	Wissenschaftliche Monographien zum Alten und Neuen Testament
WO	*Die Welt des Orients*
WTQ	*Westminster Theological Quarterly*
WUNT	Wissenschaftliche Untersuchungen zum Neuen Testament
ZA	*Zeitschrift für Assyriologie und vorderasiatische Archäologie*
ZAW	*Zeitschrift für die alttestamentliche Wissenschaft*
ZBK	Züricher Bibelkommentar

BIBLIOGRAPHY

Commentaries on the Book of Daniel

Cited by author and page

Bauer, Dieter. *Das Buch Daniel*. NSKAT 22. Stuttgart: Verlag Katholisches Bibelwerk, 1996.
Baumgartner, Walter. *Das Buch Daniel*. Giessen: Töpelmann, 1926.
Beckwith, Carl. *Ezekiel, Daniel*. RCS 12. Downers Grove, IL: IVP Academic Press, 2012.
Beek, Martinus A. *Das Danielbuch: Sein historischer Hintergrund und seine literarische Entwicklung; Versuch eines Beitrages zur Lösung des Problems*. Leiden: Ginsberg, 1935.
Bentzen, Aage. *Daniel*. HAT 19. Tübingen: J. C. B. Mohr, 1952.
Bevan, Anthony A. *A Short Commentary on the Book of Daniel for the Use of Students*. Cambridge: Cambridge University Press, 1892.
Calvin, John. *Commentary on Daniel*. Translated by T. Myers. London: Banner of Truth Trust, 1966.
Charles, Robert H. *A Critical and Exegetical Commentary on the Book of Daniel*. Oxford: Clarendon Press, 1929.
Collins, John J. *Daniel: A Commentary on the Book of Daniel*. Edited by Frank Moore Cross. Hermeneia. Minneapolis: Fortress, 1993.
Davies, Philip R. *Daniel*. OTG. Sheffield: JSOT Press, 1985.
Delcor, Matthias. *Le livre de Daniel*. SB. Paris: J. Gabada, 1971.
Driver, Samuel R. *The Book of Daniel*. CBSC 23. Cambridge: Cambridge University Press, 1900.
Goldingay, John. *Daniel*. WBC 30. Dallas: Word Books, 1989.
Goldwurm, Hersh. 1979. *Sefer Daniyel* [in Hebrew and English] = *Daniel: A New Translation with a Commentary Anthologized from Talmudic, Midrashic, and Rabbinic Sources*. ArtScroll Series. Brooklyn: Mesorah Publications. 2d ed., rev. and corrected, 1980.
Hartman, Louis F., and Alexander A. DiLella. *The Book of Daniel: A New Translation with Notes and Commentary*. AB 23. Garden City, NY: Doubleday, 1978.

Hitzig, Ferdinand. *Das Buch Daniel erklärt.* KEHAT 10. Leipzig: Weidmann, 1850.
Jerome, Saint. *Jerome's Commentary on Daniel.* Translated by Gleason L. Archer. Grand Rapids: Baker, 1958.
Keil, Carl Friedrich. *The Book of the Prophet Daniel.* Translated by M. G. Easton. CFTL 34. Edinburgh: T&T Clark, 1884.
Koch, Klaus. *Daniel.* BKAT 22. Neukirchen-Vluyn: Neukirchener Verlag, 1986.
Koch, Klaus, with Till Niewisch and Jürgen Tubach. *Das Buch Daniel.* EdF 144. Darmstadt: Wissenschaftliche Buchgesellschaft, 1980.
Lacocque, André. *The Book of Daniel.* Translated by David Pellauer. Atlanta: John Knox, 1979.
Lebram, Jürgen-Christian. *Das Buch Daniel.* ZBK 23. Zurich: Theologischer Verlag, 1984.
Lengerke, Cäsar von. *Das Buch Daniel: Verdeutscht und ausgelegt.* Königsburg: Gebrüder Bornträger, 1835.
Montgomery, James A. *A Critical and Exegetical Commentary on the Book of Daniel.* ICC. Edinburgh: Clark, 1950.
Pace, Sharon. *Daniel.* SHBC. Macon, GA: Smyth & Helwys, 2008.
Plöger, Otto. *Das Buch Daniel.* KAT 18. Gütersloh: Gütersloher Verlagshaus, 1965.
Porteous, Norman W. *Daniel.* OTL. Philadelphia: Westminster, 1965.
Riessler, Paul. *Das Buch Daniel.* KWKHSAT 3. Vienna: Mayer, 1902.
Seow, Choon-Leong. *Daniel.* WestBC. Louisville, KY: Westminster John Knox, 2003.
Smith-Christopher, Daniel L. "Daniel." Pages 19–152 in vol. 7 of *New Interpreter's Bible.* Nashville: Abingdon, 1996.
Theodoret of Cyrus. *Commentary on Daniel.* Translated by Robert Hill. SBLWGRW 7. Atlanta: Society of Biblical Literature, 2006.
Towner, W. Sibley. 1984. *Daniel.* IBC. Atlanta: John Knox.

Monographs and Articles Related to the Book of Daniel

Cited by author, plus year and/or page as needed

Ackroyd, Peter R. 1972. "The Temple Vessels—A Continuity Theme." Pages 166–81 in *Studies in the Religion of Ancient Israel.* SVT 23. Leiden: Brill.
Adang, Camila. 1996. *Muslim Writers on Judaism and the Hebrew Bible: From Ibn Rabban to Ibn Hazm.* Leiden: Brill.
Adler, William. 1996. "The Apocalyptic Survey of History Adapted by Christians: Daniel's Prophecy of 70 Weeks." Pages 201–38 in *The Jewish Apocalyptic Heritage in Early Christianity.* Edited by James C. VanderKam and William Adler. Assen: Van Gorcum.

Bibliography

Albertz, Rainer. 1988. *Der Gott des Daniel: Untersuchungen zu Daniel 4–6 in der Septuagintafassung sowie zu Komposition und Theologie des aramäischen Danielbuches.* SBS 131. Stuttgart: Verlag Katholisches Bibelwerk.

———. 2001. "The Social Setting of the Aramaic and Hebrew Book of Daniel." Pages 171–204 in vol. 1 of *The Book of Daniel: Composition and Reception.* Edited by John J. Collins and Peter W. Flint. SVT 83.1. Leiden: Brill.

Albo, Joseph. 1930. *Sefer Ha-Ikkarim [Book of Principles].* Volume 4 part 2. Edited and translated by Isaac Husik. Philadelphia: Jewish Publication Society.

Alexander, Paul Julius. 1985. *The Byzantine Apocalyptic Tradition.* Berkeley: University of California Press.

Alexander, Philip S. 2002. "Enoch and the Beginning of Jewish Interest in Natural Science." Pages 223–44 in *The Wisdom Texts from Qumran and the Development of Sapiential Thought: Studies in Wisdom at Qumran and Its Relationship to Sapiential Thought in the Ancient Near East, the Hebrew Bible, Ancient Judaism, and the New Testament.* Edited by Charlotte Hempel, Armin Lange, and Hermann Lichtenberger. BETL 159. Leuven: Peeters.

Alfrink, Bernardus. 1959. "L'idée de résurrection d'après Dan XII, 1–2." *Bib* 40:355–71.

Alshich, Moshe ben Chayim, and Rashi. 1994. *The Book of Daniel, Shield of the Spirit.* Translated by Ravi Shahar, Ephraim Oratz, and Yizchak Hirschfeld. Jerusalem: Feldheim.

Alt, Albrecht. 1954. "Zur Menetekel-Inschrift." *VT* 4:303–5.

al-Ṭabarī, Muhammad. 1987. *The Ancient Kingdoms.* Vol. 4 of *The History of al-Ṭabarī.* Translated by Moshe Perlmann. SUNY SNES. Albany: State University of New York.

Anderson, Gary A. 2009. *Sin: A History.* New Haven: Yale University Press.

Arjomand, Said Amir. 2003. "Islamic Apocalypticism in the Classic Period." Pages 380–416 in *The Continuum History of Apocalypticism.* Edited by Bernard McGinn, John J. Collins, and Stephen Stein. New York: Continuum.

Arnold, Bill. 1993. "Wordplay and Narrative Techniques in Daniel 5 and 6." *JBL* 112:479–85.

Aster, Shawn Zelig. 2012. *The Unbeatable Light: Melammu and Its Biblical Parallels.* AOAT 384. Münster: Ugarit-Verlag.

Athenaeus. 2007. *The Learned Banqueters.* Translated by S. Douglas Olson. LCL 208. Cambridge, MA: Harvard University Press.

Austin, David. 1794. *Downfall of Mystical Babylon.* Elizabethtown, NJ.

Barclay, John M. G. 1996. *Jews in the Mediterranean Diaspora.* HCS 33. Berkeley: University of California Press.

Bardill, Jonathan. 2011. *Constantine, Divine Emperor of the Christian Golden Age.* Cambridge: Cambridge University Press.

Barker, Sara. 2009. *Protestantism, Poetry and Protest: The Vernacular Writings of Antoine de Chandieu, C. 1534–1591*. SASRH. Aldershot: Ashgate.
Bar-Kochva, Bezalel. 1989. *Judas Maccabaeus: The Jewish Struggle against the Seleucids*. Cambridge: Cambridge University Press.
Barton, George A. 1899/1900. "The Story of Ahikar and the Book of Daniel." *AJSL* 16:242–47.
Barton, John. 1988. *Oracles of God: Perceptions of Ancient Prophecy in Israel after the Exile*. New York: Oxford University Press.
Basile, Giovanni Maniscalco. 1995. "Power and Words of Power: Political, Juridical and Religious Vocabulary in Some Ideological Documents in 16th Century Russia." Pages 51–79 in *Beiträge zur 7. Internationalen Konferenz zur Geschichte des Kiever und des Moskauer Reiches*. Wiesbaden: Harrassowitz.
Baynes, Leslie. 2012. *The Heavenly Book Motif in Judeo-Christian Apocalypses, 200 BCE–200 CE*. JSJSup 152. Leiden: Brill.
Beale, Gregory K. 1974. *The Use of Daniel in Jewish Apocalyptic Literature and in the Revelation of St. John*. Lanham, MD: University Press of America.
Beatrice, P. F. 1993. "Pagans and Christians on the Book of Daniel." *Studia Patristica* 25: 27–45.
Beaulieu, Paul-Alain. 1989. *The Reign of Nabonidus, King of Babylon, 556–539 B.C.* New Haven: Yale University Press.
———. 2006. "Official and Vernacular Languages: The Shifting Sands of Imperial and Cultural Identities in First Millennium B.C. Mesopotamia." Pages 186–216 in *Margins of Writing: Origins of Culture*. Edited by Seth L. Sanders. OIS 2. Chicago: Oriental Institute of the University of Chicago.
———. 2009. "The Babylonian Background of the Motif of the Fiery Furnace in Daniel 3." *JBL* 128:273–90.
Bejaoui, Fathi. 2006. "Christian Mosaics in Tunisia." Pages 93–101 in *Stories in Stone: Conserving Mosaics of Roman Africa; Masterpieces from the National Museums of Tunisia*. Edited by Aïcha Ben Abed. Los Angeles: Getty Publications.
Bekkum, Wout van Jac. 2008. "Four Kingdoms Will Rule: Echoes of Apocalypticism and Political Reality in Late Antiquity and Medieval Judaism." Pages 101–18 in *Endzeiten: Eschatologie in den monotheistischen Weltreligionen*. Edited by W. Brandes and F. Schmieder. Berlin: de Gruyter.
Bell, Catherine M. 1992. *Ritual Theory, Ritual Practice*. New York: Oxford University Press.
Benjamin of Tudela. 1907. *The Itinerary of Benjamin of Tudela*. Edited and translated by Marcus Nathan Adler. London: Oxford University Press.
Benton, Tim, and Nicola Durbridge. 1999. "O Aleijadinho: Sculptor and Architect." Pages 143–177 in *Views of Difference: Different Views of Art*. Edited by C. King. New Haven: Yale University Press.

Berg, Johannes van den. 1999. *Religious Currents and Cross-Currents: Essays on Early Modern Protestantism.* Leiden: Brill.

Berger, David. 1985. "Three Typological Themes in Early Jewish Messianism: Messiah Son of Joseph, Rabbinic Calculations, and the Figure of Armilus." *AJSR* 10:141–64.

Berner, Christoph. 2006. *Jahre, Jahrwochen und Jubiläen: Heptadische Geschichtskonzeption im antiken Judentum.* BZAW 363. Berlin and New York: de Gruyter.

Bernheimer, Richard. 1970. *Wild Men in the Middle Ages: A Study in Art, Sentiment, and Demonology.* London: Octagon.

Berquist, Jon L. 1995. *Judaism in Persia's Shadow: A Social and Historical Approach.* Minneapolis: Fortress.

Bevan, Edwyn R. 1900. "A Note on Antiochos Epiphanes." *JHS* 20:26–30.

Beyer, Klaus. 1984–2004. *Die aramäischen Texte vom Toten Meer.* 2 vols. Göttingen: Vandenhoeck & Ruprecht.

Bhabha, Homi. 1994. *The Location of Culture.* London and New York: Routledge.

Bickerman, Elias. 1967. *Four Strange Books of the Bible: Jonah, Daniel, Koheleth, Esther.* New York: Schocken Books.

———. 1979. *The God of the Maccabees: Studies on the Meaning and Origin of the Maccabean Revolt.* SJLA 32. Leiden: Brill.

Bickford, Charlene, and Kenneth R. Bowling. 1989. *Birth of the Nation: The First Federal Congress, 1789–1791.* Lanham, MD: Madison House.

Biruni, Muhammad ibn Ahmad. 1879. *The Chronology of Ancient Nations; An English Version of the Arabic text of the Athâr-ul-Bâkiya of Albîrûnî, or "Vestiges of the Past."* Edited and translated by Edward Sachau. London: William Allen.

Black, Jeremy, et al. 2004. *The Literature of Ancient Sumer.* New York: Oxford University Press.

Blasius, Andreas. 2006. "Antiochus IV Epiphanes and the Ptolemaic Triad: The Three Uprooted Horns in Dan 7:8, 20 and 24 Reconsidered." *JSJ* 37:521–47.

Blenkinsopp, Joseph. 1988. *Ezra–Nehemiah: A Commentary.* OTL. Philadelphia: Westminster.

Bøe, Sverre. 2001. *Gog and Magog: Ezekiel 38–39 as Pre-text for Revelation 19,17–21 and 20,7–10.* WUNT. Mohr Siebeck: Tubingen.

Boitani, Pietro. 1984. *Chaucer and the Imaginary World of Fame.* Suffolk: D. S. Brewer.

Borah, Woodrow. "Queen of Mexico and Empress of the Americas: 'La Guadalupana' of Tepeyac." *Mexican Studies/Estudios Mexicanos* 12 (1996): 326–39.

Bostick, Curtis V. 1998. *The Antichrist and the Lollards: Apocalypticism in Late Medieval and Reformation England.* SMRT 70. Leiden: Brill.

Bowen, Monica Jayne. 2008. "A Call for Liberation: Aleijadinho's 'Prophets' as Capoeiristas." M.A. thesis, Brigham Young University.
Bowen, Nancy R. 2001. "The Quest for the Historical Gebira." *CBQ* 63:597–618.
Boyce, Mary. 1975. *The Early Period*. Vol. 1 of *A History of Zoroastrianism*. HOS 8. Leiden: Brill.
———. 1982. *Zoroastrianism under the Achaemenians*. Vol. 2 of *A History of Zoroastrianism*. HOS 8. Leiden: Brill.
———. 1990. [1984.] *Textual Sources for the Study of Zoroastrianism*. Chicago: University of Chicago.
Boyce, Mary, and Frantz Grenet. 1991. *Zoroastrianism under Macedonian and Roman Rule*. Vol. 3 of *A History of Zoroastrianism*. HOS 8. Leiden: Brill.
Boyer, Paul S. 1992. *When Time Shall Be No More: Prophecy Belief in Modern American Culture*. SCH. Cambridge, MA: Harvard University Press.
Brading, David A. 2002. *Mexican Phoenix: Our Lady of Guadalupe; Image and Tradition across Five Centuries*. Cambridge: Cambridge University Press.
Braght, Thieleman J. van. 1853. [1660 in Dutch.] *A Martyrology of the Churches of Christ, Commonly Called Baptists, during the Era of the Reformation*. Vol. 2. Translated by Benjamin Millard. London: J. Haddon.
Brekelmans, Christianus H. W. 1965. "The Saints of the Most High and Their Kingdom." *OtSt* 14:305–29.
Briant, Pierre. 2002. *From Cyrus to Alexander: A History of the Persian Empire*. Translated by Peter T. Daniels. Winona Lake, IN: Eisenbrauns.
Brockington, Leonard H. 1973. *The Hebrew Text of the Old Testament: The Readings Adopted by the Translators of the New English Bible*. London: Oxford University Press; Cambridge University Press.
Broida, Marian. 2012. "Textualizing Divination: The Writing on the Wall in Daniel 5:25." *VT* 62:1–13.
Brooks, Joanna. 2003. *American Lazarus: Religion and the Rise of African-American and Native American Literatures*. Oxford: Oxford University Press.
Brousson, Claude. 1684. *Apologie du projet des réformez de France, fait au mois de May 1683: Pour la conservation de la liberté de conscience & de l'exercice public de religion, que les edits & traitez de pacification leur accordent*. Cologne: Pierre du Marteau.
Bullinger, Heinrich. 1849–52. *The Decades of Henry Bullinger*. 5 vols. in 4. Cambridge: Cambridge University Press.
Bungey, Darleen. 2007. *Arthur Boyd: A Life*. Crows Nest: Allen & Unwin.
Burgmann, Hans. 1974. "Die vier Endzeittermine im Danielbuch." *ZAW* 86:543–50.
Burke, Garance. 2013. "Harold Camping, 92, doomsday minister saw Rapture prediction pass." Associated Press, December 17.

Bibliography

Burnier-Genton, Jean. 1993. *Le Rêve subversif d'un sage: Daniel 7*. MdB 27. Geneva: Labor et Fides.
Camping, Harold. 1992. *1994?* New York: Vantage Press.
Cannon, Christopher. 2008. *Middle English Literature*. PCHL. Cambridge: Polity Press.
Caquot, André. 1955. "Sur les quatre bêtes de Daniel VII." *Semitica* 5:5–13.
Caragounis, Chrys. 1986. *The Son of Man: Vision and Interpretation*. Tübingen: Mohr Siebeck.
Carney, Court. 2009. "'A Lamp Is Burning in All Our Dark': Bob Dylan and Johnny Cash." Pages 39–43 in *Highway 61 Revisited: Bob Dylan's Road from Minnesota to the World*. Edited by Colleen Josephine Sheehy and Thomas Swiss. Minneapolis: University of Minnesota Press.
Carr, David. 2005. *Writing on the Tablet of the Heart: Origins of Scripture and Literature*. Oxford: Oxford University Press.
Casey, Maurice. 1979. *Son of Man: The Interpretation and Influence of Daniel 7*. London: SPCK.
———. 2010. *The Solution to the 'Son of Man' Problem*. Library of New Testament Studies 343. London: T&T Clark International.
Chatzidakis, Manolis. 1999. *Hosios Loukas: Byzantine Art in Greece*. Athens: Melissa Publishing.
Chazan, Robert. 1996. "Daniel 9:24–27: Exegesis and Polemics." Pages 143–59 in *Contra Iudaeos: Ancient and Medieval Polemics between Christians and Jews*. Edited by Ora Limor and Guy Stroumsa. Tübingen: Mohr Siebeck.
———. 2000. *God, Humanity, and History: The Hebrew First Crusade Narratives*. Berkeley: University of California Press.
Clermont-Ganneau, C. 1886. "Mané, Thécel, Pharès, et le Festin de Balthasar." *JA* 8:36–67.
Clifford, Richard J. 1975. "History and Myth in Daniel 10–12." *BASOR* 220: 23–26.
Cohen, Thomas. 1991. "Millenarian Themes in the Writings of António Vieira." *Luso-Brazilian Review* 28:23–46.
Collins, Adela Yarbro. 1976. *The Combat Myth in the Book of Revelation*. HDR 9. Missoula, MT: Scholars Press for Harvard Theological Review.
———. 1996. "Numerical Symbolism in Jewish and Early Christian Apocalyptic Literature." Pages 55–138 in *Cosmology and Eschatology in Jewish and Christian Apocalypticism*. JSJSup 50. Leiden: Brill.
Collins, Anthony. 1726. *The Scheme of Literal Prophecy Considered: In a View of the Controversy, Occasioned by a Late Book, Intitled, A Discourse of the Grounds and Reasons of the Christian Religion*. London.
Collins, John J. 1979. *Apocalypse: The Morphology of a Genre*. [In the journal] *Semeia* 14. Missoula, MT: Scholars Press.

———. 2000. "The Afterlife in Apocalyptic Literature." Pages 119–39 in *Death, Life-After-Death, Resurrection and the Life to Come in the Judaisms of Antiquity*. Part 4 of *Judaism in Late Antiquity*. Edited by A. J. Avery-Peck and J. Neusner. Leiden: Brill.

———. 2001. "Cult and Culture: The Limits of Hellenization in Judea." Pages 38–61 in *Hellenism in the Land of Israel*. Edited by G. E. Sterling. Notre Dame, IN: University of Notre Dame Press.

Colpe, Carsten. 1972. "*Ho huios tou anthrōpou* [The Son of Man]." *TDNT* 8:400–477.

Conybeare, Frederick C. 1913. *The Story of Aḥiḳar*. 2d ed. Cambridge: Cambridge University Press.

Coogan, Michael D., and Mark S. Smith. 2012. *Stories from Ancient Canaan*. 2d ed. Louisville, KY: Westminster John Knox.

Cook, David. 2002. "An Early Muslim Daniel Apocalypse." *Arabica* 49:55–96.

———. 2003. *Studies in Muslim Apocalyptic*. Princeton: Darwin.

———. 2005. *Contemporary Muslim Apocalyptic Literature*. Religion and Politics. Syracuse: Syracuse University Press.

Cook, John. 2004. *The Interpretation of the Old Testament in Greco-Roman Paganism*. Studien und Texte zu Antike und Christentum 23. Tübingen: Mohr Siebeck.

Corrodi, Heinrich. 1781–83. *Kritische Geschichte des Chiliasmus*. Frankfurt and Leipzig: n.p.

Cowley, Arthur E. 1923. *Aramaic Papyri of the Fifth Century B.C.* Oxford: Clarendon.

Cowper, William. 1782. *Progress of Error*. In *Poems by William Cowper, of the Inner Temple, Esq.* London: J. Johnson.

Coxon, Peter. 1976. "Daniel III 17: A Linguistic and Theological Problem." *VT* 26:400–409.

Cromwell, Oliver. 1901. *Speeches of Oliver Cromwell, 1644–1658*. Edited by Charles Stainer. Oxford: Oxford University Press.

Cross, Frank M. 1979. "A Recently Published Phoenician Inscription of the Persian Period from Byblos." *IEJ* 29:40–44.

Cumont, Franz. 1909. "La plus ancienne géographie astrologique." *Klio* 9:263–73.

Dalley, Stephanie. 2001. "Assyrian Court Narratives in Aramaic and Egyptian: Historical Fiction." Pages 149–61 in *Historiography in the Cuneiform World*. Part 1 of *Proceedings of the XLVe Rencontre Assyriologique Internationale* [at Harvard University]. Edited by Tzvi Abusch et al. Bethesda, MD: CDL Press.

Danker, Frederick. 1992. "Purple." *ABD* 5:557–60.

Darby, John Nelson. 1864. *Studies on the Book of Daniel: A Course of Lectures*. London: John Bateman.

Davies, J. G. 1958. *He Ascended into Heaven.* New York: Association Press.
Davies, Philip R. 1981. "Calendrical Change and Qumran Origins: An Assessment of VanderKam's Theory." *CBQ* 45:80–89.
———. 2002. "The Scribal School of Daniel." Pages 247–65 in vol. 1 of *The Book of Daniel: Composition and Reception.* Edited by J. J. Collins and P. W. Flint. SVT 83.1. Leiden: Brill.
Day, John. 1985. *God's Conflict with the Dragon and the Sea.* UCOP 3. Cambridge: Cambridge University Press.
Dearn, Alan. 2007. "Persecution and Donatist Identity in the Liber Genealogus." Pages 127–36 in *From Rome to Constantinople: Studies in Honour of Averil Cameron.* Edited by Hagit Amirav and Bas ter Haar Romeny. LAHR 1. Leuven: Peeters.
De Cleyre, Voltairine. 2004. *The Voltairine de Cleyre Reader.* Edited by A. J. Brigati. Oakland: AK Press.
De Wet, Chris L. 2009. "The Reception of the Susanna Narrative in Early Christianity." Pages 229–44 in *Septuagint and Reception: Essays Prepared for the Association for the Study of the Septuagint in South Africa.* Edited by J. Cook. SVT 127. Leiden: Brill.
Delano-Smith, Catherine. 1990. "Maps as Art and Science: Maps in Sixteenth Century Bibles." *Imago Mundi* 42:65–83.
Demiri, Lejla. 2013. *Muslim Exegesis of the Bible in Medieval Cairo: Najm al-Dīn al-Ṭūfī's (d. 716/1316) Commentary on the Christian Scriptures: A Critical Edition and Annotated Translation with an Introduction.* Leiden: Brill.
Dickey, Laurence. 2002. "*Translatio Imperii* and *Translatio Religionis*: The 'Geography of Salvation' in Russian and American Messianic Thinking." Pages 13–32 in *The Cultural Gradient: The Transmission of Ideas in Europe, 1789–1991.* Edited by Catherine Evtuhov and Stephen Kotkin. Lanham, MD: Rowman & Littlefield.
DiLella, Alexander A. 1977. "The One in Human Likeness and the Holy Ones of the Most High in Daniel 7." *CBQ* 39:1–19.
———. 1981. "Daniel 4:7–14: Poetic Analysis and Biblical Background." Pages 247–58 in *Mélanges bibliques et orientaux en l'honneur de M. Henri Cazelles.* Edited by A. Caquot and M. Delcor. AOAT 212. Kevelaer: Butzon & Bercker.
DiTommaso, Lorenzo. 2005. *The Book of Daniel and the Apocryphal Daniel Literature.* SVTP 20. Leiden: Brill.
Dittmer, Jason. 2010. "Obama, Son of Perdition? Narrative Rationality and the Role of the 44th President of the United States in the End-of-Days." Pages 73–99 in *Mapping the End Times: American Evangelical Geopolitics and Apocalyptic Visions.* Edited by Jason Dittmer and Tristan Sturm. Burlington, VT: Ashgate.

Dodds, Jerrilynn. 1993. "Islam, Christianity, and the Problem of Religious Art." Pages 27–40 in *The Art of Medieval Spain, A.D. 500–1200*. Edited by John O'Neill. New York: Metropolitan Museum of Art.

Doob, Penelope. 1974. *Nebuchadnezzar's Children: Conventions of Madness in Middle English Literature*. New Haven: Yale University Press.

Dorrien, Gary J. 1998. *The Remaking of Evangelical Theology*. Louisville, KY: Westminster John Knox.

Dossin, Georges, and Andre Finet. 1976. *Correspondence féminine*. ARM 10. Paris: P. Geuthner.

Doukhan, Jacques. 1979. "The Seventy Weeks of Daniel 9: An Exegetical Study." *AUSS* 17:1–22.

Drawnel, Henryk, ed. 2011. *The Aramaic Astronomical Book from Qumran: Text, Translation, and Commentary*. Oxford: Oxford University Press.

Droy, Alf. 2001. *Wake Up! The Lord Is Returning*. London: El Shaddai.

Duhm, Bernhard. 1897. *Das Buch Hiob*. HKAT 16. Freiburg im Breisgau: Mohr.

Dunbar, David. 1983. "Hippolytus of Rome and the Eschatological Exegesis of the Early Church." *WTQ* 45:322–39.

Eissfeldt, Otto. 1951. "Die Menetekel-Inschrift und ihre Deutung." *ZAW* 63:105–14.

Emerson, Ralph Waldo. 1990. *Ralph Waldo Emerson: Selected Essays, Lectures and Poems*. Edited by R. Richardson. New York: Bantam Books.

Emerton, John A. 1958. "The Origin of the Son of Man Imagery." *JTS* 9:225–42.

———. 1960. "Participles in Daniel 5:12." *ZAW* 72:262–63.

Emilsen, William W. 2001. "Gandhi, Scripture and the Bible." *Pacifica* 14:71–86.

Emmerson, Richard Kenneth. 1981. *Antichrist in the Middle Ages: A Study of Medieval Apocalypticism, Art, and Literature*. Seattle: University of Washington Press.

Engelke, Matthias. 2010. "Nebuchadnezzar: The King as Image of Transformation." Pages 195–202 in vol. 1 of *Kierkegaard and the Bible*. Edited by Lee C. Barrett and Jon Bartley Stewart. Burlington, VT: Ashgate.

Eph'al, Israel. 1978. "The Western Minorities in Babylonia in the 6th–5th Centuries BC: Maintenance and Cohesion." *Orientalia* 47:74–90.

Epstein, Shifra. 1995. "The Bobover Hasidim Piremshpiyl: From Folk Drama for a Purim to a Ritual of Transcending the Holocaust." Pages 237–56 in *New World Hasidim: Ethnographic Studies of Hasidic Jews in America*. Edited by Janet S. Belcove-Shalin. Anthropology & Judaic Studies. Albany: State University of New York Press.

Erdman, David. 1954. *Blake, Prophet against Empire: A Poet's Interpretation of the History of His Own Times*. Princeton: Princeton University Press.

Falk, Daniel K. 1998. *Daily, Sabbath, and Festival Prayers in the Dead Sea Scrolls*. STDJ 27. Leiden: Brill.

Farbstein, Esther. 2007. *Hidden In Thunder: Perspectives on Faith, Halachah and Leadership during the Holocaust*. Vol. 1. New York: Feldheim.
Fassler, Margot Elisabeth. 2010. *The Virgin of Chartres: Making History Through Liturgy and the Arts*. New Haven: Yale University Press.
Feldman, Seymour. 2003. *Philosophy in a Time of Crisis: Don Isaac Abravanel, Defender of the Faith*. New York: RoutledgeCurzon.
Fewell, Danna Nolan. 1991. *Circle of Sovereignty: Plotting Politics in the Book of Daniel*. 2d, rev., and extended ed. Nashville: Abingdon.
Fincke, Jeanette C. 2003. "The Babylonian Text of Nineveh: Report on the British Museum's Ashurbanipal Library Project." *AfO* 50:111–49.
Fine, Steven. 2005. *Art and Judaism in the Greco-Roman World: Toward a New Jewish Archaeology*. New York: Cambridge University Press.
Fishbane, Michael. 1988. *Biblical Interpretation in Ancient Israel*. New York: Oxford University Press.
Fitzmyer, Joseph A. 1974. "Some Notes on Aramaic Epistolography." *JBL* 93:201–25.
———. 1995. *The Aramaic Inscriptions of Sefire*. Revised edition. Biblica et orientalia 19A. Rome: Pontifical Biblical Institute.
Flusser, David. 1972. "The Four Empires in the Fourth Sibyl and in the Book of Daniel." *IOS* 2:148–75.
Fodor, Alexander. 1974. "*Malḥamat Dāniyāl*." Pages 85–160 in *The Muslim East: Studies in Honor of Julius Germanus*. Edited by Gyula Kaldy-Nagy. Budapest: Loránd Eötvös University.
Frahm, Eckart. 2004. "Royal Hermeneutics: Observations on the Commentaries from Ashurbanipal's Libraries at Nineveh." *Iraq* 66:45–50.
Francisco, Adam. 2007. *Martin Luther and Islam: A Study in Sixteenth-Century Polemics and Apologetics*. Leiden: Brill.
Frank, Richard M. 1959. "The Description of the 'Bear' in Daniel 7:5." *CBQ* 21:505–7.
Freyre, Gilberto. 1947. *Interpretação do Brasil: aspectos da formação social brasileira como processo de amalgamento de raças e culturas*. São Paulo: José Olympio.
Fried, Lisbeth. 2004. *The Priest and the Great King: Temple-Palace Relations in the Persian Empire*. Winona Lake, IN: Eisenbrauns.
Friedenberg, Daniel M. 2009. *Sasanian Jewry and Its Culture: A Lexicon of Jewish and Related Seals*. Urbana: University of Illinois Press.
Fröhlich, Ida. 1993. "Daniel 2 and Deutero-Isaiah." Pages 266–70 in *The Book of Daniel in Light of New Findings*. Edited by A. S. van der Woude. BETL 106. Leuven: Leuven University Press.
Fuller, Robert C. 1995. *Naming the Antichrist: The History of an American Obsession*. New York: Oxford University Press.
Gadd, Cyril J. 1958. "The Harran Inscriptions of Nabonidus." *AnSt* 8:35–92.

Gallé, A. F. 1900. *Daniel avec commentaires de R. Saadia, Aben-Ezra, Raschi, etc., et variantes des versions arabe et syriaque.* Paris: E. Leroux.

Gandhi, Mohandas. 1963. *Collected Works of Mahatma Gandhi.* Vol. 9. Delhi: Publications Division, Ministry of Information and Broadcasting, Government of India.

Gardiner, Alan H. 1968. *Ancient Egyptian Onomastica.* 3 vols. London: Oxford University Press.

Geissen, Angelo. 1968. *Der Septuaginta-Text des Buches Daniel 5–12: Zusammen mit Susanna, Bel et Draco, sowie Esther, Kap. 1.1a–2.15.* PTA 5. Bonn: R. Habelt.

Gera, Dov. 1998. *Judaea and Mediterranean Politics 219 to 161 B.C.E.* BSJS 8. Brill: Leiden.

Gibb, E. J. W. 1900. *A History of Ottoman Poetry.* Volume 1. London: Luzac & Company.

Ginsberg, Harold L. 1948. *Studies in Daniel.* TSJTSA 14. New York: Jewish Theological Seminary of America.

———. 1953. "The Oldest Interpretation of the Suffering Servant." *VT* 3:400–404.

———. 1954. "The Composition of the Book of Daniel." *VT* 4:246–75.

Godfrey, Richard, and Mark Hallett. 2001. *James Gillray: The Art of Caricature.* London: Tate.

Goldman, Harry Merton. 1977. "Pins and Needles: An Oral History." Ph.D. diss., New York University.

Goldstein, Bernard, and David Pingree. 1990. *Levi Ben Gerson's Prognostication for the Conjunction of 1345.* Philadelphia: American Philosophical Society.

Grabbe, Lester L. 1979. "Chronography in Hellenistic Jewish Historiography." Pages 43–68 in vol. 2 of *SBL 1979 Seminar Papers.* SBLSP 17. Chico: Scholars Press.

———. 1988a. "Another Look at the Gestalt of 'Darius the Mede.'" *CBQ* 50:198–213.

———. 1988b. "The Belshazzar of Daniel and the Belshazzar of History." *AUSS* 26, no. 1:59–66.

———. 1991. "Reconstructing History from the Book of Ezra." Pages 98–106 in *Persian Period.* Edited by Philip R. Davies. Vol. 1 of *Second Temple Studies.* JSOTSup 117. Sheffield: Sheffield Academic Press.

———. 2001. "A Dan(iel) for All Seasons: For Whom Was Daniel Important?" Pages 229–46 in vol. 1 of *The Book of Daniel: Composition and Reception.* Edited by J. J. Collins and P. W. Flint. SVT 83.1. Brill: Leiden.

Grainger, John D. 2010. *The Syrian Wars.* MSup HACA 320. Leiden: Brill.

Grayson, Albert Kirk. 1975. *Assyrian and Babylonian Chronicles.* TCS 5. Locust Valley, NY: J. J. Augustin.

Green, Rosalie B. 1948. "Daniel in the Lions' Den as an Example of Romanesque Typology." Ph.D. diss., University of Chicago.

Grelot, Pierre. 1974. "La Septante de Daniel IV et son substrat semitique." *RB* 81:5–23.

———. 1975. "Ariōk." *VT* 25:711–19.

———. 1985. "L'écriture sur le mur (Daniel 5)." Pages 199–207 in *Mélanges bibliques et orientaux en l'honneur de M. Henri Cazelles*. AOAT 215. Neukirchen-Vluyn: Neukirchener Verlag.

———. 1995. "Daniel VI dans la Septante." Pages 103–18 in *Kata tous Hebdomêkonta = Selon les Septante: Trente études sur la Bible grecque des Septante*. Festschrift for Marguerite Harl. Edited by G. Dorival and E. Munnich. Paris: Cerf.

Griffith, Sydney. 1987. "Ephraem the Syrian's Hymns 'Against Julian': Meditations on History and Imperial Power." *VC* 43:238–66.

Guinness, Henry Grattan. 1905. *History Unveiling Prophecy; Or, Time as an Interpreter*. London: Fleming H. Revell.

Gunkel, Hermann. 2006. *Creation and Chaos in the Primeval Era and the Eschaton: A Religio-historical Study of Genesis 1 and Revelation 12*. Translated by K. William Whitney Jr. Grand Rapids: Eerdmans.

Gurevich, Aron I. 1985. *Categories of Medieval Culture*. Translated by G. L. Campbell. London: Routledge & Kegan Paul.

Haag, Ernst. 1983. *Die Errettung Daniels aus der Löwengrube: Untersuchungen zum Ursprung der biblischen Danieltradition*. SBS 110. Stuttgart: Katholisches Bibelwerk.

———. 1989. "Die drei Männer im Feuer nach Dan. 3:1–30." Pages 20–50 in *Die Entstehung der jüdischen Martyrologie*. Edited by J. W. van Henten. Leiden: Brill.

———. 1993. "Der Menschensohn und die Heiligen (des) Höchsten." Pages 137–85 in *The Book of Daniel in the Light of New Findings*. Edited by A. S. van der Woude. BETL 106. Leuven: Leuven University Press.

Hachlili, Rachel. 2009. *Ancient Mosaic Pavements: Themes, Issues, and Trends*. Leiden: Brill.

Haddad, Yvonne Y., and Jane I. Smith. 2010. "The Anti-Christ and the End of Time in Christian and Muslim Eschatological Literature." *MW* 100:505–29.

Hagen, Rainer, and Rose-Marie Hagen. 2003. *What Great Paintings Say: Volume 1*. Köln: Taschen.

Hallo, William W., ed. 1997–2003. *The Context of Scripture*. 3 vols. Leiden: Brill.

Halperin, David J. 1988. *The Faces of the Chariot: Early Jewish Response to Ezekiel's Vision*. TSAJ 16. Tübingen: Mohr Siebeck.

Hamm, Winfried. 1969. *Der Septuaginta-Text des Buches Daniel Kap. 1–2 nach dem Kölner Teil des Papyrus 967*. PTA 10. Bonn: Habelt.

———. 1977. *Der Septuaginta-Text des Buches Daniel Kap. 3–4 nach dem Kölner Teil des Papyrus 967*. PTA 21. Bonn: Habelt.

Hardt, Hermann von der. 1708. *De Quatuor Monarchiis Babyloniae Pro antique Historiae Judaicae luce: Ad illustrandum Colossum in insomnio Nebucadnezaris Dan. II*. Helmstedt: Hammius.

Hartman, Lars. 1966. *Prophecy Interpreted: The Formation of Some Jewish Apocalyptic Texts and the Eschatological Discourse Mark 13 Par*. ConBNT 1. Lund: Gleerup.

Hasslberger, Bernhard. 1977. *Hoffnung in der Bedrängnis: Eine formkritische Untersuchung zu Dan 8 und 10–12*. ATSAT 4. St. Ottilien: EOS Verlag.

Hayes, John H., and Sara Mandell. 1998. *The Jewish People in Classical Antiquity: From Alexander to Bar Kochba*. Louisville, KY: Westminster John Knox.

Hays, Christopher B. 2007. "Chirps from the Dust: The Affliction of Nebuchadnezzar in Daniel 4:30 in Its Ancient Near Eastern Context." *JBL* 126:305–25.

———. 2011. *Death in the Iron Age II and in First Isaiah*. FAT 79. Tübingen: Mohr Siebeck.

Heiser, Michael S. 2001. "The Mythological Provenance of Isaiah 14:12–15: A Reconsideration of the Ugaritic Material." *VT* 51:354–69.

Heller, Roy L. 2009. "'But if not . . .' what? The Speech of the Youths in Daniel 3 and a (Theo)logical problem." Pages 244–55 in *Thus Says the Lord*. Edited by John J. Ahn and Stephen L. Cook. New York and London: T&T Clark.

Hendel, Ronald. 2008. "Isaiah and the Transition from Prophecy to Apocalyptic." Pages 261–79 in vol. 1 of *Birkat Shalom*. Edited by Chaim Cohen et al. Winona Lake, IN: Eisenbrauns, 2008.

Henze, Matthias. 1999. *The Madness of King Nebuchadnezzar: The Ancient Near Eastern Origins and Early History of Interpretation of Daniel 4*. SJSJ 61. Leiden: Brill.

———. 2002. "Nebuchadnezzar's Madness (Daniel 4) in Syriac Literature." Pages 550–71 in vol. 2 of *The Book of Daniel: Composition and Reception*. Edited by John J. Collins and Peter W. Flint. SVT 83.2. Leiden: Brill.

Herford, Robert. 1903. *Christianity in Talmud and Midrash*. London: Williams & Norgate.

Herodotus. 1987. *The History*. Translated by David Greene. Chicago: University of Chicago Press.

Hill, Christopher. 1990. *Antichrist in Seventeenth-Century England*. Riddell Memorial Lectures 41. London: Verso.

Hillers, Delbert. 1965. "A Convention in Hebrew Literature: The Reaction to Bad News." *ZAW* 77:86–89.

Himmelfarb, Martha. 2010. *The Apocalypse: A Brief History*. Malden, MA: Wiley-Blackwell.

Holm, Tawney L. 2013. *Of Courtiers and Kings: The Biblical Daniel Narratives and Ancient Story-Collections.* EANEC 1. Winona Lake, IN: Eisenbrauns.

Hölscher, Gustav. 1919. "Die Entstehung des Buches Daniel." *TSK* 92:113–38.

Hommel, Fritz. 1902. "Die Abfassungszeit des Buches Daniel und der Wahrsinn Nabonids." *TLB* 23:145–50.

Horowitz, Elliott. 1992. "Speaking of the Dead: The Emergence of the Eulogy among Italian Jewry of the Sixteenth Century." Pages 129–62 in *Preachers of the Italian Ghetto.* Edited by David B. Ruderman. Berkeley: University of California Press.

Hourihane, Colum. 2001. "'De Camino Ignis': The Iconography of the Three Children in the Fiery Furnace in Ninth-Century Ireland." Pages 61–82 in *From Ireland Coming: Irish Art from the Early Christian to the Late Gothic Period and Its European Context.* Edited by Colum Hourihane. Princeton: Princeton University Press.

Howard, Cameron B. R. 2011. "Writing Yehud: Textuality and Power under Persian Rule." Ph.D. diss., Emory University.

Howell, Thomas Bayly, and Thomas Jones Howell, eds. 1826. *A Complete Collection of State Trials and Proceedings for High Treason and Other Crimes and Misdemeanors from the Earliest Period to the Year 1783, with Notes and Other Illustrations.* Vol. 33. London: Longman, Hurst, Rees, Orme & Brown.

Humphreys, W. Lee. 1973. "A Lifestyle for Diaspora: A Study of the Tales of Esther and Daniel." *JBL* 92:211–23.

Hunt, Lucy-Anne. 2007. "Eastern Christian Iconographic and Architectural Traditions: Oriental Orthodox." Pages 388–419 in *The Blackwell Companion to Eastern Christianity.* Edited by Ken Parry. Blackwell Companions to Religion. London: Blackwell.

Husser, Jean-Marie. 1999. *Dreams and Dream Narratives in the Biblical World.* Translated by J. M. Munro. Sheffield: Sheffield Academic Press.

Huygens, Daniel Johannes. 1996. *Opposite the Lion's Den: A Story of Hiding Dutch Jews.* Rose Bay, New South Wales: Brandl & Schlesinger.

Ibn Kathīr, Ismāʿīl. 2003. *Stories of the Prophets: Peace Be upon Them.* Translated by Rashad Ahmad Azami. 2d ed. Riyadh: Darussalam.

Ibrahim, Hassan Ahmed. 2004. *Sayyid ʿAbd Al-Raḥmān Al-Mahdī: A Study of Neo-Mahdīsm in the Sudan, 1899–1956.* IA 4. Leiden: Brill.

Isakhan, Benjamin. 2013. "Heritage Destruction and Spikes in Violence: The Case of Iraq." Pages 219–48 in *Cultural Heritage in the Crosshairs: Protecting Cultural Property during Conflict.* Edited by J. Kila and J. Zeidler. Leiden: Brill.

Jacobs, Martin. "An Ex-Sabbatean's Remorse? Sambari's Polemics against Islam." *JQR* 97:347–78.

Japhet, Sara. 1993. *I & II Chronicles*. OTL. Louisville, KY: Westminster/John Knox.
Jeansonne, Sharon Pace. 1984. "The Stratigraphy of the Text of Daniel and the Question of Theological Tendenz in the Old Greek." *BIOSCS* 17:15–35.
Jellicoe, Sidney. 1968. *The Septuagint and Modern Study*. New York: Oxford University Press.
Jepsen, Alfred. 1961. "Bemerkungen zum Danielbuch." *VT* 11:386–91.
Jones, Bruce W. 1968. "Prayer in Daniel 9." *VT* 18:488–93.
Jung, Carl G. 1977. *The Symbolic Life: Miscellaneous Writings*. Translated by G. Adler and R. Hull. Princeton: Princeton University Press.
Kant, Immanuel. 1978. *Anthropology from a Pragmatic Point of View*. Translated by Victor Lyle Dowdell; revised and edited by Hans H. Rudnick. Carbondale: Southern Illinois University Press.
Kearns, Rollin. 1978–82. *Vorfragen zur Christologie*. 3 vols. Tübingen: Mohr.
Keel, Othmar. 1978a. *Jahwes Entgegnung an Ijob: Eine Deutung von Ijob 38–41 vor dem Hintergrund der zeitgenössischen Bildkunst*. FRLANT 121. Göttingen: Vandenhoeck & Ruprecht.
———. 1978b. *The Symbolism of the Biblical World: Ancient Near Eastern Iconography and the Book of Psalms*. Translated by T. J. Hallett. New York: Seabury.
———. 1998. *Goddesses and Trees, New Moon and Yahweh: Ancient Near Eastern Art and the Hebrew Bible*. Sheffield: Sheffield Academic Press.
———. 2000. "Die Tiere und der Mensch in Daniel 7." Pages 1–35 in *Hellenismus und Judentum: Vier Studien zu Daniel 7 und zur Religionsnot unter Antiochus IV*. Edited by Othmar Keel and Urs Staub. OBO 178. Freiburg, CH: Universitätsverlag.
Kellermann, Ulrich. 1989. "Das Danielbuch und die Märtyrertheologie der Auferstehung." Pages 51–75 in *Entstehung der jüdischen Martyrologie*. Edited by Jan W. van Henten. Leiden: Brill.
Kelsey, Neal, and Marvin Meyer. 1999. "Another Amulet against Fever." Page 100 in *Ancient Christian Magic: Coptic Texts of Ritual Power*. Edited by Marvin W. Meyer and Richard Smith. Princeton: Princeton University Press.
Kestenbaum and Company. 2011. *Catalogue of Fine Judaica: Printed Books, Manuscripts, Autograph Letters and Graphic Art*. Auction held on December 8, 2011.
Kim, Yang-sŏn. 2004. "Compulsory Shinto Shrine Worship and Persecution." Pages 87–120 in *Korea and Christianity*. Edited by Chai-shin Yu. Fremont, CA: Asian Humanities Press.
King, Catherine. 1999. *Views of Difference: Different Views of Art*. New Haven: Yale University Press. Citing pp. 280–81 in Gilberto Freyre, *Interpretação do Brasil*, as translated by T. Benton. Rio de Janeiro: J. Olympio, 1947.

King, Martin Luther, Jr. 1991 [1963]. "Letter from a Birmingham Jail." Pages 68–85 in *Civil Disobedience in Focus*. Edited by Hugo Adam Bedau. London: Routledge.
Kirchmayr, Karl P. 2010. "Mene-tekel-Uparsin." *VT* 60:483–86.
Kirkpatrick, Shane. 2006. *Competing for Honor: A Social-Scientific Reading of Daniel 1–6*. BibInt 74. Leiden: Brill.
Kitchen, Kenneth A. 1965. "The Aramaic of Daniel." Pages 31–79 in *Notes on Some Problems in the Book of Daniel*. London: Tyndale.
Knibb, Michael. 1976. "The Exile in the Literature of the Intertestamental Period." *HeyJ* 17:253–72.
Koch, Klaus. 1995. *Die Reiche der Welt und der kommende Menschensohn: Studien zum Danielbuch*. Edited by Martin Rösel. Neukirchen-Vluyn: Neukirchener Verlag.
———. 2000. "Die Winde des Himmels über dem Völkermeer (Dan 7:1f). Schöpfung oder Chaos?" Pages 46–55 in *"Unter dem Fussboden ein Tropfen Wahrheit": Festschrift für Johann Michael Schmidt zum 65jährigen Geburtstag*. Edited by H.-J. Barkenings and U. F. W. Bauer. Düsseldorf: Presseverband der Evangelischen Kirche im Rheinland.
Koetsier, T., and K. Reich. 2005. "Michael Stifel and His Numerology." Pages 291–311 in *Mathematics and the Divine: A Historical Study*. Edited by T. Koetsier and L. Bergmans. Amsterdam: Elsevier.
Kohen, Elli. 2007. *History of the Byzantine Jews: A Microcosmos in the Thousand Year Empire*. Lanham, MD: University Press of America.
Kohlberg, Etan. 1992. *A Medieval Muslim Scholar at Work: Ibn Ṭāwūs and His Library*. Leiden: Brill.
Kooij, Arie van der. 1993. "The Concept of Covenant (*berît*) in the Book of Daniel." Pages 495–501 in *The Book of Daniel in the Light of New Findings*. Edited by A. S. van der Woude. BETL 106. Leuven: Leuven University Press.
Koselleck, Reinhart. 2002. *The Practice of Conceptual History: Timing History, Spacing Concepts*. Translated by T. S. Presner et al. Stanford, CA: Stanford University Press.
Kratz, Reinhard G. 1991. *Translatio imperii: Untersuchungen zu den aramäischen Danielerzählungen und ihrem theologiegeschichtlichen Umfeld*. WMANT 63. Neukirchen-Vluyn: Neukirchener Verlag.
———. 2000. "Die Visionen des Daniel." Pages 219–36 in *Schriftauslegung in der Schrift*. Festschrift for Odil Hannes Steck. Edited by Reinhard G. Kratz, Thomas Krüger, and Konrad Schmid. BZAW 300. Berlin: de Gruyter.
———. 2001. "Visions of Daniel." Pages 91–113 in vol. 1 of *The Book of Daniel: Composition and Reception*. Edited by John J. Collins and Peter W. Flint. SVT 83.1. Leiden: Brill.

Kuhl, Curt. 1930. *Die drei Männer im Feur: Daniel Kapitel 3 und seine Zusätze.* Giessen: Töpelmann.

Kuhrt, Amélie. 2010. [2007.] *The Persian Empire: A Corpus of Sources from the Achaemenid Period.* London: Routledge.

Kvanvig, Helge S. 1988. *Roots of Apocalyptic: The Mesopotamian Background of the Enoch Figure and of the Son of Man.* WMANT 61. Neukirchen-Vluyn: Neukirchener Verlag.

Lacan, Jacques. 1988. *The Seminar of Jacques Lacan.* Book 2, *The Ego in Freud's Theory and in the Technique of Psychoanalysis, 1954–1955.* Edited by Jacques-Alain Miller. Translated by Sylvana Tomaselli. Cambridge: Cambridge University Press.

Ladd, William. 1831. *The Calumet: New Series of the Harbinger of Peace.* Vol. 1. New York: Dewey's Press.

Lambert, Wilfred G. 2013. *Babylonian Creation Myths.* Winona Lake, IN: Eisenbrauns.

Lamoreux, John. 1996. "Early Eastern Christian Responses to Islam." Pages 3–32 in *Medieval Christian Perceptions of Islam.* Edited by John Tolan. London: Routledge.

Land, Gary. 1998. *Adventism in America.* Berrien Springs, MI: Andrews University Press.

Lapide, Cornelius. 1717. *Commentaria In Quatuor Prophetas Maiores.* 2d edition. Venice: Jerome Albritus.

Lapsley, Jacqueline. 2000. *Can These Bones Live? The Problem of the Moral Self in Ezekiel.* BZAW 301. New York: de Gruyter.

Larkin, Clarence. 1918. *Dispensational Truth.* Philadelphia: Clarence Larkin.

Lash, Archimandrite Ephrem. 2008. "Biblical Interpretation in Worship." Pages 35–48 in *The Cambridge Companion to Orthodox Christian Theology.* Edited by Mary B. Cunningham and Elizabeth Theokritoff. Cambridge: Cambridge University Press.

Lasine, Stuart. 2001. *Knowing Kings: Knowledge, Power, and Narcissism in the Hebrew Bible.* Semeia Studies. Atlanta: Society of Biblical Literature.

Latowsky, Anne A. 2013. *Emperor of the World: Charlemagne and the Construction of Imperial Authority, 800–1229.* Ithaca, NY: Cornell University Press.

Lebram, Jürgen-Christian. 1975. "König Antiochus im Buch Daniel." *VT* 25:737–72.

Lenglet, A. 1972. "La structure littéraire de Daniel 2–7." *Bib* 53:169–90.

Lerner, Robert. 1976. "Refreshment of the Saints: The Time after Antichrist as a Station for Earthly Progress in Medieval Thought." *Traditio* 32:97–144.

Levene, Dan. 2013. *Jewish Aramaic Curse Texts from Late-Antique Mesopotamia: "May These Curses Go Out and Flee."* MRLLA 2. Leiden: Brill.

Levenson, Jon D. 2006. *Resurrection and the Restoration of Israel*. New Haven: Yale University Press.
Lévinas, Emmanuel. 1969. *Totality and Infinity: An Essay on Exteriority*. Translated by Alphonso Lingis. Pittsburgh: Duquesne University Press.
Levison, John R. 2009. *Filled with the Spirit*. Grand Rapids: Eerdmans.
Lindsey, Hal. 1970. *The Late, Great Planet Earth*. Grand Rapids: Zondervan.
Lipiński, Edward. 1978. Review of *Le livre de Daniel*, by André Lacocque. *VT* 28:233–39.
Lipschits, Oded. 2003. "Demographic Changes in Judah between the Seventh and the Fifth Centuries B.C.E." Pages 323–76 in *Judah and the Judeans in the Neo-Babylonian Period*. Edited by O. Lipschits and J. Blenkinsopp. Winona Lake, IN: Eisenbrauns.
Loewenstein, David. 2001. *Representing Revolution in Milton and His Contemporaries: Religion, Politics, and Polemics in Radical Puritanism*. Cambridge: Cambridge University Press.
Luther, Martin. 1848. *The Table Talk*. Translated by William Hazlitt. London: David Bogue.
Ma, John. 2000. *Antiochus III and the Cities of Western Asia Minor*. Oxford: Oxford University Press.
Macrobius. 2011. *Saturnalia*. Translated by Robert A. Kaster. LCL 512. Cambridge, MA: Harvard University Press.
Mailloux, Steven. 1998. *Reception Histories: Rhetoric, Pragmatism, and American Cultural Politics*. Ithaca, NY: Cornell University Press.
Maimonides, Moses. 1985. *Epistles of Maimonides: Crisis and Leadership*. Translated by Abraham Halkin. Philadelphia: Jewish Publication Society.
Malbon, Elizabeth Struthers. 1990. *Iconography of the Sarcophagus of Junius Bassus*. Princeton: Princeton University Press.
Margoliouth, David S. 1901. "Mene, Mene, Tekel, Upharsin." Pages 340–41 in vol. 3 of *A Dictionary of the Bible: Dealing with Its Language, Literature, and Contents Including the Biblical Theology*. Edited by James Hastings. New York: C. Scribner's Sons.
Massachusetts Total Abstinence Society. 1908. *The Temperance Cause* 30 (March).
Mastin, Brian A. 1992. "The Meaning of *hălāʾ* at Daniel IV:27." *VT* 42:234–47.
Matt, Daniel Chanan. 1983. *Zohar: The Book of Enlightenment*. Mahwah, NJ: Paulist Press.
Mayer, John. 1652. *Commentary upon All the Prophets Both Great and Small*. London: Abraham Miller and Ellen Cotes.
McClintock, John, and James Strong. 1896. *Cyclopædia of Biblical, Theological, and Ecclesiastical Literature*. Vol. 1. New York: Harper & Brothers.

McGarry, Eugene P. 2005. "The Ambidextrous Angel (Daniel 12:7 and Deuteronomy 32:40): Inner-Biblical Exegesis and Textual Criticism in Counterpoint." *JBL* 124:211–28.

McGinn, Bernard. 2000. *Antichrist: Two Thousand Years of the Human Fascination with Evil.* New York: Columbia University Press.

———. 2002. "Eriugena Confronts the End: Reflections on Johannes Scottus' Place in Carolingian Eschatology." Pages 3–32 in *History and Eschatology in John Scottus Eriugena and His Time: Proceedings of the Tenth International Conference of the Society for the Promotion of Eriugenian Studies, Maynooth and Dublin, August 16–20, 2000.* Edited by J. McEvoy and M. Dunne. Leuven: Leuven University Press.

McKenzie, Duncan W. 2012. *The Antichrist and the Second Coming: A Preterist Examination.* Vol. 2. Maitland, FL: Xulon.

McLay, Timothy. 1998. "It's a Question of Influence: The Theodotion and Old Greek Texts of Daniel." Pages 231–54 in *Origen's Hexapla and Fragments: Papers Presented at the Rich Seminar on the Hexapla, Oxford Centre for Hebrew and Jewish Studies, 25th July–3rd August 1994.* Edited by Alison Salvesen. Tubingen: Mohr Siebeck.

McNamara, Martin. 1970. "Nabonidus and the Book of Daniel." *ITQ* 37:131–49.

Meinhold, Johannes. 1884. *Die Composition des Buches Daniel.* Inaugural diss. Greifswald: Julius Abel.

Mendels, Doron. 1981. "The Five Empires: A Note on a Hellenistic Topos." *AJP* 102:330–37.

Metzger, Martin. 1991. "Zeder, Weinstock, und Weltenbaum." Pages 197–229 in *Ernten, was man sät: Festschrift für Klaus Koch zu seinem 65. Geburtstag.* Edited by Dwight R. Daniels, Uwe Glessmer, and Martin Rösel. Neukirchen-Vluyn: Neukirchener Verlag.

———. 1992. "Der Weltenbaum in Vorderorientalischer Bildtradition." Pages 1–34 in *Unsere Welt—Gottes Schöpfung: Eberhard Wölfel zum 65. Geburtstag am 16. April 1992.* MTS 32. Marburg: Elwert.

Mezoughi, Nouredine. 1977. "Saint-Gabriel en Provence: Réflexions sur l'iconographie de la façade et sur la signification symbolique de l'oculus." *CSMC* 8:105–36.

Miller, Patrick D. 1970. "Animal Names as Designations in Ugaritic and Hebrew." *UF* 2:177–86.

Mobley, Gregory. 1997. "The Wild Man in the Bible and the Ancient Near East." *JBL* 116:217–33.

Moore, Sean D. 2010. *Swift, the Book, and the Irish Financial Revolution: Satire and Sovereignty in Colonial Ireland.* Baltimore: Johns Hopkins University Press.

Morenz, Siegfried. 1951. "Das Tier mit den Hörnern." *ZAW* 63:151–54.

Morgan, M. Gwyn. 1990. "The Perils of Schematism: Polybius, Antiochus Epiphanes, and the 'Day of Eleusis.'" *HZAG* 39:37–76.
Mørkholm, Otto. 1966. *Antiochus IV of Syria*. CMD 8. Copenhagen: Gyldendalske Boghandel.
———. 1970. "The Seleucid Mint at Antiochia on the Persian Gulf." *AJN* 16:31–44.
Morrison, Craig E. 2004. "The Reception of the Book of Daniel in Aphrahat's Fifth Demonstration, 'On Wars.'" *Hugoye* 7:55–82.
Mosca, Paul G. 1986. "Ugarit and Daniel 7: A Missing Link." *Bib* 67:496–517.
Moss, Candida. 2012. *Ancient Christian Martyrdom: Diverse Practices, Theologies, and Traditions*. ABRL. New Haven: Yale University Press.
Mullen, E. Theodore. 1992. "Divine Assembly." *ABD* 2:214–17.
Müller, Hans-Peter. 1970. "Der Begriff 'Rätsel' im Alten Testament." *VT* 20:465–89.
———. 1977. "Die weisheitliche Lehrerzählung im Alten Testament und seiner Umwelt." *WO* 9:77–98.
Müntzer, Thomas. 1988. *The Collected Works of Thomas Müntzer*. Edited and translated by Peter Matheson. Edinburgh: T&T Clark.
———. 1993. *Revelation and Revolution: Basic Writings of Thomas Müntzer*. Edited and translated by Michael Baylor. Cranbury, NJ: Associated University Presses.
Murray, Robert P. R. 1984. "The Origin of Aramaic ʿir, Angel." *Orientalia* 53:303–17.
Myrdal, Gunnar. 1944. *An American Dilemma: The Negro Problem and Modern Democracy, Volume 2*. New York: Harper & Brothers.
Nestle, Eberhard. 1884. "Zu Daniel." *ZAW* 4:247–50.
Netanyahu, Benzion. 1998. *Don Isaac Abravanel: Statesman and Philosopher*. Ithaca, NY: Cornell University Press.
Neujahr, Matthew. 2012. *Predicting the Past in the Ancient Near East: Mantic Historiography in Ancient Mesopotamia, Judah, and the Mediterranean World*. BJS 354. Providence: Brown Judaic Studies.
Newport, Kenneth. 2000. *Apocalypse and Millennium: Studies in Biblical Eisegesis*. Cambridge: Cambridge University Press.
Newsom, Carol A. 2004. *The Self as Symbolic Space: Constructing Identity and Community at Qumran*. STDJ 52. Leiden: Brill.
———. 2010. "Why Nabonidus? Excavating Traditions from Qumran, the Hebrew Bible, and Neo-Babylonian Sources." Pages 57–80 in *The Dead Sea Scrolls: Transmission of Traditions and Production of Texts*. Edited by Sarianna Metso, Hindy Najman, and Eileen M. Schuller. STDJ 92. Leiden: Brill.
———. 2011. "God's Other: The Intractable Problem of the Gentile King in Judean and Early Jewish Literature." Pages 31–48 in *The "Other" in Second Temple Judaism: Essays in Honor of John J. Collins*. Edited by Daniel C.

Harlow, Karina Martin Hogan, Matthew Goff, and Joel S. Kaminsky. Grand Rapids: Eerdmans.

———. 2014a. "The Reuse of Ugaritic Mythology in Daniel 7: An Optical Illusion?" Pages 85–100 in *Opportunity for No Little Instruction: Studies in Honor of Richard J. Clifford, S.J. and Daniel J. Harrington, S.J.* Edited by C. Frechette, C. Matthews, and T. Stegeman. New York: Paulist Press.

———. 2014b. "The Rhetoric of Jewish Apocalyptic Literature." Pages 218–34 in *The Oxford Handbook of Apocalyptic Literature.* Edited by J. J. Collins. New York: Oxford University Press.

Newton, Thomas. 1826. *Dissertations on the Prophecies: Which Have Remarkably Been Fulfilled, and at this Time are Fulfilling in the World.* Edited by W. S. Dobson. London: J. F. Dove.

Nicholl, Colin. 2004. *From Hope to Despair in Thessalonica: Situating 1 and 2 Thessalonians.* SNTSMS 126. Cambridge: Cambridge University Press.

Nichols, Joel, and James McCarthy III. 2011. "When the State Is Evil: Biblical (Dis)obedience in South Africa." *St. John's Law Review* 85:583–625.

Nickelsburg, George W. E. 2001. *1 Enoch 1.* [On *1 En.* 1–36, 81–108.] Hermeneia. Minneapolis: Augsburg Fortress.

———. 2006. *Resurrection, Immortality, and Eternal Life in Intertestamental Judaism and Early Christianity.* HTS 56. Cambridge, MA: Harvard University Press.

Niditch, Susan. 1983. *The Symbolic Vision in Biblical Tradition.* HSM 30. Missoula, MT: Scholars Press for the Harvard Semitic Museum.

———. 1996. *Oral Word and Written Word.* Louisville, KY: Westminster John Knox Press.

Nissinen, Martti. 2009. "Pesharim as Divination: Qumran Exegesis, Omen Interpretation, and Literary Prophecy." Pages 43–60 in *Prophecy after the Prophets?* Edited by K. de Troyer, A. Lange, and L. Schulte. Leuven: Peeters.

Noegel, Scott B. 2007. *Nocturnal Ciphers: The Allusive Language of Dreams in the Ancient Near East.* AOS 89. New Haven: American Oriental Society.

Noth, Martin. 1926. "Zur Komposition des Buches Daniel." *TSK* 98/99:143–63.

———. 1955. "Die Heiligen des Höchsten." *NTT* 56:146–61.

———. 1966. [Translation of German rev. ed., 1960.] "The Holy Ones of the Most High." Pages 215–28 in *The Laws in the Pentateuch and Other Essays.* Translated by D. R. Ap-Thomas. Edinburgh: Oliver & Boyd.

Nyman, Monte. 2006. *Abomination of Desolation.* Springville, UT: Cedar Fort.

Ohm, Juliane. 2008. *Daniel und die Löwen: Analyse und Deutung nordafrikanischer Mosaiken in geschichtlichem und theologischem Kontext.* Paderborn: Schöningh.

O'Malley, John W. 1968. *Giles of Viterbo on Church and Reform: A Study in Renaissance Thought.* Leiden: Brill.

Oppenheim, A. Leo. 1970. *Ancient Mesopotamia: Portrait of a Dead Civilization*. Chicago: University of Chicago Press.
———. 2008. *The Interpretation of Dreams in the Ancient Near East*. Piscataway, NJ: Gorgias.
Otto, Bishop of Freising. 2002. [1928.] *The Two Cities: A Chronicle of Universal History to the Year 1146 A.D.* Translated by C. Mierow. Edited by A. Evans and C. Knapp. New York: Columbia University Press.
Ovadiah, Asher. 1994. "Art of the Ancient Synagogues in Israel." Pages 301–18 in *Ancient Synagogues: Historical Analysis and Archaeological Discovery*. Edited by Dan Urman and Paul Flesher. StPB 47. Leiden: Brill.
Pachomius. 1989. *Pachomian Koinonia III: Instructions, Letters and Other Writings of Saint Pachomius and His Disciples*. Edited and translated by Armand Veilleux. Kalamazoo: Cistercian Publications.
Parpola, Simon. 1987. "The Forlorn Scholar." Pages 257–78 in *Language, Literature, and History: Philological and Historical Studies Presented to Erica Reiner*. Edited by Francesca Rochberg-Halton. New Haven: American Oriental Society.
———. 1993. "The Assyrian Tree of Life: Tracing the Origins of Jewish Monotheism and Greek Philosophy." *JNES* 52, no. 3:161–208.
Patai, Raphael. 1979. *The Messiah Texts: Jewish Legends of Three Thousand Years*. Detroit: Wayne State University Press.
Pattemore, Stephen. 2004. *The People of God in the Apocalypse: Discourse, Structure and Exegesis*. SNTSMS 128. Cambridge: Cambridge University Press.
Paul, Shalom. 1993. "Decoding a 'Joint' Expression." *JANES* 22:121–27.
———. 2001. "The Mesopotamian Babylonian Background of Daniel 1–6." Pages 55–68 in vol. 1 of *The Book of Daniel: Composition and Reception*. Edited by John J. Collins and Peter W. Flint. SVT 83.1. Leiden: Brill.
———. 2004. "Daniel 12:9: A Technical Mesopotamian Scribal Term." Pages 115–18 in *Sefer Moshe: The Moshe Weinfeld Jubilee Volume*. Edited by Chaim Cohen, Avi Hurvitz, and Shalom M. Paul. Winona Lake, IN: Eisenbrauns.
Pearce, Laurie E. 2006. "New Evidence for Judeans in Babylonia." Pages 399–411 in *Judah and the Judeans in the Persian Period*. Edited by Oded Lipschits and Manfred Oeming. Winona Lake, IN: Eisenbrauns.
Peerbolte, L. J. Lietaert. 1996. *The Antecedents of Antichrist: A Traditio-historical Study of the Earliest Christian Views on Eschatological Opponents*. StPB 49. Leiden: Brill.
Pesenson, Michael, and Jennifer Spock. 2012. "Historical Writing in Russia and Ukraine." Pages 282–302 in *1400–1800*. Vol. 3 of *The Oxford History of Historical Writing*. Edited by José Rabasa, Andrew Feldherr, Daniel R. Woolf, and Grant Hardy. Oxford: Oxford University Press.

Peter, Chrysologus, Archbishop of Ravenna. 2004. *Selected Sermons*. Vol. 2. Edited and translated by William Parlady. Washington, DC: Catholic University of America Press.

Petuchowski, Jakob J. 1978. *Theology and Poetry: Studies in the Medieval Piyyut* [liturgical poetry]. Littman Library of Jewish Civilization. London: Routledge & Kegan Paul.

Pfau, Aleksandra Nicole. 2008. "Madness in the Realm: Narratives of Mental Illness in Late Medieval France." Ph.D. diss., University of Michigan.

Phillips, L. Edward. 2008. "Prayer in the First Four Centuries A.D." Pages 31–58 in *A History of Prayer: The First to the Fifteenth Century*. Edited by Roy Hammerling. CCT 13. Leiden: Brill.

Pitarakis, Brigitte. 2010. "Objects of Devotion and Protection." Pages 164–81 in *Byzantine Christianity*. Edited by Derek Krueger. PHC 3. Minneapolis: Augsburg Fortress.

Pitkin, Barbara. 2007. "Prophecy and History in Calvin's Lectures on Daniel (1561)." Pages 323–47 in *Die Geschichte der Daniel: Auslegung in Judentum, Christentum und Islam*. Edited by K. Bracht and D. du Toit. BZAW 371. Berlin: de Gruyter.

Plutarch. 1909. "Symposiacs." Pages 132–356 in vol. 6 of *The Complete Works of Plutarch*. New York: Kelmscott Society.

Podskalsky, Gerhard. 1972. *Byzantinische Reichseschatologie: Die Periodisierung der Weltgeschichte in den vier Grossreichen (Dan 2 und 7) und dem tausendjährigen Friedensreiche (Apok. 20)*. Munich: Fink.

Porter, Paul A. 1983. *Metaphors and Monsters: A Literary-Critical Study of Daniel 7 and 8*. ConBOT 20. Lund: Gleerup.

Portier-Young, Anathea. 2011. *Apocalypse against Empire: Theologies of Resistance in Early Judaism*. Grand Rapids: Eerdmans, 2011.

Postgate, J. Nicholas. 1995. "Royal Ideology and State Administration in Sumer and Akkad." Pages 395–411 in vol. 1 of *Civilizations of the Ancient Near East*. Edited by Jack M. Sasson. Peabody, MA: Hendrickson.

Powell, Marvin A., Jr. 1979. "Ancient Mesopotamian Weight Metrology: Methods, Problems and Perspectives." Pages 71–107 in *Studies in Honor of Tom B. Jones*. Edited by Marvin A. Powell Jr. and Marvin H. Sack. AOAT 203. Neukirchen-Vluyn: Neukirchener Verlag.

Priest, J. "Testament of Moses (First Century A.D.): A New Translation and Introduction." Pages 919–34 in *The Old Testament Pseudepigrapha*, vol. 1. Edited by James H. Charlesworth. Garden City, NY: Doubleday, 1983.

Pusey, Edward B. 1865. *Daniel the Prophet*. Oxford: Parker.

Pyper, Hugh. 2012. "Looking into the Lions' Den: Otherness, Ideology, and Illustration in Children's Versions of Daniel 6." Pages 51–72 in *Text, Image, and Otherness in Children's Bibles: What Is in the Picture?* Edited by Caroline Vander Stichele and Hugh S. Pyper. Atlanta: Society of Biblical Literature.

Quintus Curtius. 1946. *History of Alexander*. Translated by John C. Rolfe. LCL 368. Cambridge, MA: Harvard University Press.
Rabinowitz, Isaac. 1973. "Pesher/pittaron: Its Biblical Meaning and Its Significance in the Qumran Literature." *RevQ* 8:219–32.
Raël. 2004. *Intelligent Design: Message from the Designers*. Beauceville, Quebec: The Raëlian Foundation.
Rappaport, Uriel. 1992. "Apocalyptic Vision and Preservation of Historical Memory." *JSJ* 23:217–26.
Ratliff, Brandie, and Helen C. Evans, eds. 2012. *Byzantium and Islam: Age of Transition, 7th–9th Century*. New Haven: Yale University Press.
Redditt, Paul L. 1988. "Daniel 11 and the Sociohistorical Setting of the Book of Daniel." *CBQ* 60:463–74.
Reeves, John C. 2005. *Trajectories in Near Eastern Apocalyptic: A Postrabbinic Jewish Apocalypse Reader*. Atlanta: Society of Biblical Literature.
Reeves, Marjorie. 1969. *The Influence of Prophecy in the Later Middle Ages: A Study in Joachimism*. Oxford: Oxford University Press.
Reinhold, Meyer. 1970. *History of Purple as a Status Symbol in Antiquity*. CL 116. Brussels: Latomus.
Richard, Pablo. 1990. "El pueblo de Dios contra el imperio: Daniel 7 en su contexto literario e histórico." *RIBLA* 7:25–46.
Rigger, Hansjörg. 1997. *Siebzig Siebener: Die "Jahrwochenprophetie" in Dan 9*. TThSt 57. Trier: Paulinus-Verlag.
Ringgren, Helmer. 1983. "Akkadian Apocalypses." Pages 379–86 in *Apocalypticism in the Mediterranean World and the Near East*. Edited by David Hellholm. Tübingen: Mohr Siebeck.
Ringrose, Kathryn. 2003. *The Perfect Servant: Eunuchs and the Social Construction of Gender in Byzantium*. Chicago: University of Chicago Press.
Rizal, José. 1913. *The Reign of Greed: A Complete English Version of "El Filibusterismo" from the Spanish*. Translated by Charles Derbyshire. Manila: Philippine Education Co.
Robinson, Neal. 2001. "Antichrist." Pages 107–11 in vol. 1 of *Encyclopedia of the Qurʾān*. Edited by Jane Dammen McAuliffe. Leiden: Brill.
Roca-Puig, Ramón. 1976. "Daniele: Due semifogli del codice 967: P. Barc. inv. nn. 42 e 43." *Aeg* 56:3–18.
Rochberg, Francesca. 2004. *The Heavenly Writing: Divination, Horoscopy, and Astronomy in Mesopotamian Culture*. Cambridge: Cambridge University Press.
Root, Margaret Cool. 1979. *The King and Kingship in Achaemenid Art*. Leiden: Brill.
Rosenak, Michael. 2005. "Theological Reflections on the Holocaust: Between Unity and Controversy." Pages 161–75 in *The Impact of the Holocaust on Jewish Theology*. Edited by Stephen T. Katz. New York: New York University Press.

Rosenberg, Daniel, and Anthony Grafton. 2013. *Cartographies of Time: A History of the Timeline*. New York: Princeton Architectural Press.

Rosenblum, Jordan. 2010. *Food and Identity in Early Rabbinic Judaism*. New York: Cambridge University Press.

Rosenmüller, Ernst. 1836. *The Biblical Geography of Central Asia: With a General Introduction of Sacred Geography, Including the Antediluvian Period*. Edinburgh: Thomas Clark.

Rosenthal, Ludwig A. 1895. "Die Josephgeschichte, mit den Büchern Ester und Daniel verglichten." *ZAW* 15:278–84.

Roth, Norman. 1994. *Jews, Visigoths, and Muslims in Medieval Spain: Cooperation and Conflict*. Leiden: Brill.

Rowley, Harold H. 1935. *Darius the Mede and the Four World Empires in the Book of Daniel: A Historical Study of Contemporary Theories*. Cardiff: University of Wales Press Board. Repr., 1959, 1964.

———. 1965. "The Unity of the Book of Daniel." Pages 249–80 in *The Servant of the Lord and Other Essays on the Old Testament*. Edited by H. H. Rowley. 3d ed. Oxford: Blackwell.

Rustow, Marina. 2008. *Heresy and the Politics of Community: The Jews of the Fatimid Caliphate*. Ithaca, NY: Cornell University Press.

Sarachek, Joseph. *The Doctrine of the Messiah in Medieval Jewish Literature*. New York: Jewish Theological Seminary, 1932.

Saritoprak, Zeki. 2003. "The Legend of al-Dajjāl (Antichrist): The Personification of Evil in the Islamic Tradition." *MW* 93:291–307.

Satran, David. 1985. "Early Jewish and Christian Interpretation of the Fourth Chapter of the Book of Daniel." Ph.D. diss., Hebrew University of Jerusalem.

———. 1994. *Biblical Prophets in Byzantine Palestine: Reassessing the Lives of the Prophets*. SVTP 11. Leiden: Brill.

Scales, Len. 2012. *The Shaping of German Identity: Authority and Crisis, 1245–1414*. Cambridge: Cambridge University Press.

Schaudig, Hanspeter. 2001. *Die Inschriften Nabonids von Babylon und Kyros' des Grossen: Samt den in ihrem Unfeld entstandenen Tendenzschriften; Textausgabe und Grammatik*. AOAT 256. Münster: Ugarit-Verlag.

Scheindlin, Raymond P. 2008. *The Song of the Distant Dove: Judah Halevi's Pilgrimage*. Oxford: Oxford University Press.

Schwartz, Daniel R. 2008. *2 Maccabees*. Commentaries on Early Jewish Literature. Berlin: de Gruyter.

Scofield, Cyrus I. 1909. *The Scofield Reference Bible*. Oxford: Oxford University Press.

Segal, Alan F. 1977. *Two Powers in Heaven: Early Rabbinic Reports about Christianity and Gnosticism*. SJLA 25. Leiden: Brill.

———. 2004. *Life after Death: A History of the Afterlife in the Religions of the West*. New York: Doubleday.

Sellin, Ernst. 1910. *Einleitung in das Alte Testament*. Leipzig: Quelle & Meyer.
Sevcenko, Nancy Patterson. 2009. "Images of the Second Coming and the Fate of the Soul in Middle Byzantine Art." Pages 250–72 in *Apocalyptic Thought in Early Christianity*. Edited by Robert J. Daly. Grand Rapids: Baker Academic.
Shalev, Eran. 2013. *American Zion: The Old Testament as a Political Text from the Revolution to the Civil War*. New Haven: Yale University Press.
Shea, William H. 1982a. "Darius the Mede: An Update." *AUSS* 20:229–47.
———. 1982b. "Nabonidus, Belshazzar, and the Book of Daniel: An Update." *AUSS* 20:133–49.
———. 2001. "The Search for Darius the Mede (Concluded), or, The Time of the Answer to Daniel's Prayer and the Date of the Death of Darius the Mede." *JATS* 12:97–105.
Shepkaru, Shmuel. 2006. *Jewish Martyrs in the Pagan and Christian Worlds*. Cambridge: Cambridge University Press.
Sherwin-White, Susan M. 1987. "Seleucid Babylonia: A Case Study for the Installation and Development of Greek Rule." Pages 1–31 in *Hellenism in the East: The Interaction of Greek and Non-Greek Civilizations from Syria to Central Asia after Alexander*. Edited by Amélie Kuhrt and Susan M. Sherwin-White. Berkeley: University of California Press.
Sherwin-White, Susan M., and Amélie Kuhrt. 1993. *From Samarkhand to Sardis: A New Approach to the Seleucid Empire*. London: Duckworth.
Shuck, Glenn W. 2003. "Raëlian Movement." Pages 246–50 in *Religion and American Cultures: An Encyclopedia of Traditions, Diversity, and Popular Expressions, Volume 1*. Edited by Gary Laderman and Luis D. León. Santa Barbara, CA: ABC-CLIO.
Silver, Hillel. 1927. *History of Messianic Speculation in Israel*. New York: Macmillian.
Skemer, Don C. 2006. *Binding Words: Textual Amulets in the Middle Ages*. University Park: Pennsylvania State University Press.
Smith, Joseph. 1921. *The Doctrine and Covenants of The Church of Jesus Christ of Latter-day Saints Containing Revelations Given to Joseph Smith, the Prophet, with Some Additions by his Successors in the Presidency of the Church*. Salt Lake City: Church of Jesus Christ of Latter-day Saints.
Smith, R. Payne. 1903. *A Compendious Syriac Dictionary, Founded upon the Thesaurus Syriacus of R. Payne Smith*. Edited by J. Payne Smith. Oxford: Clarendon.
Smith-Christopher, Daniel L. 1993. "Gandhi on Daniel 6: A Case of Cultural Exegesis." *BibInt* 1:321–38.
Soden, Wolfram von. 1935. "Eine babylonische Volksüberlieferung von Nabonid in den Danielerzählungen." *ZAW* 53:81–89.

———. 1983. "Kyros und Nabonid: Propaganda und Gegenpropaganda." Pages 61–63 in *Kunst, Kultur und Geschichte der Achämenidenzeit und ihr Fortleben*. Edited by H. Koch and D. N. Mackenzie. AMI 10. Berlin: Reimer.

Sokoloff, Michael. 1976. "*'āmar něqēʾ*, 'Lamb's Wool' (Dan 7:9)." *JBL* 95:277–79.

Spier, Jeffrey. 2007. "The Earliest Christian Art: From Personal Salvation to Imperial Power." Pages 1–24 in *Picturing the Bible: The Earliest Christian Art*. Edited by Jeffrey Spier. Kimbell Art Museum. New Haven: Yale University Press.

Spronk, Klaas. 1986. *Beatific Afterlife in Ancient Israel and in the Ancient Near East*. AOAT 219. Neukirchen-Vluyn: Neukirchener Verlag.

Stamm, Johann Jacob. 1939. *Die akkadische Namengebung*. Leipzig: J. C. Hinrich.

Staub, Urs. 2000. "Das Tier mit den Hörnern." Pages 37–85 in *Hellenismus und Judentum: Vier Studien zu Daniel 7 und zur Religionsnot unter Antiochus IV*. Edited by Othmar Keel and Urs Staub. OBO 178. Freiburg, CH: Universitätsverlag.

Steck, Odil Hannes. 1980. "Weltgeschehen und Gottesvolk im Buche Daniel." Pages 53–78 in *Kirche: Festschrift für Günther Bornkamm zum 75. Geburtstag*. Edited by Dieter Lührmann and Georg Strecker. Tübingen: Mohr.

Sternberg, Meir. 1985. *The Poetics of Biblical Narrative*. Indiana Literary Biblical Series. Bloomington: Indiana University Press.

Stetzer, Frank. 2007. *Religion on the Healing Edge: What Baháʾis Believe*. Wilmette, IL: Bahaʾi Publishing.

Stevenson, James. 1978. *The Catacombs: Rediscovered Monuments of Early Christianity*. APP 91. London: Thames & Hudson.

Stone, Michael. 1959. "A Note on Daniel 1:3." *ABR* 7:69–71.

Strauss, Claudia, and Naomi Quinn. 1997. "Research on Cultural Discontinuities." Pages 210–51 in *A Cognitive Theory of Cultural Meaning*. PSPA 8. Cambridge: Cambridge University Press.

Strawn, Brent. 2005. *What Is Stronger than a Lion? Leonine Image and Metaphor in the Hebrew Bible and the Ancient Near East*. OBO 212. Göttingen: Vandenhoeck & Ruprecht.

Suh, David K. S. 2000. *The Korean Minjung in Christ*. Eugene, OR: Wipf & Stock.

Summers, Mark Wahlgren. 2000. *Rum, Romanism, and Rebellion: The Making of a President, 1884*. Chapel Hill: University of North Carolina Press.

Sundkler, Bengt. 1948. *Bantu Prophets in South Africa*. Cambridge: James Clarke & Co.

Swain, Joseph. 1940. "The Theory of the Four Monarchies: Opposition History under the Roman Empire." *CP* 35:1–21.

Tabor, James. 1998. "Patterns of the End." Pages 409–30 in *Toward the Millennium: Messianic Expectations from the Bible to Waco.* Edited by Peter Schäfer and Mark R. Cohen. Leiden: Brill.
Täubler, Eugene. 1946. "Jerusalem 201 to 199 BCE on the History of a Messianic Movement." *JQR* 37, no. 1:1–30.
Tawil, Hayim. 2002. "Hebrew *nappēṣ yad* [in Dan 12:7] = Akkadian *qāta napāṣu*: A Term of Non-Allegiance." *JAOS* 122:79–82.
Tcherikover, Victor. 1959. *Hellenistic Civilization and the Jews.* Philadelphia: Jewish Publication Society.
Thiselton, Anthony. 2010. *1 and 2 Thessalonians through the Centuries.* BBC. Malden, MA: Blackwell.
Thomas Aquinas. 2006. *Summa Theologiae, Volume 32, Consequences of Faith: 2a2ae. 8-16.* Edited and Translated by Thomas Gilby. Cambridge University Press: Cambridge.
Thomas, Samuel I. 2009. *The "Mysteries" of Qumran: Mystery, Secrecy, and Esotericism in the Dead Sea Scrolls.* SBLEJL 25. Atlanta: Society of Biblical Literature.
Tkacz, Catherine Brown. 2002. *The Key to the Brescia Casket: Typology and the Early Christian Imagination.* CJA 14. Notre Dame, IN: University of Notre Dame Press.
Toorn, Karel van der. 1992. "Ordeal." *ABD* 5:40–42.
———. 1998. "In the Lions' Den: The Babylonian Background of a Biblical Motif." *CBQ* 60:626–40.
———. 2007. *Scribal Culture and the Making of the Hebrew Bible.* Cambridge, MA: Harvard University Press.
Towner, W. Sibley. 1969. "Poetic Passages of Daniel 1–6." *CBQ* 31:317–26.
———. 1999. "Daniel, Book of." *DBI* 1:242–49.
Towns, Elmer. 1996. *Fasting for Spiritual Breakthrough.* Ventura, CA: Regal Books.
Travis, William J. 2000. "Daniel in the Lions' Den: Problems in the Iconography of a Cistercian Manuscript, Dijon, Bibliothèque Municipale, MS 132." *AM* 2/14:49–71.
Tribe, Tania Costa. 1996. "The Mulatto as Artist and Image in Colonial Brazil." *OAJ* 19:67–79.
Trotter, Jonathan. 2012. "The Tradition of the Throne Vision in the Second Temple Period: Daniel 7:9–10, 1 Enoch 14:18–23, and the Book of Giants (4Q530)." *RevQ* 99:451–66.
Tselikas, Agamemnon. 2008. "Spells and Exorcisms in Three Post-Byzantine Manuscripts." Pages 72–81 in *Greek Magic: Ancient, Medieval and Modern.* Edited by J. C. B. Petropolous. New York: Routledge.
Ulrich, Eugene. 1987. "Daniel Manuscripts from Qumran: Part 1, A Preliminary Edition of 4QDan[a]." *BASOR* 268:17–37.

———. 1988. "Double Literary Editions of Biblical Narratives and Reflections on Determining the Form to Be Translated." Pages 101–16 in *Perspectives on the Hebrew Bible: Essays in Honor of Walter J. Harrelson*. Edited by J. L. Crenshaw. Macon, GA: Mercer University Press.

———. 1989. "Daniel Manuscripts from Qumran: Part 2, A Preliminary Edition of 4QDan^b and 4QDan^c." *BASOR* 264:3–26.

———. 2000. "Daniel." Pages 239–87 in *Psalms to Chronicles*. Vol. 11 of *Qumran Cave 4*. Edited by Eugene Ulrich, P. W. Skehan, and P. Flint. DJD 16. Oxford: Clarendon.

———. 2001. "The Text of Daniel from Qumran." Pages 573–85 in vol. 2 of *The Book of Daniel: Composition and Reception*. Edited by J. J. Collins and P. W. Flint. SVT 83.2. Brill: Leiden.

Utt, Walter, and Eugene Strayer. 2003. *The Bellicose Dove: Claude Brousson and Protestant Resistance to Louis XIV, 1647–1698*. Brighton: Sussex Academic Press.

Valdez, Maria Ana T. 2010. *Historical Interpretations of the "Fifth Empire": The Dynamics of Periodization from Daniel to António Vieira, S.J.* Leiden: Brill.

Valeta, David. 2005. "Court or Jester Tales? Resistance and Social Reality in Daniel 1–6." *PRSt* 32:309–24.

van Peursen, Wido. 2011. "Daniel's Four Kingdoms in the Syriac Tradition." Pages 189–208 in *Tradition and Innovation in Biblical Interpretation: Studies Presented to Professor Eep Talstra on the Occasion of His Sixty-Fifth Birthday*. Edited by W. Th. van Peursen and J. W. Dyk. Leiden: Brill.

VanderKam, James C. 1981. "2 Maccabees 6, 7A and Calendrical Change in Jerusalem." *JSJ* 12:52–74.

———. 1992. "Ahiqar, Book of." *ABD* 1:113–15.

Vanonen, Hanna. 2011. "The Textual Connections between 1QM 1 and the Book of Daniel." Pages 223–46 in *Changes in Scripture: Rewriting and Interpreting Authoritative Traditions in the Second Temple Period*. Edited by Hanne von Weissenberg, Juha Pakkala, and Marko Marttila. Berlin: de Gruyter.

Vogel, Winfried. 2010. *The Cultic Motif in the Book of Daniel*. New York: Peter Lang.

Warren, Rick, Daniel Amen, and Mark Hyman. 2013. *The Daniel Plan: 40 Days to a Healthier Life*. Grand Rapids: Zondervan.

Watson, Carolyn J. 1981. "The Program of the Brescia Casket." *Gesta* 20:283–98.

Wernberg-Møller, Preben. 1957. *The Manual of Discipline*. STDJ 1. Grand Rapids: Eerdmans.

Whitla, William. 1922. *Sir Isaac Newton's Daniel and The Apocalypse*. London: John Murray.

Whittier, John Greenleaf. 1892. *The Poetical Works of John Greenleaf Whittier.* Vol. 1. New York: Houghton Mifflin.
Whybray, Roger N. 1974. *The Intellectual Tradition in the Old Testament.* BZAW 135. Berlin: de Gruyter.
Wiesel, Elie. 1993. *Sages and Dreamers: Biblical, Talmudic, and Hasidic Portraits and Legends.* New York: Simon & Schuster.
Wiesel, Elie, and Timothy Beal. 2000. "Matters of Survival: A Conversation." Pages 22–35 in *Strange Fire: Reading the Bible after the Holocaust.* Edited by Tod Linafelt. Sheffield: Sheffield Academic.
Williamson, Hugh G. M. 1985. *Ezra, Nehemiah.* WBC 16. Waco: Word Books.
Willis, Amy C. Merrill. 2010. *Dissonance and the Drama of Divine Sovereignty in the Book of Daniel.* New York: T&T Clark International.
Wills, Lawrence M. 1990. *The Jew in the Court of the Foreign King: Ancient Jewish Court Legends.* HDR 26. Minneapolis: Fortress.
Wilson, Gerald. 1990. "The Prayer of Daniel 9: Reflection on Jeremiah 29." *JSOT* 48:91–99.
Winston, Bill. 2010. *The Kingdom of God in You: Discover the Greatness of God's Power Within.* Tulsa: Harrison House.
Wiseman, Donald J. 1985. *Nebuchadrezzar and Babylon.* Schweich Lectures. London: Oxford University Press.
Wixom, William. 1999. *Mirror of the Medieval World.* New York: Metropolitan Museum of Art.
Wolf, Kenneth Baxter. 1996. "Christian Views of Islam in Early Medieval Spain." Pages 85–108 in *Medieval Christian Perceptions of Islam.* Edited by John Tolan. London: Routledge.
Wolters, Albert M. 1991a. "The Riddle of the Scales in Daniel 5." *HUCA* 62:155–78.
―――. 1991b. "Untying the King's Knots: Physiology and Wordplay in Daniel 5." *JBL* 110:117–22.
―――. 1995. "Belshazzar's Feast and the Cult of the Moon God Sin." *BBR* 5:199–206.
Woolever, Frank. 2011. *Gandhi's List of Social Sins: Lessons in Truth.* Pittsburgh: Dorrance.
Wright, Jacob L. 2010a. "Commensal Politics in Ancient Western Asia: The Background to Nehemiah's Feasting (Part I)." *ZAW* 122:212–33.
―――. 2010b. "Commensal Politics in Ancient Western Asia: The Background to Nehemiah's Feasting (continued, Part II)." *ZAW* 122:333–52.
Xenophon. 1968. *Cyropaedia.* Translated by Walter Miller. LCL 51. Cambridge, MA: Harvard University Press.
―――. 1998. *Anabasis.* Edited by John Dillery. Translated by Carleton L. Brownson. LCL 90. Cambridge, MA: Harvard University Press.

Young, Robert J. C. 2010. "Walking Westward." Pages 13–28 in *Back to the Future of Irish Studies: Festschrift for Tadhg Foley*. Edited by Maureen O'Connor. Bern: Peter Lang.

Yücesoy, Hayrettin. 2009. *Messianic Beliefs and Imperial Politics in Medieval Islam: The ʿAbbāsid Caliphate in the Early Ninth Century.* Columbia: University of South Carolina Press.

Zadok, Ran. 1979. *The Jews in Babylonia during the Chaldean and Achaemenian Periods according to the Babylonian Sources*. Haifa: University of Haifa.

———. 1984a. "On Five Iranian Names in the Old Testament." *VT* 26:246–47.

———. 1984b. "The Origin of the Name Shinar." *ZA* 74:240–55.

———. 2002. *The Earliest Diaspora: Israelites and Judeans in Pre-Hellenistic Mesopotamia*. Tel Aviv: Diaspora Research Institute.

Zell, Michael. 2002. *Reframing Rembrandt: Jews and the Christian Image in Seventeenth-Century Amsterdam*. Berkeley: University of California Press.

Zimmermann, Frank. 1938. "The Aramaic Origin of Daniel 8–12." *JBL* 38:255–72.

INTRODUCTION

Despite its relatively brief length, the book of Daniel has had a powerful effect on the religious imagination of Judaism and Christianity. The first part of the book (chs. 1–6) consists of a series of loosely linked but well-written short stories, describing the adventures of the exile Daniel and his three companions at the courts of Babylonian, Median, and Persian kings. In these stories Daniel and his friends confront decisions about how their fidelity to the God of Israel places limits on their participation in the life of the court and their obedience to the king's commands (chs. 1, 3, 6). Jealous courtiers use their knowledge of the Jews' religious practices to entrap them and expose their disobedience to the king. The scenes of their endangerment and deliverance in the fiery furnace (ch. 3) and the pit of lions (ch. 6) are dramatic moments for miraculous displays of divine power. Because of his God-given capacities, Daniel also figures as an interpreter of royal dreams for Nebuchadnezzar (chs. 2 and 4) and of the mysterious "handwriting on the wall" that appears to Belshazzar (ch. 5)—feats that none of the king's own sages are able to accomplish. Both types of narratives show the king encountering the surpassing power of the God of Daniel and his friends and ultimately coming to confess the sovereignty of this God and acknowledge his judgment. Although these narratives originally served to address social, cultural, and theological stresses of a Jewish Diaspora population in Mesopotamia, their memorable plots and characters allowed them to transcend their original functions and to continue to be narratives that entertained and inspired later generations.

Daniel's characterization in chs. 1–6 as a skilled interpreter of dreams also permitted him to be adapted in antiquity for a different type of role in the chapters that form the second half of the book. In contrast to chs. 1–6, chs. 7–12 are largely Daniel's own first-person accounts of revelatory encounters, involving mysterious visions and deeply disturbing angelophanies. While these chapters are not the earliest known apocalypses—the earliest stages of *1 Enoch* pre-date Daniel—they quickly became influential and contributed substantially to the development of this important type of ancient literature. In Dan 7–12 the apocalypses are focused on political events of the Hellenistic period, in particular the emergence of the kingdom of Alexander the Great and the two powerful kingdoms of the Ptolemies in Egypt and of the Seleucids in Syria and Mesopotamia that succeeded Alexander. Much of this material is specifically focused on the events of 167–164 B.C.E., when a crisis in the relationship between the Seleucid king Antiochus IV Epiphanes and the Jews of Judea led to savage violence, resulting in the ravaging of Jerusalem and the desecration of the temple and other acts of religious repression. These final chapters of the book embody a new form of resistance and a new form of hope in the face of the persecution.

Even though contemporary readers would have easily understood the coded symbolism of the apocalypses, their referents became increasingly obscure with the passage of time. But precisely because they used symbolic language, the Danielic apocalypses were able to be reinterpreted and reapplied to later periods of political crisis. This process began very early, as the apocalypses were interpreted to refer to the Roman suppression of the Jewish revolt of the first century C.E. and the Roman destruction of the temple at Jerusalem. Throughout history, however, especially in certain strands of Christian interpretation, the Danielic apocalypses have been used as a key to understand events concurrent with the interpreter. In particular, during the medieval period and during the Protestant Reformation, various factions appealed to Daniel to demonize their enemies and to vindicate their own right to sovereignty. Given this powerful history of influence, one needs to read the book not only in light of the circumstances of the times of its origin but also in light of its reception in Judaism and Christianity (see the section by Breed, below).

The Masoretic Book of Daniel in Literary Context

The book of Daniel as it appears in Jewish and Protestant canons, derived from the Masoretic Text, is only one edition of one composition of a larger Danielic literature that flourished in the Persian and Hellenistic periods. That Masoretic edition itself contains evidence of a diverse literary tradition that grew over time, as the book of Daniel consists of two different genres (narratives and apocalypses) written in two different languages, Hebrew and Aramaic. The Catholic Canon, based on the Greek (LXX) version of Daniel, preserves additional narratives about Daniel in which the focus is on the emptiness of pagan idolatry (Bel and the Dragon [better translated as Serpent]) and on Daniel's cleverness in exposing corruption (Susanna). Moreover, Dan 3 contains two long poetic prayers not included in the Masoretic edition. Moreover, the textual tradition of the LXX known as the Old Greek (OG) preserves a different literary edition of chs. 4–6. The Jewish and Christian traditions also differ on the canonical placement of Daniel, with the Jewish canon including Daniel among the Writings (*Ketubim*) and the Christian tradition placing Daniel with the Prophets.

Beyond the different editions of the canonical books of Daniel, fragmentary texts from the Dead Sea Scrolls preserve additional Danielic eschatological prophecies (*Pseudo-Daniel*$^{a\ b}$ [4Q243–44]; *Pseudo-Daniel*^{c} [4Q245]), as well as other closely related writings (e.g., *Prayer of Nabonidus* [4Q242]; *Four Kingdoms*$^{a\ b}$ [4Q552–53]). Although this commentary will focus on the Masoretic edition of the book of Daniel, it will refer to the other Danielic texts and traditions as the discussion warrants.

Texts and Versions

The Masoretic Text and Qumran

Modern editions and translations of Daniel MT are based on the Leningrad Codex (ca. 1008 C.E.), but among the Dead Sea Scrolls eight fragmentary copies of the book of Daniel were found, two from Qumran Cave 1, one from Cave 3, and five from Cave 4. According to paleographical dating, the oldest manuscripts (*Daniel*^{c} [4Q114]; *Daniel*^{e} [4Q116]) date from the late second or early first century B.C.E., little more than fifty years after the final composition of the book. The other manuscripts date from the first centuries B.C.E. and C.E. The material preserved is as follows (Ulrich 2001, 574):

Qumran Scroll and Danielic Contents	Century
1QDaniel^a (1Q71): 1:10–17; 2:2–6	first half of 1st c. C.E.
1QDaniel^b (1Q72): 3:22–30	early or mid 1st c. B.C.E.
4QDaniel^a (4Q112): 1:16–20; 2:9–11, 19–49; 3:1–2; 4:29–30; 5:5–7, 12–14, 16–19; 7:5–7, 25–28; 8:1–5; 10:16–20; 11:13–16	mid 1st c. B.C.E.
4QDaniel^b (4Q113): 5:10–12, 14–16, 19–22; 6:8–22, 27–29; 7:1–6, 11(?), 26–28; 8:1–8, 13–16	first half of 1st c. C.E.
4QDaniel^c (4Q114): 10:5–9, 11–16, 21; 11:1–2, 13–17, 25–29	late 2d or early 1st c. B.C.E.
4QDaniel^d (4Q115): 3:8–10?, 23–25; 4:5–9, 12–16; 7:15–23	mid or late 1st c. B.C.E.
4QDaniel^e (4Q116): 9:12–17	late 2d or early 1st c. B.C.E.
pap6QDaniel (6Q7): 8:16–17(?), 20–21(?); 10:8–16; 11:33–36, 38	first half of 1st c. B.C.E.
In addition, Dan 11:32 and 12:10 are cited in *4QFlorilegium* (4Q174).	mid 1st c. C.E.

Several important conclusions can be drawn from the Qumran evidence. First, the text of the Qumran fragments agrees quite closely with that of the MT, though there are a few minor differences (Ulrich 2001, 580). Second, all twelve chapters of Daniel MT are attested by the Qumran texts and citations. Third, several features that scholars have sometimes argued to be secondary are present in the Qumran fragments and thus are either original or entered the tradition at a very early stage. Thus *1QDaniel*^{a} preserves ch. 1 in Hebrew and the shift from Hebrew to Aramaic in Dan 2:4. The shift from Aramaic to Hebrew at the end of ch. 7 and the beginning of ch. 8 is attested by *4QDaniel*$^{a\ b}$. Fourth and finally, the additional narrative material and prayers that occur in the LXX versions of Daniel between MT 3:23 and 24 are not present in *1QDaniel*^{b} or *4QDaniel*^{d}.

Greek Versions (LXX)

Two Greek versions of Daniel are extant, one known as the Old Greek (OG) and the other as Theodotion (Th). The OG translation was probably made in the late second or early first century B.C.E., most likely in Alexandria (Montgomery 38; Hartman and DiLella 78). With the exception of chs. 4–6 (see below), most scholars consider Theodotion to be a revision of the OG to conform more closely to the MT (Pace 26; but see Hartman and DiLella 82; McLay). At some point early in the Christian tradition, certainly by the second half of the third century C.E., the OG was displaced by Th (Jellicoe 86–87). Since the early church fathers considered deviation from the MT to be evidence of error, they valued Theodotion more highly. In his comments on Dan 4:6, Jerome observes that "by the judgment of the teachers of the Church, the Septuagint edition [i.e., the OG] has been rejected in the case of this book, and it is the translation of Theodotion which is commonly read, since it agrees with the Hebrew as well as with the other translators" (trans. Archer).

As a consequence of this decision, the Theodotion manuscripts of Daniel LXX are numerous, but the OG is poorly attested. Indeed, for some time the OG was known only in the Hexaplaric manuscript Codex Chisianus (MS 88), and indirectly in the highly literal Syriac translation of Paul of Tella, known as the Syro-Hexapla. In 1931, however, a pre-Hexaplaric manuscript of the OG, Papyrus 967, was discovered in Aphroditopolis in Egypt. It contains portions of Ezekiel, Esther, and Daniel and is dated to the second or early third century C.E. (for critical editions, see Geissen; Hamm 1969; 1977; and Roca-Puig).

Both Greek versions differ from the MT in containing what are commonly known as the "Additions" to Daniel, that is, the Prayer of Azariah and the Song of the Three Jews plus their narrative framing, the story of Susanna, and the stories of Bel and the Dragon. They disagree as to the arrangement of the additional narratives, however. Theodotion places Susanna before Dan 1, since Daniel is introduced as a youth and is not said to be at Nebuchadnezzar's court. The OG places Susanna after Dan 12 but before Bel and the Dragon (except for Papyrus 967, which places it at the end of the book). Most scholars now assume that these additional materials were originally composed in either Aramaic or Hebrew, though there has been more controversy over the original language of Susanna. Even there, however, the preponderance of the evidence favors a Semitic original (see J. Collins 427–28).

The OG is particularly important for understanding the development of the book of Daniel, especially chs. 4–6, where the OG and Th differ significantly. Here it is evident that the OG and Th represent not only independent translations but also translations of distinct literary editions. The strongest differences appear in ch. 4. The OG does not begin with the encyclical to the nations, but presents this material in an expanded form at the end of the narrative. It also contains both plusses and minuses of a substantive nature with respect to Th, which closely follows the MT. The nature of the relationship between these two traditions in chs. 4–6 is complex. Albertz (1988, 76) and Wills (87–121) have argued for the priority of the OG, but Satran (1985, 62–68) and Grelot (1974, 22) for the priority of the MT/Th. It is unlikely that a unidirectional explanation of the differences is adequate to the evidence. John Collins (219–21) is more likely correct in arguing that both traditions "preserve variant formulations of a common story. Neither one can be regarded as the *Vorlage* of the other" (221). The divergences between the OG and MT/Th in ch. 5 are less stark but still significant and include numerous narrative and discursive differences. Among other things, the OG is significantly shorter (see comments below). In ch. 6 the differences are minor but numerous.

How is the difference between OG and MT/Th in these chapters best accounted for? It may be that the version of chs. 4–6 now present in the OG is actually older than that translation as a whole and originally circulated independently as a booklet. When the complete MT was translated into what we now know as the OG, that translator apparently preferred the older and more familiar version of chs. 4–6 to the *Vorlage* present in MT and so incorporated the existing Greek translation of these chapters into the OG version rather than preparing a new translation from the MT. The Theodotion revision of the OG, on the other hand, chose to make a fresh translation of the MT of Dan 4–6 (J. Collins 11). Thus the two versions differ much more sharply from one another in chs. 4–6 than they do elsewhere.

Non-Masoretic Danielic Compositions

The variety of Danielic compositions attested outside of the Masoretic tradition indicate how the figure of Daniel was employed for a number of different religious and cultural concerns. Of the Additions found in the Septuagint, the stories of Bel and the Dragon are most similar to the court tales of Dan 1–6 in that they take place at a royal court and feature rivalry between Daniel and other powerful figures at court. The story of the Dragon even makes use of the motif of the pit of lions known from Dan 6. Bel and the Dragon differ from the court tales of chs. 1–6, however, in that they are specifically focused on how the powerless idols and pagan deities are different from the living God of the Jews. This was an important theme in Jewish literature from the Diaspora (e.g., Isa 44; Epistle of Jeremiah). Bel and the Dragon has a more humorous tone than the Daniel MT stories and features Daniel's cleverness more than his wisdom or mantic abilities. The story of Susanna differs more sharply from the others, and it is likely that the wise youth who is its male protagonist was only secondarily identified with the figure of Daniel. It concerns false accusations brought against an innocent woman of the Babylonian Diaspora by two corrupt elders who give false testimony against her. Just as she is about to be executed, God rouses the spirit of a young man, who sequesters the witnesses and cross-examines them separately, demonstrating that their testimony is false. In both the OG and Th this figure is identified with Daniel, presumably because of the Babylonian locale and the features of cleverness and integrity that characterize Daniel in the other narratives.

The insertion of the Prayer of Azariah and the Song of the Three Jews into Dan 3 exhibits the practice of embellishing popular narratives by adding prayers and hymns. Although already attested in First Temple biblical literature (e.g., the Song of Hannah in 1 Sam 2), it becomes more prominent in Second Temple texts. Chronicles' adaptation of the Deuteronomistic History incorporates excerpts from Psalms in 1 Chr 16:8–36 and 2 Chr 6:41–42. Greek Esther includes several prayers that are not present in the less pietistic Masoretic version of the narrative. And one copy of a "reworked" pentateuchal text from Qumran (4Q365) incorporates a new Song of Miriam into the text of Exod 15. Thus the addition of the two poetic compositions in Daniel is part of a more general cultural preference to illustrate characters' piety through appropriate hymns and prayers.

Composition and Development of Daniel MT

Prior to the eighteenth century, most Christian and Jewish interpreters took it for granted that the book of Daniel derived from the sixth century B.C.E. and comprised stories about and writings by the figure of Daniel himself. Doubts about the historical origin of the apocalyptic chapters were already voiced in antiquity, however, by the pagan writer Porphyry (ca. 234–305 C.E.), who noted that the supposed prophecy to Daniel in ch. 11 was a strangely accurate account of history up until the time of Antiochus IV, at which point it diverged sharply from what was known of historical events. Thus Porphyry concluded that the book was composed in the second century B.C.E. Although Porphyry's own writings are not preserved, Jerome (15) engaged Porphyry's opinions in his own commentary and attempted to refute them:

Porphyry wrote his twelfth book against the prophecy of Daniel, denying that it was composed by the person to whom it is ascribed in its title, but rather by some individual living in Judaea at the time of the Antiochus who was surnamed Epiphanes. He furthermore alleged that "Daniel" did not foretell the future so much as he related the past, and lastly that whatever he spoke of up till the time of Antiochus contained authentic history, whereas anything he may have conjectured beyond that point was false, inasmuch as he would not have foreknown the future. (trans. Archer)

In the eighteenth century Porphyry's questions were again taken up by Enlightenment scholars in England (Anthony Collins) and Germany (Heinrich Corrodi), who also questioned the date of Daniel's composition on much the same grounds as had been laid out by Porphyry. During the nineteenth century, as the struggle between historical-critical and traditionalist scholarship raged, the book of Daniel became one of the flashpoints. The conservative scholar Pusey made it a test case:

The book of Daniel is especially fitted to be a battle-ground between faith and unbelief. It admits of no half-way measures. It is either Divine or an imposture. ... The writer, were he not Daniel, must have lied on a most frightful scale. (1)

By the late nineteenth century, however, critical biblical scholarship had been persuaded by the arguments of those who saw at least the apocalypses, if not also the narratives, as originating in the context of the Antiochene persecutions of the second century B.C.E. The author was not seen as "lying," as Pusey argued, but as engaging in the rhetorical strategy of pseudepigraphy—that is, writing under the name of another, a widespread practice in a variety of ancient genres.

Arguments about the date of the apocalyptic chapters in the book of Daniel are related to arguments about the compositional history of the book and whether it was written at one time or developed over an extended period of time. Though there were dissenting voices, most historical-critical scholars of the nineteenth century assumed the unity of the book, which they dated to the second century B.C.E. An alternative paradigm, proposed by Johannes Meinhold (1884) and further developed by Gustav Hölscher (1919), argued that the stories of chs. 1–6 originated independently and later were collected. This collection then became the core onto which the Aramaic apocalypse in ch. 7 was attached. Later, after the addition of ch. 7, the Hebrew apocalypses of chs. 8–12 were added in the Antiochene period. Although some scholars (e.g., Charles xxxviii–xlviii; Bentzen 9–10; Porteous 120–21; Rowley 1965, 249–60) have defended the unity of the book, most now adopt a theory of gradual composition and development. In part, the theory of a gradual, accretional development is an attempt to make sense of one of the most striking features of the book: its Aramaic and Hebrew bilingualism.

Complicating the attempt to understand the bilingualism of the book in relation to theories about its composition is the fact that the two languages do not coincide precisely with the two main genres of the book, the court tales of chs. 1–6 and the visions of 7–12. Although most of the narratives are in Aramaic, Hebrew is used for 1:1–2:4a. Aramaic is introduced at 2:4b, when the king's Chaldean advisers begin to speak. Aramaic is also the language used for the first vision in ch. 7, with the remainder of the visions written in Hebrew.

Various theories have been developed to account for this odd pattern, many more ingenious than persuasive (J. Collins 12–13). The most persuasive and commonly held theory is that an original pre-Maccabean corpus of narratives composed in Aramaic was expanded in the Maccabean period by a series of apocalyptic visions largely composed in Hebrew (Montgomery 88–99). What remains to be explained in this view, however, is why ch. 1 is in Hebrew and ch. 7 in Aramaic. R. H. Charles presented strong evidence that ch. 1 was originally composed in Aramaic and subsequently translated into Hebrew (xlvi–xlviii; Koch 16–18). This chapter contains a striking number of Aramaisms and can readily be retroverted into Aramaic. Moreover, ch. 1 was clearly composed as an introduction to the narratives, since it introduces the characters and explains how they came to have both Jewish and Babylonian names (cf. chs. 3–5), identifies Daniel as distinctively gifted at dream interpretation (cf. chs. 2, 4), and mentions the temple vessels, which will figure in ch. 5. The concluding reference to Daniel's continuing until the first year of Cyrus (1:21) forms an inclusio with 6:28 (6:29 MT). Also significant is that, while ch. 1 foreshadows the narratives, it does not show any awareness of the visions or serve to introduce them specifically. Thus it seems most likely that ch. 1 was composed in Aramaic before the apocalyptic visions were added. If so, then it becomes necessary to explain why the introductory chapter was translated into Hebrew. Although one cannot be certain, it may be related to the composition and addition of the Hebrew apocalyptic visions in chs. 8–12. Presumably having the book begin and end in Hebrew gives it a measure of unity.

The use of Aramaic for ch. 7 is explained differently by those who consider it to have been originally composed in the Maccabean period and those who assume that it was a pre-Maccabean apocalypse later updated to the events of that period. John Collins (24), for example, who takes it to be a Maccabean composition, assumes that ch. 7 was composed in Aramaic because of its dependence on the dream in ch. 2. By contrast, Albertz (2001, 176–79) argues that the theme of divine sovereignty and the overt establishment of God's everlasting kingdom unifies chs. 2–7 and differs from the eschatology of chs. 8–12, which emphasizes the death of Antiochus, the restoration of the temple, and resurrection. Thus he argues for an original Aramaic book of Daniel consisting not of chs. 1–6 nor 2–6 but 2–7 (cf. Lenglet). The position taken in this commentary is closer to Albertz than to J. Collins, though with some differences (discussed in the following sections).

Composition and Development of Daniel MT

Most scholars agree that the narratives in Dan 2–6 were originally composed and circulated individually, only later being drawn into a loosely linked cycle of stories (Koch, Niewisch, and Tubach 61–66; J. Collins 35–38). While it is difficult to recover the stages of development, the origins of several of the stories may go back to the end of the Neo-Babylonian period, since they contain traditions relating to Nabonidus, the last king of Babylon (556–539 B.C.E.). These stories were secondarily transferred to the more famous Nebuchadnezzar. Already by the turn of the twentieth century, scholars recognized that Belshazzar was not the son of Nebuchadnezzar (Dan 5:11–12) but of Nabonidus (Riessler 43; Hommel). Moreover, the account of Nebuchadnezzar's seven-year absence from Babylon in ch. 4 was recognized as a fictionalized version of Nabonidus's actual ten-year absence from Babylon, while he took up residence in Teima in northern Arabia (von Soden 1935). Recovery of Nabonidus's own inscriptions from Harran in 1956 revealed striking literary similarities between the inscriptions and elements in Dan 4 (Newsom 2010, 67–70). Further buttressing this connection was the discovery at Qumran of a fragmentary document called the *Prayer of Nabonidus* (4Q242), which, though not literarily directly related to Dan 4, nevertheless independently preserves similar traditions about Nabonidus. Moreover, the account of the setting up of an image and requiring worship of it in ch. 3 may be a parodic echo of Nabonidus's own notorious championing of the moon-god Sin (McNamara 144–48; Beaulieu 2009, 275–77). Though the evidence is less clear, the motif of the ominous dream in Dan 2 is prominent enough also to suggest that this narrative was originally about Nabonidus, since of all the Neo-Babylonian kings, he was the only one to concern himself with portentous dreams. He even recorded a dream from his first regnal year that betrayed his anxieties about the legitimacy of his kingship, since he was a usurper (Newsom 2010, 59–60). As it now stands, however, the story in Dan 2 cannot be earlier than the Hellenistic period, since the ominous dream contains references to a sequence of Gentile kingdoms concluding with that of Alexander and his successors. Even so, both the presence of Nabonidus traditions in the narratives and, more generally, the focus on the Babylonian court suggest that the origin of the narratives in Dan 2–6 is to be sought among the Jewish exiles in Babylonia and their descendants.

Since Nabonidus was not a king whose memory had much cultural resonance for Jews except during the time of his actual reign, it is not surprising that many of the stories originally told about him were transferred to the more historically significant Nebuchadnezzar. One cannot know how close the narratives at this stage of development were to the form in which they are now preserved in the MT or the OG, but if they concluded with the king's statements confessing the power of the Most High God, then something of their function may be discernible. Nebuchadnezzar's conquest of Judah, the destruction of the temple, and the exile of much of the ruling class was the major traumatic event in Judean history. Such experiences require cultural strategies for understanding and incorporating them into patterns of meaning. They have to be mastered. Depicting Nebuchadnezzar as an arrogant king who ultimately was humbled and came to recognize the power of the Most High God addresses a deep wound of cultural memory. Moreover, the fact that the end of the Neo-Babylonian Empire did not see the restoration of an independent Judean kingdom but incorporation into yet another Gentile empire, that of the Persians, meant that the underlying theological problem of how to understand the sovereignty of YHWH in relation to the power of the Gentile monarchs remained a live issue for Jews. While Nebuchadnezzar may have served as a symbolic figure for Gentile monarchs in general, the corpus of Daniel narratives also expanded during the Persian period to include stories about Cyrus (Bel and the Dragon) and Darius (Dan 6). Though referred to in the final form of the book as "Darius the Mede," there is evidence that the story was originally told about the Persian Darius I (559–486 B.C.E.; see commentary).

The distinctiveness of the OG version of Dan 4–6 (see "Greek Versions" above) suggests that these chapters once formed a distinctive booklet of Daniel stories and were perhaps the core of the developing collection. The strikingly similar doxological elements that stand at the beginning and end of this collection in the MT (4:1–3 [3:31–33 MT]; 6:26b–27 [27b–28]) may belong to the redactional shaping of this collection as a booklet. The booklet demonstrated the power of the Most High by featuring three different Gentile kings who were humbled or judged by God. At some later point, perhaps in the early Hellenistic period, the Danielic narrative of ch. 2 and the narrative featuring Shadrach, Meshach, and Abednego (ch. 3) were joined to the prior collection, and an introduction was composed that tied the various stories together and explained how Daniel and his three friends came to be in the court of Nebuchadnezzar (ch. 1). The incorporation of these additional narratives about Nebuchadnezzar shifted the balance of the collection, so that chs. 1–4 now might be seen as a Nebuchadnezzar cycle in which the king is slowly and painfully educated about the source of his own sovereignty in relation to that of the Most High God. In contrast to the powerful Nebuchadnezzar, both Belshazzar and Darius are presented as feckless kings. They form their own contrast pair, however, with Belshazzar as the blasphemous figure judged by God and Darius as the well-meaning king who recognizes his need of God's assistance. The collection concludes effectively with Darius's strong doxological praise of God. There is thus, contra Albertz and Lenglet, good reason for thinking that Dan 1–6 did form an intentionally shaped and edited collection of narratives.

It is also likely that ch. 7 was composed as a complement to the narrative cycle some time before the composition of chs. 8–12. Not only does it differ from the later apocalyptic visions in language (Aram. rather than Heb.), but it also has different eschatological concerns. Thus ch. 7 envisions the establishment of the kingdom of God on earth and the dispossession of Gentile sovereignty. But chs. 8–12 are concerned with the temple and its sacrifices and the fate of the "wise" (*maśkilîm*). Chapter 7 is closely related to the eschatological schema and imagery of ch. 2, much more so than with the other apocalyptic visions. These differences are significant and suggest a substantial difference in time and context between ch. 7 and what follows. While redaction-critical arguments are seldom conclusive, the references to Antiochus in ch. 7 are both intrusive and easily excised (see commentary). Thus a pre-Maccabean composition for ch. 7 is plausible, with a secondary insertion of material to update the vision for the Antiochene persecution. Where and when one should posit the first edition of ch. 7 is less clear, however. One suggestion is Judea in the period under Antiochus III (late third or early second century B.C.E.; so Lebram 21, 84; Albertz 1988, 188–90). While this is certainly a possibility, one should also consider that the development of Danielic eschatology in chs. 2 and 7 may have taken place in the Judean Diaspora in Babylon soon after the Greek defeat of the Persian Empire and the brutality of the wars of the Diadochi. Babylonian hostility toward the Greek conquerors was also expressed in historical prophecies like the *Dynastic Prophecy*, which envisions a defeat of Alexander, though there is no evidence of literary connection between these works and Daniel (see Neujahr 128–36).

The remainder of the chapters were composed after December 167 B.C.E., since they are aware of the desecration of the temple and the cessation of sacrifice (see 1 Macc 1:54–59; Gera 228), but before the end of 164, when Antiochus IV was killed at Tabae in Persia and Judah the Maccabee retook and reconsecrated the temple (1 Macc 4:46–61; some scholars date the events a year earlier, with the desecration occurring in 168; see Schwartz 536). Opinion differs as to whether one should posit a single author for all of the chapters or whether the differences in style and revelatory medium featured in the apocalypses are better accounted for by positing two or three different authors, who were responding to one another's work. Thus ch. 8 self-consciously alludes to elements from ch. 7 and was clearly composed as a companion piece. The fictional dating of both visions to the first and third years of Belshazzar further serves to group them. Also, ch. 8 has strong verbal links with chs. 10–12, and the suggestion has sometimes been made that the vision of chs. 10–12 was intentionally composed as a further explication of ch. 8 (Hasslberger 397–98). The latter vision's detailed summary of Seleucid and Ptolemaic history, however, suggests a quite different mode of composition from the symbolic vision of ch. 8, perhaps an eschatological reworking of a Seleucid historiographical document (Rappaport; Grabbe 2001, 234–45). Chapter 9 is distinct from the other apocalypses in centering on mantic exegesis of a prophetic text rather than being framed as a dream vision. Its location between chs. 8 and 10–12 interrupts the close connection between these two visions, leading some to suggest that it was the last of the apocalypses to be composed and was secondarily inserted between chs. 8 and 10–12 (so Kratz 2000, 230; Berner 21–22), but there is insufficient evidence to make a conclusive judgment. The composition of the final chapters of Daniel and its redaction into the book as we know it in the MT tradition must have been a relatively rapid process, since the earliest manuscripts from Qumran that attest this edition and textual tradition are little more than fifty years removed from the date of composition of Dan 8–12.

Genres

The Court Tales: Setting and Social Function

Toward the end of the 19th and beginning of the 20th centuries, scholars began examining similarities between the stories of Dan 1–6 and those of Joseph, Esther, Tobit, Judith, and 1 Esd 3 (see, e.g., Rosenthal; Baumgartner). With the exception of Judith, each of these stories features Jews who serve in the court of a Gentile king. Moreover, the Dead Sea Scrolls have yielded fragments of additional compositions that appear to contain similar stories. One of these, 4Q550 (*Proto-Esther*), is attested in five Aramaic copies, is set in the court of a king named Darius, and appears to tell of the exoneration and reward of a courtier named Bagasro. Much closer to the Danielic traditions themselves is the Aramaic 4Q242 (*Prayer of Nabonidus*); like Dan 4, it is narrated as a first-person account by the king, here Nabonidus. It describes his healing from a serious disease and his subsequent praise of the Most High God, communicated in an encyclical. A "Jewish diviner fr[om the exiles . . .]" plays a role, though he is not named in the extant text.

In addition to these Jewish stories, striking similarities exist between the Daniel cycle and *Ahiqar*, a narrative that describes the disgrace and exoneration of the wise courtier Ahiqar in the court of Esarhaddon. Although a copy of *Ahiqar* was discovered in a Jewish military colony serving the Persian Empire in Elephantine, Egypt, it is not a Jewish composition but probably originated in Mesopotamia (yet see Holm 78–88, 477, for discussion of a possible origin in Egypt). Nevertheless, its widespread distribution indicates the popularity of court tales and the way in which the genre became familiar among a variety of peoples in the Persian Empire.

If, as seems likely, the court tale first developed in Mesopotamia, its original social function may have been to explore and narratively resolve tensions between the king and his courtiers on the one hand and between rival courtiers on the other (Dalley 153–55). Letters from mantic experts serving in the court of Esarhaddon, as well as literary texts from Mesopotamia (e.g., *I Will Praise the Lord of Wisdom*; see Parpola 1987), clearly attest the reality of these tensions. Judging from the characterization and plot developments in *Ahiqar*, as well as recurrent elements in other narratives, the court tales provided not only a means for depicting the dangerous power and anger of the king but also for burlesquing the king as emotionally extravagant, easily duped, and none too perspicuous. With the exception of Dan 5, however, the king is not presented as a villain. That role is reserved for rival courtiers, whose evil machinations are defeated in the end, as the hero is restored to his rightful place. Either way, the narratives have a comedic structure. Although they may have served as safety valves for expressing anxieties of court life, the narratives were not subversive of the court. As Wills (21) observes, "There generally exists in court legends the idea that it is in the court where all moral conflicts have their just resolution. This is not, it should be emphasized, because the wisdom and virtue of the king render it so, . . . but because the power and centrality of the court hold absolute sway over human events, and behind this temporal power is the hand of just retribution." Indeed, according to the common ancient Near Eastern ideology of royal rule, the rule of heaven is manifest in the office of the king.

Within the court stories two typical plot lines recur with such frequency that they may be called subgenres. Lee Humphreys described these as "tales of contest" and "tales of conflict." In the tales of contest the hero—often an outsider or low-ranking figure—is able to solve a problem or interpret an enigma that the established sages are not able to resolve. The subgenre, the tale of conflict, involves tension between the hero and jealous courtiers who scheme to bring about the hero's downfall but are thwarted in the end, so that the hero is rewarded by the king. Daniel 2, 4, and 5 exhibit in stronger or more superficial form the contest plot, but chs. 3 and 6 are strongly shaped by the conflict pattern. Similarly, the tale of Ahiqar is shaped by the court-conflict pattern, though some versions of the story also incorporate a court-contest motif.

Although the court tale may have been originally developed in Mesopotamia to address tensions endemic to the courtier-and-king relationship, it was adapted to serve additional functions as other peoples of the empire took it up. Not only in the Jewish tales but also in a number of anecdotes in Herodotus that bear some resemblance to court tales, the wise counselors are ethnic outsiders in the court of the king. Wills persuasively argues that these narratives reflect what he terms a "ruled ethnic perspective" (68), in which an ethnic community told stories of the cleverness of their own counselors in the multiethnic context of the foreign king's court. Thus the narratives were vehicles for ethnic dignity and self-assertion. Although the ethnicity of Ahiqar is not explicit in narrative concerning him, a second-century-B.C.E. cuneiform list of court scholars refers to him as "Aba-Enlil-Dari, whom the Aramaeans call Ahiqar," and the case has been made that he was an Aramaic culture hero in much the same way that Daniel and his friends functioned for the Jews (Beaulieu 2006, 194–95; Holm 85). The ethnic perspective is even more strongly present in Jewish stories such as Esther and Dan 3 and 6, where the ethnicity of the protagonists and their adversaries at court is explicitly noted.

While the narratives of Dan 1–6 and Bel and the Dragon share both the concern with king/courtier relations and the often ethnically charged arena of conflict among courtiers, they differ from other pagan and Jewish court tales in having a pronounced theological focus. In the period after the fall of Judah and the destruction of the temple, the issue of Jewish claims to the sovereignty of God in relation to the reality of Gentile imperial power posed an acute theological problem. The court tales provide a particularly useful context for exploring this issue, since they already make the issue of the king's power a matter of narrative concern. Thus in the Daniel narratives, the kings are confronted by various manifestations of the ultimate power of the God of the Jews, and in several of the narratives the stories conclude with the king's confession of the power of the Most High God.

Although the Daniel narratives are most fruitfully analyzed in relation to other court tales, they can also be grouped with other sorts of narratives in ways that highlight different generic possibilities. So, for example, Hans-Peter Müller (1977) grouped Dan 1–6 with a selection of other stories that he designated as "wisdom-didactic narratives" (*weisheitliche Lehrerzählungen*). In this group he included Job, Joseph, Tobit, Esther, Dan 1–6, and *Ahiqar*. Although court tales figure prominently in this group, the court setting per se is not critical. These narratives are character-based stories in which the ethical virtues of the main character are critical. They often have exotic locales (Ur, Egypt, Nineveh, Susa, Babylon) and heroes of high status ("the richest man in the east," a vizier of Egypt, the chief purchasing agent for Sennacherib, the queen of Persia, and high-ranking ministers of the Babylonian court). In these stories the virtue of the main character is tested in a moment of decision that puts this protagonist in conflict with authorities (e.g., Tobit's decision to bury the dead, Daniel's decision not to eat the king's food or his resolve to continue to pray to God, his three friends' decision not to bow down to the statue of gold, Joseph's decision not to have sex with Potiphar's wife, Esther's decision to come unannounced before the king), though the test of virtue may not involve acts of disobedience (e.g., Job's decision to respond to loss with words of piety). It is the character's decision to act on their virtue, however, that ultimately leads to the resolution of the conflict and the restoration of a harmonious world. The wisdom-didactic narratives are morally optimistic in their worldview and comedic in their structure: they end with the hero's virtue not only intact but also instrumental in resolving the conflict and securing a world rightly ordered. Indeed, the earliest allusion to the Daniel narratives, in 1 Macc 2:59–60 in Mattathias's speech to his sons, lists Hananiah, Azariah, and Mishael along with Daniel as examples of those who were tested and found faithful. Thus Dan 3 and 6 at least were being read as didactic-wisdom narratives in the late second century B.C.E., when the context of the Maccabean revolt led to a particular interest in the feature of endangerment because of faith.

Genres

Narratives often have affinities with genres that develop subsequent to their composition, such that comparison with later genres can highlight particular features in distinctive ways. Just so, Dan 3 and 6 have frequently been compared with later Jewish and Christian martyr legends, despite the fact that none of the heroes dies in Daniel (see Kuhl; Haag 1989; Kellermann). What is relevant is the similarity between the threat to the heroes from a Gentile king because of a conflict between their faith and the religious edicts of the king, and the willingness of the heroes to die rather than to betray their God (e.g., Eleazar in 2 Macc 6 and the mother and seven sons in 2 Macc 7). Some prefer the designation "confessor legends" rather than "martyr legends" as a generic description, highlighting the way in which narratives feature the testimony of the endangered hero.

Danielic Court Tales: Accommodationist or Resistance Literature?

In 1973 Lee Humphreys wrote a highly influential article that interpreted Esther and Dan 1–6 as stories about a "lifestyle for Diaspora," arguing that these narratives were comedically structured accounts reassuring Diaspora Jews that, despite certain potential problems, they could successfully participate in the structures of empire without compromising their identities as Jews and their worship of the God of Israel. Humphreys's reading of Dan 1–6 was broadly influential and often understood in relation to the ideological self-presentation of the Persian Empire as a multicultural imperium in which all of the peoples happily joined together to support the Great King.

Since the mid-1990s, a different interpretation of the narratives of Dan 1–6 has been argued, one informed by postcolonial studies. From this perspective Humphreys's article has been seen as making too much of a case that the Daniel narratives were accommodationist literature. Instead, it is argued, the Danielic narratives are examples of resistance to imperial claims. Daniel Smith-Christopher (20–21), for example, argues that Humphreys's approach "has tended to overlook [the narratives'] potent sociopolitical power as stories of resistance to cultural and spiritual assimilation of a minority by a dominant foreign power. . . . The perspective of the book of Daniel toward foreign conquerors, even in the first six chapters, is not nearly so benign as is often thought; in fact, it is openly hostile to their authority." Reading through the lens of anticolonialist theorists such as Albert Memmi and Franz Fanon, Smith-Christopher understands Dan 1–6 as unflinching acts of resistance. This view has become much more common in recent years, and variations of it occur in the work of many other scholars (e.g., Kirkpatrick; Valeta). These authors emphasize the ways in which the kings are represented as obtuse, given to irrational rages, easily manipulated, and often subjected to humiliations within the narrative world.

What both Humphreys's and Smith-Christopher's approaches only partially perceive is the complex relationship between imperial and colonized discourse, the phenomenon that Homi Bhabha designated as "hybridity." The discourses both of imperial power and of the subordinated peoples must be worked out in relation to one another. The colonized often make use of intellectual and literary forms developed by the dominant culture but do not simply appropriate them. They hybridize them in an attempt to make space for their own agency, even as these forms may delimit the space of agency. By the same token, the imperial powers seldom have sufficient brute strength to override and ignore the cultures of the subject peoples. More often, they engage them in ways that use the subject people's own symbols for purposes of authorization of the imperium. In doing so, they implicitly acknowledge the limits of their own constructions of reality.

This cultural negotiation is the phenomenon that Wills had already partially noted in his analysis of the moral imagination of the court tales. It is key to understanding the complicated ideological positioning of Dan 1–6. As Jews of the Eastern Diaspora appropriated the court tale genre for their own purposes, they hybridized it in a variety of ways, but rarely in ways that broke its ideological commitment to the court as the place where moral conflicts find just resolution. They added ethnic and religious tensions to the professional tensions already present in the court tale genre. In the case of Dan 1–6 they also strongly theologized the genre, constructing sustained reflections on the nature and relationship of divine and human sovereignty. By doing this the stories contest the claims of power made by imperial rhetoric, asserting a counterclaim that ultimate sovereignty belongs only to the God of the Jews. This is evident not only in the plot lines of the stories, but also as the kings themselves, through their poetic doxologies in chs. 2–4 and 6, confess the power of the God of the Jews. In this way the narratives appear to function as resistance to the ideology of empire. The motif of the king's confession, however, also serves to legitimate the empire's claims to power. These Gentile kings are the ones whom God has chosen to rule "over the kingdom of mortals" (4:17 [14b]), and so their ultimate recognition and praise of God renders them worthy of the honor and rule entrusted to them. Only the sacrilegious Belshazzar is destroyed. The *system* of Gentile imperial rule is ideologically stabilized by showing how it can be consistent with claiming the ultimate sovereignty of the God of the Jews.

It is important to ask, however, whether the doxologies uttered by Nebuchadnezzar and Darius are merely fantasies of the authors of Daniel or if they have some parallel in actual imperial rhetoric. This question pertains to the debate, which cannot be engaged here, as to the authenticity of the decrees of Cyrus recorded in Ezra and 2 Chronicles, with their acknowledgment of "YHWH the God of heaven [who] has given me all the kingdoms of the earth" (2 Chr 36:23). The weight of current scholarly opinion is that the wording, if not the substance, of the decree is the product of Jewish authors (e.g., Blenkinsopp 1988, 74–76; Grabbe 1991, 99–102), though some defend their authenticity (e.g., Williamson xxiii–xxxiii). Although the Persian kings claimed kingship by virtue of the Persian deity Ahura Mazda in their own imperial inscriptions, in Babylon they were represented as authorized by Marduk. The Cyrus Cylinder, an inscription placed in the foundations of the city wall of Babylon shortly after Cyrus's conquest of the city, describes him as chosen by Marduk for kingship over Babylon (*ANET* 315; *COS* 2:315). Similarly, in Egypt Darius I represented himself as authorized by the Egyptian gods (Fried 77–78). A statue of Darius, inscribed with a trilingual text, includes in the hieroglyphic section the claim that Darius is "son of [Re], engendered by Atum, living image of Re, who has placed him on his throne.... Atum ... ordered him to conquer each of the two lands, and the goddess Neith has given him the bow she holds" (Kuhrt 478).

While it is possible that Persian kings extended this practice to the minor peoples of the empire, such as Yehud, there is no evidence outside of the contested passages in Ezra and 2 Chronicles. Nevertheless, one can see how relating the king's rule to the will of the local deity would have served both imperial power and colonized people. Such assertions would give dignity to subject peoples, while at the same time helping to secure imperial rule, since rebellion against the king would be rebellion against the decisions of the people's own deity. Whether such authorization of Persian rule was an imperial practice with respect to the minor peoples or not, the confessions placed in the mouths of the Gentile kings in Dan 1–6 are to be seen neither as merely accommodation nor resistance but as attempts to negotiate the ideological double bind of life under Persian rule.

The one element in the court tales that destabilizes the ideological compromise between an affirmation of YHWH's sovereignty and the reality of Gentile rule, as it is worked out by the plot structure and the royal confessions, is the content of Nebuchadnezzar's dream in Dan 2. The dream symbolizes an eschatological action by God to bring to an end the delegation of divine rule to Gentile powers. The four-kingdoms schema featured in the dream, representing the kingdoms of Babylon, Media, Persia, and Greece, cannot antedate the early Seleucid period. Since it is likely that the narratives of the core of Dan 1–6 were already in existence in the Persian period, presumably the dream content is secondarily inserted or significantly reworked. Its oddity in context is also suggested by the fact that, although the dream foretells the ultimate demise of Nebuchadnezzar's kingdom, along with those following him, he seems delighted with Daniel's interpretation. Whatever dream was originally present in Dan 2 is no longer recoverable, whether it was a version of the statue with a different meaning or an entirely different dream. What is of significance, however, is that the dream as it now stands challenges the compromise that the plot of the Daniel stories had made with Gentile rule. The dream and its interpretation by Daniel acknowledge that YHWH has delegated sovereignty to Gentile rule, a position already articulated in Jer 25:9–11; 27:5–7 and Isa 45:1–8. It goes beyond claims that YHWH would limit the duration of a particular king or dynasty (as, e.g., in Jer 25:12; 27:7) by envisioning the resumption of direct divine rule by YHWH and YHWH's people. The eschatological content and revelatory medium of Dan 2 thus form a bridge to the apocalyptic chapters.

The Apocalyptic Dream Visions: Origins, Genre, and Rhetoric

The book of Daniel is unique in that its apocalypses (chs. 7–12) were developed out of and grafted onto a different genre of literature: the court tale. Although other early apocalypses, such as *1 Enoch* and the first edition of the *Apocalypse of Moses*, assume that readers are familiar with traditions about those seers from Genesis and Deuteronomy, respectively, they have a literary independence from the older accounts. Not so Dan 7–12. Moreover, Daniel is the only apocalyptic seer without a pedigree in the literature that was assuming scriptural status in the Second Temple Period, namely, the Torah, the Prophets, and the Psalms. (The Dan'el of Ezek 14:14, 20; 28:3 is a different figure.) Even Ezra is associated with Torah both in the book of Ezra and in the apocalypse of *4 Ezra*, where he is presented as a second Moses. The unusual literary setting of the Daniel apocalypses as supplements to a cycle of court stories is due to the fact that the narratives provided hospitable ideological ground for the development of apocalyptic revelations through the mantic talents of Daniel and the preoccupation of the narratives with the theme of divine sovereignty.

Historically speaking, in the aftermath of Alexander's death, it was apparently the protracted violence of the wars of the Diadochi that made the symbolic accommodation of Gentile rule no longer seem plausible and thus to require some different response. One response was the redaction of the Danielic tales themselves to incorporate an eschatological element (Nebuchadnezzar's dream). But perhaps it was not seen as sufficient for God to communicate the end of the period of Gentile rule only to a Gentile monarch. In the revelation to Daniel in ch. 7, which has striking similarities with ch. 2, God reveals further secrets about the divine intention to a representative of the Jewish community, Daniel, and more explicitly points to the role of the Jewish people as embodying God's sovereign rule on earth.

If the chronology for the earliest developing stages of the Daniel apocalypse of ch. 7 assumed in this commentary is correct (see discussion above), then the first edition of Dan 7 and the Book of the Watchers in *1 En.* 1–36 were roughly contemporary developments. Although *1 En.* 1–36 is less directly political in its concerns, it has been plausibly suggested that its account of the violence wrought by the giant offspring of the angels and human women alludes to the wars of the Diadochi (Nickelsburg 2001, 63). These two texts would thus have been part of a literary development, likely taking place among the Babylonian Jewish Diaspora, that helped to establish the genre and rhetorical features of the apocalypse shortly after the end of the Persian Empire. Both also were sufficiently successful so that additional compositions were created within their respective literary traditions to address the later Antiochene crisis (the updating of Dan 7; Dan 8–12; *1 En.* 83–90).

Although the genre of apocalypse was subject to considerable variation, its basic elements proved surprisingly durable and provided a template that was appropriated by later writers for hundreds of years. The template of basic features for apocalypses was insightfully analyzed by the Apocalypse Group of the SBL Genres Project and published in *Semeia* 14. The group summarized its analysis in the following definition:

> Apocalypse is a genre of revelatory literature with a narrative framework, in which a revelation is mediated by an otherworldly being to a human recipient, disclosing a transcendent reality which is both temporal, insofar as it envisages eschatological salvation, and spatial, insofar as it involves another, supernatural world. (J. Collins 1979, 9)

The differences between Dan 7–12 and *1 En.* 1–36 were noted by the Apocalypse Group as highlighting a focus on history as revealed through prophecy *ex eventu* (Daniel) and a focus on an otherworldly journey with attention to cosmology (*1 Enoch*). These emphases, however, soon come to be complexly blended in other apocalyptic compositions, including those in the Enochic tradition.

While the literary features of the genre of apocalypse are well analyzed, less has been said about the distinctive rhetoric of apocalyptic (see Newsom 2014b). The apocalypses in Daniel are manifestly persuasive documents in attempting to convince their audience of the truth claims that they make about the intentions of God for the course of history, and especially about the resolution of the Antiochene crisis. To do this, they construct a palpable sense of reality, cause the reader to desire access to that reality, and construct the seer as a figure of authority who mediates that access. They also construct the audience as persons who are like the seer himself in important respects.

In contrast to argumentative forms of rhetoric, the Danielic apocalypses can be described as epiphanic rhetoric. They persuade by disclosing a transcendent reality in vivid terms that make it compelling. Part of this strategy is the use of first-person speech, a feature quite rare in ancient Hebrew prose. Moreover, Daniel's testimony is written down and kept secret (7:1; 12:4), so that the reader has a sense of being the intended audience for Daniel's communication. Vividness is also conveyed by the fact that Daniel not only describes what he sees; he also describes his physical and emotional reactions to the same (7:15, 28; 8:17–18, 27; 10:7–19).

Daniel's revelations generate desire for knowledge not only because they offer to provide the key to the course of political history and to predict the outcome of Antiochus IV Epiphanes' blasphemous persecutions, but also because the source of the revelations is in Daniel's privileged access to heavenly beings and scenes of the divine court, uniting the features of transcendence, hierarchy, and mystery into a rhetoric of the sublime.

The vivid description of the Ancient of Days and the overwhelming fiery strangeness of his throne (7:9–10), using details drawn from Ezekiel's inaugural vision (Ezek 1), creates an experience of the sublime for the readers. A similar sense of sublimity characterizes Daniel's description of and reaction to the angel in Dan 10, where beauty and terror are inextricably mixed.

The way revelation is presented in the book of Daniel is also a part of its rhetorical appeal. The desired knowledge is the key to the course of history and the divine intentions for history, yet this knowledge is figured as inaccessible. Most notably, it is a divine secret that is revealed only to chosen recipients (note the use of the term *rāz*, "mystery," in ch. 2). Even those who receive it are initially baffled and disturbed and require interpretation from someone higher up in the hierarchy of knowledge, as Daniel interprets for Nebuchadnezzar and an angel interprets for Daniel. The use of symbolic visions in chs. 7 and 8 also model knowledge as hidden and requiring decoding, though aspects of the symbols are often left uninterpreted, suggesting the possibility of further hidden dimensions of knowledge. Earlier prophetic texts become oracular phenomena, explicitly in ch. 9 and implicitly in the patterns of intertextual allusion that are prominent in ch. 11. Since many of the symbols and allusions would be grasped by a competent reader, the reader is configured as an insider, one of those empowered by knowledge.

In some instances, however, the knowledge conveyed by the apocalypse poses real conceptual difficulties, as in discerning the figure hidden in the complex coded history in ch. 11 or in grasping the significance of the puzzling numbers in 12:5–12. Numerical patterns of various sorts are an important part of the rhetoric of knowledge: they organize historical phenomena into discernible patterns that do not have their origin in the raw events of history themselves but in an order that transcends history. While the number four that is used prominently in chs. 2 and 7 is a common signifier of totality, other numerical patterns are drawn from ritual/liturgical orders, such as the hermeneutical use of seven as "week, heptad" to draw out hidden meaning from Jeremiah's prophecy of seventy years and to structure the final eschatological period (7:27; 9:27).

The knowledge offered in the apocalypses of Daniel is also figured as desirable through its association with books and scribes. In a culture in which few were literate, books themselves had a mysterious and authoritative status (Niditch 1996, 79; Baynes 58). Daniel, who is represented as a scribe already in the narratives (1:4, 17), consults the books of Jeremiah (9:2) and writes down his own revelatory experiences (7:1; 12:4). Moreover, the revelation is to be kept secret and sealed (8:26; 12:4), so that the reader is configured as one who now has access to secret writings from long ago. Most important, however, are the heavenly books (see Baynes). Three different types of heavenly books are mentioned: the book of deeds that records the acts of the four beasts/kingdoms (7:10); the book of fate in which predestined events of the future are recorded (10:21); and the book of life in which those who are to be granted a beatific afterlife are recorded (12:1).

The Social Location of the Authors of Daniel

The presence of Mesopotamian traditions in the Daniel narratives, the local color of the court settings, and the use of Aramaic laced with Akkadian and Persian terms suggest that the Daniel stories originated in the Eastern Diaspora, in the late Neo-Babylonian and Persian periods. Although a judgment about the provenance of ch. 7 depends on an assessment of its redactional history, the remainder of the apocalypses are intensely focused on the events of the Antiochene crisis of 167–164 B.C.E. and were almost certainly composed in Jerusalem or its vicinity.

One common assumption about the authors of the Daniel narratives is that the authors were themselves somehow connected with court life and that Daniel and his three friends represent the "fantasy selves" of the authors. Although the description of court life as depicted in the narratives is mostly superficial, a few details might suggest knowledge of court practices (see comments on chs. 1 and 5) and other details some familiarity with tropes from Babylonian and Persian literary traditions and inscriptions (see comments on chs. 2–4, 6). The fact that the heroes of the narratives are depicted as learned scribes and counselors makes it plausible that the authors were themselves scribes in the Jewish Diaspora. But is it plausible that such persons would be learned in "the literature and language of the Chaldeans" (1:4)? Or that they would have had positions, however modest, in the imperial bureaucracy (1:5; 2:48–49; 3:12; see Briant, 350–52, on the scarcity of foreigners in the Persian administration)?

These are difficult questions to answer, since very little is known about the lives and conditions of the descendants of the Babylonian exiles who largely comprised the Eastern Diaspora. The biblical accounts of the two exiles of 597 and 586 B.C.E. suggest that the Judeans who were exiled to Babylonia came from the upper classes, that is, royals and nobles, plus skilled artisans. The royal family was settled in Babylon itself, and the documents known as the Weidner tablets record payments in oil and barley to prominent political prisoners, including Jehoiachin, five of his sons, and eight retainers. Beyond the king's small household, however, there is no evidence for other Jewish exiles settled in Babylon proper, though it is highly likely that some were. Most of the exiles were settled in ethnic villages in areas of Babylonia needing redevelopment (Eph'al 81–83). The limited documentary evidence available from the sixth and fifth centuries gives an impression that these Jews and their descendants were largely poor or of modest means (Pearce; Zadok 2002, 55–56). Some were employed as "alphabet scribes" in the Persian army, which implies literacy in Aramaic, though this was a nonelite post, in contrast to cuneiform scribes (Zadok 2002, 56).

The Hebrew Bible itself provides ample evidence for a lively scribal tradition among the exiles and the later Diaspora (the book of Ezekiel, one edition of the book of Jeremiah, Isa 40–66, Esther, and Dan 1–6 itself, at a minimum). Yet the primary evidence for Jewish engagement with Babylonian scribal culture, known as *ṭupšarrūtu*, comes from the pseudepigraphical books of *1 Enoch* and the *Aramaic Levi Document* (4Q213–214), which, like the narratives of Daniel, were composed in Aramaic. The Enochic Astronomical Book (*1 En.* 72–82) reflects some familiarity with the style and contents of Babylonian astronomical/ astrological literature, whereas the Book of the Watchers (*1 En.* 1–36) contains a polemic against the forms of knowledge cultivated by the Babylonian incantation priests known as the *āšipu*—magic, medicine, and divination (Drawnel 58–59). Since the *āšipu* were a hereditary priestly class, Jews would not have been trained in this tradition. There was, however, a separate and lower-ranking class of bilingual scribes who wrote in Aramaic, the *sepīru*. Evidence exists for the interpenetration of Aramaic and Akkadian incantation and exorcistic literature (see Drawnel 59). Although no genealogies are preserved for the *sepīru*, Zadok's analysis of Judean names and occupations in Babylonian and Achaemenid era Mesopotamia concludes that "Judeans were well-represented among this special group of scribes" (Zadok 2002, 56). Thus, while the book of Daniel, along with *1 Enoch* and the *Aramaic Levi Document*, reflects the prestige of Babylonian scribal learning among the non-Babylonian scribes of Mesopotamia, it remains uncertain whether the authors of Daniel might have served in low-ranking posts in Babylonian temple or court institutions.

How one should envision the relationship between the scribes responsible for the Aramaic Daniel narratives and those who composed the Hebrew apocalyptic chapters is also uncertain. Since the profession of scribe was often hereditary, it is possible that the Danielic scribes who composed chs. 8–12 during the Antiochene crisis were descendants of the authors of Dan 1–6, whose families had returned to Judea. In light of the broad popularity of the Danielic narratives and the proliferation of different kinds of texts associated with the figure of Daniel, however, it is more likely that unrelated groups of scribes took up the popular figure for their own purposes. Scribal self-consciousness is even more marked in the apocalypses than in the narratives, with repeated references to books and writing (7:1, 10; 9:2; 10:21; 12:1, 4). Most important, the text refers to the authors and those associated with them as "the wise [*maśkilîm*] among the people," who function as teachers (11:33–35; 12:3, 10). This term is also used in the Qumran literature for an official who had teaching functions within the sectarian community, though there is no indication of a genetic link between the Danielic *maśkîlîm* and the Qumran *maśkîl*.

While scribes did not belong to the wealthiest strata of society, their expertise was a form of social capital that gave them cultural power. The apocalyptic chapters of Daniel not only demonstrate significant interpretive expertise with respect to Jewish Scriptures but also show a detailed knowledge of the political relationships between the Seleucid and Ptolemaic kingdoms (ch. 11). The material in ch. 11 may derive from a Greek source (Rappaport 223–24). These features have suggested that the *maśkîlîm* might have been scribes in the employ of the Seleucid bureaucracy (Redditt; P. Davies 2002, 258). Alternatively, the high priest's administrative staff would also be a place where one might find scribes learned in both religious literature and the political relations of the major powers.

The Historical Context of Daniel 7–12

The Danielic apocalypses of chs. 8–12 and the final form of ch. 7 respond from the midst of one of the most traumatic events in Jewish history, the violent persecutions of Jews by Antiochus IV and the beginning of the revolt against Antiochus by Judah the Maccabee. While detailed notes about particular aspects of this history relevant to understanding Dan 7–12 are discussed more fully in the commentary itself, an overview of the historical context is provided here for general orientation.

Although no historical account of the surrender of Jerusalem to Alexander exists, a legendary account in Josephus (*Ant.* 11.326–39) concerning the meeting of the high priest with Alexander suggests that this transition to Greek rule was handled peacefully. When Alexander's generals divided his kingdom after his death in 323 B.C.E., however, a period of turmoil arose. A treaty by the victorious generals in 301 awarded Syria-Palestine (known in Greek as Coele-Syria) to Seleucus I, who also ruled Mesopotamia and lands to the east. However, Coele-Syria was already occupied by the armies of Ptolemy I, the general who had established his kingdom in Egypt. He claimed it as his own "spear-won" land and refused to relinquish it to Seleucus. Over the next century a series of five wars would be fought between these two kingdoms over the control of this area. During most of these wars Judea and Jerusalem were not directly involved in the fighting. Only in the fifth Syrian war was Jerusalem a site of armed struggle in 201–200.

During the Ptolemaic period, Jews largely handled their own internal affairs. The high priest was not only the religious but also the political leader of the nation and conducted relationships with the Ptolemaic overlords, including the collection and payment of taxes. A small group of aristocratic families played various roles in the governance of the temple and the city of Jerusalem. The three best-documented families are the Oniads (the high-priestly family), the Tobiads of Transjordan, and the Sanballats, the family of Samaria's governor. These families often intermarried but at times were bitter rivals. Although this rivalry was a major factor in the events that led up to the Antiochene crisis in 167, it had its roots in conflicts in the third century concerning the authority for collecting taxes.

The Ptolemaic system of taxation, often referred to as "tax farming," authorized a local official to collect and pay the taxes required by the Ptolemaic government; any extra taxes collected were kept by the local official. The opportunities for abuse by the tax farmer are obvious. Although the high priest was initially the tax farmer for Judea, a dispute with Ptolemaic officials allowed a member of the Tobiad family, Joseph, to displace the high priest Onias II as the authorized tax farmer.

During the period of Ptolemaic rule, Judean aristocratic families had incentives to become conversant with aspects of Greek culture, mostly in order to take advantage of the economic opportunities offered by the new regime. To varying degrees they would have been educated in Greek as well as Jewish culture. Moreover, the Ptolemaic bureaucracy in Coele-Syria as well as the aristocratic families involved in governance and trade would have needed trilingual expertise (Greek, Aram., Heb.). Documentary evidence exists that the Tobiad family employed scribes competent in Greek by the middle of the third century B.C.E. (Hayes and Mandel 36). Josephus (*Ant.* 12.160–85, 196–219) depicts Joseph the Tobiad and his sons as at home in the sophisticated court circles of Ptolemaic Alexandria.

While some families like the Tobiads ingratiated themselves with the Ptolemaic powers, loyalty was based on a keen sense of who was likely to retain power. Thus pro- and anti-Ptolemaic and Seleucid factions among the Jews were undoubtedly highly fluid, based on which side was likely to be or become the overlord of Judea. During the fifth Syrian war the authorities in Jerusalem threw their support behind Antiochus III, supplying his troops with provisions. As things turned out, this was a good bet, and once the war concluded in 198 B.C.E., Antiochus III offered important rebuilding support and tax concessions to Jerusalem, along with assurances that the Jews could continue to conduct their internal affairs according to their own traditions and customs (Josephus, *Ant.* 12.138–44). The text of the decree contains such specific knowledge of Jewish customs that it was undoubtedly drafted with the help of Jewish temple scribes.

The period of Seleucid rule over Judea and Jerusalem thus got off to a good start, at least from the perspective of Jerusalem's aristocracy, who would have benefited most from the tax concessions. Hellenistic kingdoms were perennially short of money, however, and the difficult economic situation of the

Seleucid kingdom may have been exacerbated by heavy indemnities imposed on it by Rome, which checked Syrian aggression into Asia Minor in 189 at the battle of Magnesia. Whatever the reasons, the Seleucid government was always eager to extract wealth from its possessions. Since in antiquity temples often served as banking institutions as well as religious establishments, central governmental appropriation of provincial funds often involved religious trespass, robbing temples, whether carried out violently or by means of legal policy. The first documented instance of such conflict between the Seleucid state and Jerusalem occurred sometime between 178 and 175 B.C.E., when a high-ranking Seleucid minister, Heliodorus, was dispatched to implement new policies concerning temple administration that at least some Jerusalemites saw as constituting an assault on the temple (Portier-Young 78–91). As one would expect, Seleucid policy also was enmeshed with local politics, with some Jews collaborating with the Seleucids and some denouncing the policy. A highly colored account of this episode, which lays the blame primarily at the feet of a devious Jewish aristocrat, Simon, is preserved in 2 Macc 3. This same Simon attempted to blame the high priest, Onias III, for the situation. Onias went to Antioch to plead his case with the monarch, Seleucus IV.

Turbulent internal politics in Jerusalem intertwined with equally turbulent events in the Seleucid capital. In 175 B.C.E. the assassination of Seleucus IV was apparently masterminded by Heliodorus. Antiochus IV, a younger brother of Seleucus IV, quickly usurped the throne, outmaneuvering his surviving brother, Demetrius. He then married his sister-in-law, the widow of Seleucus IV, and eventually executed his nephew, the son of Seleucus IV, who was the legitimate heir. Before Onias III could make his case, Onias's brother Jason, who was serving as the caretaker high priest in Jerusalem, approached Antiochus IV with a proposal, sweetened by a monetary incentive, that he be appointed high priest in place of Onias III (2 Macc 4). For an additional fee Jason asked for permission to reconstitute Jerusalem legally as a Greek city, a *polis*, with the Greek institutions of the *gymnasion* and *ephēbeion*, which educated young men for the city. Although 2 Maccabees, our primary source of information, expresses disapproval, it also provides evidence that these innovations were enthusiastically greeted by the upper classes of Jerusalem, including the priesthood. Hellenism per se was not seen as religiously problematic by the Jewish establishment, though they did find ways around aspects of participation in Hellenistic culture that seemed to conflict with their monotheistic beliefs (2 Macc 4:18–20). Indeed, a visit by Antiochus IV to Jerusalem in 172 B.C.E. was greeted with a torchlight parade and cheers, though these were undoubtedly staged by the aristocratic families who sought to benefit from the greater incorporation of Jerusalem into the Greek system.

How events went from this mutual accommodation to persecution and rebellion (or rebellion and persecution) in five short years is a thorny historical problem. Rival theories abound. What is clear, however, is that the events were precipitated by a collision of Seleucid/Ptolemaic conflict and by internal conflicts among the rival aristocratic families of Jerusalem, with the latter probably being the more volatile element. Three years after Jason bought his high priesthood, a rival from a non-Oniad priestly family approached Antiochus IV with an offer to buy the high priesthood at a substantially higher price. This was Menelaus, who was, according to 2 Maccabees, none other than the brother of the Simon who attempted to subvert Onias III in the affair of Heliodorus (4:23–24; cf. ch. 3). He was apparently supported by elements of the Tobiad family, who had been prominent since the Ptolemaic period. Menelaus succeeded, but the result was a civil war with the supporters of Jason. Jason's followers were overcome, and Jason himself fled to Transjordan, where he took refuge with Hyrcanus, one of the Tobiad family who was at odds with his brothers. Moreover, in order to pay the sum he promised to Antiochus IV, Menelaus stole golden treasures from the temple (4:25–32). This action aroused riots in Jerusalem (4:39–42). By means of ample bribes paid to high Seleucid officials, Menelaus survived the debacle (4:43–50).

While this unstable situation in Jerusalem was developing, Antiochus IV began his invasion of Egypt. A rumor came to Judea that Antiochus had died, prompting Jason to attempt a countercoup against Menelaus in 169 (2 Macc 5:5). Although the coup failed, it apparently enraged Antiochus, who considered the province to be in revolt (5:11). On his way back from Egypt, he savaged Jerusalem and plundered the temple. Probably this was the turning point in Jewish disaffection, though the worst was yet to come.

The historical sources are so obscure and contradictory that historians are in conflict as to how to best reconstruct the events of the next two years. It is clear that Antiochus staged a second invasion of Egypt in 168, where his inconclusive campaign was brought to an end by Roman intervention. The book of Daniel suggests that he was so angered by this humiliation that he again savaged Jerusalem, desecrated the temple, and instituted the persecution of Jewish religious observances (11:30–31). There are, however, reasons to doubt that Antiochus was so dissatisfied by the outcome of events (see comments on Dan 11). Moreover, 1 Maccabees dates the events of the persecution almost a year later, in 167. So did Antiochus IV begin his persecution of Judaism in 168 or 167? Good arguments can be made for either chronology, though the position of this commentary is to see the persecutions as beginning in 167. If so, then there is something of a gap. We simply do not know what was going on in Jerusalem between mid-168 and mid-167. Although it is possible that Antiochus's punitive actions (desecration of the temple, prohibition of Jewish religious customs, and so forth) may simply have been a reaction to Jason's attempted countercoup, it is also possible that there was active rebellion after Jason fled and that this was what prompted Antiochus's further repressions.

The Historical Context of Daniel 7–12

Whatever the cause, Antiochus IV's reactions seem to indicate that he considered Judea to be in rebellion and that something about Judea's religion was critical to the causes of the rebellion. Persecution for religious reasons was basically unknown in Hellenistic culture. The extreme oddity of Antiochus's response—attacking temple practices and religious observance—has given rise to theories that the architects of the persecution must have been hellenizing Jews, who foregrounded divisive religious observances as "the problem" (so Bickerman 1979, 83–88, and so 1 Macc 1 seems to suggest). The specificity of the nature of the persecution gives some credence to this theory, but it is probably not the whole story. Others have suggested that the socioeconomic dynamics of the Hellenistic kingdoms exacerbated class tensions between the aristocracy and their retainers and the rest of the Jewish population (so Tcherikover, 151), and that one should look for economic and class-based reasons for the rebellion, which expressed itself through religious symbols. There is much to be said for this analysis also. One should recognize, however, that both Bickerman and Tcherikover were European Jews of the twentieth century who read the ancient sources through the lens of the persecution of the Jews in Europe, in both Nazi Germany and czarist and Soviet Russia. These perspectives may have sharpened their vision but also skewed it to some degree. Thus their theories should be used with some caution.

In the end, our ancient sources do not allow us to understand fully why events developed as they did or how the participants understood their causes. It is clear, however, that the authors of the book of Daniel would not have agreed with either Bickerman or Tcherikover about the origins of the conflict. For the authors of Daniel, the conflict was rooted in the anomaly of divine devolution of earthly sovereignty to Gentile kings (Dan 2, 7). While this was, for whatever undisclosed reason, God's intention for a period of time, that delegated sovereignty had been abused by the Hellenistic kings. And when that abuse had become unendurable, as it was in the actions of the current Seleucid rulers, God would act to take back sovereignty. For the authors of Daniel, the profanation of the temple is the only act that matters and that provokes God to action.

The historical moment of the apocalyptic chapters of Daniel is poised after these awful events but apparently just before Judah the Maccabee's reconquest and rededication of the temple in December 164. In that same year and perhaps at nearly that same time, Antiochus IV died, an event hopefully predicted by Daniel (11:40–45). It is clear, however, that the author of Dan 11 did not yet know of these events. The emotional and theological tension between expectation and ultimate disappointment is framed in ch. 12, which presumably knows of these historical events but does not find them to be satisfying. The author(s) of the book had expected the defeat of Antiochus IV to usher in the eschatological end of history. But that did not happen. The insertions into the final chapter of the book (12:5–12) recalculate the expected times so as to push them just barely into the future. As one read these verses, one feels as though one is reading successive editions of newspapers updating breaking events. But the final predicted event failed to happen.

So how is it that the book that so spectacularly failed to predict an eschatological culmination of history continued to have meaning for readers who were not contemporary with the events in which it was written? That is not easy to say, though probably it had to do with the rhetoric of "mystery" established in ch. 2 and developed in the apocalyptic chs. 7–12. These chapters tease the reader with the sense that historical events have a hidden pattern that only the adept can discern, though clues to this mystery are hidden in Scripture and in revelations to favored experts. This fundamental "tease" ensured the book's longevity. Readers who were persuaded that its revelations could not be false, since they were derived from the "book of truth," had to assume that their failure to be implemented in historical events lay not in their falsity but in the inability of interpreters to understand the referents of their symbols. Hence arose the millennia-long tradition of interpreting Dan 7–12 in relation to the current events of the interpreter. In this way Daniel has become a prophet for all ages.

History of Daniel's Reception, by Brennan W. Breed

Benjamin of Tudela, a Jewish world traveler who provided fascinating and detailed accounts of medieval Asia and Africa, stumbled upon a literal struggle over the legacy of Daniel when he visited the Persian city of Susa in about 1160 C.E. According to Benjamin, a river divided a community of wealthy diasporic Jews from a community of poor diasporic Jews. On the side of the wealthy Jews, along with the marketplaces full of luxurious goods for sale, was the sepulcher of the biblical Daniel. Though chapter 10 depicts Daniel on the banks of the Tigris River (10:4), Susa is the last city mentioned as a home to Daniel in the biblical book (8:2), and since at least the first century C.E., some Jewish writers have believed that it holds the tomb of Daniel (Josephus, *Ant.* 10.269–72). Eventually, some of the poorer Jews of Susa began to suspect that Daniel's proximity was responsible for their neighbors' wealth. So they asked that Daniel's tomb be relocated to their side of the river. Unsurprisingly, the wealthy neighborhood declined the request, and hostilities ensued. As Benjamin narrates:

> So war prevailed between them for many days, and no one went forth or came in on account of the great strife between them. At length both parties growing tired of this state of things took a wise view of the matter, and made a compact, namely the coffin of Daniel be taken for one year to the one side and for another year to the other side. This they did, and both sides became rich. (Benjamin 52)

There is something to be learned from this story: Daniel's legacy is indeed an enrichment to those who struggle for it. Nevertheless, these communities were missing something important. Like the Jewish communities of Susa, many inheritors of the traditions embodied in the Jewish Scriptures, including Christians, Muslims, and many others, assume that the legacy of Daniel is a singular thing that can only belong to one owner at a time. It must be wrested from some other community's hands if it is to enrich one's own community. And perhaps the only way to share Daniel is to let him go for a certain amount of time and then demand him back.

For many readers of biblical texts, this is the point of biblical criticism: to find out whose interpretation of Daniel is the right one, and therefore who is wrong. Seen from this perspective, the history of the Bible's "reception"—that is, the history of all the readings, uses, and influence of the Bible throughout history—is useful only insofar as it addresses the question of what the Bible really means. But this is finally an unhelpful way of thinking about the Bible *and* reception. Biblical texts, including the book of Daniel, were all composed, edited, and updated over a long period of time and by various communities. By the time the book of Daniel existed in a version recognizable to modern readers, it had passed through the hands of Jewish scribes in the Persian Diaspora, later scribes on the brink of the Hellenistic incursion, and still later scribes living in Jerusalem during the oppression of Antiochus IV. It is quite likely that these various groups who together wrote and rewrote the book of Daniel, separated by many miles and hundreds of years in time, did not understand the text in exactly the same way. The first "complete" version of the book of Daniel already contained within itself a tension about what this biblical text really means—as evidenced in the vast difference between the court stories in chs. 1–6 and the apocalyptic texts in chs. 7–12. Fighting over Daniel's bones, or even just agreeing to pass them back and forth every now and then to avoid fisticuffs, is not the best interpretive strategy.

But Benjamin of Tudela recounts another chapter of the tale that offers an alternative mode of appropriating Daniel's legacy:

> When this great Emperor Sinjar, king of Persia, saw that they took the coffin of Daniel from one side of the river to the other, and that a great multitude of Jews, Mohammedans and Gentiles, and many people from the country were crossing the bridge, . . . he said, "It is not meet to do this ignominy unto Daniel the prophet, but I command you to measure the bridge from both sides, and to take the coffin of Daniel and place it inside another coffin of crystal, so that the wooden coffin be within that of crystal, and to suspend this from the middle of the bridge by a chain of iron; at this spot you must build a synagogue for all comers, so that whoever wishes to pray there, be he Jew or Gentile, may do so." And to this very day the coffin is suspended from the bridge. (Benjamin 53)

Emperor Sinjar argues that it is disrespectful to disturb Daniel's bones every year. He orders the various communities to split the difference and keep Daniel in the middle ground, suspended in the middle of the bridge between them. And at that spot, Sinjar commands an interfaith place of prayer to be built "for all comers." This ending appeals to those with postmodern sensibilities: all must share Daniel equally, and as such he exists in a noncommittal space that is property of no particular group. We can all approach and reverently remember Daniel, paying homage to his legacy in the space of many others who pay homage in their own ways.

But there is a problem with this construal of Daniel's legacy, too: Daniel hangs above a bridge upon which no one lives, inhabiting an interstitial space that is at once accessible but also uninhabitable to all others. Sinjar's power allowed him to wrest Daniel from communities who treasured him in their own particular ways and place him in a sanitized and impersonal space simply designed to reduce friction. Some interpreters of the Bible likewise seek out this space of reverence and sharing: reception history can simply become a place to try to understand and connect with a diverse group of communities over time, and one can witness a variety of Daniels; this supposedly demonstrates that all readers share Daniel in their own way. One might even go so far as to claim that all interpretations and uses of Daniel are good ones, and that all should strive to share Daniel equally with all other readers. Some interpreters hold this belief for ethically defensible reasons—it does, in fact, often reduce strife—but it likely does so at the expense of honesty. Everyone does not share the same Daniel.

Not everyone shares the same book of Daniel, either: even in the late Second Temple period, the book of Daniel existed in a variety of forms. A number of different versions of the book of Daniel existed at the time of the Dead Sea Scrolls, and these different books of Daniel continue to exist today. Some communities read the stories of Susanna and the Elders and Bel and the Dragon as integral parts of the book, and other communities see them as extracanonical additions. Yet Dan 7–12 is an addition to an earlier core of Danielic court stories that one finds in chs. 2–6, so an addition after chs. 7–12 were composed is merely one more step in a long process of composition. Where does the book of Daniel end? What is the correct version of the book? There are no objective, universally valid, uncommitted answers to this question. Different religious communities have made decisions on this matter, but these decisions are not binding for those outside of each community. There is no uninhabited space suspended in the middle of a bridge from which to read and interpret the book of Daniel. Any construal of the text demands that the reader pick a place.

Yet the story of Daniel's resting place in Susa is not exhausted by Benjamin of Tudela's travelogue. Muḥammad Abūʾl-Qāsim Ibn Ḥawqal, a tenth-century-C.E. Muslim chronicler, tells another conflicting version of the story of Daniel's bones (Rosenmüller 318). Several Muslim chroniclers relate that the companion of Muhammad and military commander Abu Musa al-Ashʿari found the hidden tomb of Daniel in Susa in 638 C.E. The townspeople prized Daniel's remains because they brought rains whenever they were consulted during a drought. Upon learning of the story of Daniel, Abu Musa consulted with Ali, cousin of Muhammad, who told Abu Musa to remove the bones of Daniel "to some place where the people of Susa could no longer enjoy the possession of" them (Rosenmüller 314). As Ibn Ḥawqal tells it, Abu Musa reburied Daniel in a riverbed "so that it could not be viewed. A bay or gulf of the river came over this grave, which may be seen by anyone who dives to the bottom of the water" (Rosenmüller 318).

This is an arresting image: Daniel's body is buried under the running water, slowly dispersing itself within the Karkheh River, feeding into the Tigris and then the Persian Gulf, eventually flowing into the Indian Ocean and throughout the world. Daniel is made available to those who will dive to the bottom of the water—those who are not struggling with each other to claim him so much as struggling with the current long enough to see him in his discontinuous pieces. Daniel is neither trapped in a particular community nor sequestered in a universally accessible yet uninhabitable space. Rather, Daniel circulates around the globe, at home everywhere and always moving on to somewhere else.

A series of Muslim legends also recount stories of Daniel recovering a book of primordial wisdom, perhaps even the book that bears his name, that falls into the sea. The tale of the "Queen of the Serpents," found in the complex *One Thousand and One Nights* tradition, contains a story about an extremely wise and prolific Greek sage named Daniel, who lived through a shipwreck that destroyed all his work save five parchment pages full of esoteric wisdom, which he bequeathed to his foolish son, Hasib (Gibb 431). In 1430 C.E. Musa, an Ottoman poet, wrote a *mesnevi* (a series of rhyming couplets) titled *Jamasp-Name*, or the *Book of Jamasp*, which retells this story (Gibb 432–33). Musa draws from the Persian tradition that of the ancient sage-king Jamasp, who "possessed knowledge of the stars and made correct predictions about them," and from the subsequent tradition that Jamasp was the biblical prophet Daniel's son (Kohlberg 374). In Musa's story, the prophet Daniel has a book that prescribes effective remedies against every illness, including death. The recipe for the tonic of immortality features herbs that grow on the far side of the Oxus River, which Daniel crosses in hopes of completing his batch. But God dispatches Gabriel to thwart Daniel's progress, and Gabriel confronts Daniel on the bridge over the Oxus. Gabriel, disguised as a fellow traveler, asks Daniel if he has a book of magic medicines; Daniel naively admits this and displays it, allowing Gabriel to throw the book into the river. Daniel can only recover a few leaves of the text, which he passes on to his child, named Jamasp, who is the protagonist of a lengthy story that follows. In a sixteenth-century Ottoman miniature that illuminates this story of Jamasp, one sees Gabriel arresting Daniel's progress on the narrow bridge, inquiring about the status of the magical book, while a fish jumping out of the river foreshadows the fate of Daniel's book (see fig. 1).

Figure 1. A sixteenth-century C.E. Ottoman miniature depicting the angel Gabriel confronting Daniel on the bridge over the Oxus River. © The British Library Board (Add 24962. F. 11v).

In these legends, the waters both preserve the text for all eternity and separate it from any fixed location or community. This image provides the metaphor for the approach to reception history followed in this commentary. Instead of arguing over the identity of the real or true Daniel, or agreeing to share him in harmony by finding common ground between variant traditions, this history of reception will trace the very different ways in which Daniel has traveled through the flux of time and space and allow them to coexist in their irreconcilable particularities. Daniel's legacy is incredibly complex. Susa is not Daniel's only traditional burial spot: some claim he died elsewhere in Persia, others that he died in Babylon, or Kirkuk, or Muqdadiyah, or Samarkand, or back in Judah. Daniel has always been, and will always be, a field of discontinuous trajectories filled with uncounted capacities and potentials. Daniel will forever continue to circulate, regardless of attempts to hem him in. In the reception-historical segments that follow, the guiding question is not "What has the book of Daniel meant?" but rather "What can the book of Daniel do?"

COMMENTARY

Daniel 1–6
Exiled Jews and Gentile Kings: Lessons in Knowledge and Power

Daniel 1–6 is unified by the characters of Daniel and his three friends. They are introduced as prisoners brought to Babylon by King Nebuchadnezzar, who selects them to be trained for royal court service. The three friends figure prominently only in ch. 3, so it is primarily the figure of Daniel himself who unifies chs. 1–6. While one can certainly read these narratives in light of the challenges posed to the Jewish characters—and that has primarily been how the history of reception has read these stories—a good case can be made that the true focus is on the figure of the Gentile king. The drama of the stories can be grasped in terms of whether and how the Gentile king will recognize the true nature of eternal divine sovereignty and the actual source of his own, delegated sovereignty. Daniel and his friends enter the various kings' courts ostensibly as prisoners who are granted special training so that they may become courtiers and administrative officials. But their most significant role is to be conduits of the power of the Jewish God—the "God of Heaven," the "Most High." The encounter between the power of the Most High and of the Gentile kings will establish that it is actually the God of the Jews who is in control of history and who delegates and eventually takes back sovereignty over the earth. How the Gentile kings learn this lesson is the burden of each of the narratives.

Daniel 1:1–4:37 (34) The Education of King Nebuchadnezzar

Although the earliest collection of Danielic narratives may have had different emphases (see the introduction), in the form of the book as it appears in the MT the first four chapters form a kind of *Bildungsroman* for Nebuchadnezzar, a story of his "education." Thus ch. 1 presents him as a character who thinks he is the prime agent in history. But the style and plot of the story show the reader that it actually is God who gives him his victories. Indeed, though he does not realize it, even the superiority that Nebuchadnezzar recognizes in the young Jewish sages is not the result of his own mandated program for them but rather is the effect of God's actions.

In ch. 2 Nebuchadnezzar's sense of control is abruptly disturbed by a dream, which can be understood as a communication from a divine power. Issues of sovereignty are complexly configured in this chapter. In contrast to the failure of the Babylonian sages, the Jewish Daniel is able to recount and interpret the king's dream because of the power of his God, who is confessed by Nebuchadnezzar to be a "revealer of mysteries." In the dream itself, Nebuchadnezzar's own sovereignty over all the earth is affirmed. But it is contextualized in an account of future events that describes the transfer of sovereignty from one Gentile kingdom to another until the fourth kingdom (that of the Greeks) acts with unprecedented violence. At that point the Most High intervenes to bring to an end the succession of Gentile sovereignties, and God's own sovereignty manifests itself on earth. Nebuchadnezzar's response to Daniel's interpretation of the dream seems to suggest that he grasps the implications of the fact that Daniel's God is "Lord of kings." But the following stories will suggest that he has not yet fully understood.

Although ch. 3 may originally have been independent from ch. 2, the redactor's coordination of the two accounts encourages readers to see Nebuchadnezzar's erecting of an "image of gold" as his response to having been identified as the "head of gold" on the imposing statue of his dream in ch. 2. If so, he has not grasped the message of that dream. The plot of the story explicitly sets up a conflict between the sovereign power of the king, who demands obeisance to the image he has set up, and the sovereign power of the God of the Jews, who implicitly forbids such obeisance. The utter frustration of the king's attempt to burn up the Jews in a fiery furnace is a metaphorical rendering of the impotence of his sovereign command versus the sovereignty of the Most High God. Once again, Nebuchadnezzar seems to grasp the meaning of the encounter in acknowledging the God who saved those who "disregarded the word of the king." But his further action in attempting to use his own power to protect this God from the indignity of blasphemy suggests that he may not have truly understood the relations of power.

Chapter 4 differs from the rest in being narrated in the first person by Nebuchadnezzar. His full-throated confession of the Most High God in the opening verses suggests that what he is about to relate will explain his final transformation from someone who did not fully grasp the implications of divine sovereignty to someone who does. The story that Nebuchadnezzar tells is one of his own humiliation, transformation, and restoration. Because this is not only a story of inappropriate hubris but also a story of God's ultimate control of the world powers and their dominion, it is vital that Nebuchadnezzar be presented

Agency, Knowledge, and Power

as a king whose dominance extends over the whole earth. Though he undergoes temporary displacement from his kingship, what changes at the end is not his status but his understanding of his status. Once he realizes that the Most High is the source of his kingship, then even greater glory is added to him. For the time in which the Most High chooses to exercise sovereignty through delegation to Gentile monarchs, their honor and glory, if exercised in humility and pious awareness, is worthy of great glory. Only when they think that they themselves are the authors of their own glory—or that their own gods are—do they become objects of punitive judgment.

Daniel 1 Agency, Knowledge, and Power

1 In the third year of the reign of Jehoiakim, king of Judah, Nebuchadnezzar,[a] king of Babylon, came to Jerusalem and besieged it. 2 And the Lord[b] gave Jehoiakim, king of Judah, into his power, along with some of the vessels of the house of God, and he brought them[c] to the land of Shinar,[d] to the house of his god;[e] the vessels he brought to the treasury of the house of his god. 3 The king commanded his head of staff, Ashpenaz,[f] to bring some of the Israelites, specifically from the royal family and the nobles,[g] 4 young men in whom there was no defect, attractive in appearance, proficient in every form of wisdom, knowledgeable and perceptive, and who were capable of serving in the king's palace—and to teach them the literature and language of the Chaldeans. 5 And the king assigned them a daily allotment from the king's portion[h] and from the wine that he drank. They were to be educated[i] for three years, after which[j] they would enter the king's service.

6 Among them, from the tribe of Judah, were Daniel, Hananiah, Mishael, and Azariah. 7 The head of staff decided on names[k] for them. For Daniel he decided on "Belteshazzar"; for Hananiah, "Shadrach"; for Mishael, "Meshach"; and for Azariah, "Abednego." 8 Daniel decided in his mind that he would not defile himself with the king's portion or with the wine that he drank, so he sought permission from the head of staff that he not have to defile himself. 9 And God caused Daniel to receive favor and sympathy from the head of staff. 10 The head of staff said to Daniel, "I am afraid of my lord the king, who has assigned your food and drink. Otherwise, he will see you looking haggard compared with the young men who are in your group, and then you will have made me liable to the king."[l]

11 So Daniel said to the supervisor,[m] whom the head of staff had appointed over Daniel, Hananiah, Mishael, and Azariah, 12 "Test your servants for ten days and let us be given vegetables[n] to eat and water to drink. 13 Then let our appearance and the appearance of the young men

who eat the king's portion be examined by you, and deal with your servants according to what you observe." 14 He listened to them with respect to this matter and tested them for ten days. 15 At the end of ten days it was observed that their appearance was better and plumper than all the young men who had been eating the king's rations. 16 So the supervisor continued to take their portion and the wine they were to drink and would give them vegetables instead. 17 And to these young men, the four of them, God gave knowledge and proficiency in all literature and wisdom; and Daniel understood every sort of vision and dreams.

18 At the end of the period that the king had set for them to be brought in, the head of staff brought them into the presence of Nebuchadnezzar. 19 And when the king spoke with them, none of them was found to be like Daniel, Hananiah, Mishael, and Azariah; so they entered the king's service.[o] 20 In every matter requiring insightful wisdom[p] concerning which the king inquired of them, he found them ten times better than all the mantic experts[q] and exorcists[r] in his whole kingdom. The king honored them and showed them the affairs in his whole kingdom.[s] 21 And Daniel was there until the first year of Cyrus the king.

a. *Nebuchadnezzar*. In Akkadian the Neo-Babylonian king's name is *Nabû-kudduri-uṣur*, meaning "Nabu has protected the son who will inherit" (Stamm 43). In the MT the more accurate spelling Nebuchadrezzar occurs in Ezekiel and all but six instances in Jeremiah. In other books the form Nebuchadnezzar reflects dissimilation of *r* to *n* (Koch 1).

b. Heb. *ʾădōnāy*. Except in the prayer in ch. 9, Daniel otherwise always uses *hā-ʾĕlōhîm* for God. A few MSS read *yhwy* in 1:2, which may well be original.

c. *waybîʾēm*. OG, Th, and Vg translate the suffix as a neuter, indicating that the phrase refers to the vessels, not to Jehoiakim as well as the vessels, but this interpretation is contextually unlikely.

d. *Šinʿār*. A relatively rare term for Babylon(ia) in the MT. Most of the contexts carry negative connotations (e.g., Gen 10:10; 11:2; 14:1, 9; Zech 5:11), though it is also mentioned as one of the places from which the remnant of the people will return to the land (Isa 11:11). The word probably derives either from Akk. *Šanḫara*, originally the name of a region in Syria, or from *Samḫarû*, a Kassite tribe in Babylonia in the mid-second millennium. See *HALOT* 1607; Zadok 1984b.

e. *bêt ʾĕlōhāyw*. This phrase is missing in the OG but could represent the translator's attempt to reduce redundancy. MT itself may be the result of the combination of two alternative readings: "and he brought them to Shinar to the house of his god" and "the vessels he brought to the treasury of the house of his god."

f. *ʾašpĕnaz rab sārîsāyw*. The word *ʾašpĕnaz* derives from Old Persian *ašpinja*, having to do with hospitality and accommodations (Koch 2–3); as a title for a court official, it designates someone in charge of household arrangements (Lipiński 238). Apparently this meaning had become obscure for the tradents of Dan 1, who appear to take it as a personal name (so also the versions; Montgomery 124). The following phrase, *rab*

Agency, Knowledge, and Power 37

sārîsāyw, serves as a clarifying gloss. That expression ultimately derives from Akk. *ša rēši*, "the one at the head" (cf. 1 Kgs 22:9; 2 Kgs 18:17; 23:11). It later develops the nuance of "eunuch" (Isa 56:3; Esth 1:10; etc.), though it continues to designate a high official in the court bureaucracy, without regard to sexual status.

g. While it is possible to read the phrase as identifying three categories ("Israelites and members of the royal family and nobles"; so Stone), the sequence rather suggests that "Israelites" is a comprehensive term, with the latter phrases specifying which kinds of Israelites (so Montgomery 125; Goldingay 5; Koch 3). "Nobles" (*partĕmîm*) derives from the Old Persian *fratama* ("noble"), designating persons of high rank (Lipiński 236–37; Koch 3–4).

h. *pat-bag*. Derived from Old Persian *patibaga*, "portion." The Greek derivative *potibazis* refers to honorific gifts from the royal table (Montgomery 127). Hebrew tradition divides the word to reflect a popular etymology that related the word to Heb. *pat*, "piece, fragment" of food.

i. *ûlĕgaddĕlām*. The infinitive with lamed is parallel to *lĕhābîʾ* in v. 3 and *ûlălammĕdām* in v. 4, all of which depend on the initial *wayyōʾmer* in v. 3. Verse 5b is grammatically intrusive and may be taken as a narrative aside or arguably as a redactional seam.

j. *ûmiqṣātām*. Depending on whether one takes the suffix to refer to "years" (3rd masc. suf. with 3rd fem. pl. antecedent; GKC 135o) or to the young men being trained, the phrase may be a temporal expression ("after which") or a statement about selection ("and some of them"). The reference to the three-year training period in v. 5 supports the former alternative. The phrasing of v. 19, which focuses on the selection of Daniel and his friends, supports the latter.

k. *wayyāśem lāhem . . . šēmôt*. An uncommon expression for naming (Judg 8:31; 2 Kgs 17:34; Neh 9:7). With the exception of Judg 8:31, it refers to the giving of a replacement name. The translation chosen here tries to capture both the deliberateness of the act of renaming and the wordplay between vv. 7 and 8.

l. Lit., "made my head liable to the king," though not necessarily implying a capital offense, as OG and S interpret the phrase.

m. *melṣar*. Probably derived from Akk. *manṣāru/maṣṣāru*, "watcher," "guard" (*CAD* 10/1:341). OG reads "*Abiesdri*, the chief eunuch who had been appointed over Daniel," assuming that the *melṣar* is the same official as in v. 3.

n. *zērōʿîm* (in v. 16 *zērʿōnîm*, though 4QDan^a has *zērōʿîm*). Whether the word means "vegetables" in general or "seeds" is uncertain (see Montgomery 135; Koch 8–9).

o. Lit., "and they stood before the king."

p. Instead of the common word pair *ḥokmâ ûbînâ* (reflected by G and Vg), MT preserves the unusual construct phrase *ḥokmat bînâ*, which is to be preferred as the more difficult reading (Plöger 37; Koch 10).

q. *ḥarṭummîm*. A word ultimately deriving from Egyptian *ḥr.tp*, originally a lector priest without mantic functions (Gardiner 1:56). The word was taken into Akkadian as *ḥarṭibi*, used to designate some kind of Egyptian mantic expert, usually identified as "dream interpreter," who served in the Mesopotamian courts in the Assyrian period and presumably later (*CAD* 6:116; Oppenheim 2008, 238). In biblical texts *ḥarṭummîm* are presented as magicians (Exod 7:11, 22; 8:7, 18–19 [8:3, 14–15 MT]; 9:11) or as dream interpreters (Gen 41:8, 24; Dan 2:2).

r. *'aššāpîm*. From Akk. *āšipu*, "exorcist" (*CAD* 2:431), a specialist who primarily diagnosed disease from bodily signs and offered incantations. The pairing of an Egyptian term and an Akkadian term suggests less a specific reference to their technical specialties than an inclusive reference to the experts of the two most ancient and sophisticated cultures of the ancient Near East (similarly Montgomery 137).

s. So Papyrus 967. 4QDan^a contains a lacuna that requires a longer text than that preserved in the MT. Cross, cited in J. Collins 129, suggests [*bkl mlkwtw wykbdm hmlk wyr'm b*]*kl d*[*br*] *bmlkwtw*. The omission in MT is due to homoioteleuton.

Overview and Outline

Chapter 1 introduces the book as a whole, the story cycle in chs. 1–6, and the Nebuchadnezzar cycle in chs. 1–4. Moreover, it is a story in its own right, although one with a less developed plot than those that follow. As an introduction to the whole book, it presents the characters and the themes that will be important throughout Daniel. The sovereignty of the God of Israel over political and historical processes, which is thematically central to both parts of the book, is subtly but clearly articulated, as is the complex relationship between knowledge and power.

This ch. 1 appears to have been originally composed as an introduction to chs. 1–6 only and not significantly changed when chs. 7–12 were added. Not only is there no foreshadowing of chs. 7–12, as there is of chs. 2–6, but there is also a tension between the chronological notice that concludes ch. 1 ("And Daniel was there until the first year of Cyrus the king," v. 21) and the chronology of 10:1, which refers to Daniel's vision in the third year of Cyrus. Thus the functions of ch. 1 should be understood primarily in relation to the story cycle. One change was made, however, to adapt ch. 1 to the expanded book. Linguistic evidence suggests that the chapter was originally composed in Aramaic and translated into Hebrew when the Hebrew chs. 8–12 were incorporated into the book (Charles xlvi–xlviii; Koch 16–18).

Chapter 1 prepares the reader for the stories that follow. Even though Daniel's three friends play no independent role in ch. 1, they are introduced and an explanation is given for the foreign names by which they will be known in ch. 3. Daniel's Babylonian name, which appears to be original to the story in ch. 4, is similarly introduced here. The origin of Daniel's expertise in dream interpretation and superiority to Nebuchadnezzar's own court experts, central to the plot of chs. 2 and 4, is explained. Moreover, the vessels from the Jerusalem temple, which will figure prominently in ch. 5, are also mentioned. Even the plot of ch. 1, which involves quiet resistance to the king's will, anticipates the more dramatic conflicts of chs. 3 and 6. Finally, the chronological notice of 1:21 forms an inclusio with the reference to Cyrus in 6:28 (29).

Even though there is evidence that chs. 4–6 may have circulated independently at an early stage of the development of the Daniel traditions (see

Agency, Knowledge, and Power

introduction), the focus in ch. 1 on the figure of Nebuchadnezzar also appears to be part of a redactional strategy to distinguish chs. 1–4 from the remaining narratives and to form them into a cycle of stories concerning the slow and painful education and transformation of the king. At every stage of the compositional process, however, redactors have been content to allow tensions and inconsistencies to remain, so that the chapters never achieve the integration of a novella like the Joseph story in Genesis but remain an episodic story cycle.

Despite the redactional functions that ch. 1 fulfills, it is also a well-written story in its own right, containing elements of both the court contest and court conflict plots, though in a relatively muted form. The superiority of Daniel and his friends to the other trainees when Nebuchadnezzar examines them, as well as the honor that the king consequently shows them, gives the conclusion of the story something of the shape of the court contest (cf. chs. 2, 4–5). The dramatic action of the plot, however, largely revolves around the Jews' resistance to the king's command concerning their food (cf. chs. 3 and 6). In terms of narrative structure, ch. 1 is composed of a series of balanced scenes in a roughly chiastic pattern, with the two central ones introducing and resolving the primary narrative conflict:

A. Introduction: Historical and geopolitical setting (1:1–2)
  B. Nebuchadnezzar's instruction to the head of staff concerning the Israelites (1:3–5)
    C. Encounter between the head of staff and Daniel (1:6–10)
    C^1. Encounter between Daniel and the supervisor (1:11–17)
  B^1. Nebuchadnezzar's interview of the trainees (1:18–19)
A^1. Conclusion: Proleptic overview of chs. 1–6 with concluding historical note (1:20–21)

Comments

[1–2] Although the genre of ch. 1 is that of the court tale, the introductory verses gesture toward a different genre: historiography. The notation of Jehoiakim's regnal year, the summary narration of the siege of Jerusalem, and the deportation of the king and the temple vessels imitate the style of Kings, Chronicles, and the historiographical narratives in Jeremiah. The phraseology of the verse is close to that of Jer 39:1. Despite the stylistic similarity to historiography, however, the events described are fictitious. Since Jehoiakim's accession to the throne is usually dated to 609 B.C.E., and Nebuchadnezzar did not become king until 605, the synchronism of v. 1 is impossible (cf. Jer 25:1). Moreover, no evidence exists for a Babylonian siege of Jerusalem before 598/97, as both 2 Kgs 25 and the Babylonian Chronicle independently attest (Grayson 102). Nevertheless, the author of Dan 1 is not being cavalier with history. The verse reflects an older though historically erroneous tradition that has its origin in the Chronicler's account of Jehoiakim's reign (see Japhet 1065–66, for a refutation of attempts to argue for the historicity of the Chronicler's account). According to 2 Chr 36:6–7, "Nebuchadnezzar, King of Babylon, came up against him [i.e., Jehoiakim], and he bound him with fetters in order to take him to Babylon. And Nebuchadnezzar brought some of the vessels of the house of the LORD to Babylon, and he put them in his palace in Babylon" (AT).

A possible source for the Chronicler's tradition may lie in the book of Jeremiah, both in Jeremiah's prediction in 22:10–12 that Jehoiakim would die in exile, and in 25:1–11, where the synchronism between Jehoiakim's fourth year and the first year of Nebuchadnezzar serves as an introduction to a prophecy of a forthcoming invasion of Judah by Nebuchadnezzar. Daniel 1:1 may arrive at its date of the third year of Jehoiakim through an attempt to harmonize the account in Chronicles with the note in 2 Kgs 24:1 that "In his [i.e., Jehoiakim's] days Nebuchadnezzar the king of Babylon came up, and Jehoiakim became his servant for three years; then he turned and rebelled against him." Although the allusion in 2 Kgs 24:1 is to Jehoiakim's revolt in 601 B.C.E., it does not specify the date and so leaves open the possibility for a reader to assume that the revolt came in the third year of his kingship. Since the stories in Dan 1–6 show no further interest in the particularities of Judean history, it seems likely that it was not the author of Dan 1 himself who worked out this synthesis (*pace* Koch 1995, 21–22) but rather that he drew on a historiographical interpretation of the sources that had already become current.

This historiographical introduction serves several purposes in Daniel. The paired dates in v. 1 (third year of Jehoiakim) and v. 21 (the first year of Cyrus) situate the Daniel cycle within the chronological framework of the beginning and end of exile. Moreover, the focus on the encounter between the two kings foregrounds the author's theological concern with kings and kingdoms. (The term "king" occurs some 187 times in Daniel and the related word "reign" 69 times; Bauer 68). Koch (36–37) overinterprets, however, when he sees here the transfer of universal kingship from the house of David to Nebuchadnezzar. As the symbolism of the king's dream in ch. 2 will make clear, Israel's succession to universal kingship follows rather than precedes the sequence of Gentile empires.

The reference to the temple vessels not only sets up the story of Belshazzar's feast in ch. 5 but also associates the Daniel stories with the significant concern in Second Temple Judaism for the fate of the temple vessels, the portable symbol of divine presence in a culture that rejected physical representation of the deity (2 Kgs 24:13; 25:13–17; Jer 27:16–22; 28:1–9; 2 Chr 36:7, 10, 18). Only in Ezra (1:7–10; 5:14) and in Daniel, however, are the vessels said to have been deposited by Nebuchadnezzar in a Babylonian temple. While the return of the vessels to Jerusalem by Cyrus is the concern of Ezra, which sees the temple vessels as a marker of continuity between the first and second temples, in Daniel the vessels serve as a physical symbol of divine power, much as they do in Jeremiah.

Two key verbs establish a critical claim about historical agency. Ostensibly, Nebuchadnezzar is the powerful actor, associated three times with the verb *bôʾ* in both its Qal and Hiphil forms. He "comes" to Jerusalem and "brings" his captives and spoil to Babylon. But although Nebuchadnezzar is said to besiege Jerusalem, the author never says that Nebuchadnezzar takes Jerusalem. Rather, it is God who "gives" (*nātan*) Jehoiakim and the temple vessels into Nebuchadnezzar's power. Throughout the rest of the story, Nebuchadnezzar and his officials are associated with the verb *bôʾ* (vv. 3, 18 [twice]), whereas God is consistently associated with the verb *nātan* (vv. 9, 17). Thus the reader knows what Nebuchadnezzar does not know: the God of Israel is the effective agent in history, not Nebuchadnezzar.

While the issue of access to and possession of knowledge is a recurrent thematic element in the book of Daniel, it also serves an important narrative function. Authors distribute knowledge to the participants in their stories in different ratios. One character may be in possession of knowledge that another lacks. Characters may possess knowledge that the reader lacks, or as here, the narrator may grant the reader knowledge that a character lacks. This differential access to knowledge is often crucial to the tension that fuels the plot. Correspondingly, the resolution of the plot will be effected when access to crucial knowledge is equalized and the reader and all of the characters share the same understanding of reality (Sternberg 176–79). Thus vv. 1–2 initiate a narrative tension generated by just such a knowledge gap concerning the true agent of history, a gap that will not be closed until ch. 4: "until you [Nebuchadnezzar] understand that the Most High is sovereign over the dominion of mortals, and he gives it to whomever he wishes" (v. 25b [22b]).

The reference to God's giving Jehoiakim and the temple vessels into the power of Nebuchadnezzar evokes the similar statement in Jer 27:6 ("Now, I am giving all these lands into the power of Nebuchadnezzar, king of Babel" [AT]). Indeed, Dan 1–6 is indebted to Jeremiah for its characterization of Nebuchadnezzar and his divinely sanctioned role in world events. It provides the impetus for Daniel's novel representation of Nebuchadnezzar as a redeemed Gentile king.

[3–5] With v. 3 the focus shifts from the panoramic view of world events to a private interview between Nebuchadnezzar and the head of his household staff concerning the disposition of some of the deportees, who are to be selected for particular qualities, given provisions, and trained. The king's description provides the reader with the first characterization of Daniel and his three friends. Because the author uses the style of free indirect discourse, incorporating the characteristics of Nebuchadnezzar's speech into the narration without rendering it as a direct quotation, these verses also serve to characterize Nebuchadnezzar himself. Not incidentally, even though two persons are present in the scene, only Nebuchadnezzar speaks. He is a king accustomed to commanding and making things happen (the perspective in his implied view of the events of vv. 1–2). Moreover, he is represented as a knowledgeable and even detail-oriented king who knows the qualifications he wants for the personnel who will serve in his court, as well as the training and support necessary to produce them. He is represented as pragmatic and perhaps even benevolent, incorporating the deported Israelites into his court bureaucracy rather than dealing punitively with them.

Although both the scene and the scenario are fictitious—there is no historical evidence for Judean deportees being incorporated into the higher-ranking levels of the bureaucracy of the Neo-Babylonian court—the author's description of the process is strikingly similar to much-older accounts describing how war captives were to be incorporated into positions within Mesopotamian court households (see fig. 2). Whether this is coincidental or reflects a standard procedure that operated more or less unchanged for centuries is impossible to know. In a letter sent from Zimri-Lim, king of Mari, to his wife Shibtu (18th c. B.C.E.), Zimri-Lim outlines his intentions for a group of war captives from the city of Ashlaka (ARM X 126; Dossin and Finet 184–85; Paul 2001, 62–63). In instructions that are similarly meticulous and detailed, Zimri-Lim instructs Shibtu to select up to thirty female weavers who have a good physical appearance ("who, from the fingernails to the hair of the head, do not have any flaw"), to entrust them to Warad-ilišu, who is to train them as musicians, and to allocate sufficient food rations for them to ensure "that their appearance not change." A second official, Mukannišum, is mentioned in relation to the food rations. Similarly, in Dan 1 there is a selection according to physical appearance without any flaw (v. 4), training in an area of professional expertise (vv. 4–5), and the provision of foods that will preserve a healthy appearance under the direct supervision of a subordinate official (vv. 5, 10–15).

Nebuchadnezzar's instructions begin with the social status of the young men to be selected: members of the royal family and nobles. Although the author never specifies the exact social status of Daniel and his friends, later Jewish tradition assumed that Daniel and his friends were of the family of King Zedekiah (Josephus, *Ant.* 10.188). Isaiah's prophecy to Hezekiah that some of his sons would serve as eunuchs in the palace of the king of Babylon (Isa 39:7) appears to be the basis for these traditions that assume Daniel and his friends were members of the royal family (*b. Sanh.* 93b). The king also specifies the intellectual qualities and accomplishments they should have. The piling up of the terms rather serves to underscore the superlative aptitude and excellent previous training of the young men to be selected. The emphasis, however, is thematically important, for knowledge plays a crucial role in the book. The description is also similar to that of the ideal scribe in the Egyptian Papyrus Anastasi: "choice of heart, persevering in counsel, . . . a youth distinguished of appearance and

Agency, Knowledge, and Power

Figure 2. A group of prisoners of war, playing lyres, depicted in a stone relief from the palace of the Neo-Assyrian king Sennacherib (705–681 B.C.E.). © The Trustees of the British Museum.

pleasing of charm, who can explain the difficulties of the annals like him who composed them" (*ANET* 475). Although very few individuals in the ancient Near East received advanced scribal training (see fig. 3), it was customary for aristocratic youths to be given an education that included basic literacy and the memorization of a standard set of classic texts (Carr 20–21). The socialization and enculturation of such education prepared the highborn youths for service in the royal administration, as is reflected in the final qualification that Nebuchadnezzar specifies: "capable of serving in the king's palace" (lit., "to stand in the king's palace"; cf. 1 Kgs 1:2; 10:8; 12:8; etc.). Undoubtedly the expression derives from the physical postures that denoted hierarchy in court etiquette: the king seated with his advisers standing before him (cf. 1 Kgs 22:19).

The purpose for the selection is announced only at the end of the long, syntactically complex enumeration of the desired qualifications: training in "the literature and language of the Chaldeans." The term "Chaldean" originates as an ethnic designation for a group of tribes in southern Mesopotamia that rose to political dominance in the Neo-Babylonian Empire founded by Nabopolasar in

Figure 3. Neo-Assyrian scribes recording war booty. One beardless scribe, probably a eunuch, writes in cuneiform with a stylus. The other scribe writes on a papyrus or leather scroll. From the Palace of Sennacherib (705–681 B.C.E.). © The Trustees of the British Museum.

626 B.C.E. In the Hebrew Bible it most often refers to Babylon and the Babylonians (e.g., 2 Kgs 25:4; Isa 47:1; Jer 21:4; Ezek 1:3); so also in Dan 5:30; 9:1. By the Hellenistic period, however, and perhaps earlier, the word developed a secondary meaning, referring to a class of Babylonian divinatory experts. The popular image of Chaldeans is expressed by Diodorus Siculus in this manner:

> For being assigned to the service of the gods, they spend their entire life in study, their greatest renown being in the field of astrology. But they occupy themselves largely with soothsaying as well, making predictions about future events, and in some cases by purifications, in others by sacrifices, and in others by some other charms they attempt to effect the averting of evil things and the fulfillment of the good. They are also skilled in soothsaying by the flight of birds, and they give out interpretations of both dreams and portents, (2.29.2–3; LCL, trans. Oldfather)

The term is used in this professional sense here and elsewhere in Daniel (except 5:30; 9:1). The language and literature of the Chaldeans would thus refer to the technical literature of these divinatory experts, composed and transmitted in Akkadian cuneiform.

Babylonian astrological and divinatory knowledge enjoyed a high degree of cultural prestige throughout the Persian and Hellenistic periods. Both Alexander the Great and Seleucid kings consulted Chaldean experts (Diodorus Siculus 17.112–14; frg. 21). Although Dan 1 is historically implausible in suggesting that foreigners would be formally trained in this highly esoteric Babylonian field of expertise, the more important question is why the Jewish author presents his fictional characters as receiving such training. The issue involves the ambivalent relationship of displaced and colonized peoples toward the intellectual accomplishments of the imperial power. Such specialized knowledge is, on the one hand, both highly attractive and often unattainable. The roughly contemporary early Enochic literature (esp. *1 En.* 1–36 [Book of the Watchers] and 72–82 [Astronomical Book]) reflects the appropriation and adaptation of traditions concerning antediluvian Mesopotamian sages and rather out-of-date astronomical lore (P. Alexander 230–42). On the other hand, such knowledge evokes cultural resistance and an insistence that one's own traditions are superior (Drawnel 58–59). Much as in Isa 44:25–26, the author of the Daniel stories proclaims the superiority of YHWH's servants and the failures of the Babylonian diviners. The entire imagined world of the Daniel story cycle is a complex cultural negotiation, involving the desire for aspects of the imperial culture but also a need both to resist it and to incorporate certain aspects of it on the Jews' own terms (see introduction).

The instructions concerning the training of the youths are interrupted in v. 5b by specifications for food rations. The provision of food by the king and even the phraseology (*dĕbar-yôm bĕyômô*) also evoke the arrangements made for the exiled Jehoiachin by the Babylonian king Evil-merodach in 2 Kgs 25:29–30, though Jehoiachin's provisions are not explicitly said to come from the king's own food. Eating at the same table (1 Sam 20:30–34; 2 Sam 9:9–13) or providing food from one's own portion (Gen 43:34) signifies both an honor conferred and an expectation of loyalty. While the practice of the king's supplying rations for a variety of dependents is well attested in ancient Mesopotamia (Oppenheim 1970, 104), the notion that it is specifically the king's own food and wine that is shared with these court dependents reflects Persian rather than Babylonian court life (Montgomery 122; Koch 52–53). Both the magnificent luxuriousness of the king's table and the king's largesse were elements of Persian royal self-presentation that captured the imagination of the peoples of the empire (Briant 200, 286–92). It is not known whether a three-year period of specialized training was typical of Persian court practice or is simply an invention of the storyteller.

[6–10] The scene shifts with the introduction of new characters, the four from among the larger group of deportees with whom the story will be concerned.

Here they are identified as Judahites rather than Israelites, as in v. 3 above. The names of all four are attested elsewhere, predominantly in postexilic works, and are all theophoric: Daniel ("God has judged"; cf. Ezra 8:2; Neh 10:6 [7]); Hananiah ("God has been gracious"; Ezra 10:28; Neh 3:8); Mishael (of uncertain meaning, perhaps "Who is what God is?" Exod 6:22; Neh 8:4); and Azariah ("God has helped"; Ezra 7:1; Neh 3:23). Although not an explicit part of the king's instructions, the first act taken by the head of staff is to assign new names to the Judeans. The names are somewhat garbled versions of Babylonian, Persian, and Aramaic names. "Belteshazzar" is likely from Akkadian *Balāṭ-šu-uṣur*, "protect his life"; or *Balāṭ-šar-uṣur*, "protect the life of the king." The most plausible suggestion for the origin of "Shadrach" is Old Persian *cithra*, plus the afformative -*ka*, meaning "shining," "brilliant" (Koch 6; Lipiński 234). Although the precise meaning of "Meshach" is obscure, it incorporates a version of the name of the Persian god Mithra (Greek: Mithras). Moreover, the name *Mi-iš-ša-ak-qa* is attested at Persepolis (Lipiński 234). "Abednego" is an Aramaic name containing a distorted version of the name of the Babylonian god Nebo; it would thus mean "servant of Nebo." The meaning of these foreign names would probably not have been transparent to the original audience of Dan 1 and would simply have sounded like names from the privileged linguistic registers of the multiethnic imperial society of the Persian era.

From the perspective of redaction history, the account of the renaming serves to integrate traditions originally about other characters into the Daniel cycle. The name Belteshazzar appears to be the original name of the character in ch. 4. Elsewhere Daniel is the preferred name for the main character, generally used by the narrator and by Belshazzar, the queen mother, and Darius. Belteshazzar is used only in direct speech by Nebuchadnezzar in ch. 4 and in explanatory glosses in 2:26 and 5:12. Shadrach, Meshach, and Abednego are the only names used in ch. 3, the story in which the three friends are the protagonists, and are likely the traditional names for the characters. The Hebrew names appear only in chs. 1 and 2, in which the three figure only peripherally. Thus the Hebrew names appear to be secondary. Ironically, if anyone can be said to give these characters new names, it is the redactor rather than the Babylonian head of staff.

Although redactional activity may have been the occasion for the double names, it does not account for their significance in the narrative. The renaming of the characters is the first stage in what is intended to be a thoroughgoing transformation of their identities and roles. Fewell (15–18) has aptly compared the process with that of a rite of passage. There is separation and seclusion, a liminal period during which instructors teach specialized knowledge required for filling new roles, special food, and new names. Entering as young deportees from Judah, the characters will graduate as members of the Babylonian administration. Despite the assertions of some commentators (e.g., Bentzen 20), there is no indication that the assignment of new names is regarded negatively in the narrative. Many prominent Jews of the exilic and postexilic period are known by Babylonian names, including Sheshbazzar (Ezra 1:8) and Zerubbabel (3:2). The Jewish characters in the book of Esther have Babylonian names incorporating references to Babylonian deities (Mordecai/Marduk; Esther/Ishtar); and Esther herself also has a Hebrew name, Hadassah (Esth 2:7). Later in the Hellenistic period, Jews often bore Greek names as well as Hebrew ones (e.g., Joshua/Jason in 2 Macc 4:7; Josephus, *Ant.* 12.239). Thus the phenomenon of double names was part of the multicultural reality of life under the great empires, especially in the Diaspora but increasingly in Judah as well.

Explicit acts of renaming by kings and their representatives have an additional connotation, however. It is simultaneously an honor conferred by the king to mark the recipient's new status and a sign of the expectation of loyalty to the king who bestows the name. See, for example, Pharaoh's naming Joseph as Zaphenath-paneah when he appoints him over all of Egypt (Gen 41:45); Neco's giving Eliakim the throne name Jehoiakim (2 Kgs 23:34); and Nebuchadnezzar's assigning Mattaniah the throne name Zedekiah (2 Kgs 24:17). A nonbiblical source attests the same practice in Seleucid Babylonia. An inscription from 244 B.C.E. reads "Anu-uballit son of Anu-iksur, of the Ah'utu family, šaknu (governor) of Uruk, on whom Antiochus, King of Lands, bestowed the other name Nikarrchos" (Sherwin-White and Kuhrt 150). The social significance of the names given to the young Judeans by the head of staff would be a similar marker of their new status within the court.

Whatever the function of the new names within the Babylonian court context, the double names are an index of the double identities experienced by all exiles, immigrants, and colonized peoples, who must continually negotiate the sometimes-conflicting claims of the two cultures to which they belong. The complexity and ambiguity of these tensions are exquisitely represented in this narrative. While neither the new names nor the enculturation in the Babylonian language and divinatory literature appears to be objectionable, the problem arises from another source: the food provided by the king. The author emphasizes the tension through a subtle wordplay, using the same verb in vv. 7 and 8 (*śîm*) to describe the head of staff's decision about new names ("he decided") and Daniel's determination not to defile himself with the king's food and drink ("Daniel decided"). Each is negotiating the cultural divide: the head of staff is diminishing the "foreignness" of the Judean exiles in their new Babylonian context, and Daniel is asserting a nonnegotiable marker of Judean identity.

Why Daniel should consider the king's food defiling has never been definitively explained. The word translated "defile" (*gāʾal*) occurs in late texts with a cultic or ritual significance (Isa 59:3; Mal 1:7, 12; Ezra 2:62; Neh 7:64; 1QM 9.8). Thus Daniel is concerned specifically about an aspect of his religious identity. But while one may suggest reasons why the king's meat might be objectionable (e.g., if offered to a Babylonian god or slaughtered without proper draining of the blood), no biblical basis exists for an avoidance of Gentile wine (though such a prohibition develops later; see *m. ʿAbod. Zar.* 2:3; 4:8–12; 5:1–12). Some have suggested that what is objectionable is that the food comes from the king's own supply (Seow 26; Koch 64–65), but that would not explain the choice of the word *gāʾal*, "to defile." That a specific explanation cannot be found is actually a key to understanding the situation. No commonly and clearly accepted rules existed for the situation in which Daniel and his friends found themselves. While some of the food laws now found in the Torah may be of considerable antiquity, it is unclear to what extent they were or were not broadly embraced, even in the postexilic period. Ample evidence exists that, especially in the Diaspora, there was a range of opinions on the significance of food laws as boundary markers between Jews and Gentiles. Thus 2 Kings sees nothing objectionable in Jehoiachin's receiving rations from the Babylonian king (25:27–30). Esther dines with King Ahasuerus and Haman (Esth 5:4–8; 7:1–2). And it is unlikely Nehemiah could have filled the position of cupbearer to Artaxerxes if he could not taste the king's wine (Neh 2:1). Both Daniel and the book of Tobit (1:10–11) suggest a situation in which Jews decided for themselves on more or less rigorous food practices. Apparently the other young Jews, apart from Daniel and his three friends, saw no need to reject the king's food. Similarly, Tobit is explicit in contrasting his avoidance of "eating the food of the Gentiles" with the practices of his relatives and fellow Israelite deportees (1:10). Because restrictive food practices serve as powerful boundary markers between ethnic communities, it is not surprising that as one moves further into the Hellenistic period, references to the avoidance of Gentile food or eating with Gentiles become more common and more explicit (Jdt 12:1–4; Esth 14:17 OG; 1 Macc 1:62–63; *Jos. Asen.* 7:1; *Jub.* 22:16; Josephus, *Life* 3.14). But even in the *Letter of Aristeas* (180–86), the Jewish priests are represented as eating at the table of the Egyptian king. While it is no longer possible to reconstruct the halakic logic that governed the understanding of Daniel concerning defiling foods, the fact that a decision had to be made is part of the *internal* negotiation of cultural identity ("What does being a Jew in a foreign land require of me?") that precedes the negotiation with the Gentile authorities.

The exchange between Daniel and the head of staff has a curious quality that speaks volumes about the realities of power in the royal court. After Daniel goes to the head of staff to seek permission not to defile himself with the food, the narrator notes that God gave Daniel "favor and sympathy" before him. While such statements about Jewish heroes in Gentile courts are almost a cliché (Gen 39:21; Neh 1:11; Esth 2:9, 15, 17; cf. 1 Esd 4:42; *T. Jos.* 2:3), the claim generates an expectation that Daniel's request will be granted. Yet the head of staff does not grant the request when he replies in v. 10. To grasp what is going on, one must think about the dynamics of life at the royal court, of what can be said and what needs to be left unsaid. How it is that the head of staff's words are in fact an expression of favor and sympathy? In v. 10 the head of staff replies by describing the dangers posed by the power of a displeased king. Kings do not expect to have their explicit commands disobeyed, and what Daniel has asked requires just that. But if the head of staff does not agree to Daniel's request, neither does he deny it. He simply underscores his critical concern. If Daniel and his friends end up looking haggard, they will have endangered the head of staff. With that the interview ends. What goes unsaid is the tacit permission the head of staff gives Daniel to work out a behind-the-scenes solution.

[11-17] In each exchange in the story, only one character's words are reported directly. In vv. 3–5 only the king's words are reported; in vv. 8–10, the words of the head of staff; and in vv. 11–14, Daniel's words. What Daniel says in v. 12 would make sense as a direct reply to the head of staff; but the words are addressed to another, lower-ranking official, the supervisor. Even though the exchange between Daniel and the officials is divided between two different conversations, it is part of the same negotiation. In this scene the interplay between knowledge and power and the differentiation between the space "before the king" and the space away from the king are critical. Even though the king is theoretically the most powerful actor, his commands can be abrogated—but only so long as the king does not know (cf. the similar dynamics in chs. 3 and 6). The king's lack of knowledge creates a space where individuals can exercise their own power. But whoever possesses knowledge about the violation of the king's commands becomes dangerously empowered. Thus words must be used with caution. Not only does the head of staff show Daniel sympathy and kindness by not using his knowledge of Daniel's proposed resistance against him, but he also protects himself by replying to Daniel with the words of an impeccably loyal servant of the king who respects the king's commands. At the same time, by focusing only on the criterion of Daniel's appearance rather than explicitly denying Daniel's request, he gives the courtier's equivalent of a wink. Daniel has been given space to pursue his request, so long as the criterion of good appearance can be met—and so long as the head of staff does not have to know about the arrangements.

Daniel's scrupulousness in protecting the vulnerability of the head of staff and the supervisor is reflected in his request for a very brief test: only ten days out of a period of three years. Moreover, Daniel explicitly leaves the evaluation of the experiment in the supervisor's hands (translating either "according to what you observe" or "as you see fit"). The food that Daniel requests is identified by a rare word, spelled *zērōʿîm* in v. 12 and *zērʿōnîm* in v. 16. Although clearly related to the Hebrew word for "seed" (*zeraʿ*), it is not certain whether *zērōʿîm/zērʿōnîm* refers to a diet of seeds (i.e., legumes) or to vegetables in general, that is, things grown from seed. While it is not impossible that the author's word choice reflects a specific halakic understanding of the resistance of seeds to contracting ritual impurity (Ginsberg 1954, 256), it seems unlikely.

In addition to the less problematic nature of vegetable foods in relation to ritual impurity, the contrast between the two diets sets up other symbolic contrasts. The king's food represents power, both because of its source and because of the nature of the food itself. Meat, a rarity in the diet of ordinary persons in antiquity, would have been part of the king's rations. Even Greek writers were impressed by the predominance of meat in the Persian court diet (Briant 289). As anthropologists have often noted, meat, because it is food produced by slaughter, is particularly associated with power. Wine, too, is a food that connotes power, not only because of the labor involved and the mysterious process of fermentation, but also because of its inebriating effect (cf. 1 Esd 3:17b–24). Thus even though the narrator does not elaborate the details of the foods in question, the symbolic contrast between the two diets is one between "strong" foods and "weak" foods. By feeding the young men from his own rations, Nebuchadnezzar directs to them some of the abundant strength that flows from a powerful king.

Despite modern nutritional assumptions, the outcome of the ten days' test is no argument for the health benefits of a diet rich in fruits and vegetables. Although the narrator simply presents the results of the test in terms of the appearance of Daniel and his friends, the completely counterintuitive results would signal to the reader the presence of a power far stronger than Nebuchadnezzar at work behind the scenes. As with the opening verses of the chapter, the author subtly creates a narrative world in which the ironic structures of power are explored, as God's control of events manifests itself to Daniel and the reader in ways that are invisible to the king.

Although the head of staff may be motivated by "favor and sympathy" toward Daniel, no such motive is ascribed to the supervisor. The narrative logic suggests less lofty incentives for this lower-ranking official, as the versions imply (Montgomery 131; 1:16 OG: "he was taking to himself"). For three years the supervisor receives four portions of very high quality food and wine in exchange for much less costly vegetables and water. The two short scenes in vv. 11–16 suggest quite economically the complex world of the court, where favors may be granted so long as positions are protected, and where mutually beneficial exchanges can be made, so long as knowledge of it is kept from superiors. The dramatic situation in ch. 1 is thus quite similar to that of chs. 3 and 6, where the Jews seek, quietly and privately, to avoid a royal decree that would compromise their identity as Jews. Here in ch. 1, when the young men are obscure figures in the court, they receive the cooperation of Gentile officials. In the later chapters, when they themselves have become high-ranking figures, the intrigue of their rivals will maneuver their conflict into a public confrontation with the king.

What was implicit about the source of effective power in the test of the diet is made explicit in v. 17. For the third time (cf. vv. 2, 9) the narrator uses the phrase "God gave." Nebuchadnezzar's command concerning the education of the young men in v. 5 clearly assumed that the instruction he provided, like the food, would produce the results he desired. Here, however, their proficiency in the learned literature of the Babylonian curriculum comes from God. A second note distinguishes Daniel from his three companions through his special competency in understanding visions and dreams, gifts he will display in chs. 2 and 4. The interpretation of dreams was never a particularly important part of Mesopotamian manticism and was not a specialized technical divinatory practice (Husser 27–29, 38) nor a consistent concern of Mesopotamian monarchs, although the Neo-Babylonian king Nabonidus was preoccupied with revelatory dreams (Beaulieu 1989, 108–13). The focus on dreams and visions as means of divine revelation in Daniel reflects more the interests of emergent Jewish apocalypticism and may be seen as part of the author's negotiation with the cultural context of the Mesopotamian Diaspora. Even as the story cycle acknowledges the status of Babylonian divinatory science, it imaginatively creates a world in which the knowledge that the king vitally needs is the kind of knowledge cultivated not by Babylonian diviners but by *Jewish* manticism. Thus the narrative shifts the cultural contest to a framework in which the Jewish figures have a divinely granted advantage.

[18–19] Paralleling the scene in which Nebuchadnezzar commanded the head of staff concerning the preparation of the young men (vv. 3–5) is the scene in which the head of staff brings them "before the king" for his examination. That Nebuchadnezzar himself conducts the interview and evaluates the candidates not only characterizes him as an intelligent and discerning monarch but also as someone who likes to be in control of the process from beginning to end. The delicious irony of the story, of course, is that the reader knows what the king does not know, that in the space away from his presence his underlings have acted contrary to his express commands. The king who would be always in control does not, in fact, control his servants in all respects. Moreover, there is another monarch, far more powerful and far more in control of events than Nebuchadnezzar, who has prepared these exceptional young men for his service. The narrative ends with an imbalance of critical knowledge between Nebuchadnezzar and the Jewish characters, and between Nebuchadnezzar and the reader, thus suggesting that, despite the resolution of the immediate tensions of the narrative, the story is far from over. Indeed, the narrator seems intentionally to fashion conclusions to the stories in chs. 1–3 that include both elements of closure and elements that suggest unresolved issues.

[20–21] Since the initial interview concerned only the examination of the Jewish trainees, v. 20 is best taken as a proleptic summary of Nebuchadnezzar's subsequent evaluation of Daniel and his friends in relation to his own experts. Both chs. 2 and 4 serve as demonstrations of Daniel's superiority to these other interpreters. The clause about the honor bestowed on the young men and

Nebuchadnezzar's disclosure of the affairs of his kingdom (see note on v. 20c), omitted from the MT through textual error, also anticipates the honors and political promotions received by Daniel and his friends in 2:46–49 and 3:30. The final chronological notice marks as a narrative horizon the end of the Judean exile, which in Jewish understanding was also not the result of mere imperial political calculations but the effect of God's intentions expressed through Cyrus (Isa 45:1–8; Ezra 1:1–4; 2 Chr 36:22–23).

History of Daniel's Reception, by Brennan W. Breed

Daniel's Identity

If one sees an image of the biblical character Daniel or his three companions, there is a good chance that the figure in the image will look quite young. He will likely appear beardless and with long hair. If he is not naked, then he will be wearing a long cloak held together in the middle of his chest by a large bejeweled clasp, a tunic covered in precious stones, leggings fitted into knee-length boots, and a conical cap with the top tilted forward, adorning his head. This typical depiction of Daniel signifies several things: first, it identifies him as a young person working in a foreign court. In Greco-Roman visual art, as in the art of the Byzantine Empire and Latin West, the Phrygian cap typically identified its wearer as a non-Greek from the East. Daniel's Phrygian cap thus signals his diasporic location: he lives out of place. Second, Daniel's lavish garb communicates his relatively high status in the empire: he works in the court of the foreign king. Third, in many contexts his beardless face, handsome visage, and court status suggest his particular identity as a court eunuch; foreign youths serving in many imperial courts throughout history were not typically allowed to do so unless they had been castrated, and many readers have assumed the same rule held for Daniel.

Immediately, the image of Daniel confronts the viewer with one of the central tensions of the book of Daniel—indeed, a tension that underlies much of disaporic literature throughout history: how does one maintain cultural and religious identity while surviving in a dominant culture that threatens to undermine that identity? Many readers of Daniel understood this text, and especially ch. 1, to instruct them in their own construction and maintenance of identity.

One can trace Daniel's identity problem to the biblical text itself. Is Daniel a wise courtier, as depicted in chs. 1–6, or is he an interpreter of visions, as depicted in chs. 7–12? Within Second Temple and early rabbinic Judaism, Daniel's confusing identity sparked disagreement. In 1 Macc 2:59–60, Daniel is listed among the ancestors of the faith, but he is absent in Ben Sira's song in praise of the ancestors. Judging from the number of extant manuscripts, Daniel was certainly popular at Qumran, but the book of Daniel was also generative of a number of different genres of Danielic texts, suggesting that his role proved difficult to label.

Daniel the Prophet?

Some rabbis believed that Daniel was a prophet (*Pesiq. Rab.* 4; *Qoh. Rab.* 2.2), and Josephus argued that Daniel was "one of the greatest prophets," and that "now that he is dead, he has an immortal reputation: all the books that he wrote and left behind are read by us even now, and from them we have the belief that Daniel spoke with God" (*Ant.* 10.266–68). Nevertheless, in the Jewish tradition Daniel is often called the "beloved one" instead of "the prophet" (Dan 10:11; cf. *b. Sanh.* 93a–b), and many rabbinical interpreters strenuously argue that he was not a prophet: "[Haggai, Zechariah, and Malachi] are more important than [Daniel], because they are prophets and he is not a prophet" (*b. Meg.* 3a). The traditional Jewish division of the Hebrew Bible places Daniel in the Writings, not the Prophets (*b. B. Bat.* 14b), which suggests the importance of this opinion.

Medieval rabbinic interpreters continued to debate Daniel's identity: Naḥmanides (*Comm. Gen.* 18.1) argued that Daniel was not a prophet, while Maimonides (*Guide* 2.45) wrote that Daniel was not quite a full prophet but nevertheless was of a lesser order of prophets. Since Daniel was not mentioned in the Qur'an but was nevertheless an important figure in Muslim tradition, some Muslim interpreters also concluded that he was a lesser prophet (Rosenmüller 318). Christian interpreters, on the other hand, as a rule include Daniel among the prophets, seen in Jesus' comment in Matt 24:15 as well as the Christian canonical placement of the book among the major prophets (cf. Hippolytus, *Comm. Dan.* 1.28.5; Clement of Alexandria, *Strom.* 1.122.4; Augustine, *Civ.* 18.34). Some Christians used this disagreement with rabbinical readers as a pretense for anti-Jewish polemics. Theodoret, for example, argued that Jewish interpreters engage in "impious blasphemy" when they "place this divine prophet outside the prophetic corpus, despite learning by experience the truth of the prophecy" (Theodoret 327). Christian interpreters unanimously agree that Daniel was righteous; Origen argues that, in spite of his confession in chapter 9, the book of Daniel omits any mention of Daniel's sin (*Comm. Rom.* 6.9; cf. Dan 6:5), while Augustine detects so-called Pelagian tendencies in this comment and claims that Daniel did in fact sin (*Nat. grat.* 42).

Sometimes Daniel's prognostication was lauded even when his prophetic status was denied. Jews, Christians, and Muslims all revered Daniel's wisdom, which tended to include both pious insight and elements of mantic, astrological, and magical powers. Some books associated with Daniel's name include esoteric knowledge and predictions of the future (see comments on Dan 2 and 9). A series of loosely related late medieval Muslim and Christian apocalyptic astrological texts called *Malḥamat Dāniyāl* embody this tradition (Fodor). Daniel's association with esoterica explains his name's appearance in Jewish, Christian, and Muslim magic spells to protect individuals from wild animals (cf. Dan 6), judges (cf. Susanna), and other opponents (cf. Dan 3; Tselikas 75).

Daniel and Food

In most of the Hebrew Bible, eating food with and from foreigners does not seem to present a difficult problem. By the Hellenistic era, however, the shift from the Judahites as an ethnicity to the Jews as a political and religious group required new boundary-marking practices to construct and maintain a distinct Jewish identity (Rosenblum 35–37). Some Jewish readers interpret Daniel's food restrictions as an expression of priestly food purity laws, perhaps leading to his identification in OG Bel and the Dragon as a priest (*y. Šabb.* 1.4, 3d; Ibn Ezra, *Comm. Dan.* 1:5; note his discussion of the naturally healthy lifestyle that flows from this diet in 1:15). Others have understood Daniel to reject the temptation to idolatry that would come from table fellowship with Gentiles (Gersonides, *Comm. Dan.* 1.5), and some argued that Daniel's refusal only applied to his circumstances and was not necessarily a model for all others to follow (cf. Shmuel in *b. ʿAbod. Zar.* 36a). Some Jewish interpreters understood Daniel's act in light of widespread Jewish dietary mourning for the loss of the temple (*b. B. Bat.* 60b; cf. Josephus, *Ant.* 4.137; *Vita* 13–14). These readers generally do not seem to understand Daniel's act as overt resistance, but rather as an attempt to retain something of his Jewishness in light of his changed location, political allegiance, language, and name.

Christians, on the other hand, tended to read Daniel's food choices as expressions of his quest for a pure faith, not his religious and communal identity. Especially after the time of Constantine, many late antique and medieval Christians did not need to mark their identity against the dominant culture, so this act of resistance made more sense as a rebellion against the forces of temptation marshaled by the devil that rule this present world. Tertullian, for example, described Daniel's diet as a "partial fast" and claimed that this practice cultivates spiritual development, wisdom, and esoteric knowledge (*Jejun.* 9), and many early and medieval Christian interpreters agreed.

Because the Hebrew word for "vegetable" derives from the root meaning "seed," both Theodotion and the Old Greek translation of Dan 1:16 present the Jewish youths as eating edible seeds; the resulting tradition in both Jewish and Christian communities understood Daniel to eat pulse crops, such as lentils. Thus fifth-century Byzantine author Mark the Deacon writes of the novice Salaphtha who, in the tradition of Daniel, maintained an "ascetic regimen during the Lenten period" that "excluded even bread and salt, allowing only soaked pulse and raw vegetables" (Satran 1994, 91). Due to this interpretive tradition,

History of Daniel's Reception

by the medieval period soaked pulse became the normal fare of Byzantine monks. Even in the modern period, this association continues: in *Progress of Error*, William Cowper (215) writes, "Daniel ate pulses by choice—example rare!" For these readers, Daniel's spare and thus self-denying diet increased his holiness. In writing an order for monastic women, Leander of Seville, a sixth-century bishop, counseled the nuns to "learn temperance and parsimony from the prayer and examples of ancients. . . . Daniel scorned the feasts of kings and lived on vegetables in order to teach others. . . . Do not become a cause for scandal to those to whom you wish to set an example by encouragement and proof of a good life" (*FC* 62:208).

Many Christians understood Daniel's refusal of the king's wine to be an example particularly worthy of emulation. For example, the seventeenth-century Dutch Anabaptist Thieleman J. van Braght stressed the example of sobriety set by Daniel and his companions (291). Likewise, the modern temperance movement has often cited Dan 1:8–16 as an example of the spiritual, moral, intellectual, and health benefits of a sober lifestyle. An anonymous poem written by a member of the early twentieth-century American temperance movement reads:

Daniel's Band
In the Book of Daniel we read that when the young Hebrew was offered wine to drink, he voted " No." He persuaded three of his friends to vote "No." Let us all join Daniel's Band.
    Daniel said " No,"
    And we will do so.
    Daniel won three,
    And so will we!
                     (Massachusetts Total Abstinence Society)

Likewise, in the Mormon community, Daniel and his three friends' refusal to eat "defiling" food is often mentioned in relation to the "Word of Wisdom," section 89 of *Doctrine and Covenants*, which forbids tobacco, alcohol, and habit-forming drugs. And in recent years, evangelical Christians have introduced many different forms of "Daniel fasting," pursued sometimes for increased spiritual insight and sometimes for weight loss; these varying plans often include a strict diet of vegetables and water (Warren, Amen, and Hyman).

Identity and Resistance

Readers in minority communities have often sought to emulate Daniel's rejection of the king's food and wine through analogous acts of subtle resistance against dominant cultures. For example, during the First Crusade in 1096 C.E., Christians began a wave of persecutions of Jews throughout Europe. In the

Rhineland area of Germany, Crusaders attempted to force the conversion and baptism of Jews, and when they resisted, the Crusaders attacked the Jewish communities. At least eight hundred Jews were murdered in the town of Worms alone. In the midst of this persecution, the Daniel story emerged as a locus of hope that encouraged the faithful to reject the waters of baptism offered by the foreign rulers (Chazan 2000, 175–90).

Centuries later, Daniel emerged as an important text for those marginalized by colonial empires in Africa, Asia, and the Americas. Antônio Francisco Lisboa, pejoratively nicknamed Aleijadinho, "The little disabled one," was a famous sculptor and architect in the Portuguese colony of Minas Gerais in Brazil. An illegitimate son of a Portuguese carpenter and an African slave woman from the Azores, Aleijadinho was considered a low-standing mulatto in colonial society (Benton and Durbridge 173–77). Moreover, Aleijadinho suffered from a debilitating disease that limited the use of his hands and feet. Nevertheless, he was the most talented and celebrated sculptor in colonial Brazil. The visages and mannerisms of his figures exhibit surprisingly strongly non-European features, likely aided by the African descent of his two assistants (see fig. 4). Many at the time, and still many today, interpreted Aleijadinho's hybrid art as an "expression of revolt against the social situation" (Gilberto Freyre, via Benton and Durbridge 175).

Aleijadinho's greatest work, the 1805 sculptures of the *Twelve Prophets* lining the staircase at the entrance to the sanctuary Bom Jesus de Matosinhos in Minas Gerais, subtly embraces the fomenting anticolonial revolutionary movement. The figures of the prophets, including one of Daniel, encouraged resistance to Portuguese oppression by mimicking movements from a martial art invented by Africans working on Brazilian plantations (*capoiera*) that disguised itself as a dance form (M. Bowen). Capoiera was officially banned by the colonial penal code, and thus the gestures carried a significant antislavery sentiment. The prophet Daniel stands in a gesture that suggests he has just finished a dramatic capoierain kick in resistance against the empire's lions that crouch at his feet, and a laurel wreath on his head connotes his God-granted victory over oppressive powers. Daniel holds a scroll inscribed with the words "Israel Shall be Saved," which is a general statement of hope that God's sovereignty assures the eventual liberation of those oppressed, such as diasporic Judahites and, by implicit analogy, colonized Brazilians. This sculpture seems to be a direct encouragement to those who fought in the unsuccessful 1798 rebellion in the region that their struggle was not in vain; eventually their cause would succeed (Tribe 67–79).

One can find examples of Daniel's legacy of subtle resistance even in recent times. During the Imperial Japanese occupation of Korea in the early twentieth century, the Japanese practices of imposing the Japanese language, renaming

Fig. 4. Daniel the Prophet by Antônio Francisco Lisboa ("Aleijadinho"), from the Bom Jesus das Matosinhos in Minas Gerais, Brazil (nineteenth century C.E.). Aleijadinho sculpture. © Brian J. McMorrow. Used by permission.

Koreans with Japanese names, and forcing worship at Shinto shrines seemed to some Korean Christians to parallel the Babylonian practices of Daniel 1:1–7 (Kim). In response, Korean Christians told the stories in the books of Daniel and Exodus to encourage resistance to perceived idolatry and the hope for both survival and eventual deliverance. As a Western missionary in Korea described the situation, "Neither the preacher nor the teacher would speak directly about the Korean people under the Japanese rule. They only spoke of the people of Israel. . . . Not surprisingly, the Old Testament and more particularly the book of Exodus and the book of Daniel were most disliked by the Japanese authorities and later banned from the church" (Suh 22). Fifty years later, a group of South African theologians produced the Kairos Document, a theological rejection of the apartheid regime and a call for resistance that highlights the importance of civil disobedience, citing (among other texts) the book of Daniel as a scriptural example of such action, emphasizing Dan 1 (Nichols and McCarthy 613).

Daniel and Gender Identity

To many interpreters, one aspect of Daniel's identity in particular has proved unsettling: his gender. Daniel and his companions were foreign youths working in the court of the king, and the text notes that they were handsome (1:4), invested with much authority (1:19), and given over to the palace eunuch (the head of staff) for training (1:3–7). There is no mention of any wives or children for any of these characters. Early interpreters observed that Daniel and his companions were likely made eunuchs, which was taken to be a fulfillment of Isaiah's prophetic message to Hezekiah in Isa 39:7, "Some of your own sons who are born to you shall be taken away; they shall be made eunuchs in the palace of the king of Babylon" (cf. *b. Sanh.* 93b; Josephus, *Ant.* 10.186).

Some rabbinic interpreters, troubled by the low status and negative stereotypes associated with eunuchs, noted that the youths were said to be "without physical defect" (Dan 1:4), which might mean that they were never made eunuchs (*b. Sanh.* 93b). Other rabbinic readers argued that Daniel and his companions were so chaste that they merely seemed to be eunuchs, or that it was idolatry itself that was castrated in their time (*b. Sanh.* 93a–b), while still others interpreted the reference to a lack of physical defect to apply only to the time before their capture or perhaps to the miraculous aftermath of the fiery furnace and the lions' den (*Song Rab.* 4). The inclusion of eunuchs in the assembly of Israel in Isa 56:4–5, which promises faithful eunuchs "an everlasting name that shall not be cut off," signified for some talmudic interpreters the unending reception history of the book of Daniel itself (*b. Sanh.* 93b).

Jerome learned of the rabbinic assumption that Daniel was a eunuch and passed this information on to other Christians (Jerome, on 1:13; *Jov.* 1.25), who were also generally uneasy about Daniel's gender. The Roman model of the *pater familias* as well as the Christian idea of celibate struggle both assumed the normative model of a potent male; eunuchs took an easy way out of the ascetic spiritual fight. Throughout late antiquity, moreover, eunuchs existed on a low rung of the social ladder.

Thus for the fourth-century archbishop of Constantinople John Chrysostom, Daniel was clearly a righteous Judahite prophet, merely "dressed in Persian garments," and he goes to great exegetical lengths in an attempt to prove that Daniel was not a eunuch (Ringrose 87–110). Though Chrysostom knows that meatless meals are associated with eunuchs, he says that it is a miracle that Daniel looks so masculine after eating them. It seemed important to John to protect Daniel, proclaimed as a precursor of Christ and one of the most important figures in the Christian East.

Yet over time in the Byzantine Empire, eunuchs rose in both political and religious stature. They became associated with holiness and positive powers of boundary crossing, such as the ability to mediate between kings and the populace, between men and women, and between the sacred and profane spheres, even becoming associated with angelic beings (Ringrose 90–94). By the 10th century, Byzantine author Symeon Metaphrastes argued that Daniel was a eunuch *and* a holy man, but he did not characterize Daniel as particularly prophetic (Ringrose 92). And in the 12th century, Theophylatikos of Ohrid, a Byzantine archbishop, simply assumes that this biblical hero was, of course, a eunuch, asking, "What is Daniel to you?" (Ringrose 87). By the 14th century in the Latin West, Daniel's status as a eunuch failed to raise any eyebrows, as Daniel's appearance in the Monk's Tale in Geoffrey Chaucer's *Canterbury Tales* proves—and one can also witness a seemingly unproblematic 14th-century visual representation of Daniel's castration in an illuminated *Bible Historiale* manuscript in the Hague (KB 71A23, f. 222v).

Daniel 2 Nebuchadnezzar's Dream: The End of Divine Delegation of Sovereignty

1 In the second year[a] of the reign of Nebuchadnezzar, Nebuchadnezzar dreamed dreams. His spirit was troubled and his sleep fled[b] from him. 2 The king commanded that the mantic experts[c] and the exorcists,[d] the diviners[e]—that is, the Chaldeans[f]—be summoned in order to explain to the king his dreams. So they came and stood before the king.

3 The king said to them, "I dreamed a dream, and my spirit is troubled to know the dream." 4 The Chaldeans said to the king (*Aramaic*),[g] "O king, live forever! Tell the dream to your servants, and we will make known the meaning." 5 The king answered the Chaldeans, "The word is decreed[h] by me: If you do not make known to me the dream and its meaning, you will be torn limb from limb,[i] and your houses will be made into public toilets![j] 6 But if you make known the dream and its meaning, you will receive gifts, reward,[k] and great honor from me—only[l] tell me the dream and its meaning!" 7 They answered a second time and said, "Let the king tell the dream to his servants, and we will make known the meaning." 8 The king answered, "I know of a certainty that you are trying to control the moment,[m] because you see that I have decreed[n] 9 that if you do not make known the dream to me, there is one verdict for you. You have conspired together to speak a lying and deceptive word to me until the times change. Only[o] tell me the dream, and I will know that you are able to explain its meaning to me." 10 The Chaldeans answered the king and said, "There is no human upon dry land who is able to make known what the king asks,[p] for no great and powerful king[q] has ever asked such a thing as this of any mantic expert or exorcist or Chaldean. 11 The thing that the king requires is so extraordinary that there is no one else who could make it known to the king except the gods, whose dwelling is not with flesh." 12 Thereupon the king became furiously angry and commanded that all the sages of Babylon be killed.

13 The decree went forth, and the sages were about to be killed.[r] They sought Daniel and his companions in order to kill them. 14 Then Daniel responded wisely and judiciously[s] to Arioch,[t] chief of the royal executioners[u] who had gone out to kill the sages of Babylon. 15 He said to Arioch, "Officer of the king, why is the decree from the king so peremptory?" Then Arioch explained the matter to Daniel. 16 So Daniel went in and[v] requested of the king that he give him time so that he could tell the meaning to the king.

17 Then Daniel went to his house, and he explained the situation to Hananiah, Mishael, and Azariah, his companions, 18 that they might seek mercy from the God of heaven concerning this mystery, so that Daniel

and his companions would not perish together with the rest of the sages of Babylon. 19 Then in a night vision the mystery was revealed to Daniel, and Daniel blessed the God of heaven. 20 Daniel said,

"Blessed be the name of the great[w] God from everlasting to everlasting, for wisdom and power[x] are his.
21 He changes times and seasons,
    removing kings and setting up kings.
He gives wisdom to the wise
    and understanding to those who have insight.
22 He reveals the deep and hidden things;
    he knows what is in darkness
    and the light dwells with him.
23 To you, O God of my fathers, I give thanks and praise,
    for you have given me wisdom and power,
and now you have disclosed to me what we asked of you,
    for you have disclosed to us what concerns the king."

24 Thereupon, Daniel went[y] to Arioch, whom the king had appointed to destroy the sages of Babylon, and he spoke to him in this manner: "Do not destroy the sages of Babylon. Bring me before the king, and I will explain the meaning to the king."

25 Then Arioch rushed Daniel before the king and said to him, "I have found a man among the Judean exiles who can disclose the meaning to the king!" 26 The king said to Daniel, whose name was Belteshazzar, "Are you indeed able to disclose to me the dream that I saw and its meaning?" 27 Daniel answered the king and said, "No sages, exorcists, mantic experts, or astrologers[z] are able to explain the mystery about which the king asks. 28 But there is a God in heaven who reveals mysteries, and he has disclosed to King Nebuchadnezzar what will happen at the end of days. Your dream[aa] upon your bed was this:

29 "As for you, O king, as you were in bed your thoughts welled up concerning what will be after this, and the revealer of mysteries disclosed to you what will happen. 30 Now as for me, it is not by means of any wisdom within me more than in any other living being that this mystery was revealed to me, but so that the meaning might be disclosed to the king and that you might understand the thoughts of your mind. 31 You, O king, were looking, and there before you was a single large statue. That statue—enormous and with an extraordinary brilliance—was standing before you, and its appearance was awe inspiring. 32 That statue—its head was of fine gold, its chest and arms of silver, its belly and hips of bronze, 33 its legs of iron, its feet partly of iron and partly of pottery. 34 You kept watching as a rock was hewn out, not by human hands, and it struck the statue on its feet of iron and pottery and shattered them. 35 Then, all

Nebuchadnezzar's Dream: The End of Divine Delegation of Sovereignty

together, the iron, pottery, bronze, silver, and gold shattered and were like the chaff from the summer threshing floors. And the wind lifted them up, and they were nowhere to be found.[bb] But the rock that struck the statue became an enormous mountain and filled all the earth.

36 "This was the dream. Now we will declare its meaning before the king.

37 "You, O king, king of kings—to whom the God of heaven has given a kingdom of power, might, and glory;[cc] 38 and into whose hands he has given, wherever they dwell, human beings, the beasts of the field, and the birds of the air; and who has made you ruler over all of them—you are the head of gold. 39 After you will arise another kingdom, inferior to you, and another kingdom, a third one, of bronze, which will rule over the whole earth. 40 The fourth kingdom will be strong like iron. Just as iron shatters and breaks everything,[dd] all these it will shatter and crush.[ee] 41 As for the fact that you saw feet,[ff] partly of potter's clay and partly of iron, it will be a divided kingdom, and some of the firmness[gg] of iron will be in it, just as you saw iron mixed with earthenware. 42 And as for the toes of the feet, partly of iron and partly of pottery, part of the kingdom will be strong, and part of it will be brittle. 43 As for the fact that you saw the iron mixed with potter's clay, they will mix by marriage,[hh] but they will not hold together, this to that, just as iron does not mix with pottery. 44 In the days of those kings the God of heaven will set up a kingdom that will not be destroyed throughout the ages, and dominion will not pass to another people. It will shatter and put an end to all these kingdoms, but it will stand through the ages, 45 just as you saw that from a mountain a rock was hewn out, not by hands, and that it shattered the iron, the bronze, the pottery, the silver, and the gold.[ii]

"A great God has disclosed to the king what will be hereafter. The dream is certain, and its interpretation trustworthy."

46 Then King Nebuchadnezzar prostrated himself and paid homage to Daniel. He commanded that a grain offering and incense be offered to him. 47 The king said to Daniel, "Truly, your god is God of gods and Lord of kings, and a revealer of mysteries, since you have been able to reveal this mystery." 48 Then the king exalted Daniel and gave him many great gifts and gave him authority over all the province of Babylon and made him chief prefect over all the sages of Babylon. 49 At Daniel's request, the king appointed Shadrach, Meshach, and Abednego over the administration of the province of Babylon, while Daniel remained in the king's court.[jj]

a. Papyrus 967 reads "twelfth," presupposing *šĕtêm 'eśrēh*.

b. MT *ûšĕnātô nihyĕtâ 'ălāyw* would mean "and his sleep came upon him," i.e., he fell asleep again, though it is an odd way to express the idea. While Th, MS 88, and Syro-Hexaplar reflect the MT, Papyrus 967 omits the phrase. More likely the verb is a corruption of *nādĕdâ*, "fled" (Vg *fugit*; cf. 6:19). An alternative suggestion by Koch (139) would relate *šĕnātô* to Akk. *šunatu/šuttu(m)*, which means "dream" (*CAD* 17/3:405–7). Repointing to *šunātô*, the phrase would mean "the content of his dream lay (depressingly) on him."

c. See notes to 1:20.

d. See notes to 1:20.

e. Related to Akk. *kaššāpu*, "sorcerer" (*CAD* 8:292).

f. See comments on 1:5. Although the syntax suggests that the Chaldeans are a fourth group, it is more likely a comprehensive term for the various specialists (cf. 2:4–5).

g. The word *ʾărāmît*, which does not appear in the extant text of 1QDan^a, may be a scribal notation of the change in language from Heb. to Aram. If so, it should not be translated as part of the narration. Alternatively, some take the word adverbially, "in Aramaic."

h. *ʾazdāʾ*. A loanword from Old Persian, it is debated whether the sense is "made public, promulgated" or "certain, decided" (see *HALOT* 1808; Lipiński 238).

i. Lit., "you will be made pieces," from Old Persian *handāma*, "member, piece" (Lipiński 237).

j. *nĕwālî*. A word of uncertain meaning and derivation. Perhaps, as traditionally rendered, "dunghill" (cf. 2 Kgs 10:27) or "rubbish heap." The proposed meaning "ruins," from Akk. *nabālu/nawālu*, "to destroy" (Montgomery 148), is not supported by Assyriologists (Koch 90).

k. *nĕbizbâ*. Although the general meaning is clear from the context, the derivation and precise nuance is uncertain. Recent commentators favor a Persian derivation (Koch 90; J. Collins 148).

l. *lāhēn*. Although some ancient translations render "therefore" (Papyrus 967; Vg), attempts to provide a linguistic justification seem strained (Montgomery 150; Koch 90; *HALOT* 1907). More likely is the well-attested adversative meaning.

m. Lit., "buying the time." The connotation in English of "buying time," i.e., stalling, does not fit the context. The issue is control. See the comments.

n. See note h above.

o. See note l above.

p. Lit., "the matter of the king."

q. *šallîṭ* may be construed as an adjective or as a noun ("no great king or ruler"; so OG and Th).

r. The participle *mitqaṭṭĕlîn* could also be translated "were being killed," but see v. 24.

s. The euphony of the elegant phrase *ʿēṭāʾ ûṭʿēm* defies translation. The nuance, as Plöger (22) observes, is "to find the right word at the decisive moment." Cf. Prov 26:16.

t. *Arioch* is probably the Old Persian name *Ăriyuka* (Grelot 1975, 715) or *Ăryă-va(h)u-ka* (Zadok 1984a, 246). The name occurs in Gen 14:1 and Jdt 1:6.

u. The title that Arioch bears is literally "chief of the slaughterers." While that phrase aptly describes his present task, the term was also used as a general court title meaning something like "captain of the guard." In the MT it is used to designate Potiphar (Gen 39:1), a prison warden (Gen 40:3–4; 41:10–12), and Nebuzaradan (2 Kgs 25:8–20; Jer 39:9–14; 52:12–30), Nebuchadnezzar's assistant who organized the exile of the Judeans.

v. Th and Syr lack "went in and."

w. Reading with 4QDan[a], *lhw' šmh dy 'lh' rbh mbrk*.

x. Although *gĕbûrâ* is commonly translated "power," in certain contexts, as here, it has the connotation of intellectual power (Wernberg-Møller 74). Cf. Job 12:13; Prov 8:14. In CD 13.8 *gbwrwt pl'w* corresponds to *rzy pl'* in 1QS 9.18. Appropriately, some MSS of Th translate *gĕbûrâ* here with *synesis*, "intelligence." In v. 23 the same phrase is rendered by OG as *sophian kai phronēsin*.

y. Rather than read one occurrence of *'al* as a verb and one as a preposition, omit one occurrence of *'al* as dittographic. Cf. 4QDan[a].

z. In both Heb. and Aram. the root *gzr* ("to cut") develops the meaning "to decide." Thus *gāzĕrîn* are "(fate) determiners," through whether the technique used is astrology or the examination of entrails (Vg: *aruspices*) is uncertain (Montgomery 163).

aa. Omit *wĕḥezwê* as a gloss. There is no space for the phrase in 4QDan[a]. Moreover, *dĕnâ hû'* presumes a singular subject.

bb. Lit., "and no place was found for them." There is no need to translate *'ătar* as "trace." Cf. *Ahiqar* 97, *bkwl 'tr*, "everywhere."

cc. Although *ḥisnā'*, *toqpā'*, and *yĕqārā'* are nouns, Koch (100) is surely correct that *malkûtā'* is the comprehensive category qualified by the following words. Similarly, J. Collins (151), "a mighty and glorious kingdom."

dd. Omit *ûkparzĕlā' dî-mĕrā'a'*. MT preserves a double reading.

ee. Although MT takes *kol-'illên* as the object of *mĕrā'a'*, it is more likely to be taken with the following verbs (so Goldingay 35).

ff. Omit *wĕ'eṣbĕ'ātā'*, an addition in MT and Th that does not appear in OG and apparently not in 4QDan[a] (see J. Collins 151).

gg. *niṣbĕtā'*, lit., "plant, planting," with the nuance of "firmness" apparently deriving from the notion of a plant's rootedness.

hh. Lit., "by human seed."

ii. The sequence appears disordered (cf. v. 35). The versions mostly place "pottery" at the beginning of the sequence, although Papyrus 967 reads "iron, pottery, bronze."

jj. Lit., "in the gate of the king" (cf. Esth 2:19, 21; 3:2).

Overview and Outline

Chapter 2 is distinct among the court tales in Dan 1–6. Although each of the stories uses the genre of the court tale to make imaginatively persuasive the claim that the God of Israel is sovereign over all earthly kings, only in ch. 2 does this claim extend beyond the frame of the immediate events of the story to encompass the course of history itself. Here and only here in these court tales does an eschatological horizon envision an end to the long succession of Gentile empires. The difference is so striking that some have tried to reconstruct a hypothetical earlier version in which the eschatological elements were not present and to interpret the four parts of the symbolic statue as referring originally to four Neo-Babylonian kings rather than four kingdoms (so Kratz 1991, 55–62). While such hypotheses are not impossible, they are speculative. Certainly in its present form the story can be dated no earlier than the first decades of the

Seleucid Empire (late 4th to early 3d centuries B.C.E.). Nevertheless, there are intriguing hints that the roots of the story might go back to the period of transition from the Neo-Babylonian Empire to that of the Persians. (See introduction and comments on ch. 4.) Granted that this chapter may well bear within it the traces of nearly two hundred years of "recycled" materials, the primary cultural horizon within which the framework of the story developed would have been that of the Jewish Diaspora in the Persian Empire. "King Nebuchadnezzar" thus serves as a figure for Gentile monarchs in general.

Although Dan 2 is a story of religious and cultural resistance to the claims of imperial power, the extent to which it conducts its resistance from within the very linguistic and cultural world of Persian imperial imagination is striking. The language in which the author primarily writes is not Hebrew but Aramaic, the *lingua franca* of the Persian Empire. The genre of the court story enjoyed international popularity in the Persian Empire, as witnessed by the distribution of the *Ahiqar* story and traditions (VanderKam 1992, 113–15). Most significantly, the concept of a divine world dominion as represented in Dan 2 is, as Koch has argued, a perspective developed within Persian thought (1995, 61). Most explicitly, the four-kingdoms schema of the dream and its interpretation has its roots in a Persian historiographical understanding of the transfer of imperial rule from one people to another (Swain). This intellectual orientation should not be surprising. The Jewish Diaspora constituted a tiny minority within a culturally imposing Persian imperium. To make sense of their situation required engaging the Persian imperial thought world. The author of Dan 2 does not simply absorb this discourse, however, but finds creative ways to resist and subvert it, reinscribing Jewish values within the literary forms, schemas, and concepts he engages. Nevertheless, the price of appropriating the Persian historiographical schema in order to turn it against the current Seleucid imperial power is a retrospective validation of the legitimacy of the preceding Gentile imperial powers as part of God's intentions for history. This legitimation includes the Neo-Babylonian Empire as it is embodied in the figure of Nebuchadnezzar, the destroyer of the Judean kingdom and the temple of Jerusalem.

The extent to which the entertaining genre of the court tale has been put to more serious purposes is evident when one compares Dan 2 with the similar story of Joseph interpreting Pharaoh's dreams in Gen 41. In both, the king has an ominous dream that his regular mantic experts are helpless to interpret but that is explained by a Jew who had been originally brought to the court as a prisoner or slave. In both, the Jewish interpreter is rewarded with a high political rank in the kingdom. The two stories even share similar phraseology and verbal expressions, and it is possible that the author of Dan 2 knew the Joseph story (cf. Gen 41:8 and Dan 2:1, 3; Gen 41:25 and Dan 2:28–29; Gen 41:22 and Dan 2:31). In Daniel, however, not only is the dramatic tension much greater, with the king demanding to be told the dream itself and threatening horrific violence if the interpreters do not comply, but also the content of the dreams is of a different order. Whereas Pharaoh's dream concerns a pragmatic problem that needs to be addressed in the immediate future (planning to cope with a famine), Nebuchadnezzar's dream extends far into the future and concerns the nature and status of imperial dominion itself. The dream has not been sent to warn the king to take some specific action but to make known to the king the mystery and meaning of the historical process. The concerns of the story can also be identified by observing the frequency of key words, which disproportionately have to do with kingship (*melek*, 46×; *malkû*, 10×) and with wisdom, revelation, and interpretation (*yĕdaʿ*, 19×; *pĕšar*, 12×; *ḥăwâ*, 10×; *rāz*, 9×; *ḥakkîm*, 9×; *gĕlâ*, 7×; *kaśdîm*, 5×; *ḥokmâ*, 4×; plus the lists of mantic experts in 2:2, 10, 27).

Thus Dan 2 is no simple court tale but a highly sophisticated exploration of the relationship between knowledge and power. The interplay between these two phenomena is what drives the plot, but it is also the way in which the story serves to negotiate real tensions in the social world of the Jewish Diaspora. Within the story world, Nebuchadnezzar is the ultimate recipient of the revelatory knowledge. But the true recipient of the revealed knowledge is the reader, who gains a measure of empowerment in the world through access to this knowledge. Even more so than in ch. 1, much of the artistry of the narrative has to do with the ways in which knowledge is given, withheld, or deferred, both with respect to the various characters and with respect to the reader. This narrative strategy has the effect of making the reader into an active interpreter, thereby coming to resemble Daniel himself.

The story unfolds in three major scenes:

Scene 1: The king's dream and his unsuccessful consultation with his
    mantic experts (2:1–12)
        Narrative setting (2:1–2)
        First exchange (2:3–4)
        Second exchange (2:5–7)
        Third exchange (2:8–12)
Scene 2: Daniel's intervention with Arioch and the disclosure of the
    mystery to Daniel (2:13–24)
        Daniel's encounter with Arioch (2:13–16)
        Daniel seeks understanding (2:17–18)
        Revelation to Daniel and doxological response (2:19–23)
        Daniel seeks out Arioch to request interview with the king
            (2:24)
Scene 3: Daniel's appearance before Nebuchadnezzar (2:25–49)
        Introduction of Daniel to the king and Daniel's preliminary
            address (2:25–30)
        Daniel recounts the dream itself (2:31–35)
        The interpretation of the dream (2:36–45)
        The king's response and reward of Daniel (2:46–49)

Comments

[1] The chapter begins with a date notice that apparently contradicts the story in ch. 1. If Nebuchadnezzar's disturbing dream occurs in the second year of his reign, it would happen during the time that Daniel and his three friends were still in training to become sages, according to ch. 1. At the end of ch. 2, however, the four are promoted to leading positions in the kingdom, so that they could hardly be called up for their "final examination" by Nebuchadnezzar at the end of their third year of training, as 1:18–19 describes. Two solutions to this conundrum are possible. One is that the MT involves a textual corruption: instead of "second," one should read "twelfth," as does Papyrus 967. That would not only resolve the temporal contradiction but would also suggest an intriguing correlation between Daniel and traditions in Jeremiah. According to Jeremiah's chronology of Judean/Babylonian reigns, Nebuchadnezzar's twelfth year would correspond to Zedekiah's fourth year (calculated from the synchronism in Jer 32:1). The fourth year of Zedekiah is the year in which a scroll written by Jeremiah, describing the ultimate punishment of Babylon, was to be carried to that city, read aloud, and thrown into the Euphrates as a symbol of Babylon's ultimate destruction (Jer 51:59–64). It was also the year in which Jeremiah opposed Hananiah's optimistic prophecy of an early return of the first exiles to Babylon (Jer 28:1–11) and in which Jeremiah declared that YHWH had given Nebuchadnezzar sovereignty over the nations "and even the wild beasts" (Jer 28:14), a claim to which Dan 2:38 alludes. Thus Dan 2 would represent a divine disclosure to the Babylonian king parallel to the prophetic word from YHWH to Jeremiah. This fit between the texts is perhaps a bit too neat, however, and it is more likely that the Greek translator himself found a clever exegetical resolution to a perplexing contradiction in his source text. If this exegetical reconciliation is the work of early interpretive tradition, then the Greek text of Papyrus 967 is important testimony to an early attempt to correlate the Daniel narratives with the book of Jeremiah.

If the MT reading of the "second year" is correct, it is probably an indication that the Daniel stories were originally composed independently of one another. Although many of the details (such as the varying personal names of the characters) were coordinated with one another as the stories were brought together, not all of the details in the individual stories have been harmonized.

The reference to the "second year" as the time of a disturbing dream makes good sense dramatically. Kings in the ancient Near East often faced threats to the establishment of their reigns, especially at the time of their accession to the throne. The date would be particularly apt if this chapter does have its roots in an old Jewish story told originally about the last Babylonian king, Nabonidus, who came to power as a usurper. In an inscription probably written in the middle of his first regnal year, Nabonidus describes an astronomical dream in which he is assured by a young man who appears within his dream that the sign is not an evil portent. As the dream continues, Nabonidus has a conversation with his illustrious (but now dead) predecessor Nebuchadnezzar, who also reassures him (Beaulieu 1989, 22, 110–11; Schaudig 514–29). Clearly Nabonidus was concerned about the legitimacy and stability of his kingship. If there is a historical source behind the story of Dan 2, it is presumably this public inscription of Nabonidus. But in Dan 2 the narrative has been recast as one about the great king Nebuchadnezzar.

A further comparison with Gen 41 points to a significant aspect of narrative artistry here. In Gen 41 the author describes to the reader the content of Pharaoh's dream as he dreams it (vv. 1–7). In Dan 2 the reader's knowledge of the content of the dream is repeatedly deferred, even as various hints are given. Thus the reader is invited to make surmises about the dream—to engage in acts of interpretation and decipherment of the meager information that is given—surmises that must be revised as further information is disclosed. In v. 1 the reader knows only that Nebuchadnezzar has a dream early in his reign that disturbs him and robs him of sleep. The sense of ominousness coupled with the date invites the supposition that the dream has to do with some threat to the security of his reign.

[2] The following scene closely parallels Gen 41:8 and may well be a stock motif: the disturbed king summons his mantic experts to interpret his ominous dream. Although the Babylonian king Nabonidus attributed particular significance to dreams, most Neo-Babylonian kings did not. Unfortunately, little is known directly about the role of dreams in the Persian court. The Greek historians, however, suggest that the Persian kings may well have treated symbolic dreams as significant portents, as they recount a number of dreams attributed to Persian kings. The closest parallel to Nebuchadnezzar's anxiety-producing dream is one attributed to the Median king Astyges, who is said to have dreamed of a vine growing from the womb of his own daughter that "shaded all Asia." His Magi interpreted it to mean that "the child of his daughter [i.e., Cyrus] would become king in his place," an eventuality that Astyges attempted, unsuccessfully, to prevent (Herodotus 1.107–8).

The terms used for the mantic experts summoned by the king in v. 2 are drawn from several cultural and linguistic realms (see notes on 1:20). The "magicians" (*ḥarṭummîm*) were a category of mantic experts imported from Egypt to the Neo-Assyrian court (Oppenheim 2008, 238). They also appear in the Joseph story as functionaries of Pharaoh's court (Gen 41:24). The term "exorcists" (*ʾaššāpîm*) derives from a specific class of Babylonian experts skilled at diagnosing and combating evil powers that attacked a person (*CAD* 1/2:431). "Diviners" (*mĕkaššĕpîm*) derives from a Hebrew verb that refers to sorcery or conjuring (related to Akk. *kašāpu*). "Chaldeans" (*kaśdîm*), a word that originally referred to a southern Babylonian tribe but came to be a term for

Babylonian mantic experts, is apparently used here as a summary term for the entire array of specialists summoned by the king. The picture is thus that of a king who can command the whole spectrum of mantic experts from all of the national and ethnic traditions of the empire.

[3–12] The interview between the king and his experts unfolds in a series of three exchanges (vv. 3–4, 5–7, 8–12), characterized by mutual misinterpretation and ending in potential disaster.

[3–4] The king's initial request appears straightforward but is actually full of ambiguity. He says that he has dreamed a dream and is anxious *lādaʿat ʾet-haḥălôm*. Since the verb *yĕdaʿ* can mean "to understand" (e.g., v. 30) as well as "to know," the mantic interpreters assume that he means he wants to understand the meaning and significance of the dream. Moreover, in Mesopotamian practice the telling of the dream was part of the therapeutic process for dispelling the evil effects that come from having an ominous dream (Oppenheim 2008, 218).Thus the court experts make the innocent request that the king tell them the dream (cf. Gen 41:8b) so that they can cause him to understand its meaning (*pĕšar*). The exact significance of *pĕšar* is difficult to capture in English. Like its Akkadian cognate *pišru*, it can refer to the "translation" of obscure symbols into straightforward language, a type of interpretation. But the term also refers to what Rabinowitz describes as "the presage or prognostic of the dream, its life-and-death prefiguring of the future" (223). Perhaps one can come close to the nuance of *pĕšar* by thinking of it as what the dream *signifies.*

The mantic experts' direct speech to the king is the place at which the narrative switches from Hebrew to Aramaic, marked in the text by the apparent scribal notation *ʾărāmît* (see note to 2:4). Their polite address to the king echoes a common ancient Near Eastern royal greeting, attested in biblical (1 Kgs 1:31; Neh 2:3), Akkadian, and Persian sources (J. Collins 156). Here, however, it has an unintentionally ironic resonance, since Nebuchadnezzar may well be anxious about just how long he will live.

[5–7] In the second exchange with the experts, Nebuchadnezzar makes it clear that his demand is not simply for the interpretation but also for "the dream *and* its interpretation" (vv. 5–6). Although some early and modern interpreters (e.g., Josephus, *Ant.* 10.195; Jerome, on 2:3; cf. Goldingay 46; Bauer 81) have thought Nebuchadnezzar's request meant that he had forgotten the dream, it is much more likely that the demand has to do with the balance of power and knowledge that obtains between the king and his advisers. Nebuchadnezzar possesses knowledge that the advisers lack: the content of the dream. But he does not possess the skill to interpret the dream. Thus the advisers possess a power of expertise that the king lacks. Moreover, the king recognizes that he cannot judge whether the interpretation the experts render is truthful. His anxiety reflects the ambivalence of royal power in general, which is ostensibly all powerful but in fact often at the mercy of others (Lasine 1–9). The

Nebuchadnezzar's Dream: The End of Divine Delegation of Sovereignty

Neo-Assyrian king Ashurbanipal boasted of his personal grasp of the scribal arts, which limited the ability of his experts to manipulate him (Fincke 122). Here Nebuchadnezzar uses the knowledge that he possesses (the content of his dream), as well as his power as king to punish or reward, to set a test that he thinks will establish the veracity of the interpreters.

This scene also contributes to the characterization of the king. In court tales kings are often depicted as impetuous, capable of quick and deadly rage if thwarted, but also of extravagant generosity when pleased (e.g., Pharaoh in Gen 40:1–3, 13, 19; Ahasuerus in Esth 1:12; 4:11; 6:1–11; 7:5–10; Neh 2:1–2; *Ahiqar* 3:32–33). Such displays of power were also part of royal self-presentation. As Darius proclaimed in the Behistun Inscription, "Among these peoples, the man who was loyal, him I rewarded; he who was faithless, I punished" (DB §8; Kuhrt 143). Dismemberment and the destruction of houses are occasionally mentioned as particularly horrific punishments (Ezek 16:40–41; 2 Macc 1:16) and serve to heighten the dramatic tension. To make a house into a common toilet (if that is the correct translation; see notes) would be a further humiliation (cf. 2 Kgs 10:27).

The mutual misunderstanding continues, however. As if they do not grasp the king's demand, the experts repeat their request that the king tell them the content of the dream, though they phrase the request in slightly more polite language (a jussive verb rather than an imperative).

[8–12] The intense anxiety of the king concerning the dream manifests itself in the way he interprets the behavior of the mantic experts as conspiracy. What the king accuses them of is less clear than is often assumed. He claims certain knowledge that "you are buying ʿiddānāʾ." Most translators render this phrase as "buying time," but as Goldingay (33) rightly observes, it is not the equivalent of the English idiom. The word ʿiddānāʾ does not refer to duration (*pace* BDB) but to a set time or defined period of time (so the CAL). In the phrase the word is also marked as definite ("the time"). Since the sages are willing to interpret the dream as soon as the king tells it to them, their request can scarcely be interpreted as a stalling maneuver. The next part of the king's statement (vv. 8b–9a) indicates that he sees the sages motivated by the certainty of the king's ultimatum and decree. Thus to "buy the time," that is, to possess or own it, seems to be an idiom designating a strategy to gain control of the situation. In v. 9b Nebuchadnezzar clarifies his accusation and again uses the term ʿiddānāʾ, accusing the sages of conspiring together to concoct a misleading interpretation of his dream "until the time changes." Later in the chapter in Daniel's doxology, "changing times and seasons" is parallel to "removing and installing kings" (v. 21). "Until the time changes" may be a euphemistic way of referring to the king's demise and replacement by another monarch. Now Nebuchadnezzar's anxiety becomes clear. In Mesopotamian culture evil dreams could often be rendered harmless by engaging in the appropriate rituals (Oppenheim 2008, 218,

302). Nebuchadnezzar apparently fears that the possibly conspiratorial sages will give him a falsely benign interpretation of an ominous dream. Relying on their advice, he would then fail to take the necessary measures that could deflect the evil portent, thus leading to his overthrow and death. His demand that the sages relate the dream itself is a test of the accuracy of their interpretation. Herodotus (1.120, 128) recounts an analogous situation in which the ominous dream of Astyges (see comments on v. 2) is reinterpreted by his Magi as having been innocuously fulfilled, so that he need not kill his grandson Cyrus. When it turns out that the dream did indeed foretell his displacement by Cyrus, Astyges has the Magi executed because their reassurances prevented him from killing the young Cyrus. But by then it is too late to prevent the fulfillment of the dream.

The author portrays the emotional panic of the sages through a shift in their verbal style. Formerly terse and businesslike, the sages now become loquacious. The beginning and end of their response to the king emphasizes the human impossibility of the task ("no one on dry land," "no one . . . except the gods"), thus setting up a contrast between the limits of their technical expertise and the knowledge communicated through divine revelation to Daniel (vv. 27–28; cf. Isa 44:25–26). In point of fact Mesopotamian sages did on occasion invoke the gods for assistance (Oppenheim 2008, 221), but the story is interested in constructing a contrast between the Chaldean sages and the Jewish Daniel. Less often noted but equally important for understanding the author's perspective is the sages' emphasis on the absolutely unprecedented nature of the request (v. 10b). The fact that Nebuchadnezzar eventually does have his request answered makes him unique among "great and powerful kings" (cf. vv. 29–30). Why the story elevates the figure of Nebuchadnezzar is discussed below.

[13–23] Tensions between vv. 13–16 and 24–28 have led many scholars to suggest that the present version of Dan 2 has undergone revision (so J. Collins 158; Hartman and DiLella 139; Bauer 85; Wills 82–83; but cf. Goldingay 42, 44; Koch 159). In vv. 13–16, the officials seek out Daniel and his friends as members of the sages who are to be executed, and Daniel himself goes to the king to request an audience, suggesting that he is someone with access to the court. In vv. 24–25, however, Daniel approaches Arioch, who then brings Daniel before the king and introduces him to the king as someone he has "found," "a man from the Judean exile," which suggests that he is neither a court sage nor someone previously known to the king. The narrative tension may point to an earlier version of Dan 2 in which Daniel was portrayed as a wise youth, similar to his role in Susanna, or like Joseph in Gen 41 (so J. Collins 158). Since the narrative reads intelligibly without vv. 13–23, these verses may have been composed to adapt the older story to the present cycle, incorporating references to Daniel's three friends (vv. 17–18), representing the Jews as already members of the professional sages (v. 13–16), and including a thematically important poetic blessing (vv. 19–23).

[13–16] The character of Arioch is reminiscent of the cooperative officials who assist Daniel in ch. 1. There, as here, Daniel's ability to speak diplomatically prevents misfortune. In the present form of the narrative, Daniel takes initiative independently of Arioch (v. 16). Like Esther (Esth 4:11), he goes unbidden to the king, though the narrator does not dramatize the moment. Josephus, in an attempt to establish more continuity in the story, has Daniel ask Arioch to approach the king for him (*Ant.* 10.202). A similar concern may account for the readings of Theodotion and the Syriac Peshitta, which omit the words "went in and," thus allowing for the interpretation that Daniel makes his request through Arioch.

[17–19a] The contrast between what an author chooses to dramatize and what the author only briefly narrates is an important clue to the story's central concerns. What happens in vv. 17–19a might have been seen as the key moment in the narrative: the Jewish sages, under a death threat, pray to their God (i.e., "seek mercy; cf. Ps 25:6) and receive a revelatory disclosure that will resolve the conflict between the king and his sages. But the author does not dramatize the scene nor give the text of the prayer. Were he to do so, emphasis would be placed on the Jewish sages themselves. In this story, however, it is not the relationship between God and the Jewish characters that is central so much as the relation between God and the king. Nevertheless, the brief scene is artfully rendered.

The scene forms a narrative and thematic bridge between the framing of the action in the first part of the story (the death threat) and in the second part (the communication of the dream to the king). Realistically, the narrator presents Daniel's motivation to discover "this mystery" simply as the desire that he, his friends, and the rest of the sages not be killed. The content of the dream is not yet the concern to Daniel that it is to the king. The author's use of the term "mystery" or "secret" (*rāz*) is strategic, however. Previously, the king's dream has simply been referred to as "the matter" or "thing" (*millĕtā'*, vv. 10, 11, 15). The term *rāz* is a Persian loanword that enters both Aramaic and Hebrew in the Second Temple period (Thomas 245–51). While it can refer simply to something that is kept hidden (Sir 8:18), which is presumably how the character Daniel intends it in v. 18, the word also can refer to cosmic and eschatological mysteries, as it often does in texts from Qumran (Koch 165–67; Thomas 136–86), and as it is used later in this chapter. Thus the author may have chosen the word in order to foreshadow the content of the dream itself.

The influence of the Persian milieu is also seen in the terminology used for the deity: "God of Heaven" (cf. vv. 18, 37, 44). Although attested earlier (Gen 24:3, 7), it only becomes popular in Persian Period literature (esp. Ezra, Nehemiah, and Chronicles). Its frequency in official correspondence (Ezra 5:12; Cowley, nos. 30:2, 27–28 [= *TAD* 1.A 4.7]; 31:2, 26–27 [= *TAD* 1.A 4.8]; 32:3–4 [= *TAD* 1.A 4.9]; 38:5 [= *TAD* 1.A 4.3]) and in the decree of Cyrus in Ezra 1:2 suggests that it developed as the term by which the Persians designated the God of Israel (J. Collins 159). Here again, one sees the cultural negotiation that takes place between the imperial power and its subordinate peoples. In identifying the God of Israel as the "God of heaven," the Persians highlight features that YHWH and the Persian god Ahura Mazda share in common, including a concern for cosmic order and its manifestation on earth (Berquist 136–37). Part of the Persian ideology was the representation of the many peoples of the empire as coordinated supporters of the great king and his unlimited sovereignty (Briant 171–81). In Ezra 6:8–10, the decree attributed to Darius represents the king as supporting the rebuilding of the temple of the "God of Heaven" in Jerusalem as a place where the Jews may "pray for the life of the king and his sons" (NJPS).

How King Nebuchadnezzar's dream is revealed to Daniel is not entirely clear. The narrator describes it as a "vision of the night" (v. 19a), which is a term often used with the meaning of "dream," as in v. 28 (cf. Isa 29:7). Thus it is possible that Daniel redreams Nebuchadnezzar's dream. This is the second occasion when the narrator might have chosen to disclose the dream, allowing the reader access to the content of the dream as Daniel receives it. Instead, this knowledge is teasingly deferred. The reader is given only hints about the dream, as these are suggested by Daniel's doxology in vv. 19b–23.

[19b–23] In form-critical terms Daniel's prayer can be characterized as an individual thanksgiving with hymnic elements (Plöger 50; Towner 1969, 319; Goldingay 38–39). The prayer is quite carefully composed, both in terms of content and poetics, making extensive use of parallelism and repetition both between lines and within lines. The two main parts of the prayer are parallel to one another. In the first part, Daniel opens in v. 20 with a blessing of the name of God, using a third-person jussive verb (cf. Ps 113:2; Job 1:21). The second part, in v. 23, opens with confession and praise of God in the first person. The reason given for the praise is parallel in each part. In v. 20, it is God's possession of the qualities of wisdom (*ḥokmâ*) and power (*gĕbûrâ*). In v. 23 it is because God has given just these qualities to Daniel himself. Although *gĕbûrâ* can refer to physical or political power, it also has the connotation of intellectual power (Wernberg-Møller 74), a range of meanings that is exploited in the chapter's exploration of the relationship between power and knowledge. Thus the prayer gives examples of the manifestation of these divine qualities in vv. 21–22. Divine power is first exemplified by God's ability to "change times and seasons," to move history from one epoch to another (a topic extensively developed in various apocalyptic texts and Qumran literature). Such epochs, the text suggests, are marked by "removing kings and setting up kings."

Verse 21b introduces new characters, however. Parallel to the kings are the "wise" and those who "have insight." Thus the two categories of human agents in the story (kings and sages) appear to manifest respectively the two featured characteristics of God. What God reveals to the sages is specifically the type of transcendent hidden wisdom suggested by the term "mystery" (*rāz*) in v. 19. While the darkness and light referred to in the final part of v. 22 may simply be a merism, expressing totality, the difference in the relationship of God to darkness and to light suggests an incipient dualism, perhaps under the influence of Persian thought (Koch 175–76). The balance between kings and sages suggested by the prayer's symmetry is undercut in v. 23, however, as Daniel specifically thanks God for giving him both "wisdom and power" in having made known to him "what concerns the king." Now the reader must reassess the nuance of *gĕbûrâ*, recognizing the way in which knowledge *is* power in this chapter. Yet, as Daniel will explain in v. 28, the purpose of the revelation is so that the king himself might know the divine secrets. The story world will only reach equilibrium when both sage and king understand the divine revelation. At this point in the narrative the reader's knowledge stands somewhere between the king's ignorance and Daniel's full understanding, for the reader has only the clues that can be gained from overhearing Daniel's prayer. Although the reader can rightly surmise from v. 21a that the king's dream had to do with the removal and replacement of rulers, the reader might well assume, as Nebuchadnezzar's anxiety suggests he did, that the dream foretold his imminent downfall.

[24–30] As noted above, these verses seem to presuppose a different version of the story than that presumed by vv. 13–16 and ch. 1, a version in which Daniel is not a sage of the royal court but, as Arioch introduces him to the king, simply "a man from the Judean exiles" (v. 25).

Narratively, the scene unfolds as a contrast parallel to the interview between Nebuchadnezzar and his court experts in vv. 3–11. Perhaps suggesting skepticism, the king asks if Daniel is "able" to make known the dream and its interpretation (v. 26). Daniel's reply in v. 27 is a reprise and even a heightening of the sages' earlier assertion of the impossibility of the task (vv. 10–11). By characterizing the king's request as a "mystery" (*rāz*), Daniel further implies its inaccessibility. Rhetorically, the main purpose of this statement is to highlight the exceptional nature of what Daniel is about to do, but it also serves to clear the king's sages of the imputation that they were behaving in a conspiratorial fashion, as Nebuchadnezzar has imagined. Indeed, throughout the story Daniel shows solicitude for his fellow sages (vv. 18, 24). But v. 28 draws a sharp contrast between the sages' and Daniel's sources of knowledge. Whereas they grounded the impossibility of complying with the king's command in the fact that such knowledge was accessible only to the gods, "whose dwelling is not with flesh" (v. 11), Daniel is able to tell the dream because there is just such a "God in heaven" whose intention it is to disclose a revelation to King Nebuchadnezzar (v. 28).

Once again the author teases the audience with a hint of the content of the dream by summarizing its contents as "what will happen at the end of days," a phrase that could simply mean "in the future" (cf. Gen 49:1; Num 24:14; Deut

4:30; 31:29), though in most cases a future that is significantly distant (e.g., Isa 2:2; Mic 4:1). As Driver (26) aptly analyzed the phrase, it "denotes the *closing period* of the future, so far as it falls within the range of view of the writer using it" (italics original). Here in Dan 2 it is arguably used for the first time with an eschatological sense (Lacocque 45), a usage repeated in the latter chapters of the book (cf. 8:19; 10:14; 12:8).

The apparent redundancy between v. 28 and vv. 29–30 leads many commentators to assume that the verses are either ancient doublets (so Montgomery 162; J. Collins 162; Hartman and DiLella 140) or evidence of redaction (Kratz 1991, 55–57), though Koch (118) sees it as an example of the chapter's characteristic use of retarding devices. Given that the text would read smoothly without vv. 29–30 and that these two verses emphasize important thematic elements, they may well be a redactional expansion. Whatever the case, one should inquire as to how their content emphasizes a thematic aspect of the narrative. Daniel minimizes his own wisdom and casts himself as merely the facilitator of a communication from the divine "revealer of mysteries" to King Nebuchadnezzar. Despite many readers' tendency to focus on the character of Daniel, these verses suggest that the story is primarily about Nebuchadnezzar.

Why is it so important to the author that Nebuchadnezzar be the recipient of this divine revelation? While the ultimate recipient of the knowledge is the reader, Nebuchadnezzar's knowledge is also crucial, for the narrative serves as an attempt to negotiate the cognitive dissonance created by belief in the sovereignty of the God of Israel and the reality of Gentile sovereignty on earth. Over several centuries Israelite prophetic and historiographical literature attempted a variety of resolutions to this conundrum (Newsom 2011). They identified Gentile monarchs as agents of the divine will for specific purposes (e.g., Sennacherib in Isa 10:5–6), but also ascribed arrogant false consciousness to them (Isa 10:7–14; cf. 37:21–29). Or they envisioned a monarch's kingship as ordained by YHWH (Nebuchadnezzar in Jer 27:5–8 and Ezek 17:11–21) without raising the question whether the monarch was aware of the source of his rulership or not. The motif of the king's awareness first appears with respect to Cyrus, whose military success occurs "so that you may know" that it is YHWH who has chosen him for a purpose (Isa 45:3–5). This change of emphasis probably reflects the competitive propagandistic environment in which the Babylonian priests represented Cyrus as acknowledging the receipt of his kingship from Marduk (*ANET* 315; *COS* 2:315). Later, in the absence of the Davidic dynasty, Jewish thinking partially assimilated the Persian monarchy to the roles previously played by the Judean kings (e.g., Ezra 6:1–12; 7:11–26; 2 Chr 36:22–23). Here too, the narratives in Dan 1–6 contribute to this effort of imaginatively appropriating the Gentile monarchies for the religious and political self-understanding of emergent Judaism by representing Nebuchadnezzar not only as a proud and arrogant monarch who ultimately comes to understand

Nebuchadnezzar's Dream: The End of Divine Delegation of Sovereignty 75

and publicly acknowledge the supreme sovereignty of Israel's God but also as someone to whom God entrusts knowledge of the plan for the epochs of world history that Nebuchadnezzar has initiated. That the stories do this by falsifying historical reality raises complex issues in narrative ethics. Is the imaginative "redemption" of Nebuchadnezzar that takes place in Dan 2–4 a betrayal of the suffering of those who endured the destructions and oppression of the sixth century? Or is it a way of creatively triumphing over the past in the name of a yet-to-be-unfolded future?

[31–35] Daniel demonstrates the reliability of his information by narrating the dream just as it occurred in the king's own experience, making reference to the king's unfolding perception of the dream ("you were looking, and there before you was . . ." v. 31; "you kept watching as . . ." v. 34). While dream narration in the Bible frequently makes use of the grammatical particle that focuses vision (Heb. *hinnēh*; Aram. *ʾălû*), only in Daniel is the dreamer's experience of looking at the dream images emphasized (Dan 4:10, 13 [7, 10]; cf. 7:2–13). This feature does, however, sometimes occur in prophetic visions, though with different grammatical devices (Amos 7:8; 8:2; Jer 1:11, 13; Zech 1:18; 2:1 [2:1, 5 MT]; 4:2; 5:1, 9; 6:1).

The verbs of seeing divide the dream account into two parts. In the first part the static image of the statue is described, first in its overall appearance (v. 31), then according to each of its four parts, proceeding downward from the head to the feet (vv. 32–33). The second verb of seeing introduces both the action sequences of the dream and the second major image, the stone (vv. 34–35). The initial description of the image stresses its overwhelmingness, without giving specific details. One often-overlooked detail is that the statue is described as "standing before you" (v. 31). That is, Nebuchadnezzar not only experiences the dream but is himself a figure within the dream as the observer of the statue and what happens to it.

The detailed description of the statue makes use of two intersecting symbolic schemata: the parts of the human body and a series of metals. While the image of the body suggests totality, the sequence that moves from head to foot is a symbolic movement from the most to the least noble parts of the body. Similarly, the metals are allocated in a sequence that moves from the most noble to the least, with the feet described as partly of a base, nonmetallic material: terracotta. In some sense a value judgment is made by means of the image itself, though in the interpretation the emphasis is not as much on the declining scale per se as on the contrast between the first and fourth elements. In particular, the mixture of iron and pottery suggests an inherent incompatibility or instability (Smith-Christopher 55, citing Sir 13:2–3).

What else might a culturally informed reader of the period surmise from the imagery itself? In the ancient Near East statues mostly represented either gods or kings, and the term *zîv* ("brilliance") often describes the appearance of gods or kings (*HALOT* 1864; *CAD* 21:119). Also of significance is the fourfold division of the statue and the correlation of the parts with different metals. One need not attempt to look for precise parallels to such statues in the art of the ancient Near East. The imagery is symbolic. The number four is a widespread figure for totality, reinforcing the sense of totality also connoted by the "single statue" (v. 31). The differentiation among the elements, however, suggests change and thus serves as a trope for temporal sequence.

Parallels from other symbolic accounts in antiquity suggest possible sources for the imagery, though each differs from the dream of Dan 2 in significant ways (see J. Collins 162–65; Koch 126–38). Whether the author was directly aware of any of these is a question that cannot be answered with certainty. More likely, such symbolic schemas were widely distributed. The most well known of these is Hesiod's figure of the five ages of humankind (gold, silver, bronze, unidentified material, iron) in *Works and Days* 1.109–201. Since the general sequence of the ages is one of decline, interrupted only by the unidentified heroic fourth age, it is most probable that Hesiod is adapting an earlier schema of four declining ages, each identified with a metal (similarly J. Collins 162). While the metals are the same as those used in Dan 2, the interpretation will make clear that Daniel is concerned with kings and kingdoms, not with the ages of humankind.

Much more likely as a source of influence on the imagery of Dan 2 is a Persian tradition now preserved only in ninth-century-C.E. Pahlavi documents, the *Zand-i Vohuman Yasht* (ch. 1; also known as the *Bahman Yasht*) and the *Denkard* (9.8). Despite the late attestation, many of the traditions in these documents are believed to be quite ancient (Boyce 1990, 2). In the *Zand-i Vohuman Yasht* the god Ahura Mazda discloses "the wisdom of all-knowledge" to Zarathustra in a vision. Zarathustra sees a tree with four branches, one of gold, one of silver, one of steel, and one of mixed iron. The four branches are identified as four periods of time constituting the Zoroastrian millennium, each of which is identified with a particular king, sage, or sovereignty. The first three are positively identified, with the fourth of mixed iron representing the "evil rule of the devs (= demons) with disheveled hair" (Boyce 1990, 92). The *Denkard* gives a similar interpretation, although it identifies the periods somewhat differently and suggests more of a religious than a political periodization. Even though the metals differ slightly from those used in Dan 2, the distinctiveness of the "mixed iron" for the fourth period and its negative evaluation in contrast to the other periods strongly suggest a genetic link between the two traditions (for an extended discussion, see Flusser).

In Daniel, the action sequence of the dream begins in an appropriately surreal fashion, with the contrasting image of the rock, cut out (from what is not specified) without human agency (v. 34). Although Dan 2 recounts a literary dream, not an actual one, the symbolic processes of meaning making are similar. Rock and statue contrast with one another in significant ways. A statue is a carefully crafted artifact; a rock is a natural object, especially one not shaped by human hands (cf. Plöger 52). Attention is first focused on the action sequence. What kind of plot can develop from bringing together a statue and a rock? Most naturally, one in which the rock strikes the statue. The prior description of the statue with its culminating account of the unstable feet makes it logical that the feet will be the place of impact.

Dream logic is not that of the ordinary world, however, and the effect of the rock's impact is not simply to break the feet but to "pulverize" them. Indeed, retracing the parts of the statue in reverse order, v. 35 insists that all of the metal parts of the statue are similarly pulverized "all together." This effect underscores the sense that, although made of different parts, the statue represents one thing. In a second trope of destruction, the remains of the statue are likened to the chaff from a threshing floor, blown away by the wind. Whether the association was conscious or unconscious, the imagery evokes Isa 41:14–15, where Israel is likened to a threshing sledge that turns mountains and hills into chaff (Seow 47).

Only with the final action sequence describing the rock is its full symbolic significance suggested. The rock that becomes a great mountain (Aram. *ṭûr*; cognate with Heb. *ṣûr*) evokes the imagery of Zion as a high mountain rising above all others (Isa 2:2; Mic 4:2). YHWH is also frequently referred to as Israel's *ṣûr* (e.g., Deut 32:4; 1 Sam 2:2; 2 Sam 22:32//Ps 18:31 [32]; Isa 44:8; Hab 1:12), and just as the mountain "fills the earth," so YHWH's glory fills the earth (Isa 6:3). The clustering of imagery from Isaiah in the dream further suggests that the phrase "hewn-out stone" might also evoke the address to the Judean exiles in Isa 51:1: "Look to the rock from which you were hewn" (Seow 47–48; different verbs are used, however). In literary as in actual dreams, images may have multiple, overlapping resonances that cannot be reduced to a univocal meaning.

[36–45] Although the general sense of the dream's meaning would be decipherable to a culturally literate reader, the interpretation adds further specificity. Given Nebuchadnezzar's anxiety, the elaborate rhetoric of vv. 37–38, which delays the pertinent information to the end of the sentence, is a tension-raising device. It also serves to define Nebuchadnezzar's significance and to establish a thematically central point of political theology. The positive representation of Nebuchadnezzar as a monarch given his dominion by the God of heaven derives from a similar characterization of him in Jeremiah (25:9; 27:5–8; 28:14), though the function is somewhat different. In Jeremiah, the characterization of Nebuchadnezzar is part of Jeremiah's argument against other prophets concerning an urgent military-political decision: whether King Zedekiah should rebel against or submit to Babylonian domination (Jer 27–28). By the time when the cycle of stories in Daniel was composed, however, the events of the early sixth century belonged to a distant past. Here the characterization of Nebuchadnezzar plays a role in a comprehensive theory of political dominion that will be articulated explicitly in Dan 4:14, 22, 29.

As in Ezek 26:7, Nebuchadnezzar is described as "king of kings," a title often used by Neo-Assyrian kings, though not by Nebuchadnezzar himself. It designates him as the legitimate overlord of other kings (Lebram 51), a central concept for the author of Dan 1–6, who is concerned with the issue of the divine delegation of sovereignty to Gentile kings. Note that all of the verbs in vv. 37–38 are active, with God as the subject, and describe the God of heaven as the source of Nebuchadnezzar's royal authority (cf. Dan 1:2). Ancient Near Eastern kings regularly attributed their kingship to the will of a god, normally the dynastic god of their own line, although for political purposes in a conquered land they might attribute their kingship to the chief god of that nation. Thus in an inscription composed by the priests of Marduk in Babylon, Cyrus is presented as chosen by Marduk (*ANET* 315; *COS* 2:315). Similarly, after the conquest of Egypt, Cambyses assumed the pharaonic title that represented him as the living Horus (Boyce 1982, 73). The Seleucid kings also invoked the Babylonian gods as the granters of their kingship (*ANET* 317). Whether or not the decree of Cyrus in Ezra 1:2–4//2 Chr 36:23 is fully historical, it participates in this rhetorical tradition. In this ideological exchange, the adherents of the deity in question receive the symbolic empowerment that comes through attributing the king's authority to the will of their deity; the king in turn receives the political stability that comes from the endorsement of the deity of the subject people. While the narrative of Dan 2 is to be understood against the general background of this negotiation of power between the imperial authority and colonized subjects, the specific idealized monarch in Dan 2 belongs to the distant past and serves as a foil for the base, violent, and unstable fourth kingdom described in vv. 40–43. As will become clear, for the author of Daniel the divine authorization of Gentile rulers is both conditional and temporary.

The details with which Nebuchadnezzar's sovereignty is described are developed from Jer 27:5–7 and 28:14, where not only the nations but also the wild beasts serve him. In ancient Near Eastern art the king was often represented as hunting or subduing wild animals, which represented chaotic forces (Keel 1978a, 63–81). The Babylonian kings also demonstrated their power over such forces by establishing game parks where wild animals were kept (Oppenheim 1970, 46). The addition here of "birds of the air" may be inspired by the imagery of Nebuchadnezzar's dream in Dan 4:12 (9 MT), but it also evokes Gen 1–2, which describe the dominion of the primal human over other creatures (1:26; 2:19–20). The OG certainly heard this echo, since it adds "fish of the sea" to the list. These allusions represent Nebuchadnezzar as an almost mythic figure. Ezekiel, too, knew of traditions that likened kings to the primal human in Eden, though he used this tradition in a satirical fashion against the king of Tyre (28:11–19). In Dan 2, however, the details corroborate Daniel's

Nebuchadnezzar's Dream: The End of Divine Delegation of Sovereignty

identification of the first part of the symbolic image of Nebuchadnezzar's dream. Nebuchadnezzar is not, as he feared, represented by the whole statue. Rather, he is the golden head.

Throughout the history of interpretation the four parts of the statue have most commonly been understood to represent four successive kingdoms or empires. But because Nebuchadnezzar himself rather than the Neo-Babylonian kingdom is identified as the head of gold, a minority of interpreters, beginning in the eighteenth century (von der Hardt; discussed in Rowley 1935, 166–73), have instead suggested that the statue represents four kings. Some scholars argue that the four parts of the statue represent the last four kings of the Neo-Babylonian kingdom (Nebuchadnezzar, Amel-Marduk, Neriglissar, and Nabonidus or Nabonidus/Belshazzar), while the rock represents Cyrus (so Davies 48; Fröhlich 268; cf. Kratz 1991, 62). Thus the dream would originally be an anti-Babylonian oracle roughly contemporary with Isa 40–55, which also gives Cyrus a prominent role as YHWH's anointed who will overthrow Babylon (Isa 45:1–8). Yet there are problems with this interpretation. Nebuchadnezzar was succeeded by four, not three, further kings (Labashi-Marduk ruled briefly after Neriglissar). Moreover, the imagery of the rock becoming a mountain and ruling as an eternal kingdom would seem an odd claim for a Jewish writer to make about Cyrus. Most significantly, the details of the three successors to Nebuchadnezzar given in the interpretation by Daniel do not fit well with what is known about the remaining kings of the Neo-Babylonian dynasty. Neriglissar, the son-in-law of Nebuchadnezzar, had some military success but can scarcely be said to have ruled over the whole earth. Nor would it be appropriate to describe the relationship between Nabonidus and Belshazzar as a divided kingdom. Nabonidus retained the status of king throughout his absence from Babylon.

An alternative interpretation assumes that the four kings are those named in the stories of Daniel itself—Nebuchadnezzar, Belshazzar, Darius the Mede, and Cyrus—with the rock representing either the Judean exiles or God (Goldingay 51; Seow 46–47). While somewhat more plausible, this proposal cannot explain why the fourth kingdom would receive such a negative description in Dan 2:40–43, since Cyrus is mentioned in Daniel only in passing (in 1:21; 6:28 [29]; 10:1) and in rather positive fashion elsewhere in biblical tradition. Finally, the redactional additions in vv. 42–43 assume that the dream and its interpretation concern four empires, not four kings. That this was also the original meaning of the symbolic dream seems most plausible. The kings and kingdoms mentioned in the book of Daniel are, however, key to the identification of the kingdoms in Nebuchadnezzar's dream. In Dan 1–6 the Babylonian kingdom, represented by Nebuchadnezzar and Belshazzar, is replaced by that of Darius the Mede (5:30–31 [5:30–6:1]), which in turn is followed by that of Cyrus the Persian (6:28 [29]). Although the story cycle does not refer to a later kingdom, the king of Greece (i.e., Alexander) is identified as defeating the Medes and Persians in Dan 8:20–21. Thus the sequence of Gentile kingdoms presupposed in Dan 2 is best understood as Babylonia, Media, Persia, and Greece. Since the eschatological destruction of the Hellenistic kingdoms did not occur, later Jewish and Christian writers identified the fourth kingdom with Rome, combining the Medes and the Persians as a single kingdom (cf. *4 Ezra* [2 Esd] 13; Josephus, *Ant.* 10.206–10; Jerome, on 2:31–40).

Excursus 1: Origin and Development of the Four-Kingdoms Schema

Concern about the significance of the transfer of kingship from one city, dynasty, or nation to another was a long-standing preoccupation in the ancient Near East. It is reflected in the Sumerian King List (*ANET* 265–67), as well as in the Egyptian dynasty lists (e.g., the Abydos and Karnak king lists). In the first millennium, interest was directed to the series of international empires that ruled one after the other. Although the earliest evidence for this historiographical schema is found in two Greek authors, Herodotus (5th c. B.C.E.) and Ctesias (4th c. B.C.E.; preserved in Diodorus Siculus 2.1–34), the schema is not of Greek but of Persian origin. Herodotus himself indicates that he relies on Persian sources (1.95), and Ctesias was the court physician to Artaxerxes II (404–359). Both Herodotus and Ctesias describe the transfer of sovereignty as proceeding from the Assyrians to the Medes and then to the Persians. While Herodotus gives a historically sober account, Ctesias describes the three as holding vast world empires. Both the grandiosity of the schema and its apparent function of legitimizing Persian domination are consistent with other aspects of Persian imperial ideology (Briant 172–83). This sequence of Assyria, Media, and Persia is also reflected in the book of Tobit (14:4), which was likely composed in the Eastern Diaspora, and in the Jewish *Sibylline Oracles* 4:49–101.

Despite the fact that Alexander presented himself in many ways as the successor to the Persian kings, there is no indication that Greek historians added Greece as the fourth kingdom in an attempt to appropriate the schema as legitimizing propaganda for any of the Hellenistic kingdoms. Roman historians, however, did use the historiographical schema in sources attested from the second century B.C.E. onward (Polybius 38.22; Dionysius of Halicarnassus 1.2.2–4; Tacitus, *Hist* 5.8–9; Appian, *Hist. rom.*, Preface, 9). Arguably the earliest account is that of Amelius Sura (so Swain 2–3; but see Mendels):

> The Assyrians were the first of all races to hold power, then the Medes, after them the Persians, and then the Macedonians. Then when the two kings, Philip and Antiochus, of Macedonian origin, had been completely conquered, soon after the overthrow of Carthage, the supreme command passed to the Roman people. (via Swain 2–3)

The schema found in Dan 2, however, differs in structure and function from that used by the Romans. Like the Persians, the Romans were interested in legitimizing their empire as the successor to the series of world empires in a simple schema of continuity. In Daniel, however, there is sharp discontinuity between the four Gentile kingdoms represented by the statue and the quite different kingdom represented by the statue-shattering rock.

Thus there appears to be a strategic difference between the way in which the schema is used by empires and by those who were subjugated by empires.

Daniel also partially adapts the sequence of kingdoms to the Jewish experience of history. Instead of the sequence "Assyria, Media, Persia," which reflects the actual transition of power from the Persian perspective, Daniel substitutes Babylon for Assyria as the first kingdom ("Babylon, Media, Persia"), thus creating a historically incoherent sequence, since Media did not rule after Babylon. It is not clear, however, that the Jewish author of Daniel was the first writer to transform the historiographical schema into a model of resistance. Other examples of historical schemas used as resistance literature from roughly the same period do exist, although their interpretation is problematic because they have been updated after their original predictions failed. *Sibylline Oracles* 4 appears to have been structured according to a four-kingdoms schema (Assyria, Media, Persia, Macedonia), which is finally brought to an end by an eschatological judgment. In the present form of the *Sibylline Oracles,* however, the Macedonian kingdom shares its space as the fourth kingdom with Rome, suggesting an updating of the original oracle. The *Dynastic Prophecy*, written in the dialect of late Babylonian, was apparently originally a prophecy *ex eventu*, written from the Persian perspective shortly after the conquest of Alexander the Great, since its attempt to project the future predicts that the once-defeated Darius III will rally to defeat Alexander, a desired event that did not take place. But this text, too, was later updated to chronicle the further reigns of Alexander's successors (so Neujahr 58–71). The phenomenon of updating has left its mark on Daniel as well. The interpretation in vv. 42–43 adds details not warranted by the original description of the image but prompted by unfolding events at some distance from the time of the original text.

Although the four parts of the statue receive brief but equal attention in the presentation of the dream imagery itself, they are not evenly treated in the interpretation. After the long description of Nebuchadnezzar in vv. 37–38, the second and third kingdoms are only briefly described. Neither of them has explicit divine authorization like that given to Nebuchadnezzar, but neither are they represented in particularly negative terms. Of the second all that is said of it is that it is "inferior to you," literally, "earth in comparison with you" (v. 39). The third kingdom, by contrast, is described in terms of its unique breadth of power, as one which will "rule over the whole earth." Apparently, the author of Dan 2 knows little with which to characterize the Medes. Although a few biblical texts refer to the Medes as potential successors to the Babylonians (Isa 13:17; Jer 51:11, 28), they do not loom large in Jewish tradition. By contrast, the immense empire of the Persians was that within which the Jewish communities both in Yehud and in the Diasporas of Egypt and Syro-Mesopotamia lived for over two hundred years. From that vantage point, the Persian Empire was one that truly ruled "over the whole earth."

The author of the chapter, however, is living in the Hellenistic period, after the conquest of the Persian Empire by Alexander the Great, since the sequence as he represents it concludes with a fourth kingdom. This fourth kingdom is seen as the turning point in history. Its difference from the others is represented in terms of its destructiveness. Its symbolic material, iron, is identified as that which "shatters and breaks everything" (v. 40a), reflecting the rapid, violent, and destructive impact of the Hellenistic conquest of the Persian Empire (Portier-Young 49–54). Curiously, the fourth kingdom is said to "shatter and crush *all these*" (v. 40b), referring to the three previous kingdoms. Although Ginsberg (1948, 6) tried to find a historical context in which all three kingdoms could be said to exist in some residual form, his approach is too literalistic. The imagery has both a cultural and a symbolic significance. In some sense the Hellenistic Empire was seen to constitute a break from the previous sequence of Near Eastern kingdoms (cf. Dan 7:7) and thus to represent a particularly significant moment in the historical process, a judgment that many modern historians share. More importantly, the action of the fourth kingdom in destroying all its predecessors anticipates what is ascribed to the everlasting kingdom (vv. 35, 44). Through this imagery the fourth kingdom is framed as the definitive counterpart to the final kingdom that the God of heaven will raise up. It is the negative shadow of that kingdom.

If it is correct that the biblical writer appropriated an original Persian oracle that represented the fourth kingdom as "mixed iron," adapted in Daniel as "partly iron and partly terra-cotta," then v. 41 would belong to the interpretation of the original oracle and not to a later updating, except perhaps for the phrase "and the toes," which does not appear in Papyrus 967 and apparently was not present in 4QDan[a]. In identifying the mixture of materials as a "divided kingdom," the author alludes to the division of Alexander's empire among his primary generals after his death. From the perspective of the Near East, the two most important were Ptolemy, who ruled from Egypt, and Seleucus, whose base of power was in Mesopotamia and Syria.

Since the dream mentions only legs and feet, vv. 42–43, which describe toes, may be later redactional additions, updating the original prediction in light of subsequent historical events. None of the ancient versions agrees fully with the MT, and it is no longer possible to reconstruct the sequence of supplementary additions with certainty (for attempts, see Koch 102–3; Jepsen 387–89). Verse 41 comments upon the inherent instability of a divided kingdom, though emphasizing the residual strength represented by the element of iron. In comparison, v. 42 emphasizes equally the strength and weakness of the two parts of the kingdom, perhaps alluding to the shifting balance of power between the Ptolemaic and Seleucid kingdoms (cf. ch. 11). Reinterpreting a phrase from v. 41 concerning the "mixing" of iron and pottery as (lit.) "mixing by human seed but not clinging together," v. 43 provides the most salient clue to particular historical events. This imagery most plausibly refers to the dynastic intermarriages between the Ptolemies and the Seleucids, those of Antiochus II to Berenice in 252 B.C.E. and of Ptolemy V Epiphanes to Cleopatra, daughter of Antiochus III,

Nebuchadnezzar's Dream: The End of Divine Delegation of Sovereignty

in 193–92, neither of which achieved a lasting detente between the two kingdoms. Both marriages are referred to in Dan 11:6, 17.

[44–45] The active role of the God of heaven resumes in v. 44, "set[ting] up" yet another kingdom. The differentiation of this kingdom from the others is marked in several ways. First, it is not called the "fifth" kingdom, implying that it does not belong to the sequence. Second, in contrast to the others, it is described as an everlasting rather than a temporary sovereignty. And third, it is explicitly said to "shatter and put an end to all these kingdoms." As noted above, although the verb "shatter" (*dĕqaq*) is taken from the action in the dream sequence (v. 35), which is briefly repeated in v. 45a, it is also one of the verbs used to describe the violent action of the fourth kingdom (v. 40), which was also said to have destroyed its predecessors. Delineating resemblance between opposites is a common trope, one that becomes very common in the dualistic imagery of apocalyptic literature.

The text says little about the nature of the final kingdom apart from its everlastingness. In the concluding description the text adds one detail to the dream imagery, describing the rock as cut out from "a mountain" (v. 45a). This detail led early interpreters to interpret the rock as a symbol of the awaited messiah (*4 Ezra* [2 Esd] 13:6–7; Luke 20:18; also Irenaeus [*Haer.* 5.26] and Jerome [on 2:40]; see Towner 1999, 243). That, however, is an anachronistic interpretation. There is no messianic expectation in the book of Daniel itself, although aspects of its imagery are later reinterpreted in messianic contexts and play a significant role in the construction of messianic imagery (see comments on ch. 7).

The more difficult question is whether the rock represents a final universal sovereignty exercised by a revived kingdom of Israel—or is rather the direct sovereignty of the God of heaven directly manifested on earth (so Koch 219). The explicit reference to the "people of the holy ones of the Most High" and their kingdom in 7:27 is not by itself definitive. That verse could be seen as a later interpretation of the more general language in 2:44. Moreover, the reference to the kingdom not being left to another people might suggest that the discontinuity with the previous kingdoms indicates that this sovereignty is of a wholly different order (Plöger 54; Goldingay 52, 59). On balance, however, it seems more likely that the author envisions the rulership of the God of heaven being manifest through the earthly sovereignty of a revived kingdom of Israel. In 4:3 (3:33 MT); 4:34 (31); and 6:26 (27) both Nebuchadnezzar and Darius praise the sovereignty of the God of heaven as already a present and everlasting reality in terms that explicitly echo the language of 2:44. Thus the *future* event alluded to in Nebuchadnezzar's dream must refer to something of a different nature. The image of the rock "cut out" from the mountain (v. 45) or from some undefined entity (v. 34) also fits more naturally as an image of Israel or perhaps of the Diaspora community itself as the nucleus of the new Israelite kingdom.

Daniel's final words form an inclusio with v. 28, attesting the certainty of the events revealed in the dream and the authenticity of his interpretation but also underscoring the purpose of the dream as a revelation to Nebuchadnezzar of the course and goal of future history. In terms of the narrative, it appears that an equilibrium has been reached in terms of access to knowledge. Daniel, the king, and the reader all now know the content and the interpretation of the dream. But the balance has actually shifted. The reader, who began as the least empowered in terms of access to knowledge, now has more understanding than either the king or Daniel. Since the dream is a *vaticinium ex eventu*, the reader who is able to make the interpretive connections knows the specific identities of the kingdoms that Daniel refers to only in the most general terms. Thus the reader becomes a figure like Daniel, capable of interpreting revealed mysteries.

[46–47] In contrast to the Joseph story, where Joseph not only interprets Pharaoh's dream but also advises him on the course of action he should take (Gen 41:33–36), Daniel does not tell Nebuchadnezzar what to do with the revelation. The dream is not a warning so much as it is a disclosure of a profound reality. Nebuchadnezzar's response is neither puzzling nor incongruous. It is precisely the right response, as both his actions and words indicate. As Jerome already observed in his comments on Dan 2:46, Nebuchadnezzar's actions in bowing before Daniel and commanding that sacral offering be made to him is not worship of the human Daniel but of the God whose power has been manifest through him. The action is similar to what Josephus reports in the apocryphal story of the encounter between Alexander and the Jewish high priest. According to Josephus, when Alexander saw the high priest, he recognized him as the figure who appeared in a dream announcing that he would conquer Asia, and so Alexander prostrated himself before the high priest, who represented the power of a great god who had revealed the future to him (*Ant.* 11.329-39). While this is not an action that would be proper for a Jew, it is how certain Jewish authors envisioned Gentile kings responding to manifestations of divine power. Nebuchadnezzar's words similarly interpret his actions: he praises not Daniel but "your god." The three phrases he uses characterize this deity in three sets of relationships. Calling him "God of gods" (cf. Deut 10:17; Ps 136:2), Nebuchadnezzar recognizes him as powerful over other deities. "Lord of kings," a title known from a Persian-era inscription (Cross; cf. Deut 10:17; Ps 136:3), indicates that Nebuchadnezzar grasps this deity's control of the history of earthly sovereignties. Calling him "revealer of mysteries" (cf. 1QH^a 26.14–15) affirms that this is a divine revelation (vv. 28, 45). The king's response is not a "conversion" (*pace* Hartmann and DiLella 150; contrast 2 Macc 9:17). Rather, it is, or appears to be, a recognition by Nebuchadnezzar of the Jewish God as ultimate source of knowledge and sovereignty, the central concern of the cycle of stories in Dan 1–6. Although at the conclusion of this chapter Nebuchadnezzar seems to have understood matters clearly, the events of chs. 3 and 4 will show that he has not yet grasped the full implications of what he has affirmed.

[48–49] Having first honored Daniel's God, Nebuchadnezzar turns to the business of honoring the man Daniel. The reward and promotion of the clever or faithful sage is a stock element in court tales (Gen 41:37–45; Esth 8:2; 10:2–3). Here Daniel is given two distinct posts, the governorship of the "province of Babylon" and the professional leadership of "the sages of Babylon." The various categories of mantic experts in Assyria and Babylonia were headed by leaders with the title of *rabû*, although apparently there was no general head of sages (Koch 239). The final verse, like v. 17, serves to incorporate references to Daniel's three friends into a narrative in which they play no significant role, thereby setting up the story in ch. 3, in which they play the prominent role. Lacocque's (54–55) suggestion that v. 49 serves to explain why Daniel is not present in ch. 3 is ingenious but finally unconvincing. Daniel does not decline the political office for himself but asks that his friends be appointed to his staff. Daniel has authority "over the whole province of Babylon" whereas they are appointed "over the administration of the province of Babylon." The "gate of the king" is an expression from Persian court protocol, referring to those who attended upon the king in proximity to the royal palace and chambers (Xenophon, *Cyr.* 8.1.6; cf. Herodotus 3.120; Esth 3:2) and suggests the high status of Daniel at the court.

History of Reception, by Brennan W. Breed

The Four-Kingdoms Schema

The four-kingdoms schema found in Dan 2 and 7 has proved to be one of the most influential time-structuring devices in all of world history. One tradition, exhibited by third-century-C.E. Neoplatonic philosopher Porphyry and evident in the Peshitta version of the book of Daniel as well as the exegetical work of several Syriac Christians, interprets the text in a manner similar to contemporary biblical scholars (van Peursen 195; note, however, that Porphyry denotes the third empire as Alexander's and the fourth empire as those of the Diadochoi). Outside of these rare readers, there is a consistent tendency for empires to legitimate their own rule and emphasize historical continuity with this schema, whereas those subjugated by empires use the trope to emphasize the illegitimacy and discontinuity of their current political states of affairs. For almost all Jews until the Arab invasions of the seventh century C.E. and for most Christians until the time of Roman emperor Constantine, the Danielic four-kingdom schema represented the kingdoms of (1) Babylon; (2) some combination of Media and Persia; (3) Greece or Macedonia, usually including Alexander's Hellenistic Empire and the resulting kingdoms of the Diadochoi; and (4) Rome.

Due to Rome's unprecedented size and power, as well as its destruction of the Jerusalem temple, it became the centerpiece of discussion in both communities.

In the first-century-C.E. Jewish pseudepigraphic work *4 Ezra* (2 Esd) 11–12, Ezra has a series of visions, one of which shows an eagle with twelve wings. An angel interprets as follows: "The eagle which you saw coming up from the sea is the fourth kingdom which appeared in a vision to your brother Daniel. But it was not explained to him as I now explain or have explained it to you" (12:11–12; *OTP*, trans. Metzger; cf. *2 Bar* 39). Thus the angel updates the schema to include the new colonial power, a pattern that would continue in Jewish communities living outside of Rome's fluctuating borders. Josephus, who was attempting to interpret the Jewish people for a Roman audience, was in a more delicate position. In his discussion of the book of Daniel, he explained that "our nation suffered these things under Antiochus Epiphanes, according to Daniel's vision, and what he wrote many years before they came to pass. In the very same manner Daniel also wrote concerning the Roman government and that our country should be made desolate by them" (*Ant.* 10.276). Josephus praised the invulnerability of the kingdom of iron—for him, Rome—and he did not mention the detail of iron mixing with clay. As for the stone that smashed the statue in Nebuchadnezzar's dream, Josephus equivocates: "And Daniel also revealed to the king the meaning of the stone, but I have not thought it proper to relate this, since I am expected to write about what is past and done and not of what is to be" (*Ant.* 10.210).

Early Christians followed the same line of interpretation: the New Testament book of Revelation reworks images from Dan 7 to create a new beast from the sea, which symbolizes the oppressive power of Rome (13:1–10), and by the second century Christian exegetes treated the Roman reading as commonplace (Irenaeus, *Haer.* 5.26.1; Hippolytus, *Comm. Dan.* 4.3–4). As Hippolytus explains, "However, the now-ruling animal is not one nation, but it is a collection of all languages and generations of humankind and is prepared to be a multitude of warriors, who are all called Romans, but do not originate from one country" (*Comm. Dan.* 4.8). For these interpreters, the fourth kingdom, Rome, embodies evil itself. Hippolytus, for instance, insists that the antichrist will emerge from the kingdom of Rome (*Comm. Dan.* 4.10; cf. Dan 7:8).

Imperial Use

After Constantine's decision to privilege the Christian religion in the early fourth century, Christian exegetes reinterpreted the significance of the fourth empire, though they did not contest that it described Rome. The court stories in Dan 1–6 demonstrate a desire that the foreign monarch should recognize the sovereignty of YHWH (cf. Dan 6:26), and many post-Constantinian Christians decided to read Dan 2 and 7 with this concern in mind rather than the apocalyptic destruction of world empires signified in Dan 7–12. Eusebius, Constantine's court theologian, declared that Constantine was the "first Christian emperor," and that he "alone of all the Roman emperors has honored God the all-sovereign with exceedingly godly piety; he alone has publicly proclaimed to all the word of Christ" (*Vit. Const.* 75). In a sermon in praise of Constantine, Eusebius applied Dan 7:18 ("the holy ones of the Most High shall receive the kingdom") to the transition of Roman imperial power from Constantine to his sons, thus reinterpreting the fourth kingdom as one that transitions seamlessly into the fifth empire of the saints (Podskalsky 13). In Eusebius's view, the empire's ruler acknowledged the sovereignty of the true God, and thus the fourth kingdom had been sanctified, inaugurating a universal peace. The promised future fifth kingdom would then be merely a continuation and spiritualization of this fourth kingdom, which would rule until the end of time. Roman Christians were nearly unanimous in their support of this interpretation (Cyril of Jerusalem, *Catech.* 15.12; Eusebius, *Dem. ev.* 25; Lactantius, *Inst.* 7.16; Victorinus of Pettau, *Comm. Apoc.* 17.9), and Jerome's discussion of the four kingdoms in his Daniel commentary (on 2:31–40; 7:4–8) became the standard interpretation through the medieval period through its adoption in the *Glossa ordinaria*.

Non-Roman Christians and those living near the borders of Rome, however, had more complex opinions, even if they supported the empire. For example, Ephrem, a fourth-century Christian theologian, lived in Nisibis, a Syrian city on the border of the Roman Empire and Sassanian Persian Empire. Ephrem supported Rome as the defender of Christianity, but celebrated when his city of Nisibis fell to the Sassanians, because the retreating Roman army carried with it the body of the dead emperor, Julian "the Apostate," who had rejected Christianity and returned to traditional Roman religion. As the Persian flag rose over Nisibis, Ephrem wrote a series of hymns against Julian that used the kingdom schema of Daniel to declare the Persian victory to be a necessary cleansing of the holy empire (Griffith). Julian, Ephrem argued, had returned to the pagan gods and thus reverted from the fourth empire to the third Greek kingdom:

> He rejoiced God, and gladdened Daniel:
> a king, the Hellenic king, has been rebuked,
> for he angered God and denied Daniel,
> and there near Babylon he was judged and condemned.
>   (*Adv. Jul.* 1.18–20; Griffith 251)

With the decline of the Roman Empire in the fifth century, Roman Christians faced a new historiographical dilemma with regard to the four-kingdom schema. Augustine's book *City of God,* for example, tried to distinguish between the merely worldly empire of Rome and the spiritual kingdom of God, which would never perish. In his discussion of Daniel, Augustine brushes past speculation on the schema, agreeing to its basic interpretation but downplaying its significance: "There are some expositors who take the four kingdoms to be the Assyrian, Persian, Macedonian, and Roman Empires. This is an excellent suggestion, as anyone can see who will study the scholarly and carefully written work of the priest, Jerome, on Daniel" (*Civ.* 20.23).

Yet overwhelmingly Christian exegetes chose to reinterpret the schema rather than relinquish it. Western European Christians argued that the end of time had not arrived, and thus the kingdoms emerging from the Roman Empire's demise had restarted or somehow inherited the status of the holy fourth, and final, kingdom. Many Christians believed that the Byzantine Empire, whose inhabitants called themselves Romans, were seamless inheritors of the fourth-kingdom status (Himmelfarb 129–30). In the wake of the Byzantine empress Irene's usurpation of her son's throne in 797 and resulting fears of the collapse of the Byzantine state, Pope Leo III decided to crown Charlemagne the "Emperor of the Romans" on Christmas Day in 800. This act was designed to protect Rome from the Lombards, but it also attempted to transfer the fourth-kingdom status from the Byzantine Empire to a Western European monarch in order to defer the apocalypse that would result from the demise of the fourth kingdom (Latowsky 13–15). Notker Balbulus, a ninth-century Frankish monk, opened his hagiographical *Deeds of Charlemagne* with the claim that God moved from East to West through the four kingdoms, and Charlemagne's kingdom offers a new, glorious start: "He who ordains the fates of kingdoms and the march of centuries, the all-powerful Disposer of events, having destroyed one extraordinary image, that of the Romans, ... then raised up among the Franks, the golden head of a second image, equally remarkable, in the person of the illustrious Charles" (McGinn 2002, 10). In the tumultuous century that followed Charlemagne's death, his kingdom was divided into several pieces that vied for centuries to claim the status of inheritor of the fourth kingdom. In 962, Otto I of Saxony managed to consolidate power in Germany and was crowned emperor and successor of Charlemagne's kingdom by Pope John XII, and shortly thereafter medieval German chronicler Adam of Bremen argued that, through Otto, the Germans had proved their inheritance of Daniel's fourth-kingdom status (Scales 282).

The legacy of Charlemagne gave rise to the influential medieval concept of *translatio imperii* ("transfer of rule"), which traced the lineage of the fourth kingdom. Otto of Freising, a twelfth-century German bishop and chronicler, wrote his world history in order to demonstrate that the *translatio imperii* proceeded from Rome to Byzantium after the fall of Rome, then to the Franks in 800, and from there to the Lombards and finally the Germans, where he claimed it resided at his time (155). Otto was, however, worried about the strength of the fourth kingdom, and suggested that at his time it had developed feet of clay, intimating that the apocalypse was near (94). In the thirteenth century, the German kings crowned by the pope were said to rule over the "Holy Roman Empire," the German continuation of the fourth kingdom.

By the fourteenth century, it was commonplace to advocate for one's own locality as the fourth kingdom, as this status, when recognized by others, especially if by the Roman pontiff, granted actual authority (Scales 279). This is evident in Konrad von Megenberg's polemical *Lament* from the 1330s, in which a pope urges a personified church: "If you grant the [imperial] eagle to this rude people [the Germans], you can if you wish take it up again" (Scales 280). The twelfth-century French poet Chrétien de Troyes suggested that the *translatio imperii* as well as the *translatio studii* ("transfer of knowledge"), a closely linked concept, moved from Greece to Rome and finally to France (Gurevich 131), while Richard of Bury, fourteenth-century bishop of Durham, argued that the title had passed from Rome to Paris and, finally, to Britain (Boitani 149).

The medieval abbot Adso of Montier-en-Der adopted a Byzantine motif of the Last World Emperor, the final monarch of the Danielic fourth empire, in his influential apocalyptic work on the antichrist (Valdez 211–12). Adso used this motif to justify the increase in power of the Carolingian monarchs relative to the Roman pontiff. Resulting French and German versions of this legend differed, leading to friction that manifested itself in jostling over claims for the title "fourth kingdom." The fourteenth-century French Franciscan friar Jean de Roquetaillade, for example, wrote a commentary on the medieval "Cyrillic Prophecy" (by Cyril of Constantinople, d. ca. 1235) that described the German emperor Frederick II Hohenstaufen as the antichrist, referring to Dan 7:8, and suggested in turn that the French king Charles of Anjou would be the blessed Last World Emperor (Valdez 217). Friction between various monarchs and the Roman pope led to a discussion about the nature of the "Rome" presumed in the fourth kingdom; from the Investiture controversy of the eleventh century until the Reformation, church officials such as Giles of Viterbo argued that the Roman Church was the fourth kingdom (O'Malley 104), while political leaders and humanists such as the fifteenth-century German scholar Conrad Celtis argued that Italy had long ago passed its temporal authority northward (Dickey 15). Martin Luther drew on this biblical trope to justify his argument that the Roman pontiff was attempting to exercise improper authority in Germany; in the 1520s, Luther argued that the "providence of God" arranged for the "transfer" of empire, learning, and religion from Latins to Germans (Dickey 16). Luther writes that God's "words and grace" are "a traveling object. . . . It was with the Jews, but away it went. . . . Rome and the Latin lands have also had it, but away it goes and now they have the Pope" (Dickey 17).

Early historians of the Reformation, such as Johannes Carion and Johannes Sleidanus, used Luther's twist on the four-kingdoms schema as the basis for their histories as they argued that Protestantism was the new identity of the fourth kingdom (Dickey 17). John Calvin shifted the terms of the discussion with his insistence that the fourth monarchy was not Rome but the Seleucids, and that the Christian era was, as a whole, to be identified with the stone cut without human hands; many later Reformers followed his interpretation (Pitkin 326). Catholic exegetes from the Counter-Reformation period generally defend the identification of the Roman Church by distinguishing between "heathen Rome" and "Christian Rome," of which the latter is represented by the Roman pontiff (Lapide 13–15). In an attempt to defuse religious tensions, Hugo Grotius advocated for a historical understanding of the fourth kingdom as that of the Seleucids, and nothing more, though his argument that the millennium began with Constantine suggested a subtle Roman interpretation (Berg 96).

In the early modern era, the four-kingdom schema manifested itself in striking visual terms. "Daniel's Dream Map," an image from the early sixteenth century that was in constant use until the mid-seventeenth century, depicts a Ptolemaic map of the world with each continent assigned to a beast and an image of the Turkish army threatening Europe, which is represented with the third beast (see fig. 5). This image accompanied printed versions of Luther's commentary on Daniel and his sermon against the Turks, as well as many German printed Bibles; the Turkish army appears in the image because of its 1529 siege of Vienna, which threatened to end the Holy Roman Empire (Delano-Smith). In the 1570s, the Catholic priest Jean Boulaese, professor of Hebrew at Paris, created a popular chart that displayed the history of the world according to the four-kingdom schema, which Boulaese thought predicted the impending apocalypse (Rosenberg and Grafton 52). And in 1585, Lorenz Faust published a book titled *Anatomia statue Danielis* (Anatomy of Daniel's statue), which included a woodcut depicting the statue from Daniel's dream (Rosenberg and Grafton 56). The statue's face resembles the king of Saxony, August I, perhaps because Faust believed he was the Last Emperor. On the statue's body are inscribed the names of world rulers throughout history, with the names of Mesopotamian rulers on the statue's head, Median and Persian rulers on the chest, Roman emperors on the skirt, and Byzantine and Ottoman rulers on the right leg, with the Holy Roman emperors on the left leg. Faust positions the rulers purposefully according to the statue's anatomy and explains his choices: Darius appears over the lung because he gave breathing space to the Jewish people, and Heliogabalus (Elagabalus), the notoriously immoral emperor whose dead body was disposed of in a sewer, is located "at the exit from the rear" (Rosenberg and Grafton 56). The work serves to justify the current status of the Holy Roman Empire in the sixteenth century and to advocate for its impending war against the Ottoman Empire.

In the seventeenth century, the combination of the Thirty Years' War, the Ottoman threat to Europe, and the colonization of the "New World" created a widespread sense of apocalypticism throughout Europe, of which the Portuguese Jesuit author António Vieira, who spent much of his life in Brazil, provides one conspicuous index. Following the prophecies concerning the Fifth Kingdom made by Gonçalo Anes Bandarra, a sixteenth-century Portuguese shoemaker who had been commanded to cease writing by the Inquisition, Vieira argued

Figure 5. "Daniel's Dream Map," from Martin Luther, *Eine Heerpredigt wider den Türken*, Wittenburg, 1542. The fourth beast, located in Africa, represents the Turkish Empire. The head on its central horn is an interpretation of the little horn and the "mouth speaking arrogantly" (Dan 7:8). Courtesy of the Richard C. Kessler Reformation Collection, Pitts Theology Library, Candler School of Theology, Emory University.

that Portugal was the fifth kingdom mentioned in Daniel, and that it must unite the world through its conversion of all peoples to Christianity (Cohen).

Meanwhile, Puritans saw the so-called New World as a divinely ordained place of refuge for them; they appropriated the trope of *translatio imperii* to help them express their conviction. Seventeenth-century English Puritan Thomas Hooker wrote that God's gospel was a "traveling object," like Luther's description, that was moving relentlessly toward America (Dickey 19). The eighteenth-century Anglo-Irish philosopher, Bishop George Berkeley, wrote a poem titled "Verses on the Prospect of Planting Arts and Learning in America" that ended with this stanza:

> Westward the course of empire takes its way;
> The first four Acts already past,
> A fifth shall close the Drama with the day;
> Time's noblest offspring is the last.
> (Young 21)

This poem expresses the widely held notion that the progression of empires in Daniel had continually moved from East to West, and that the direction of *translatio* had continued to the present day, ending in America (the "fifth"). The notion of the Westward expansion of empire deeply influenced the leaders of the early United States of America, convincing them that the divinely ordained destiny of America included ownership of all lands to the Pacific Ocean, and even later into the Pacific Islands (Bickford and Bowling 77–86).

In the Christian East, the Byzantine Empire identified itself as the original Roman Empire and thus believed that Rome transferred its kingdom to Constantinople with Emperor Constantine, its founder. With the advent of the Muslim invasions in the seventh century, the Byzantine faithful began producing a series of apocalyptic works to help them justify their empire and believe that it would survive; they appropriated Daniel's four-kingdoms schema to convince themselves that the Arab invasions did not constitute another world empire that would upset the schema (Himmelfarb 129–30). Near the year 690, an anonymous Syriac Christian wrote an apocalypse now known as *Pseudo-Methodius,* which quickly became popular throughout the Christian world; it claims that after the death of Alexander the Great, his mother, an Ethiopian woman named Kushet, married Byzas, the founder of the city Byzantium, and their daughter Byzantia married Romulus, the founder of Rome. In this way, *Pseudo-Methodius* links the Byzantine Empire directly to Alexander's empire, and there is no need to understand Rome as the fourth kingdom. Thus the Byzantine Empire remains the last empire before the apocalypse in the "succession of kingdoms" (Paul Alexander 13–32). Soon afterward the Byzantine *Visions of Daniel* tradition developed, which includes thirteen extant Greek apocryphal Danielic apocalypses, including *Diegesis Danielis, Seven-Hilled Daniel,* and *Last Daniel* (DiTommaso 96–97). In all of these texts, the Byzantine Empire is presented as the fourth and final human kingdom. As *Pseudo-Methodius* asks: "Which is the power or kingdom of people below heaven that is mighty and strong in its power and will be able to prevail over the great power of the Holy Cross in which the kingdom of the Greeks, that is of the Romans, possesses a place of refuge?" (Paul Alexander 42–43).

In 1453, when Constantinople fell to the Ottoman Turks, the Russian kingdom centered in Moscow was quick to assume the mantle of the fourth empire. Nestor Iskander, the pseudepigraphical author of the sixteenth-century work *Tale of the Taking of Tsargrad,* integrated Dan 2 and 7 to argue that Constantinople had transferred its Roman power to Russia, whose Tsars ("Caesars") had already begun to interpret an ancient Byzantine legend to predict that they would "free" Constantinople from Turkish control (Basile). The sixteenth-century monk Philothetus of Pskov wrote that Moscow was "Third Rome," after Rome itself and Constantinople, thereby instilling a sense of imperial messianism that continues to motivate Russia's foreign policy (Dickey 25). And

History of Reception

in the seventeenth century, Nicolae Milescu Spafarii, a Moldovan author who wrote in support of the Russian tsar, concluded from his reading of Dan 2 and 7, "The Westerners claim that the Greek kingdom was replaced by the German. Similarly, the Turks say that according to God's will the Greek kingdom was bequeathed unto them. We insist that the Russian monarchy is the only successor to the Greek, not only due to its piety but also because of the monarch's direct descent from Anna of Constantinople," who was the sister of Byzantine Emperor Basil II and wife of Vladimir, the first Christian monarch of Kiev and ancestor to Romanov Tsar Aleksei Mikhailovich (Pesenson and Spock 295).

Anti-Imperial Use

Many readers of Dan 2 and 7 sought to question and even subvert the rule of the empires in which they lived. Late antique and medieval Jewish exegesis, for example, continued the early Jewish interpretive tradition that the fourth kingdom, Rome, was evil and soon to be condemned by God. As *Exodus Rabbah* claims, "Gold refers to Babylon, silver refers to Media; brass refers to Greece; Rome, that destroyed the temple, is likened to iron" (35.5); talmudic sages even referred to Rome as "the wicked kingdom" (note R. Johanan's comments in *b. Šeb.* 20 and *b. ʿAbod. Zar.* 2b; *b. Yoma* 77a; *b. Meg.* 11a; *b. Qidd.* 72a; *Lev. Rab.* 13.5). As Rashi (1040–1105) writes: "The fourth empire is that of the Romans" (Gallé 26). The Roman interpretation was so strong that even rabbis living in non-Roman territory believed that Rome would eventually conquer all; in *b. Yoma* 10a, for example, Rav argues that the Sassanian Empire must temporarily lose its land in Mesopotamia to Rome before the coming of the messianic age, since Rome is the final kingdom (J. Reeves 94).

For some Christians, especially those who had been persecuted by either the Roman or Byzantine Empires for their nonconciliar theological convictions, the fourth kingdom was evil and deserving of chastisements. For example, after persecution by the Byzantine emperor Heraclius, the Monophysites argued that the subsequent Arab invasions of the seventh century were the result; this is argued implicitly in the Palestinian *Doctrine of Jacob Recently Baptized*, which criticized the weakness of the Byzantine Empire through images taken from Dan 2 and 7 (van Peursen 202). The seventh-century Syriac apocalypse *The Gospel of the Twelve Apostles* claimed that the powerful Ummayad dynasty, described as the fourth kingdom from Daniel, would collapse in civil war and then a northern king, not a Byzantine emperor, would ultimately take power, suggesting that the author did not see Byzantine victory as desirable (van Peursen 192).

In the early days of the Arab invasions, some Jewish residents of the Byzantine Empire saw a hope for liberation. *Pirqe Rabbi Eliezer* 28 reads Gen 15:7–21 in light of the four-kingdoms schema, in which the animals sacrificed typologically represent the peoples who will one day oppress the Jewish people; one manuscript interprets the turtledoves as the "Ishmaelites," or Arab Muslims (J. Reeves 14). In this version, the scheme begins with Rome, and then moves to Greece—understood to be Byzantium, the Greek-speaking Roman East—and then to the Sassanian Persian Empire, and then finally to "Ishmael," thus matching up with the succession of empires who had ruled over Jews in the Middle East from late antiquity to the medieval period. In the eighth century, Pinhas the Priest, a liturgical poet, interpreted each of the four "ages" as two kingdoms, with the last composed of the Arabs and Rome:

> You have torn apart the kingdom of Babylonia and Chaldea by strife,
> You have moved away Media and Persia, Greece and Macedonia,
>   Qedar and Edom;
> You will now set to destruction. . . .
> Four prevailed against four in shrewdness until iron was crushed into dust.

Pinhas ends his poem with a prediction against both powers: "Your people will break the bars of their yoke" (Bekkum 115). A tradition of medieval Hebrew apocalypses purporting to be the work of Simeon bar Yochai present the events of the seventh century through the Crusades by using the framework of the four-kingdoms schema, with the struggle between Rome ("Edom") and the Muslim kingdoms ("Ishmael") fulfilling the final stage of world history: "The Ishmaelites will do battle with the Edomites. . . . They will do battle with the Ishmaelites and kill many of them and assemble themselves at the camp at Acco. Iron shall crumble clay, and its legs will break down to the toes, and they shall flee naked without horses" (J. Reeves 99).

The Karaite Jewish community offers an alternative understanding of the four-kingdoms schema, with the Muslim rulers constituting the fourth monarchy and aiding in the conflict between rabbinic Jews and the Karaites, as described by tenth-century scholar Daniel al-Qumisi:

> The Rabbinites were princes and judges, in the days of the kingdom of Greece, the kingdom of the Romans and the Persian Magians, and those who sought the Torah could not open their mouths with the commandments of the Lord out of fear of the rabbis . . . until the arrival of the kingdom of Ishmael, since they always help the Qaraites to observe the Torah of Moses, and we must bless them. . . . For by means of the kingdom of Ishmael God broke the rod of the rabbis from upon you. (Rustow 117)

Yet other Karaites, such as Yefet ben Ali of Basra, berated the Muslim rulers of Baghdad in particular because of their oppression of Mesopotamian Jewry; Yefet argued that the fourth kingdom was constituted by the Muslim empires, but the little horn was the elite of Baghdad (cf. Dan 7:8; Roth 208).

Abraham ibn Ezra, writing in twelfth-century Iberia ruled by the Almohad Caliphate, agreed that the third kingdom was Rome; he argued that the Romans and the Greeks are culturally and ethnically similar, but the fourth kingdom must be Islam, because it is the most powerful empire to have existed (Goldwurm 108). Judah HaLevi, a contemporary of Ibn Ezra, lamented the particularly oppressive actions of the Almohads against the Jews. HaLevi wrote a poem hoping for an upending of the political order, presented as a dream recited to "Hagar's son" and claiming,

> Yea, thou the clay mixed with iron feet,
> come at the end of days, in pride uprisen—
> haply He hath hurled the stone, smashed the effigy,
> requital for thine ancient misdeeds given.
> (Scheindlin 89)

Likewise, the seventeenth-century Egyptian Jewish chronicler Sambari wrote a series of polemics directed at the Muslim rulers of Egypt in the guise of historical narratives laced with the four-kingdoms schema. He interpreted the kingdoms as Babylon, Egypt, and Constantinople, which he says emerged "after our magnificent temple had been destroyed," thus referring to the Muslim caliphates of the Abbasids, Fatimids, and Ottomans, the Muslim powers who occupied those cities in his day (Jacobs 356).

In early modern Northern Europe, Jewish authors and artists adapted many ideas of the Renaissance to their own theological and political agendas, including Christian construals of the four-kingdoms schema. An early eighteenth-century Northern European Jewish manuscript adaptation (see fig. 6) of Lorenz Faust's woodcut from *Anatomia statue Danielis* serves as an example. Like Faust's woodcut, the image depicts Mesopotamian kings on the helmet, Persian kings on the chest, Hellenistic rulers on the midsection, Roman emperors on the kilt, and Byzantine and Ottoman rulers on the right leg, as well as Holy Roman emperors on the right; both legs are multicolored to reflect the mixing with clay. However, the rulers have been updated to the years 1711–14, including Charles VII in the Holy Roman Empire, indicated by "Ashkenaz" on the big toe (Kestenbaum 98–99). The image includes a detailed key with astrological symbols that correspond to certain traits of each ruler, from the perspective of Jewish subjects: the sign for Saturn indicates a magnanimous ruler, Venus indicates an evil ruler, and so on. It is clear that these rulers are being judged and have been "found wanting" (Dan 5:27). Faust's Christian image depicts Christ emerging from the heavens opposite an apparently immobile giant rock resting on the ground, which suggests divine guidance and perhaps even approval. The Hebrew version of the image, however, depicts a mobile rock falling toward the statue from the heavens, inscribed "pure stones," indicating the hope that the Jewish people, "the holy ones of the Most High," would inherit the kingdom after all of these empires expire (cf. Dan 7:27).

Likewise, minority Christian groups throughout Europe and the Americas have consistently used the four-kingdoms schema as a critique of European

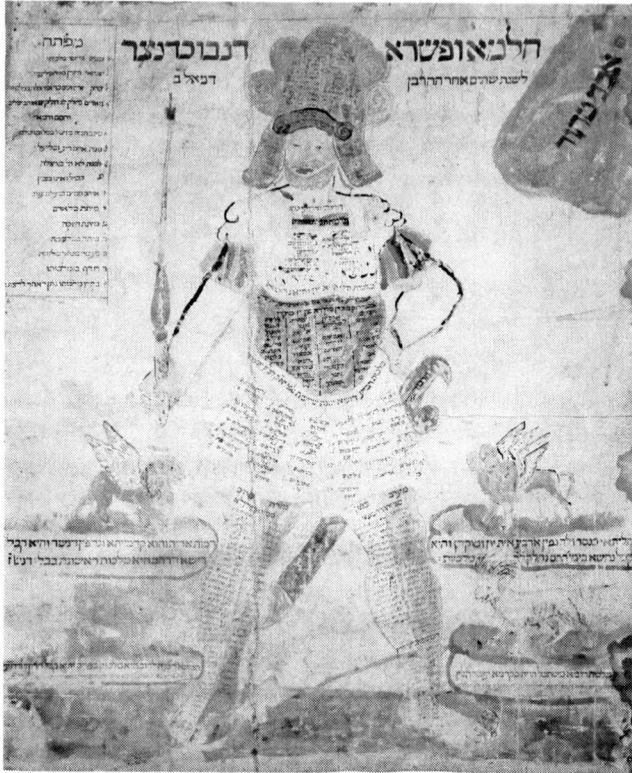

Figure 6. An illuminated vellum sheet of northern European Jewish provenance, 1711–14. It depicts an adaptation of Lorenz Faust's rendering of Nebuchadnezzar's dream and its interpretation from *Anatomia statue Danielis*. Kestenbaum & Company Actioneers, New York. Used by permission.

Christian imperialism. For example, the stories about the Virgin of Guadalupe concerning Mary's apparition at Tepeyac, Mexico, in 1531, written first in Spanish by the priest Miguel Sanchez in 1648, subtly incorporate the four-kingdoms schema. In the sacred image, the Virgin of Guadalupe is depicted as the apocalyptic "woman clothed with the sun" from Rev 12:1. The original apparition of Mary reportedly spoke to Juan Diego in Nahuatl, an Aztec language, and the early texts concerning this event conveyed that "the Virgin had selected the Creoles to be the basis of her new kingdom and so exalted them beyond all other people" (Borah 332). As Miguel Sanchez wrote, "This New World has been won and conquered by the hand of the Virgin Mary, . . . [who had] prepared, disposed, and contrived her exquisite likeness in this her

The Statue of Gold: A Clash of Sovereignties

Mexican land, which was conquered for such a glorious purpose" (Brading 58). And in more recent times, Liberation theologian Pablo Richard wrote about the Nicaraguan resistance to the military influence of the United States in 1980s Latin America: "Today we live in a situation very similar to that experienced by God's people in the times of Daniel. Today we also live in the midst of a confrontation between the *Empire* and the *People*. . . . This confrontation is lived out within the social and popular base movements. It is in this context that reading and re-reading Daniel helps us discern God's Kingdom in our history" (Richard 45).

Daniel 3 The Statue of Gold: A Clash of Sovereignties

1 King Nebuchadnezzar made an image of gold.[a] Its height was sixty cubits, its breadth six[b] cubits. He erected it in the plain of Dura in the province of Babylon.[c] 2 Then Nebuchadnezzar the king sent to assemble the satraps, the prefects, and the governors, the counselors, the treasurers, the judges, magistrates, and all the provincial officials[d] to attend the dedication of the golden image that Nebuchadnezzar the king had erected. 3 Then the satraps, prefects, and governors, the counselors, the treasurers, the judges, the magistrates, and all the provincial officials assembled themselves at the dedication of the image that King Nebuchadnezzar had erected, and they stood before the image that Nebuchadnezzar had erected. 4 The herald proclaimed in a loud voice: "You are commanded, O peoples, nations, and languages, 5 at the time that you hear the sound of the horn, the pipe, the lyre, the trigon, the harp, the tambour, and the whole musical ensemble, you shall fall and prostrate yourselves to the image of gold that King Nebuchadnezzar erected. 6 Whoever does not fall and prostrate himself—immediately[e] he will be thrown into the burning fiery furnace." 7 Accordingly, at that time, when all the peoples heard the sound of the horn, the pipe, the lyre, the trigon, the harp, and the whole musical ensemble, all the peoples, nations, and languages fell and prostrated themselves to the image of gold that King Nebuchadnezzar had erected.

8 Accordingly, at that time certain Chaldeans[f] approached and denounced[g] the Jews. 9 They said to King Nebuchadnezzar, "O king, live forever. 10 You, O king, issued a command that every person who heard the sound of the horn, the pipe, the lyre, the trigon, the harp, and the tambour, and the whole musical ensemble should fall and prostrate himself before the statue of gold. 11 And whoever did not fall and prostrate himself would be thrown into the burning fiery furnace. 12 There are certain Jews whom you appointed over the administration of the province of Babylon—Shadrach, Meshach, and Abednego—these men do not pay

attention to you, O king; they do not revere your god,[h] and they do not prostrate themselves to the image of gold that you erected."

13 Then Nebuchadnezzar in a furious anger issued an order to bring Shadrach, Meshach, and Abednego. Thereupon these men were brought before the king. 14 Nebuchadnezzar said to them, "Is it true, Shadrach, Meshach, and Abednego, that you do not revere my god[i] and that you do not prostrate yourselves to the image of gold that I erected? 15 Now if you are ready, so that at the time when you hear the sound of the horn, the pipe, the lyre, the trigon, the harp, and the tambour, and the whole musical ensemble, you fall down and prostrate yourselves to the image that I made . . . ;[j] but if you do not prostrate yourselves, you will be thrown immediately into the burning fiery furnace. And what god is there who can save you from my hands?"

16 Shadrach, Meshach, and Abednego replied to King Nebuchadnezzar,[k] "It is not necessary for us to answer you concerning this matter. 17 If our God, whom we revere, is able to save us from the burning fiery furnace and from your hand, O king, he will save us.[l] 18 But if not, be it known to you, O king, that we will not revere your god, and we will not prostrate ourselves to the image of gold that you erected."

19 Then Nebuchadnezzar was filled with rage, so that the appearance of his face was changed toward Shadrach, Meshach, and Abednego. He commanded that the furnace be heated seven times more than it was customary to heat it. 20 He ordered some of the strongest men who were in his army to bind Shadrach, Meshach, and Abednego in order to throw them into the burning fiery furnace. 21 Then they bound these men in their trousers, their shirts, their hats,[m] and all their clothes, and they were thrown into the burning fiery furnace. 22 Because of this, because the command of the king was urgent and the furnace had been excessively heated, these men who brought up Shadrach, Meshach, and Abednego—the fire killed them![n] 23 And these three men, Shadrach, Meshach, and Abednego, fell into the burning fiery furnace bound.

24 Then King Nebuchadnezzar was startled and rose in haste,[o] saying to his counselors, "Did we not throw three men into the fire bound?" They answered the king, "Certainly, O king." 25 He replied, "Look! I see four men, walking around loose in the midst of the fire, with no sign of harm on them—and the appearance of the fourth is like a god!"[p]

26 Then Nebuchadnezzar drew near to the gate of the burning fiery furnace. He said, "Shadrach, Meshach, and Abednego, servants of the Most High God, come out—come here!" Then Shadrach, Meshach, and Abednego came out of the fire. 27 The satraps, the prefects, the governors, and the counselors of the king gathered together and were looking at these men over whose bodies the fire had no power, and the hair of whose heads

The Statue of Gold: A Clash of Sovereignties 99

was not singed, and whose cloaks were not affected, and to whom the smell of smoke did not even cling. 28 Nebuchadnezzar said, "Blessed be the God of Shadrach, Meshach, and Abednego who sent his angel and saved his servants who trusted in him and who disregarded the word of the king and gave their bodies so that they would not revere and not prostrate themselves to any god except their God. 29 I hereby issue a decree that any people, nation, or language who speaks blasphemy against the God of Shadrach, Meshach, and Abednego shall be dismembered and his house made into a public toilet, because there is no other god who is able to deliver like this."

30 Then the king promoted Shadrach, Meshach, and Abednego in the province of Babylon.

a. OG and Th add the date: "the eighteenth year of Nebuchadnezzar," i.e., 586 B.C.E., the year Nebuchadnezzar captured Jerusalem, according to Jer 52:29. The effect is to emphasize the rivalry between Nebuchadnezzar and the God of Israel.

b. Papyrus 967 reads "twelve."

c. Alternatively, take dwr° as a common noun, "wall," and $mdynh$ in its later meaning, "city," and translate "in the plain of the wall of the city of Babylon," i.e., the space between the inner wall and the great outer wall of Babylon, Nimit-Enlil, built by Nebuchadnezzar (see Herodotus 1.178–82). OG translates dwr° as $peribolou$, "enclosure."

d. The lists of officials differ in number and arrangement among the versions, including 4QDan[a]. Koch (245) suggests that OG interprets the list in reference to the administrative structures of Ptolemaic Egypt, while Th reflects Roman Syria.

e. Lit., "in that hour."

f. See comments on 1:4.

g. Lit., "ate their pieces," an idiom also attested in Akkadian.

h. Kethib: "gods"; Qere: "god." Th renders the plural, "gods"; OG the singular, "your idol."

i. The Aram. is ambiguous and might be translated either as a true plural or as a plural of majesty. OG and Th construe the word as plural ("gods"), but the context suggests that it be taken as a singular.

j. The king leaves his thought uncompleted, breaking off the sentence without stating the apodosis. The technical term for this device is aposiopesis.

k. The accentuation in MT has the three address the king without his title (". . . replied to the king, 'O Nebuchadnezzar'"). OG and S include the title.

l. The versions appear to be troubled by the theological implications of MT and render the verse as an assertion. Th: "For there is a God, whom we serve, able to save us." OG: "There is a God in heaven, our one Lord, whom we fear, who is able to save us."

m. The identification of the first two terms is contested, but see Rosenthal §189. All three are items of Persian dress.

n. Th omits the account of the soldiers being burned up, apparently through haplography, but translates v. 23. In place of MT's vv. 22–23, OG reads: "The men who readied and bound them and brought them to the furnace threw them into it. Then these men who bound those with Azariah—the flame from the furnace burned them and killed them—

but they [Azariah and his companions] were protected." OG and Th then introduce the Prayer of Azariah at this point.

    o. OG connects the king's reaction to the Jews' singing and fills in narrative detail. "When the king heard them singing hymns and, standing up, saw that they were alive...." OG omits the king's conversation with the officials, apparently by haplography.

    p. Lit., "a son of gods," i.e., a divine being.

Overview and Outline

Daniel 3 is preserved in two literary editions, one found in the MT and the other in the Greek versions. Some of the minor variations reflect different stylistic sensibilities. For example, the MT enhances the literary feature of repetition, whereas the Old Greek tends to minimize it. The major differences, however, concern the scene in which the three Jews are cast into the fiery furnace. The scene is tersely narrated in the MT, with the narrative focused on the king's perception of events. In both Greek versions (OG and Th), short narrative sections direct the focus to the events inside the furnace and to the mechanism by which the angel of God protects the three (vv. 24–25, 46–50). The major difference, however, is the inclusion of two long poetic compositions, the Prayer of Azariah and the Song of the Three Jews. While the basic narrative is the same in each edition, the differences significantly change the emphasis and alter the generic affinities of the story.

Scholars identify the genre of Dan 3 variously, most commonly as a court-conflict tale, martyr legend, or wisdom didactic tale. The court-conflict tale contributes the most significant generic features to Dan 3: the basic plot structure of the fall and rehabilitation of the courtiers, the jealousy of rival courtiers and their manipulation of the king, as well as the characterization of the king as emotionally mercurial (cf. *Ahiqar*; Esther; Tob 1–2; Dan 6). But Dan 3 can also usefully be compared with the wisdom didactic tale, a story of character contested and confirmed in a world that first seems to be hostile to the heroes' virtue but that eventually honors it. This framework draws attention to the character of the heroes and to the happy ending, which comes about precisely because the heroes chose to exercise their virtue at a time of testing or conflict. Finally, the martyr legend (or as some prefer, the confessor tale) focuses on the specific issue of fidelity to God in the face of religious oppression and threatened death. In actual martyr stories, of course, the salvation of the martyr is postmortem rather than a rescue from death.

Although Dan 3 evokes all three genres, it also alters genre conventions in ways that contribute to its own distinctive purposes. In the MT the author shifts the focus from the Jewish characters to Nebuchadnezzar. He is the only individual character; all others are collective characters (the three Jews, certain Chaldeans, the group of officials, the soldiers). He is also the only character

The Statue of Gold: A Clash of Sovereignties

to undergo change and to display a variety of emotions. At a crucial moment in the plot, the story is narrated from his point of view. Thus, in contrast to all three of the genres the story invokes, the Gentile king rather than the Jewish courtiers or confessors becomes the protagonist. This role for Nebuchadnezzar is underscored by the placement of Dan 3 amid a series of stories that trace the gradual and at times painful education of the king.

Daniel 3 is an originally independent story secondarily adapted for inclusion in the Daniel cycle. Not only does Daniel not figure in it as a character; no effort is even made to account for his absence. At the same time both Dan 1 and 2 have anticipated Dan 3 by including references to Daniel's three friends, even though they do not play an active role in those narratives.

Clues to the date of the story are elusive. The presence of Greek terms for musical instruments (vv. 5, 7, 10, 15) have sometimes been taken to argue for a date in the Seleucid period (e.g., Driver lviii–lix; Bentzen 38), but Greek and ancient Near Eastern cultures intermingled long before the conquests of Alexander the Great (Kitchen 44–49; Koch 272). Specific political terminology is more likely an indication of the milieu of the story's creation, and the prominence of Persian terms, coupled with the absence of Hellenistic ones, suggests that the story developed during the time of the Persian Empire. The story may also make use of older traditions about the Babylonian king Nabonidus. Nabonidus's attempt to foster worship of the moon-god Sin evoked strenuous opposition from the priests of Marduk, who wrote a scathing satire in verse. Part of the poem describes Nabonidus as making an image of the god and placing it upon a pedestal (*ANET* 313). For the Jewish tale, however, Nebuchadnezzar, the conqueror of Jerusalem, becomes the king whose arrogance is burlesqued.

Even though ch. 3 is originally an independent story, it is well integrated with the other Daniel tales: it continues the development of Nebuchadnezzar's character, the exploration of the interplay of power and knowledge, and the difficult negotiation of Diaspora identity in an imperial context. Power and perception are central to this story. Nebuchadnezzar's exercise of royal power and the surprising limits it encounters form the basic plot. The story focuses on the way in which Nebuchadnezzar's false perceptions about the nature and source of power are progressively dismantled during the course of events. The interplay of knowledge and power also characterizes the actions of the Chaldean courtiers who attempt to exercise power by using what they know about the Jews and by manipulating what the king knows and how he perceives it. It is no accident that the crucial scene in the narrative is one that involves the king's seeing something, generating a new perception that transforms all that he thought he knew.

One should not overlook, however, the extent to which the very telling of the story itself engages the relationship of power and perception in an act of resistance to the claims of imperial rule. To tell a story is to create a world where the storyteller has a kind of sovereign power. But even fictional stories, such as Dan 3, draw on materials from and make reference to the real world. In so doing, they are a means of acting upon the real world, a means of exercising power by encouraging readers to perceive reality differently. For this reason artists are often feared by oppressive regimes. Thus it is not simply the king's perceptions of power that are transformed but also those of many readers. For Diaspora Jews the telling of such a story is a way of acknowledging the fearful power of the kings of the Persian and Hellenistic Empires while at the same time asserting the merely provisional reality of their claims to power. There is a Sovereign beyond and above these earthly monarchies.

The story develops in four scenes, which may be outlined as follows:

Scene 1: The officials are commanded to worship Nebuchadnezzar's image of gold (3:1–7)
    Erection of the statue (3:1)
    Summons to officials and their assembly (3:2–3)
    The herald's command and the officials' compliance (3:4–7)
Scene 2: Conflict: The Jews endangered (3:8–12)
    The Chaldeans plot against the Jews (3:8)
    Address to the king (3:9–11)
    Accusation against Shadrach, Meshach, and Abednego (3:12)
Scene 3: Confrontation: The three Jews before Nebuchadnezzar (3:13–23)
    Nebuchadnezzar's ultimatum (3:13–15)
    The three Jews' defiance (3:16–18)
    Attempted execution in the fiery furnace (3:19–23)
Scene 4: Resolution: Deliverance and confession by Nebuchadnezzar (3:24–30)
    Nebuchadnezzar and his court witness the divine protection of the Jews (3:24–27)
    Nebuchadnezzar confesses the power of God and issues an edict against blasphemy (3:28–29)
    Nebuchadnezzar promotes the three Jews (3:30)

Comments

[1–7] The story begins abruptly, foregrounding the action of King Nebuchadnezzar in making and setting up a statue of gold. Even though the story was originally independent of the other Daniel stories, it has been carefully situated. Does the juxtaposition of the stories imply that Nebuchadnezzar performs this action as a consequence of the dream in ch. 2? The lack of a date notice in MT allows the supposition that the events in ch. 3 follow closely upon those of ch. 2. Moreover, several verbal echoes encourage a connection. The same term

The Statue of Gold: A Clash of Sovereignties

(*ṣĕlēm*) is used to describe the image in the dream (2:31–32) and the image Nebuchadnezzar sets up. Nebuchadnezzar was represented in the dream by the head of gold (2:38), and now he makes a statue of gold. Already in the third century C.E., Hippolytus (*Comm. Dan.* 2.15) assumed that Nebuchadnezzar's actions were motivated by the pridefulness induced by his identification with the head of gold, which is then mirrored in some sense by the image of gold.

While these suggestive connections may explain why the author incorporated the story of Nebuchadnezzar and the image of gold, no attempt has been made to fully assimilate the story to that of Dan 2. As eventually becomes evident in vv. 12, 14, and 18, the image does not represent Nebuchadnezzar himself but "his god." The king's desire to have the statue worshiped makes it an embodiment of his own royal will, as indicated by the frequent repetition of the phrase "the image that King Nebuchadnezzar erected" (vv. 2, 3, 5, 7, 12, 14, 18). Within the story the most important thematic symmetry is between Nebuchadnezzar's command concerning the worship of the image of his god (vv. 4–6) and his command concerning the prohibition of blaspheming the god of Shadrach, Meshach, and Abednego (v. 29). In each case the king's power ostensibly serves to honor the god in question but in fact eclipses the deity.

The odd proportions of the golden image, 60 × 6 cubits or approximately 90 × 9 feet, have bothered interpreters from earliest times. The Greek translator of Papyrus 967 gives the breadth as 12 cubits, apparently a rationalizing change. Commentators sometimes similarly try to rationalize the information, suggesting that it was an obelisk or a stele with an engraved image at the top and that it was gold plated rather than made of solid gold (e.g., Montgomery 196; Hartman and DiLella 160), but surely the point is precisely the fantastical nature of the image. The information exaggerates the popular legends about extraordinary statues that were common in the Persian and Hellenistic periods, such as Herodotus's report about the statue of Bel in Babylon, which was "a statue of solid gold, fifteen feet high," requiring some 800 talents of gold to make (1.183; trans. Greene). More significantly, it parodies the tradition of monumental architecture and sculpture itself, which was a fundamental method of royal propaganda, advertising the power and wealth of a king who could command such material and human resources and create such wonders.

The setting of the events in Dan 3 is described rather vaguely as "in the plain of Dura in the province of Babylon." Since Dura (Akk. *dūru*, "city wall") is part of the name of many Mesopotamian locations (e.g., Dur Sharrukin), it is not the specific location but the characteristics of the place that are relevant. It is a place near Babylon with a broad, open expanse sufficient to accommodate the spectacle that Nebuchadnezzar is organizing.

From antiquity to the present, royal and state power has advertised itself through public spectacle, as reflected, for example, in Leni Riefenstahl's notorious documentary of the 1934 Nazi Party Congress at Nuremberg, *Triumph of the Will.* What makes public spectacle a powerful instrument of propaganda is its combination of spectatorship and choreographed participation. As ritual studies have shown, the engagement of the body has a strong effect on the inner persuasiveness of the ritual activity (Bell 215). To engage one's own body in an activity coordinated with masses of others' bodies is to experience a sense of participation in something transcendent and powerful, something to which it seems natural to give one's allegiance. Although all of the kingdoms of the ancient Near East made use of such public spectacles, the Persian Empire was exceptional in its self-conscious use of such displays. The reliefs at Persepolis, the ceremonial capital, depict the peoples of the empire bringing gifts to the great king in a choreographed pageant of great dignity (see fig. 7). Similarly, the carefully staged reviews of the ethnically diverse units of the Persian army were, as Briant observes, "neither more nor less than stagings of the Empire," a means "to hand the Great King a mirror in which to contemplate his own power" (198). Although Dan 3 sets its story during the reign of Nebuchadnezzar, it is most likely this fearful but seductive representation of Persian imperial power that Dan 3 engages and resists.

Verse 2 introduces one of the signature stylistic features of Dan 3, the lengthy and often repeated lists of functionaries and musical instruments. Elaborate lists of various sorts—of royal titulature, officials, conquered nations, items of booty, materials used in the construction of palaces, and so forth—were a staple of ancient Near Eastern royal inscriptions and iconography (Koch 276; Briant 172–73) and gave verbal and visual testimony to the power of the great king. Here the author of Dan 3 provides an administrative list. Although the precise meanings of some of the terms are uncertain, the syntax of the list appears to differentiate between the first group of major officials and a second group of minor ones. "Satraps" (Aram. *ʾăḥašdarpĕnayyāʾ*) is a Persian loanword meaning "guardian of the realm" and refers to the highest-ranking official who served as a personal representative of the king (Briant 65). "Prefect" (Aram. *signayyāʾ*), and "governor" (Aram. *paḥăwātāʾ*) are terms derived from Akkadian that refer, respectively, to a kind of undersatrap and to a variety of provincial administrators. The second group is composed of terms derived from Old Persian, which appear to refer to various classes of financial, legal, and police officials (Koch 246). Taken together, the two groups form a merism of officialdom, from highest to lowest, as the summary phrase "all the provincial officials" makes clear. That the author should be familiar with this administrative taxonomy is not surprising: as Smith-Christopher observes, "All minority peoples learn the vocabulary of authority very quickly" (62).

These officials are given a second characterization when they are addressed by the herald in v. 4. There they are referred to not in their administrative capacities but as "peoples, nations, and languages," that is, as representatives of the many ethnic groups comprising the empire. A prominent aspect of Persian

The Statue of Gold: A Clash of Sovereignties

Figure 7. The presentation of tribute to the Persian king, depicted in limestone relief from the east stairway of the Apadana in Persepolis (fifth century B.C.E.).

imperial ideology was the representation of the ethnic diversity of the empire. The royal throne was depicted as being upheld by the various peoples of the empire, whose distinct ethnic dress and hairstyles were meticulously represented (Root 152–53, 160). Reliefs showing gift-bearing emissaries from all the nations of the empire similarly delight in depicting with exacting detail the range of peoples doing homage to the great king (Briant 176–81). The diversity of languages of the empire was also reflected in the multilingual decrees of Darius, such as the Behistun Inscription, which also stipulated that it be publicized throughout the provinces (§70; Kuhrt 149). The politico-ideological purpose of these representations was, as Briant remarks, "to depict every country and every people of the Empire united in harmonious cooperation organized by and surrounding the king" (178). One could scarcely ask for a more apt summary of what the author of Dan 3 represents in vv. 1–7.

When one prunes away the lists and repeated phrases to examine the actual plot structure of vv. 2–7, what appears is a pair of command and execution sequences. Nebuchadnezzar orders the officials to assemble (v. 2), and they assemble (v. 3). The herald commands them to prostrate themselves at the sound of the music (v. 4–5), and the officials do so, just as they were commanded (v. 7). The "harmonious cooperation" that Briant and others see modeled in the aesthetics of the Persepolis reliefs is here given a literary representation in the choreography of the officials' bowing down as one at the signal of the carefully enumerated musical instruments. Although in actual fact an enormous number of individual preparations, journeys, acts of coordination, and so forth would have been entailed for the event to take place, all of this activity is hidden from view. Similarly, the actual time required is collapsed. All that remains is command and obedience. The verbal icon is strikingly similar to that of the Priestly writer in Gen 1:3: "God said, 'Let there be light'; and there was light." Or, to invoke a text more closely related to Israel's countering of the claims of imperial control, compare Isa 40:26: "Lift high your eyes and see: Who created these? He who sends out their host by count, Who calls them each by name: Because of His great might and vast power, Not one fails to appear" (NJPS).

The only verse in vv. 2–7 that falls outside of the command and execution sequence is the herald's announcement of the punishment to be inflicted on anyone who does not prostrate himself (v. 6), foreshadowing the conflict to come. The threatened punishment owes more to the folkloric plot than to reality, since there is no clear evidence of the death penalty for religious disobedience prior to the persecution of Antiochus IV Epiphanes (J. Collins 185). But because the story of Dan 3 imagined such a danger, the narrative became an important model for Jewish resistance against Antiochus's decrees (1 Macc 2:59).

Why the author chooses the particular motif of death in a furnace of blazing fire is uncertain. Burning was not a common mode of execution in the ancient Near East (though see Gen 38:24; Lev 21:9; Laws of Hammurabi, §§25, 110, 157; Herodotus 1.86). A Babylonian school text from the early sixth century B.C.E. reports a king's punishment of blasphemous temple officials with the command: "Destroy them, burn them, roast them. . . . to the cook's oven, . . . make their smoke billow, bring about their fiery end with the fierce flame of the box-thorn!" (Beaulieu 2009, 284). It is not impossible that this dramatic motif was known by Jewish scribes in Babylon. Given the influence of the book of Jeremiah upon Daniel, however, it is likely that the motif is picked up from Jer 29:21–23, which refers to two Jewish prophets, Ahab and Zedekiah, who were "roasted in the fire" by Nebuchadnezzar.

[8–12] The first scene was panoramic in its scope, inviting the reader to visualize a vast outdoor scene with a cast of thousands, an orchestrated sound track, and synchronized movements of the assembled officials. In the second scene the focus narrows to a small group identified only as "certain Chaldeans" and their private interview with King Nebuchadnezzar (v. 8; cf. the similar technique in 1:1–2, 3–5). Yet the action of the two scenes is carefully coordinated, as the text indicates by using the same introductory phrases in vv. 7 and 8: "accordingly, at that time." The coordinated temporal phrases suggest that the Chaldeans did not just happen to notice the actions of the three Jews but had been intentionally watching them, presumably knowing that the Jews might not comply with the king's command (cf. Dan 6:11–12). That their motive is hostility to the three

Jewish courtiers rather than disinterested concern for the king's command is further implied in the colorful expression used for their denunciation: "They ate the pieces" of the Jews (v. 8, lit.). The phrase is borrowed from Akkadian (*CAD* 1/1:255, *karsu* + *alāku*), and though its origin is obscure, its aggressive connotations are evident.

Whether the Chaldeans' motives are professional or ethnic is uncertain and perhaps a false alternative. The term "Chaldean" can refer either to the ethnic group of southern Babylonians to which the royal family of the Neo-Babylonian Empire belonged or to the mantic experts who served the king. Although in ch. 2 the term is clearly used in its professional sense, the parallel between the terms "Chaldeans" and "Jews" in v. 8 might suggest an ethnic as well as a professional dimension to the rivalry. In Esth 3:1–11, the rivalry between Mordecai and Haman similarly involves both elements. Unfortunately, little is known directly about the relations between ethnic groups in the Persian Empire, when these stories were probably developed. To be sure, the motif of Jews as highly placed officials in both Esther and Daniel is simply part of the fiction. Almost all of the high positions at court were held by Persians. Nehemiah, cupbearer to Artaxerxes I (reigned 465–425 B.C.E.), is the only Jew known to have held a significant position at court under the Achaemenids (Neh 2:1). The greatest ethnic diversity is attested among the low-ranking *kurtaš*, who were laborers and craftsmen in the Persian administrative apparatus (Briant 433), though no Jews are mentioned in the surviving records. It is possible, however, that the authors of Daniel and Esther used their fictions about highly placed characters to deal with issues of interethnic and administrative tension that their audience experienced in more mundane walks of life.

The location of the scene in vv. 8–12 is not specified, but presumably it takes place at the king's ceremonial station, from which he has observed the spectacle, since his subsequent command to the three Jews presumes the proximity of the orchestra and golden image (v. 15). The Chaldeans' report introduces a discrepancy between what the king thinks he has seen, represented in the panoramic point of view of the narrator in v. 7, and what has actually happened on the ground. It is not the case that "*all* the peoples, nations, and languages fell and prostrated themselves to the image of gold." This short scene deftly captures the role that the control of information plays in the life of power at the royal court. Despite his ostensibly panoptic perspective, the king does not see everything. Those who have information can use it to their own advantage by manipulating what the king perceives and knows (cf. 1 Kgs 1; Fewell 44–46; Lasine 3–4). The jealous Chaldean courtiers are thus the dangerous counterparts to the cooperative and discreet officials of ch. 1 who help the Jews by concealing information that could put them at risk.

The Chaldeans' rhetoric is carefully crafted. Although their words to the king are mostly a repetition of the herald's announcement in vv. 4–6, they frame them in terms of the king's own will and authority: "You, O king, issued a command" (*'antĕh malkāʾ śāmtā ṭeʿēm*). The accusation proper frames the situation by identifying the miscreants not only by name but also by ethnicity ("certain Jews") and by the king's personal role in advancing them to office ("whom you appointed"), perhaps indirectly disclosing the sources of the Chaldeans' jealousy. In the Chaldeans' speech the actual misdeed the Jews are alleged to have done is the very last element mentioned. The information is preceded by two comments that interpret the significance of the act for the king. The Chaldeans represent the Jews' refusal to prostrate themselves as disdain for the king's own authority. The syntax is so peculiar (*lāʾ-śāmû ʿălāk malkāʾ ṭeʿēm*) that some commentators suggest emending the text (Charles 66; but see J. Collins 186; cf. Dan 6:13 [14]). The expression is rhetorically effective, however, since in Aramaic it explicitly parallels their opening words about the king's command. What the Jews have done is presented as first and foremost a challenge to the king's majesty. The actual act of the Jews, not bowing down before the image of gold, is also given a more comprehensive interpretation: they do not revere or worship Nebuchadnezzar's god. While the facts that the Chaldeans report are presumably true, they have framed them in such a way that they sound sinister to the king.

Daniel 3 illustrates the dilemmas that might occur to Jews employed in the royal administration in which political positions could entail participation in a pagan cult. Already 2 Kgs 5:17–19 considers an analogous situation, though it concerns the Aramaean commander Naaman, who explains to the prophet Elisha that, although he will henceforth worship only YHWH, his official position requires that he go through the motions of bowing down in the temple of Rimmon, an accommodation that the prophet accepts as appropriate.

The specific situation described in Dan 3, a forced act of homage to a state-sponsored cult image, does not correspond to the realities of ancient Near Eastern monarchies, though Jews did sometimes experience analogous situations in the Greco-Roman period. Imagined stories, however, may sharpen and dramatize more diffuse social and psychological anxieties precisely to illumine what issues are at stake. Although sole worship of YHWH that excluded acknowledgment of other deities may have been a long-standing practice in Israelite religion, it was by no means the understanding of all Jews, even in the sixth century, when many considered that worship of YHWH might be combined with veneration of other deities (e.g., Jer 44:15–25; and during the Persian period, in the Jewish colony at Elephantine). Thus the exiles and their descendants may have been of several minds as to the appropriateness or inappropriateness of paying homage to the deities of the peoples among whom they lived (cf. Deut 4:27–28). The vigor of the polemics in Isa 40–55 concerning the nothingness of other gods and the folly of worshiping cult images (Isa 40:18–20; 41:6–7, 21–24; 44:6–20) strongly suggests that the issue may have

The Statue of Gold: A Clash of Sovereignties

been unsettled in the early Diaspora. While monotheism and an abhorrence of idol worship eventually became markers of Jewish religious distinctiveness, there is ample evidence from the Hellenistic and Roman periods that some Jews continued to assimilate to the pagan religious cultures in varying degrees (e.g. 1 Macc 1:11; 2 Macc 4:18–20; Barclay 103–24, concerning Egyptian Jews). It is quite possible that Dan 3, like Dan 1 concerning food practices, draws the limits of acceptable Jewish actions with a bright line precisely because there was no consensus as to what a Jew might or might not do.

[13–18] The king does not reply to the Chaldeans, though his actions demonstrate that their words have had their effect. The king's "furious anger" is a stock motif in court tales (see 2:12; Esth 1:12; *Ahiqar* 2:28–3:39), though Lebram (63) argues that his anger is actually appropriate to his responsibilities, since a public disrespect for state gods threatens the order of the kingdom. The narrator relates the summoning of the three Jews as a command-and-execution sequence, underscoring the culture of prompt obedience that characterizes the court. In contrast to the depiction of King Ahasuerus in Esther, who seems to be easily manipulated by his courtiers, Nebuchadnezzar pursues information brought to him and makes his own judgments. He does not punish the Jews simply upon the allegations of the Chaldeans. But even though he asks the Jews directly, "Is it true?" he also does not wait for their reply but commands the act of homage to be performed in his sight. Nebuchadnezzar will judge from actions, not words. Although Nebuchadnezzar incorporates part of the Chaldeans' speech into his own (an aspect of the story's strongly repetitive style), he does not cite all of it. He does not ask the Jews directly if they pay no attention to his commands, the issue that the Chaldeans foregrounded, but refers only to the other two charges. His renewed command to them in v. 15 is itself the test of how they regard his authority.

Nebuchadnezzar's concluding rhetorical question, "And what god is there who can save you from my hands?" serves several narrative functions. As an intertextual echo of the words of "the great king, the king of Assyria" in 2 Kgs 18:28–35, it serves to characterize Nebuchadnezzar as the type of arrogant king whose pretensions will be exposed. His words also serve the storyteller's purposes by disclosing to the reader that the true antagonists in the narrative are not Nebuchadnezzar and the three Jews but Nebuchadnezzar and YHWH, as the second intertextual echo underscores. In Deut 32:39 YHWH declares, "There is no god besides me. I kill and I make alive; I wound and I heal; and no one can deliver from my hand."

The confrontation between the king and the three Jews is the first of two dramatic high points in the narrative and enables the three to articulate their actions in a confessional statement. The encounter with the ruler later becomes a regular feature of martyr legends (e.g., 2 Macc 7; 4 Macc 8–13; Josephus, *J.W.* 1.312–13; *Ant.* 14.429–30). Just what the three Jews say to the king has occasioned disagreement from the earliest translations to the present. What is "this matter" to which they say they have no need to reply? Th renders "these words," whereas OG translates "this injunction." Montgomery (206; Heller 248) thinks it is the indictment itself to which they refer, John Collins the offer of reprieve (187). More likely, in view of their following words, it is the king's rhetorical question to which they refer (so Goldingay 71; Koch 284), since they do in fact reply to the offer of reprieve in v. 18. Understanding their statement in this fashion keeps the focus on the theological confrontation between the king's power and that of their god. Early translators were apparently scandalized by v. 17, for rather than rendering it as a conditional ("if our God, whom we revere, is able to save us"), they make it into a positive statement (OG: "For there is a God in heaven, our one lord whom we fear, who is able to save us"; Th: "For there is a god, whom we worship, capable of saving us"; similarly, the Vulgate and the Peshitta). Although some early twentieth-century commentators continued trying to find alternative translations that put a more confident statement in the mouths of the three Jews (e.g., Driver 41; followed by NJPS), the linguistics of the passage require the conditional translation (see Coxon 406–9). Considerations of narrative art also support the judgment that the focus is on whether there is a God with such power. Just as Nebuchadnezzar laid out the alternatives offered to the Jews as paired positive and negative conditional statements in v. 15 (" if . . . and if not," *hēn . . . wĕhēn lāʾ*), so in vv. 17–18 their reply is phrased in paired positive and negative conditionals ("if . . . and if not," *hēn . . . wĕ hēnlāʾ*). Just as Nebuchadnezzar did not pause for an answer after his question to them in v. 14 ("Is it true . . . ?"), but instead seeks the truth in their actions, so they declare that they have no need to answer his rhetorical question ("What god is there . . . ?") with words but will let subsequent events reply. Such a statement also adds to the narrative excitement, since it ostensibly leaves open the question whether the story will end with their death or deliverance.

The concluding words of the three Jews have long been admired, as the storyteller certainly intended, as a defiant statement of uncompromising fidelity to God in the face of terrible threats. What is less often noted is what this stance discloses about the dynamics of power. Their refusal to comply with the king's order, despite the threat of the worst that he can inflict, exposes the limits of dictatorial power. Nebuchadnezzar literally has no power to enforce his command, to make the Jews behave like all the rest of his officials. He can kill the three Jews; but he cannot make them worship his god. Even if they should not be saved, in this matter they have more power than the mighty king of Babylon. The recognition of this unforeseen reversal is what fuels Nebuchadnezzar's rage in v. 19. An observation by the philosopher Emmanuel Lévinas clarifies the dynamics of such situations. "I can wish to kill only . . . [that] which exceeds my powers infinitely, and therefore does not oppose them but paralyzes the very power of power. The Other is the sole being I can wish to kill" (198). The

The Statue of Gold: A Clash of Sovereignties

refusal of the three Jews exceeds Nebuchadnezzar's power infinitely. Hence he desires to exterminate them.

[19–27] The details of the events that follow are the expression of Nebuchadnezzar's desire to annihilate what he cannot control. In antiquity the king's visage was not just a matter of personal appearance but was also itself a manifestation of his almost numinous power, which could bestow either grace or terror (Aster 86–89). The changing of the king's visage from openness to hostility would be feared by any courtier. Since a furnace at ordinary temperature would be sufficient to kill human beings, the king's hyperbolic command to heat it seven times hotter serves to represent both his annihilating rage and the extent of his power, since it is impossible to imagine how such an increase in temperature could be accomplished except in the story world of folklore. The narrative pace is breathless, as everything seems to happen in an instant. This is apparently the significance of the detail that the three were bound while still wearing their clothes, since it was customary for prisoners about to be executed to be stripped (Hartman and DiLella 162–63). The list of items of clothing is part of the stylistic signature of the story, and as with the list of officials, the precise meaning of the terms, except for "hat" (*karbĕlâ*), is disputed (see trans. notes). The terms are all derived from Persian, however, and add to the local color of the story, suggesting that everyone was dressed in court regalia (Montgomery 210). The climactic detail of the incineration of the soldiers as they carry out the king's order underscores the terribleness not only of the fire but also of the king's own power.

The transition from v. 23 to vv. 24–25 is abrupt, and the Greek versions reflect a somewhat longer narrative that some have argued might represent the original text. But it is likely that the more detailed narratives are secondary, filling the gap (J. Collins 189–90). The aesthetics of the MT narrative are carefully crafted to serve its thematic concerns. Verses 19–23 are intensely visual, as the reader's eyes are directed to each detail leading to the execution of the three Jews. The last detail described is the falling of the three into the furnace, so that the reader's eye tries to follow the scene into the furnace itself. At that moment, however, the point of view changes from that of the omniscient narrator to that of Nebuchadnezzar. Now it is not a matter of what the reader sees but of what Nebuchadnezzar sees, and the reader is dependent on his report in order to know what has happened.

Although the furnace has not been described physically, it appears to have been open at the top, since the Jews were lifted or carried up (*sĕlaq*) and fell (*nĕpal*) into the furnace. The king, however, seems to be looking into the furnace from the side (*tĕra'*, "gate," "hatch"), and the three Jews come "out" (*nĕpaq*) rather than "up" from the furnace in v. 26. Montgomery suggests that it may be envisioned as analogous to the structure of a lime kiln with both top and side openings (202).

The king's cognitive dissonance is vividly rendered through his conversation with his courtiers, as he first seeks confirmation of what he knows has just happened and then reports what he now sees. In contrast to the Greek versions, which try to rationalize the situation by describing the agency by which the three escape being burned up (an angel who shakes out the flame), MT highlights the sheer uncanniness of the situation, as it is perceived by Nebuchadnezzar. Though three were thrown in, four are visible; though they were bound, they are now unbound; though the soldiers were burned up from the mere proximity to the flames, the figures in the furnace are walking around unharmed in the midst of the flames. In the MT the fourth figure is never said to do anything and plays no role in the subsequent events of the narrative. Nor is it even clear what or who this fourth figure is. In v. 25 Nebuchadnezzar reports that its appearance is like that of a divine being, literally, "a son of god(s)" (*bar-ʾĕlāhin*). The phraseology facilitated later Christian interpreters to perceive the figure as the preexistent Christ (Montgomery 215; J. Collins 190). The original audience would likely have associated it with the angel of YHWH (see v. 28; cf. Gen 16:7; Exod 14:19; 1 Kgs 19:5–8; 2 Kgs 19:35), the figure that often manifests divine power and presence to those for whom YHWH has a particular concern. The imagery of the fire that does not burn, however, most directly evokes the theophany of God to Moses in Exod 3:1–3, represented there also by the angel of YHWH.

For whom does this mysterious figure appear? In contrast to Dan 2, there is no revelatory message to Nebuchadnezzar in this story. Whatever transpired in the furnace between the divine figure and the three Jews is not disclosed by the narrator, which is a gap that the Greek versions cannot resist filling. But for the MT the focus is on Nebuchadnezzar. Like a Peeping Tom, he has seen an event in which he is not a participant, taking a glimpse into a different reality and forms of power that nullify his own. Appropriately, it is not the narrator but Nebuchadnezzar who interprets the events and their significance. The first hint concerning his interpretation comes in the words with which he commands the three to come out of the furnace, for he identifies them not only by name but collectively as "servants of the Most High God." This divine epithet is a common title for the supreme deity in the Hellenistic period among both Jews and Gentiles (in Greek, *hypistos*). In the Bible it is characteristically used by pagans (e.g., Melchizedek in Gen 14:19; Balaam in Num 24:16; the king of Assyria in Isa 14:14; Cyrus in 1 Esd 2:3; the pagan slave girl in Acts 16:17; see Montgomery 215–16) and thus is appropriate in Nebuchadnezzar's mouth. In vv. 15–18 the tension between Nebuchadnezzar and the three Jews was framed in terms of which god they would worship. Nebuchadnezzar's characterization of them here already signals his recognition of the rightness of their choice.

In the opening scene of the story, the extraordinary golden image that Nebuchadnezzar had erected was the focus of a spectacle designed to be awe inspiring. Here in the concluding scene many of the same officials, including the highest ranking, are again present and witness a far more awe-inspiring spectacle. The three miraculously preserved Jews serve as the symbolic counterpart to the golden image, that is, as the physical manifestation of a sovereign's power. The miraculous details of their appearance are described by the narrator in free indirect discourse, that is, as the narrator's rendering of the amazed comments of the spectators as they examine the bodies, hair, clothes, and smell of the three. Nothing but a supernatural power could account for this miraculous state of affairs.

The conclusion of the story simultaneously provides a satisfying resolution of the conflict and a disturbing note of irresolution. In Dan 2, after Daniel had interpreted the king's dream, Nebuchadnezzar responded with a word of praise about the God of Daniel ("Truly, your god is God of gods and Lord of kings"; 2:47). Despite his words, for most of ch. 3 Nebuchadnezzar has been represented as someone who has not understood what "Lord of kings" implies. Now at the end, Nebuchadnezzar utters a public blessing of "the God of Shadrach, Meshach, and Abednego" that explicitly acknowledges the thwarting of his own power by this deity. Nebuchadnezzar includes all three of the issues raised by the Chaldeans in v. 12, and in the same order: the disregard of his command, the Jews' worship of no god but their own, and their refusal to bow down. If the story ended there, it would appear that Nebuchadnezzar had fully grasped the relation between divine and human sovereignty. But Nebuchadnezzar gives another command, one parallel in disturbing ways to the one he issued at the beginning. Although his first command was a positive order requiring worship of the golden image, this second command is a negative one prohibiting blasphemy of the God of Shadrach, Meshach, and Abednego. Both are addressed to the entire kingdom ("any people, nation, or language") and both are to be enforced by threat of gruesome execution. Both make the king the protector of the deity, thus confusing the issue of the nature, source, and uses of royal and divine power. Although Nebuchadnezzar answers his own earlier rhetorical question about the existence of a God who can save persons from his hand, the irony of his second command and the lack of understanding it reflects shows that the truth remains hidden from him. Despite the apparent resolution of the conflict, the education of King Nebuchadnezzar is not yet complete.

History of Reception, by Brennan W. Breed

Faithful Resistance

Rabbi Meïr Leibush ben Jehiel Michel Wisser, known by his acronym Malbim, was a profound interpreter of Scripture in Eastern Europe during the nineteenth century. In his commentary on the book of Daniel, Malbim notes an important symbolic effect of burning by fire: if successful, it erases any trace of what it consumes (Goldwurm 117). In Dan 3, then, the burning of the three Jewish youths was an attempt by Nebuchadnezzar to erase not only the Jewish people but also any memory of their resistance against the Babylonian Empire. But the Jews survived this attempt to extinguish their memory as well as their resistance to assimilation, just as the community has survived every such attempt throughout the past several millennia. The stories crafted during the exile and early Diaspora, including the book of Daniel, have provided encouragement and justification for this survival, and the reoccurrence of the story of the three youths and the fiery furnace at crucial junctures of Jewish history is testament to their ongoing effectiveness. As Elie Wiesel, a Jewish survivor of the Holocaust, explains: "Survival is living through. In Hebrew, the word is *sarid*. . . . *Sarid* is one who does not escape—the battle or the slaughter, for example—but survives it, lives through it." The story of the three youths models survival as opposed to escape, since the youth "live through" the furnace. And for Wiesel, the study of the Hebrew Scriptures "is a matter of survival. I study these texts in order to survive" (Wiesel and Beal 22–23).

The absence of Daniel at the fate of Hananiah, Mishael, and Azariah has always attracted interpretive interest. In one rabbinic telling, God made Nebuchadnezzar send Daniel elsewhere in the kingdom on business so that Daniel's holiness and merit did not overshadow the faith of the three youths; this shows that one does not need to attain Daniel's status as a special hero to resist the powers of this world (*b. Sanh.* 93a). Some interpreters have suggested that the youths died in Babylon soon after the event of the fiery furnace, while others claimed that the youths survived and returned to the land of Israel after the edict of Cyrus (*Song Rab.* 5.1).

For centuries, readers of the Daniel cycle continued to compose additions to this already-adapted story. The Prayer of Azariah and the Prayer of the Three Jews, found in Dan 3:24–90 LXX but not in the MT, includes two long prayers offered during the fiery furnace event as well as a short narrative interlude. A reference to the "most wicked" king "in the world" is likely a reference to the political and religious oppression of Antiochus IV, and thus a clue to the timing of the composition and possible inclusion of these additions (Dan 3:32 LXX). One or both of these prayers may have been extant before their addition to Dan 3 LXX; a reference to the lives of the faithful as a substitute for the penitential sacrifice of a whole burnt offering (Dan 3:40 LXX), understood as the youths' sojourn in the furnace, may have led to the inclusion of the Prayer of Azariah. A direct reference to the three youths (Dan 3:88 LXX) suggests that this prayer of praise once functioned as an independent reminder of their courage and God's deliverance of the faithful. In the narrative addition, an angel visits the youths in the furnace and brings a cool wind that makes the bottom of the furnace tolerable (Dan 3:46–50 LXX); later rabbinic interpreters said that this wind, signifying God's presence and help, also knocked down Nebuchadnezzar's statue and continued across the plain of Dura, where the Tower of Babel once stood, to a certain valley at the precise moment when the prophet Ezekiel commanded the wind to blow the breath of life into the newly reconstituted bodies that once were dry bones (Ezek 37:9–10; *Song Rab.* 7.14). The themes of these earliest-known additions to the story of the fiery furnace—resistance to contemporary political oppression, faithful self-sacrifice, and spiritual and bodily restoration—comprise the most common interpretive trajectories of this text to the present day.

Resistance

Throughout history, most readers of Dan 3 have been nearly unanimous on one point: the three youths encourage similar acts of religious, political, and cultural defiance in the contemporary world of the reader. Early readers, however, were divided about the specifics of Nebuchadnezzar's command. Was the statue an image of Nebuchadnezzar himself, and thus the demand for symbolic political submission? Or was it an image of a deity, and thus the demand for idolatrous worship?

Jews and Christians in antiquity often depict the Roman Empire as posing both issues simultaneously. As Josephus relates, when Pilate attempted to set up effigies of Caesar in Jerusalem, many Jews assembled to protest, baring their throats to demonstrate their complete devotion to the cause of anti-idolatry (*Ant.* 18.55–59). In 40 C.E., the Roman emperor Caligula sent an army to place statues of himself in the Jerusalem temple, which elicited a similar response of mass protest and the eventual abandonment of the effort by the Syrian governor (*Ant.* 18.263–67). In several early midrashic texts, a Roman official, variously named as Trajan and Marainus, mocks two Jews named Papos and Lullianus before executing them. He says: "If you come from the people of Hananiah, Mishael, and Azariah, let your God come and save you from my power" (*b. Taʿan.* 18b; *Sipra* 9.5; *Sem.* 8.15). Papos and Lullianus respond that the three youths "were perfectly righteous men, and they merited that a miracle should be done for them, and Nebuchadnezzar was also a king worthy for a miracle to be done through him, but as for you, you are a common and wicked man and not worthy, ... and as for us, we have deserved of the Omnipresent that we should die" (*b. Taʿan.* 18b). The Jewish God, Papos and Lullianus maintain, controls all things through providence, including the end of the narrative: "At the end," they claim, "the Omnipresent is going to demand the penalty of our blood from your hand."

Another midrashic retelling of Dan 3 underscores the issue of sovereignty in light of the youth referring to the king as "O Nebuchadnezzar" rather than

"O king" (Dan 3:16): "If it is to pay taxes, then you are king, but for this thing which you are ordering us to do, you are simply Nebuchadnezzar (*Lev. Rab.* 33.6). And in an intriguing inscription in a synagogue floor dating from the fifth century C.E. in ʿEn Gedi, the names Hananiah, Mishael, and Azariah accompany Abraham, Isaac, and Jacob with the phrase "peace over Israel" (Hachlili 234–35). This inscription also contains a cryptic prohibition of revealing the community's secret to the Gentiles, which underscores the tensions felt by Jews living under foreign powers and suggests a source for the popularity of Daniel's companions.

Early Christian interpreters likewise read Dan 3 in light of Roman imperial temptations to both idolatry and improper political subservience. The book of Revelation, for example, depicts an idolatrous veneration of an image of a beast, signifying Rome, that seems to draw from Dan 3 (13:7–8, 14–15). Before Constantine's privileging of Christianity in the Roman Empire, Christian theologians often dealt with questions of proper submission to secular authorities in light of idolatry with recourse to the story of the three youths (e.g., Tertullian, *Idol.* 15). But after Constantine, Christians shifted their interpretation of Nebuchadnezzar. Augustine, for instance, understood Dan 3 as a prophecy of the eventual conversion of the Roman Empire due to the faith of the early Christian martyrs (*Ep.* 93; *FC* 18:65). Aside from individuals in immediate crisis or those identifying with schismatic groups, Christian interpretation from that point onward tended toward a spiritualization of the themes in Dan 3.

Medieval Jews, on the other hand, faced a constant struggle for ethnic and religious survival in the presence of oppressive powers and thus relentlessly revisited the example of the three youths in its literal sense. One talmudic story, meant to explain the need to recite certain psalms at the Passover meal, claims that Abraham was also thrown into a furnace by his brother Nahor because he wouldn't bow to Nahor's idols, and God rescued Abraham directly as a foreshadowing of the deliverance of the three youths (*b. Pesaḥ.* 118a). This story extends the event of the fiery furnace back to the moment of Israel's birth, which presents similar political and religious oppression as a constant struggle throughout the history of the Jewish people. By including the first progenitor of the Jewish people in the furnace, as well, the talmudic rabbis seem to include every Jewish community into the story, including those in their contemporary setting. The continuing endurance of the Jewish people, the sages claim, is reason to sing the Hallel Psalms (113–118).

Some Jewish readers emphasize the cultural and political dimensions of oppression evident in Dan 3. Like many other readers, the medieval Jewish interpreter Saadiah noticed the intriguing transition from a dream of a statue in Dan 2 to a story of an actual statue in Dan 3. Nebuchadnezzar feared the prophecy of a Jewish kingdom that would eclipse his Babylonian Empire, Saadiah asserted, and so he tried to entice the Jews to become idolatrous so that God would refrain from honoring them and destroying the Babylonian Empire in turn (Goldwurm 112). Rashi claimed that the too-narrow statue of Nebuchadnezzar kept falling "until they brought all the gold in Jerusalem and poured layers [as a base] for its feet, to fulfill what was said [Ezek 7:19], 'and their gold will be for an impure object'" (Alshich 127). This gold had been taken from Jerusalem during its destruction, and thus the statue represented the Babylon Empire's foundations resting on the shattered remains of the Judahite state (Goldwurm 113). And in the tenth century, the Byzantine ruler Basil I began a severe repression of his Jewish subjects. He attempted to make all Jewish people abandon their religion by forcibly baptizing them and selling them into slavery. A Hebrew manuscript called the *Vision of Daniel* recounts Basil's terror and the attempted Jewish resistance, which included "crypto-observance," much like the avoidance practiced by the three youths in the opening verses of Dan 3 (Shepkaru 110).

From the medieval to the modern world, the attempts to eradicate the Jewish people have continued. At times, scriptural interpretation itself was the resistance to political and religious oppression. In the midst of the Holocaust, Rabbi Simcha Gardom of Kutno, a prisoner in the concentration camp in Konin, Poland, knew that those who could not work would be first to be killed. He explained to Rabbi Joshua Aaronson, who recorded the events of the Konin camp in his diary, that torture and forced labor were worse than death. Citing the talmudic opinion "Had Hananiah, Mishael, and Azariah been lashed [instead of thrown into the furnace], they would have worshiped the image," the rabbi decided to refuse work and study Torah instead, which was an avoidance that was tantamount to accepting death. He claimed that he wanted to die studying Torah as an act of defiance: "I would rather go to the World of Truth with a page of Gemara than with a spade" (Farbstein 306). The enactment of the three youths in Jewish communities continues to bring hope in the face of trauma and oppression today, as seen in the Purim plays of the Bobover Hasidic community in Brooklyn, New York, which have attempted to wrestle with the experience of the Holocaust. In a play first performed in 1971, Nebuchadnezzar tries to convince the three youths that God is unimportant and ineffectual, and then pleads with them to renounce their ethnic and religious identity and join the majority culture (Epstein 240–49).

The story of the three youths has likewise given hope to many other marginalized and oppressed people throughout history and is a common trope found in the literature of Christian people who are put at risk because of their religious affiliation. In early modern Europe, a series of religious and political conflicts between Catholic and Protestant rulers led to many oppressed minorities on both sides claiming the legacy of the three youths. The French Reformed pastor Antoine de Chandieu, for instance, wrote a play titled *Tragi-comedie* that included a portrayal of the three youths in the fiery furnace as a meditation on his seemingly miraculous release from prison in the aftermath of the French king Henri II's crackdown on Protestantism in Paris in 1557 (Barker 115–23). Likewise, the nineteenth-century Quaker poet and activist John Greenleaf Whittier wrote a poem about two seventeenth-century Quaker children in Massachusetts who were ordered by a Puritan judge to be sold into slavery in Barbados. The children were found guilty of failure to pay a fine imposed for nonattendance at Puritan church services. In honor of their faithful resistance by nonobservance of secular authorities' rules, the God "who cooled the furnace around the faithful three" intervened and made all slave traders refuse them passage, whereby the children were miraculously set free (Whittier 65).

Yet the story of the three youths has also been used by those in power. Thus some contemporary accounts claim that Pope Urban II's 1095 call for Crusade, against Muslims to reclaim the Holy Land, included references to Daniel and the three youths as examples of biblical role models who risked everything for God. These biblical examples took hold in the European Christian mind and occurred regularly in literature promoting the Crusades (Shepkaru 165). But some were more circumspect about the applicability of this story. John Calvin, who had seen many religious and secular leaders justify their actions through reference to Daniel and the three youths, cautioned the faithful to be suspicious of political rulers of all stripes when they flaunt their religion as Nebuchadnezzar had done in Dan 3. As Calvin argues, political rulers primarily look out for their own interests and thus use religion for their own purposes. As he writes in his comments on Dan 3: "[Political rulers] traffic in the name of God to attract greater reverence toward themselves. . . . Religion, then, is to the kings of the earth nothing but a pretext; but they have neither reverence for God in their minds, as the language of this profane king [Nebuchadnezzar] proves" (Calvin 218).

In the modern world, the three youths continue to offer communities hope amid adversity as well as a pattern by which to interpret survival against the odds. In the African American community during the years following the abolition of slavery in the nineteenth century, the popularity of the names Shadrach, Meshach, and Abednego testify to the community's self-understanding as a group of faithful people who overcame traumatic oppression by means of God's help. And their example of civil disobedience was a theological and narrative resource for Martin Luther King Jr. as he wrote a defense of his methods of protesting segregation and racism during the civil rights movement from his own imprisonment in a Birmingham jail: "Of course, there is nothing new about this kind of civil disobedience. It was seen sublimely in the refusal of Shadrach, Meshach, and Abednego to obey the laws of Nebuchadnezzar because a higher moral law was involved. . . . We can never forget that everything Hitler did in Germany was 'legal' and everything the Hungarian freedom fighters did in Hungary was 'illegal'" (M. King 74).

Martyrdom

The issue of martyrdom looms large in the interpretation of Dan 3. In the narratives of Daniel 1–6, God rescues the faithful who resist because of their religious commitments. It does not seem to encourage the faithful to openly risk their lives, as one sometimes sees in the developed theology of martyrdom. Likewise, in the story of the seven children murdered for their faith in 2 Macc 7, the children's deaths are not presented as events of martyrdom, but rather as a punishment for communal sin (7:18). In the Roman era, however, the fusion of the Jewish theme of trust in God during religious conflict with the Roman concept of the "noble death" drove the development of martyrdom for both Jews and Christians (Shepkaru 57). In the book of 4 Maccabees, for example, the earlier story of the seven brothers is retold as a martyr story, and the brothers are understood to adumbrate the "three youths in Assyria" (13:9). Their mothers' parental love for these martyrs is described as more fierce than the lions who threatened Daniel or the furnace that threatened Mishael (16:3), and she counsels her sons to endure their torture "for the sake of God" just as the biblical examples did (16:19). Josephus also explained that "Since [Daniel's] death, his memory lives on eternally" because of his heroic deeds (*Ant.* 10.266). Thus in the Roman period, the stories of the Persian and Hellenistic eras were reinterpreted as the foundations of Jewish and Christian martyrdom.

In late antique and early medieval midrash, some rabbis encouraged those facing oppressive rulers to see their own deaths as in some way a gift to God. One rabbi called the odor emanating from the fiery furnace as "a pleasant smell," interpreting the burning as a sacrifice pleasing to God (*Gen. Rab.* 34.9). Another rabbinic reader believed the three youths to have sealed a covenant with God on their way down to the flames (*b. Sanh.* 110b), and others related the willingness to give one's life to cultic sacrifice by reading Ps 50:5: "Gather to me my faithful ones, who made a covenant with me by sacrifice!" This attempt to legitimate voluntary death, however, is somewhat unusual in Jewish tradition. Vicarious and expiatory approaches to death are more often found in Christian exegesis. While sometimes passive resistance required the willingness to give up one's life, many rabbis argued that if there was another possible course of action, it must be pursued (Goldwurm 180). Rabbi Aaron ha-Cohen of Lunel, for example, who was expelled from France in 1306 and came to Majorca, Spain, argued fervently that one should not seek out martyrdom, and one should certainly not kill oneself in search of it. To make his case he pointed to the three youths in the furnace, who were not hurt in part because they did not seek to harm themselves (Shepkaru 268). Yet God saved the three youths; what does this say for later martyrs who actually die? One talmudic sage claimed that God avenges the blood of martyrs but had to spare Nebuchadnezzar, and thus the empire, because the youths survived (*Lam. Rab.* 1.16).

Some Jewish readers have emphasized the faith of the three youths in the Jewish God regardless of whether or not that God will save them (Dan 3:18). In one medieval reading, Hananiah, Mishael, and Azariah approach Daniel to discover what they should do in light of Nebuchadnezzar's decree to worship the image. Daniel sends them to Ezekiel, who can use his prophetic powers to discern God's will. God tells Ezekiel, "I will not stand by them," meaning that the three youths will not be saved, and even the prophet's tears and arguments could not change the divine decision. The youths, upon hearing the news, decide to embrace martyrdom. When they leave, God tells Ezekiel that it was all a ploy and that "of course" God will protect them, but God desired that they approach the act with perfect faith (*Song Rab.* 7.13). This pure faith was so powerful, some rabbis claimed, that God redeemed Israel from Egypt because it possessed the potential to generate such incredible piety (*Midr. Ps.* 114:5), and even the angel Gabriel followed the youths around in the fire as "a disciple walks with his master" (*Pesiq. Rab.* 35).

André Neher, a twentieth-century Jewish scholar and philosopher, reinterpreted the youths' acceptance of possible divine abandonment in his meditations on God's silence in the wake of great tragedies. Neher observes that the youth in Dan 3:18 begin with the Aramaic phrase *hēn-lāʾ*, literally meaning "if no," or as Neher interprets the phrase, "yes-no"; he argues that this is an equivocation amounting to an admission of divine silence. For some interpreters, the divine silence is deafening in its ethical and theological implications: what sort of God would refuse to save if it was possible? Yet for Neher, God's silence creates the space for true human freedom. Neher admits that this is a shocking and unsettling state of affairs, but nevertheless that even if God is "silent and remote, we shall serve him." The possibility of martyrdom requires divine absence and the possibility, even assumption, of abandonment of the righteous in the end (Rosenak 170).

Some communities have marked this seeming divine absence in their interpretation and use of Dan 3. Medieval Jews, for example, saw a disturbing rise in incidents of ethnic and religious acts of violence in response to the anti-Semitic call for the Crusades in the late eleventh century, and many of these Jews described themselves in terms of the three youths and the fiery furnace. In 1171, a French nobleman's servant in Blois, France, accused a Jewish leatherworker named Isaac ben Eleazar of murdering and skinning a Christian child. The town, already upset at the Jewish community for an affair between a local noble and a Jewish woman, launched more accusations. In response, the secular and religious authorities quickly tried and executed the Jewish community. Prosecutors refused to accept a large ransom for the thirty-two Jews of Blois and instead sentenced them to death by burning. A Hebrew account tells of three rabbis—Yehiel bar Rabbi David the Priest, Yequtiel bar Judah the Priest, and Judah bar Aaron—who escaped after their bonds were miraculously burned but their bodies were spared. The prosecutors put the three back into the fire several times, but the fire continually refused to burn them. After execution by the sword, the men's bodies finally remained in the fire but were not consumed. The other Jews perished but their bodies, as well, did not burn, and until their death they sang "in a pleasant voice," similar to the three youths' prayer added to Dan 3 LXX (Shepkaru 225–26). This story, and many other stories from European Jews who suffered in the anti-Semitic pogroms of the late medieval and early modern period, never fail to highlight the faith and courage of the martyrs, but they also share another intriguing quality: in these stories, God never appears. Though they draw from Dan 3 and 6, in which God plays a definite role, these medieval Jewish martyr stories depict a faithful people acting courageously without a hint of whether the Divine is simply silent or altogether absent (Chazan 2000, 179).

A medieval Jewish poet named Isaac bar Shalom crafted a liturgical poem, called a *piyyut*, after the massacres that Christians inflicted following the call for the second crusade in 1147. The poem begins with a shocking accusation: "There is none like you among the mute, / keeping silence and being still / in the face of those who aggrieve us." The poem juxtaposes praise of God's past actions and deep pain about God's present negligence, ending each stanza with the phrase: "Do not keep silence!" One of the stanzas mentions "a charred and overflowing pile, / like an oven both uncovered and unswept," which holds "those falling in God's fire," for which "all Israel weeps," but then ends with a recollection of one of God's miracles for those threatened by flame: "Like Hananiah, Mishael, and Azariah: / Do not keep silence!" (Petuchowski 71–83). Isaac's words of both praise and condemnation resonated so fully with his community that Ashkenazic Jews still recite this *piyyut* on the first Sabbath after Passover.

Christian martyrdom, on the other hand, followed a different path. In the New Testament, allusions to the three youths along with Daniel's sojourn in the lions' den are listed among models of faith (Heb 11:33–38). Their exemplar status continued with *1 Clement* 45.6–7, which mentions Daniel and his companions as models for Corinthian Christians of the first century. In late antiquity, the fiery furnace became a template for Christian martyr stories. The *Martyrdom of Polycarp* tells of the execution by fire of an early Christian bishop who confessed his belief in Christ even though the civil authorities told him that to do so meant certain death. Like Hananiah, Mishael, and Azariah in Dan 3 LXX, Polycarp offers a prayer just before his execution that refers to himself as a burnt offering (14.1–2; Dan 3:24–27 LXX). The story of Dan 3, as well as the story of the lions' den in Dan 6, became important to Christians not only as a story of faithful sacrifice but also of trust that God would resurrect the martyrs in return; this connection is made explicit in the many frescoes of the three youths and the lions' den in Christian catacombs and sarcophagi from late antiquity (Moss 38; cf. Irenaeus, *Haer.* 5.5.2). In these frescoes and sarcophagi, Daniel and the youths are often depicted as standing naked in the orans prayer pose, which connects the image of the faithful deceased biblical character with the faithful deceased occupant of the tomb. They are stripped bare at the moment of death as they were at the moment of birth, awaiting the new life that was inaugurated at the moment of baptism, which was also experienced in the nude in the early Christian church. The three youths became associated with the cult of martyrs, and soon their own relics and cult centers in Egypt and Mesopotamia became popular; among others, Theophilus, archbishop of Alexandria in the early fifth century, built a shrine to honor some of the relics of the three youths.

Restoration

Especially after the conversion of Constantine, new martyrs were rare until the early modern religious wars in Northern Europe. Thus Christians tended to spiritualize the story of the three youths, interpreting it as a story of the trials inflicted by the devil and the struggle to remain faithful in one's everyday life (Origen, *Comm. Rom.* 4.10; Gregory of Nazianzus, *Or. Bas.* 1.5). The use of the fiery furnace motif and the lions' den in catacomb art, as well as their inclusion in the *Commendatio Animae*, the early Christian prayer for the dead, led to their common use in Christian visual art to denote the protection of souls after death, such as in the medieval wall mosaics of the Byzantine monastery of Hosios Loukas (Chatzidakis 39, 48). Some icons of the three youths in the Christian East, a very popular motif in the sixth and seventh centuries, depict them wearing scapulars, articles of monastic clothing, among their regular Persian court garb. The visual connection with monasticism implies that the youths were a model of perseverance for the Christian monks, whose cells were sometimes called "furnaces" in which they might catch a glimpse of the "Son of God" (Ratliff and Evans 54–55). These monks endured penitential prayer and introspection for the sake of spiritual purification, hoping to emerge as faithful and whole as the three youths did. Thus the youths signified bodily and spiritual restoration for the Christian faithful.

In medieval Christian Nubia, as in Coptic Egypt, the motif of the three youths in the furnace was extremely popular, occurring in almost all extant Nubian church decorations. The Nubian frescoes generally follow the Byzantine iconography, with the three youths in Persian court dress flanked by an angel, likely Michael, holding a large cross-staff, which calms the fire that surrounds them. In the cathedral at Faras, Nubia, a tenth-century fresco depicts the three youths and Michael in the furnace (Hunt 410–11; see fig. 8). At the time, there was peace and prosperity in Christian Nubia due to healthy relations between the Nubians and the Egyptian Fatamid rulers. It was not likely a

Figure 8. A tenth-century C.E. fresco from Petros Cathedral in Faras, Nubia, depicting the three youths and the angel Michael in the furnace, Sudan National Museum, Khartoum. © Brian J. McMorrow. Used by permission.

reference to martyrdom: it most likely signified the struggle of the human soul for purification and the hope of resurrection for the deceased.

Many Christians and Jews believed in the efficacy of the three youths for concrete bodily and social restoration, as well. One particular late antique Jewish Aramaic incantation bowl, for example, contains a magical spell seeking to ensure that two men from the community would persevere despite a barrage of curses from over thirty people in the community; it opens with the story of the three youths surviving the furnace, which was supposed to contain power "to affect the annulment of curses" (Levene 97). In medieval Coptic magical texts, the three friends are also named several times in both their Hebrew and Babylonian names; these texts ask for an extinguishing of the flames of sickness in an individual's body just as the flames were extinguished for the youths in the furnace (Kelsey and Meyer). And in modern South Africa, a scholar visiting a service of the Christian Zion Sabbath Apostolic Church in northern Zululand in the 1940s noticed how the leader of the congregation repeatedly prayed for several sick people, including his own desperately ill son: "We pray to the God of Meshach, Shadrach and Abednego, that he will be fit again soon" (Sundkler 184, 187).

One story ties together these themes of subjugation, martyrdom, and restoration. In 1793, an epidemic of yellow fever raged through Philadelphia. Benjamin Rush, a physician who spearheaded the response effort, falsely believed people of African descent to be immune to the virus. He asked the Free African Society, an ecumenical Christian organization founded by two ex-slaves, Richard Allen and Absalom Jones, for aid. Allen and Jones agreed to lead their community in an effort to tend to the sick and dying throughout the city, as well as removing corpses from the area. After the fever passed, white Philadelphians began accusing the Free African Society and the black nurses of starting the epidemic and then profiting from its terror by stealing from the population, even though the black community had volunteered their efforts. In response, Allen and Jones wrote *A Narrative of the Proceedings of the Black People, during the Late Calamity in Philadelphia, in the Year 1793*, which explained their role in the city's recovery and interpreted the black community's history as one of divine intervention and faithfulness to the divine covenant. As Allen and Jones wrote: "We found a freedom to go forth, confiding in him who can preserve in the midst of a burning fiery furnace, sensible that it was our duty to do all the good we could to our suffering fellow mortals" (Brooks 168–69).

Daniel 4 (3:31–4:34) Hubris and Humiliation, Arrogance and Understanding

1 (3:31) King Nebuchadnezzar to all peoples, nations, and languages who dwell throughout the earth: May your well-being be great. 2 (3:32) It seems fitting to me to relate the signs and wonders that the Most High God has done for me. 3 (3:33) How great are his signs, how powerful his wonders! His kingship is an everlasting kingship, and his dominion endures from generation to generation.

4 (1) I, Nebuchadnezzar, was living contentedly in my house, flourishing in my palace. 5 (2) I had a dream, and it frightened me. The thoughts while I lay in bed and the images in my head terrified me. 6 (3) I issued an order to bring all the sages of Babylon to me, so that they might let me know the meaning of the dream. 7 (4) Then the mantic experts, the exorcists, the Chaldeans, and the astrologers entered, and I told them the dream. But its meaning they could not make known to me. 8 (5) Finally, Daniel—whose name is Belteshazzar,[a] after the name of my god, and in whom is a holy divine spirit[b]—came before me, and I told him the dream:

9 (6) "Belteshazzar, head of the mantic experts, I know that a holy divine spirit is in you and that no mystery is too difficult for you. Consider the dream[c] that I saw, and tell me its meaning. 10 (7) These are the images that were in my head[d] upon my bed: I was looking, when suddenly—[e]

> A tree in the center of the earth.
> Its height was immense.
> 11 (8) The tree grew large and strong.
> Its top reached the heavens,
> and it was visible to the ends of the earth.
> 12 (9) Its foliage was beautiful,
> and its fruit abundant;
> in it was food for all.
> Beneath it the animals of the field found shade;
> in its branches dwelt the birds of the sky;
> and all flesh fed from it.

13 (10) "I kept looking at the visions of my head while I was in my bed, when suddenly a watcher, a holy one, was descending from heaven, 14 (11) calling out loudly. And thus he said:

"Chop down the tree
and lop off its branches.
Strip off its foliage
and scatter its fruit!
Let the animals flee from beneath it,
and the birds from its branches!
15 (12) But leave the stock of its root[f] in the ground,
in a fetter of iron and bronze,
in the grass of the field.
Let him be bathed with the dew of heaven,
and with the animals be his provision
among the plants of the earth.
16 (13) Let his mind be changed from that of a human,
and let the mind of an animal be given to him,
while seven times pass over him.
17 (14) By the decree of the watchers is the edict,
and the decision is the word of the holy ones,
so that the living may know
that the Most High is powerful in the dominion of humankind.
To whomever he wishes, he gives it,
and the lowest of persons he can establish over it."

18 (15) "This was the dream that I, King Nebuchadnezzar, saw. You, Belteshazzar, tell its meaning,[g] because all the sages of my kingdom have not been able to make known the meaning to me. But you are able, because a holy divine spirit is in you."

19 (16) Then Daniel, whose name was Belteshazzar, was dumbstruck for a time,[h] and his thoughts alarmed him. The king said, "Belteshazzar, do not let the dream and its meaning alarm you." Belteshazzar answered and said, "My lord, may the dream be for your enemies and its meaning for your foes! 20 (17) The tree that you saw, which grew great and strong, and whose height reached the heavens and which was visible to the whole earth, 21 (18) and whose foliage was beautiful and whose fruit was abundant, and which had food for all in it, under which dwelt all the animals of the field, and in whose branches nested all the birds of the sky— 22 (19) it is you, O king, who have grown great and become strong. Your greatness has increased and reached to the heavens and your dominion to the end of the earth. 23 (20) And insofar as you saw, O king, a watcher, a holy one, coming down from heaven and saying, 'Cut down the tree and destroy it; but leave the stock of its root in the ground, with a band of iron and bronze, in the grass of the field. Let him be bathed with the dew of heaven, and let his provision be with the animals of the field until seven times pass over him.' 24 (21) This is the meaning, O king: It is the decision of the

Most High that has befallen my lord, the king. **25 (22)** You will be driven from humankind and with the animals of the field will be your dwelling. You will be fed grass like oxen, and you will be drenched with the dew of heaven. Seven times will pass over you until you understand that the Most High is sovereign over the dominion of mortals, and he gives it to whomever he wishes. **26 (23)** Insofar as they said to leave the stock of the root of the tree, your kingdom will be established for you from the time that you understand that Heaven is sovereign. **27 (24)** But, O king, may my counsel be pleasing to you: Redeem your sin by almsgiving and your iniquity by showing mercy to the poor; perhaps there will be a lengthening of your tranquility."

    28 (25) All this came upon King Nebuchadnezzar. **29 (26)** At the end of twelve months he was walking about on the roof of the royal palace of Babylon. **30 (27)** The king said, "Truly[i] this is Babylon the great, which I myself built as a royal residence by my powerful might and for my glorious majesty." **31 (28)** While the utterance was still in the king's mouth, a voice from heaven came down, "To you it is announced, King Nebuchadnezzar, that the kingship has passed from you. **32 (29)** From humankind you will be driven away, and with the animals of the field will be your dwelling. You will be fed grass like oxen, and seven times will pass over you until you understand that the Most High is sovereign over the dominion of mortals, and he gives it to whomever he wishes." **33 (30)** At that moment the decree was fulfilled upon Nebuchadnezzar. He was driven away from humankind, and he ate grass like oxen, and his body was drenched with the dew of heaven until his hair grew long like the feathers of vultures and his nails like the talons of birds.

    34 (31) At the end of the days, I, Nebuchadnezzar, lifted my eyes to heaven, and my reason returned to me, and I blessed the Most High, and I praised and glorified the one who lives forever, because his sovereignty is an everlasting sovereignty, and his kingdom endures from generation to generation. **35 (32)** All the inhabitants of the earth are considered as nothing, and he does as he pleases with the host of heaven.[j] There is no one who can restrain his hand or say to him, "What have you done?"

    36 (33) At that moment, my reason returned to me, and for the sake of[k] my royal dignity, my splendor and my radiance also returned to me. My counselors and my nobles sought me out. I was reestablished[l] over my kingdom, and still more greatness was added to me. **37 (34)** Now I, Nebuchadnezzar, praise and magnify, and glorify the King of heaven, all of whose deeds are right and whose ways are just, and who is able to humble those who walk in pride.

    a. See the comments on 1:6–10. The author assumes a false etymology, associating the first syllable of the name with Bēl ("Lord"), the title of the Babylonian god Marduk.

Hubris and Humiliation, Arrogance and Understanding

b. The word *ʾĕlāhîn* might be taken as a plural of majesty and so be translated "spirit of the holy God" (cf. Josh 24:19).
c. The phrase "my dream vision" appears to be the object of the verb "tell." In contrast to ch. 2, however, Nebuchadnezzar himself relates the content of the dream. Thus, following Montgomery (228), instead read the imperative, *ḥăzî*, "perceive, see."
d. Th lacks "the visions of my head," which may be a gloss from vv. 5, 10 (2, 7). The syntax in MT is awkward.
e. Here *ʾălû* directs attention. In the context of dream narration, it indicates the sudden appearance of new visual elements.
f. Both *ʿiqqar* and *šĕrōš* mean "root." The "root of its root" presumably means the part from which the tree emerges, hence "stock."
g. Reading with the Qere ("its meaning") rather than with the Kethib ("the meaning"). So also in v. 19c (16c).
h. Lit., "for about an hour."
i. Here *hălāʾ* is an asseverative particle (Mastin 247).
j. Omitted here: "and the inhabitants of the earth," a dittography.
k. The function of *lamed* here can be interpreted in a variety of ways. It may topicalize ("and as for my royal dignity") or express purpose ("and for the sake of").
l. The Aram. is not intelligible as it stands. The simplest change is to repoint the verb to the first-person singular from the third-person feminine singular.

Overview and Outline

Daniel 4 plays a climactic role in the sequence of stories in Dan 1–6. Although deriving from originally independent traditions, chs. 1–4 have been carefully edited together to provide an extended account of the gradual transformation of Nebuchadnezzar's consciousness from a king who considers himself to be the most powerful figure in his kingdom to one who recognizes that his extraordinary greatness is but a gift from the Most High God. Chapter 5, which in the MT has been closely linked to ch. 4 through an extended summary of those events (5:11–12, 18–21), uses the redeemed Nebuchadnezzar as a foil over against his weak and arrogant son, Belshazzar. Chapter 6, though about Darius the Mede, recapitulates the theme of the supremacy of the Most High, concluding with a doxology that strongly echoes those in Dan 4. Some evidence exists that at one stage chs. 4–6 circulated as a separate collection (see introduction). The skillful redactor of the MT has preserved these linkages while constructing a larger and more complex narrative cycle.

In Dan 4, the artistry of the redactor can be recognized, thanks to the unusual wealth of comparative materials extant. The OG of Dan 4 preserves a significantly different version of the story. Although the basic plot is the same, the framing of the story and many of the details and thematic emphases are different. Scholars in the past have debated whether the OG (Wills 87–113; Albertz 1988, 147–56) or the MT (Satran 1985, 62–68; Grelot 1974, 22) preserved the more original form of the story. Now, however, an emerging consensus recognizes that both the OG and the MT are independent developments from an earlier Aramaic *Vorlage* that is no longer extant (Ulrich 1988, 107–8; J. Collins 216–21; Henze 1999, 40). In addition to the OG, clues to the prehistory of Dan 4 come from texts relating to the last Babylonian king, Nabonidus. Already early in the twentieth century, on the basis of new cuneiform documents from Mesopotamia, scholars had proposed that behind Dan 4 was a story originally told about Nabonidus and only subsequently reconfigured as a narrative about Nebuchadnezzar (Riessler 43; Hommel; Soden 1935, 81–89). It was recognized that Belshazzar was the son, not of Nebuchadnezzar, but of Nabonidus. Moreover, Nabonidus was absent from Babylon for a period of ten years, in the Arabian desert oasis of Teima, and he was the object of harsh polemics from the priests of Marduk in Babylon because of his advocacy of the supremacy of the moon-god Sin. He was also, uniquely among Neo-Babylonian monarchs, known for his interest in revelatory dreams. Most significant, however, was the 1956 discovery of the Harran Inscriptions by Nabonidus and his mother, Adadguppi, in Harran in northern Mesopotamia. One of these inscriptions, Harran 2, A and B (Gadd), exhibits striking similarities with the structure and narrative details of Dan 4 MT (see below).

That there was a tradition of Jewish storytelling about Nabonidus was confirmed by the discovery of the *Prayer of Nabonidus* (4Q242) among the Dead Sea Scrolls. In first-person style this fragmentary Aramaic text relates how Nabonidus suffered from a serious ailment for seven years in Teima, praying unsuccessfully for relief from idols. He was, however, healed by the Most High God. When an unnamed Jewish exorcist disclosed to him the source of his healing, he prayed to the Most High and then composed the account of his healing. Despite the numerous features in this text similar to the narration in Dan 4, there are enough differences to indicate that neither story was a direct source for the other. Both, however, draw on a common stock of traditions about Nabonidus (see Newsom 2010).

When and why might Jews have composed stories about Nabonidus (see fig. 9), and why would some of them be later transferred to the figure of Nebuchadnezzar? As the last king of Babylon, Nabonidus reigned from 556 to 539 B.C.E., when he was captured by Cyrus II, king of Persia. His reign was one of considerable conflict. Nabonidus came to the throne in a *coup d'etat*, probably led by his son Belshazzar (Beaulieu 1989, 90–98). Nabonidus's championing of the supremacy of the moon-god Sin soon brought him into conflict with the priests of Marduk, the dynastic god of the Neo-Babylonian kingdom.

Why Nabonidus left Babylon for a ten-year sojourn in Teima is unclear. In his inscription he refers to conflict with the people of Babylon and other cities (Harran 2, A and B, 1.14–22; Gadd, 57–59) as a precipitating cause. Modern historians suggest that both military and economic aspects of the important southern trade routes may have been a reason for his extended activity in this

Figure 9. A basalt stele representing King Nabonidus with the symbols of the moon-god Sin, the planet Venus, representing Ishtar, and the winged sun-disk of Shamash. Sixth century B.C.E. Provenance unknown. © The Trustees of the British Museum.

region. Whatever the reason, one of the effects of his absence from Babylon was that the annual Akītu Festival, the Babylonian (spring) New Year's festival, could not be performed. This disruption would have exacerbated bad relations with the priests of Marduk. Indeed, the priests of Marduk apparently welcomed the conquest by Cyrus and composed propaganda on his behalf, asserting that he had been chosen to rule by Marduk himself (*ANET* 315; *COS* 2:315). Nabonidus returned to Babylon in 543 B.C.E. (Beaulieu 1989, 165). In the Harran B inscription he attributes this return to the will of the moon-god Sin. But presumably concerns about the increasing Persian military threat would have played an important role in his decision. Despite the enmity he elicited, Nabonidus was not without his supporters. After the Persian conquest, two revolts were led by individuals claiming to be his sons (Briant 120). They would not have made such claims if the name and memory of Nabonidus were unlikely to garner support.

One can only speculate as to why Jewish authors would have been interested in composing stories in which Nabonidus recognizes the supremacy of the God of Israel. But it is important to remember that the Jewish exile community in Babylon was intensely aware of unfolding military and political events in the late 540s. Possibly, just as the Babylonian community was divided between those who supported Nabonidus and those who welcomed Cyrus, so the Jewish community may have been divided. The prophet known as Second Isaiah (Isa 40–55) was an articulate supporter of Cyrus, arguing that YHWH had chosen Cyrus, anointing him and giving him military victory so that he might rebuild

Jerusalem and the temple and allow the exiles to return to Judah (Isa 44:24–45:13). The polemical tone of Second Isaiah's references to Cyrus suggests that some in the exile community resisted this interpretation of divine preference for Cyrus. It is conceivable that stories representing Nabonidus as having been chastised, redeemed, and reinstated by YHWH as king over Babylon served as counterinterpretations of current events and attempted to rally support for him. Just as Second Isaiah engages in harsh polemics against Babylonian idolatry, the *Prayer of Nabonidus* represents that king as rejecting the idols of gold, silver, and other materials. In these traditions Nabonidus is the idealized Gentile monarch. Even the contrasting portrayals of Nabonidus as redeemed king and Belshazzar as condemned king (although secondarily enhanced in the MT) make sense within the politics of the era, since there was apparently a rupture between father and son (Beaulieu 1989, 63–65, 203–5). While it is not possible to go beyond speculation, the highly charged situation of the Jewish community in Babylon in the late 540s and early 530s seems the likeliest context for the development of such traditions concerning Nabonidus (Newsom 2010, 58–72).

The narrative as we now have it in Dan 4, however, contains at best only "ghost memories" of Nabonidus. Nebuchadnezzar has replaced Nabonidus as the protagonist. The reason is not difficult to discern. Although Nabonidus became culturally irrelevant soon after the end of his reign, Nebuchadnezzar had left a wound of memory in the consciousness of Jews in the Diaspora and in Judea. Telling this story of his belated recognition of the power of the Most High was a means of redressing that memory. Yet the story undoubtedly served another and more immediate purpose. After the Persians defeated the Babylonian Empire, Jewish political sovereignty was not restored. They remained a people subject to new imperial power. Thus Nebuchadnezzar served as a symbol for all Gentile rulers. Indeed, some of the particular details of the narrative seem to reflect aspects of Persian rather than Babylonian ideology. Through its literary reworking, Dan 4 becomes something of a palimpsest, reflecting traditions both of Neo-Babylonian and Persian royal traditions. At every layer, however, it functioned as a narrative means by which Jews in the Diaspora and in Judea negotiated their dual relationships to the sovereign God of heaven and the earthly monarchs of the Gentile empires.

Excursus 2: The Harran B Inscription and Daniel 4

Harran B is a building inscription commissioned by Nabonidus to commemorate his restoration of Ehulhul, the temple of the moon-god Sin, which he completed after his return from Teima. The striking similarities in structure, sequence, and detail between Harran B and Dan 4 MT strongly suggest that the author of the *Vorlage* of Dan 4 MT was aware of this Harran Inscription and shaped his own composition in light of it. As the editor of Harran B noted, "The clear purpose of these inscriptions was publicity"

(Gadd 90). Although the largely illiterate population could not read the inscription itself, writings designed for the public were communicated by public reading (Toorn 2007, 11–14). Much about the dissemination of this inscription remains unknown: whether, for instance, copies of it were also circulated in Babylon or in Teima, and thus where and how Jewish communities would have become aware of it (Koch 1995, 98). Since the *Vorlage* of Dan 4 MT is no longer extant, allowance must also be made for the further development of the narrative when it was adapted as a story about Nebuchadnezzar. Nevertheless, the pattern of similarities between the two texts is significant, as the following outline indicates:

Harran B Inscription	**Daniel 4**
1. First-person address to unspecified public	First-person encyclical to "all peoples, nations, and languages" (4:1 [3:31])
2. Announcement of "the great miracle of Sin," which is the act of calling Nabonidus to kingship	Announcement of "the signs and wonders that the Most High God has done for me" (4:2 [3:32]), which includes the humiliation and final exaltation of Nebuchadnezzar to even greater royal honor, as he acknowledges the sovereignty of the Most High God (4:34–35 [31–32])
3. Self-description as "the lonely one who has nobody, in whose heart was no thought of kingship"	The goal of the events is to demonstrate that the Most High gives kingship "to whomever he wishes, . . . the lowest of persons" (4:17 [14])
4. The action in the narrative is a revelatory dream. Sin commands the rebuilding of Ehulhul. What prevents the immediate fulfillment of the divine command is the sinful and rebellious behavior of the populace of Babylonia.	The revelatory dream foretells the humiliation of the king until he learns the source of human kingship (4:10–17 [7–14]).
5. Sin makes Nabonidus leave Babylon for remote Arabia for ten years. Sin and the other deities care for him and ensure his success during this time.	Nebuchadnezzar is "driven away from human society" (5:21) in Babylon and lives a bestial existence for seven years. His kingdom, however, is preserved for him (4:24–27 [21–24]).
6. The period in Teima comes to an end with the fulfillment of the predicted period (*adannu*) of ten years.	Nebuchadnezzar's exclusion from human society comes to an end with the fulfillment of the set period of seven times (4:34 [31])
7. Hymnic praise of Sin	Hymnic praise of the Most High God (4:34–35 [31–32])

Harran B Inscription	Daniel 4
8. Nabonidus takes the road to Babylon. Just before the reference to the completion of the ten-year period, Nabonidus notes that his subjects "turn[ed] again to me so that they began to serve me."	Counselors and nobles seek out Nebuchadnezzar to restore him to his throne (4:36 [33])
9. Nabonidus fulfills the command to build anew the Ehulhul and concludes with final praise of Sin and an address to "whoever you be whom Sin will (later on) name to kingship."	Nebuchadnezzar concludes with praise of "the King of heaven" (4:37 [34])

Excursus 3: *Prayer of Nabonidus* (4Q242)

The words of the p[ra]yer which Nabonidus, king of [Baby]lon, [the great] king, prayed [when he was smitten] with a bad disease by the decree of G[o]d in Teima. [I, Nabonidus, with a bad disease] was smitten for seven years and sin[ce] G[od] set [his face on me, he healed me,] and as for my sin, he remitted it. A diviner (he was a Jew fr[om among the exiles) came to me and said:] "Pro[cla]im and write to give honour and exal[tatio]n to the name of G[od Most High," and I wrote as follows:] "I was smitten by a b[ad] disease in Teima [by the decree of the Most High God.] For seven years [I] was praying [to] the gods of silver and gold, [bronze, iron,] wood, stone, clay, since [I thoug]ht that th[ey were] gods [. . .] their [. . .] apart from them. I was made strong again [. . .] from it he caused to pass. The peace of [my] repo[se returned to me. . .] my friends. I was not able [. . .] how you are like [. . .]. (trans. Collins in *DSSR* 6)

Structure, Literary Features, and Outline

In contrast to the other narratives in Dan 1–6 and to the OG version, Dan 4 MT is framed as a public letter sent by Nebuchadnezzar to the peoples of his empire. Doxologies at the beginning (4:3 [3:33]) and end (4:37 [34]) provide an inclusio. When chapter divisions of the Vulgate were established in the medieval Christian tradition, the first three verses of the narrative were mistakenly assigned to ch. 3. The versification of the MT also includes these verses with ch. 3. Although modern Christian translations have rejected this division, it is followed in printed editions of the MT and the NJPS translation. The confusion over the placement of these verses was apparently caused by the occurrence of doxological elements at the conclusion of several of the narratives (2:47; 4:37 [34]; 6:26–27 [27–28]). Manuscript evidence from antiquity supports the understanding of 3:31-33 MT as the beginning of Dan 4 rather than the end of Dan 3 (see Montgomery 224).

The structure is fairly straightforward, although complicated by a shift between first-person and third-person narration:

Epistolary introduction and doxology (4:1–3 [3:31–33], first person)
Narrative setting; dream and request for interpretation (4:4–8 [1–5], first person)
Account of the dream (4:9–18 [6–15], first person)
Daniel's reaction and interpretation (4:19–27 [16–24], third person)
Fulfillment of predicted punishment (4:28–33 [25–30], third person)
Nebuchadnezzar's restoration (4:34–36 [31–34], first person)
Concluding doxology (4:37 [34], first person)

The alternation between first- and third-person narration is a literary feature, not redactional (*contra* Koch 1995, 85–89; Haag 1983, 19–20), and it well serves the narrative and thematic purposes of the story cycle. The narratives have traced Nebuchadnezzar's gradual and erratic awareness of the nature and power of the God of Daniel, as the king moves from ignorance (1:17–20) to cognizance of this deity's ability to reveal mysteries (2:47), then to a recognition of his power to thwart the king's decree and save his devotees (3:28–29). Yet it has not been clear that Nebuchadnezzar has actually grasped the full implications of his own statement that this deity must therefore be the "Lord of kings" (2:47). The first-person narration in ch. 4 takes the reader into Nebuchadnezzar's own mind and makes him the primary witness to the transformation in understanding that he has undergone. Thus he develops into a fully rounded character in a way that none of the others do. Commentators have long suggested that the switch to third-person narration in vv. 28–33 [25–30] serves to avoid the awkwardness of having the king narrate his own madness, yet the third-person narration also characterizes vv. 19–27 (16–24). In this section of the story, the point of view is largely that of Daniel. Not only is it literarily smoother to have this section framed by third-person narration, but the shift serves another purpose. Since Nebuchadnezzar's understanding in chs. 2 and 3 was demonstrably flawed, a wholly first-person narration in ch. 4 might leave the reader uncertain as to whether Nebuchadnezzar's account could be fully trusted. The third-person sections allow critical aspects of the meaning of Nebuchadnezzar's experience to be framed by Daniel and the anonymous narrator.

While the introductory verses cast the story as the contents of an encyclical letter, the core of the narrative is a dream report, interpretation, and fulfillment. The MT lightly shapes the narrative as a court contest tale by having the king summon the sages of Babylon, who fail to interpret the king's dream (vv. 6–7 [3–4]), setting up Daniel's successful interpretation. These verses are not present in the OG and clearly represent the MT redactor's attempt to assimilate the narrative to the court contest tale of Dan 2. That this is not the primary genre of the story is evident from the fact that Daniel vanishes from the story after giving his interpretation. The climax of the narrative is the restoration of Nebuchadnezzar and his confession.

That the narrative was not even originally about the character Daniel is suggested by the fact that the name by which Nebuchadnezzar addresses the Jewish dream interpreter is Belteshazzar (vv. 8, 9, 18, 19 [5, 6, 15, 16]). The two names are correlated when the character is introduced (v. 8 [5]) and at the beginning of the third-person narration (v. 19 [16]). Otherwise in the narratives the name Belteshazzar occurs only in 1:7 (where the origin of the Jewish characters' Babylonian names is explained), in 2:26, and in 5:12, where the queen mother describes Daniel to Belshazzar. These references are clearly redactional details serving to accommodate the Belteshazzar story in ch. 4 to the Daniel cycle.

Comments

[4:1–3 (3:31–33)] The epistolary introduction is not present in the OG, which instead records the king's epistle at the end (4:37b–c [34b–c]). The OG may have moved the epistle and doxology from the beginning in order to assimilate the form of the story to the other Daniel narratives.

The epistolary address is modeled after typical Aramaic conventions with the name of the sender and addressee, followed by an initial greeting, expressing a desire for the well-being of the recipient (Fitzmyer 1974 211, 214; cf. Ezra 4:11, 17; 5:7–8; 7:12). The addressees ("peoples, nations, and languages") are identified by the same terminology used in 3:4 and 29 for the recipients of Nebuchadnezzar's decrees and in 6:25 (26) for Darius's letter. The terminology is a rhetorical imitation of Persian imperial ideology, which stressed the multiethnicity of its empire (Briant 172–75; cf. Esth 1:22; 3:12; 8:9). The letter is thus political and will deal with what is essentially a political issue: the nature and source of sovereign power. That the issue is, as Koch suggests (1995, 110), an ideology of *universal* kingship may be implied in the author's hyperbolic description of Nebuchadnezzar's realm as including those "who dwell throughout the earth."

The content of the letter is summarized in 4:2 (3:32) as "signs and wonders," a phrase common in the Hebrew Bible, but most frequently used in relation to the exodus tradition, often with specific reference to Pharaoh (Exod 7:3; Deut 6:22; 7:19; 26:8; 29:2–3; 34:11; Jer 32:20–21; Pss 105:27; 135:9; Neh 9:10). Thus the Egyptian Pharaoh and the Babylonian Nebuchadnezzar are paralleled as monarchs who experience the power of the Israelite God. The opening also echoes the beginning of Nabonidus's Harran Inscription with its reference to "the great miracle of Sin," which is that "Sin called me to kingship" (*ANET* 562). Persian inscriptions also typically open with praise of Ahura Mazda and a statement that he has made the writer king (Koch 1995, 111). At each stage of its redactional development, the opening of the story would have served to position the Gentile monarch as confessing the power and sovereignty of the God of the Jews.

Hubris and Humiliation, Arrogance and Understanding 135

The epithet "Most High God" (*ʾĕlāhāʾ ʿillāʾâ* or *ʾĕlāhāʾ ʿillāyʾâ*) corresponds to Hebrew El Elyon, an ancient title attested not only in the Hebrew Bible (e.g., Gen 14:18–20, 22; Deut 32:8–9; 2 Sam 22:14; Pss 7:17; 97:9) but also in Ugaritic, Phoenician, and Aramaic sources. It became particularly popular, however, in the postexilic period. The Aramaic term was also used to render the Persian epithet for Ahura Mazda, *baga vazraka*, "great god" (Koch 1995, 111). In Daniel, except for 3:26 and 7:25, the epithet occurs only in this narrative (4:2 [3:32], 17, 24, 25, 32, 34 [14, 21, 22, 29, 31) and in its summary in 5:18, 21. Thus it has particular thematic significance, which is made explicit in the poetic doxology in v. 36 (33) that completes the introduction. In that verse the terms "signs" and "wonders" are paired with the political terms "kingship" (*malkût*) and "dominion" (*šolṭān*). What distinctively characterizes the Most High's sovereignty is its duration (*dār wĕdār*; *ʿālam*); the key terminology is apparently drawn from the praise of God in Ps 145:13: "Your kingship is an *eternal* kingship, and your rule for *all generations*" (AT). What distinguishes divine sovereignty from human sovereignty is its everlastingness. The doxology is repeated almost verbatim in 4:34 (31) at the very moment when Nebuchadnezzaar's reason is restored to him. He has finally understood the significance of the first dream vision in 2:31–35, 44, which visually contrasted the transitory nature of human sovereignties with the eternal quality of divine dominion. Where the dream in Dan 2 has an eschatological aspect, however, Dan 4 does not. It is a narrative about the present conditions for the authorization of a Gentile imperium. The recognition by the king of the *eternal* (and therefore ultimate) divine sovereignty becomes the basis for the divine authorization of a *universal* but temporary human dominion. What Persian ideology described as Ahura Mazda's authorization of the Great King's rule the author of Dan 4 redescribes from the perspective of the conquered as the conditional authorization of such rule by the Most High (similarly, Koch 1995, 112–16). Thus the narrative embodies a complex act of simultaneous accommodation and resistance to Persian imperial claims about reality.

[4:4–8 (1–5)] The narrative proper begins in 4:4 (1). The terms "house" and "palace" anticipate the crucial scene described in vv. 29–30 (26–27), when Nebuchadnezzar utters the fateful words that precipitate his punishment. Here, however, he describes his situation as "contented" (*šĕlēh*) and "flourishing" (*raʿnan*), a term that literally describes trees or other vegetation and metaphorically refers to humans (Pss 37:35; 52:8 [10]; 92:14 [15]; Jer 17:8), apparently chosen in anticipation of the tree imagery of the dream.

The king's disturbing dream is a stock motif, not only in Jewish court tales (Gen 41; Dan 2) but also in traditions about the Median king Astyges in Herodotus (1.107–8). Verse 5 (2), however, is awkward and redundant, and it is likely that either the phrase "the thoughts while I lay in bed" or "the images in my head" has been secondarily added (see Montgomery 227; Plöger 70).

The perfunctory account of the summoning of the dream interpreters and their failure is absent from the OG and is apparently a redactional element in the MT designed to increase the similarity between Dan 2 and 4. No other elements evoke the subgenre of court contest tale, such as a reward of Daniel. The list of experts is similar to that in 2:2, though here "astrologers" (*gāzrayyāʾ*) substitutes for "diviners" (*mĕkaššĕpîm*), and the sequence differs slightly. Note that here the king does not ask for the interpreters to tell him the dream, as in ch. 2, but only to give its meaning.

In ch. 4 the reader first encounters Daniel through Nebuchadnezzar's characterization of him. The equating of the two names in v. 8 (5) is, as noted above, probably an indication that the story was originally about a Jewish interpreter named Belteshazzar. The narrative, however, gives a false etymology for the name. The first element is "*bēlṭ*," rendering Akkadian *balāṭu* ("life"), not "*bēl*" for Akkadian *bēlu* ("lord"), an epithet of the dynastic god Marduk (see also comment on 1:7). The false etymology plays a thematic role in the story, however, since what Nebuchadnezzar will learn is that his kingship comes not from Marduk but from "the Most High," that is, the God of Israel.

Nebuchadnezzar characterizes Daniel/Belteshazzar as someone in whom is a *rûaḥ-ʾĕlāhîn qaddîšîn*, a phrase that might be translated as "a spirit of the holy gods," "a spirit of the holy god," or "a holy divine spirit." A similarly ambiguous phrase is used by Pharaoh to describe Joseph in Gen 41:38. The first option would highlight Nebuchadnezzar's pagan perspective. The so-called "plural of majesty" is regularly used to refer to the God of Israel, and the equivalent Hebrew phrase *ʾĕlōhîm qĕdōšîm* is applied to YHWH in Josh 24:19. Whichever translation is preferred, Nebuchadnezzar's characterization of Daniel/Belteshazzar refers back to ch. 2 and Daniel's success in interpreting the dream, which Nebuchadnezzar attributes to the god of Daniel, who is "a revealer of mysteries" (2:47). This gives Nebuchadnezzar the confidence that "no mystery is too difficult for you" (4:9 [6]; cf. 2:30).

The language of "spirit" (*rûaḥ*) requires further clarification. As an anthropological term, it can refer to what makes sentient beings different from nonsentient beings, that is, what animates them (cf. Gen 2:7 and 6:3). It also refers to a person's dispositions and emotional state (e.g., Ps 77:3 [4]) and, as a synonym for *lēb* ("mind"), is a term for the self (e.g., Ps 77:6 [7]). "Spirit" also has a qualitative dimension, denoting a person's abilities, native talents, or aptitude (e.g., Num 27:18). It is in this sense that the word "spirit" is used here, as also of Joseph in Gen 41:38. The whole phrase, "a spirit of the holy god(s)" or "a holy divine spirit," could refer either to the quality of Daniel's spirit, or to his ability as a "god-given" talent, or both. Elsewhere, Daniel's abilities are described with the term "extraordinary spirit" (*rûaḥ yattîrâ*; 5:12; 6:3 [4]; see the thorough discussion of such phrases in Levison 34–86).

[9–18 (6–15)] In this section Nebuchadnezzar shifts from narration addressed to the epistolary audience to cite his direct speech to Daniel, including his requests for an interpretation (vv. 9, 18 [6, 15]), which form an inclusio, and his recitation of the dream itself (vv. 10–17 [7–14]). As many have noted, the recitation of the dream is strongly parallelistic in its style. Scenes are introduced with prose elements (vv. 10, 13 [7, 10]), and in places editorial activity may have disrupted the poetry (vv. 15, 17c [12, 14c]). Thus scholars differ in their specific analysis (see, e.g., Goldingay 78; Montgomery 229–30; DiLella 1981), but as the stichometric presentation in the translation above indicates, the parallelism is striking, with both bicola and tricola used throughout the dream account. The poetic style does not necessarily indicate an older piece incorporated into the chapter, though given the eclectic tendencies of the composition, it is possible that the dream description is a piece of recycled tradition now put to a new use. By comparison with the MT, the OG is much more discursive and less poetic and seems to represent expansionistic tendencies (contra Wills 106–7).

[10–17 (7–14)] The dream is divided into two parts. Verses 10–12 (7–9) give a highly visual but static description of the tree itself, characterized by many nominal phrases. Verses 13–17 (10–14) contain the pronouncement of judgment, couched in imperatives and jussive clauses. The final verse identifies the authorization of the decree and its purpose.

The image of "the great tree" is an ancient and widespread symbol in the ancient Near East, attested as early as the fourth millennium B.C.E. and found in artistic and textual representation from the civilizations of the Indus valley to Egypt and Greece (Parpola 1993, 161; see the illustrations in Metzger 1992, 13–30; Keel 1978b, 28–29, 48–51, 135–36, 140–43, 186–87). Its precise meaning and significance are often difficult to determine, and in all likelihood it could be used to represent a variety of values. Most commonly, the tree has associations with fertility and flourishing, often represented by flanking animals and birds who feed on it or take shelter beneath it (Metzger 1992, 2, 13–30; Keel 1998, figs. 2–3, 13, 34–36, 65–67, 77). A number of Middle Bronze Age Syrian seals represent the tree alongside the hieroglyphic ankh symbol, ⚥, denoting life (Metzger 1992, 12; cf. Keel 1998, figs. 33–34), and the mythical tree of life in Gen 2–3 (see also Prov 3:18) is a variation of this tradition (cf. DiLella 1981, 255–58, on parallels between Dan 4 and Gen 2–3). Many depictions of the tree, however, represent it more as a "world tree," a symbol that connects and integrates the spheres of the cosmos. The tree is frequently depicted with a winged sun above it, representing heaven, and in a number of instances it is associated with the waters under the earth (e.g., Ezek 31:4). Or it may be situated on a stylized cosmic mountain (Metzger 1992, 6–8).

Not surprisingly, the tree came to be associated with royal power and thus became an important symbol in imperial ideology. Although attested earlier, this connection is most pronounced in Neo-Assyrian iconography, where the tree often is positioned under the winged sun-disk that represents the god Ashur and is flanked by images of attendant winged *apkallu* genies. Sometimes the king appears between the genies and the tree, and in some examples the king actually replaces the tree (Parpola 1993, figs. 2–4 and n. 31). Thus Parpola seems correct in suggesting that the ensemble represents divine world order and the king's vital place in mediating that order. The tree as imperial symbol "not only provided a legitimation for Assyria's rule over the world, but it also justified the king's position as the absolute ruler of the empire" (Metzger 1992, 10–11; Parpola 1993, 168—yet his speculations about the relation of this symbolism to Jewish kabbala are to be regarded with great skepticism).

In the Hebrew Bible the Davidic dynasty is sometimes likened to a tree, with its individual kings designated as "branches" (e.g., Isa 11:1; Ezek 17:1–8). The biblical texts that most closely resemble the ancient Near Eastern traditions, however, are the poems concerning foreign kings in Ezek 31 and Dan 4. Although the great tree continued as a motif in Neo-Babylonian art, and there is evidence for sacred trees in Persian royal practice (Briant 232–38), it is not clear that Ezekiel or Daniel is responding directly to Neo-Babylonian or Persian royal self-representation. Rather, the imagery may have become familiar from the long period of Assyrian dominance in the ancient Near East and eventually appropriated as something of a cliché for imperial self-representation of any nationality. It is generally agreed that there is no direct literary dependency between Dan 4 and Ezek 31 and similar texts. Yet Metzger's comparative analysis suggests the existence of a common poetic tradition, including not only a repertoire of stock motifs concerning the tree (cosmic dimensions, symbolic location, source of shade or protection, provider of sustenance and dwelling) but also perhaps certain poetic tropes, such as the distinctive use of tricola and chiasm (Metzger 1991, 229).

[10–12 (7–9)] The dream is introduced much as the dream in 2:31, with a compound verb denoting gazing ("you were/I was looking"), the particle of focalization ("there" or "suddenly"), and a description of the image in short, almost staccato phrases. The "world tree" characteristics of the image are identified immediately in v. 10 (7) by its location "in the center of the earth" (*bĕgôʾ ʾarʿāʾ*; cf. Gen 2:9) and its enormous height (cf. Ezek 31:3–5), which "reached the heavens" (v. 11b [8b]). The final colon in v. 11c (8c) completes the spatial imagery by noting that it was visible "to the ends of the earth." Thus both vertical and horizontal axes are employed to describe the tree. The verbs in v. 11a (8a) can denote either process (e.g., "grew large and strong" until it "reached") or state, but as in Dan 2, the dream appears to be structured through the representation first of a static image and then by an account of its destruction. The OG includes additional cosmic imagery, referring to the sun and moon as dwelling in its branches.

Two series of tricola in v. 12 (9) describe the significance of the tree for the inhabitants of the world. Again, the account is highly visual. In the nominal clauses of v. 12a–c (9a–c), the first colon draws the eye first to the foliage and the aesthetic satisfaction it provides; the next draws the eye closer to the abundant fruit nestled in the foliage. Finally, the third identifies the tree not simply as *a* source of food but as the source of food "*for all.*" In the tricolon of v. 12d–f (9d–f), the first two cola introduce the motif of protection and a dwelling place for animals and birds. In the last colon the topic returns to the tree as the source of nourishment. The expression "all flesh" might be a summary term for the animals and birds, or it could refer to humans, thus completing the sequence of animals, birds, humans (cf. Ezek 31:6). In either case the imagery is clear. The dream evokes the deep symbol of the tree as the source of wellbeing for all the world.

The association of this image with the king, which will be made explicit in v. 22 (19), expresses a widespread royal ideology. As noted above, Neo-Assyrian reliefs sometimes represented the king and the tree as interchangeable symbols. Although the imagery is somewhat different, Ps 72 similarly associates the just rule of the Davidic king with the flourishing of nature, so that both the social and the natural world are part of the harmonious divine order mediated by the rule of the king (cf. Postgate 408, on the Assyrian king). While the ensemble of imagery is highly positive, several of the terms in Dan 4:10–12 (7–9) have connotations that could sound a disturbing note to a Jewish audience. Terms for height frequently are associated with the kind of pride that elicits divine judgment (e.g., Isa 2:12–17; Ezek 17:24; Job 40:11–12). The phrase "its top reached the heavens" is also evocative of the description of the Tower of Babel with "its top in the heavens" (Gen 11:4).

[13–17 (10–14)] Verse 13 (10) introduces the second, dynamic stage of the dream with a repeated reference to looking (cf. 2:34) and the focalizing particle. As in ch. 2, the second scene is one of destruction of the image, though here the destruction is commanded rather than enacted. The agent of the announcement is described by a hendiadys as "a holy watcher," literally, "a watcher and a holy one." While there is no question that this is an angelic figure, the origin and connotation of the term "watcher" (*ʿîr*) remains somewhat uncertain. Daniel 4:13 (10), 17 (14), 23 (20) are the only attestations of the term in the MT, though it also occurs frequently in Aramaic texts from Qumran (such as *1 Enoch* 10:9; 12:3; 13:10; 22:6; 93:2; 4QEnGiants^a [4Q203] frg. 7a 7; frg. 7b 1.4; 4QEnGiants^d [4Q532] frg. 2 7; 1QapGen [1Q20] 2.1, 16; 6.13; 7.2; 4QAmram^d [4Q546] 22.1). In Hebrew it occurs in the *Damascus Document* (CD 2.18), and lies behind the Ethiopic of *Jubilees* 4:15, 22; 7:21; 10:5. Not infrequently, the term is paired with "holy one." Although many of the instances refer to the fallen watchers, the angels who descend to earth to mate with human women (*1 En.* 10–16, a development of Gen 6:1–4), the term itself has no negative connotations and is applied to other angelic figures (*1 En.* 22:6; 93:2). The etymology assumed by the Greek translators of these texts derives the term from the Semitic root *ʿwr*, "to wake up," for they render *egrēgoroi* "wakeful ones," and the angels are sometimes described in terms of their wakeful vigilance

(*1 En.* 20:1; 39:12–13; 71:7). An alternative interpretation derives the term ʿwr from the Ugaritic root *ģyr*, "to protect." The two functions are not unrelated, even if the etymologies are (cf. Ps 121:1–5), and the English term "watcher" preserves the ambiguity. (For speculations about possible mythic backgrounds for the term, see Kvanvig 304–12; Murray.)

In Dan 4 the angelic figure performs the familiar function of herald and messenger. It is not clear to whom the plural imperatives are addressed. The fact that the king sees the angel "descending" might suggest that the command is to be carried out by human functionaries, as the tree in Ezek 31:11–12 is cut down by the nations. But the announcement might also be made to other members of the divine council. The ambiguity is probably simply part of the convention of divine pronouncement. The addressees of the announcement of comfort in Isa 40:1–5, with its plural imperatives and complementary jussives, are similarly ambiguous.

The four imperatives in Dan 4:14b–e (11b–e) describe the progressive destruction of the tree, beginning with its trunk and sequentially moving to its smaller component parts—branches, foliage, fruit—just as the description had begun with the totality of the tree and then directed attention to the smaller elements (*pace* Koch 1995, 100–101, who sees the activity as a kind of pollarding, so as to produce a tall, standing trunk; see below). The sheltering of the animals and birds in v. 12d (9d) is similarly reversed in v. 14f–g (11f–g). The imagery of utter destruction is, however, suddenly and surprisingly halted by the angelic command of 15a–c (12a–c), requiring preservation of the base of the tree. That the preservation of some part of the tree is a sign of the possibility of renewal is later made clear in v. 26 (23). But in the dream account itself, it is an ambiguous image. Although trees were known for their powers of regeneration (Isa 11:1; Job 14:7), the images that follow simply suggest that the remains of the tree are subjected to further humiliation.

The remainder of the imagery in v. 15 (12) is difficult in the extreme. At some point the underlying image shifts from being that of a tree to being the human figure of Nebuchadnezzar himself. But where? And what is the referent and significance of the "band of iron and bronze"? One line of interpretation, since the suggestion of Lengerke in 1835 (cited in Montgomery 233), has been to see in the band a kind of protective device to keep the base of the tree from splitting. This suggestion has two problems, however. First, the word ʿiqqar simply means "root" and does not imply that a sizeable trunk was left. Second, no evidence exists for such a practice in antiquity. A variation on this line of thought has been to explore the phenomenon of wooden poles with multiple metal bands representing sacred trees in Mesopotamia (Kvanvig 479) or even the wooden stave with metal bands carried by Nabonidus (Koch 1995, 104–9). But the parallels seem far-fetched since the tree has been cut down and the band applied only after its destruction.

An alternative line of interpretation, going back to Jerome (on 4:15 [12]), has been to see the reference to the "band of iron and bronze" as the fetter by which a madman is restrained. The introduction of such imagery seems very abrupt, although the OG does refer twice to Nebuchadnezzar being "bound" (v. 33a [30a]) with "shackles and bronze manacles" (v. 17a [14a]). In each case the imagery is associated with his eating grass with the animals. Given the complex compositional history of Dan 4 and the wide variety of traditions upon which it drew, it seems most likely that this reference in the MT is a motif from an alternative account of Nebuchadnezzar being restrained during his time of madness (cf. Wills 92–97). Though the transition in the MT may be the result of awkward editing, it does provide the dream account with an appropriately surreal morphing of images. Indeed, the masculine gender of both "tree" and "Nebuchadnezzar" would permit one to translate "it" throughout the passage, thus leaving the imagery as fluid as dreams often are.

Verse 16 (13) identifies the critical aspect of the king's punishment. In ancient Near Eastern thought, the world contains three basic types of beings: deities, humans, and animals. Each is distinguished by its relation to knowledge and rationality. Indeed, Gen 2–3 is a mythic account of how an original two types of being (divine beings and nondivine beings) became three. When the originally animal-like first woman and man ate from the tree of knowledge, they became "like gods" but not fully divinized. That is, they became a type of being intermediate between deities and animals. According to Sumerian tradition, in primordial time, before the gifts of civilization, people lived like animals—not wearing clothes or eating cooked food but rather eating grass (see "The Debate between Grain and Sheep," Black 225–29). In the Gilgamesh Epic, Enkidu is represented as just such a prehuman, one who shares in the lot of animals and whose hair is long and shaggy. Although Enkidu's loss of his ability to run with the animals as he becomes fully human is described with some pathos, the animalized human was largely viewed with abhorrence, as in the ethnic slurs directed against the Amorites, describing them as living like animals rather than like civilized humans ("The Marriage of the God Martu," discussed in Henze 1999, 93–99). Nebuchadnezzar's punishment is even more appalling, however, because kings occupied a distinctive and exalted status. They were intermediaries between the divine and human realms and were even spoken of as the "image" of god (Parpola 1993, 168n33), an idea that influences the reference to humans as made "in the image" of God in Gen 1. For the king Nebuchadnezzar to have his human mind replaced by an animal mind removes him from a nearly superhuman status to a subhuman rank.

The duration of this punishment is announced in advance as "seven times," perhaps signifying seven years. If Dan 4 does indeed draw on old Nabonidus sources, then this detail may be the author's adaptation of the Harran Inscription's statement that Sin decreed a period of ten years for Nabonidus's sojourn in Teiman, yet seven is the more common symbol of completion in Jewish tradition. More significant for the narrative, the announcement of the duration in advance gives a distinctive quality to the punishment. Unlike the dream in Dan 2, which described an ultimate destruction of the image and the Gentile kingdoms it represented, the limited duration of this punishment is linked to its different purpose, which, as v. 17 (14) indicates, is educative (cf. vv. 25, 34–35 [22, 31–32]). Slight differences occur between the punishment described in v. 17 (14) and Daniel's interpretation in v. 25 (22). Verse 17 (14) attributes the decree to the "watchers" and the "holy ones," whereas Daniel's interpretation in v. 24 (21) says it is a "decision [NRSV: decree] of the Most High." These are essentially synonymous expressions, however, as the angelic beings are part of the divine council, a concept that has ancient roots in Israelite and ancient Near Eastern thought (cf. 1 Kgs 22:19–23; Jer 23:21–22). Similarly, v. 17 (14) refers to "the living" as the ones who are to understand, whereas v. 25 (22) identifies the king himself as the recipient of the lesson. The two elements are complementary: the king's own recognition leads to the general letter to all the peoples that constitutes Dan 4.

What the king and the people come to recognize through the events recounted in the encyclical is the nature and source of political sovereignty. To say that "the Most High is sovereign" is in one sense a very traditional claim. The psalms are replete with references to such divine sovereignty over human kings and all peoples (e.g., Pss 2; 93; 95–98). More striking is the collective phrase *malkût ʾănāšāʾ*, "the human dominion." In contrast to the multiple "kings" and "nations" of the psalms, this phrase posits a universal imperium, all of humanity considered as a single domain (Koch 1995, 83, 114). This shift in conceptualization reflects the ideological context of the Persian period, in which the cycle of stories most likely took shape. The sense of a universal kingship under a single high god is reflected in the stereotypical style of Achaemenid royal inscriptions. For example, "A great god (is) Ahura Mazda, who created this earth, who created yonder heaven, who created men, who created blissful happiness for man, who made Xerxes king, one king of many, one lord of many. I (am) Xerxes, the great king, king of kings, king of countries containing many peoples, king on this great earth far and wide, son of Darius, the king, an Achaemenian" (Kuhrt 244). Although somewhat analogous rhetoric was used in Neo-Assyrian royal inscriptions, it was not characteristic of the Neo-Babylonian style. Daniel 4 is thus an attempt to respond to a new conception of kingship and to incorporate it into its own theological perspective.

In vv. 10–17 (7–14) one sees the complexity of this engagement with Persian imperial ideology. The text assumes the Persian understanding of the scope and nature of kingship but implicitly contests kingship's source and origin. In doing this, the author alludes to and builds on two earlier biblical texts: Isa 45 and Jer 27. Second Isaiah's claim that YHWH has summoned and authorized

Hubris and Humiliation, Arrogance and Understanding 143

Cyrus's kingship and conquest was explicitly tied to the purpose "so that they may know, from the rising of the sun to its setting, that there is none apart from me" (Isa 45:6 AT; the phrase in 45:3c "so that you [sg.] may know" is secondary, though its addition makes the passage even more similar to Dan 4:25 [22]). The phrase "he gives it to whomever he wishes" in Dan 4:17 (14) echoes Jer 27:5, where, as part of the oracle authorizing the kingship of Nebuchadnezzar, YHWH says, "I give it to whomever seems fitting to me" (AT). Thus Dan 4 stands in a tradition of texts that have attempted to deal with the cognitive dissonance of the power of the Gentile empires by incorporating them into the divine intentionality of YHWH.

The one detail from v. 17 (14) that does not have an antecedent in this biblical tradition is the reference to "the lowest of persons." Although Nebuchadnezzar's future punishment will make him just that, it seems an odd way to describe his status in general. The OG does not have a parallel to this line in v. 17 (14), though when the punishment actually commences, the voice from heaven tells Nebuchadnezzar that "the kingdom of Babylon has been taken away from you and is given to another, to a despised man in your household" (v. 31 [28], trans. J. Collins 211). Thus this detail may be the remnant of a similar threat that has been largely eliminated in the editorial shaping of the MT (so Albertz 1988, 55–57). Or it may simply be an idiom alluding to the sovereign freedom of the Most High, similar to the play on "high" and "low" in Ezek 17:24.

[18–27 (15–24)] Following Nebuchadnezzar's repeated request to Daniel to interpret the dream in v. 18 (15), the first-person narration switches to third person as the point of view shifts from Nebuchadnezzar to Daniel. That Daniel should be psychologically disturbed is an unusual detail. While it is typical for the recipient of a dream to be upset because of uncertainty as to what the dream or vision portends (Gen 40:6; 41:8; Dan 2:3; 4:5 [2]; 7:15; 8:27), the interpreter is usually represented as unperturbed, even when he has to deliver bad news (Gen 40:18–19). Daniel's wish that the dream might be for the king's enemies is an apotropaic gesture, intended to avert the threat from its object. Yet as his interpretation makes clear, there is no avoiding the judgment portended by the dream. Nevertheless, Daniel's reaction and the mutually solicitous exchange between the king and Daniel suggest a degree of genuine affection between them (cf. Neh 2:1–2). The function of these details appears to be to orient the reader's attitude toward the king. In the preceding chapters Nebuchadnezzar has been ambivalently portrayed. The dream of judgment implies divine displeasure, and yet the purpose of the narrative is to depict the redemption of the king. Thus Daniel's concern for the king encourages a sympathetic inclination toward him, which will be rewarded by the king's confession at the end. Early Christian interpreters, notably Hippolytus (*Comm. Dan.* 3.7) and Jerome (on 4:19 [16]), interpreted the relationship more or less in this way. Hippolytus describes Daniel as an adviser "who, like a good physician, wishes to heal his wounds" (Henze 1999, 106). Yet for the rabbis, for whom Nebuchadnezzar was above all the destroyer of Jerusalem and the temple, Daniel's response was inexplicable. Various midrashim suggest that Daniel was either dissembling or that his response was part of a scheme to seek relief for the exiles (Henze 1999, 108–14).

Just as the account of the dream was divided into two scenes, so Daniel's interpretation takes up each part in turn, as Daniel first summarizes the content (vv. 20–21, 23 [17–18, 20]) and then gives the interpretation (vv. 22, 24–26 [19, 21–23]). The summaries are partly literal repetition, partly selective and periphrastic. In the interpretation, too, some details are ignored, some are relocated, and others are elaborated in ways that introduce features not specifically included in the description. These differences should not be given too much significance, as they may simply be stylistic features that prevent excessive repetition.

[20–22 (17–19)] In his interpretation of the tree as the king, the appearance of the tree rather than its location or provision of food is the focus. More specifically, the vertical and horizontal dimensions of the tree represent respectively the king's greatness and his sovereignty. Nothing in the summary or the interpretation in vv. 20–22 (17–19) explicitly indicates that there is anything wrong about either quality. Indeed, the description of Nebuchadnezzar is not so different from what Daniel says of his greatness and dominion in 2:37–38 (cf. 4:36 [33]).

[23–26 (20–23)] The summary of the scene of punishment in v. 23 (20) is somewhat elliptical, with details paraphrased and the reference to the king's mind omitted. Yet it is clearly Nebuchadnezzar's animalization that is the focus of the interpretation in v. 25 (22). His being driven away from human habitation is a detail that probably has its ultimate origin in the Nabonidus traditions and hostile speculations about the reasons for his absence from Babylon, though even the hostile Verse Account of Nabonidus (*ANET* 312–15) does not accuse him of madness. Daniel's interpretation also adds the note that Nebuchadnezzar will be fed grass like cattle, a detail about diet that was a commonplace in the Mesopotamian traditions about those who were not truly human (see above). Do these details, coupled with the reference to the fetter in v. 15 (12), suggest a picture of Nebuchadnezzar as restrained but cared for by his courtiers during the time of his madness? (cf. Wills 95). It is difficult to say with certainty what the text intends.

Daniel's account of the purpose of the punishment (v. 25b [22b]) takes up the final words of the watchers (v. 17 [14]) and relates them specifically to Nebuchadnezzar: his failure to recognize that Heaven is sovereign is the flaw in his kingship. Although the use of "Heaven" (v. 26 [23]) as a term for the deity becomes common in Hellenistic and Roman era literature (e.g., 1 Macc 3:18–19; 2 Macc 7:11; Matt 21:25; Luke 15:18; John 3:27; *m. 'Abot* 1.3; 2.12), this is its only occurrence in the Hebrew Bible. Its use here is artful, for it underscores the irony that though the king's greatness reached to heaven, he did not truly understand that "Heaven" was sovereign over him. The OG makes Nebuchadnezzar's destruction of the temple in Jerusalem an example of the king's arrogance (4:22 OG), but the MT is concerned only with the relationship between Nebuchadnezzar and the Most High. Changing the order of the elements in the dream, Daniel reserves the image of the root stock until the end (v. 26 [23]) and disambiguates it as a sign of hope for restoration, dependent upon the king's recognition of the true source of sovereignty.

[27 (24)] The advice with which Daniel concludes his speech to the king has often puzzled readers since it seems unrelated to the problems that the dream and its interpretation have identified. First, one should recognize that Daniel does not suggest that this course of action will avert the judgment. The decree is irrevocable. This stance is at odds with the Mesopotamian understanding of ominous dreams and signs. Indeed, the purpose of mantic experts was both to interpret the omen and to advise on the appropriate course of action for deflecting the fate (Oppenheim 2008, 239; see comments on 2:8–12). Here, however, Daniel offers only the possibility of delaying the time before the judgment is executed and thereby extending Nebuchadnezzar's present state of tranquil contentment (cf. 4:4 [1], where the same word, "content/tranquil," is used [$šlh$]).

Second, Daniel's suggestion of "almsgiving" and "showing mercy to the poor" are not actions directly correlated with Nebuchadnezzar's failure to recognize the sovereignty of the Most High. Although the term $ṣidqâ$ has the broader meaning of "righteousness, right conduct" in earlier Aramaic (and in its Biblical Heb. cognate), it comes to mean "almsgiving." Here the parallelism with "showing mercy to the poor" indicates that it has that more specific meaning, and this is how both the OG and Th translate it. During the Second Temple period almsgiving became the premier social virtue and was assumed to have general efficacy in softening the heart of the Deity (cf. Sir 3:30). In the book of Tobit, too, almsgiving is distinctly emphasized (4:5–10; 12:6–10; for a history of this development, see Anderson).

The scene ends abruptly with Daniel's words of advice. Nebuchadnezzar's reaction is not given, nor does Daniel appear further in the narrative. Did Nebuchadnezzar heed Daniel's advice? The fact that the punishment does not occur until twelve months later (v. 26) suggests that he may have done as Daniel advised and so delayed the judgment. Nevertheless, just as Nebuchadnezzar in previous narratives both understands and fails to understand the significance of the divine revelations to him, his subsequent actions indicate that he has not grasped the full import of the dream.

[28–33 (25–30)] The next scene, continuing in third-person narration, describes the punishment. The setting, with Nebuchadnezzar "on his palace," presumably on the roof or the surrounding walls, and receiving a divine pronouncement of judgment, is evocative of an ancient tradition about Nebuchadnezzar by the Greek historian Megasthenes, reported by Abydenus and preserved by Eusebius (*Praep. ev.* 9.41.6). In this account Nebuchadnezzar stands on his palace and himself prophesies the destruction of the Neo-Babylonian Empire by the "Persian mule" Cyrus. (Cyrus was the son of a Persian king and a Median princess.) Nebuchadnezzar utters the wish that Cyrus would be driven into the desert to wander among wild beasts. Then Nebuchadnezzar disappears. While the two stories are quite different in their import, the similarities suggest that the author of Daniel may have been aware of traditions about Nebuchadnezzar that he mined for dramatic details in the composition of his own tale.

[30 (27)] In Dan 4, Nebuchadnezzar's words on the roof of his palace are not a prophecy but a boast concerning his achievements as a builder and what they represent. The Neo-Babylonian dynasty, from Nabopolassar to Nabonidus, was composed of avid builders, but Nebuchadnezzar's long reign allowed him the most scope for massive construction works. He built a palace for himself, restored the Esagila (temple of Marduk), and built a series of massive fortification walls, among many other projects (Wiseman 51–73; see fig. 10). The royal pride in these achievements is amply on display in the inscriptions. He describes his palace as "the seat of my royal authority, a building for the admiration of my people, a place of union for the land" (trans. Langdon, cited in Wiseman 55).

The magnificence of Babylon became legendary throughout the ancient world, as indicated by Herodotus's extensive and awestruck descriptions, though he attributes the building of Babylon to two legendary Assyrian queens (1.178–86). The Hellenistic-era Babylonian historian Berossus correctly credited Nebuchadnezzar (summarized by Josephus in *Ag. Ap.* 1.134–41).

These building projects, although they served social, religious, and military purposes, were also material propaganda for the imperial power of the king. The Persians, even more than the Babylonians, emphasized this element in the royal building projects. Indeed, the Persian imperial ideology can be best understood through an analysis of its art and architecture (see Root). In the inscriptions that accompany these magnificent buildings, the king always represents himself as the pious servant of his god (the Babylonian Marduk and Persian Ahura Mazda, respectively) and his kingship as deriving from the will of the god. The grandeur of the palaces, temples, and fortifications thus stands as a testament to the power of the god as manifested on earth through his chosen king. It is this aspect of royal ideology that Dan 4 addresses in having Nebuchadnezzar boast of the building of Babylon, though the words attributed to him refer only to his own royal glory and not to his dynastic god.

[31a (28a)] Although no figure is seen, the voice from heaven is undoubtedly the "holy watcher" of v. 23 (20). For a similar use of a "voice" announcing a divine decree, see Isa 40:3, 6. Such disembodied divine voices become a

Hubris and Humiliation, Arrogance and Understanding

Figure 10. Artist's reconstruction of the ceremonial Ishtar Gate of Babylon. Preserved portions of the gate are displayed in the Pergamon Museum in Berlin. BPK (Bildarchiv Preussischer Kulturbesitz), Berlin; Art Resource, New York.

familiar trope in later Jewish and Christian literature (Josephus, *Ant.* 13.282; *2 Bar.* 13:1; 22:1; Matt 3:17; Mark 1:11; Luke 3:22). In rabbinic tradition the heavenly voice known as the *bat qôl* was a means of communication from heaven after the supposed cessation of prophecy (*t. Soṭah* 13.3).

[31b–32 (28b–29)] Nebuchadnezzar's punishment is summarized as the loss of kingship. The OG is more expansive at this point, elaborating on the transfer of Nebuchadnezzar's kingdom to a "despised person" in his house (perhaps an interpretation of the phrase "the lowest of persons" in v. 17 [14]; so J. Collins 231). The MT, however, with more artistry and thematic focus, attends only to the condition of the king. The summary of the punishment follows closely the phraseology of Daniel's interpretation in v. 25 (22), thus adding authority to his words. Although the voice refers to the "seven times" and to the ultimate result of the punishment ("until you know/understand"), it says nothing about the preservation of the kingdom for Nebuchadnezzar.

[33 (30)] Just as the divine voice spoke at the instant when Nebuchadnezzar uttered his boastful words (v. 31 [28]), so the decree is enacted "at that moment." The narrative summary of the punishment repeats elements of the voice's pronouncement, including the detail of being drenched by the dew (vv. 15, 25 [12, 22], omitted by v. 32 [29]). It also adds a new feature, the description of the king's hair and nails growing long, so that he resembled a vulture (v. 33 [30]). While this detail is part of the larger symbolism of the king's animalization, it carries additional connotations. In Mesopotamia, demons and the dead were described as having birdlike features, a motif that can also be detected in Israelite literature (Hays 2007, 309–10, 316–17). Similarly, in the Syriac version of *Ahiqar*, the hero is hidden in a pit. When he is later brought up from the pit, he describes himself, saying, "the hair of my head had grown down on my shoulders, and my body was foul with the dust, and my nails were grown long like an eagle's" (Conybeare 116). Thus Nebuchadnezzar's period of punishment is described with imagery that likens it to a time of death.

[34–37 (31–34)] Nebuchadnezzar's suffering is not merely educative but also transformative (*contra* Pace 117). That is, he does not gradually come to an understanding of divine sovereignty through his humiliation and suffering. Instead, just as predicted, his suffering endures for a set period of time, and when that time is completed, he is restored; but he receives a new understanding. Although the OG has the king supplicate God *before* he is restored (v. 33c [30c]), the MT describes the event in ways more in keeping with the king's animalistic state. He cannot speak, but he signals as an animal might, by directing his eyes to heaven. In response to this gesture of acknowledgment, his reason is restored.

Physically, the restoration of Nebuchadnezzar to his kingship is accomplished by the counselors and nobles who "sought him out," just as he had been "driven out" at the onset of his madness. The more decisive aspects of his restoration, however, have to do with the consequences of Nebuchadnezzar's new understanding, which he articulates in the doxology of vv. 34b–35 (31b–32). Since these verses are marked off by a resumptive repetition ("My reason returned to me"), they may be a redactional element related to the other doxologies in chs. 2–6; but they are critical to the final form of ch. 4. Poetically, the first lines are a close variation of 4:3 (3:33), the doxology that opens Nebuchadnezzar's letter. The emphasis on the eternal nature of the divine rule is also underscored by the reference to God as "the one who lives forever" (v. 34 [31]; 12:7; Sir 18:1; cf. Gen 21:33). The rest of the doxology emphasizes the incomparable power of God, using phrases evocative of Isaiah (34:12; 40:17; 45:9).

Even before the counselors and nobles arrive, however, Nebuchadnezzar has been restored to kingly status by the return of his "splendor and radiance," the charisma that makes a king godlike (cf. 2:31). Three of the terms used in v. 36b (33b) also appear in Nebuchadnezzar's boast in v. 30 (27). They are thus not negative qualities in and of themselves; what had made them problematic was Nebuchadezzar's failure to understand their true source. Far from being a diminished king after his experiences, Nebuchadnezzar appropriately observes that "still more greatness was added to me," since he now understands that the Most High is the one who was pleased to establish him over the dominion of humankind (v. 17 [14]). That Nebuchadnezzar has not yet again misunderstood the purpose of the divine revelation, as he seemed to do in chs. 2 and 3, is confirmed by the concluding verse of the chapter. Not only does Nebuchadnezzar refer to the Most High explicitly as the *"King* of heaven," a term unique in the Hebrew Bible (cf. 5:23); he also praises God precisely because of God's ability to humble the arrogant.

The structure of Nebuchadnezzar's experiences can be likened to a rite of passage. First, he is stripped of his status and separated from society. The seven seasons constitute a liminal period in which he experiences privations and humiliations, but in the end he receives new knowledge. Finally, he is reintegrated into society, but now he has a transformed status as he recognizes that he holds his kingship as a fiefdom from the Most High. The focus on the transformation of the king in Dan 4 is also part of a broader interest in Persian and Hellenistic Jewish literature on the moral psychology of arrogance and the transformed understanding. The closest parallel to the dynamics of this narrative are to be found in the Chronicler's account of Manasseh's captivity, suffering, and recognition that "YHWH indeed was God" (2 Chr 33:10–16; cf. Prayer of Manasseh). Variants of the motif are found in 1 Macc 6 and 2 Macc 9 concerning Antiochus IV Epiphanes. The dynamics are also similar to those of the prideful man described by Elihu in Job 33, a connection noted first by Duhm (159) and discussed by Plöger (79) and Haag (1983, 108–9). Representing Nebuchadnezzar according to this pattern allows the Jewish audience to address the wound of memory created by Nebuchadnezzar's destruction of Judah and the temple. Significantly, in the MT tradition, in contrast to the OG, no explicit reference is made to these actions of Nebuchadnezzar. Though possibly repressed, they are never truly absent when his name is invoked. Like Jer 27:6–7, thus Dan 4 deprives Nebuchadnezzar of his role as an autonomous agent in history. In contrast to Jeremiah, however, which takes no interest in his character, Dan 4 humanizes Nebuchadnezzar and indeed presents him in the positive role of the redeemed sinner, completing the development of his character begun in ch. 1. That this depiction of him was controversial is indicated by the resistance to Dan 4 in rabbinic interpretation of this chapter (see Henze 1999, 109–14).

A similar moral ambiguity attends the way in which this narrative addresses the cultural context of the Persian period. The imaginative work performed by the Nebuchadnezzar cycle as a whole and ch. 4 in particular acknowledges political realities that cannot be changed (Gentile imperial rule in the Persian and early Seleucid periods), yet at the same time subverts the claims of the imperial ideology by constructing a counternarrative. The intellectual bargain struck by such a strategy, however, is that the rule by the regime in power is implicitly validated as the will of God. As the following chapter will indicate, however, that validation leaves room for sharp prophetic critique.

History of Reception, by Brennan W. Breed

Political Sovereignty and the Foreign King

From the ancient world to the modern, a major interpretive problem for Jews concerns Daniel's apparently overzealous service to the king of Babylon. Daniel, who in verses 19 (16) and 27 (24) expresses concern that the king's prosperous reign would continue, strikes many readers as a sycophant at best and a traitorous collaborator at worst. Some sages asked if Daniel was culpable for aiding an idolatrous blasphemer (*b. B. Bat.* 4a). If Daniel had given Nebuchadnezzar poor advice, could he have hastened the demise of the oppressive empire? For his disloyalty, some rabbinic interpreters claimed, God allowed the conquering Persians to demote Daniel to a mere court attendant, where he met and served Esther as her eunuch (Esth 4:5). He had been renamed "Hathach," these interpreters claimed, because his power had been cut down in punishment (reading *ḥătāk*, "to divide," for the name *hătāk*); others even went so far as to claim Daniel's trip to the lions' den was punishment for his collaboration (*b. B. Bat.* 4a).

Yet other rabbinic readers defended Daniel, saying that he intended to help his own people. Thus one rabbinic midrash argues: "Do not think that the righteous Daniel would offer this advice to Nebuchadnezzar, who hated the Omnipotent one, if he had not known that Israel was wasting away from hunger as it wandered in exile. Hence he gave this advice to him because of his concern for them, and because he knew ultimately Nebuchadnezzar's soul would suffer" (*Tanḥ. Mishpaṭim* 4). In other words, the precarious state of the Jews afforded them no protection if Daniel incurred the king's wrath, and in any case Nebuchadnezzar would merit punishment with or without Daniel's advice. Still others, such as the seventh-century Talmudist Shmuel Eidels, known as Maharsha, agreed that Daniel's intentions were pure, but his collaboration was nevertheless improper (Goldwurm 149).

Christian interpreters tended to think more from the perspective of the ruler than from the diasporic minority. In the early church, Christians seemed to use Dan 4 to convince themselves that God's providence guided secular rulers (Hippolytus, *Comm. Dan.* 3.4.1–4). After Constantine, the image of the penitential ruler was significant in the Christian conception of secular power. By the early sixth century, a Christian legend emerged that described Constantine, baptized and cured of leprosy by Pope Sylvester I, humbling himself penitently and abandoning idolatry (Satran 1994, 92). Augustine, among others, was convinced that Nebuchadnezzar's humbling foretold Constantine's supposed conversion: "The earlier time of that king [before Nebuchadnezzar's humility] represented the former age of emperors who did not believe in Christ, at whose hands the Christians suffered because of the wicked; but the latter time of that king represented the age of the successors to the imperial throne, now believing in Christ, at whose hands the wicked suffer because of the Christians" (*Ep.* 93.3.9). For Augustine, the conversion of the king to the proper religion changes the targets of imperial power, but perhaps not the methods—notably, making those who do not conform to the king's religion to suffer. Yet the motif of the penitent king served as a check on the power of medieval kings. A famous story of Holy Roman Emperor Henry IV's barefoot penitential trek through the snowy Alps to make amends with Pope Gregory VII serves as one example of the power that this motif held in medieval European culture; Thomas Aquinas, in his *Summa theologiae,* juxtaposes "holy men faithfully serving masters who were unbelievers, for instance, Joseph Pharaoh, Daniel Nebuchadnezzar, and Merdecai Ahasuerus," with Gregory VII's decree that absolved those who serve excommunicated persons, such as Henry IV, from their duties; as Thomas concludes, "in her early days the Church was not yet capable of checking the earthly princes, so she allowed the faithful to obey" (Thomas 100–103).

In Eastern Christianity, the link between Nebuchadnezzar and Christendom was quite strong. The *History of the Armenians,* a fifth-century story about the conversion of the kingdom of Armenia to Christianity in 301, describes the pagan Armenian king being knocked from his chariot by a divinely sent demon who possessed the king and drove him to "rave and eat his own flesh. And in the likeness of Nebuchadnezzar, king of Babylon, he lost his human nature for the likeness of wild pig" (Satran 1994, 94). The story claims that Gregory the Illuminator, a Christian evangelist in Armenia, helped the king to recover, and in response the king converted to Christianity, ordered the Christianization of his empire, and committed himself to uprooting other religious practices in his kingdom. In this story, Gregory functions as a spiritual director as well as healer, encouraging the king to eat an ascetic diet of pulse, the same diet that Eastern Christians understood Daniel to have requested in ch. 1 (Satran 1994, 96). Christians understood these kingly conversions to be types of the conversion of Nebuchadnezzar in Dan 4, which made many of them comfortable with the very concept of Christendom.

Nebuchadnezzar's story possesses interpretive power in Islamic tradition as well; in general, Nebuchadnezzar's animal transformation served as a warning to kings. Muhammad ibn Jarir al-Tabarī, a tenth-century Persian scholar, tells of Nebuchadnezzar's anger with Daniel and his three companions because of their refusal to eat impurely slaughtered royal meat. Nebuchadnezzar then threw them into a trench with six lions, who miraculously did not devour them; upon returning, the king noticed a seventh form, an angel, in the trench with the men. As al-Tabarī relates the story: "Then the seventh man came forth. It was an angel, and he slapped Nebuchadnezzar, who turned into a wild beast for seven years" (al-Tabarī 106–7). This story condenses several stories from Dan 1–6 into a compact lesson for secular rulers: if you threaten the lives of the religious scholars, God will intervene on their behalf.

Some interpreters understood the text to speak to political rulers more generally. The early Jewish midrash *Mekilta de-Rabbi Ishmael* understood Isa 14:4–20, a speech about an anonymous Babylonian king, to be a discourse about Nebuchadnezzar as characterized particularly by Dan 4 (Henze 2002, 551). Since the poem ends with the world's shocked appraisal of the king's fall (Isa 14:16–17), the rabbinic readers seem to imply the universal example that God has set for all political leaders. Aphrahat, a fourth-century Syriac Christian monastic author, followed the *Mekilta* and argued that Dan 4 taught that the wicked rulers of the earth are merely instruments of the divine will, and they will eventually be destroyed (Henze 2002, 552).

In the era of the Reformation and Counter-Reformation in Europe, religious wars led to a shift in Christian discussions of political sovereignty. Especially for Christians who were members of a denomination or sect that was in conflict with the local political ruler, it was increasingly common to question the ruler's sovereignty. Martin Luther wrote that Nebuchadnezzar's punishment in Dan 4 was intended "as a comfort to the miserable and imprisoned Jews, and also for those who today and forevermore are plagued by tyrants or suffer injustice." Yet Luther claimed that the faithful should "patiently suffer such tyrants" because "of their future judgment" (Beckwith 292). Luther was careful to state his support for even tyrannical temporal rulers in light of the peasant uprising of Thomas Müntzer, who rejected the leaders of his day. John Calvin, himself a temporal authority for a time in Geneva, agreed that although Nebuchadnezzar "was a cruel tyrant and had harassed and all but destroyed God's church, yet since he was under his sway, [Daniel] was bound to pray for him. . . . They knew him to be the executor of God's just vengeance and to be their sovereign ruler" (268). Calvin believes that Daniel and the rest of the diasporic community knew and understood the lesson of God's providence found in Dan 1:2.

Yet some within Christendom did use Nebuchadnezzar's transformation, and in particular the motif of Nebuchadnezzar's "madness" in Dan 4, to critique secular power. At times readers connected this event to the mental illnesses of actual regents. In 1393, for example, King Charles VI of France, a beloved young monarch, suffered a severe episode while he led his army in search of Pierre de Craon, who was responsible for a failed assassination attempt. Charles was impatient and angry because the army was moving slowly, and when he was accosted by a barefoot leper who told him to abandon his quest, Charles suddenly killed several of his nearby troops and tried to kill his own brother before he collapsed in a coma. This public trauma at the height of his power and popularity led his detractors to label him "Nebuchadnezzar." Jean Froissart, a French chronicler who was patronized by members of the English royal court, suggested that Charles had been transformed like Nebuchadnezzar into an animal-like state because of his hubris, and that his unchecked pride threatened all the subjects of France (Pfau 60).

King George III of England offers another famous case of "Nebuchadnezzar's madness." In 1788, George began a long public struggle with mental illness. American preachers had made the comparison between George and Nebuchadnezzar in sermons even before this event (Shalev 61), but British subjects were more reticent due to the possible accusation of treason. Yet in 1817, the High Court of Edinburgh brought charges of sedition against the politically active independent Universalist minister Neil Douglas for the crime of interpreting Nebuchadnezzar's madness as a symbol of King George III. As the prosecutor explains: "That he did presume to draw a parallel between Nebuchadnezzar and our sacred sovereign, admits not a doubt; . . . it was impossible to allege a single point of resemblance, between his most sacred majesty and the personage mentioned in Scripture, without seditious criminality" (T. B. Howell and T. J. Howell 675).

William Blake, an English Romantic poet and artist who supported both democracy and social equality, created a famous image of Nebuchadnezzar's transformation in 1790 for a book titled *The Marriage of Heaven and Hell;* it depicts the emperor dethroned, naked, unshorn, and with eyes cast down. This image strongly resonates with the events of the French Revolution, in which the French people deposed the monarchy. Blake's Nebuchadnezzar evokes the contemporary status of the French ex-king as it attempts to reveal the true mortal, humble nature of every person posing as a sovereign. Blake was careful not to insinuate any connection to King George III and his mental illness, but viewers at the time would not have missed the potential link, as well as the implicit critique of the modern emphasis on rationalism (Erdman 193).

And in recent times, the connection between Nebuchadnezzar's instability and political leaders continues to be effective. Famously, Saddam Hussein, president of Iraq in 1979–2003, was obsessed with the figure of the ancient Mesopotamian ruler Nebuchadnezzar and even considered himself to be the king's successor. When Hussein rebuilt the ancient area of Babylon, "he insisted that every brick be emblazoned with the inscription 'To King Nebuchadnezzar in the reign of Saddam Hussein'" (Isakhan 224). Hussein used the image of Nebuchadnezzar to invoke the historical legacy of military expansion and empire as well as the destruction of Jerusalem. But Nebuchadnezzar also provided metaphors for those who questioned Hussein's psychological health, as well as fodder for those who believed that the American invasion of Iraq aligned with the "end times" supposedly foretold in Nebuchadnezzar's dream in Dan 2 (Droy 78).

Some interpreters noticed a special attention to justice, and particularly economic justice, in the advice given by Daniel in 4:27 (24). Daniel tells Nebuchadnezzar that giving money to the poor and showing favor to the oppressed might prolong his own prosperity. *Midrash Tanḥuma*, an early medieval Jewish interpretation of the Torah, presents a rabbinical reading of Nebuchadnezzar's question, "Is this not magnificent Babylon?" (4:30 [27]). At this time, according to *Tanḥuma*, Nebuchadnezzar heard the tumult of the poor and oppressed who had assembled at the gates to his palace, to receive the aid that Nebuchadnezzar had promised in compliance with Daniel's advice. But Nebuchadnezzar told his servants to turn away the poor, and then he justified his action by pointing out that wasting his money on aid to the poor would hamper his spectacular building campaign (*Tanḥ. Vayera* 17).

According to fifteenth-century Portuguese Jewish political leader and biblical commentator Isaac ben Judah Abrabanel, Nebuchadnezzar's sin of unparalleled pride could only be redeemed by the particular humbling act of altruistic solidarity with the oppressed within his empire (*Mayenei HaYeshua* 6.4). The notion of balancing one's ethical and religious debt to God by giving money to the poor, and thus investing funds in one's depleted heavenly "bank account," existed in Second Temple Judaism and beyond (Anderson 135–51, 160). But Abrabanel, a successful financier who served for a time as the treasurer to King Afonso V of Portugal, spoke from his own experience. Several times contemporary Jews called him "as wise as Daniel" because of his ability to work with Gentile kings (Netanyahu 88). He also had a talent for amassing wealth—and also for using it to protect the oppressed Jewish populations of Iberia and beyond by, among other things, redeeming Jews sold into slavery. In response to these actions, Abrabanel's contemporaries called him "a savior of the oppressed from the hands of their enemies" because he had "rescued Jews from the lions," an obvious reference to Daniel's rescue in Dan 6 (Netanyahu 89).

Many Jews and Christians have also emphasized the spiritual and redemptive functions of almsgiving. The ancient Rabbis Meir and Akiba were both reported to have said that God does not support the poor, so that "through [giving alms to] them we may be saved from the punishment of Gehinnom" (*b. B. Bat.* 10a). Early Christian leaders such as John Chrysostom and Cyprian, who in his discussion of Dan 4 argues that "our petitions become effective by almsgiving" and that we "are delivered from death by almsgiving" (Cyprian, *Eleem.* 5), also supported the redemptive quality of almsgiving. In the era of the Reformation and Counter-Reformation, Protestants and Catholics used Dan 4 to debate the theological relationship between works and salvation. John Mayer, a seventeenth-century English Reformed theologian, claimed that Daniel's advice nevertheless teaches us to "be charitable and give abundantly of your goods to the poor. . . . It may well be proved that no one is a true convert, or shall find favor at God's hands, who turns not . . . from hard-heartedness to charitableness" (531–32). Yet others, such as Swiss Reformed theologian Heinrich Bullinger, argued that Dan 4:27 (24) merely gives advice about running an empire, not about personal salvation; according to Bullinger, Daniel's message is merely that Nebuchadnezzar should "embrace justice" and relinquish oppression throughout his empire because that is a natural way to prolong it (Bullinger 3:92).

Personal Sovereignty and the Foreign King

Readers have argued over the precise nature of Nebuchadnezzar's transformation. Was it only Nebuchadnezzar's body that changed, while his mind stayed intact? Or did he change in mind and body? Some readers interpreted Nebuchadnezzar's dream in Dan 4 in light of Daniel's vision of a lion who is given the wings of an eagle and the heart—that is, mind—of a person (7:4), which would contradict 4:16 (13). The early medieval rabbinical tradition holds that Rabbis Nahman and Eleazar argued over this point: Nahman believed that Nebuchadnezzar had the mind of an animal and thus did not comprehend his situation, while Eleazar believed that, in order for this to be a punishment, Nebuchadnezzar had to be aware of his condition, and thus he read with Dan 7:4 (*Lev. Rab.* 13.5). Likewise, the Christian theologians Jerome and Ephrem the Syrian believed that he had lost his ability to think rationally. With the rise in scientific approaches to medical research in the early modern period, there was a widespread interest in diagnosing Nebuchadnezzar's particular affliction; Giovanni Diodati, a Swiss-Italian Reformed theologian from the seventeenth century, agreed with others who suggested the appearance of "a disease called lycanthropy, which is a kind of frenzy and madness" in which a person believes that oneself has transformed into an animal, but also suggested that demonic possession played a role (Beckwith 289). Carl G. Jung, as a psychoanalyst naturally interested in dreams and their interpretation, argued that Nebuchadnezzar's unchecked sense of self-aggrandizement led to a compensatory response by his psyche, which cut him down to size like the tree, since the king had become "a complete regressive degeneration of a man who has overreached himself" (110).

Many interpreters, however, have understood Nebuchadnezzar's narrative restoration as a symbol of repentance (cf. Cyril of Jerusalem, *Catech.* 2.17–19). The early Christian theologian Tertullian (*Paen.* 12.7–8) and the Jewish historian Josephus (*Ant.* 10.242) believed that only Nebuchadnezzar's body changed during his period of metamorphosis; for Tertullian, this is important because he reads this episode as highlighting Nebuchadnezzar's repentance, which requires his mental capacities. Such interest derives from the translational choices of Dan 4 OG, which subtly suggests the motif of repentance (Henze 1999, 190). Ephrem, a Syriac theologian from the fourth century, compared

Dan 4 to Gen 1–3 in his *Hymns on Paradise* and observed that both stories involve the concept of human dominion (cf. Gen 1:28), human relationships to animals, and a "fall" that prompted a longing for redemption (Henze 2002, 556). While Adam's fall was in some sense final, Nebuchadnezzar embodies the possibility of transformation through penance, which rereads God's punishment in Dan 4 as instead a careful administration of pedagogical pain.

Ephrem's interpretation was influential in the creation of a unique form of Syriac monasticism; his influence can be seen in early Syriac monastic texts such as the *Letter to the Mountaineers*, whose anonymous author cites Dan 4 as an encouragement to live as a hermit-monk in the wilderness, to let one's unkempt appearance resemble Nebuchadnezzar's, and to search for penitential transformation (Henze 2002, 566–70). In this trajectory of Syriac and later Byzantine interpretation that includes the *Vita Danielis*, Daniel plays the role of a spiritual counselor who instigates a transformative moment in the lives of his patients.

Yet this transformative aspect of Nebuchadnezzar's mental illness does not always figure as penance. Mental instability has often been interpreted not only as a punishment for sin but also as a liminal state in which the afflicted may see themselves and the world in a new light, leading to insight, love, and sometimes penance. John Gower's fourteenth-century poem "Confessio Amantis" and the anonymous Middle English poem "Cleanness" both use the trope of Nebuchadnezzar's mental illness and compare it to the instabilities and insights felt by one in love (Doob 162–63). And the nineteenth-century Danish theologian Søren Kierkegaard revisited the theme of Nebuchadnezzar's madness several times, most famously in his book *Stages on Life's Way*, to confront the reader with an example of someone who was faced with a religious crisis and decided to embark upon a journey to a new stage of personal psychological, ethical, and religious development (Engelke). In a similar vein, nineteenth-century American Transcendentalist author Ralph Waldo Emerson writes that humans "are, like Nebuchadnezzar, dethroned, bereft of reason, and eating grass like an ox. . . . A man is a god in ruins" (53).

Sovereignty and Chaos

For some readers, particularly those in the modern world, Nebuchadnezzar's disorientation does not model any particular person or political role; rather, it images a world that has lost its meaning. The twentieth-century Australian painter Arthur Boyd, for example, created a series of paintings, from 1966 into the 1990s, that revolved around the episode of Nebuchadnezzar's transformation in Dan 4. Boyd moved to the Hampstead area of London in 1960, and on a stroll through the Tate Modern Art Gallery, he was arrested by the image of

Figure 11. An oil painting depicting Nebuchadnezzar's madness by Australian painter Arthur Boyd, titled *Nebuchadnezzar with Blue Flowers and White Dog* (1969). Reproduced with permission of Bundanon Trust.

Nebuchadnezzar by William Blake (Bungey 416). His *Nebuchadnezzar* series crystallized when he witnessed a self-immolation that he interpreted as a protest of the Vietnam War (Bungey 428). Boyd's series explores the existential and ethical crises of his day through dystopic images of a ghostly Nebuchadnezzar screaming in pain (*Nebuchadnezzar in a Fire*, 1969), flying through the air like a napalm bomb toward a source of life (*Nebuchadnezzar on Fire Falling over a Waterfall*, 1966–68), and decomposing on the ground with a tree emerging from his midsection (*Nebuchadnezzar's Dream of the Tree*, 1969). One image, *Nebuchadnezzar with Blue Flowers and White Dog* (1969; see fig. 11), depicts the naked king trudging ahead with head cast downward, looking beyond the blue flowers in his enormous hands toward his inhuman feet. His black hair, grown for years on end, drapes over his back and floats over a similarly ghostly dog who bays at the moon. Upon inspection, the pastoral sunset in the background depicts a rhinoceros mating with a small four-legged animal. Nebuchadnezzar's flowers are merely aesthetic distractions from the harsh, irrational, and seemingly hopeless scene.

There is perhaps no less interpretable manner of death than an innocent noncombatant killed in an act of political terrorism, such as the 2002 murder of American journalist Daniel Pearl by a group that called itself the National Movement for the Restoration of Pakistani Sovereignty. In order to explore the events of Pearl's life as well as his death, American composer Steve Reich wrote a four-movement musical piece titled *Daniel Variations,* which juxtaposes two lines of Dan 4 spoken by Nebuchadnezzar ("I saw a dream, images upon my bed and visions in my head frighten me") and Daniel ("Let the dream fall back onto the dreaded") with two lines spoken by Daniel Pearl. The music varies between major and minor keys as the words alternate between existential terror and deep hope.

Daniel 5–6 The Education of Feckless Kings

The final two chapters in the cycle of narratives concern the successors of Nebuchadnezzar: Belshazzar, who is represented as the son of Nebuchadnezzar; and Darius the Mede, who overthrows Belshazzar. Since the cycle of stories concerning Nebuchadnezzar effectively developed the themes of divine and human sovereignty and of moving from illusion to true understanding, chs. 5 and 6 might seem redundant. Even as they reiterate the theme, however, they do so with kings whose characters differ sharply from that of Nebuchadnezzar and from each other. Whereas Nebuchadnezzar was associated with conquests and the exercise of terrifying power, both Belshazzar and Darius are represented as rather feckless kings. Yet though they are both weak in certain respects, only Belshazzar is presented as actively blasphemous in treating the vessels from the Jerusalem temple with disrespect and pressing them into service for praising other gods. He is thus the only king in the cycle whose reign and life is taken away by divine judgment. In this respect he forms a foil for the sympathetically presented Darius. Darius's weakness manifests itself as gullibility and a willingness to be flattered by his courtiers. Although the decree he signs, forbidding petition to any god or human except himself, could as readily be taken as a mark of blasphemy as Belshazzar's behavior, he is not judged in the story. In contrast to Belshazzar's arrogance, Darius is represented as humbly aware of his powerlessness and as respectful of Daniel's God (6:16 [17]). Whereas Belshazzar's story ends with his death, the end of ch. 6 is Darius's decree directing all of his subjects to show reverence to the God of Daniel. Even Nebuchadnezzar's encyclical was only an expression of his personal praise of the Most High God. But Darius's decree requires the universal recognition of the sovereignty of Daniel's God. It thus brings the cycle of narratives to a satisfying conclusion.

Daniel 5:1–31 (6:1) Belshazzar and the Handwriting on the Wall: A Lesson Belatedly Learned

1 King Belshazzar[a] held a great feast[b] for his thousand nobles, and he was drinking wine in the presence of the thousand. 2 Under the influence of the wine,[c] Belshazzar commanded that the gold and silver vessels that his father had taken from the temple in Jerusalem be brought in, so that the king and his nobles, his consorts and his concubines might drink from them. 3 Then they brought in the vessels of gold and silver[d] that had been taken from the temple, which is the house of God,[e] in Jerusalem, and the king and his nobles, his consorts and his concubines drank from them. 4 They drank wine and praised the gods of gold and silver, bronze, iron, wood, and stone. 5 At that moment the fingers of a human hand came forth and before the lamp began writing upon the plaster of the wall of the king's palace, so that the king saw the palm of the hand that was writing. 6 Then the king's face went deathly pale,[f] his thoughts alarmed him, the knots of his loins loosened,[g] and his knees knocked together. 7 The king cried aloud to bring in the exorcists, the Chaldeans, and the astrologers. The king said to the wise men of Babylon, "Whoever can read this inscription and tell me its meaning will wear the purple, and a golden chain upon his neck. He will rule as third in rank[h] in the kingdom."

8 Then all the king's sages came in, but they were not able to read the inscription or to make known its meaning to the king. 9 Then King Belshazzar became highly agitated. His face went pale, and his nobles were dismayed. 10 Because of the situation of the king and his nobles, the queen came to the banquet hall. The queen said, "O king! Live forever! Do not let your thoughts alarm you, and do not let your face be pale. 11 There is a man in your kingdom in whom is a holy divine spirit.[i] In the days of your father he was found to have enlightenment, insight, and wisdom like the wisdom of the gods, and King Nebuchadnezzar, your father,[j] established him as chief of the mantic experts, exorcists, Chaldeans, and astrologers, 12 because an extraordinary spirit, knowledge, and insight for interpreting[k] dreams, explaining enigmatic oracles, and loosening knots was found in him, in Daniel, whom the king named Belteshazzar. Now, let Daniel be summoned, and he will make known the interpretation."

13 Then Daniel was brought in before the king. The king said to Daniel, "Are you Daniel, one of the Judean exiles whom the king, my father, brought from Judah? 14 I have heard concerning you that a spirit of the gods is in you, and that you possess enlightenment, insight, and exceeding wisdom. 15 Just now the wise men and the exorcists were brought in before me so that they might read this inscription and make known to me

its meaning, but they were not able to make known the meaning of the thing. 16 I have heard concerning you that you are able to make interpretations and to solve enigmas. Now if you are able to read this inscription and to make known to me its meaning, you will wear the purple and a chain of gold upon your neck, and you shall rule as third in the kingdom."

17 Then Daniel answered and spoke before the king: "May your gifts be for yourself; give your rewards to others. But I will read the inscription and make known to the king its meaning. 18 As for you, O king, the Most High God gave the kingdom and greatness and glory and honor to Nebuchadnezzar, your father. 19 On account of the greatness that he gave to him, all the peoples, nations, and languages trembled and feared before him; for whomever he wished he would kill, and whomever he wished he made live, and whomever he wished he raised up, and whomever he wished he brought low. 20 And when his heart had become arrogant and his spirit hardened to the point of insolence, he was cast down from the throne of his kingdom, and the honor was taken away from him. 21 He was driven away from human society, and his mind became like that of an animal. With the wild asses was his dwelling. He was fed grass like cattle, and his body was drenched with the dew of heaven until he understood that the Most High God is sovereign in the kingdom of humans and that he raises up over it whomever he wishes. 22 But you, his son Belshazzar, have not humbled your heart, even though you knew all this. 23 Against the Lord of heaven you exalted yourself, and the vessels of his house were brought before you, and you and your nobles, your consorts and your concubines drank wine from them, and you praised the gods of silver and gold, bronze, iron, wood, and stone, which neither see nor hear nor understand. But the God in whose hand is your breath and all your ways, him you did not glorify. 24 Then from his presence a hand was sent forth, and this inscription was written.

25 "This is the inscription that was written: 'A mina,^{l} a sheqel, and half-minas.'^{m} 26 This is the interpretation of the matter: 'Mina': God has reckoned your kingdom and paid it out. 27 'Sheqel': You have been weighed in the scales and found wanting. 28 'Half-Mina': Your kingdom has been assessed and given to Media and Persia."

29 Then Belshazzar gave the command, and they clothed Daniel in purple, with a chain of gold upon his neck, and they proclaimed about him that he would be the third ruler in the kingdom. 30 In that very night Belshazzar, king of the Chaldeans, was killed. 31 (6:1) And Darius the Mede received the kingdom when he was sixty-two years old.

a. *bēlša'ṣṣar*. This spelling of the name is used throughout ch. 5, except in v. 30, where the erroneous spelling *bēl'šaṣṣar* occurs, a spelling also found in 7:1 and 8:1.

Belshazzar and the Handwriting on the Wall: A Lesson Belatedly Learned

b. Lit., "made bread." This unusual idiom also occurs in Eccl 10:19.

c. Although the noun *ṭěʿēm* usually occurs in Biblical Aram. with the sense of "command" or "advice," the meaning "taste" is attested in other Aram. dialects (*HALOT* 1885). Thus one could also translate "at the taste of the wine," i.e., "when he had tasted the wine," referring to the custom of sending round the wine after the meal (so Montgomery 251).

d. Reading with Th; the MT is missing "and silver."

e. This slightly awkward phrase serves to highlight the author's perspective and concern for the confrontation between Belshazzar and God (Arnold 482).

f. See comments on the verse.

g. See comments on the verse.

h. See comments on the verse.

i. See notes to translation and comments on 4:8 (5).

j. The phrase "your father the king" at the end of the verse appears to be an alternative reading to "King Nebuchadnezzar your father."

k. The participles *měpaššar* and *měšārēʾ* may function as verbal nouns (Emerton 1960). Alternatively, they could be repointed as infinitives, as they appear in v. 16.

l. The MT repeats the word *měnēʾ*. Five of the six ancient witnesses (OG, Th, Vg, Josephus [*Ant.* 10.243–44] and Jerome [on 5:25–28]) indicate only three terms. Only the Peshitta agrees with the MT. If the MT is retained, then the first occurrence of the word should be interpreted, following Eissfeldt (109), as a passive participle, "counted as a mina."

m. As Rosenthal (§45) notes, "The dual is preserved only in remnants." Thus the plural form here may be taken as a dual (Goldingay 102), which is suggested by the context. See comments below.

Overview

The abrupt beginning of ch. 5 ("King Belshazzar held a great feast . . .") creates a gap between itself and the preceding chapter. At the end of ch. 4, Nebuchadnezzar, humbled and aware of the source of his sovereignty in the Most High God, had been restored to his kingdom. Now it appears that he is dead and that another king rules in his place, one who in the course of the narrative will be identified as his son. Apparently the story circulated in several versions, two of which are preserved in the Old Greek translation, and one of which is represented in the MT and the closely related Theodotion translation. All three versions establish a contrast between the figure of Nebuchadnezzar, who ultimately acknowledged the sovereignty of the Most High God, and Belshazzar, who praises idols. Whereas Nebuchadnezzar was restored to his kingdom, Belshazzar's kingdom is taken away from him. All three versions also involve a mysterious detached hand that miraculously appears and inscribes a message of judgment on the palace wall. The stories differ, however, in the extent to which they develop the contrast between Nebuchadnezzar and Belshazzar; the MT makes this comparison the most detailed and explicit.

The OG, the MT, and Narrative Variation

A comparison of the three accounts helps one both see how traditional stories tend to exist in variant versions and appreciate how the author of the MT carefully developed details to enhance the themes of the Daniel MT cycle. One should not necessarily assume a linear evolution of the text, however. Certain details in the Masoretic version may well be earlier than their counterparts in the OG. Typologically, however, the simplest version is contained in a preface to the OG of Dan 5. It may be a summary of a longer version. This preface identifies the occasion for Belshazzar's feast as the dedication of his palace and the number of guests as two thousand. The feast is possibly to be identified with the (spring) New Year's Akītu Festival (so Wills 123–24; but see Delcor 126; and Haag 1983, 56). In high spirits from the wine, Belshazzar praises the idols of the nations but not the Most High God. Nothing is said of the temple vessels from Jerusalem, however. Thus his sin is idolatry, not sacrilege. The fingers of a hand appear and write an inscription on the plaster opposite the light. The inscription consists of three words: *Mane, Phares, Thekel*, which the narrator interprets: "*Mane*: it has been numbered; *Phares*: it has been taken away; *Thekel*: it has been established." If this summary represents the story in its totality, then there is no mystery as to the meaning of the words, no court contest, and indeed, no Daniel. Of course, it is possible that the scribe responsible for these verses in the OG text may simply have included portions of the alternative version, not the entire story.

The main story of Belshazzar's feast in the OG is closer to the MT version but less developed and dramatic. The OG narrative does not mention the occasion for the feast but has Belshazzar call for the vessels from the Jerusalem temple that Nebuchadnezzar had taken, so that he and his companions may drink from them. Here sacrilege compounds idolatry. In response to this act the fingers of a hand appear and write on the plaster wall. Words that the hand writes are not specified, but in contrast to the first account, the king's emotional reaction is recorded, heightening the tension. The motifs of the baffled interpreters and the offer of reward are also present in this version. The king himself summons the queen, who reminds him of Daniel and Daniel's role in explaining difficult meanings to his father, King Nebuchadnezzar. When Daniel is brought in and offered the king's reward, he reads the inscription as "it has been numbered; it has been reckoned; it has been taken away," a sequence that is implicitly different from the first summary version, even though the Aramaic words are not cited. Daniel relates the judgment to the king's blasphemous and idolatrous actions at the banquet and expands upon the interpretation, including the prediction that Belshazzar's kingdom is to be given to the Medes and the Persians. Daniel receives his reward, and the narrator relates that the oracle was fulfilled, though it does not specify when, and gives the name of the Median king who succeeded Belshazzar as Xerxes.

The MT version of Belshazzar's feast follows the basic outline of the main OG story, but it is crafted in ways that heighten the contrast between the redeemed Nebuchadnezzar and the condemned Belshazzar, as well as enhancing other literary features. It expands the description of the idols and the expressions of the king's fear, heightens the dramatic juxtaposition of events by having Belshazzar killed the very night of the banquet, and gives the queen a more commanding role. The most striking difference, however, is the recasting of Daniel and his address to the king. In this version Daniel's surpassing wisdom is described more fully by the queen, a description repeated by Belshazzar. But Daniel himself is cast as much in the role of prophet as sage. Not only does Daniel reply to the king's offer of reward with a dismissive word; he also delivers a lengthy prophetic indictment of Belshazzar, contrasting him with his father, Nebuchadnezzar, and retelling much of the story of ch. 4. In contrast to both OG versions, the mysterious writing consists of four terms (*Mene, Mene, Tekel, u-Parsin*), and the riddling quality of the oracular words is emphasized.

Babylonian and Greek Accounts of the Fall of Babylon

Just as the existence of various versions of the story indicates a complex history of narrative development, so the existence of various Babylonian and classical sources sheds light on the way in which cultural memories of the end of the Babylonian kingdom have been taken up into the narrative of Dan 5. Although some conservative biblical scholars have attempted to argue for the historicity of Dan 5, that is to misunderstand the role of these details in the story. (See Shea 1982a; 1982b; 2001; and the refutations by Grabbe 1988a; 1988b) The story is historical fiction that uses sometimes distorted memories of events to construct an alternative narrative about the end of the Babylonian Empire, an account that would have religious significance for the Jews of the Eastern Diaspora.

Five ancient sources refer to the events of the fall of Babylon in 539 B.C.E.: (1) the Babylonian Chronicle, the most trustworthy historical source (Grayson 104–11); (2) the Cyrus Cylinder, a propagandistic document probably composed on Cyrus's behalf by priests of Marduk, the principal god of Babylon (*ANET* 315–16; *COS* 2:315); (3–4) the accounts of the Greek historians Herodotus (1.190–91) and Xenophon (*Cyr.* 7.5.1–36); and (5) the account of Berossus, a Hellenistic-era Babylonian historian whose work is excerpted by Josephus (*Ag.Ap.* 1.151–53). In addition, numerous cuneiform documents make reference to Belshazzar. None of these documents should be used to reconstruct historical events without attention to their own purposes and biases, of course.

Belshazzar was the son of the last king of Babylon, Nabonidus, and thus not related to Nebuchadnezzar. Although never holding the status of king, Belshazzar served as subregent for Nabonidus during the ten years that Nabonidus was in residence at Teima in Arabia. Because he was not king, he was not authorized to conduct the yearly Akītu Festival in honor of the god Marduk (Bēl). When Nabonidus returned to Babylon, he apparently resumed sole royal authority, and the Akītu Festival was resumed (Beaulieu 1989, 186–87). The status of Belshazzar after Nabonidus's return is unclear.

With respect to the fall of Babylon in 539, the Babylonian Chronicle refers to a battle at Opis on the bank of the Tigris River. Afterward, Sippar fell without a battle, Nabonidus fled, and the army of Cyrus entered Babylon without opposition. Nabonidus was later captured. According to Berossus, Cyrus spared his life, resettling him in Carmania, a satrapy of the Persian Empire near the straits of Hormuz. Nothing certain is known of the fate of Belshazzar. The Greek sources give a rather different account, suggesting that Cyrus captured the city by deflecting the course of the Euphrates River and taking Babylon by surprise, though this seems to be a literary embellishment. Herodotus says that the Babylonians "had a festival going on at the time, and they continued dancing and enjoying themselves until they learned the truth all too well" (1.191; trans. Greene; cf. Xenophon, *Cyr.* 7.5.25). Xenophon gives an even more highly colored account, having Cyrus attack when he had "heard that a certain festival had come round in Babylon, during which all Babylon was accustomed to drink and revel all night long" (*Cyr.* 7.5.15; trans. Miller). In Xenophon's account the king of Babylon is killed in a surprise attack on the palace where the feasting was going on (7.5.29–30). This tradition appears to be reflected also in the Jewish description of Belshazzar's feast. Although Beaulieu (1989, 226), followed by Wolters (1995, 200–201), has suggested that the tradition of a festival on the night that Babylon fell might be a historical memory of an actual Akītu Festival for the moon-god Sin, it is also possible that this is simply a stock motif (so Goldingay 108). In either case the patterns of similarity and difference among these accounts help one see how Dan 5 participates in the creation of cultural memories about the end of the Babylonian Empire and attempts to give that event religious significance.

Genre, Literary Structure, and Outline

As a literary entity Dan 5 is a court tale with a court contest motif (cf. ch. 2). But in the MT version it also has elements of a prophetic legend, as Daniel's indictment of the king is evocative of other biblical stories of prophet-king conflict (1 Sam 2:27–36; 15:13–26; 2 Sam 12:7–12; 1 Kgs 21:20–24; 22:19–23). The contrast between a strong king who builds up a kingdom that his weak and vain son loses also reminds one of the way in which 1 Kings represents Solomon and Rehoboam (1 Kgs 12:1–20). A final stock motif is the critique of idols by stressing their inert materiality (cf. Isa 44:9–20; Jer 10:3–5; Epistle of Jeremiah; *Prayer of Nabonidus* [4Q242]). These additional elements, largely absent from the OG version, are indicative of the literary creativity of the MT author.

Unlike most of the other Daniel narratives, ch. 5 does not divide sharply into different scenes, and commentators differ somewhat in analyzing the structure. The following outline is largely based on the introduction of new elements into the scene or the change in speaker:

> The king's banquet and the mysterious oracle (5:1–6)
>> Setting the scene: The king's command to bring the sacred vessels (5:1–2)
>> The desecration of the vessels (5:3–4)
>> The supernatural hand that writes upon the wall and the king's reaction (5:5–6)
>
> Attempts to interpret the oracle (5:7–12)
>> The king's summons of the sages, who fail to interpret the writing (5:7–9)
>> The queen's appearance and recommendation of Daniel (5:10–12)
>
> Daniel before Belshazzar (5:13–29)
>> Belshazzar's address to Daniel (5:13–16)
>> Daniel's rebuke of Belshazzar (5:17–23)
>> Daniel's interpretation of the hand and its inscription (5:24–28)
>> Daniel's reward (5:29)
>
> Conclusion: Belshazzar's death and Darius's accession to the kingdom (5:30–31 [6:1])

Comments

[1–2] Banquets in antiquity, especially royal banquets, were not simply festive occasions. They were occasions for extravagant display that were as much symbolic as material (Briant 286–92). Indeed, recent anthropological studies emphasize the formal etiquette and ritual-dramaturgical dimensions of banquets (Wright 2010a, 214). Solomon's table service is specifically mentioned as one of the primary things that persuades the Queen of Sheba of Solomon's dominance (1 Kgs 10:4–5 [NJPS: "She was left breathless"]; cf. 5:2–3). Lavish banquets also positioned the king as a powerful benefactor and bound his subordinates more closely to him. To eat the king's food was to take the king's gift literally into one's own body and with that act to acknowledge a social bond and a social debt (cf. 2 Sam 3:20–21; 1 Chr 12:38–40 [39–41]; 2 Chr 18:1–3). (Although the young men in Dan 1 were not invited to a banquet, receiving food from the king's table involved a similar symbolic transaction.) Another indication of the political significance of royal banquets is the fact that they were a popular subject for artistic representation in reliefs, wall paintings, inlays, and seals (Wright 2010a, 223–32). Although royal banquets were characteristic of most ancient court societies, the Achaemenid rulers, during whose time the

Daniel narratives most likely received their primary shaping, were particularly adept at using banquets as an instrument of political control.

The thousand nobles may simply be a round number suitable to the style of a tale, though royal feasts were quite large, and food was often distributed widely. The Assyrian king Ashurnasirpal II inaugurated the building of his new capital with a banquet that he claimed lasted 10 days and entertained 69,574 persons (*ANET* 560)! Some have suggested that the thousand guests at Belshazzar's banquet is inspired by the Persian institution of the royal bodyguard, which was referred to as "the thousand" (so Lebram 73).

Seating arrangements at royal banquets were part of the choreography of the banquet. Many depictions of banquets in ancient Near Eastern art show the king enthroned, lifting a cup of wine, facing his nobles and military officers (see fig. 12). Such seems to be the scene in v. 1, which describes Belshazzar drinking wine "before the thousand" (cf. 2 Kgs 25:29; Jer 52:33). According to Athenaeus (*Deipn.* 4.145b–c), Persian kings normally ate in a separate chamber, but for special banquets they would sit at a separate table and face their guests.

The beginning of v. 2 could be translated either as "when tasting the wine" or "at the command of the wine," that is, "under the influence of the wine." Montgomery (251), followed by Seow (78), prefers the first option, taking it to be a technical term for banqueting customs in which wine circulates after the meal (Aelian, *Var. hist.* 12.1). Most, however, assume that Belshazzar acts with drunken bravado: indeed, the OG represents him as "in high spirits from the wine." Royal banquets were often occasions on which excessive amounts of wine were drunk, and the Babylonians and Persians were noted in both classical and biblical sources as particularly heavy drinkers (Esth 1:8, 10; Herodotus 5.18; Quintus Curtius 5.1; Athenaeus, *Deipn.* 4.144a; on the power of wine, see 1 Esd 3:17–24).

The cups used at royal banquets were particularly important vehicles for the king's display of wealth and power, and the Persians in particular were known for their love of golden vessels (Briant 294–97). Belshazzar tries to impress his guests and display his prowess by arranging for a unique set of drinking vessels to be used: the sacred vessels from the temple in Jerusalem. Part of the contrast between Belshazzar and Nebuchadnezzar is to be seen in their different treatment of the temple vessels. In 1:2, when "the Lord gave Jehoiakim, king of Judah, into his [Nebuchadnezzar's] power, along with some of the vessels of the house of God," this king of Babylon treated them respectfully, placing them in the treasury of the temple of his god. Though he sees himself as exerting power over them, Nebuchadnezzar does not subject them to dishonor. Belshazzar, however, treats them like royal tableware, a blasphemous gesture. Because the Judean religion did not have a cult statue of YHWH, the temple vessels play a particularly important role in metonymically representing YHWH and

Figure 12. The Standard of Ur, a Sumerian work from the third millennium B.C.E. The upper register depicts a royal banquet. © Trustees of the British Museum

his sovereignty. In the texts relating to the period of the exile, they become, as Ackroyd described them, a symbol of continuity (166). Like the people themselves, they were taken into exile (2 Kgs 24:13; 25:13–17; Jer 52:17–23; 2 Chr 36:7, 18), then returned to Jerusalem by the command of Cyrus (Ezra 1:7–11). Isaiah 52:11 depicts the exiles as purifying themselves in order to carry the sacred vessels back to Jerusalem.

This verse also mentions that the king's wives and concubines were present at the banquet. The terms used for the women are rare, but the first, šēgal, appears to be derived from the Akkadian term ša ekalli, "she of the palace," and to be a term for the king's wife (Neh 2:6; Ps 45:9 [10]), though not necessarily the highest-ranking wife. The word for concubine, lĕḥēnâ, is apparently also of Akkadian derivation (alaḫḫinatu) and originally referred to a woman in the court of the queen (CAD 1/1:294). Other biblical texts also assume two classes of women in the king's harem (1 Kgs 11:3; Song 6:8), though the terminology is different.

Evidence is mixed as to whether the presence of women at banquets was customary or not. In Esther, the king entertains the men at a banquet while Queen Vashti holds a separate banquet for the women (1:9). Some classical sources suggest that concubines at least were present at banquets (Plutarch, *Quaest. conv.* 1.1; Macrobius 7; Xenophon, *Cyr.* 5.2.28). Herodotus records a story about the Persians at the Macedonian court who tell their hosts that it is Persian custom to dine with wives and concubines, though this account is clearly part of a lascivious ploy on the part of the Persians and not a trustworthy description of Persian customs. As the Persians get drunk, they become amorous with the women (Herodotus 5.18). Here, too, the presence of women at the banquets along with abundant wine is meant to imply an atmosphere of drunken rowdiness and sexual libertinism (cf. 1 Esd 4:29–31).

[3–4] The author's stylistic fondness for lists is evident, as the catalog of the persons present ("the king and his nobles, his consorts and his concubines") is repeated from v. 2. Moreover, in the act of drinking, which would have included libations to Babylonian gods (Bentzen 47), the author refers to them as "the gods of gold and silver, bronze, iron, wood, and stone." The rhetorical ploy of focusing on the materials that made up the statues of the gods is common in Judean anti-idolatry polemics (cf. Deut 4:28; Isa 44:9–20; Jer 10:3–5; Ps 115:4–7; Epistle of Jeremiah). It is often used in conjunction with the claim that the statues cannot see or hear or eat or smell and thus evidently have no power when compared to the living God, a point that will be made in Dan 5:23. In the broader Daniel tradition, the closest parallel to this list is to be found in the *Prayer of Nabonidus* (4Q242). There the healed and forgiven Nabonidus writes an encyclical in which he explains that during the seven years he suffered from an illness, "[I] was praying [to] the gods of silver and gold, [bronze, iron,] wood, stone, clay, since [I thoug]ht th[ey were] gods" (lines 7–8; trans. Collins; see comments on Dan 4). The Danielic stories of Bel and the Dragon also make fun of idols by drawing attention to their status as things made of "clay inside and bronze outside" (v. 7) or mere animals that can be killed if fed a mixture of pitch, fat, and hair (v. 27). Thus one is in no doubt that Belshazzar's praise of these gods, which is carried out in the very act of desecrating the sacred vessels of the Most High God, will be exposed as deadly folly.

[5–6] The eerie drama of the disembodied hand writing its mysterious message on the wall of the banquet hall has challenged artists over the centuries, though none has captured the sublime terror as well as Rembrandt (see fig. 13). The first dramatic element is the temporal immediacy of the divine response ("at that moment"). The second is the disembodied hand. Elsewhere in the story cycle, divine communications occur either by dreams (2:1; 4:5 [2]), by means of a heavenly voice (4:31 [28]), or by an apparition of a divine figure (3:25). Here what is seen is only a hand from fingers to wrist (*ʾeṣbeʿān, pas yĕdâ*). This is, of course, the part of the body involved in holding a reed pen for writing. That the message is delivered not orally but as a written text adds to its mystery and power. Few people in the ancient world were literate, yet kings publicly displayed monumental texts recording their accomplishments. The written text was itself a sign of power. Moreover, it was the custom, at least in Mesopotamia, for public readings of official texts to be held, so that the contents were communicated to the audience (Toorn 2007, 13–14). Thus the scene enacted here parallels the royal use of the written word.

This message, however, is intended for those in the banquet hall, especially the king himself, and the detailed description of its location underscores this intention. At night in a large hall illuminated only by lamps, the lighting would be uneven, with bright and dark areas, a feature that Rembrandt exploits in his painting. That the writing is clearly visible is ensured by the author's statement

Belshazzar and the Handwriting on the Wall: A Lesson Belatedly Learned   169

Figure 13. Rembrandt's depiction of Belshazzar's Feast, oil painting ca. 1636–38.
© National Gallery, London; Art Resource, New York

that the hand writes on the smooth plaster of the wall illuminated by a lamp. The precise details not only encourage the reader's visualization of the scene but also align the reader's focalization with that of the king. The narrator does not give the reader any privileged information about the nature or content of the writing. As in ch. 2, the reader will learn the meaning only when the king does. The only hint the reader receives is the choice of the verb *něpaq* to describe the appearance of the hand, since that verb was twice used in a different conjugation in vv. 2–3 to refer to the "bringing out" of the temple vessels. The wordplay is a signal that the mysterious hand is a direct response to Belshazzar's blasphemy (Arnold 482).

Verse 6 focuses only on the emotional reaction of the king, especially as this manifests itself in physical symptoms. It is difficult to give an adequate translation for the first phrase, which also occurs in vv. 9, 10, and 7:28. The Aramaic word *zîw* refers to a person's appearance or countenance. It is cognate with the Akkadian word *zīmu*, which can be used to describe the glow of stars. In some Aramaic and Hebrew dialects, *zîw* also refers to the blossoms of flowers and as the name of a month in which flowers bloom (1 Kgs 6:1, 37). It thus suggests the normally healthy, glowing appearance of a person, with cheeks suffused with blood like the color of a flower. To say that someone's *zîw* changes is to suggest an unhealthy appearance, hence the translation here: "he became deathly pale" (cf. Jer 30:6, also describing terror). A cognate expression in Job 14:20 describes the changed appearance of someone who is literally dying.

The knocking of the knees is a familiar manifestation of deep fear, but considerable disagreement exists as to what the loosening of the knots of the loins refers to. This phrase is strategically chosen, for it is used in a different sense in vv. 12 and 16, where it refers to an aspect of Daniel's intellectual prowess. Here, however, it is a physical phenomenon. But what precisely does it mean? Al Wolters (1991b) has argued that the word for "knots" (*qiṭrîn*) does not otherwise describe joints. Thus he suggests the word refers to the sphincter muscles of the urethra and anus, which tighten and loosen to control bodily wastes. Persons in antiquity would be familiar with such anatomical details in part because containers for liquids were often made from animal skins that had to be tied off precisely where those orifices had been. Thus the scene depicts the humiliating incontinence of the king, much to the enjoyment of the Jewish audience. The later use of the phrase to describe Daniel's ability to "untie knots" would be a double entendre that enhanced the scatological humor of the story.

As appealing as that interpretation is in some respects, ch. 5 otherwise does not have the bawdy style that fits such a narrative detail. The stories of Bel and the Dragon do engage in such cartoonish effects, with the serpent exploding after eating the "food" Daniel has prepared for it. But the narrative in Dan 5 does not otherwise strike that tone. Thus the alternative interpretation of Shalom Paul (1993) seems more likely. Paul situates the king's reaction as part of an ancient Near Eastern literary convention, a trope originally analyzed by Delbert Hillers (1965). In a variety of genres, including myths, royal inscriptions, and literary texts from Mesopotamia, Ugarit, and Israel, the recipient of disturbing news exhibits fear that expresses itself as a bodily reaction. For example, Paul cites Esarhaddon's description of a king's reaction to his missive: "(When) he [the king] heard my royal message which burns the enemies like a flame, his hips collapsed, his heart was seized (by fear), his legs trembled, . . . his countenance looked bad" (122). A similar description occurs in Nahum's description of the fear of the defenders of Nineveh: "Hearts melt, knees tremble, writhing is in all the loins, and every face grows pale" (2:10 [11] AT). The description of Belshazzar in Dan 5:9 invokes this trope, and the choice of the term "knots," though somewhat unusual, is motivated by the wordplay that the author develops in vv. 12 and 16.

[7–9] That the king calls for mantic experts to read and interpret the inscription indicates that he understands it to be an omen, a form of divine writing that communicates the will of the gods in coded fashion. This is quintessentially a Mesopotamian concept of divine communication. Astronomical omens were referred to as "heavenly writing," and omen priests would pray that the god's answer to an inquiry would be found "written" on the liver of the sheep they were about to examine (Broida 4; Rochberg 48). The genre of *mukallimtu* commentaries textualized omens and interpreted them according to a variety of sophisticated hermeneutical techniques (Frahm 46–47), some of which are similar to those used by Daniel (see below). This means of communicating the divine will is sharply different from what prevails in preexilic Israelite and Judean contexts. There the favored means is the prophetic oracle, which is generally not coded, though occasionally symbols may be used (e.g., Amos 7:7–9; 8:1–2). That a Jewish author should represent divine communication in this fashion suggests the ways in which a Diaspora people in an imperial setting might appropriate and hybridize aspects of the dominant religion. The assumptions and interpretive techniques that one sees in this narrative are further developed in Jewish scriptural interpretation at Qumran and in certain forms of rabbinic exegesis. In both cases the Scriptures are treated as esoteric communications from God requiring expert interpretation (for the nuances of the term *pišrāʾ*, see comments on 2:4). The categories of mantic experts called by the king are a subset of those named in 2:2; 4:7 (4); 5:11 (see comments on 2:2).

The gifts promised by the king have particular significance. Clothing and ornaments coded social status in antiquity. The purple garment in particular was a sign of high status. Such objects were often given as tribute or bestowed as royal gifts (Danker 558; Reinhold 9–12). Gold, of course, has also long been valued as a status symbol and sign of royal favor, and the two are often associated (see Esth 8:15; 1 Esd 3:6–7; cf. Gen 41:42). Herodotus (3.20) reports that Cambyses sent the Ethiopians gifts "including a purple cloak and a twisted gold necklace." The term used for necklace or collar here is *hamnîkâ*, a Persian loanword that refers to an ornament worn by high-ranking Persian nobility, often a present from the king (Xenophon, *Cyr*. 2.4.6; 8.5.15; *Anab*. 1.2.27; 1.5.8; 8.29).

The political status offered is that of a *taltî*, literally, "third," cognate with Hebrew *šālîš*. Originally it apparently referred to the third man in a three-man chariot, who supported the soldier who actually did the fighting. Later the term was used more broadly to refer to a high official or aide to the king (2 Kgs 7:2, 17, 19; 9:25; 15:25). Some take it to mean that Daniel would be third in rank in the kingdom. While it seems unlikely that the term was used with a numerical sense, that may be how the author of Dan 6 takes it, since he has Darius appointing Daniel as one of three ministers to oversee the 120 satraps, apparently honoring Belshazzar's promise to Daniel.

The failure of the king's experts to read the inscription is a stock motif in a court contest tale (cf. 2:2–12; 4:6–7 [3–4]; Gen 41:8). It does not require the ingenious but unsupported suggestions of some that the inscription was written with cuneiform numerical symbols or in some other special script (e.g., Alt; Lebram 76; Grelot 1985, 205–7; Goldingay 109; Kirchmayr). Nor is there any indication that the inscription is invisible to everyone but the king, as Lacocque (95) suggests. Yet the inscription does have a riddle-like quality, facilitated by the ambiguities inherent in an Aramaic writing system that represents consonants only.

The king's fear is described in terms that echo v. 6a, with the addition of a note about the dismay of his courtiers as well. The scene invites a comparison with the reaction of Nebuchadnezzar in 2:12, who meets the similar failure of his wise men with towering rage and an edict of mass execution. While neither king is portrayed positively, the contrast highlights Belshazzar's weakness.

[10–12] As has been recognized since antiquity, the queen who enters the banquet hall is not to be understood as Belshazzar's wife but as his mother (so Jerome, on 5:10–12) or grandmother (so Josephus, *Ant*. 10.237), since she recalls information from the time of his father's reign. The queen mother held a place of authority and dignity in the ancient Near East, though, of course, the extent of her power depended a great deal on the force of her own personality and ambition. A queen mother was most likely to be influential if she had played a role in helping her son to achieve the kingship. Such is the case with Bathsheba, who strategizes with the prophet Nathan to ensure that Solomon and not Adonijah succeeds David (1 Kgs 1; for other references to the queen mother, see 1 Kgs 15:13; 2 Kgs 11:1–3; 24:12; Jer 13:18; cf. the cautionary arguments of N. Bowen). In the Neo-Babylonian Empire, too, Adad-guppi, the mother of Nabonidus and grandmother of Belshazzar, was a very powerful figure who fostered her son's career and probably influenced his religious devotion to the moon-god Sin. Her inscription (*ANET* 311–12) gives a sense of her strong personality. Herodotus names the mother of the last king of Babylon (i.e., Labynetus, a corruption for Nabonidus) as Nitocris and credits her with great wisdom, which she used to plan and execute the formidable defenses of Babylon (1.185–87).

In the OG version of Daniel, Belshazzar himself sends for the queen mother, but the MT, adding yet another detail to the depiction of Belshazzar as hapless, simply has her appear while Belshazzar and the nobles are in a state of confusion. Though the courtly greeting with which she greets the king is a stock phrase ("O king, live forever"; cf. 2:4; 3:9; 6:6, 21 [7, 22]), it has a special irony for those who know that this story will end with Belshazzar's death on that very night.

The story gives no reason why Belshazzar does not seem aware of Daniel, but the logic of the court contest narratives requires that Daniel not have been among the sages first summoned by Belshazzar (cf. 2:2–12, 25–28). For the reader there is also an echo of the trope of the "king . . . [who] knew not Joseph" (Exod 1:8 KJV). The queen mother's description of Daniel's wisdom contains an ambiguous phrase that can be translated as "spirit of the holy God," "spirit of the holy gods," or "a holy divine spirit" (see comments on 4:8–9 [5–6]). The point seems to be to acknowledge that Daniel's wisdom surpasses that which can be obtained by human skill alone, since she reiterates that his wisdom is like that of the gods (Levison 74–80). Finally she draws attention to Daniel's particular expertise. His ability to interpret dreams was mentioned already in 1:17 and demonstrated in the interpretation of Nebuchadnezzar's dreams in chs. 2 and 4. The second power is often translated as "explaining riddles." While the Aramaic term (*ʾăḥîdâ*) and its Hebrew cognate (*ḥîdâ*) can refer to riddles of the sort used by monarchs to test each other's cleverness (1 Kgs 10:1; Josephus, *Ant.* 8.143), here the term refers rather to an enigmatic or coded oracle (Müller 1970, 474–75; cf. Ezek 17:2), which is precisely what the handwriting on the wall is. The third ability, "loosening knots" (*měšārēʾ qiṭrîn*), may be a term for unbinding or dissolving magical spells (so Bevan 103–4; Charles 130), though that is not a talent that Daniel is called upon to display. In this context, it is probably better to take it as a synonymous expression for "explaining enigmatic oracles" (so Montgomery 259). Though redundant, the phrase is used for comic effect, since the same phrase was used to describe Belshazzar's physical response to the disturbing phenomena in v. 6.

[13–16] Belshazzar's words to Daniel cast doubt on the impression created earlier that he has been unaware of Daniel's existence, since he supplies details about Daniel's being one of the Judean exiles brought to Babylon by Nebuchadnezzar. (In the OG it is the queen mother who supplies this information in v. 10.) The detail adds psychological complexity to the portrait of Belshazzar, since it suggests that his apparent lack of knowledge of Daniel was more of a repression of knowledge than true ignorance. Moreover, the phrase "whom the king, my father, brought from Judah" recalls the references to the temple vessels being taken from Jerusalem and brought to Babylon (1:2; 5:2–3). Daniel and the temple vessels—all brought from Jerusalem by Nebuchadnezzar—now once again come together in a dramatic setting that will reveal the power of the God who gave them into the hands of Nebuchadnezzar in the first place.

Verses 14–16 are largely repetitions of what the king, the queen, and the narrator have said in vv. 7–8 and 11–12. The fondness for repetition is a trait of the MT edition. The OG is much shorter, with the king merely asking Daniel if he is able to interpret the writing and offering the reward.

[17] The contrast between Daniel's interaction with Belshazzar and with Nebuchadnezzar could not be more marked. Daniel speaks with courtesy and modesty to Nebuchadnezzar in 2:27–30 when asked if he can interpret the dream. In 4:18–19 (15–16) the interchange between Nebuchadnezzar and Daniel seems to reflect mutual concern between the king and his sage. Here, however, the abrupt rejection by Daniel of the king's gifts presages the rebuke he will address to Belshazzar. Indeed, as has been often recognized, Daniel's tone is more like that of a prophet delivering a word of judgment than like that of a sage (cf. Elijah in 1 Kgs 21:20–24).

Daniel's statement that he can interpret the mysterious writing contrasts with his need to seek divine assistance in interpreting Nebuchadnezzar's dream in 2:16–23 and is more like his immediate grasp of the meaning of the dream in ch. 4. In narrative terms it heightens the drama and the contrast between the powerlessness and fear of Belshazzar and his wise men alongside the power of Daniel and his God.

[18–21] The OG has neither the initial response of Daniel to the king, nor the long retelling of Nebuchadnezzar's experiences as a foil to Belshazzar's own conduct, demonstrating again the MT's concern to shape the story in a way that highlights the contrast between a humbled and redeemed Gentile king and an arrogant and blasphemous one.

The construction of v. 18 is a clever intertextual play with 2:37, where Daniel opened his interpretation of the dream of the great statue with (a) an address to the king ("you, O king") and (b) a description of the royal gifts that the God of heaven had given him ("a kingdom of power, might, and glory"). Here, similarly, Belshazzar is addressed as "you, O king." The following words, "the kingdom and greatness and glory and honor," do not turn out to be what the Most High God has given to Belshazzar but rather to his father, Nebuchadnezzar. Verse 19 similarly evokes the story in ch. 3 through its use of the phrase "all the peoples, nations, and languages" (3:4, 7; 4:1 [3:31]) and its emphasis on the power of life and death wielded by the monarch. Of course, in ch. 3 the people who do not fear and tremble before Nebuchadnezzar and whom he in fact cannot kill are the three Jews who will not bow down to his statue. In ch. 5, however, Daniel emphasizes only the power with which Nebuchadnezzar was entrusted, not its limits. The power to kill or let live and to raise up or bring low are ordinarily powers ascribed to God (cf. Deut 32:39; 1 Sam 2:6–7; Ps 75:7 [8]), as thematic in the earlier chapters of Daniel (cf. 2:21; 4:17, 32, 37 [14, 29, 34]).

Verses 20–21 retell the story of Nebuchadnezzar's hubris and subsequent humbling (4:1–37 [3:31–4:34]). The "exalted heart" is a stock phrase for arrogance (cf. Deut 8:14; 17:20; Ezek 31:10), and the verb "grew strong" (*tĕqap*) is used by *Targum Onqelos* to describe the hardening of Pharaoh's heart in Exod 7:13, 22; etc.). Nebuchadnezzar's arrogance is present in every story about him, but it is thematic in chs. 3 and 4. In ch. 3 he sets himself up as more powerful than any god (3:15); and even in recognizing the power of the God of Shadrach, Meshach, and Abednego, he asserts himself as this god's protector (3:29). The dream of ch. 4 uses the imagery of the great tree to address both Nebuchadnezzar's God-given greatness and his arrogance (cf. Ezek 31), yet it also has him make a prideful boast (Dan 4:30 [27]) that triggers his punishment. Daniel recounts that punishment with phrases largely drawn from ch. 4, though with some variation in detail: "driven away from human society" (4:25, 32–33 [22, 29–30]); "his mind became like that of an animal" (4:16 [13]); "with the wild asses was his dwelling" (cf. 4:25 [22], "with the animals of the field"); "he was fed grass like the cattle" (4:25, 32–33 [22, 29–30]); "his body was drenched with the dew of heaven" (4:25, 33 [22, 30]). The result, that Nebuchadnezzar must recognize God's sovereignty and ability to set over "the kingdom of humans" whomever he pleases, is also a near quotation of 4:25, 32 (22, 29).

[22–24] The narration of Nebuchadnezzar's experience sets up the radical contrast with Belshazzar's character and actions. Belshazzar's own arrogance is all the more blameworthy because he had knowledge of Nebuchadnezzar's humbling as a model and yet failed to learn from it. The reflexive verb, "exalt oneself" (*hitrômamtā*), will also be the key expression used of Antiochus's arrogance in setting himself above all gods (11:36). The comparable action by Belshazzar is the sacrilege of drinking from the temple vessels while praising idols. In keeping with the author's fondness for repetition, the accusation repeats phrases from vv. 3–4, including the lists of those who drank from the vessels and the various materials of the idols. What is added to this description at the end thus receives special emphasis. It is the contrast between the idols and God. Just as Belshazzar failed to understand the significance of Nebuchadnezzar's experience, so he utterly fails to understand the difference between the idols and the Lord of heaven. As in other idol polemics (cf. Deut 4:28; Isa 44:9–20; Jer 10:3–5; Ps 115:4–7; Epistle of Jeremiah), the idols are described as insensate objects, not true gods. By contrast, everything that exists can be traced back to the power of God. Nothing is more a part of the self than breath, yet even that is in God's power (cf. Job 12:10). Similarly, persons perceive themselves to be agents who direct their own actions. But, Daniel claims, the reality is otherwise (cf. Jer 10:23; Prov 16:9). To a large extent this claim about the role of God in relation to human life and agency is simply an expression of appropriate humility before God, a humility that Belshazzar conspicuously lacks. Later, however, in certain of the Dead Sea Scrolls it will become part of a complex theological anthropology that emphasizes the predestinarian implications of these ideas (Newsom 2004, 211–14).

Montgomery (261) is certainly correct that the introductory word of v. 24 (*bēʾdayin*, "then") is simply temporal, not causal as Theodotion takes it. Daniel's narration of the events of the evening leads him back to the inscription and the interpretation that in v. 17 he promised to provide.

[25–28] The inscription that Daniel reads and interprets does have the quality of a riddle. Since ancient Aramaic was written without vowel points and often without word divisions, the one who reads has to make a variety of interpretive decisions merely in order to pronounce what is written (for a list of possibilities, see Wolters 1991a, 159–60). Even as pointed in the text, the first two terms retain a certain ambiguity since they can be taken either as passive verbs or as nouns. Because the third word is a plural or dual noun, however, it is best to take Daniel's reading of the words as three nouns, which is also how Josephus ("number," "weight," "a break," *Ant.* 10.243–44) and Jerome (on

5:26–28: "number," "a weighing out," "removal") already understood them. But it appears that these ancient interpreters missed the riddling quality of the inscription. In 1886 Clermont-Ganneau recognized that the three nouns are actually terms for weights: *měnēʾ* is a mina (= 60 sheqels; Ezek 45:12); *těqēl* is a sheqel; and *parsîn* means half-minas. The word *pěrēs* would simply and literally mean "a divided portion," but it is attested with the specific meaning of half-mina on inscribed weights from Babylon (Clermont-Ganneau 44–45), in the eighth-century-B.C.E. Panamuwa Inscription (*COS* 2:158–60), as well as in later Rabbinic Hebrew (*m. ʿEd.* 3.3). A few commentators, troubled by the fact that the weights are not in descending order, have argued that *parsîn* should here be taken as "half-sheqels" (cf. Plöger 89; Goldingay 111), but the evidence for half-minas is stronger. The spelling *těqēl* for sheqel raised some problems when Clermont-Ganneau first made his suggestion, since it is more commonly spelled with a *shin*, but the spelling with a *taw* is now attested in the Elephantine papyri (see Cowley 30 [#10.5]; Beyer 1984, 100).

Thus the mysterious hand wrote on the wall: "a mina, a sheqel, and [two] half-minas." Here is an enigmatic oracle in the form of a riddle. What does it mean? In the ancient Near East, weights were not simply abstract concepts but were physical objects, usually made of stone, sometimes with the word designating the standard weight inscribed on them (Powell 107). The concreteness of their differing size and weight facilitated a metaphorical extension of their meaning, and the use of mina and half-mina as figurative valuations of personal character is attested in the Babylonian Talmud (*b. Taʿan.* 21b: "It is more proper that a mina [i.e., a scholar] son of half a mina [i.e., a nonscholar] should go to a mina, son of a mina, than that a mina son of a mina should go to a mina, son of half a mina" [AT]). Following this possibility, Clermont-Ganneau suggested that the riddle was not an original composition of the author of Daniel but went back to a late Neo-Babylonian or early Persian period popular saying that evaluated the last kings of Babylon. This suggestion has been widely accepted by other scholars, though there is a considerable variety of proposals for which kings were originally intended by the riddle (see J. Collins 251; Wolters 1991a, 162n44). As the riddle is taken into the book of Daniel, however, the reader would be inclined to solve the riddle by inserting the identities of the four kings named in Dan 1–6. Nebuchadnezzar would be the mina, as he is both chronologically first and is highly evaluated within the narratives (2:37–38; 5:18–21). The hapless Belshazzar would be the low-valued sheqel, and the two half-minas would be the sympathetically presented Darius the Mede (Dan 6) and Cyrus the Persian, whose presentation in biblical literature is similarly positive (cf. Isa 45:1–8; Ezra 1:1–4; 2 Chr 36:22–23). As in chs. 2 and 4, the reader is enlisted in the hermeneutical work of "untying knots."

Daniel, however, will prove more perceptive and insightful than the reader, for he does not interpret according to this rather obvious allegorical hermeneutic. Instead, Daniel uses a technique of double reading, what Noegel (24–26) calls a "punning hermeneutic." Although occasionally used in preexilic bibical texts (cf. Jer 1:11–12; Amos 8:1–2), it is a standard technique in many types of Mesopotamian divinatory literature (Noegel 11–26) and reflects the Jewish Diaspora's absorption of aspects of Mesopotamian religion and culture. Similarly, just as Neo-Assyrian scholars would introduce the interpretation of astronomical omens with the phrase *anniu piširšu*, "this is its interpretation," so Daniel uses the phrase *děnâ pěšar-millětāʾ*, "this is the interpretation of the matter" (Nissinen 47–49). Daniel cites each word in its nominal form but then interprets it as a verb. Thus the noun *měnēʾ* (mina) is interpreted as the verb *měnâ*. The Hebrew cognate verb ordinarily refers to counting or enumerating, and that is also the ordinary usage in many Aramaic dialects (see CAL under *mny*). Hence many translations take the expression as elliptical for "he has numbered (the days of) your kingdom" (NJPS). But the verb in Hebrew (Sir 40:29) and Syriac (see R. P. Smith 281) can mean "account," or "reckon." Given the governing trope of weights, this is more likely the sense here. Similarly, though the second verb can mean "brought to an end," the trope of weighing Belshazzar's kingdom on a scale suggests that the other nuance of this verb, "hand over" or "pay out," is to be heard here (Montgomery 265; Wolters 1991a, 171).

The second noun, *těqēl*, is interpreted as the cognate verb "to be weighed" (*těqal*), though in the second-person passive, "you have been weighed in the scales." To be "found wanting" (*ḥassîr*) means that Belshazzar's heft does not even weigh as much as a sheqel does. While that meaning continues the trope of the riddle, the author may be testing the reader's powers to "untie knots." The interpretation may not simply be derived from the trope but also can be generated by a secondary reading of the letters written on the wall as *tiqqal*, from *qělal* ("to be light"; so Wolters 1991a, 173–74). The author could have used the word *tiqqal* itself in the interpretation, but that would have deprived the cleverest of readers of the reward of figuring out the hermeneutical principle Daniel is implicitly using. Rashi discerned this play on words and rendered, "You have been weighed before him and have been found light in every way" (cited in J. Collins 252).

When Daniel comes to interpret the third word, he does not cite the plural form of the inscription itself but rather the singular *pěrēs* in order to facilitate the double wordplay. The meaning of the verb (*pěras*), here rendered in the passive, is taken by most commentators as "divided," which is the meaning of the cognate verb in Hebrew. That meaning is not well attested in other Aramaic dialects, however. Moreover, the Neo-Babylonian Empire was not in fact divided between Media and Persia. Nor does the book of Daniel elsewhere seem to assume that to be the case, since it appears to take Median and Persian rulership to be successive rather than simultaneous empires (2:37–39; 7:5–6). To be sure, the translations of Th and the Vulgate support the meaning "divided," as does Josephus, but this only indicates that they assumed the verb had the same meaning as the more familiar Hebrew cognate. Wolters (1991a, 169), following a suggestion of Margoliouth (341), observes that *Targum Onqelos* uses *prs* with the sense of "assess," a meaning similar to the previous two verbs of Daniel's interpretation. That way of understanding the verb keeps closer both to the governing trope of "weights and measures" and to the way in which the book of Daniel construes the relationship of the Median and Persian kingdoms as successive sovereign powers in the sequence of kingdoms. As in the preceding interpretations, the initial word is interpreted with not just one but two decipherments. The word *pĕrēs* is reinterpreted not simply through the verb "assessed" but also through the noun "Persia" (*pārās*). This highly intricate wordplay, which would have been accessible to the original audience, became genuinely puzzling to readers and translators several centuries later and has only been recovered as modern scholarship has recognized the nuances of words whose meanings had been lost.

The significance of the wordplay requires comment. Though modern readers may tend to see it as merely a clever device displaying the wit of the author, ancient understandings of the relationship between words and realities were different. Especially in oracular situations, words were understood to participate in the reality of the thing they described. The polysemy of words allowed connections to be made between different levels or aspects of reality. The interpreter's construction of punning meaning was not a display of wit but a perception of hidden realities and, indeed, an act of power (cf. Noegel 40).

[5:29–31 (6:1)] Following this intense and intellectually demanding scene of Daniel's confrontation with the king and interpretation of the oracular writing, the narrative denouement is both swift and enigmatic. Where the author had been at pains to describe Belshazzar's emotional reaction to the mysterious message in vv. 6 and 9, here, even as Belshazzar hears the news of the impending end of his kingdom, no reaction of his is recorded other than his fulfillment of the promise of the reward that Daniel had earlier rejected (v. 17). It is difficult to know what to make of this terse narrative depiction of the king. Perhaps this event is simply the narrator's fidelity to the logic of the court story that requires the fulfillment of the promised reward (cf. 2:48–49; 3:30). But it is also possible that the narrator gives Belshazzar a moment of dignity. The braggart son, who had no military accomplishments to give him status, sought to attain it through aggressive and sacrilegious actions toward the sacred vessels of the God of the Jews. Though fearful when confronted by a divine omen, once the reality of his situation is revealed to him, he meets his fate with dignity and shows respect toward the very emissary of the deity at whose hands he will die.

There is no reliable historical evidence as to the fate of Belshazzar in the events of 539 B.C.E., though Xenophon (*Cyr.* 7.5.24–30) reports that a group of soldiers under the command of Gobryas and Gadatus entered the palace quarters and killed the king and those with him. A similar tradition seems to be assumed by Daniel. Literarily, the final verses also establish a transition to ch. 6. There Daniel will be one of the three chief rulers under the king Darius the Mede, suggesting that he honored Belshazzar's promotion of Daniel to be a "triumvir."

The identity of the enigmatic figure of Darius the Mede is discussed in connection with ch. 6. It is not at all evident why the text gives the age of Darius as sixty-two. As some have noted, this may be close to the age of Cyrus when he took Babylon (J. Collins 253). Literarily, it may make it plausible that the Median rule would be short and that Daniel could easily survive into the time of Cyrus's rule over Babylon (cf. 1:21).

History of Reception, by Brennan W. Breed

Interpreting Divine Judgment

"The writing is on the wall." This phrase, common now in many cultures around the world, most often describes a situation in which a decisive event seems certain to happen, whether it be the end of a political regime or a couple's eventual marriage. Yet in the book of Daniel, the foreboding signal is notable for its inscrutable nature: not only can the participants at the feast not understand the writing; the Babylonian scholars are equally stymied. Readers of Dan 5 have taken up various pieces of this puzzle as they struggled to make sense of this story's historicity, its message, and its usefulness in their contemporary contexts. And as they do so, these readers enact the generative interpretive process that Dan 5 depicts—and that also brought the text itself into being.

Interpreting History

One of the thorniest issues of interpretation for the book of Daniel, and for much of biblical literature, is the relationship between the biblical text and the historical record. The story of Belshazzar's feast brings this interpretive question to the fore because it was plainly problematic even for ancient readers. An early rabbinic reader noticed the chronological issues that arose between the last verse of ch. 4 and the first verse of ch. 5 and asked: "What happened to Evil-merodach?" (*Gen. Rab.* 85.2). This absence is important because Evil-merodach was at times admired by various interpreters for his release and favorable treatment of the Judahite king Jehoiachin (2 Kgs 25:27–29; Goldwurm 156).

Some rabbinic readers sought to interpret the text in a way that reflects history more accurately. Rashi claimed that Belshazzar was Evil-merodach's son, necessitating the interpretation of the word *'ăbûhî* in Dan 5:2 as "his grandfather" rather than "his father" (Alshich 272). Likewise, some Christian readers, such as Jerome (on 5:1), pored over ancient historiographical sources such as Josephus, Berossus, and Xenophon to deduce how the biblical text might bend but not break the historical facts. Many other rabbinic readers followed the talmudic opinion that the Torah, for pedagogical reasons, does not always follow chronological sequence (*b. Pesaḥ.* 6b). Rabbi Eleazar proposed that Belshazzar in Dan 5 follows abruptly on the heels of Nebuchadnezzar in Dan 4 to "juxtapose the story of one wicked person with the story of another," since the slightly better Evil-merodach would muddle the ethical point of the text; Rabbi Samuel bar Nahman, however, concluded that the gap helpfully juxtaposed Nebuchadnezzar's destruction of Judah with the end of Belshazzar's kingdom (*Gen. Rab.* 85.2).

Some Christian readers, such as the fifth-century Theodoret of Cyrus, who was usually consumed with proving the surface meaning of Scripture to be coherent and historical, followed these rabbinic suggestions, stating that Daniel omitted Evil-merodach "since he was composing not history pure and simple but prophecy—hence his not recording everything done by Nebuchadnezzar, either, but only those things of which mention was required with a view to bringing benefit" (Theodoret 135).

The motif of interpretation seems to be carefully woven throughout the text of ch. 5, and some readers have understood small textual details in this light. According to the Talmud, Belshazzar timed his feast to coincide with the end of the seventy years prophesied by Jeremiah (25:11–12). The Babylonian kings had not yet desecrated the temple vessels because they feared that it would bring the wrath of YHWH, but with the final passing of the seventieth year, Belshazzar understood himself to have prevailed over the Jewish God, and celebrated by defiling the temple wares. Yet, as Rava explains, "Belshazzar calculated the seventy years of exile but made a mistake" (*b. Meg.* 11b). The Gemara explains that Belshazzar started counting the seventy years at Nebuchadnezzar's accession to the throne, and Ahasuerus began counting with the exile of Jehoiachin, but God began the seventy years with the destruction of Jerusalem (*b. Meg.* 11b; cf. *S. ʿOlam Rab.* 28).

The character of the queen, the only female character in Daniel MT to have a speaking role (5:10–12), has attracted much attention because of her dramatic entrance to the festivities, her knowledge of and admiration for Daniel, and her long memory of Nebuchadnezzar's reign. According to Jerome (on 5:10), the third-century-C.E. philosopher Porphyry mocked the book of Daniel at this point because it dared to show a woman knowing more than her husband; Jerome's response shows his own discomfort with this, however, as he cites Josephus and Origen, who believe the queen to be Belshazzar's grandmother and mother, respectively, and "therefore knew about previous events of which the king was ignorant." Theodoret of Cyrus (141) explains that the king's wives were already in attendance (5:2), so the queen mother, who "being old" was

History of Reception 181

"probably not a party at that stage to the drunkenness or the antics or dancing," reentered the party to recommend Daniel's interpretive skill. Throughout history, many readers have supplemented the Bible at this point with the ancient Greek scholar Herodotus. He describes a clever and cunning Babylonian queen near the end of the empire's rule named Nitocris, who led the defensive fortification of Babylon—and also left a deceptive riddle on her tomb, placed above a gate to the city, suggesting to the Persian armies that within her tomb a treasure was buried. As Herodotus writes, to Darius "it seemed a monstrous thing that he should be unable to use one of the gates of the town, and that a sum of money should be lying idle, and moreover inviting his grasp, and he not seize upon it. Now he could not use the gate, because, as he drove through, the dead body would have been over his head. Accordingly he opened the tomb; but instead of money, found only the dead body" (1.185–88). Many influential works, such as Handel's oratorio *Belshazzar* (1774), have simply taken for granted that the queen in Dan 5 is Nitocris of Babylon.

Interpreting Words

Why could the king's Babylonian scholars not read the writing on the wall or interpret its message? The Talmud (*b. Sanh.* 22a) offers an array of responses. Rav argued that the letters were written in the ancient Hebrew athbash code, used in Jeremiah (5:1; 25:26; 51:41), in which the last letter of the alphabet is substituted for the first, the second-to-last for the second, and so on. Thus the Babylonian scholars did not know the proper code. Other rabbinic sages argued that the letters were arranged in an uncharacteristic manner, and thus the scholars failed to understand the proper direction in which to read the text. The Mishnaic sage Shmuel the Small claimed that the letters were organized into three distinct words, with the first letters of each word in order forming the first word of the divine message, the second letters forming the second word, and so on. Other rabbinic interpreters have suggested that the code required every fifth letter to be read, or that the letters were organized into a particular grid in which the letters had to be read top to bottom, and then right to left in columns (Goldwurm 163).

The famous early modern Jewish scholar Rabbi Menasseh ben Israel, resident of Amsterdam, proponent of Jewish dialogue with the Christian world, and neighbor and friend of Rembrandt van Rijn (the painter), gave his own theory of the writing on the wall in a Latin treatise named *De termino vitae*, which sought to explain Jewish ideas of divine providence to a Gentile and mostly Calvinist audience. Menasseh argued that God's prophecies are purposefully obscure, but they must be interpreted properly by humans in order that they may manifest themselves in the world, and thus God's plans for Babylon's destruction required the proper interpretation by Daniel before they could be carried out (Zell 67). Menasseh argued that humans played a precise role in providence that required their hermeneutical acumen. In his book, Menasseh depicted Belshazzar's inscription in five columns and three rows that spelled out the message, moving from top to bottom and right to left.

It seems that Menasseh explained his interpretation of this text to his friend Rembrandt, because the famous painter depicted the inscription in an identical manner—save for his mistaking the final letter as a zayin instead of a nun—in his ca. 1636–38 painting *Belshazzar's Feast* (Zell 59; see fig. 13 above). Rembrandt's use of Hebrew in his painting is somewhat unusual in the history of Christian art, which has tended to either ignore the phrase or depict it in Latin. But in the context of early modern Christian discourse, Rembrandt's interest in Hebrew mirrors that of Christian Hebraist scholars. Rembrandt shows Belshazzar, the queen, and several courtiers in shock as they stare at the inscription before Daniel has been summoned. Rembrandt's naturalistic style can be seen in the realistic faces and the honest surprise that lacks typical royal decorum. Like other Netherlandish painters, Rembrandt depicts the table setting, including the temple vessels, in very lifelike detail; as in other still-life paintings, these naturalistic images convey the richness but also the brevity of life. And for the Dutch viewers, the confiscation and misuse of the Jews' treasures, figured by the lavish cups and plates on the table, would evoke thoughts of the excesses of the Spanish Empire, which had ruled the Netherlands—and seized much Dutch wealth in the process (Hagen and Hagen 244).

Many readers, however, have not labored as much over the letters but have instead puzzled over the words themselves and their meanings. Among other interpreters, Alshich noticed that Daniel only accounted for one occurrence of "mina." He wrote in response: "The word *menei* was written twice, as if to signify that Belshazzar was being repaid measure for measure. Belshazzar had 'counted' the number of years in which his dynasty should last, and arrogantly declared that although seventy years had passed, his kingdom still stood. In return, God 'counted' the number of years pertaining to his rule.... In response to your 'counting,' God has 'counted' your kingship" (Alshich 315–16). *Parsîn*, the word for "half-mina," is a plural form in Dan 5:25, which some rabbinic readers took as a hint to read the last word of the inscription twice, just as the first word occurred twice. Both Rashi and Abraham ibn Ezra (d. 1164) took the first *parsin* to refer to the act of breaking the kingdom, and the second to refer to the Persians—thus interpreting Daniel's double interpretation as his use of the dual form of the word (Goldwurm 173).

Those interested in the theory or art of interpretation have often thought of Daniel's reading of the writing on the wall, and perhaps none have ruminated more on the dynamics of interpretation than those who developed the form of talk therapy known as psychoanalysis in the nineteenth and twentieth centuries. Jacques Lacan, an idiosyncratic follower of Sigmund Freud, referred to

"Mene, Tekel, Uparshin" several times in his writings and seminars. Lacan taught that symptoms should not be "read" as if they were disposable, conscious messages for some deeper, unconscious meaning. Instead they encode and constitute the very unconscious truths that people often assume lies behind or beyond the symptoms. Like Menasseh ben Israel, Lacan argues that the message on the wall similarly enacts the doom that it represents, and he claims that this is analogous to symptoms that manifest in a patient's speech. Lacan uses Mene, Tekel, Uparshin to teach psychoanalysts what it might mean to read their patients' speech "like one reads coffee grounds," because "the very manner in which it is spelt out, its enigmatic, hermetic nature, is in fact the answer to the question of meaning" (Lacan 158). Lacan relates the writing on the wall to the self-referential Islamic formula "There is no God but God," because "there is no other word, no other solution to your problem, than the word."

Interpreting the Times

Daniel 5 has intrigued many readers throughout history precisely because it is the only story in the court tales (Dan 1–6) to describe the actual demise of an oppressive monarch. Chapter 2 foretells the destruction of the four kingdoms, but ch. 5 alone enacts a destruction. For that reason, this story has been particularly interesting to those facing a powerful enemy or oppressor. In the medieval period, for example, the eighth-century commentary on Revelation by Beatus of Liébana became quite popular throughout the Iberian Peninsula because of Christian apocalyptic fears stemming from the rise of Islam. One particular illuminated manuscript of this commentary, the Morgan Beatus, also included a commentary on Daniel's apocalyptic texts. It depicts Belshazzar's feast taking place underneath a type of arch characteristic of Muslim architecture, well known through its conspicuous use throughout the Great Mosque of Cordoba, which was the symbol of Muslim dominance over the Iberian region (Dodds 30). By analogy with the biblical story, this artist suggests that the opulent and powerful Umayyad rulers in Cordoba were perched on the edge of disaster. Centuries later, the British caricaturist James Gillray would depict his nation's bitter enemy, the emperor Napoleon Bonaparte, at a banquet while the divine hand inscribes the proverbial writing on the wall (see fig. 14). On the table before him lies the most important parts of the British government and economy arrayed like molded desserts, labeled carefully ("St. James' Palace," "The Bank of England," etc.) Napoleon's wife, Josephine, drinks heavily, while his sisters stand behind, dressed quite provocatively; Gillray uses Napoleon's female family members as ciphers for improper desire, playing on the reference to Belshazzar's wives and concubines at the feast (5:2). Gillray depicts grenadiers holding bloody sabers, symbolizing the brutal war that Napoleon continued to unleash on Europe. Behind Napoleon, the divine hand holds a set

Figure 14. British caricaturist James Gillray's engraving of Napoleon Bonaparte as Belshazzar, fearful of the handwriting on the wall, published August 24, 1803. Public domain (Library of Congress Archives)

of scales, in which the crown of Louis XVII, the deposed and executed French monarch, outweighs the red cap characteristic of the French revolutionaries. This print was published in 1803 in response to Napoleon's boast that, if it would only fog in London for three straight days, he could invade and conquer the country (Godfrey and Hallett 124). Thus, just when Napoleon thinks that he can dominate England, his vast empire will collapse. In light of the commercial ideology of the British Empire, it seems telling that Gillray depicts the political and economic centerpieces of the British Empire as analogous to the vessels of the Jerusalem temple.

Many within the British Empire itself offered criticism of the centrality of elite structures of political and financial power through the image of Belshazzar's feast. In 1720, for example, the Anglo-Irish priest, politician, and writer Jonathan Swift published a poem titled "The Run upon the Bankers," which attacked the banking system promoted by the British that collapsed earlier in the year due to rampant speculation and then squeezed the Irish people to pay their debts. Swift often criticized the British government for abusing and unfairly profiting from the Irish people; in "The Run upon the Bankers," Swift compares the financial system to corrupt and stagnating blood that hinders the communal body's health (Moore 69–71). The poem ends with the warning that, in the end, the British financiers will be judged by the scales of righteousness, and when they inevitably offer heaps of "bills and gold" to cover their end of the balances, the heavenly voice will echo Dan 5: "Weigh'd in the balance and found light!"

In the United States as well, Belshazzar's feast was often a powerful metaphor for the evils of social and political inequality. In the tightly contested presidential election of 1884, the Republican candidate James G. Blaine held a $50-per-head fund-raising banquet at Delmonico's, an expensive restaurant, which gave traction to his political rivals' accusations that he pandered to the rich and ignored the poor. The next day, Walt McDougall published a cartoon based on Gillray's caricature of Napoleon in the *New York World* newspaper titled "The Royal Feast of Belshazzar, Blaine and the Money Kings." It depicts Blaine and his wealthy donors feasting on desserts labeled "lobby pudding," "monopoly soup," and "Navy contract," indicating the various aspects of crony capitalism, while a poor family begs for bare sustenance from the table. In the context of the very close race, it is likely that this last-minute scandal cost Blaine the presidency (Summers 286–87).

Belshazzar's feast has proved to be particularly important for those advocating radical political opposition. For example, José Rizal, a Filipino author and activist who was executed by the Spanish army in 1896 for sedition, wrote a novel titled *El filibusterismo*, which criticized the colonial government for its oppression and encouraged the Filipino people to revolt. In a pivotal part of the plot, one of the main characters plants a bomb at the wedding party of an elite family and leaves a handwritten note on his way outside that reads, "Mene Thecel Phares" (Rizal 332). And in 1911, the radical American author Voltairine de Cleyre, an advocate for anarchism early in her life and for communism near its end, began her last poem, titled "Written—in—Red" and dedicated to the working-class revolution taking place at the time in Mexico. She references the writing on the wall, but reverses the direction of the message: de Cleyre depicts the peasants as the authors of the message and the wealthy "gods" as the recipients:

> Written in red their protest stands,
> For the Gods of the World to see;
> On the dooming wall their bodiless hands
> Have blazoned "Upharsin," and flaring brands
> Illumine the message: "Seize the lands!
> Open the prisons and make men free!"
> (De Cleyre 216)

Twenty years later, in the midst of the Great Depression, a predominately Jewish ladies' garment workers union in New York City wrote a musical revue while on strike; they named it *Pins and Needles*, and it became a major Broadway hit. One of its numbers, penned by the Jewish songwriter Harold Rome, was titled "Mene, Mene, Tekel" and uses the figure of Belshazzar's feast to criticize the bellicose political powers of the world and the economic systems that they support. The lyrics describe a rich feast attended by the autocrats and fascist dictators of the world, made possible by the labor of the Israelite "scamps" who were sent "all to makin' bricks in concentration camps." Daniel then tells the dictator Belshazzar the news ("King stop your frolic and your flaunting. . . . The Lord don't like dictators or dictators' ways") and predicts the perseverance of the working-class Israelites after the empire crumbles (Goldman 206, 221).

Interpreting Oneself

Throughout history many readers have looked more to individual or spiritual reform than economic and political. Ancient and medieval Christians tended to read Belshazzar's feast typologically as a reference to the last judgment, in which each individual will be called to account for their actions. In a fifteenth-century Belgian manuscript illumination of the "Typological scenes from the life of Jesus" (Morgan M. 649, fol. 7r), the artist juxtaposes an image of Daniel addressing a seated, crowned Belshazzar while pointing at a wall inscribed with "MANE THECEL PHARES" alongside an image of Christ seated on a rainbow, accompanied by angels holding trumpets, calling the dead to rise out of the ground. A hell-mouth lurking in the lower left-hand corner of the frame reminds the viewer that these resurrected individuals will immediately face judgment.

Likewise, the Middle English poem titled "Cleanness" uses Belshazzar's feast as an example of God's judgment upon an individual's sin (Cannon 157). The American poet Emily Dickinson wrote a poem with similar import that begins "Belshazzar had a letter," and concludes with the claim that this single correspondence can be read "without glasses" by the "conscience of us all," suggesting that the writing on the wall is a call to ethical introspection applicable to every individual (Mailloux 45–46). Johnny Cash's song "Belshazzar," written before his musical stardom while he was in the Air Force, also retells the biblical story as a morality tale, but Bob Dylan refashioned the song on his 1975 album *The Basement Tapes* into a "damning example of unresolvable mystery," thus aligning the message with its ancient origins in the text of Dan 5 (Carney 40).

Daniel 6:1–28 (2–29) Darius and the Pit of Lions: A Lesson Gratefully Learned

1 (2) It pleased Darius to establish over the kingdom one hundred and twenty satraps throughout the entire kingdom. 2 (3) And over them were

Darius and the Pit of Lions: A Lesson Gratefully Learned

three chief ministers, of whom Daniel was one. These satraps reported to them, and so the king was not bothered.[a] 3 (4) Then this man Daniel distinguished himself over the other chief ministers and the satraps, because of his extraordinary abilities,[b] and the king was inclined to appoint him over the entire kingdom. 4 (5) Then the chief ministers and the satraps began seeking to find some grounds for indictment against Daniel concerning affairs of state, but they were not able to find any grounds for indictment or corruption, because he was trustworthy, and so no act of negligence or corruption was found against him.[c] 5 (6) Then these men said, "We will not find any grounds for indictment against this Daniel unless we find something against him in the law of his God."[d]

6 (7) Then these chief ministers and satraps all barged in[e] upon the king and spoke to him thus: "O King Darius, live forever! 7 (8) All of the chief ministers of the king, the prefects, the satraps, the counselors, and the governors have taken counsel together that the king should establish a decree and make it legally binding[f] that if anyone shall petition any god or human for thirty days, except you, O king, he will be thrown into the pit of lions! 8 (9) Now, O king, issue a prohibition and put it in writing,[g] so that it will be unchangeable according to the law of the Medes and the Persians, which cannot be annulled." 9 (10) Accordingly, King Darius, wrote the decree and prohibition.

10 (11) As for Daniel, when he learned that the decree had been written, he entered his house, where in his upper chamber he had windows that opened toward Jerusalem. Three times a day he would kneel and pray and give thanks to his God, because this was what he had been doing previously.

11 (12) Then those men barged in and found Daniel petitioning and seeking mercy from his God. 12 (13) Then they approached the king and said, "O king,[h] did you not put in writing a prohibition that any person who petitioned any god or human for thirty days, except for you, O king, would be thrown into the pit of lions?" The king said, "Indeed, the matter is like the law of the Medes and the Persians, which cannot be annulled." 13 (14) Then they replied to the king, "Daniel, who is one of the Judean exiles, has not paid attention to you, O king, nor to the prohibition that you have written. Three times a day he makes his petition." 14 (15) Then, when the king heard the matter, he was very upset, and he set his mind upon saving Daniel. Until the sun went down, he kept trying to rescue him. 15 (16) Then those men barged in upon the king and said to the king, "Know, O king, that it is a law of the Medes and the Persians that every prohibition and ordinance that the king has issued cannot be changed." 16 (17) Then the king gave the command, and Daniel was brought and cast into the pit of lions. The king said to Daniel, "Your god whom you

worship continually—he must save you."ⁱ 17 (18) A stone was brought and placed against the mouth of the pit, and the king sealed it with his signet ring and with the signet rings of his nobles, so that nothing might be changed concerning Daniel.

18 (19) Then the king went to his palace and spent the night without food, nor was any diversionʲ brought to him, and his sleep eluded him. 19 (20) Then at dawn the king rose at first light and went in anxious haste to the pit of lions. 20 (21) And when he drew near to the pit, he cried out to Daniel with a voice full of anxiety. The king said to Daniel, "Daniel, servant of the living God, has your God whom you worship continually been able to save you from the lions?" 21 (22) Then Daniel spoke to the king, "O king, live forever! 22 (23) My God sent his angel and closed the mouth of the lions. They did not harm me because I was found innocent before him, and also to you, O king, I have done no harm." 23 (24) Then the king was immensely pleased, and he commanded that Daniel be brought up from the pit. Daniel was brought up from the pit, and no harm was found on him, because he had trusted his God. 24 (25) The king commanded that those men who had maligned Daniel, their children, and their wives be brought and cast into the pit of lions. They did not reach the bottom of the pit before the lions overpowered them and crushed all their bones.

25 (26) Then King Darius wrote: "To all peoples, nations, and languages who inhabit all the earth: May your peace be great. 26 (27) I have hereby issued a decree that in the whole domain of my kingdom there shall be trembling and awe before the God of Daniel.

> He is a living God,
>   who endures forever;
> his kingdom is indestructible,
>   and his dominion lasts until the end.
> 27 (28) He saves and delivers,
>   he makes signs and wonders
>   in the heavens and upon the earth,
> for he saved Daniel from the power of the lions."

28 (29) So this man Daniel prospered during the reign of Darius and during the reign of Cyrus the Persian.

---

a. In the Haphel the verbal root *nzq* means "to suffer harm" (Ezra 4:13–15, 22) but the versions render the Peal here as "to be bothered." This nuance is also attested for the Akk. cognate, *nazāqum*, "to become irritated, to be concerned" (*CAD* 11/2:136).

b. Lit, "because an extraordinary spirit was in him."

c. The final clause is not attested in Th and may be a variant worked into MT. OG differs significantly. See comments on the verse.

d. Although in other contexts *dāt* can refer to the Torah (e.g., Ezra 7:12), here it has more of the sense of customary religious practice. The translation "law" is retained, however, to emphasize the wordplay with the "law of the Medes and Persians" that Daniel breaks.

e. The nuance of the verb is difficult to capture, and the versions employ a variety of terms to translate the three occurrences of the word in this chapter (see Montgomery 272; J. Collins 265–66). In other contexts the Aram. and its Heb. cognate variously connote haste, hostile agitation, and coordinated activity (*HALOT* 1978–79).

f. The Aram. phrase is the equivalent of the Akk. expression *riksa dunnunu*, "to make legally binding" (Paul 2001, 58).

g. Others take the phrase to mean "sign the document" (Hartman and DiLella 195).

h. The MT reads "concerning the prohibition of the king." Not only is this redundant, but it would have the courtiers beginning their address to the king abruptly, without a greeting. The translation above follows the Greek and Syriac versions, which omit the phrase "concerning the prohibition." It is found, however, in 4QDan^b.

i. Although the verb is imperfect and not jussive (so Hartman and DiLella 195), Goldingay (121) is correct that a modal sense of some sort is required in light of Darius's anxiety during the night.

j. The meaning of *daḥăwān* is unknown. The Greek versions use terms for food, suggesting that the phrase complements the previous reference to fasting. Other suggestions have included "musical instruments" (Ibn Ezra), "tables" (Rashi), and more recently "concubines" (see *HALOT* and references there). "Diversions," an intentionally vague term, follows the translation of NJPS.

Overview

Daniel 5 and 6 are closely connected narratives, so much so that the Jewish and Christian traditions disagree as to where one ends and the other begins. The Jewish tradition concludes ch. 5 with the notice of Belshazzar's death in v. 30 and opens ch. 6 with the notice that Darius the Mede received the kingdom, despite the coordinating conjunction "and" that connects the two verses. The Christian tradition, which is generally followed by modern scholars, treats that verse as the conclusion to ch. 5 (v. 31), and begins the following story with Darius's decision about the administrative organization of his kingdom. Yet without the preceding notice, one would not know who Darius is or the circumstances by which Darius came to the throne. This redactional link, which connects two originally independent narratives, invites comparison between Belshazzar and Darius. Both kings are presented as ineffectual, and both are involved in a situation in which the issues of idolatry and the power and status of the king are central to the plot of the narrative. They are, however, presented as a study in contrasts. Belshazzar arrogantly asserts himself over the symbols of the Most High God and never confesses the power of this God. Darius passively accepts a temporary status that exalts him over all gods and humans but is grieved by the consequences and utters the strongest confession of the Most High's sovereignty in the whole cycle of narratives. Although the story functions well as an independent narrative, it has been fashioned by the redactor to serve as the conclusion to the cycle of chs. 1–6.

The Relation of Daniel 6 and Daniel 3

Chapter 6 is also structured in a fashion that invites comparison with ch. 3, and it is possible that it may have been modeled on it. Like ch. 3, Dan 6 invokes several genres, each of which draws attention to different aspects of the narrative. The plot draws from the court-conflict tale in which the hero's high status at court makes him the object of jealousy and intrigue, resulting in his fall and threatened execution, although the hero is ultimately restored (cf. *Ahiqar*). Since the hero is endangered because of his faithfulness to God, the story can also be read as a confessor tale, in which the endangerment and rescue serve to demonstrate the power of God and to provide an occasion for characters to praise God's power and graciousness (cf. 3 Maccabees; *L.A.B.* 6). Similarly, the story can be read as a wisdom didactic tale in which the hero's exercise of a particular virtue initially appears to imperil him but ultimately saves him (cf. Job 1–2; 42).

Quite apart from their generic affinities, a dense network of similarities and contrasts in plot, characterization, and motif link Dan 6 with the story of Shadrach, Meshach, and Abednego in Dan 3. In both narratives jealous rivals imperil the Jewish hero(es) by exploiting or manipulating their religious values and practices in a way that exposes their disobedience to a royal command or law. In both the king orders an execution, though in Dan 3 Nebuchadnezzar is arrogant and challenges the heroes' God in a direct confrontation with the three Jews, whereas in Dan 6 Darius is as much trapped as Daniel by the law he approved. Indeed, he appeals to Daniel's God for help (cf. 3:15 and 6:16 [17]). In both stories, the form of execution involves a separated space where an element other than a human executioner is the agent (fire, lions). In both, a divine figure is involved in the deliverance of the hero(es). In both, either the executioners or the enemies of the hero(es) are killed by the same means that had been prepared for the hero(es). Finally, in both accounts the climax of the narrative is a dramatic confession of the power of the God of the hero(es), though the confession of Darius goes far beyond that of Nebuchadnezzar in 3:28–29, and draws upon the language of 4:1–3 (3:31–33), which introduces the final Nebuchadnezzar story. Thus it provides a fitting conclusion for the sequence of narratives about Gentile kings.

Stylistically, the most noticeable characteristic of the narrative is its use of repeated key words and self-conscious repetition. The temporal flow of the narrative is underscored by the use of the introductory word "then" (*ʾĕdayin/ bēʾdayin*) some 14 times. The repetition of words for "seek" (*bĕʿâ*, 5 times) and "find" (*hištĕkaḥ*, 8 times) underscore aspects of the development of the plot and theme (Arnold 483). Also, as Lacocque (107) notes, "the king" (*malkāʾ*) occurs 31 times, "Daniel" 21 times, "the kingdom" (*malkûtāʾ*) 10 times, "throw into a pit of lions" (*mirmēʾ lĕgōb ʾaryāwātāʾ*) 4 times with slightly differing syntax, "pit" (*gōb*) 6 times, and "lions" (*ʾaryāwātāʾ*) 9 times. While some of these repetitions are simply a part of the storyteller's art, others point to the thematically central issue of sovereignty. More significant is the strategic reuse of certain words, especially those involving the terms "living God" (*ʾĕlāhāʾ ḥayyāʾ*, vv. 20, 26 [21, 27]), and various forms of the verbs "save" (*šêzib*, vv. 16, 27 [17, 28]) and "harm," "destroy" (*ḥabbēl*, vv. 22–23, 26 [23–24, 27]). Of these, "harm" is the key to the ideological tension and resolution addressed by the narrative. Do Daniel's religious practices "harm" the king in a way that makes them incompatible with the king's sovereignty? Since the king does *not* wish Daniel to be harmed but is incapable of saving Daniel himself, the actions of the living God in saving Daniel align God's sovereign power with the wishes of the king and show Daniel's religious practices to be in harmony with, rather than in opposition to, the well-being of the king.

Structure, Literary Features, and Outline

The structure of Dan 6 can be analyzed as follows:

Introduction: Daniel's advancement (6:1–3 [2–4])
A conspiracy to entrap Daniel (6:4–9 [5–10])
    Daniel's vulnerability identified (6:4–5 [5–6])
    The trap laid by manipulating the king (6:6–9 [7–10])
Daniel (and the king) entrapped (6:10–17 [11–18])
    Daniel found at prayer by the conspirators (6:10–11 [11–12])
    The conspirators spring the trap (6:12–14 [13–15])
    The conspirators demand Daniel's execution (6:15–17 [16–18])
Daniel delivered and the conspirators executed (6:18–24 [19–25])
    The king's anxiety (6:18–20 [19–21])
    Daniel's reassurance of the king (6:21–23 [22–24])
    The conspirators executed (6:24 [25])
The king's proclamation (6:25–27 [26–28])
Conclusion: Daniel's continuing success (6:28 [29])

Comments

[1 (2)] The figure of Darius the Mede has posed an interpretive puzzle since antiquity because his existence cannot be reconciled with other historical sources. Josephus struggles to make sense of the contradictions, maintaining that he was a son of Astyages, which would make him Cyrus's cousin (*Ant.* 10.248–49). Jerome, who follows Josephus, adds that Darius must have heard of the portent disclosed to Belshazzar and Daniel's interpretation of it and so joined with Cyrus to attack Babylon. Thus Jerome says, "No one should be troubled by the fact that Daniel is said in one place to have lived in Darius's reign, and in another place in the reign of Cyrus" (on 6:1; trans. Archer). Josephus's and Jerome's attempts at harmonizing the sources, however, cannot stand up to historical scrutiny. Rowley's extended study, *Darius the Mede and the Four World Empires in the Book of Daniel* (1935), examined a variety of attempts to identify Darius the Mede with known historical figures, demonstrating why each was a false identification. More recently an attempt has been made by Koch (1995, 125–39) to revive the argument that Darius the Mede is to be identified as Ugbaru/Gubaru (= Gobryas in classical sources), the governor of Gutium who sided with Cyrus and who actually took Babylon for Cyrus, according to the Nabonidus Chronicle (Grayson 109–10). He seems to have had administrative responsibilities over Babylon for a short period of time. Since Gutium was closely associated with Media in Babylonian sources, the traditions behind Daniel may have assumed that he was a Mede (Koch 1995, 130). Though in some respects ingenious, this argument is ultimately unpersuasive since it does not account for the name Darius in Dan 6. Nor, as has been demonstrated, did Ugbaru/Gubaru ever hold the title "King of Babylon" (Grabbe 1988a, 201–4).

It is far more likely that when the narrative of Dan 6 circulated as an independent story (see introduction), it was told about the third monarch of the Persian Empire, Darius the Great, son of Hystaspes, 522–486 B.C.E., (see fig. 15) a very important figure in the cultural memory of the Jews since it was during his reign that the temple was rebuilt (Hag 1:1; 2:1). Darius was remembered in classical sources for his administrative reforms, including the organization of the kingdom into a number of satrapies (Herodotus 3.89), a detail that leaves its trace in the claim of Dan 6:1 (2) that Darius appointed 120 satraps over his whole kingdom. The number is a folkloristic exaggeration (cf. Esth 1:1; 8:9; 1 Esd 3:2), since Darius's own inscriptions make reference variously to 23 (Behistun Inscription; Kuhrt 141) or 29 satrapies (Naqš-i Rustam, reliefs and inscriptions; Kuhrt 502).

How and why did Darius the Persian become "Darius the Mede" as the narratives were transmitted? This change was perhaps facilitated by the prophetic tradition that the Medes would be the ones to attack and destroy Babylon (Isa 13:17; Jer 51:11, 28). Furthermore, the schema of the sequence of four kingdoms in Nebuchadnezzar's dream (Babylon, Media, Persia, Greece) created the need for the story cycle to represent a Median dominion succeeding that of the Babylonians and preceding that of Cyrus. Similar to the case of the Nabonidus traditions that were recast as Nebuchadnezzar stories in chs. 3–4, a faint historical memory of Darius the Persian can be discerned behind the wholly fictitious character of Darius the Mede.

[2 (3)] The reference to "three chief ministers" does not reflect any known administrative body of the Persian Empire. First Esdras 3:9 makes reference to "three nobles" who advise the king, whereas Esth 1:14 and Ezra 7:14 refer to a group of seven. These are likely conventional tropes, though in the case of Daniel the number may be influenced by Belshazzar's making the interpreter of the writing a *taltî* (Dan 5:7, 16, 29), which the author of Dan 6 may have interpreted as one of three administrators under the king. Their responsibilities include supervising the satraps. The purpose of this structure is debated and depends on how the word *nāziq* is to be understood (see textual notes). If the phrase is translated "not be bothered," then the detail contributes to the characterization of Darius as someone who does not wish to be personally bothered with the details of running the kingdom. Such a depiction would be consistent with the way in which his ministers initiate the law they propose to him and his carelessness in not thinking through its implications (vv. 6–9 [7–10]). If, however, the phrase is translated "not be harmed," then it sets up an irony, since the conspiring officials try to use their posts to harm Daniel and in so doing deprive the king of his best administrator. Although a different word for "harm" is used in vv. 22–23 (23–24), the concept of harm is thematically important in the narrative.

[3–5 [4–6]] The narrator attributes Daniel's preeminence among his administrative colleagues to the fact that "an extraordinary spirit" was in him (see comments on 4:9 [6]). Just as Nebuchadnezzar rewarded Daniel's exceptional talents by making him "chief prefect over all the sages of Babylon" (2:48; cf. 4:9 [6], "head of the mantic experts"), so Darius intends to make Daniel the chief administrator of his kingdom. There was no such position in the historical Persian Empire, though the Greek sources seem mistakenly to have attributed such power to the court officer known as the *hazarpatiš* ("commander of a thousand," chiliarch), whose actual role had to do with regulating audiences with the king (Briant 258–59). The role of chief administrator is a literary motif, modeled probably on Joseph's status in Pharaoh's court, according to Gen 41:40–43. The function of this motif is to motivate the jealousy and hostility of the other administrators. Such conflicts among courtiers were undoubtedly common at many courts where position and livelihood depended on the favor or disfavor of the king, though they are particularly well documented in Neo-Assyrian letters between scholar-advisers and the king (Parpola 1987). The fateful conspiracy of rivals figures as a critical motif in the highly influential Babylonian literary composition *Ludlul bēl nēmeqi* (see Toorn 1998, 634–35). It is quite possible that the author of Dan 6 was familiar with the tropes of this literary tradition, even if not the actual compositions (see comments on v. 7 [8] below).

While the OG version attributes the conspiracy against Daniel only to the other two chief administrators, which seems more realistic, the MT also includes the satraps (all 120 of them?), lending the narrative a quality of comic exaggeration. The king's high estimation of Daniel's qualities receives ironic confirmation from the fact that the jealous conspirators are not able to find any grounds for accusation against Daniel in matters of state. His vulnerability can only be connected with "the law of his God." As Lebram (81) observes, this is one of the earliest texts in which a religious stance is presented as the distinguishing mark of Judaism, and it is no accident that it occurs in a text describing a Jew of the Diaspora. The Persian loanword *dāt* ("law," "decree," "customary practice") can refer to public legislation, a royal command, or normative religious practice. Since there is no scriptural command to pray three times a day, the contextual meaning is that of religious practice. But the wording sets up the conflict as one between the *dāt* of God and the *dāt* of the king. The deliberate manipulation of an aspect of Jewish religion to create such a conflict goes beyond the unintentional dilemma created by the king's food in ch. 1 or the opportunistic exploitation of the three Jews' refusal to bow down in ch. 3. It more closely resembles the staged conflict in the martyrdom stories of 2 Macc 6–7. Yet in Dan 6 the underlying conflict is not religious; religion is simply a means to dispose of an object of jealous professional rivalry.

[6 (7)] Verses 6–9 (7–10) not only set the trap for Daniel; they also serve to characterize the king. Though the verb that describes the courtiers' action in v. 6 (7) (*hargišû*) could simply refer to their coordinated activity (cf. Hartman and DiLella, "came in collusion"; see trans. notes above), in other Aramaic dialects it often has more aggressive overtones (see *HALOT* 1978–79). As the narrative unfolds, it appears that the courtiers regard the king as someone who is weak and can be manipulated, perhaps even bullied—something that was certainly not true of the historical Darius Hystaspes.

It is worth observing how knowledge is distributed among the characters and the reader in the story. The king knows nothing of the motives of the courtiers. The reader knows the motives of the courtiers and knows that their conspiracy has something to do with Daniel's religious practices, but the narrator has not further described their plans. Thus the king and the reader both hear the words of the courtiers at the same time, though the reader listens with a suspicion that is not part of the king's reception. Indeed, the king's credulity plays a major role in the plot.

[7 (8)] The courtiers represent the proposal they are about to make as the result of deliberative counsel conducted among all levels of government officials. If taken at face value, then the entire kingdom is in league against Daniel. More likely it is a self-serving lie. Certainly there is one key courtier who is not party to the agreement, though the king does not notice the absence of Daniel and its possible significance. While this inattention is necessary for the plot of the narrative, it also further serves to characterize Darius as not particularly shrewd or discerning. The proposal itself is nonsensical and at home only in folkloric fiction. Preventing the petitioning of any god or person except the king would wreak havoc on the religious and social order of the kingdom. This absolute decree, however, is to be in effect for only thirty days, so it cannot be an attempt to change the nature of the kingdom permanently. Thus, though the courtiers offer no rationale or purpose for the decree, it can only be understood as an act of flattery toward the king, a symbolic way of marking him out as superior not only to all other humans but even to the gods themselves. Such a notion would have horrified the actual monarchs of the Persian Empire as blasphemous, for they did not ascribe any divine honors to themselves. Even the later Seleucid monarchs, who did claim certain aspects of divine status (Ma 219), would not have entertained such a decree. Its absurd extravagance, however, effectively captures the issue at the heart of the narratives of Dan 1–6. From the perspective of the Jews, Gentile imperial power effectively represents itself as absolute. The aesthetic and theological work of the narratives is to articulate the lurking contradiction between the claims of that power and the power of the God of the Jews. It is resolved by having the king confront the limits of his power and be led to acknowledge the sovereignty of the Most High God. It does not matter that the king may be personally benign and favorable to a character like Daniel; the danger lurks in the very structure of Gentile imperial power and its tendency to absolutize itself.

The particular punishment attached to violation of this command, to be thrown into a pit of lions, has never been satisfactorily explained. No record exists of such a punishment in the ancient Near East. Lions were trapped in pits, but they were either killed outright or left to starve (Toorn 1998, 637). If they were to be kept, they were put in cages or kept in zoological gardens (cf. Ezek 19:2–9). As v. 17 (18) will make clear, the author of Dan 6 thought of the pit of lions as a subterranean chamber with a narrow opening at the top small enough to be closed with a large stone. While this punishment may be simply the creation of the author's imagination, it does seem to draw on various literary tropes. Lions are regularly used in biblical and Mesopotamian texts as images of vicious forces arrayed against a suffering person, and the focus is often on their mouths and teeth (e.g., Pss 22:13 [14]; 57:4 [5]); Strawn 50–54). Protection from woes was similarly imagined as a god closing the mouth of the lion, as in *Ludlul*: "Marduk put a muzzle on the mouth of the lion that was devouring me" (cited in Toorn 1998, 636; cf. Dan 6:22 [23]). In this light it is noteworthy that the only other literary reference to a "pit of lions" is in the letter of the "forlorn scholar" Urad-Gula to Ashurbanipal: "Day and night I pray to the king in front of the lion's pit" (Toorn 1998, 632). Although the context is broken, there is a reference two lines later to his "colleagues," who might be the referent of the metaphor. Thus van der Toorn makes the plausible suggestion that the phrase "pit of lions" is a metaphor for the scholar's ravening and hostile colleagues, a metaphor that may well have been known to the educated author of Dan 6. One need not imagine, however, that Dan 6 shows "misrecognition of a metaphor" (Toorn 1998, 638). It may rather be a clever choice to take a well-known metaphor and to literalize it for artistic purposes in a fantastic story. The motif proved popular since it was also used in the other Daniel narrative of Bel and the Dragon. Opinion is divided as to whether the motif was simply an independent bit of tradition that each author appropriated separately, or whether one of the Daniel narratives borrowed the motif from the other.

The origin of the motif does not exhaust its symbolic resonance, however. Lions were often tropes for royal power (Strawn 54–58). Here, as a means of execution for violating a royal decree, the lions ostensibly serve as a metonym of the terrifying sovereign power of the king, much as the fire does in Dan 3. Here, as there, the power of the living God disempowers the king. In Dan 6, however, the disempowering is fervently desired by the king.

[8–9 (9–10)] As the courtiers urge the king to issue the decree, they emphasize that it should be put in writing and associate this action with making it unalterable. Writing played a somewhat different role in ancient cultures than it does in fully literate societies. Royal decrees were customarily written and might be publicly displayed, but since most of the populace could not read, they were communicated by public readings (Toorn 2007, 12–13). Archival copies of such decrees were kept in treasuries, where they could be consulted (cf. Ezra 6:1–2). Thus the written nature of the decree was associated with its authority. There is no historical basis, however, for the reference to the laws of the Medes and the Persians being unalterable once issued. This trope, which also appears in Esth 1:19 and 8:8 (and implicitly in a narrative in Diodorus Siculus 17.30), functions as a reflection on the ironies of power. In Esther, the unalterableness of the decree that Haman has been allowed to issue against the Jews (3:10–14) means that it can only be countermanded by issuing a second unalterable decree allowing the Jews to defend themselves (8:8–14). The episode in Diodorus is closer to the use of the trope in Dan 6, showing a king trapped by his own unwise decree, as it represents Darius III condemning a man to death, then realizing his innocence but being unable to reverse a decision made by royal authority.

[10 (11)] Daniel's response to the decree is described slightly differently in the OG and the MT, which alters the dynamics of the story in each version. Both mention Daniel's knowledge of the decree. Thus his actions represent a conscious decision. The OG (also Vulgate), however, uses an active verb to describe Daniel opening his windows, implying that he intentionally made his violation of the king's decree public. In the MT (and Th) the description of Daniel's room simply says that it had windows that opened toward Jerusalem. Here Daniel is characterized as doing nothing different from his customary practice, not actively advertising his behavior but also not concealing it. Readers, however, even when they are reading the MT or translations based on it, sometimes subtly recast the action as the OG does. Smith-Christopher (94) notes that Gandhi read the episode this way and cited Daniel as an example of the "soul force" of nonviolent resistance, or *satyagraha*.

The development of daily prayers by laity occurred gradually during the Second Temple period as a custom of popular piety, not a requirement of torah. Practices varied with respect to frequency and prayer postures. The orientation toward Jerusalem appears to have developed in the wake of the exile and is well attested (1 Kgs 8:30, 35, 38, 42, 44, 48; 2 Chr 6:34; 1 Esd 4:58), and Tob 3:11 also attests the open window of an upper room as a place for prayer. Daily private prayer seems first to have been coordinated with the morning and evening sacrifices at the temple, perhaps with the notion that the smoke of offerings and incense carried the prayers of the faithful to God (e.g., Jdt 9:1). Lay prayers may have been offered in imitation of the practices of the Levites at the temple (1 Chr 23:30). Another developing practice was the coordination of prayer times with the movement of the sun (perhaps attested in Ps 55:17 [18]). The overlap and merger of these practices eventually led to the thrice-daily practice that became standard in Judaism (Falk 47–49, 114–16).

Postures for prayer also varied and included standing (1 Chr 23:30; Neh 9:3; Matt 6:5; Mark 11:25; Luke 18:11, 13; *m. Ber.* 5.1), kneeling (1 Kgs 8:54; Ezra 9:5; 2 Chr 6:13; Luke 22:41; Acts 9:40), and prostration (Josh 7:6; Matt 26:39; see Keel 1978b, 308–23). The description in Daniel is likely influenced by the model of Solomon in 1 Kgs 8, since both kneeling and orientation toward Jerusalem are prominent there.

[11 (12)] Just as the conspirators were described as "barging in" upon the king in v. 6 (7), so the same verb is used to describe their interruption of Daniel at prayer. A subtle difference exists between the narrator's description of Daniel's prayer in v. 10 (11) and when it is perceived through the eyes of the conspirators in v. 11 (12). In v. 10 (11) the first verb for prayer is very general (*mĕṣallē'*), though it may refer to petition (cf. Ezra 6:10), and the second (*môdē'*) refers specifically to praise and thanksgiving. But in v. 11 (12), as the scene is focalized by the conspirators, the prayers are described as "seeking mercy" (*mitḥannan*) and "petitioning" (*bā'ē'*)–the very act prohibited by the royal decree. The conspirators see what they came to see.

[12–14 (13–15)] Kings are powerful persons, but courtiers are skilled at controlling and manipulating royal power. Here the conspirators set the stage by asking the king if he has not issued a ban on petitions to anyone but the king. When he not only affirms the existence of the ban but also characterizes it as unchangeable, they are ready to spring their trap. Their rhetoric is strikingly similar to that used by the enemies of Shadrach, Meshach, and Abednego in Dan 3:8–12. There the Chaldean courtiers similarly rehearse before the king the command he issued and the punishment for disobedience. In both places the ethnicity of the accused is highlighted, as the three are called "certain Jews" and Daniel is identified as "one of the Judean exiles." The act in question is framed in identical terms as a personal slight to the king ("They pay no attention to you").

Nebuchadnezzar's reaction to the accusation is rage (3:13). Darius's reaction is also distinctly negative. The displeasure or upset that he feels is expressed in an idiom (lit., "it seemed greatly bad to him") that is the mirror opposite of the expression in v. 1 (2) (lit., "it seemed good to Darius"). But as the reader soon learns, it is not Daniel's behavior that upsets Darius but the danger in which Daniel is placed. Thus Darius serves as a contrast character to Nebuchadnezzar. And yet both encounter the limits of their power. Nebuchadnezzar will fail to kill the three Jews. Darius can find no way to save Daniel.

[15–17 (16–18)] For the third time the verb "barging in" is used to characterize the peremptory actions of the conspirators (vv. 6, 11 [7, 12]), marking their determination to control the situation. In contrast to their speech to the king in v. 12 (13), which was cast as an interrogative ("Did you not . . . ?"), here they speak to the king with an imperative ("Know, O king . . ."), as they remind him of the unalterableness of the decree, which he himself had affirmed in v. 12 (13). Thus he is trapped and forced to do what is most repugnant to himself: give the command to have Daniel thrown into the pit of lions. Once again, the author seems to intend a comparison with ch. 3. When Nebuchadnezzar prepared to condemn the three Jews, he said, "What god is there who can save you from my hands?" (3:15). By contrast, Darius affirms that it is only Daniel's God who can save him.

As noted above, the way the pit of lions is imagined is deeply odd and belongs to the literary imagination rather than to any ancient Near Eastern reality. The opening is small enough that it can be closed by rolling a rock over it. It is not clear how one would affix a seal to the rock. Clay might be put around the rock and a seal impressed upon it. Or a length of cord might be stretched across the rock and closed with a clay bulla and seal. The purpose of the seals is to prevent tampering during the night. Here the rock is secured with seals of both the king and the nobles. This double sealing reflects the conflict between the king and his courtiers. Implicitly, the king fears that the courtiers might take Daniel out and kill him themselves. For their part, the courtiers want to prevent the king from rescuing Daniel and then resealing the pit. The use of both seals ensures that neither can tamper with the pit. This is how the OG interprets the detail: "So that Daniel might not be removed by them or the king pull him up from the pit."

[18–19 (19–21)] To increase suspense, the narrative point of view does not follow Daniel into the pit of lions but follows Darius. Although the exact translation of the verse is uncertain (see trans. notes), Darius's evident fondness for Daniel is expressed through his anxiety, which makes him unable to eat, distract himself, or sleep during the night, and which sends him rushing anxiously to the pit at first light. By contrast, the lions' den scene in Bel and the Dragon (vv. 33–39) narrates the scene from within the pit, describing Daniel as eating the meal miraculously brought to him by the prophet Habakkuk. The later artistic

Figure 15. An agate cylinder seal and impression with the inscription, "Darius the Great King," depicting the Persian king shooting arrows at a lion (sixth to fifth centuries B.C.E). The Persian King Darius I is the monarch upon whom the literary figure of Darius the Mede is modeled. © The Trustees of British Museum.

tradition, too, tends to focus not on the king's anxiety but on the miraculous scene of Daniel with the lions (see fig. 16).

The narrator continues to dramatize the king's anxiety in the anguish of his voice as he calls out to Daniel. Verse 20 (21) alludes back to v. 16 (17). There the king had admitted that only Daniel's God could save him. Here, in words closely similar, he rephrases his statement as a question. The conspirators had set their trap in a way that would pit Daniel's loyalty to his God against his loyalty to the king. In both vv. 16 (17) and 20 (21) Darius highlights Daniel's relation to his God with the phrase "whom you worship continually," adding here the characterization of Daniel as "servant of the living God." The phrase "living God" is relatively common in other biblical texts, but normally in the mouth of an Israelite, often in contexts of tension between Israelite and Gentile powers or idols (e.g., Josh 3:10; 1 Sam 17:26; 2 Kgs 19:4, 16; Jer 10:10). Here, even though it seems premature for the king to say it, the phrase aptly captures what is at stake: the issue of the effective power of Daniel's God.

[21–23 (22–24)] Daniel's reply to the king reframes the situation not simply as one of salvation from danger but as a judgment. The conspirators had presented the king with a situation in which Daniel was guilty of violating the binding decree issued by the king. Daniel did not deny his actions, and Darius never questioned that he was guilty. Darius merely hoped that Daniel would be spared from punishment. Daniel, however, casts the night in the pit of lions not as a punishment but rather as a judicial ordeal. Psalm 17:3, 15 may refer to an ordeal that takes place at night, from which the psalmist emerges acquitted at dawn.

Figure 16. *Daniel in the Lions' Den* (ca. 1614/16), oil painting by Peter Paul Rubens. Courtesy National Gallery of Art, Washington, DC.

Daniel's words carefully parallel his relationship to God, his relationship to the king, and his own fate: just as he was found "innocent" (*zākû*) with respect to God, he has done no "harm" (*ḥăbûlâ*) with respect to the king. Daniel was in fact guilty of breaking the foolish law, but his actions did not harm the king. Consequently, the lions did not harm him (*ḥabbĕlûnî*). The wordplay demonstrates the logic of the justice of God's judgment, which trumps the foolish law the king decreed, much to the king's delight (v. 23a [24a]).

The mechanism of Daniel's salvation echoes that of the three Jews in Dan 3. An angel sent by God closed the mouths of the lions, much as the figure who looks like a divine being walking with Shadrach, Meshach, and Abednego in the fiery furnace in Dan 3:25 represents God's power to keep them safe. Just as they are seen to have suffered no damage from the fire upon emerging from it (3:27), so also when Daniel is brought up, no harm (*ḥăbāl*) is found on him (6:23d [24d]). Just as the narrator explains here that this was because "he had trusted his God," so Nebuchadnezzar uses a similar phrase to describe the reason for God's deliverance of the three Jews (3:28).

[24 (25)] In contrast to ch. 3, where those who had maligned (lit., "eaten the pieces"; cf. 3:8; 6:24 [25]) the Jews are simply forgotten, here the conspirators receive the punishment they devised for Daniel (cf. Bel and the Dragon). While the punishment of a man's family for his crime is occasionally attested in biblical narratives (e.g., Num 16:27–33; Josh 7:10–26; 2 Sam 21:5–9; Esth 9:13–14), it was not a part of ordinary ancient jurisprudence and was sometimes explicitly forbidden (e.g., Deut 24:16 and its application in 2 Kgs 14:6). Here the action belongs rather to the topos of the king's wrath, which one finds expressed in various extravagant ways (cf. Nebuchadnezzar in Dan 1:10; 2:5, 12; 3:13, 19). Presumably the author is thinking here just of Daniel's two administrative colleagues, not of the entire roster of satraps who joined the conspiracy. Otherwise one would have the improbable spectacle of several hundred people being devoured by lions before they hit the floor.

[25–27 (26–28)] The narrative is brought to an end with the king's praise of God, as also occurs in chs. 2–4. Darius's proclamation is closest to that of Nebuchadnezzar in 4:1–3 (3:31–33) and may well have been constructed from phrases used in the earlier narratives. The address in v. 25 (26) is a verbatim citation of 4:1 (3:31). The introduction of the royal decree also echoes 3:29, though the content of it goes beyond Nebuchadnezzar's intent to punish blasphemy against the God of the Jews. Here Darius makes a positive command that the God of Daniel should be met with "trembling and awe." Although Darius's decree does not mean, as Lebram (83) suggests, that all peoples subject themselves to the laws of Daniel's God, it proclaims the unique power and sovereignty of this God.

In the poetic doxology that constitutes the justification for his decree, Darius first characterizes the nature of God, then the nature of God's sovereignty, and finally the nature of God's acts, focusing on the act that Darius has personally witnessed. The first colon again uses the phrase "living God" (cf. v. 16, 20 [17, 21]), which in biblical discourse distinguishes the God of Israel from the ineffective gods of the nations and especially their representation as lifeless idols (cf. Jer 10, esp. v. 10). The second colon paraphrases 4:3b (3:33b), but it uses a term of particular significance for this narrative, as the expression "indestructible" literally means "cannot be harmed" (*lā' tiṯhabbal*). The third colon (6:27a–b [28a–b]), which describes the "signs and wonders," picks up language from 4:3a (3:33a) but concretizes it with terms used earlier in ch. 6. As Darius had acknowledged in v. 16 (17) that only Daniel's God could save him (*šêzib*), so now he uses that word both to characterize God's actions generally and specifically for God's action in saving Daniel from the power of the lions.

[28 (29)] In the concluding notice, which does not properly belong to the narrative itself, the author alludes back to the notice with which ch. 1 concluded, tying Daniel to the reign of Cyrus, the king who would bring an end to the exile, with which the cycle of Daniel stories began (1:21). This comment, when taken together with the characterization of Darius as the king most well disposed to a Jewish character and the content of his exceptional decree requiring respect and awe for the God of Daniel, serves to give a strong sense of closure to the narrative cycle. The tensions that were introduced have largely been resolved through the iterative but progressive accounts of the confrontation between the Gentile kings and the power of the God of the Jews. A reader finishing ch. 6

would perhaps not expect to turn the page and discover that the book continues for six more chapters. The apocalypses break open this closure and make room for themselves in the book in part by connecting the revelatory visions of Daniel to the transition between kingdoms, dating chs. 7 and 8 to the reign of Belshazzar, ch. 9 to that of Darius, and chs. 10–12 to that of Cyrus. They also exploit the unresolved tension of the revelation to Nebuchadnezzar in ch. 2, which promised an end to the sequence of Gentile kingdoms, an end that the narrative cycle does not depict. (See the introduction for further discussion of the relation of the apocalypses to the narrative cycle.)

History of Reception, by Brennan W. Breed

Survival as Resistance

Early interpreters tended to focus on the exemplary faith of Daniel and the three youths in the fiery furnace as a model of courage under trial; at times, they emphasized the willingness to die for one's beliefs (4 Macc 13:9; 16:3, 21; 18:12–14), and at other times they stressed that God can miraculously save those who faithfully petition (Josephus, *Ant.* 10.257–58). As a result of these motifs of faithful courage and miraculous survival, Daniel was a popular figure in Christian and Jewish art of late antiquity. In the sixth-century-C.E. Palestinian synagogue in Naʿaran (north of Jericho), for example, a mosaic panel with a frontal scene of Daniel standing between two lions with hands raised in the typical position of prayer, often called the orans position, appears on the floor just in front of the shrine that would have held the Torah scroll. While the figural parts of these images were defaced sometime in the medieval period, the inscription "Daniel shalom [peace]" makes clear the subject matter. At the time, the ruling Byzantine Christians were particularly aggressive toward Jews residing in their dominion; the sixth-century emperor Justinian passed legislation that banned all non-Christian houses of worship in North Africa, including synagogues, forbade the reading of the Torah in Hebrew and the reading of the Mishnah, Gemara, and midrashim altogether (Kohen 46). Ironically, poor implementation of these policies allowed for an expansion of synagogue building in Palestine. Amid these hostile state policies that threatened their religious practices, directly before the Torah shrine the Jews of Naʿaran depicted Daniel as persevering and even flourishing in shalom amid Darius's lions (Ovadiah 310). The iconography of Daniel, standing orans between two lions, was borrowed from earlier Christian iconography, but his prayer stance and proximity to the Torah shrine symbolically depicts his prayer toward Jerusalem, whose temple the shrine represents. And during the communal liturgy, the prayer leader would have stood before the Torah shrine, directly over the image of Daniel, and raised his hands in prayer in a similar manner. Thus the prayer leader, and by extension the community, reenacted and enlivened the Daniel story at every prayer service (Fine 187). The Byzantine-era depictions of Daniel on a Torah shrine base from the synagogue at En Samsam in the Golan, as well as the mosaic of Daniel at Susiya in Mount Hebron, likely functioned in a similar manner (Hachlili 80–83).

Early Christians also depicted Daniel in the lions' den as an icon of survival, but clearly emphasized that it foreshadowed individual resurrection rather than the survival of the community. Daniel is shown by many frescoes in numerous catacombs around Rome, usually appearing naked in the frontal orans prayer pose, flanked by lions, surrounded by other images of miraculous deliverance such as the three youths in the furnace, Jonah and the fish, Noah's ark, and Job (Stevenson 80). Daniel's consistent nudity in images from late antique Western Europe likely symbolizes the linked experiences of death and birth, as well as the liturgical practice of baptism, which signifies both the death of the old life and the new life in Christ. Thus the bereaved who visited the body of their loved one would see Daniel in prayer, who adumbrates the inexplicable salvation wrought by the power of God for those in distress. In that context, Daniel offers hope for both the deceased, who yearns for resurrection, and the mourning family, who may not yet see the possibility of forging a new life in the wake of death. Likewise, Daniel appears between lions in orans pose on many early Christian sarcophagi, as do the three youths of Dan 3. Perhaps the most famous example is found on the fourth-century sarcophagus of Junius Bassus, a Christian Roman senator, which depicts eight biblical scenes that highlight themes of trial, sacrifice, and salvation (Malbon 429–30). In the catacombs and on sarcophagi, Daniel is often accompanied by Susanna, a character from a story dating to the second century B.C.E. that developed from the earlier Daniel traditions. The story of Susanna was incorporated into the Old Greek and Theodotionic versions of the book and so was considered canonical by the Eastern Orthodox Churches and deuterocanonical by the Roman Catholic Church. As someone who also survived the threat of death, Susanna's appearance on catacomb walls in the orans pose functioned as a type of the deceased in a manner similar to Daniel (De Wet).

The image of Daniel in the lions' den also appears in early Christian churches, such as the sixth-century floor mosaic from southern Tunisia, now in the Bardo National Museum (in Tunis), which shows Daniel naked in prayer and surrounded by four lions (Bejaoui 96–99). This motif can also be found in fifth-century wall paintings and carvings from Spain to Persia, on reliquaries and other liturgical boxes, and depicted on pottery, oil lamps, seals, crosses, manuscripts, and even belt buckles (Hachlili 80; Friedenberg 58–60; Green 58–62; Travis). Some images include Daniel with the lions in a paradisiacal garden, linking him to the eschatological beatific afterlife, such as the fourth-century casket from Pannonia (Ohm).

Daniel, the three youths, and Susanna are also mentioned in the Commendatio Animae ("commendation of the soul"), an early Christian prayer for the dead that asks for the power of God to deliver the deceased: "Deliver, Lord, the soul of your servant, as you did deliver . . . Daniel from the den of lions, . . . the Three Children from the furnace of burning fire and from the hand of the wicked king, . . . Susanna from the false accusation" (Tkacz 116–17). Images of the various characters mentioned in the Commendatio Animae and direct quotes from the prayer are found engraved on a fourth-century bowl from Montenegro, which may have served a memorializing function (Spier 9–10). References to the Commendatio Animae that mention Daniel in the lions' den are also found on medieval apotropaic amulets (Skemer 257). One double-sided Byzantine metal amulet from thirteenth-century Constantinople, for example, bears an image of Daniel in the lions' den on one side and an image of the archangel Michael on the other (see figs. 17–18). In the Christian East, Daniel was not depicted naked; rather, he always wore his distinctive Persian court garb. On the Constantinople amulet, Daniel looks at the viewer and raises his hand in blessing as the lions lick his feet in subservience. Most Eastern Christians believed that icons opened a channel of communication between the religious figure depicted and the devotee who prayed with the image; thus the amulet was worn around the neck by an individual seeking Daniel and Michael's protection, and it is smooth from years of use (Wixom 94). Daniel owes his life to the vigilance of the angel, here understood to be Michael, who watches guard over his life with a drawn sword and military garb (Pitarakis 178–79).

Christians have also interpreted the story of Daniel and the lions as a typological reference to Jesus Christ. Sometimes interpreters saw this event as a type of Jesus' death and resurrection (Aphrahat, *Demonstrations* 21.18), and other times to his last judgment (Travis 53). In the Annunciation sermon in his famous work *Speculum ecclesiae,* Honorius of Autun sparked a long-lasting interpretive tradition when he suggested that the lions' den prefigured the virgin birth, since the seal of the king was not breached and yet an angel passed through, much as Christ entered Mary's womb without breaking the seal of her virginity. Images depicting this interpretation appear in the facade of the tenth-century Romanesque church of St. Gabriel in Provence, the twelfth-century western façade of the cathedral in Laon, and the twelfth-century illuminated Stammheim Missal (Mezoughi).

Prayer and Survival

In rabbinic exegesis, the story of the lions' den surfaces an existential issue faced by many Jewish communities throughout history: for what is one obligated to sacrifice oneself when being oppressed by Gentile powers? One rabbinic tradition teaches that in normal circumstances, only idolatry, immorality,

Figure 17. Serpentine amulet from Constantinople (thirteenth century C.E.) depicting Daniel in the pit of lions. © The Metropolitan Museum of Art.

and murder require one to let oneself be killed rather than transgress. However, if an oppressor's coercion tries to force a Jew to convert, then one must sacrifice one's life for any custom at all; otherwise one must abandon customs, since the Torah stresses that the Jewish tradition intends to give life (Lev 18:5; Goldwurm 180). Thus Alshich asked, "Why didn't Daniel pray in hiding instead of flouting the king's decree and pray in a place which was visible to all? Isn't this tantamount to endangering one's life?" But Alshich answers: "To prevent our thinking that Daniel was placing himself in danger, the verse [v. 10 (11)] tells us that he did indeed attempt to hide his deeds. Daniel surely prayed daily with a minyan in a synagogue or study hall. However, when Daniel heard of the decree, . . . he chose to pray alone in his home. He had no idea that his enemies were watching his every move" (Alshich 336–37). In a similar manner, Jerome (on 6:11) cautioned that Daniel's private prayer in his own chamber teaches

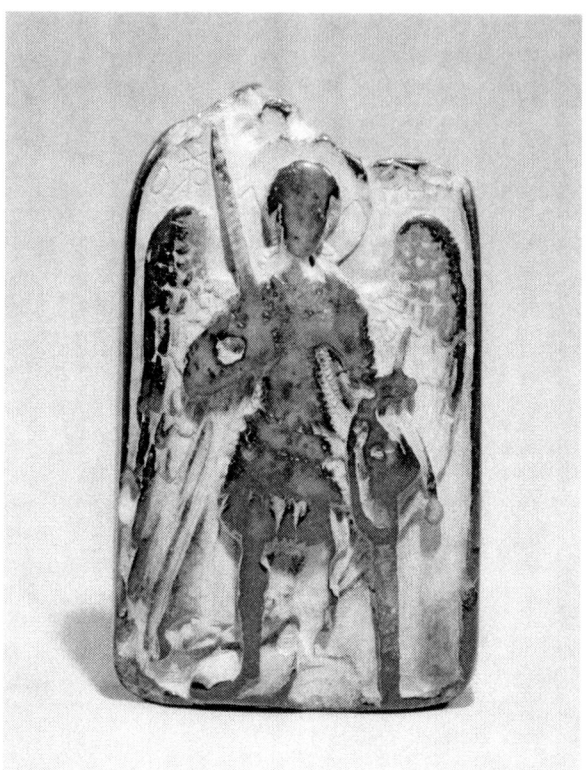

Figure 18. The archangel Michael depicted on the back side of the amulet. © The Metropolitan Museum of Art. Art Resource, New York.

that Christians "are not to expose ourselves rashly to danger, but so far as it lies in our power, we are to avoid the plots of our enemies" in order to stay alive.

Daniel 6 plays a crucial role in the creation and maintenance of the pattern of regular prayers in both Jewish and Christian traditions. Many interpreters used this text along with 1 Kgs 8:46–50 to justify the practice of praying toward Jerusalem (Rambam, *Hilchot Tefillah* 1.5; cf. Jerome, on 6:10), and others used this text as a basis for regulating the architecture of the rooms in which one offers regular prayers, including the existence and position of windows (*b. Ber.* 34b; *Hilchot Tefillah* 5.6). But most importantly, rabbinical interpreters understood Daniel's story as a lesson in the timing and frequency of regular prayers, which, though not a Torah obligation, are nevertheless either a rabbinical or a beneficial practice (*b. Ber.* 31a). While some interpreters take the regular prayers to be a substitute for temple sacrifices that were halted at the time of the exile,

Rambam claims that the postexilic Ezra instituted the official practice of thrice-daily prayer, and thus the exilic Daniel's earlier practice must have merely been his personal habit (*Hilchot Tefillah* 1.5). Others claim that Daniel's thrice-daily prayer was already his custom at the time of the exile (cf. 6:10 [11]), and thus the practice was already widespread at the time (*b. Ber.* 31a).

Christians used this text to justify the practices of fixed-hour prayer in both East and West (Jerome, on 6:10; Theodoret 163). Early fifth-century Roman monastic John Cassian wrote: "In the monasteries of Palestine and Mesopotamia and all the East, the services of the above-mentioned hours are ended each day with three psalms apiece, . . . for at these three seasons we know that Daniel the prophet also poured forth his prayers to God day by day in his chamber with the windows open" (*Institutes* 3.3 [*NPNF*² 11:213]). These prayers were thought to have important effects, as described by Peter Chrysologus, fifth-century bishop of Ravenna: "Daniel's thrice a day prayers are an instruction for us, but also he got his foreknowledge of the future from his prayers, and also merited the freedom of his people held captive for so long" (95).

Resistance through Prayer

Another Danielic story incorporating the motif of the lions' den was incorporated into the Greek versions of the book of Daniel (as ch. 14). This tale, often called Bel and the Dragon but better translated as Bel and the Serpent, dates from around the second century B.C.E. Bel and the Dragon juxtaposes three narratives, the first two of which deal with the issue of idolatry. The third narrative begins when the king hands Daniel over to an enraged mob, who then throw Daniel into a lions' den for six days. An angel in Judah then takes the prophet Habakkuk by the hair and carries him along with his dinner of stew to the lions' den in Babylon. There the starved Daniel eats Habakkuk's meal before Habakkuk miraculously returns to Judah the same way. When the king arrives to mourn Daniel's presumed death, Daniel emerges alive, and the king worships "the God of Daniel." The juxtaposition of Daniel's public attacks on idolatry with his confinement in the lions' den is at odds with Dan 6, in which Daniel finds himself in trouble merely because he privately perseveres in his own practices. The tension between these two versions of the lions' den—either a public attack on the structures of an oppressive majority or a private and non-aggressive refusal to obey authority—can be felt throughout the history of the reception of the book of Daniel.

Some Jews and Christians believed that Daniel desired to be indicted for his rebellious prayers. One talmudic tradition claims that Jews should sacrifice their life for any religious obligation, and some interpreters understand Daniel's righteous example to be his open defiance of Darius's decree (Goldwurm 181). Rashi, for example, interprets the phrase "until sunset" in 6:14 (15) as follows:

"Until sundown he [Darius] made efforts to save him. But when the time came for prayer, Daniel kneeled down to God and prayed. Then the king no longer could open his mouth to save him" (Gallé 66). Thus, according to Rashi, Daniel publicly chose to perform the evening *minḥâ* ("evening") prayer in front of the royal court, at which time Darius's defense collapsed. Likewise, Theodoret of Cyrus claimed that Daniel signaled "piety and courage" by his actions: "When he got news of the passing of the law, he had great scorn for it and continued openly doing the opposite. . . . He said his prayers not in secret but openly, with everyone watching, not for vainglory but in scorn for the impiety of the law" (163). Centuries later, John Calvin claimed that, since "the principal sacrifice which God requires, is to call on his name," Daniel "was obliged to persevere in the holy practice to which he was accustomed, unless he wished to be the very foulest apostate!" (359–60). Calvin's message was doubtless aimed at any early Protestants who hid their religious convictions out of fear.

Many later stories involving the motif of Daniel's visit to the lions' den are meant to provoke resistance against antagonistic authorities. In early Christian culture, martyrs were often described and depicted with domesticated lions as companions because of Daniel's miraculous survival, which was meant to encourage Christians in an environment many perceived to be oppressive. Some were even said to have tamed the lions themselves; in the story of Thecla, she was paraded with a lion and then thrown to the wild animals, only to have a lioness fight the other animals for her (Moss 39; cf. Josephus, *Ant.* 10.257–58). Thecla and Menas—as well as many later Christian saints, such as the Ethiopian Gabra Manfras Qeddus—were depicted in iconography with lions and revered through devotional items that used lion imagery through association with Daniel (Moss 39).

The stories of Daniel and the lions' den have proved to be popular in Islamic traditions, where Daniel's resistance to power also comes to the fore. In the *Stories of the Prophets*, the fourteenth-century scholar Ismāʿīl ibn Kathīr relates a legend similar to the story of Bel and the Dragon. Instead of Habakkuk, however, it is the prophet Jeremiah who miraculously attends to Daniel's hunger, and it is Nebuchadnezzar who throws Daniel in the den but is later foiled (518). Another Muslim story of Daniel, related by al-Tabarī, retells the episode of the lions' den but includes the three youths of Dan 3; the story ends with the angel who had shut the mouths of the lions slapping Nebuchadnezzar, who then "turns into a wild beast for seven years," as in Dan 4 (106–7). And yet another story from al-Tabarī ends with Daniel converting Cyrus to "the faith of the Israelites," which allows him to disburse funds to rebuild the Jerusalem temple (51).

From the early modern period until the present day, Dan 6 has been a crucial text in the discourse of nonviolent resistance (cf. Ladd 554). In the early modern period, Claude Brousson organized coordinated Huguenot nonviolent resistance, including public practice of their religion, in response to violent repressions by King Louis XIV (Utt and Strayer 23–24). In his 1684 publication *Apology for the Project of the French Reformed*, Brousson explained his logic and theological convictions to the general public; he repeatedly used the images of Daniel's prayer and his subsequent experience in the lions' den to explain his use of public worship as an act of resistance (16–17, 112, 291). One can also see Daniel used in more subtle ways to advocate for resistance: one famous African American spiritual asks in the refrain, "Didn't my Lord deliver Daniel, and why not every man?" The image of deliverance in this song signifies spiritual salvation as well as earthly freedom from slavery (Myrdal 993).

And in 1909, after being released from imprisonment in South Africa for refusing to carry official papers, Mahatma Gandhi gave a speech in which he claimed that he had "found much consolation in reading the book of the prophet Daniel" in jail. He learned that "Daniel was one of the greatest passive resisters that ever lived," and thus the Indian people in South Africa "must follow his example.... They must sit with their doors flung wide open and tell those gentlemen [the South African authorities] that whatever laws they passed were not for them unless those laws were from God" (Gandhi 220). Gandhi interprets the verb "open" (*pĕtîḥān*) in Dan 6:10 (11) to be in the active voice, which led to Gandhi's claim that Daniel wanted to flaunt his transgression of the immoral law. Though the verb *pĕtîḥān* is in the passive voice in MT, it is—albeit unbeknownst to Gandhi—active in the OG and Ethiopic versions (Smith-Christopher 1993, 329). And some of Gandhi's contemporaries noted his inspiration from the book of Daniel. One important facet of Gandhi's anti-British boycotts was his advocacy for local production of homespun cloth; Gandhi even developed a portable spinning wheel to encourage all people to join the effort to produce local cloth. In 1930, just after the enormously effective salt marches that led to British decolonization, a German political cartoonist named Erich Schilling, for the Munich-based weekly *Simplicissimus*, shrewdly connected Daniel's prayer resistance with Gandhi's spinning-wheel resistance. Schilling depicted Gandhi with one of his portable spinning wheels, meditating calmly, while a host of lions look on befuddled (Woolever 14).

Some interpreters of Daniel have understood his call to resist to apply to any authority whatsoever who acts unjustly—including God. Elie Wiesel, for example, retells a talmudic conversation about how Daniel uttered a string of adjectives for God that was almost identical to Moses' in Deut 10:17, but which omitted the word "mighty" in his prayer (Dan 9:4; *b. Yom.* 69d). Wiesel connects this omission to Daniel's travails in the lions' den: "The Talmud says, 'Moses said, ... God who is great and heroic and mighty.' Along came Daniel, who declared, Heroic, He? His children are oppressed by strangers—where is his might, his bravery?" Daniel's omission, the sages claim, is meant to question God's might in light of the events of the exile. Wiesel adds, "The greatest among the great dared to take the side of Jews, even against God.... Daniel said, 'If You do not save your people, I will cease to praise you.' The one who had decided to pray, even at the risk of his life, was going to curtail his prayers. ... Is this why Daniel is remembered in our sacred liturgy of the High Holidays? '*Mi sheana le-Daniel begot haarayot*—He who answered Daniel in the lions' den, may He answer our prayers!' But in the text, we find no indication of a divine response! Daniel must have prayed, that is certain—but we are not told that God answered him. We are told only that Daniel survived the danger. Is that God's reply?" (Wiesel 113–14).

Daniel 7–12
The Eschatological Clash
of Sovereignties

Although the book of Daniel as a whole can be characterized as an extended meditation on the relation between divine and human—especially Gentile—sovereignties, the complex development of the book leaves a number of disparate perspectives in unresolved tension. The narrative thrust of chs. 1–6, with its accounts of the education of three quite different monarchs, underwrites a worldview in which the eternal sovereignty of the God of the Jews can be consistent with the temporal exercise of sovereignty by Gentile monarchs, so long as these monarchs can be imagined as recognizing the ultimate sovereignty of the God of the Jews. The violent transfer of sovereignty, as in the end of the story of Belshazzar, is figured as God's judgment on a blasphemous king who is incapable of recognizing that his kingship comes from the Most High God.

While this "political imaginary" served reasonably well during the Persian imperium, it apparently was no longer plausible in the wake of the very violent conquests of Alexander and the even more violent wars among his generals after his death. Consequently, the tradents of the book of Daniel made use of other patterns that could configure the relationship between divine and Gentile sovereignties. The most important of these was the concept of the "transfer of sovereignty," originally developed by the Persians as a means to legitimate their own kingship as succeeding that of the Assyrians and the Medes, but developed by Jews and perhaps other subject peoples as a means of envisioning the end of such transfer of sovereignty among mighty empires (the four-kingdoms model; see comments on ch. 2). This perspective first makes its appearance in the book of Daniel by means of the updating of the narrative of Dan 2 to configure Nebuchadnezzar's dream as one in which the God of the Jews first delegates temporal sovereignty to a sequence of four Gentile kingdoms and then intervenes to bring this sequence to a close and to replace it with an eternal divine kingdom.

The apocalyptic chapters of Dan 7–12 develop this more critical perspective on the Gentile imperium. While most of these chapters (chs. 8–12 and certain verses of ch. 7) are written during the crisis of the Antiochene persecution of 167–164 B.C.E., there is good reason for thinking that the original form of ch. 7 was largely composed not too long after the violent outbreak of the wars between Alexander's successors. This chapter takes up the model presented in

Nebuchadnezzar's dream and reworks it in different symbolic terms, making more explicit the role of divine judgment and the Jewish identity of the eternal kingdom that succeeds Gentile rule.

Perhaps equally important, the tradents of the Daniel tradition change the genre within which to reflect on divine and human sovereignties. The largely comedic narratives of redeemed kings gives way to puzzling apocalypses that shift the focus to an inquiry into the fundamental structures of the historical process. Chapter 8, though clearly alluding to Daniel's dream vision in ch. 7, recasts the symbolism and uses a new pattern by which to understand history— the ironic structure of power being most vulnerable at the point of its apparently most triumphant moment. Chapters 10–12, which show many connections to ch. 8, develop an extraordinarily detailed analysis of the clash of the two major Hellenistic kingdoms, again modeling the telling of history by attempting to discern a hidden pattern of events. Chapter 9 is the most unusual of the apocalypses, both because of its featuring of an extended prayer of penitence (more appropriate to the literary setting of the chapter at the end of the exile than to the time of composition), and because of its use of a schema of liturgical time (weeks and Jubilee periods) to structure and interpret history. What underlies all of the efforts in these different apocalypses, however, is a serious intellectual attempt to use insights into the fundamental structures of reality to understand history and to predict the future.

Daniel 7 Revisiting the End of Divine Delegation of Sovereignty in a New Context

1 In the first year of Belshazzar,[a] King of Babylon, Daniel had a dream— visions in his head while he was in bed. Then he wrote down the dream. The beginning of the account:[b]

2 Daniel said, "In my vision in the night I was watching, when suddenly, the four winds of heaven were stirring up the great sea. 3 And four immense beasts were coming up from the sea, each different from the other. 4 The first was like a lion, but it had the wings of an eagle. I kept watching until its wings were plucked off, and it was lifted up from the ground and made to stand upon two feet like a human. And a human mind was given to it. 5 Then suddenly, another beast, a second one, resembling a bear. It was raised up on one side, and three ribs[c] were in its mouth between its teeth. And thus it was commanded: 'Arise! Eat much meat!' 6 After this, I kept watching, and suddenly another one, like a leopard. But it had four bird's wings upon its sides, and the beast had four heads. Dominion was given to it. 7 After this, I kept watching in visions of the night, and suddenly, a fourth beast, dreadful and terrifying, and exceedingly strong. It had enormous iron teeth. It was devouring and crushing—

and the remains it was trampling with its feet. It was different from every beast that preceded it. And it had ten horns. 8 I was contemplating the horns when suddenly another, small horn came up[d] among them. Three of the previous horns were uprooted before it. And there were eyes like human eyes in that horn, and a mouth speaking arrogantly.

> 9 I kept watching until
> thrones were set up,
> and one Ancient of Days took his seat.
> His clothing was like white snow,
> and the hair of his head like lamb's wool.[e]
> His throne was flames of fire,
> and its wheels blazing fire.
> 10 A river of fire was flowing
> and streaming out from before him.
> A thousand thousands served him,
> and ten thousand times ten thousand stood before him.
> The court was seated
> And books were opened.

11 I kept watching then,[f] from the time of the utterance of the arrogant words that the horn was speaking. I kept watching until the beast was killed, and its body destroyed, and it was consigned to the consuming fire. 12 As for the rest of the beasts, their dominion was taken away, but length of life was given to them for a time and a season.

> 13 I kept watching in visions of the night,
> and suddenly, with the clouds of heaven,
> one in the likeness of a human was coming.
> He approached the Ancient of Days,
> and he was presented before him.
> 14 To him was given dominion and glory and sovereignty,
> and all peoples and nations and tongues must serve him.
> His dominion is an everlasting dominion that will not pass away,
> and his kingdom one that cannot be destroyed.

15 As for me, Daniel, my spirit was distressed within me,[g] and the visions of my head disturbed me. 16 I approached one of those who stood in attendance, and I asked him about the truth of all this. He told me that he would explain the meaning of these things to me. 17 'These immense beasts, which are four in number: four kings[h] will arise from the earth. 18 But the holy ones of the Most High[i] will receive the kingdom forever, and forever and ever.' 19 Then I wanted to have certainty concerning the fourth beast, which was different from all the rest of them—exceedingly

frightful, with iron teeth and bronze claws, devouring and smashing, and trampling the remains with its feet. 20 And I wanted certainty concerning the ten horns that were on its head, and the other one that came up and before which three fell.[j] That horn had eyes and a mouth speaking arrogantly, and its appearance was greater than its companions. 21 I kept watching, and that horn made war on the holy ones, and it prevailed against them 22 until the Ancient of Days came and judgment was given for the holy ones of the Most High. The time had arrived, and the holy ones took possession of the kingdom.

23 Thus he said: 'As for the fourth beast—a fourth kingdom shall be on the earth that will be different from all other kingdoms. It will devour all the earth, and it will trample it and crush it. 24 And as for the ten horns— from that kingdom ten kings will arise, and another will arise after them. He will be different from the ones preceding him, and three kings he will bring low. 25 He will speak words against the Most High, and he will wear out the holy ones of the Most High. He will intend to change the times set by decree, and they will be given into his power, for a time and times and half a time. 26 But the court will sit, and his sovereignty will be taken away, to be utterly annihilated and destroyed. 27 Then the kingdom and the dominion and the grandeur of the kingdoms under all of heaven will be given to the people of the holy ones of the Most High. Its kingdom will be an eternal kingdom, and all the dominions will serve and obey it.'"

28 Here is the end of the account. As for me, Daniel, my thoughts disturbed me greatly, so that my face grew pale. But I kept the matter to myself.

a. Here is *bēl'šaṣṣ'ar*, as also in 8:1. Spelled *bēlša'ṣṣar* in ch. 5, except in v. 30.

b. Omit *'ămar*. The Greek versions omit one or both of the introductory phrases here and in v. 2.

c. *'il'în*. Hartman and DiLella (205) argue for the meaning "fangs." The evidence, however, is insufficient.

d. *silqāt*. A mixed form which should be corrected either to a participle or to a third-person fem. sg. perfect. The perfect occurs in v. 20.

e. *nĕqē'*. While the traditional translation "pure wool" is possible, "lamb's wool" is better attested in Aram. dialects. See Sokoloff.

f. *ḥāzēh hăwêt bē'dayin*. Normally, *bē'dayin* occurs at the beginning of a sentence, but cf. 1QapGen (1Q20) 22.2 and the analogous construction in Ezra 5:16 (Goldingay 145; Montgomery 302). Also, the repetition of "I kept watching" in v. 11b is unusual, and the Greek versions have only one occurrence. The repetition may indicate a redactional seam. See comments on v. 11.

g. *bĕgô' nidneh*. Repoint the noun to *nidnāh* with a feminine 3d sg. sf. Literally, "within its sheath," i.e., body. 1QapGen 2.10 provides attestation for the meaning, rendering emendation unnecessary.

Revisiting the End of Divine Delegation of Sovereignty in a New Context

h. The OG, Th, and the Vg all read "kingdoms," though that may be an interpretive translation. John Collins (275), however, notes that in Aramaic script *mlkyn* ("kings") could easily be confused with *mlkwn* ("kingdoms").

i. *qaddîšê ʿelyônîn*. The *nomen rectum* (absolute form) is most likely a plural of majesty, with *ʿelyôn* as a Hebraizing equivalent of Aram. *ʿillāyāʾ*. So Montgomery 307; J. Collins 312; contra Goldingay 146.

j. This sentence fragment logically depends on "Then I wanted to have certainty..." in v. 19. Verse 20 may be a redactional addition. See comments thereon.

Overview

A reader, working sequentially through the book of Daniel, would find several things to give pause as this chapter unfolds. The dating of the event recalled does not follow chronologically from the date of ch. 6, set during the early years of the reign of Darius the Mede, but rather doubles back to the first year of Belshazzar's reign. Such a date would locate the account in ch. 7 chronologically between chs. 4 and 5. Formally, too, the chapter no longer recounts a court tale but is structured entirely as a first-person symbolic dream report by Daniel himself. The content of the vision, with its account of four human kingdoms succeeded by a fifth eternal kingdom, is strongly evocative of ch. 2. Like the narratives in chs. 2–6, here ch. 7 is in Aramaic. Following ch. 7, however, are five chapters in Hebrew, recording three further apocalyptic visions revealed to Daniel. Any account of the peculiarities of ch. 7 must attend not only to issues of the growth and development of the book of Daniel over time, but also to the effect of the sequence of chapters as they are presented in the final form of the book.

Date, Provenance, Structure, and Outline

Widespread agreement exists that the narrative cycle of Dan 1–6 circulated as a coherent collection before the composition of ch. 7 and the following apocalypses (see discussion in the introduction). When, where, and for what purpose ch. 7 was composed, however, remains a matter of dispute. The final form of the chapter clearly assumes the context of the persecutions of Antiochus IV Epiphanes (in 167–164 B.C.E.). What is sharply disputed, however, is whether ch. 7 was originally composed earlier than the Antiochene crisis to articulate resistance against the new empire of the Greeks and then later updated to address the Antiochene persecutions (so Sellin 233–34; Hölscher 119–21; Noth 1926, 145–47; et al.), or whether it was only composed in that later time period (so Montgomery 94–96; Plöger 106–7; J. Collins 278–80; Goldingay 156–57; et al.). Arguments about redactional development of texts where no independent evidence exists are of necessity somewhat circular and are never conclusive.

Even so, a persuasive case exists for positing a two-stage development of ch. 7, even if the details remain contestable.

The primary puzzle is that, like the core of the narrative cycle (chs. 2–6), Dan 7 is composed in Aramaic; but like the chapters that follow, it is form-critically an apocalypse. What is often overlooked, however, is that the focus of the eschatological expectations of ch. 7 differentiate it from the following apocalypses. Like ch. 2 but unlike chs. 8–12, here Dan 7 is focused on the expectation of an eternal dominion by the earthly representatives of the Most High God. The concerns and expectations of chs. 8–12, by contrast, have to do with the fate of the temple and its sacrifices and the fate of "the wise" (*maśkîlîm*). Political dominion by Israel as a representative of God's sovereignty on earth is no longer a topic in chs. 8–12. Moreover, within ch. 7 the phrases and passages concerning the horns, and in particular the little horn, strike many readers as intrusive and disruptive. These considerations, taken together, make it plausible that ch. 7 was originally composed as an eschatological complement to the cycle of Daniel narratives in chs. 1–6, perhaps as early as the late fourth or early third century B.C.E., as a response to the violent wars of Alexander the Great's successors, the Diadochi. Although commentators often assume that the place of composition was Judea and often date the apocalypse to the time of Antiochus III (cf. Lebram 21, 84; Albertz 2001, 188–90), the Eastern Diaspora is equally if not more plausible. Hostility to Alexander and the Macedonians is evident in contemporary Babylonian texts such as the *Dynastic Prophecy* (Sherwin-White and Kuhrt 8). Antigonus in particular treated Babylonia as enemy territory (311–308 B.C.E.; see the *Babylonian Diadochi Chronicle*; Grayson 26, 118). As Sherwin-White and Kuhrt observe, "The impact of the army on territories newly subjugated, or in the process of being conquered, was horrendous and brutal; . . . pillage, destruction, mass enslavement were the norms of war" (58–59). Given the likely composition of Dan 1–6 in the Eastern Diaspora, it is quite plausible to envision the composition of Dan 7 as a response to these events by Babylonian Jews parallel to that of their Babylonian counterparts who composed the *Dynastic Prophecy*. As an anti-Seleucid text, proto-Dan 7 subsequently provided an attractive locus for updating and reapplication in response to the persecutions of Antiochus in 167–164 B.C.E. This updated text is the version preserved in MT.

Even among scholars who assume a two-stage composition for Dan 7, disagreement exists as to the particular elements that are secondary (see Koch, Niewisch, and Turbach 68–71). The following, however, may be suggested as the simplest model of base text and secondary elements:

Introduction (7:1–2a)
Account of the dream vision (7:2b–14)
    The four beasts (7:2b–7e)
    [*Antiochene addition: Horns (7:7f–8)*]

The court convenes (7:9–10)
The court's judgment on the beasts (7:11–12)
[*Antiochene addition: Horn speaking (7:11b)*]
The humanlike one and the transfer of sovereignty (7:13–14)
Narrative bridge: Request for interpretation (7:15–16)
Interpretation of the four beasts (7:17–18)
Inquiry about the fourth beast (7:19)
[*Antiochene addition: About the horns (7:20–22)*]
Interpretation of the fourth beast (7:23)
[*Antiochene addition: Interpretation of the horns (7:24–25)*]
Judgment of the fourth beast (7:26)
Sovereignty for the people of the holy ones of the Most High (7:27)
Conclusion (7:28)

Literary and Traditio-Historical Features

Form-critically, the composition is a report of a dream vision with the typical structure of such reports: (1) indication of a vision (vv. 1–2a); (2) description (vv. 2b–14); (3) request for interpretation (vv. 15–16, 19–22); (4) interpretation (vv. 17–18, 23–27); and (5) conclusion (v. 28) (cf. Niditch 1983, 184). The pattern is similar to that found in the visions of Zech 1–8.

The source and nature of the symbolism used in the chapter has evoked considerable discussion. With the recovery of ancient Near Eastern texts from Mesopotamia and Ugarit during the late nineteenth and early twentieth centuries, scholars noticed mythic overtones in the symbolism in Dan 7, first comparing aspects of it to the Babylonian creation epic, the *Enuma Elish*, which records the battle of the god Marduk with the chaotic sea, Tiamat, and the monstrous beings that come from her (see Gunkel 205–13; Lambert 50–133). With the discovery of the cycle of Baal myths from Ugarit, however, scholars claimed to see a more striking similarity between that mythic pattern and the figures and events in Dan 7 (Emerton 1958; Day 280–94). In the Baal myth, the Sea (Yam) is the first of two enemies who threaten Baal, and with him, the security of the world. When Baal, often described as the Rider of the Clouds, offers to defeat Sea, he is acclaimed by the craftsman god Kothar-wa-Ḥasis: "Now, your enemy, Baal, now you will kill your enemy, now you will annihilate your foe. You will take your eternal kingship, your dominion forever and ever" (*CTU* 1.2 IV 9–10; trans. follows Coogan and Smith). The aged god El, who is called *ab šnm* (*ʾabu šanima*), commonly understood as Father of Years, is the deity who grants kingship, though no scene involving Baal's appointment is preserved, and El actually appears resistant to Baal's appointment. Nevertheless, the similarities with Dan 7 are suggestive, including the figures of the older and younger divine figures, their epithets, and the theme of kingship.

One of the problems faced by scholars who champion the influence of the mythic pattern on the composition of Dan 7, however, is to account for how the author of this text from the Hellenistic period could have known the outlines of a myth attested only in second-millennium-B.C.E. sources. Attempts have been made to demonstrate the vitality of the (weather god) Baal-Hadad cult even into the Hellenistic period (Kearns 3:46–57), though no accounts of this myth are known from that period. Others have suggested that the mythic pattern was preserved in Israelite religious thought in the royal psalms, which make use of some of these motifs while presenting the Davidic line as the representative of YHWH's sovereignty on earth (see Ps 89:9–10 [10–11]). In this view, Dan 7 would be a remythologization of this tradition in an apocalyptic context (so Mosca). One can also argue that, even though the mechanism for the transmission of the myth can no longer be identified, the similarities are themselves evidence that the mythic pattern influenced the author of Dan 7, whether consciously or unconsciously (J. Collins 294).

Skeptics of this interpretation have pointed out that there are significant elements in Dan 7 that have no parallel in the Ugaritic myths: the sequence of four kingdoms represented as monstrous animals, the defeat of the hostile forces through a court judgment rather than through battle, and the nonparticipatory role of the humanlike figure coming with the clouds until he is granted sovereignty. No one suggests that the mythic pattern was taken over as a whole, but rather that it was creatively adapted to the needs of the author of Dan 7. Nevertheless, the discrepancies are sufficient to raise doubts as to whether or not a mythic *pattern*, as opposed to common mythic *elements*, has in fact played a role in structuring the vision (Newsom 2014a).

Methodologically, one needs to distinguish between what one might call a compositional or authorial intertextuality on the one hand and intertextual connections made by a reader on the other hand. In the case of Dan 7, a modern scholar, steeped in comparative ancient Near Eastern mythology, may be primed to recognize similarities with the Baal myth, and more distantly with *Enuma Elish*, because these texts loom large in modern scholars' sets of mental reference texts. But that is not evidence that these were actually constitutive elements in the composition of Dan 7.

While it is difficult to demonstrate conclusively how an author goes about creating a text from existing cultural materials, it is important to begin by cataloging the most clearly attested connections, those for which intentional use is most likely. When those have been identified, then one can better judge whether influence of the Baal myth is needed to account for the narrative pattern and thematic elements of Dan 7. Obviously, the author of Dan 7 draws explicitly on the schema from ch. 2 of four Gentile kingdoms succeeded by a fifth kingdom that manifests divine sovereignty. Equally evident is the use of a court judgment scene, variously attested via the Enoch tradition in the Book of the Watchers

(*1 En.* 14:18–23), the *Book of the Giants* (4Q530), and the Animal Apocalypse (*1 En.* 90:20; see below for an analysis of the relationships of these texts and traditions).

After accounting for the contribution of these stock elements, what remains? First, the image of the sea stirred up by winds. The sea as a figure of chaos belongs to the common ancient Near Eastern mythic repertoire. Its presence does not evoke the Baal myth per se. Moreover, in Dan 7 the mythic pattern of a battle with the sea is *not* represented. The sea is presented as acted upon by the winds rather than being a personified, autonomous agent. The final element to be accounted for is the description of the humanlike one as "coming with the clouds" and receiving sovereignty from the Ancient of Days. Though movement with the clouds is a characteristic of divine beings and is associated with both YHWH (Isa 19:1; cf. Deut 33:26; Pss 68:33 [34]; 104:3) and Baal (*CTU* 1.2 IV 8, 29; etc.), angels within the book of Daniel are elsewhere described in terms drawn from the descriptions of God (cf. 10:5–6). Such *elohization* of angels is also strongly present in certain Qumran literature as well, including *Melchizedek* (11Q13) and the *Songs of the Sabbath Sacrifice* (4Q400–407; 11Q17; Mas1k). The phrase in Daniel does not necessarily point back to a distinctively "Baal-shaped" role for the humanlike one. As for receiving sovereignty, there is similarly no need to invoke Baal mythology.

The basic issue with which this chapter is concerned, as with the dream in ch. 2, is God's decision to delegate universal sovereignty to Gentile empires for a period of time and then to take back that sovereignty. The notion of delegated Gentile sovereignty is variously expressed in a number of exilic and postexilic texts (such as Jer 27:5–7; Isa 45:1–9; 2 Chr 36:22–23; Ezra 1:1–4) and informs the political theology of Dan 1–6 (esp. 2:38; 4:29–34). In conceptualizing the end of the delegated Gentile imperium, Dan 2 uses imagery of inanimate objects to suggest the contrast between the nature of the Gentile kingdoms and the eschatological one: a statue and a rock that crushes it and becomes a mountain. But in Dan 7, the use of monstrous beasts from the sea to represent the Gentile empires naturally invites the development of contrasting imagery: a humanlike figure from the heavens (i.e., an angel) to whom the delegated sovereignty can be entrusted. The angel serves as a heavenly counterpart to the kingdom of Israel on earth (v. 27).

While the author of Dan 7 need not have been dependent on any external model, it is possible that the overall dynamics of Dan 7 are informed by the ideology of Davidic kingship, such as one finds it in Ps 2. In that psalm "kings of the earth" attempt to act autonomously ("Let us break the cords of their yoke," vv. 2–3 NJPS) and are confronted by the enthroned Lord (v. 4), who announces the installation of "my king on Zion, my holy mountain" (vv. 5–7 NJPS). Though the kings are threatened with possible destruction (v. 9), they are finally admonished to serve in fear (v. 11), which is similar to the role of "all the dominions" in Dan 7:27 (cf. 7:12), which are to "serve and obey" "the people of the holy ones" to whom God has given sovereignty as the earthly counterpart to the reign of the holy ones in heaven. Thus the dynamics of Davidic kingship might be deflected upward as a model for the angelic kingship envisioned in Dan 7. But there is no need to invoke influence from the Ugaritic Baal myth, especially in light of the numerous, marked differences between the Baal myth and Dan 7.

Comments

[1–2a] Why the vision should be dated to the first year of King Belshazzar is not entirely clear. Since Daniel's dream vision is a recasting of Nebuchadnezzar's dream in Dan 2, dated to the second year of his kingship, one might have expected that this vision report would be dated to a later year in the same king's reign. Belshazzar's first year, however, marks a regnal transition, and such a time may be symbolically suited for a vision report that looks forward to the ultimate transfer of sovereignty. Moreover, Belshazzar is the only king in the narrative cycle who is destroyed for his arrogant impiety by the command of God. Thus his own narrative foreshadows the judgment enacted against the fourth beast in ch. 7.

Daniel's experience is referred to in v. 1 both as a "dream" (*ḥēlem*) and a "mental vision," literally, "visions of his head" (*ḥezwê rēʾšēh*; cf. 2:28). Since certain visions involved a sense of spiritual transportation (e.g., Ezek 8:3; 11:24; 37:1; 40:1–2; *1 En.* 14:8), it is possible that the phrase "visions of the head" designates visions in which the recipient sees images but is not transported. But even though Daniel does not describe an experience of transportation, he does appear to be in the heavenly court.

Writing down a prophecy is already attested in the prophetic books (e.g., Isa 8:16; 30:8; Jer 30:2; Hab 2:2), where it serves as a future witness to the reliability of what has been announced. In apocalyptic books, the writing down of visionary experiences is common and similarly serves to preserve the revelation for future readers (Dan 12:4, 9; cf. *2 Esd* 14:42; *1 En.* 81:6; 82:1; *T. Mos.* 1:16; Rev 21:5). Although the expression *rēʾš millîn* (lit., "head of the words") resembles the phrase *rōʾš-dĕbārĕkā* ("the 'head' or 'sum' or 'essence' of your word"; Ps 119:160 AT), the corresponding phrase in v. 28, "here is the end of the account" (*ʿad-kâ sôpāʾ dî-millĕtāʾ*), suggests rather that the expressions mark the beginning and the end of the account (cf. Oppenheim 2008, 187).

[2b] The phrase "I kept watching" occurs eight times in this chapter (vv. 4, 6, 7, 9, 11, 13, 21), introducing critical elements in the dream. The interjection *ʾărû/ʾălû* (here translated "suddenly") often accompanies the phrase (vv. 6, 7, 13), though it may also occur on its own (vv. 5, 8). Compare the similar use of *rāʾâ* plus *hinnēh* to introduce visionary accounts in Zech 1:8; 2:1, 5; 5:1; 6:1.

The account mimics the actual dynamism of a dream in which different images succeed one another in rapid succession.

The symbolism in the dream is rich and evocative, but also tinged with ambiguity. Much of the scholarly argument as to whether the symbol of the sea and the winds means this *or* that misses the genuine polyvalence of powerful imagery and the strategic nature of the ambiguity. At least since Gunkel, the majority of interpreters have understood the sea in v. 2 to represent the cosmic sea that figures as the opponent of the creator god in many ancient Near Eastern mythic traditions (e.g., *Enuma Elish*; the Baal Cycle; Isa 51:9–11). Although the term "the great sea" can be used to refer to the Mediterranean (e.g., Josh 1:4), here the cosmic resonances are clear. Ambiguity enters the picture with the symbol of the four winds of heaven and the nature of their activity, "stirring up" the great sea. The contrast terms "heaven" and "sea" certainly seem to point to the background of a cosmic conflict. However, Montgomery's suggestion (285), that the winds are the *product* of the sea, as "hurricanes and mighty tempests" spawned by Chaos, seems unlikely.

The designation of "four" winds probably signifies totality, since elsewhere in Daniel the four winds seem to refer to the four points of the compass (8:8; 11:4; cf. Zech 2:6 [10]; 6:5). Certainly the four winds (Jer 49:36) or a particular wind (Exod 14:21; 15:8) may be used as a weapon of YHWH (cf. Marduk's use of four winds as weapons against Tiamat), and hence many readers understand the imagery to evoke cosmic battle (J. Collins 294; Bauer 141). Theodotion's translation explicitly takes it in that fashion ("the four winds kept assaulting the great sea"). But the Aramaic participle *měgîḥān* complicates matters. The sea is not represented as *itself* roiling or surging in an aggressive fashion. Here the sea is being *acted upon* by the winds. This leads some commentators to recognize an allusion to Gen 1:2, in which a divine wind sweeps over the surface of the cosmic waters as the first activity of creation (Burnier-Genton 150–60; Koch 2000, 46–49; Hartman and DiLella 211; Goldingay 160).

The full meaning of the imagery can only be grasped if one hears both elements—sovereign creation and conflict—in play at the same time. What will emerge from the sea is the political history of the four Gentile kingdoms. The echo of Gen 1:2 connotes that this process is part of God's creative control of historical as well as of cosmic processes. But the more distant echo of the chaotic sea and of the combat myth indicates that there is something inherently unruly and dangerous in the Gentile kingdoms, which will ultimately have to be dealt with by force. This imagery articulates the classic apocalyptic response to the mystery of evil. It is understood as never fully autonomous but as playing a designated role in a divine drama, a drama that leads to evil's ultimate destruction and elimination.

[3–7] The next section describes the four monstrous beasts that rise from the sea: one like a lion, one like a bear, one like a leopard, and one described as "different." The background for the imagery is obscure. Israelite mythic tradition knows of sea monsters like Leviathan, Rahab, and the *tannînîm*, which may either be envisioned as sea animals (Gen 1:21; Ps 104:26; Job 41 [40:25–41:26]) or as figures engaged in a cosmogonic struggle with YHWH (Isa 27:1; 51:9–10; Pss 74:13–14; 89:10 [11]). But they bear no similarities to the beasts of Dan 7 other than being associated with the sea. In the *Enuma Elish*, however, Tiamat prepares for battle with the gods by creating an army of monstrous beings:

> Mother Hubur, who forms everything, supplied irresistible weapons, and gave birth to giant serpents. . . . She created the Hydra, the Dragon, the Hairy Hero, the Great Demon, the Savage Dog and the Scorpion-man, fierce demons, the Fish-man, and the Mighty Bull, carriers of merciless weapons, fearless in the face of battle. (2.19–20, 27–30; trans. Lambert).

Many of these creatures combine elements of different animals and so bear some resemblance to the creatures in Daniel's vision. Especially if one considers an Eastern Diaspora origin for Dan 7, then perhaps the Mesopotamian motif of the army of monstrous beasts was known to the author.

The problem with this comparison, however, is that the monstrous beasts in Dan 7, even though they are ultimately judged, do *not* engage in a cosmogonic battle with God. Rather, they are subject to certain actions and authorized to do certain things—except for the fourth beast, which appears to act autonomously. As with the reference to the winds and the sea in v. 2, the author is blending two conceptions. The myth of cosmogonic struggle is very generally evoked through the association of the monstrous beasts with the sea. This evocation serves both to give a negative characterization to the beasts and to anticipate their ultimate demise. But the author overwrites the mythic plot of battle and defeat with a schema of political historiography, which describes the divine plan for the succession of imperial kingdoms until they are displaced by the eternal divine kingdom. The two plots will be coordinated again at the end (v. 11) with the destruction of the body of the fourth beast and the award of eternal sovereignty to the humanlike figure. The blended narrative shifts the interest from the cosmogonic conflict itself to the plan of God for the history of the world (cf. Haag 1993, 163).

There still remains the problem of accounting for the specific animals named in the vision. Although ingenious attempts have been made to associate the lion, bear, and leopard with elements of Babylonian astral geography (Caquot) or with Babylonian omens concerning monstrous births (Porter), these are largely unconvincing. While ancient Near Eastern art exhibits a variety of composite creatures, there are no close parallels to the types in Dan 7 (Keel 2000, 8–14). Composite animals are a feature of the imagination in many cultures since such monstrous figures connote supernatural power, whether for good or ill. Probably the motivation for the particular animals named in Dan 7 can be found in intrabiblical allusions. Often cited is Hos 13:7–8, which compares YHWH's own violence against Israel to the threats posed by a lion (*šaḥal*), a leopard (*nāmēr*), a bear (*dōb*), a lion (*lābîʾ*), and an unnamed animal (*ḥayyat haśśādeh*). This intertextual echo again suggests that the events of history are in some way expressions of YHWH's intentionality.

There may be similar intertextual motivation to associate Babylon with the lion sporting eagles' wings, since these are both considered the noblest animals in their domains and the first kingdom here corresponds to the "head of gold" in Dan 2 (so J. Collins 297). Moreover, Babylon is compared to both animals in prophetic poetry (lion: Jer 4:7; 50:17; eagle: Ezek 17:3; Hab 1:8). There seems no particular reason for associating the other beasts with specific kingdoms.

More significant than the individual identifications is the pattern. The first and the third beasts are both felines with bird wings, the first (lion-eagle) being more noble and powerful than the third (leopard-bird). The text associates both with positive characteristics (human mind, dominion). The second and fourth beasts are both associated with violence that focuses on the mouth (ribs or fangs between the teeth, iron teeth that devour), though the fourth also tramples its food with its feet. Whether this pattern reflects specific judgments about the four kingdoms is difficult to say. In the Daniel tradition, the Babylonian Nebuchadnezzar is represented as a redeemed king authorized by YHWH to rule (Dan 2:37–38; 4:1–3 [3:31–33]; 5:18–22). In biblical tradition, Cyrus is authorized by the God of Israel (Isa 44:24–45:8; Ezra 1:1–4), and the later Persian kings are positively represented (Ezra 6:1–12; Neh 2:1–8). Although Darius the Mede appears as an amiable fellow in Dan 6, the Medes as a nation are represented primarily as violent (Isa 13:17; Jer 51:11, 28), though to be sure, they do not figure often in biblical texts. In Dan 2 and 7, Greece, the fourth kingdom, is distinguished by its excessive violence (2:40; 7:7, 19).

[4] Although some commentators have suggested that the plucking of the wings disempowers the first beast (J. Collins 297; Smith-Christopher 102), it is more likely part of the humanization process that the rest of the verse describes (Goldingay 161–62; Plöger 104). The passive voice obscures the agent who does these things to the beast. While that technique adds to the mysteriousness of the dream, there is no doubt that this is the divine passive and that God is the ultimate agent who authorizes and controls the beasts. The reference to a "human mind" is an allusion to the narrative in ch. 4, in which Nebuchadnezzar's reason was restored after his period of madness. Here, however, no mention is made of the king's humiliation, only of his being made more like a human. Given the basic symbolic contrast of Dan 7 between beasts (Gentile imperiums) and one like a human (divine imperium), the humanization of the first beast is a startlingly positive image. It is, however, in keeping with the treatment of Nebuchadnezzar in the narratives (2:37–38; 4:33–34). The emphasis on the positive aspects of the first beast serves to enhance the contrast with the fourth.

[5] The imagery of the bear is obscure in two related respects. It is said to be "raised up on one side," though it is not clear whether one should take this phrase to mean that it has one front paw lifted, with its weight on the opposite side of its body, or if it has reared up on its hind legs. In either case the posture appears to be threatening. (For a survey of other less likely interpretations of the phrase, see Goldingay 162.) In biblical tradition bears were particularly associated with ferocity and often paired with lions (1 Sam 17:34–37; 2 Sam 17:8; 2 Kgs 2:24; Hos 13:8; Amos 5:19; Prov 28:15; Lam 3:10). The second obscurity concerns the translation of the word ʿilʿin. It is the common word for "ribs," in which case the bear already has dismembered prey in its mouth. Thus the posture and behavior of the bear is an enactment of the command that is given to it to "Arise! Eat much meat!" Attempts to identity specific historical entities represented by the three ribs (of which there have been many) are inconclusive. Probably the detail is simply meant to contribute to the general image of a voracious creature. Less likely, but to be given serious consideration, is the translation of the word as "fangs." Already reflected in the Vulgate (*tres ordines erant in ore eius*), the reading was also championed by Saadiah, apparently on the basis of metaphorical meanings of the Arabic cognate ḍlʿ, though there is no independent evidence of this metaphorical usage in Aramaic (Frank). The redundancy of "in its mouth, between its teeth" might be taken as a clarifying gloss for an obscure usage of the word. If that is the correct understanding of the image, then the second and the fourth beasts are similar not just with respect to their violence, but more specifically by means of the figure of terrifying teeth.

[6] The third beast, like the first, is a feline with wings, in this case a leopard with the wings of a bird. In the Bible leopards are, not surprisingly, noted for their speed (Hab 1:8) and their predation (Isa 11:6; Jer 5:6; Hos 13:7). The distinctive feature of this beast is its association with the number four (four wings, four heads). Although some commentators have suggested an allusion to the four Persian kings known to biblical tradition (e.g., Hartman and DiLella 213), the number four here, as in v. 2, more likely connotes universality (so most commentators). This interpretation is supported by the close relation of this vision to that of ch. 2, where the third kingdom is said to "rule over the whole earth" (*tišlaṭ bĕkol-ʾarʿāʾ* [2:39]). Here the third beast is explicitly given "dominion" (*šolṭān*).

[7a–e] As in Dan 2, the vision reaches its climax with the fourth kingdom. There attention was given to the "divided" nature of the fourth kingdom, suggesting that it referred to the two major successors to Alexander's kingdom, the Ptolemaic and Seleucid dynasties. In ch. 7, however, the fourth beast appears to be more specifically identified with the Seleucid kingdom. In contrast to the other beasts, the fourth one is not said to resemble a particular animal but is introduced through a chain of three adjectives describing its fearsomeness and power and summarized by the comment that it was "different" from the others. The details of the description focus on two aspects of the beast. First are its great iron teeth (*šinnayin dî-parzel*) that eat and crush (*maddĕqâ*), apparently an interpretation of the detail of the fourth kingdom in 2:40 as strong like iron that crushes (*parzĕlāʾ mĕhaddēq*). It is also, however, said to trample the remains with its feet, leading a number of interpreters to speculate that the much-feared Seleucid war elephants are the inspiration for this creature (Staub; Bauer 151–53; Goldingay 163). If so, then the (dual) "great teeth" may refer to the two tusks. An elephant would be rightly described as different from the traditional fearsome animals that form the basis for the other creatures. What is most important in the description, however, is the shift from the divine control over the first three beasts, represented through the use of the divine passive and direct command—and the fact that this different beast acts autonomously, signified by active verbs: eating and crushing and trampling.

[7f–8] The final statement in v. 7 is the notice "and it had ten horns." Although this comment may be part of the original description of the fourth beast, the fact that it is not included with the other details of the beast's appearance but occurs only after the summarizing comment about the beast being different suggests that it is the beginning of the interpolation that updates the vision to address the situation under Antiochus IV Epiphanes. In either case, what do the horns represent? Horns are a common figure for royal power in the Bible (e.g., Ezek 29:21; Zech 1:18 [2:1]; Ps 132:17) and elsewhere in the ancient Near East, the earliest attestation being the Mesopotamian horned crown that is worn by deities and adopted by Naram-Sin in the famous victory stele from the third millennium B.C.E. (*ANEP* #309). The early Seleucid kings were particularly fond of the motif, and on their coinage both Seleucus I and Antiochus I depicted themselves as wearing bulls' horns (Morenz; Staub 54–69). Thus it would be a fitting image, but not an image necessarily drawn from Seleucid iconography.

The details associated with the "little horn" throughout ch. 7—its blasphemy and arrogance, its war against the holy ones, and its attempt to change "the times set by decree"—point to Antiochus IV Epiphanes and the persecutions of 167–164 B.C.E. (Rowley 1935, 120–21). That being the case, ingenious attempts have been made to identify the ten horns with successive Seleucid kings preceding Antiochus. (See the chart of alternative suggestions in Blasius 544–46.) These calculations run into problems, however, since only seven kings preceded Antiochus IV in the Seleucid line. The number ten is, however, like the numbers four and seven, a number that represents totality and is often used in apocalyptic schemas for designating successive periods (e.g., *1 En.* 91:11–17; 93:1–10 [the Apocalypse of Weeks]; *Melchizedek* [11Q13] 2.7; *Sib. Or.* 2:15).

Antiochus is not depicted simply as one among the other horns. Even as the fourth beast represented a break with the sequence of beasts that preceded it, so Antiochus is different from the preceding horns, and his appearance signals a decisive moment in the drama of history. While it is possible, as John Collins (299) suggests, that the designation "little horn" is a slighting reference (cf. 11:21), the trope is primarily a dramatic one of the sudden appearance and growth of this figure who "comes up" among the other horns. In the interpretation in v. 20 it is described as larger than the other horns. Interpretation remains unsettled re the three horns that are uprooted before this last horn. In contrast to the symbolic round number of ten, it is likely that a specific historical allusion is intended here. Porphyry identified the three with Ptolemy VI, Ptolemy VII, and Artaxias of Armenia—kings whom Antiochus defeated in battle (so also Hartman and DiLella 216). A variant of this thesis identifies the three as Ptolemy VI, Cleopatra II, and Ptolemy VII (so Bickerman 1967, 104; Blasius). Here the little horn is not said to do the uprooting (but see v. 24). The passive verb may even suggest that he is given a place through divine agency (similarly, Goldingay 164). Antiochus IV, the brother of the reigning monarch, Seleucus IV, was not in line for the throne. When Seleucus IV was murdered by Heliodorus, one of his officials, the heir to the throne, Demetrius, was being held as a political hostage in Rome. Thus Antiochus IV was able to usurp the kingship, ostensibly reigning as coregent with Seleucus's remaining son, also named Antiochus. Antiochus IV had the child murdered after a few years. Thus the three horns that were uprooted in order to make way for Antiochus IV are probably to be identified with Seleucus IV and his two sons (so Plöger 116–17; J. Collins 320–21).

The final sentence in v. 8 describes the little horn. Like the first beast, it has features like those of a human. But whereas the first beast had a human mind, a positive feature, the horn has "eyes" and "a mouth speaking arrogantly" (cf. 11:36). In Israelite wisdom tradition, body parts, including the mouth and the eyes, are used as indicators of character and elements that must be properly directed and controlled. The mouth of the wicked or of the fool is often associated with duplicity, conflict, violence, and destruction (Prov 10:6, 11, 32; 11:11; 15:28; 18:6; 19:28; cf. Obad 12). Although the eyes in the horn are not specifically characterized, haughty eyes are a figure of arrogance (Prov 6:17; 21:4; Isa 2:11; 5:15). Moreover, the figure of the boastful king has a prototype in the depiction of Sennacherib in Isa 37:23, where his loud voice and haughty eyes are specifically paired as a trope of his arrogance. Antiochus is also characterized as speaking boastfully in 1 Macc 1:24.

[9–10] These verses shift the seer's attention from the fourth beast and its horns to the inauguration of judgment by the divine council. While much of Dan 7 is rhythmic prose, these verses have the regular parallelism of poetry, and it is possible that they are a quotation from an older composition. The concept of a divine council that meets to decide policy and render judgment is a commonplace in the ancient Near East, attested in Mesopotamian and Ugaritic sources, as well as in the Hebrew Bible (e.g., 1 Kgs 22:19; Isa 6; see Mullen).

Excursus 4: The Divine Throne, Judgment Scenes, and Daniel 7:9–10

The motif of the divine throne and its many attendants becomes a popular element in apocalypses, as does speculation about the elements of the throne itself (e.g., *1 En.* 14; 60:1–2; 90:20; *Songs of the Sabbath Sacrifice* [4Q405 frg. 20 2]; *Giants* [4Q530 2.16]; Rev 4). In these texts several details describing the divine throne show an evident debt to Ezek 1 and 10 (the seated figure, the presence of fiery phenomena, the wheels and creatures of the throne). Although this general tradition provides background for Dan 7:9–10, these verses show a striking resemblance to a distinct subset of passages: *1 En.* 14:18–23; 90:20; 4Q530 2. More precisely: (1) 4Q530 2 and *1 En.* 90:20 share with Dan 7:9–10 an action sequence concerning judgment; (2) *1 En.* 14:18–23 and Dan 7:9–10 provide details concerning the divine throne and the appearance of God; and (3) 4Q530 2; *1 En.* 14:18–23; and Dan 7:9–10 enumerate the angelic attendants. The following two charts indicate the similarities (sequence rearranged to show comparison; trans. of *1 Enoch* from Nickelsburg 2001, adapted; trans. of 4Q530 from *DSSR*).

The Action Sequence

Daniel 7	4Q530	*1 Enoch* 90:20
Thrones were set up.	Thrones were arranged.	A throne was erected.
An Ancient of Days took his seat.	The Holy Great One took his se[at].	The Lord of the Sheep sat upon it.
A thousand thousands served him, a myriad myriads attended him.	[A hundred hun]dreds served him, a thousand thousands [prostrated themselves].	
The court sat, and books were opened.	[Boo]ks were opened, and judgment pronounced.	He took the sealed books and opened them.

The Divine Throne

Daniel 7	*1 Enoch* 14:18–23	4Q530
I looked	I was looking	And behold
until thrones were set up.	and I saw a lofty throne.	the seats were arranged.
An Ancient of Days took his seat.	The Great Glory sat upon it.	The Great Holy One sat do[wn].
His apparel was like white snow.	His apparel . . . was whiter than much snow.	
His throne was flaming fire; . . . a river of fire . . . went out.	From beneath the throne issued rivers of flaming fire.	

Daniel 7	1 Enoch 14:18–23	4Q530
Its wheels were burning fire.	Its wheels were like the shining sun.	
A river of fire was flowing and streaming out before him.	Flaming fire encircled him, . . . a great fire stood by him.	
A thousand thousands served him, a myriad myriads stood before him.	A myriad myriads stood before him.	[One hundred hun]dreds served him, one thousand thousands [prostrated themselves; al]l [of them] in front of him were standing.

Much ink has been spilled in attempting to specify the relationship among these texts, yet with little consensus (see the judicious review by Trotter). The complexity of the relationships among the four texts, including the mix-and-match nature of the elements that appear in different combinations and the different degrees of elaboration, argue against a model of direct literary dependence among these texts. More likely, descriptions of the divine throne and its attendants and descriptions of divine court judgment scenes were traditional, formulaic set pieces within apocalyptic literature that could be adapted for a variety of purposes. The lower number of angelic attendants in 4Q530, however, does appear to represent a more primitive form of the tradition, since numbers tend to inflate.

The location of the scene that begins in v. 9 is unspecified. Although many assume that the location is in heaven (e.g., Hartman and DiLella 217), the only other references to thrones being "set up" are explicit that the location is on earth. In 4Q530 2.16–17, "The ruler of the heavens descended to earth, and thrones were set up, and the Great Holy One sa[t down]." Similarly, *1 En.* 90:20 specifies that "a throne was erected in a pleasant land," that is, Israel. Presumably in heaven the furniture is already in place (cf. 1 Kgs 22:19; Rev 4:2–4). As Goldingay (164) observes, although the divine council regularly meets in heaven, when God is engaged in judgment, the scene is usually on earth. The closest parallels to Dan 7:9 are Jer 49:38: "I will set up my throne in Elam and destroy king and officials from that place" (AT); and Joel 3 (4):2, 12: "I will gather all the nations and bring them down to the valley of Jehoshaphat, and I will enter into judgment with them there, . . . for there I will sit to judge." The background for the imagery is the practice of victorious kings or generals to sit in the gate and receive their troops or judge the defeated rebels (2 Sam 19:8 [9]; Jer 39:3; cf. Ps 122:5). Thus here, too, the judgment of the four kingdoms takes place on earth.

As in 4Q530, a plural but unspecified number of thrones are set up. But who sits down? Here Dan 7:9 refers only to the Ancient of Days taking his seat, leading some (e.g., Montgomery 296; Goldingay 165) to assume that only God sits. Israelite tradition does sometimes depicts only YHWH as seated, with other attendants standing before him (1 Kgs 22:19; Isa 6:1–2). Indeed, a later rabbinic tradition in *Genesis Rabbah* 65.21 concluded from an interpretation of Ezek 1:7; Dan 7:16; Isa 6:2; and 1 Kgs 22:19 that "there is no sitting in heaven" and that angels have no knees! (Halperin 149). The separate reference in Dan 7:10 to "the court" as "seated," however, suggests that first the presiding God sits, and then those who are members of his council (cf. the "princely thrones" of the council in the Ugaritic Baal epic; *CTU* 1.2. I 24–29). In various apocalyptic traditions, certain angelic beings do sit in the presence of God, including the elevated Elect One or Son of Man in the Similitudes of Enoch (*1 En.* 45:3; 62:3, 5) and the Son of Man and the twelve disciples in Matt 19:28. In those cases, as in Dan 7, the role of those seated is to pass judgment. With a different function, the twenty-four elders in Rev 4:4 have thrones in heaven, as does the speaker of the Self-Glorification hymn from Qumran, who boasts of "a mighty throne in the congregation of the gods" (*War Scroll*, 4Q491 frg. 11 1.12). The role of divine counselor, which was assumed in texts like 1 Kgs 22:19–20, however, is seen in later texts as theologically inappropriate (*1 En.* 14:23; cf. Isa 40:14). Consequently, the majority of the angels are represented as standing in attendance and serving or worshiping (*1 En.* 14:22; 4Q530 2.17–18; Dan 7:10). The details of the scene in Daniel thus combine two traditions about heaven: the myriad attendants represent the worship of God, while the seated court foregrounds the judicial function.

Physical descriptions of God are exceedingly rare in the Hebrew Bible. Given the reticence of the tradition to represent the deity (e.g., Exod 33:18–23; Deut 4:15–20), the descriptions of God in apocalyptic literature are audacious and probably function as part of their claim to unique revelatory authority. Moreover, though they ostensibly give concrete details, they overwhelm the senses in such a way that the transcendent mystery of the divine is preserved. Although the author of Dan 7 borrows details from Ezek 1 for the description of the throne, he has a different description of the body of God. The epithet "Ancient of Days," suggests an aged deity, evocative of Ugaritic El, who was known as the ᵓab šnm ("Father of Years," *CTU* 1.1 III 24; 1.4 IV 24; 1.6 I 36; 1.17 VI 49). See also other similar descriptions of YHWH as "God of Ages" (ᵓēl ʿôlām, Gen 21:33; ᵓĕlōhê ʿôlām, Isa 40:28), "Lord of Ages" (*Genesis Apocryphon* [1Q20] 21.2, mārēᵓ ʿalmayyāᵓ), and "the ancient God" (ᵓĕlōhê qedem, Deut 33:27).

More specifically, the awe-inspiring wholly otherness of the divine being is suggested imagistically through the motifs of whiteness for the Deity and fire for his throne. The garment is white and the hair "like lamb's wool." Although traditionally translated as "pure wool," the meaning "pure" for *nĕqēʾ* is attested only in later dialects of Aramaic. The connotation of "lamb's wool" is apparently also that of whiteness, for in spite of the fact that sheep can come in a variety of colors, the poetic tradition often used wool as a symbol of whiteness (e.g., Ps 147:16; Isa 1:18). Similarly, in *1 Enoch* 14:20 the garment of the "Great Glory" is described as shining like the sun and whiter than any snow. While the color symbolism might connote more than one thing, the primary emphasis seems to be on shining brightness as characteristic of the Deity (similarly Goldingay 165; in the NT, cf. Matt 28:3; Mark 9:2–3). Linen garments, presumably white, are also characteristic for angelic figures (Ezek 9:2; 10:2; Dan 10:5; 12:6–7). The function of this imagery is apparently to emphasize the difference between the human, which is fleshly and opaque, and the divine, which is of a different substance more akin to light and fire.

Indeed, fire and fiery phenomena are often associated with the Deity, including the theophany of the burning bush (Exod 3:2), the pillar of fire that leads the people (Exod 13:21–22; 14:24; Num 14:14; Neh 9:12, 19), the divine descent to Sinai in fire (Exod 19:18), and the fiery phenomena coming from the body of God in Ps 18:8 (9). Here in Dan 7:9 the fiery nature of the divine throne is most closely derived from the description of God's chariot throne in Ezek 1 (vv. 4, 13–14), although the details differ. That the throne has wheels is a detail derived from Ezek 1:15–21. The depiction of a river of fire proceeding from the presence of the Deity (Dan 7:10) has no parallel in Ezek 1 but may be related to the image of the river of water that Ezekiel sees issuing from the visionary temple in 47:1. A close parallel is found in *1 Enoch* 14:19, where "streams o[f fire]" (*šĕbûlîn d[î nûr]*) issue from beneath the throne. Similarly, the Qumran *Songs of the Sabbath Sacrifice* refer to "rivers of fire" (*nāhărê ʾûr*) in the vicinity of the holy of holies of the heavenly temple (4Q405 frg. 15 2; frg. 16 2–3). Moreover, the *Songs of the Sabbath Sacrifice* interpret the fiery phenomena that moves back and forth within the chariot throne in Ezek 1:13–14 as angelic spirits who have the appearance of "streams of fire" (*šĕbûlê ʾēš*, 4Q405 frg. 22 10). Fiery chariots and streams of fire become standard elements of the imagery of later merkabah and hekhalot mysticism (cf. *3 Enoch*, passim). Since fire is deadly to humans, the association of the divine presence with fire underscores its transcendent otherness.

The overwhelming sublimity of the divine presence is completed with a reference to the thousands and myriads of angelic figures who stand in attendance and serve him. Although the ultimate background to this notion is the council of spiritual beings who attend the divine king to discuss matters of importance (cf. 1 Kgs 22:19–22 and discussion above), here the number of such beings has been extravagantly expanded. Even the more modest numbers in 4Q530 ("hundreds . . . thousands") suggests that these attendants no longer serve as members of a functional divine council. The high numbers may also draw on a second tradition that associated God with huge heavenly armies (Ps 68:17 [18]: "The chariotry of God are twice ten thousand, many thousands twice over" [AT]), though the angelic figures have no explicit military function in this scene (but cf. Dan 8:10; 10:13). Here the image serves to suggest the unlimited power and splendor of the divine court.

With the conclusion of the description of God and the divine throne, the action sequence resumes with the reference to the seating of the court, presumably a subset of high-ranking angels, and the opening of books (v. 10b). Although written documents and records were important aspects of royal administration from earliest times (cf. the scribes and recorder mentioned among Solomon's officials in 1 Kgs 4:3 and the regularly mentioned "annals" of the kings of Israel and Judah in 1–2 Kings), the use of writing as an instrument of state control became much more prominent in the Persian Empire (Howard 62–75). In Jewish literature from the Persian period onward, there are several references to records specifically consulted by kings in order to inform proper decisions (e.g., Esth 2:23; 6:1–2; Ezra 4:15; 5:17–6:5; cf. Isa 65:6). Perhaps the closest parallel to this verse is the comparable judgment scene in *1 En.* 90:20, in which sealed books are opened and used as the basis of judgment against the "seventy shepherds" who had been given permission to pasture the Judean "sheep" since the time of the fall of Judah. As the preceding chapter in *1 Enoch* makes explicit, God has specifically charged a recording angel with documenting the extent to which the seventy shepherds exceeded the terms of their commission. In light of the preceding divine commands given to the beasts in Dan 7:4–7, it is likely that the books consulted here also document the extent to which they fulfilled or exceeded their commissions.

The reference to the books opened for the court is part of a larger "scribalization" of heaven that becomes pronounced in the religious imagination of Judaism in the Hellenistic period. The bureaucratic archives of heaven contained a variety of documents. In addition to books of deeds, such as one has here, there were also books of fate that recorded the plan of history, including eschatological events (Dan 10:21; *1 En.* 93:1–3; 103:2; Rev 5), books of heavenly laws (*Jub.* 5:12–19; 16:29; 23:32), and books of life containing the names of persons scheduled for eschatological deliverance (Dan 12:1; Luke 10:20). For earlier references to heavenly books, see Exod 32:32–33; Isa 4:3; 65:6; Mal 3:16; Ps 139:16. (For further discussion, see Baynes.)

[11–12] As elsewhere in this chapter, a reference to Daniel's own perception (cf. vv. 9, 13) introduces a new scene in the vision. Here, however, the phrase "I kept watching" occurs twice, which is most likely a resumptive repetition marking a redactional addition, since the reference to the words of the arrogant horn belongs to the updating of the vision to make it specifically applicable to Antiochus IV. Those who argue for the unity of the chapter often omit the second instance of the phrase on the basis of the Greek versions (so J. Collins 275). The meaning of the final form of the text is obscured by the difficult syntax of *bēʾdayin min*. Montgomery (302; followed by Goldingay 145; J. Collins 275; and others) argues that the phrase is equivalent to Hebrew *mēʾāz*, "from the time of." Thus Daniel would be temporally connecting the preceding scene, when he observed the little horn, with the present judgment ("I watched then from the time when I heard the sound . . . , watched as the animal was killed" [Goldingay 142]). Alternatively, if one construes *min* to have causal force, then Daniel either explains that his attention was riveted by the arrogant words (so NRSV; NIV: "Then I continued to watch because of the boastful words the horn was speaking. I kept looking until the beast was slain") or claims that the basis for the judgment and execution of the fourth beast is not simply its violent excess, but specifically the arrogant words of the little horn, that is, the arrogance of Antiochus IV (so NJPS: "I looked on. Then, because of the arrogant words that the horn spoke, the beast was killed"). The latter option seems unlikely. The arrogant words are simply one part of the culpable behavior of the beast. The awkward syntax is an attempt to coordinate Daniel's perception of two scenes taking place concurrently: the culpable behavior of the fourth beast (vv. 7–8) and the session of the court (vv. 9–10).

The divine sovereignty over the powers represented by the beasts is conveyed in several ways. Instead of a direct account of the carrying out of the court's judgment, the verbs are passives that do not explicitly name the agent, though the execution and disposal of the beast's body is obviously the fulfillment of the judgment of the court. The same technique was used in the commissioning of the beasts in vv. 4–6 and creates a subtle air of mystery. The reader sees, but not everything. The phrase "consuming fire" (*yĕqēdat ʾeššāʾ*) echoes the description of the fiery furnace from Dan 3:6, 11, 15, 20–23. Whereas Nebuchadnezzar's superheated fire had no power over the bodies of the three young men (3:27), the fire of divine judgment destroys the body of the beast representing the fourth kingdom. Although Dan 7 does not specify the source or location of the fire into which the beast is thrown, it is likely that the fire is to be connected with the river of fire issuing from the throne of God. Similarly, in Ezek 10:1–8, the fire of the coals from the chariot throne is the source of the fire of judgment that destroys Jerusalem. Although fire is occasionally mentioned as a means of execution in earlier texts (e.g., Gen 38:24; Lev 20:14; 21:9; Josh 7:15), it often figures metaphorically as an image of divine judgment (Deut 32:22; Isa 33:11–12; 66:15–16), especially in eschatological scenarios, where it comes to be more literally envisioned as the means of punishing sinners (Isa 66:24; Ezek 38:22; 39:6; Joel 2:3; *1 En.* 91:9; 100:9; 102:1; Matt 3:12; 13:42; Mark 9:43, 47–48). The closest parallel to Dan 7:11, however, is the judgment scene in *1 En.* 90, where the stars (renegade angels), seventy shepherds (angels of the nations), and the blinded sheep (apostate Jews) are all cast into an abyss of fire (90:24–27). In the imagination of *1 Enoch*, however, the punishing fire is not associated with the throne of God but is a cosmic abyss identified in *1 En.* 18:11 and 21:7 as the fiery prison for the stars who transgressed in primordial times.

Perhaps the most striking thing about the judgment in Dan 7:11–12 is the differentiation between the fourth beast and the first three. In the corresponding dream of Nebuchadnezzar in Dan 2, the rock that smashes the statue smashes it altogether, and the wind carries off every particle. In that dream even though a differentiation had been made between the first three kingdoms and the fourth, which was noted for its particular violence (2:37–40), all suffer the same contemporaneous judgment. The Gentile imperium as such is destroyed. What does it signify that, in contrast to the total annihilation of the fourth beast in ch. 7, the dominion of the other three is taken away but "length of life" is granted to them for an indefinite time (v. 12)? Ginsberg's (1948, 7) ingenious attempt to find a historical basis for the attenuated continuation of the Babylonian, Median, and Persian kingdoms mistakes the nature of the imagery. It is not a wooden allegory but evocative imagery that expresses evaluative judgments. Given the almost certain dependence of Dan 7 on the dream in ch. 2, the discrepancy in imagery is to be taken as a revision of the political judgment expressed in that dream and the development of a different eschatological scenario. Since it seems unlikely that a nostalgia for the earlier Gentile empires is in play here, the intent appears to be to intensify the claim that the fourth kingdom is of a distinctly different and more horrible nature, a point that is made both in the initial description (v. 7) and in the specific focus on it in the interpretation (vv. 19, 23), even before the interpolations concerning Antiochus IV are added.

What role is there, however, for the first three beasts/kingdoms in this symbolic world? Genteel retirement in a home for displaced monarchies? In contrast to the eschatological scenario of Dan 2, in which the stone that becomes a mountain is all that exists at the end (2:35, 44–45), Dan 7 retains more of the model of imperial rule, in which "all [i.e., all former] dominions will serve and obey" the "people of the holy ones of the Most High" (v. 27). A similar scenario is depicted in *1 En.* 90:30, where the Gentiles bow down, pay homage, petition, and obey the Jews. Yet *1 Enoch* goes even further than Daniel in having the Gentiles eventually become transformed into righteous Jews (symbolized in the allegory as white cattle [*1 En.* 90:37–38]). Both scenarios are in keeping with various earlier expectations about the nations' recognition of YHWH and service to YHWH's people (e.g., Isa 2:2–6//Mic 4:1–3; Isa 49:22–23; Zech 14:16).

[13–14] Again, a reference to Daniel's looking marks the transition to a new scene. Although many set vv. 13–14 as poetry, v. 13 at least might be better described as rhythmic prose, since it lacks the regular parallelism of vv. 9–10. The language is sufficiently stylized, however, to lend the passage an air of formality. The content of this scene, with its reference to "one in the likeness of a human," has given rise to intensive interpretive activity, both in antiquity and in modern scholarship. (See Colpe for an extensive review.)

In contrast to the eschatological imagery of Dan 2, in which the same symbolic object that destroys the statue becomes the kingdom of God's rule, here judgment and the transfer of dominion are distinct. This separation of function is one of the reasons for doubting that the mythic pattern of the Baal myth underlies the narrative movement of Dan 7 (see discussion above). Nevertheless, cosmic imagery, involving the three spheres of heaven, sea, and earth, is very much in play. Daniel's vision began with an image of the four winds of heaven stirring up the great sea (v. 2). Through this action heaven initiates the action sequence of the entire chapter. Though they come from the sea, the four beasts exercise their dominion on earth, and it is on earth, as argued above, that their judgment takes place. The symbolic symmetry of the vision is completed by having the clouds of heaven deliver to the presence of the Ancient of Days the one who is to receive dominion forever. Thus heaven brings the course of events to a close.

Verse 14 is replete with echoes from the narratives of chs. 1–6. The sequence "dominion, glory, and sovereignty" recalls the description of the rule delegated to Nebuchadnezzar in 2:37 ("a kingdom of power, might, and glory") and 5:18 ("kingdom and greatness and glory and honor"). The sequence "peoples, nations, and languages" also occurs in 3:4, 7, 29; 4:1 (3:31); and 6:25 (26), where it signifies the king's universal control. Thus the new dominion is in these respects similar to that which God had previously delegated to the earthly kings. Unlike them, however it does not "pass away" (*yeʿdēh*), the same verb used in v. 12 to describe the removal of dominion from the three first beasts. Nor will his kingship be destroyed; although the verb used here (*tiṭḥabbal*) is different, the fourth beast itself was destroyed. Positively, the lasting and indestructible nature of the new dominion not only echoes what is said about the final kingdom in 2:44, but also what is said about God's present and future sovereignty in the doxologies of 4:3 (3:33), 34; and 6:26 (27). Thus what had been a tension between the eternal dominion of God and the temporary exercise of delegated dominion by Gentile powers is now resolved in an eternal dominion of God, manifested in the eternal dominion delegated to the humanlike figure.

The identification of this humanlike figure has generated centuries of debate. The one who comes with the clouds needs to be interpreted both from within the symbolic system of the imagery of the chapter and in relation to its referent. The grammatical construction used, *bar X*, like the comparable Hebrew expression, *ben X*, designates an individual member of a species. Thus a "son of oxen" is an ox, the "sons of Israel" are Israelites, and a "son of a human" (*bar ʾĕnāš*) is a human being. The phrase *bar ʾĕnāš* occurs elsewhere in Aramaic with this generic sense in the eighth-century-B.C.E. treaty inscribed on the Sefire Stela

(3.16; Fitzmyer 1995, 154), and in the probably second-century-B.C.E. texts of *Genesis Apocryphon* (1Q20) 21.13 and *Targum of Job* (11Q10) 9.9; 26.2–3. The comparable expression in Hebrew, also with a generic meaning, occurs in Ps 144:3 (*ben-ʾĕnôš*). Very common is the similar phrase *ben-ʾādām* (e.g., Num 23:19; Jer 49:18; Ps 8:4 [5]; Job 25:6; and often used as a term of address in Ezekiel, as in 2:1). With the preposition *kĕ-* the phrase does no more than to describe this figure as human*like*, paralleling the description of the first three beasts as *like* a lion, *like* a bear, and *like* a leopard. Thus in the symbolism of the vision, origin from the (chaotic) sea is represented by beastlike figures, and origin from heaven is represented by humanlike figures. The parallel between the humanlike figure and the beasts is also manifest in their functions. Although the term "dominion" (*šolṭān*) is only used explicitly with the third beast (v. 6), it is clear that each of the four exercises dominion (v. 12). In v. 14 dominion is now given to the humanlike figure, though this dominion is qualitatively unlike theirs in that it is permanent and indestructible. Moreover, even though in the symbolic vision the humanlike figure is not instrumental in destroying the Gentile kingdoms, with respect to the exercise of dominion, he occupies the same role as the rock cut out without human hands that becomes a mountain and fills the earth in 2:34–35, 44–45. This much is evident. But to what reality does the symbolism point? By whom will the dominion of God be made manifest?

Two viable options exist. The figure could be taken as (1) a symbolic representation of the people Israel; or it could be taken as (2) a heavenly figure, the archangel Michael, who is Israel's guardian. Initially, either interpretation seems plausible, with the construal of the figure as a symbolic representation of Israel perhaps the most natural. Since the beasts represent earthly kingdoms, their counterpart might also be assumed to be an earthly kingdom. The qualitative difference identified in the beast/human contrast, as well as their respective identifications with the sea or the clouds of heaven, would allude simply to their different relationships to the Most High God, since Israel is God's people in a way that the Gentile nations are not. This identification of the figure as a symbolic representation of Israel became the consensus position of critical scholarship from the end of the nineteenth century until the last quarter of the twentieth century (see Driver 101–10 for a list of the scholars holding this position) and still finds articulate defenders (e.g., Hartman and DiLella 101–2; Delcor 155; Casey 1979, 24–25; Keel 2000, 22–23).

The alternative interpretation, that the figure represents an angelic being, specifically the archangel Michael, was originally proposed by Nathaniel Schmidt in 1900 and has been vigorously championed by Day (167–77) and John Collins (310), among others. As Collins has argued, not all of the figures in the vision are simply allegorical depictions to be decoded. The Ancient of Days is a mythic-realistic figure. And so too, according to this interpretation, should the humanlike figure be understood. The fact that this figure "comes with the clouds of heaven" should not be treated as a mere statement about a transport mechanism. Clouds are often associated with divine theophanies. YHWH "makes the clouds his chariot" and "moves on the wings of the wind" in Ps 104:3 (NJPS; cf. Ps 18:10–12). Thus the imagery associates something godlike with the figure, and as noted earlier, divine characteristics are often extended to angelic descriptions in Second Temple Judaism, most pertinently in Dan 10:5–6.

The case for identifying this figure with an angelic being, specifically the archangel Michael, is strong, since angels play a critical role in the apocalyptic sections of Daniel. In Dan 12:1, Michael is identified as "the great prince who stands over your people." The angelology of Dan 10:13, 20–21 similarly understands Gabriel and Michael as engaged in battle with the angelic princes of Persia and Greece, the time of whose dominion is coming to an end. The earliest implicit interpretation of Daniel's angelic kingdom is to be found in the Qumran *War Scroll*, which is in many ways deeply influenced by the book of Daniel. The *War Scroll* explicitly identifies this figure as Michael. Although it envisions the eschatological events as a war rather than a forensic judgment, it describes the outcome as the time when God will "raise up the authority of Michael among the angels and the dominion of Israel among all flesh" (1QM 17.7–8).

[15–16] With the conclusion of the description of the dream vision, the account turns to the reaction of Daniel. The alarm of the dreamer of a mysterious dream is a literary trope, as the reactions of both Pharaoh (Gen 41:8) and Nebuchadnezzar (Dan 2:3; 4:5 [2]) suggest. In those instances, however, the alarm is experienced after the dreamer has awakened. Here the pattern is influenced by the postexilic prophetic vision tradition, where the request for interpretation is made within the context of the vision itself (Niditch 1983, 174). The closest parallels are the night visions of Zechariah (1:8–10; 2:1–4; 4:1–7; 6:1–8). In later chapters of Daniel (8:16; 9:21), the task of interpretation is explicitly identified with the archangel Gabriel. Here, however, the interpreter is simply one of the angelic beings from among the myriads standing in attendance (v. 10). See the comments on 2:4 for a discussion of the term *pĕšar*, "meaning."

[17–18] The angel's reply is terse compared with the rich details of the dream vision. In contrast to Dan 2, where the sequence of kingdoms itself was of interest, here they are simply grouped: four beasts = four kings. Even though the figures are called kings rather than kingdoms in this verse, the king is simply the symbolic representation of the kingdom (the term "kingdom" is used in v. 23). In Dan 2 also a fluctuation exists between individual kings and kingdoms, as Nebuchadnezzar rather than the Neo-Babylonian Empire is designated as the "head of gold," though the succeeding regimes are referred to as kingdoms.

The angel pays no attention to the initial setting of the vision and does not mention the sea at all, stating rather that the kings arise "from the earth." Thus the dream retains a surplus of uninterpreted data and so retains a certain mysteriousness that the further interpretation will only partially dispel. The reader is responsible for deducing the meaningfulness of these details. For the interpreting angel, the central meaning of the dream is the transfer of sovereignty from the four earthly kingdoms to "the holy ones of the Most High." In light of this phrase, the angel's identification of the four kings as "from the earth" may simply be a contrast with the heavenly associations of the holy ones of the Most High.

For those commentators who interpret the humanlike figure as a collective symbol for the people of Israel, the term "holy ones" is assumed to refer to the people (or a subset of them), despite the fact that it is only occasionally used in such a sense in the Hebrew Bible. Montgomery (307), for example, draws attention to its rarity in this sense and claims it is found only in Dan 7; 8:24; Pss 16:3; 34:9 (10), though the reference in Ps 16:3 is contested. More recent defenders of this line of interpretation similarly point to Ps 34:9 (10) as warranting such a reference (e.g., Keel 2000, 22). Literature later than Daniel does sometimes use the term "holy ones" to refer to human communities (*1 En.* 38:4–5; 100.5; 1 Cor 14:33; Phil 1:1), and it is not difficult to see how traditional interpretation read this usage back into Daniel. But it has long been recognized that the more common referent of "holy ones" (*qĕdōšîm*) in the Hebrew Bible is to angels (e.g., Ps 89:5 [6]; Job 5:1; 15:15; Zech 14:5; and probably Deut 33:2; Prov 30:3). Moreover, that is also the common meaning of the term in noncanonical writings contemporary with or only slightly later than Daniel (e.g., Sir 42:17; 45:2; *Jub.* 17:11; *T. Levi* 3:3; *1 En.* 12:2; 14:23). Most significantly, in the book of Daniel itself, the term is clearly used to refer to angelic beings in 4:13, 17, 23 (10, 14, 20). Since the influential article by Martin Noth in 1955, the identification of the *qaddîšîn* with angelic beings has been increasingly accepted, though there continue to be those who reject this interpretation (most recently, Keel 2000, 22; see also DiLella 1977; Brekelmans). The Dead Sea Scrolls have provided extensive additional evidence for the use of the term "holy ones" for angels (1QapGen 2.1; 1QS 11.7–8; 1QS^b 1.5; 1QM 1.16; 10.11–12; 12.1, 4, 7; 15.14; 1QH^a 3.21–22; 10.35; 1Q36 1; 4QShirShabb, passim; 11QMelch 1.9; 4Q181 frg.1 2.4). Some ambiguous referents in the Dead Sea Scrolls reflect the distinctive belief of the sect that its members actually participated in community with the holy angels (see J. Collins 314, who provides an exhaustive discussion of the evidence). While it is most likely that *qaddîšîn* semantically refers to the angelic host, functionally the transfer of sovereignty to the patron angel of Israel (Michael?) and to the angelic figures associated with him in heaven also entails transfer of sovereignty to Israel, as v. 27 will specify.

The interpreting angel, to be sure, does not show any interest in identifying the humanlike one with any specific leader of the holy ones. But even if the humanlike one is originally a collective symbol for the angels, the subsequent visions in Daniel reinterpret this figure with increasing specificity, as prince of the host (8:11) and as Michael (10:21; 12:1; Willis 77).

[19–20] Just as the vision itself stressed the difference of the fourth beast from the other three, so Daniel is not satisfied with the generality of the angel's interpretation and presses for additional information about the fourth beast. In the pre-Antiochene version of the chapter, this request was answered in v. 23 with an interpretation of the actions of the fourth beast/kingdom, followed in v. 26 with an account of its judgment and destruction, and in v. 27 with an account of a transfer of sovereignty to "the people of the holy ones of the Most High." The Antiochene additions in vv. 20–22 narrow attention to the actions of Antiochus IV in 167 B.C.E.

The details that Daniel specifies about the fourth beast are a paraphrase of the description in v. 7, with the addition of a new detail that it had bronze claws. There is no reason to think that this phrase was originally part of the description; it is not unusual for the interpretation of a vision to elaborate. Moreover, since the list of the beast's activities described two actions, one performed with the mouth (devouring and crushing) and one with the feet (trampling), the addition of a note about the appearance of the feet complements the detail about the iron teeth. "Iron and bronze" are also a fixed pair of terms that can be used for various purposes (see 4:15 [12]; 1QS^b 5.26). Verse 20, which describes the ten horns and the "other one," similarly paraphrases v. 8, with the addition that the new horn appeared larger than the others. Since it was originally identified as "a small horn" (v. 8), this detail suggests its dynamic and aggressive nature.

[21–22] Oddly, v. 21 is no longer a summary of the previous vision but a further visionary account, introduced by the reference to Daniel's looking, and adding an action sequence that would fit narratively between vv. 8 and 9. The initial vision had identified the horn's actions only as arrogant speaking. Here, however, his aggression is cast as war against the "holy ones." Even Noth (1966, 226), who championed the interpretation of "holy ones" as angels, was disconcerted by the notion that a human figure, the little horn, could not only make war on the angels but even prevail for a time, thus leading him to take this instance of "holy ones" as a reference to the human community. This is not so odd a notion as might first appear, however. Even a text as ancient as the Song of Deborah conceptualizes aggression by a human foe against Israel as also involving the response of YHWH's heavenly armies, here represented as the stars, and joined by the active participation of the river Kishon (Judg 5:20–21). Biblical literature includes various human kings who are envisioned as opponents of YHWH, including Pharaoh (Exod 15) and Sennacherib (Isa 37:21–29). Their defeat, whatever the actual mechanism, is understood as occurring through the exercise of God's power. Thus earthly and heavenly realities thoroughly interpenetrate in all these contests.

What is novel in Dan 7 is the framing of the conflict in terms of the aggression of the king and his temporary success, rather than focusing only on the moment of divine victory. This aspect of Antiochus's hubristic aggression is developed in 8:9–12. Although Daniel may be the earliest attested text to use this tension-building technique, a similar scenario is more highly developed in the Qumran *War Scroll*'s account of the eschatological battle. There the forces of Light and the forces of Darkness are composed of both angelic and human combatants. Moreover, victory and defeat are evenly balanced between the two forces until the decisive seventh battle.

> On that day the congregation of the gods and the congregation of men shall engage one another, resulting in great carnage. The Sons of Light and the forces of Darkness shall fight together to show the strength of God. . . . In three lots the Sons of Light shall stand firm so as to strike a blow at wickedness, and in three the army of Belial shall strengthen themselves so as to force the retreat of the forces. . . . In the seventh lot the great hand of God shall overcome. (1QM 1.10–13; trans. *DSSR*)

There is likely a more specific reference implied in the claim that Antiochus prevailed against the holy ones, however. This phrase should be understood as an allusion to Antiochus's violation of the holiness of the Jerusalem temple (1 Macc 1:20–24), where, upon his return from Egypt in 169 B.C.E., he entered the sanctuary and despoiled it of much of its cultic equipment. In contemplating the destruction of the first temple by the Babylonians, Ezekiel interpreted the event as YHWH's own act of destruction of a polluted sanctuary (Ezek 8–11), a destruction made possible only because the divine presence had abandoned the sacred space. Since that theological option is not pursued by Daniel, Antiochus's violation must be construed as a temporary victory over the angelic forces that ordinarily protect the sacred space. These assumptions are illustrated by 2 Macc 3:22–30, which recounts how the Seleucid official Heliodorus had earlier (sometime in 178–175 B.C.E.) tried to plunder the temple treasury, only to be met by an apparition of armed angelic forces, who beat him to the ground and thus preserved the sanctity of the temple (see Portier-Young 80–93). Although 2 Maccabees was composed after Daniel, it is likely that this conception of angelic protection was a widely shared belief.

In the Aramaic of v. 21, the information about Antiochus's prevailing over the holy ones is not the complete sentence, but only the first part of one, which is completed in v. 22 by a repetition of the scene of judgment first narrated in vv. 9–12. Thus Antiochus's temporary advantage is merely prelude to his destruction. The language changes back from military to juridical, casting the conflict as one for "possession" of the kingdom. Significantly, one new phrase makes an appearance: "The time had arrived." The theme of times controlled and perhaps preordained by God for different nations to exercise sovereignty is deeply rooted in the narratives of Dan 1–6. In Dan 2, upon receiving the revelation of Nebuchadnezzar's dream, Daniel praises God as one "who changes times and seasons, removing kings and setting up kings" (v. 21). Similarly, in ch. 4, Nebuchadnezzar's reason and kingship are restored "at the end of the days" that had been decreed (vv. 32, 34 [29, 31]). The reference here to the time that has arrived deprives Antiochus's temporary victory of even a semblance of autonomous achievement. He could act only so long as the Most High had determined that he might.

[23–25] As noted above, v. 23 originally followed v. 19 as the interpretation of the fourth beast. Whereas the angel's initial interpretation of the beasts was as "kings" (v. 17), here the fourth beast is identified as a fourth "kingdom," that is, the Hellenistic kingdom of Alexander the Great, and the object of its devouring is identified as nothing less than "all the earth." Similarly 1 Macc 1:1–4 describes Alexander's conquests in universal terms. Indeed, between the beginning of his campaign in 334 and his death in 323 B.C.E., Alexander's armies conquered Asia Minor, Syria-Palestine, Egypt, Babylon, and Persia, with military campaigns also into what is now Iran, Afghanistan, and Pakistan. As the reaction of Dan 7 suggests, his power was seen as of a different dimension than the empires that had preceded him. The subsequent actions of Antiochus IV solidified the notion that the actions of the Hellenistic kingdoms exceeded the bounds of YHWH's mandate to Gentile sovereigns.

Verse 24 interprets the interpolated material in vv. 7f–8, 20 (re "ten horns"). The symbolic nature of the ten kings as a group and the likely historical allusion to the three kings is discussed in the notes to vv. 7f–8. Where v. 8 used a passive expression ("were uprooted"), here Antiochus is expressly the agent ("bring low"). The words of arrogance and the aggression against the holy ones are repeated from vv. 8, 20–21, though with a different verb ("wear out" rather than "prevail against"). The arrogant words are sometimes interpreted in light of the divine titles (e.g., "God manifest [Epiphanes]") used by Antiochus on some of his coinage (so J. Collins 321–22; Bauer 163; Willis 84). Yet the underlying dynamic of human kings who challenge YHWH in any fashion is an implicit claim to equality, if not divinity, and so it is likely the totality of Antiochus's actions and decrees that are symbolized by the arrogant words.

What is new in the account of Antiochus's behavior is the claim that he will intend to change "times and law" (*zimnîn wĕdāt*, v. 25). The referent of this phrase is debated. Most often it is taken to refer specifically to Antiochus's decree prohibiting the observance of Sabbaths and other cultic feasts (1 Macc 1:45; 2 Macc 6:6; so Lebram 91; J. Collins 322 ; Bauer 163). This is certainly a possible interpretation, and one might then render the phrase "times set by law," that is, cultic observances required by torah. The verb used with the expression, however, is *sĕbar*, "to intend" or "hope." Since Antiochus actually accomplished the prohibition on Jewish cultic observance, it seems an odd locution. The phrase has also been argued to refer to changes in the cultic calendar itself, specifically a change from a 364-day solar calendar to a 360-day lunar calendar (so VanderKam 1981, 55–60; Lebram 92; Portier-Young 193–201; but see the strong critique by P. Davies 1981). Calendrical issues otherwise do not seem to be a preoccupation of the book of Daniel, and this interpretation would also raise the same issue about the suitability of the verb *sĕbar*.

The third and most plausible interpretation is to situate the phrase in relation to the book's preoccupation with the divine power to determine times (2:21, 44–45; 4:16–17, 23, 25, 31–32, 34 [13–14, 20, 22, 28–29, 31]). The issue of the right time for the transition of sovereignty has already been raised in v. 22: "Judgment was given for the holy ones of the Most High. The time [*zimnāʾ*] had arrived, and the holy ones took possession of the kingdom." Although the terms used are not identical, the semantic fields of *dîn* ("judgment," v. 22) and *dāt* ("law/decree," v. 25) overlap (Beyer 1:544, 588). Antiochus's attack on the holy ones, and thus on the Most High himself, is a challenge to the Most High's power to determine who shall exercise sovereignty (similarly Goldingay 181). In this matter, Antiochus *intended* something that he was not able to accomplish. The following line (v. 25d) also speaks about time in this sense as divinely determined, in that the time allotted for Antiochus to exercise power over the holy ones is specified as "a time, and times, and half a time," probably to be understood as three and a half years. Although the violations of the temple and the disruption of cultic life, along with the violence against the people, are concretely the matters that provoke the sense of crisis in the Antiochene edition of Dan 7, the conceptual terms within which the author casts these matters have to do with the issue of who controls the historical process and in particular the determination of sovereign power. Although Antiochus *intends* to change the time set for his exercise of sovereignty, it is the Most High who is in control. Even Antiochus's apparent victories are not his own. The fact that the holy ones are said to "be given into his power" (*yityahăbûn*, v. 25c) is a claim that it is the Most High, not the little horn, who actually controls events (cf. 1:2).

[26–27] This part of the angel's interpretation summarizes the action sequence of the judgment scene in the vision (vv. 12–13) and the investiture scene (v. 14), though with slightly different terminology. The one significant difference is the designation of the recipient of the everlasting kingdom. Now, instead of the "one like a human being" (vv. 13–14) or "the holy ones of the Most High" (v. 22), the recipients are "the people of the holy ones of the Most High." The relation of the "one like a human being" to the "holy ones of the Most High" was discussed above. Here the issue is whether the phrase "people of the holy ones of the Most High" (*ʿam qaddîšê ʿelyônîn*) is equivalent to "holy ones of the Most High" (*qaddîšê ʿelyônîn*) or is to be distinguished from it.

There is no clear instance of the term "people" (ʿam) being used to refer to an angelic group. The two cases that have been suggested, 1QH 11.22–23 (olim 3.21–22; ʿmṣbʾ qdwšym) and 1QM 12.8 (ʿm qdwšym), are inconclusive. In 1QH 11.22–23, the word is more probably the preposition ʿim ("with"). In 1QM 12.8 the phrase might be rendered in any of three ways: as a preposition ("together with the holy ones," referring to angels); as a substantive in construct with the following noun, equivalent to an adjectival construction ("a people [consisting of] holy ones"); or as a substantive in construct, equivalent to a possessive construction ("the people of the holy ones," identifying the earthly community as related to the angelic community). In Dan 7:27 the Masoretic punctuation places a disjunctive accent under lěʿam, perhaps suggesting that they took it as an appositive, "to the people, the holy ones of the Most High," which would accord with the collective understanding of the humanlike one and the holy ones as representing Israel. But the Masoretic interpretation cannot be dispositive for the original meaning of the text. In light of the strong evidence for the use of "holy ones" to designate angels, and in view of the lack of evidence for the use of "people" as a term for angels, the clearest way in which to make sense of the phrase is as a possessive, "the people of the holy ones of the Most High" (similarly J. Collins 317). That is to say, Israel assumes sovereignty on earth, as do God's angels in heaven (cf. 1QM 17.7–8).

[28] The brief notice of the end of the account parallels the notice of its beginning in v. 1. It has the effect of putting Daniel's first-person reference to his psychological and physical state outside of the account he has written down. This is somewhat odd, since the narrative framework introducing the dream report began in the third person (v. 1). The psychological reaction parallels those of Pharaoh in Gen 41 and of Nebuchadnezzar in Dan 2 and 4, but with an important difference. In those accounts the recipient is disturbed because he does not understand the dream. When it is interpreted to him, even though the contents may be troubling, the psychological disturbance is dispelled. Here, however, the dream has already been interpreted, and the threat apparently posed by the fourth beast and the little horn has been shown to be completely under the control of the Most High. Thus from Daniel's perspective, the dream is clearly interpreted to have a happy outcome. Why, then, is he so troubled that he becomes pale? It is possible that the reaction is simply to the violent audacity of the fourth beast and the little horn. But it seems better to seek an explanation in keeping with the traditional function of such a motif. The angelic interpreter, even with Daniel's persistence, has interpreted only a portion of the mysterious symbols and has certainly not made an explicit identification of the beasts and horns. Thus the dream and its interpretation still contain a significant reservoir of mystery. This is what generates the remaining anxiety for Daniel. But rather than seeking a further interpretation, as one might expect in the genre of dream reports, Daniel reports that he kept the matter to himself. The written account is thus his only communication of the dream to a potential interpreter. And the only ones who can fulfill this role and supplement the laconic angel's interpretation with more specific details are the audience for the written account, the readers of Dan 7. They must resolve the lingering anxiety by relating the revelation to historical events.

History of Reception, by Brennan W. Breed

The Humanlike One and the Stone Cut without Hands: Corporate Deliverance and Rule

As with the four-kingdom schema (see ch. 2), an important interpretive trajectory mostly preserved in the Syriac Christian community understands the "humanlike one" (usually translated "son of man," Dan 7:13–14) to refer to the events leading up to the Maccabean revolt (Casey 1979, 51–69). Throughout history many readers have assumed that, because of the structural similarities between chs. 2 and 7, the comments about the humanlike one refer also to the stone cut "not by human hands" that smashed the statue in Nebuchadnezzar's dream (2:34–35, 44–45). But in this interpretive trajectory the reference to the "end of days" in 2:28 OG and Dan 2:45 Peshitta allowed many readers to distinguish the two images: while the stone's smashing was seen as an eschatological event, the humanlike one was treated as a reference to the corporate deliverance of the Jewish people from Seleucid rule.

According to Jerome (on 7:17), the third-century-C.E. Neoplatonic philosopher Porphyry argued in his treatise *Against the Christians* that the rock and the "son of man" both refer to the Jewish people after the Maccabean victory over the Seleucid forces—though it is possible that Porphyry thought that the latter referred to Judas Maccabee (Beatrice 37). A similar corporate interpretation appears once in the rabbinic tradition to explain the humanlike one's presentation before the Ancient of Days (7:13): "the angels lead [the Israelites] to the border of their camp, and the Holy One, blessed be he, stretches out his hand and leads them himself" (*Midr. Ps.* 21.5). The fourth-century Syriac Christian Aphrahat refers to the "holy ones" (7:18, 21, 25, 27) as "Judah [Maccabee] and his brothers" who were "fighting on behalf of their people and living in secret places" (*Demonstrations* 5.20). Aphrahat, however, combines this interpretation with anti-Jewish polemic: "Have the children of Israel received the kingdom of the Most High? Certainly not! Or has the people come on the clouds of heaven? That has passed away from them." He points to the Jewish defeat by the Romans as proof (*Dem.* 5.21). Ephrem, writing slightly later than Aphrahat, claims that the holy ones are the "priests who kept the Law of the Most High" who were "oppressed and persecuted" until the actions of "the house of Maccabeus" (Casey 2010, 85). Yet a number of early and medieval Eastern

Christian interpreters couple their historical reference to the Jewish people at the time of the Maccabean revolt with a typological reference to Jesus. Ephrem, for example, writes that "while the significance of [the humanlike one] was prefigured in the sons of the people in that they subdued the Greeks and all the surrounding kingdoms, its consummation was perfected in our Lord [Jesus]" (J. Cook 2004, 189). Also, the eighth-century Syriac theologian Theodore bar Koni writes that "in the historical context these words refer to the Maccabees, but their essential quality is fulfilled in our Lord the Messiah" (Casey 2010, 8). And according to fifteenth-century Spanish Rabbi Joseph Albo, in the preceding century Rabbi Hayyim Galipapa claimed that "all prophecies of Daniel refer to the second temple only," that the reign of the holy ones refers to the "short and definite time during which the Hasmoneans ruled," and that the phrase "ancient of days" refers to "Mattathias the high priest, who was the head of the Hasmoneans, a very old man, all of whose sons reigned after him" (Albo 418).

Some Christian interpreters have seen a collective element in the stone from Dan 2, as well as in the humanlike one and the holy ones from Dan 7, usually as an extension of the person of Jesus by means of Paul's comments about the unity of believers in the body of Christ (cf. 1 Cor 12:12–27). Augustine, for example, sees the stone's universal expansion (2:35) to refer to the universal church (*Ennarat. Ps.* 42.4; 98.14). The twelfth-century Bishop Otto von Freising, writing in the immediate wake of the investiture controversy that pitted the pope against many kings of Europe, claimed that the stone in Dan 2 "was clearly the Church that smote the kingdom near its end. . . . The Church smote the kingdom at its weak spot when the Church decided not to reverence the king of the City as lord of the earth but to strike him with the sword of excommunication," referring to the 1076 excommunication of Holy Roman Emperor Henry IV by Pope Gregory VII that successfully broke the secular control over local bishops and created an opportunity for massive ecclesiastical reform (Otto 401–2). In response to the Protestant Reformation, Catholic interpreters, such as the influential seventeenth-century Flemish Jesuit Cornelius à Lapide, claimed that the descending rock cut without human hands should be understood as both "the birth of Christ, [who] descended in the same way into the womb of the Virgin," and "the spiritual kingdom of Christ that executes judgment upon all the kingdoms of the world, and subdues all the nations to Christ and the Church" (Lapide 955–56).

Others understood this text in a political sense as referring to a violent uprising that claims mundane power. In his 1523 letter to Frederick the Wise, Thomas Müntzer wrote that, in response to unrighteous rule by the temporal powers, "the sword will be taken from them and will be given to the people who burn with zeal so that the godless can be defeated, [as in] Daniel 7; and then that noble jewel, peace, will be in abeyance on earth," understanding the holy ones as a reference to the zealous peasantry (Müntzer 1988, 69). And in his "Sermon to Princes," Müntzer made this connection clear in his interpretation of the stone from Dan 2: "The stone torn from the mountain without human touch has become great. The poor laity and the peasants see it much more clearly than you do. Yes, God be praised, the stone has become so great that, already, if other lords or neighbors wanted to persecute you on account of the gospel, they would be overthrown by their own subjects. This I know to be true. Indeed the stone is great!" (Müntzer 1993, 108–9). Later radicals, such as the Puritan English Fifth Monarchy Men, used Dan 7 to refer to their own seizure of power as the "holy ones." Oliver Cromwell himself gave a speech in which he justified revolution by means of this text: "We are at the threshold, and therefore it becomes us to lift up our heads and to encourage ourselves in the Lord. And we have some of us thought it our duty to endeavour this way, not vainly looking on that prophecy in Daniel, And the Kingdom shall not be delivered to another people. Truly God hath brought it into your hands by his owning and blessing, and calling out a military power" (Cromwell, 113–14). And this radical political trajectory culminates in the nationalism of the modern era, captured well in Presbyterian millenarian David Austin's 1794 discussion of the United States' role in dethroning European powers and instilling universal peace: "Behold the *regnum montis*, the kingdom of the mountain, begun on July 4, 1776, when the birth of the MAN-CHILD—the hero of the civil and religious liberty, took place in those United States. . . . Behold, then, this hero of America wielding the standard of civil and religious liberty over these United States. . . . Is not the Stone now rolling against the feet and toes of the mighty image?" (Austin 390, 392–93).

The Humanlike One and the Stone Cut without Hands: The Messiah

The overwhelming majority of interpreters understand the humanlike one as an eschatological messianic figure—human, angelic, or divine—in a manner similar to the Similitudes of Enoch (in *1 En.* 27–71), *4 Ezra*, and the New Testament books of Mark (13:26; 14:62) and Revelation (1:7). For rabbinic Jewish readers throughout history, the humanlike one from Dan 7:13–14 is often identified with both the stone in Dan 2 and the Davidic Messiah, who will establish the kingdom of the righteous (*b. Sanh.* 98a; *Num. Rab.* 13.14). In ʾ*Aggadat Berešit* 23.1, the Messiah is said to "spring up from the gates of Rome; then you will rejoice, for thus says Daniel: 'Behold, with the clouds of heaven there came one like a son of man and you shall see him and your heart shall rejoice'" (Caragounis 132). Messianic speculation also fuels the discussion of Anani, the last name in David's genealogy in 1 Chr 3:10–24, in the midrashic text *Tanḥuma Toledot* 20: the question "Who is Anani?" is met with the response "He is the King Messiah! See Daniel 7:13: Behold, there came with the clouds of heaven one like a son of man." The midrash links these texts by means of the linguistic similarities between the Aramaic word for "clouds of" (*'ănānê*) and the Hebrew name Anani (*'ănānî*). And in *b. Sanh.* 96b, Rabbi Nahman is reported to have called the Messiah the unusual name "Bar Nafle" because the LXX (Greek) translation of the Aramaic word "clouds of" in Dan 7:13 is *nephelōn*, which sounds like the Hebrew word for "fallen" and allows Nahman to read the rather limp description of the Davidic house in Amos 9:11 MT (*nōpelet*) instead as a veiled messianic reference to Dan 7:13 (Caragounis 134). Like many Jewish readers, Rashi (d. 1105) is careful to guard both the messianic and the corporate national sense. In response to Dan 7:13, Rashi comments: "This is the King Messiah. The nations are beasts, but the Israelites are the children of Adam, because of their humility and perfection" (Gallé 78). Ibn Ezra (d. 1164) sees both present through the distinction between the human-like one and the holy ones: "R. Yeshua said that this is the Messiah. . . . The holy ones refers to Israel" (Gallé 80). The sixteenth-century Alshich likewise interprets the stone in Dan 2 as the "rock of Israel," which he connects to the messianic sprout in Isa 11:1. Many interpreters have wondered why Daniel does not give Nebuchadnezzar a precise interpretation of the stone. Alshich offers this thought: Daniel "didn't want to arouse the king's jealousy, or appear to be guarding the interests of his own people. Thus he concealed from the king the identity of the kingdom which will never be destroyed, to be established by God" (Alshich 120).

One can see evidence of a rather widespread use of the phrase "the son of man" in a cautionary fashion to denote messianic pretensions; Rabbi Abbahu (third–fourth century) is said to have warned people with a reference to both Num 23:19 and Dan 7:13: "If a man says 'I am God,' he lies; 'I am the Son of Man,' he will finally regret it; 'I ascend to heaven,' he will not be able to fulfill it" (Herford 62–64). While Abbahu's comment criticizes the Christian understanding of Jesus' self-designation as the "Son of Man," it also discounts contemporary claims of messiahship. Likewise, Maimonides in his *Epistle to Yemen*, written in the twelfth century to the small Jewish Yemeni community during a time of persecution, warns against a local messianic preacher who taught a syncretistic form of Judaism and Islam. Maimonides further refers to an affair in Lyon, France, in the preceding century, when a messianic claimant was

> supposed to have performed the following miracle. On moonlit nights he would go out and climb to the tops of high trees in the field and glide from tree to tree like a bird. He cited a verse from Daniel to prove that such a miracle was within the power of the Messiah: *And, behold, there came with the clouds of heaven one like a man.* . . . Many who witnessed the miracle became his votaries. The French discovered this, pillaged and put many of his followers to death, together with the pretender. Some of them maintain, however, that he is still in hiding until this day. (Maimonides 130)

History of Reception

Messianic pretenders were not the only theological problems inherent in the interpretive history of Dan 7:13-14. The possibility of a second power in heaven that would also sit on a throne (7:9) was troublesome to both Jewish and Muslim interpreters, who together criticized the Christians for the apparent violation of monotheism in the Second and Third Persons of the Trinity. A rabbinic tradition repeated in several midrashic texts defends Dan 7:9-14 against these sorts of interpretations, as well as purported misuses within the Jewish community, especially from mystical sects, by claiming that the various manifestations of divinity merely reveal different aspects of the single, unified divine essence (*Mek. R. Ishmael, Baḥodesh* 5; *Shirta* 4; *Mek. R. Simeon b. Yohai, Bashalaḥ* 15; *Pesiq. Rab Kah., Piska* 21.100b).

Another tradition presents Rabbi Akiba, famous for supporting Bar Kochba's second-century-C.E. failed messianic revolt against Rome during which Akiba was martyred, as interpreting Dan 7:9 to say that the plural "thrones" includes one throne for God and another "for David," indicating the Davidic Messiah. In response, Rabbi Yosi the Galilean claims that setting a human next to the divine treats "the divine presence as profane," and thus Daniel's vision must include only thrones for multiple aspects of the divine, "one for justice and one for grace," such that God would sit in one throne when issuing harsh judgments and the other for offering mercy. One version of this exchange ends with Akiba accepting this interpretation over his own—which suggests that later rabbis dealt with their own ambivalence toward Akiba's support for a messianic revolt by depicting him changing his mind (*b. Ḥag.* 14a; Segal 1977, 49).

Other views include the possibility that the thrones are for the watchers (Dan 4:17 [14]) who function as the divine court, or that one throne is a seat and the other is a footstool (*b. Sanh.* 38a). Both Abraham ibn Ezra (d. 1164) and Pseudo-Saadia, a rabbinic interpreter active in the thirteenth century, understand the verb *rĕmîw* in Dan 7:9 to mean "thrown" although it is usually rendered as "set" in English, Thus Pseudo-Saadia interprets the phrase to mean: "The Creator will throw down the kings of the people of the world from their thrones" (Gallé 76). Ibn Ezra offered a further solution by interpreting the Ancient of Days as Michael, the archangel: "[The unseating of the kings' thrones] will be accomplished when Michael, the great prince, rises up, as it explains. He is the ancient of days. In prophetic visions, it seems that he appears aged" (Gallé 76). Some interpreters avoided this issue altogether with allegorical interpretations, such as Malbim, who argued that people must work to better themselves to perform spiritual ascent and thus "elevate themselves to heaven," after which time God will use the divine power to bring humanity to righteousness where the clouds, representing the Torah and mitzvot, will surround them (Goldwurm 206). And some interpreters have drawn moral lessons from this text, such as the second-century Christian theologian Clement of Alexandria, who thought that the image of white hair (7:9) should teach people the importance of not using artificial colorings on one's own hair (*Paed.* 3.16.4).

Because of the doctrine of the Trinity, Christian exegetes were generally happy to use the figures of the stone in Dan 2 and the humanlike one in Dan 7 to depict divine plurality. As Jerome wrote, "None of the prophets has so clearly spoken concerning Christ as has this prophet Daniel" (*Expl. Dan.*, Prologue). The final words of the *Didache,* a Christian pastoral manual of the late first or early second century, refer to the eschatological second coming of Jesus Christ with an allusion to Dan 7:13: "Then shall the world see the Lord coming upon the clouds of heaven" (16.8). Many other Christians understood the reference to the clouds to contrast the meekness of his first advent with the power and terror of his return (Justin Martyr, *1 Apol.* 51.9; *Dial.* 14.8; 31:1; Tertullian, *Adv. Marc.* 3.7.4), and many interpreters understand the judgment scene in Dan 7:9–10 to refer to the last judgment (Cyril of Jerusalem, *Catech.* 10.4; Irenaeus, *Haer.* 3.19.2; 4.33.1).

One detail particular to the judgment scene in Dan 7:10, the river of fire, seems to have found widespread representation in Christian theology and visual art (cf. *1 En.* 71:2). In the iconography of the last judgment in both the Western Latin church and the Eastern Orthodox church, one sees a river of fire snaking through the scene, often emanating from the base of the throne occupied by Christ. This can be seen, for example, in the early fourteenth-century frescoes of the *parekklēsion* (chapel) in the Church of the Holy Savior in Chora, in Istanbul. In the eighth century a plea directed at the iconoclastic emperor Constantine V to understand the power of images by looking at a last judgment scene describes "how [Christ] comes in his glory, and the myriad crowd of angels standing before his throne with fear and trembling, the river of fire that flows from the throne and consumes the sinners" (Sevcenko 258). The river of fire also appears in Byzantine liturgical poetry for Lent (Lash 39).

One also sees clouds accompanying Christ in the iconography of the last judgment, such as in the tympana of the west portal at the twelfth-century Romanesque church of St. Foy in Conques, France; the south portal at the Romanesque Abbey church at Beaulieu-sur-Dordogne, which also depicts Daniel in the lions' den being fed by Habakkuk; and the Sistine Chapel's Last Judgment fresco painted by Michelangelo. In many medieval illuminated manuscripts depicting scenes from Dan 7, the four beasts are combined with the traditional last-judgment iconography, including a frontal-facing Christ seated on a throne in a cloud-lined mandorla, holding the book of life in his left hand, with his right hand raised in blessing. One can see many such images in the various extant copies of the popular and influential medieval Spanish illuminated Beatus tradition. From the ninth through the thirteenth centuries, an illuminated copy of Jerome's *Commentary on Daniel* often accompanied manuscripts of Beatus of Liebana's eighth-century commentary on the book of Revelation, which was important because of the Spanish efforts at reconquering the Iberian peninsula. The Las Huelgas Beatus (see fig. 19), a thirteenth-century manuscript, offers an example of this lively iconographical tradition that links Dan 7 and the last judgment. Instead of a duality between the Ancient of Days and the Son of Man, Christ's role as judge conflates these characters.

Christ and the Ancient of Days are often conflated in medieval theology and iconography because of the textual variant in Dan 7:13 OG that depicts the humanlike one approaching "as," instead of "up to," the Ancient of Days. This conflation informs the imagery used to describe the divine figure in Rev 1:7, and it led to a long dispute in some Christian communities over the nature of these figures. In the Coptic *Fourteenth Vision of Daniel* of the eighth–twelfth century, for example, the Son of Man and the Ancient of Days are understood to be identical (DiTommaso 179–84). And the conflation of these figures did not stop there: in the nineteenth-century Mormon book of *Doctrine and Covenants* 27.11, a list of those who have received the gospel includes "Michael, or Adam, the father of all, the prince of all, the ancient of days," which conflates the biblical characters of the first human and the chief angel (J. Smith 41). Joseph Smith clarified this teaching: "Daniel in his seventh chapter speaks of the Ancient of Days; he means the oldest man, our Father Adam, Michael, he will call his children together and hold a council with them to prepare for the coming of the Son of Man. He [Adam] is the father of the human family. . . . The Son of Man stands before him, and there is given him glory and dominion. Adam delivers up his stewardship to Christ" (Nyman 111). Thus Smith interprets Dan 7 as a transmission of authority from Adam/Michael to Jesus as the rightful ruler of the earth.

An interpretive trajectory that took hold in North African early Christianity understood Dan 7:13–14 as a prophecy of the resurrection, ascension, and exaltation, which seems to draw from Rev 1:7. Cyprian, the third-century bishop of Carthage, claimed that Dan 7:14 described the power that Christ received at his resurrection (*Test.* 2.26), while the fourth-century Numidian Lactantius claimed that Dan 7:13 depicts Christ's ascension on the fiftieth day after the resurrection (*Epit.* 4.21). Some influential medieval Christian interpreters, such as Hugh of St. Victor and Peter of Blois, accepted this reading (J. Davies 1958, 163).

Many Christian interpreters read Dan 7:13 in light of 2:34–35 and 2:44–45, which were more commonly understood as a prophecy of the incarnation (Cyril of Jerusalem, *Catech.* 1.8; Irenaeus, *Haer.* 5.26.2; Tertullian, *Adv. Marc.* 4.10.9; Augustine, *Tract. Ev. Jo.* 1.12). Justin Martyr, a second-century Christian theologian, argued that the word "like" in Dan 7:13 indicated that this figure must be something more than human, suggesting divinity (*Dial.* 76). The famed ninth-century liturgist Amalarius of Metz wrote about a particular reading and responsory, Isa 1:4–6 and Dan 7:13–14, for the first Sunday in Advent,

Figure 19. The Las Huelgas Beatus (thirteenth-century Spain), depicting the seated Christ with the book of life, surrounded by the four beasts from Daniel 7. Pierpont Morgan MS M. 429, fol. 163r. © The Morgan Library & Museum. Used by permission.

and interpreted these texts as a dialogue. The first voice, Isa 1, "asked if Christ would be the one to rule over the people Israel," and then Dan 7 responded with references to both "the human nativity" (v. 13) and the everlasting kingdom (v. 14) that would follow, "not only that he might reign among the people Israel, but so that the Judaic tribe, and the people Israel, and all tongues might serve him" (*Liber ordine* 8.7; Fassler 71). In the Byzantine East, the sixth-century monk Cosmas Indicopluestes said that both the stone in Dan 2 and the clouds in Dan 7 symbolized the virgin birth: "For in the one passage he said 'without hands,' meaning without the seed of a man, and in the other 'on the clouds of heaven,' which, without human hands, bear and bring forth the rains as from a womb" (Casey 1979, 68). Yet some saw this as a prophetic preview of Christ's incarnation, not the event itself: as third-century Roman theologian Hippolytus put it, "Who was in heaven but the Word unincarnate? . . . [He] was called from the beginning the Son of Man on account of what he was to be, although he was not yet human" (*Noet.* 4). Martin Luther also disagreed with the interpretation that Dan 2 foreshadowed the incarnation, saying that it was "not an unchristian thought," but that it was more likely that "the mountain is the entire Jewish kingdom from which Christ came, who is their flesh and blood, and yet now he has been torn from them, and has come to the nations" (Beckwith 260).

In Islamic eschatology, the second coming of Jesus, called the "sign of the hour" in the Qur'an (43.61), precedes the day of judgment. There are many diverse traditions involving Jesus and his relationship to messianism and "the Mahdi," another sometimes-messianic figure in Islam. In the *Tafsir* (10.115), the Prophet's companion, ʾAbu Allah ibn ʾAbbas, "associated the coming down of Jesus with the apocalyptic smoke amidst which he herds people into the place of resurrection" (Arjomand 383). One of the traditional signs heralding the final day of judgment in Islam is the forty-day-long descent of thick clouds of smoke (Qur'an 44); ibn ʾAbbas seems to interpret that smoke in light of Dan 7:13–14, and its use in New Testament apocalyptic texts, as a sign of Jesus' return. But this eschatological use of Dan 7 is quite different than Muslim interpretation of the stone in Dan 2, which is generally seen as a prophecy of the Prophet Muhammad's political, military, and theological successes. According to the ninth-century Persian scholar Ibn Qutayba, in a book about Scripture edited by the eleventh-century Andalausian Ibn Hazm, the rock in Dan 2:44–45 represents "a prophet who would unite all nations, and whose rule would extend to all the horizons. Now then, has there ever been a prophet apart from Muhammad who has united all nations regardless of their diversity and of the difference between their languages, religions, kingdoms, and countries?" (Adang 160–61). Likewise, Najm al-Dīn al-Ṭūfī, a Muslim scholar working in Cairo in the fourteenth century, wrote in his comments on the book of Daniel: "Some commentators from the People of the Book have claimed that this 'stone which became a great mountain' refers to the people whom God made prevail over the kingdom of the Greeks," perhaps referring to the Romans. But Ṭūfī argues that the text refers to Muhammad because the phrase "without humans hands" refers to how Muhammad "appeared alone and singly without backing or power" before his success, whereas the Romans "were not like that, but rather, they came about with vigor, power, and supremacy" (Demiri 418–19).

Muslim interpreters also at times accused Jewish and Christian interlocutors of "anthropomorphism" based on Dan 7. The tenth-century Muslim scholar Abu Nasr Mutahhar ibn Tahir, known as al-Maqdisi ("the Jerusalemite"), claimed to have a conversation with a Jew who "goes so far as to declare that the one he worships is an old man with grey hair, arguing that he [is] found in the book of Daniel: 'I have seen the ancestor of the fathers seated on the throne'" (Adang 257).

Modern apocalyptists have also found these texts to be generative. Recent radical Muslim apocalyptic preachers, for example, following in the influential footsteps of Egyptian Saʾid Ayyub, have returned to biblical texts such as Daniel and Revelation to explain what they see as the approaching end of the world. Many of these preachers link the humanlike one in Dan 7:13 and the stone cut without hands in Dan 2 to Muhammad. Bashir Muhammad ʾAbdallah, an Egyptian apocalyptist, exegetes Dan 7 thoroughly and argues that the Ancient of Days is a reference to the Mahdi who will give "sovereignty to the saints," meaning "the Muslims," by means of the "continuing victory they will have in the establishment of the Islamic caliphate" (Cook 2005, 42). And after the second Intifada in 2000, the Saudi Safar al-Hawli charted all the symbolic elements of Dan 7, along with their modern identities, and argued that the "Son of Man who will come in the latter days" can be none other than Muhammad, as Christ is the son of a woman who announced the advent of the true great messenger; for al-Hawli the Christian obsession with the idea that Jesus is the "Son of God" effectively disqualifies him from being the "Son of Man" (Cook 2005, 48).

Daniel 8 Ironies of Power: Breaking the Horn That Challenges Heaven

1 In the third year of the reign of King Belshazzar a vision appeared to me, Daniel (after the one that appeared[a] to me previously).

2 I saw in the vision, and I was[b] in the fortified city of Susa, which is in the province of Elam,[c] and I was at the Ulai Canal.[d] 3 I lifted up my eyes and looked, and suddenly there was a ram[e] standing before the gate, and it had two horns. Both horns were long, but one was longer than the other, and the long one was coming up later. 4 I watched the ram charging to the east[f] and to the west and to the north and to the south. None of the animals could stand before it, and there was no one who could rescue from its power. It acted as it pleased and did great things.

5 And as I was contemplating this, suddenly a he-goat was coming from the west over all the earth, not touching the ground. And the goat had a conspicuous horn between its eyes. 6 It approached the ram that had the two horns that I had seen standing before the gate, and it ran at him with its powerful fury. 7 I watched it close in on the ram. It was enraged against it and struck the ram and shattered its two horns. The ram had no strength to stand before it, and it threw (the ram) to the ground and trampled it. And there was no one to deliver the ram from its power. 8 The goat grew very great, but when it had become strong, the great horn was shattered, and four came up[g] in its place toward the four winds of heaven. 9 From one of them came forth a single small[h] horn, and it grew excessively great toward the south and toward the east.[i] 10 And it grew as great as the host of heaven, and it hurled down to earth some of the host and some of the stars, and it trampled them. 11 And it became as great as the prince of the host, and from him[j] the daily sacrifice was removed, and the place of his sanctuary was thrown down. 12 In the course of rebellion, a host was given over in addition to the daily sacrifice.[k] It cast truth to the ground, and in everything that it did, it was successful.

13 Then I heard some holy one speaking, and some other holy one said to whoever was speaking, "How long is the vision of the daily offering and the transgression that desolates, his giving over of the sanctuary and a host to be trampled?"[l] 14 And he said to him,[m] "For two thousand and three hundred evenings and mornings, and then the sanctuary will be made right."

15 And while I, Daniel, was observing the vision and seeking understanding, suddenly standing before me was someone with the appearance of a man. 16 And I heard a human voice from the midst of the Ulai,[n] and it called out and said, "Gabriel, make this one understand the thing he has seen." 17 He came to where I was standing, and as he approached, I was terrified, and I fell upon my face. But he said to me, "Understand, O mortal, that the vision is for the time of the end." 18 And when he spoke with me, I entered a trance, prostrate upon the ground. Then he touched me, and he lifted me up to where I had been standing.

19 He said, "See, I am letting you know what will happen at the close of the wrath for the children of your people,[o] for it pertains to the appointed time of the end.[p] 20 The ram that you saw that possessed two horns: these are the kings of Media and Persia. 21 The shaggy goat is the kingdom[q] of Greece, and the great horn that was between its eyes, that is the first king. 22 As for the one that was shattered, and four came up in its place: four kingdoms[r] will arise from his nation,[s] but without his strength. 23 In the latter part of their reign, when their transgressions are complete,[t] a king who is hard-faced and skilled in understanding riddles will arise.

24 His power will grow strong,ᵘ
and he will plan marvelous things,ᵛ
and he will succeed in what he does.
He will destroy those who are strong,
and his plotting will be against the holy ones.ʷ
25 Deceit will prosper in his hand,
and he will become great in his own mind.
He will destroy many while they are unsuspecting.
Even against the Prince of princes he will take his stand,
but he will be broken, and not by hands.

26 The revelation of the evenings and the mornings that has been told is certain. As for you, seal up the vision, for it is for a distant future.'ˣ

27 I, Daniel, was distraughtʸ and was sick for days. Then I arose and I did the king's business. But I was appalled by the vision, without understanding it.ᶻ

a. The feminine participle does not agree in gender with the noun it modifies, the first of many instances of gender nonagreement in this chapter.

b. The MT has two phrases, "and I saw in the vision" plus "and while I was looking," which may be remnants of alternative introductions to the vision. 4QDanᵇ contains the phrase "and while I was looking" and has room for the other phrase. The OG has "I saw in the vision of my dream," but Th lacks references to seeing.

c. MT and 4QDanᵇ include yet another reference to seeing, "and I saw in the vision," probably the result of dittography.

d. The word ʾûbāl occurs only here and in vv. 3, 6. It may be a cognate of Akk. *abullu* ("city gate"), which is taken up in a number of Aramaic dialects. This is also how the versions tend to interpret the word. Context, however, suggests it is better understood as a by-form of *yûbal* ("canal, watercourse"). See the comments below.

e. Here 4QDanᵃ, 4QDanᵇ, and Papyrus 967 add the adjective "great," anticipating the verb "did great things" in v. 4.

f. "East" is present in Papyrus 967, MS 88, and the Syro-Hexapla, though it not present in Theodotion and MT. A case can be made for either reading. The four cardinal directions are important elsewhere in the chapter (v. 8) and elsewhere in Daniel (7:2).

g. Here *ḥāzût* ("conspicuousness") is intrusive and does not fit the syntax.

h. Here *miṣṣʿîrâ* appears to be pointed as a noun ("smallness") plus a preposition ("from"). Perhaps it should be understood as an otherwise unattested *mem*-prefixed noun, *maṣʿîrâ* (so Brockington 243) or *miṣʿārâ* (Hartman and DiLella 221), meaning "smallness."

i. The MT includes a third term "to the beautiful" (*haṣṣebî*). As pointed, this odd expression evokes the phrase "the beautiful land" from 11:16, 41. Instead of "the beautiful," the OG translates "the north," assuming *haṣṣāpôn*; Th translates "the host," assuming *haṣṣābāʾ*. It is difficult to say which of the three readings is most likely original. The OG does appear to be smoothing out a difficult text. Montgomery (339; cf. Plöger 122) assumes that the phrase "to the host" (*ʾel-haṣṣābāʾ*) was an alternative reading for

Ironies of Power: Breaking the Horn That Challenges Heaven   255

"up to the host" (*'ad-ṣĕbā'*) in v. 10, later misread and repointed under the influence of the phrase "the beautiful land" in 11:16, 41. This seems the most likely explanation.

j. Reading with the Qere (so also the OG and Th). The Kethib takes the verb as active ("and he removed the daily offering from him") and is reflected in the Vg and the Peshitta. Given the following passive verb, it seems likely that the passive was also intended here.

k. Verse 12a is extremely difficult. The problems concern the meaning and referent of *ṣābā'* ("heavenly host," "human army," or "tribulation"), the unusual construal of the noun as feminine (but see Isa 40:2), and the nuance of the phrase *tinnāṭēn 'al* ("placed over," "given over in addition to"). The Greek versions do not reflect *ṣābā'* and take "transgression" as the subject of the verb. John Collins (334–35) reviews and evaluates the numerous proposals for construing or emending the MT. Also compare the discussion of Willis 93–94; Bauer 170–71. The translation given above generally follows their suggestions. The alternative is to take the clause as an explanatory gloss, as Goldingay (197) suggests, and to understand it as including information about what occurred in Jerusalem, in line with the accounts of 1 Macc 1:45–46; 2 Macc 6:4–5. Thus "and an army [the troops of Antiochus] was set over the daily sacrifice in an act of transgression." Compare Delcor 174; Lebram 94. None of the approaches is without problems.

l. The MT is unintelligible without emendation. Emend *heḥāzôn* to a construct (*ḥāzôn*) and emend *tēt wĕqōdeš* ("giving and a/the sanctuary") to *tētô qōdeš* ("his giving over a/ the sanctuary"). "To be trampled," lit., "a trampling place."

m. Heb., "to me." The versions read "to him."

n. The preposition *bên* ("between") seems odd, though perhaps it suggests a location between the banks of the Ulai. Cf. 12:6–7.

o. As J. Collins (327) notes, the phrase "children of the people," attested in Papyrus 967, has apparently been lost from the MT by homoioteleuton (*z'm . . . 'm*). See 12:1 for a similar phrase.

p. Alternatively, the final part of verse may be translated "for there is an appointed time for the end."

q. Lit., "king." As in Dan 2, the terms for "king" and "kingdom" are used somewhat interchangeably.

r. The plural is pointed as in Mishnaic Heb. Note the lack of agreement with the verb.

s. Emending *miggôy* to *miggôyô*, following the OG.

t. MT reads "transgressors" with a Hiphil verb, "when the transgressors have completed (their transgressions)"; but OG and Th read, "when their transgressions are completed," reflecting *kĕtām piš'êhem*.

u. MT adds "but not through his power," apparently an intrusion from v. 22 not reflected in OG or Th. It is also possible that the phrase is an interpretive gloss.

v. The double appearance of the verb *šāḥat* is suspicious. Moreover, the verb goes awkwardly with *niplā'ôt*. More likely is the suggestion of Charles (218) that the verb *yaḥšōb* ("he will plan") should be read here.

w. The text of the end of v. 24 and the beginning of v. 25 appears to be corrupt. Perhaps *w'm* (pointed *wĕ'im*) and *wĕ'al* were alternative readings which a copyist has misunderstood. See J. Collins (340–41). A later scribe incorporated both readings and made sense of the resulting text by taking *'m* as *'am* ("people"), echoing the phrase "people of the holy ones" from 7:27 and taking *w'l śklw* with what follows.

x. Lit., "for many days."

y. Montgomery (355) takes *nihyêtî* from the root *hāwâ* ("ruin"), a suggestion already made by Rashi and Kimchi. Alternatively, the form may be a corruption of the following verb.

z. Or, "and there was no one to explain it."

Overview

If Dan 7 was originally composed in the third or possibly even late fourth century B.C.E. and only lightly updated to address the events of the Antiochene crisis that erupted in 167 B.C.E., then ch. 8 is the first freely composed text that attempts to comprehend and respond to that crisis. Even though ch. 8 is written in awareness of ch. 7 and borrows some of its symbolism, it differs in striking ways from that earlier composition. First, the language of choice is not Aramaic but Hebrew. Second, the author of Dan 8 makes extensive use of intertextual allusions to a variety of prophetic texts in order to ground the vision in earlier authoritative words. Third, in contrast to the divine authorization of at least the first three kingdoms depicted in ch. 7, all the historical powers act on their own initiative in ch. 8. Fourth, although the vision is framed in terms of kings and kingdoms, it is the temple and its fate, not the exercise of political sovereignty, that is the deepest concern of the chapter. Finally, the representation of the Deity in these two chapters and the emphasis given to various elements of the basic plot differ sharply. In ch. 7 the Ancient of Days and his throne are vividly described, and the doxological praise of the kingdom of the one like a *bar ’ĕnāš* and the people of the holy ones gives a triumphant air to the account. Approximately the same amount of space is given to the description of these realities as to the actions of the fourth beast and the little horn. In ch. 8, however, the Most High God and the heavenly hosts are presented largely as the objects of the little horn's violent aggression, and there is no visual representation of God and the hosts. The vision proper does not even describe the downfall of the "little horn." Although this information is briefly supplied by the interpretation (v. 25f), there is virtually no description of the outcome for Israel and its temple other than the brief comment that the temple will be "made right" after a set time (v. 14). The emotional tone of ch. 8 is thus decidedly more somber than that of ch. 7. What ch. 8 shares with its predecessor, however, is a conviction that the historical process can be understood in terms of a meaningful pattern. But whereas ch. 7 made use of the somewhat arbitrary four-kingdoms schema, ch. 8 tries to identify some internal logic to political power per se as it manifests itself in history. In addition, mythic narrative patterns guide perceptions of the historical structures of events and are fundamental to the chapter's hermeneutics of history.

Because the composition does not know of the recapture and rededication of the temple in 164 B.C.E., it is generally assumed to have been composed before that date, most likely shortly after the desecration of the temple in 167. Modern readers, separated by more than two thousand years from the original context of Dan 8, have to make an effort to realize what a powerful act of intellectual courage and resistance is represented in the work of this chapter, as it wrestles the brutal and terrifying events of 167 into a symbolic framework that is able not only to acknowledge the devastating nature of what has happened but also to project grounds for certainty that the evil will be overcome in the near future. The period from 175 to 170 had already seen instability in the high-priestly succession, the assassination of the popular high priest Onias III at the instigation of the usurping high priest Menelaus, and the theft of golden vessels from the temple by Menelaus, events that were followed by a systematic plundering of the temple by Antiochus IV on his return from his first campaign in Egypt in 169. During Antiochus's second campaign against Egypt in 168, a rumor that he had died sparked an attempt by Jason, brother of Onias, to oust Menelaus, resulting in a civil war within Jerusalem. In 167 a massacre and enslavement of the populace was carried out by Apollonius at Antiochus's orders, and a permanent military colony was established in the city (1 Macc 1:16–40; 2 Macc 5). Such events, though terrible, were not unparalleled examples of Seleucid state terror. But in a move that represented an utter departure from previous practices, Antiochus's decrees attempted to extirpate Judaism itself: the temple and altar were deliberately polluted and rededicated to Zeus Olympios (= Syrian Baal Shamayin), traditional sacrifices were abrogated and replaced by pagan sacrifices, the practice of circumcision forbidden, and copies of the Torah destroyed, while prominent citizens were forced to make pagan sacrifice and to eat pork (1 Macc 1:41–64; 2 Macc 6). Though some of the details undoubtedly represent an exaggeration of the atrocities actually committed, there is no doubt that the situation was one of utter terror and cognitive dissonance. The deeds of Antiochus were intended not only as physical punishment but also as symbolic proof of his absolute power over Jerusalem and its inhabitants (see Portier-Young 140–222). His desecration of the temple and forbidding the people to carry out the commandments of the Torah were acts of psychological and spiritual warfare that were intended to demonstrate the impotence of the God of Israel. In the face of this paralyzing terror, the author of Dan 8 tried to find ways to refuse the construction of reality that Antiochus's brutality asserted.

With this context in mind, it is understandable why the author of Dan 8, with the freedom to compose a new visionary account, made some of the choices he did. First, he chose to write in Hebrew rather than Aramaic. As many commentators have observed, the quality of the Hebrew in ch. 8 is idiosyncratic at best and in some cases simply ungrammatical. Although various explanations have been offered, it may well be the work of an author who would have been more comfortable writing in Aramaic but who chose to compose in Hebrew as an act of resistance. Hebrew is the language of Torah, and in this composition the author lets the language of Torah speak words that counter Antiochus's arrogant claims. Second, the fact that the violence was directed specifically toward the temple and Torah—and through them toward God and the heavenly host—serves to displace Jewish political sovereignty (the concern of Dan 7) as the most urgent issue. Third, the brutality of persecution renders untenable the model of the fourth kingdom as merely a "rogue" state, in contrast to earlier Gentile sovereigns who were divinely authorized. Seen as the culmination of Gentile power, Antiochus's persecutions eliminate any intellectual place for divinely authorized Gentile power. Interest shifts instead to analyzing the historical patterns of the rise and fall of Gentile political powers as they interact, providing the basis for predictive claims about the present. Fourth, Scripture itself supplies critical models for this insight into history. The mythic pattern of the "rebellious subordinate deity," ultimately deriving from Canaanite mythology but drawn most directly from Isa 14, provides a narrative structure that is capable of taking Antiochus's own implicit narrative about his kingship and reframing it in a way that disempowers him and predicts his downfall. Similarly, allusions to other prophetic texts, especially the visions of Ezekiel and Zechariah, imbue the vision in Dan 8 with persuasive power and authority. In contrast to these prophets, however, the author of Dan 8 does not speak in his own persona but appropriates the newer model of pseudepigraphical revelatory literature, pioneered in the third century B.C.E. by the early Enochic works (*1 En.* 1–36; 72–82) and by Dan 7 within the Daniel tradition. By framing his composition as a vision of Daniel, the author attaches his work to a well-known and popular figure already associated with the themes of divine and human sovereignty.

Literary Features and Outline

The form of the chapter is that of a vision report. One of the oddities of its structure is that it is somewhat difficult to say where the vision ends and the interpretation begins. The vision of the ram, the goat, and the little horn ends with v. 12, but following that, Daniel overhears an angelic conversation (vv. 13–14) that refers to and even begins to interpret the vision, though the angels appear unaware of Daniel's presence. In v. 15 Daniel makes reference to his seeing the vision and attempting to understand, apparently including the conversation of the angels as part of the visionary experience. Only in v. 16 is Gabriel commanded to interpret the vision for Daniel. The chapter may be outlined as follows:

Introduction (8:1)
The vision of the ram and the goat (8:2–14)
    Setting in Susa (8:2)

The career of the ram (8:3–4)
The career of the goat and its horns (8:5–12)
    Its overpowering of the ram (8:6–7)
    The aggression of the small horn (8:8–12)
Angelic conversation: "How long?" (8:13–14)
The encounter with Gabriel (8:15–19)
Gabriel's interpretation of the vision (8:20–25)
    The ram and the goat (8:20–21)
    The four horns and the small horn (8:22–25)
Concluding evaluation and instructions (8:26)
Daniel's reaction and response (8:27)

One of the literary and hermeneutical devices used by the author is the repetition of key words and expressions. Variations of the phrases "none could stand before it" (vv. 4, 7), "no one to rescue from its power" (vv. 4, 7), and "did great things" or "grew great" (vv. 4, 8, 9, 10, 11, 25), "become strong" (vv. 8, 24), "cast to the ground and trampled" (vv. 7, 10, 12, 13), and "succeed" (vv. 12, 25)—all these characterize the power of the Gentile kings, while repetition of "shattered" or "broken" describes their sudden demise (vv. 7, 8, 25). The time to which the events refer is identified as "the time of the end" (vv. 17, 19) and "the close of the wrath/their reign" (vv. 19, 23). These repeated expressions serve to indicate that what is happening at any moment is not a unique or unexpected event but is both part of a repeated pattern in political history and an event that has a foreordained end. Thus the repetition is one means by which the terror of the situation is brought under control. Although the chapter is composed primarily in prose, poetic parallelism is used to emphasize the climactic section of the interpretation, vv. 24–25, which describe the events of the end.

Comments

[1] The account opens with an introduction in the first person (cf. third person in 7:1) and specifically identifies the following vision as subsequent to "the one that appeared to me previously," that is, the one in ch. 7, thus establishing an intentional connection between the two accounts. As in ch. 5, the sacrilegious Belshazzar, who deliberately used the Jerusalem temple vessels in a royal banquet where idols were praised, makes an apt parallel to Antiochus, whose violation of the temple will be described in the vision. Why the specific date is given as "the third year" of Belshazzar is less clear. Daniel 8 stands in some narrative tension with ch. 5. That story occurs at the end of Belshazzar's reign, and it appears that Daniel has not been an active member of Belshazzar's court (5:10–16), though the conclusion of Dan 8 has Daniel arising to attend to the king's business.

[2] Where is Daniel? Josephus interpreted the verse as indicating that Daniel himself was in Susa, an Elamite city some 225 miles east of Babylon that was only a provincial fortress during the Babylonian Empire. He claims that Daniel himself built a fortress there (*Ant.* 10.264). In medieval times a legendary tomb of Daniel was venerated in Susa, and it remains there to this day. The syntax of the verse, however, suggests that Daniel was not bodily in Susa but only there in spirit: he reports what he saw "in the vision," including the fact that he seemed to be in Susa. This is how most of the ancient versions understand the reference. Susa is an apt location for the vision since the events described have to do with the conflict between the Medo-Persian Empire and that of Greece, and Susa was one of the chief residences of the Persian king Darius the Great. It was assumed to be the Persian capital by Nehemiah (1:1) and Esther (1:2).

The visionary transportation from Babylon to another city is probably modeled after Ezek 8:1–3, where the prophet is transported in spirit from Babylon to Jerusalem. The visions of Ezekiel influence the details of this chapter in several ways (see below). Just where in Susa Daniel finds himself is more difficult to say. Ulai is the name of a watercourse often identified with the modern Disful Karun, several miles east of Susa (Hartman and DiLella 224). The problem is with the word *'ûbal*. It was taken by the ancient versions as meaning "gate" (cf. Aram. *'ăbûl*), a loanword from Akkadian *abullu*, "gateway." If this is correct, then Daniel is standing at the city gate where the road led to the Ulai River (so Hartman and DiLella 224; Goldingay 196). The spelling of the Hebrew, however, suggests that the word may be a by-form of the rare word *yûbal* (Jer 17:8; 1QH^a 16.8, 11), meaning "stream" (so the majority of modern commentators). Just as Ezekiel's initial vision took place by the Chebar Canal, so Daniel's would be at the Ulai River/Canal. Similarly, the vision in ch. 10 takes place on the bank of the Tigris River.

[3] Political and military leaders in antiquity were often symbolized by powerful and aggressive animals. Ezekiel 34:17 uses "rams and goat-bucks" to designate the leaders of Israel (for rams: Exod 15:15; 2 Kgs 24:15; Ezek 31:11; for goats: Isa 14:9; Jer 50:8; Zech 10:3; see also Miller). Similarly, "horn" is a frequent metaphor for strength and so is eminently suitable as a symbol for kings. That Daniel is in Susa and sees the horns of the animal actually growing, with the second and longer horn coming up later, would probably suffice to alert an ancient reader that the two horns represent the kingdoms of Media and Persia, a conclusion confirmed in v. 20. Although the dream visions of Dan 2 and 7 treat these as separate kingdoms, the two peoples were closely related, as the alternating figures of Median and Persian nobles on the reliefs of Persepolis testify. Similarly, the book of Esther makes frequent references to "Persia and Media" (1:3, 14–19) and to "the annals of the kings of Media and Persia" (10:2). Already in Dan 6:12 (13) there is a reference to the "law of the Medes and the Persians," as though they were one culture. The superior

strength of the Persians, who displaced the Median Empire, is represented by the comparative length of the horns.

Why a ram should represent the Median-Persian kingdoms is not self-evident. Cumont suggested that the ram and the goat might be interpreted in light of a correlation of signs of the zodiac with nations attributed to Teucer of Babylon (presumed first century C.E.), an interpretation that has been widely accepted. But there are several problems with this suggestion. Teucer postdates the composition of Daniel, and it is not known if he draws on an older tradition or if such a correlation was widely known. Moreover, though the ram is associated with Persia in his system, the goat (v. 5) is associated not with Greece but more specifically with the Seleucid kingdom.

[4] The ram is represented as all-powerful. His charging in the four cardinal directions (see textual note) symbolizes the universal sweep of his aggression. The paired negative phrases "none . . . could stand" and "no one who could rescue" underscore his dominance (cf. Deut 32:39; Hos 5:14). Fittingly, though the phrases imply the defeat of opponents, none is actually depicted. The ram alone occupies the stage. In striking contrast to the depiction of the Median and Persian kingdoms in 7:5–6, where their actions were authorized by divine command, here the ram is explicitly said to do "as he pleases" (cf. 11:3, 16, 36).

Although the ram specifically represents the Median and Persian kingdoms, in a more profound sense he is the template for all imperial rulers, who characteristically represent themselves as all-powerful. The sense of all-powerfulness is evident in the way Persian kings typically open their inscriptions: "I (am) Darius the great king, king of kings, king of countries, king on this earth. . . . Auramazda gave me his support; that which I wished to do, he made it succeed for me" (Kuhrt 495). How may one contest such claims? The book of Daniel repeatedly contrasts the power of the king with the power of the sage. Already the narratives in chs. 1–6 have shown that though the kings can wield the power of violence, the sage wields the power of God-given knowledge. And so it is here. The author of Dan 8 possesses knowledge about the dynamics of power. Presented as a revelatory vision, the chapter is a theory of political power as it manifests itself in the historical process. Whereas v. 4 depicts power much as the kings themselves represent it in their public pronouncements, triumphant and unchallenged, in the following verses the author shows that this all-powerfulness is only a moment in a larger narrative pattern.

[5–7] In contrast to the earlier models of succession of empires in Dan 2 and 7, which framed the topic in terms of a divinely commissioned process, here the naturalistic imagery of the he-goat and the ram suggests another type of explanation. The goat is given no motive for his attack. He simply runs at amazing speed at the ram and crashes into it, though his emotional state is characterized as rage and fury. Something very elemental is being described. Although the two animals are of different species, the clash of the two bovids is modeled on the dominance challenges that occur among males before the breeding season. That is to say, the author of Dan 8 represents the clash as intrinsic to the nature of dominance itself. In contrast to animal behavior, however, here the clash is to the death.

Ancient readers would have had no trouble recognizing the he-goat with a single conspicuous horn as a symbol for the Macedonian army and its king, Alexander the Great. Not only the direction (from the west) but also the reference to the goat's speed would be markers for Alexander's swift destruction of the Persian Empire, which made a profound impact on the ancient world (cf. 1 Macc 1:2–4). Crossing the Hellespont in 334 B.C.E., Alexander defeated the Persian forces at Granicus. During 333 and 332 he conquered Palestine and Egypt, chasing down and defeating Darius III at Gaugamela in 331. The speed of victorious armies in general was a trope in biblical imagery, as Habakkuk says of the Babylonians (1:6–8) and Second Isaiah says of Cyrus the Great (41:3).

While the analogy with animal behavior illumines one dimension of the nature of royal power, the author makes a second, subtler claim through the near repetition in v. 7 of phrases from v. 4 ("could not stand before it," "none to rescue from its power"). In retrospect, what was said about the ram's surpassing power in v. 4 was not actually true. Or rather, it only appeared to be the case at that moment in time. Thus the author suggests that dominant power has an ironic structure. Just when it looks most powerful is when its fragility will be exposed, as the following verse makes explicit.

[8–9] Much as Alexander's rapid victory over the Persian Empire impressed the ancient world, so his sudden death in Babylon in 323 B.C.E., apparently of a fever, was emblematic of the ephemeral nature of power. The author of Dan 8 represents his sudden death with a passive expression: "the horn was shattered." As with the use of passive constructions in 7:4–6, 11–12, 26, the implication is that the agent is God. Naturalistic and divine explanations of the historical process are simply two sides of the same coin.

The four horns that sprout in the place of the great horn represent the Diadochi, the generals among whom Alexander's kingdom was divided. In fact, there were more than four who contested for power, but for a second-century Judean author the most important would have been Ptolemy Lagus (Egypt), Philip Aridaeus (Macedonia), Antigonus Monophthalmus (Asia Minor), and Seleucus Nicator (Mesopotamia/Syria). The actual struggle for succession was, of course, much more complicated and protracted than the schematic account in v. 8c suggests, involving decades of war by the generals and their successors. The author of Dan 8 is less interested in the specifics of political history, however, than he is in the symbolism. The four kings/kingdoms represent a totality, as they are oriented to the "four winds of heaven" (cf. 7:2; more generally, the "four kingdoms" of 2:37–40 and 7:3–7 are also a way of representing the totality and unity of Gentile imperial rule).

Ironies of Power: Breaking the Horn That Challenges Heaven

The author's primary interest, however, is in the "little horn" that emerges from one of them, the Seleucid king Antiochus IV Epiphanes. While the phrase "little horn" is appropriated from 7:8, it is fitted well into the governing tropes of ch. 8, for the *little* horn is immediately said to *become great*. The root *gdl* in the Qal and Hiphil forms occurs several times in this chapter (vv. 4, 8, 9, 10), characterizing the exercise of aggressive royal power. But as the pattern of greatness quickly followed by downfall has already been established in the preceding verses, the little horn enters the stage already marked for defeat by the very fact that it has grown great.

The directions in which the little horn exerts itself are perplexing (see trans. notes). The reference to "the south" refers to Antiochus's campaigns against Egypt in the Sixth Syrian War, which began in 170. The reference to "the east" is unclear. Antiochus's campaign against Parthia did not begin until 166–165, after the attack on Jerusalem and the decrees of persecution, alluded to in the following verses. It is possible, however, that the chapter was composed after Antiochus had begun his Parthian campaign and that the details are not intended to be chronological. Bauer (169) suggests that "to the east" refers to Antiochus's turning back toward Palestine after his largely successful war against Egypt was brought to an end by the intervention of the Roman army. But this hardly seems the most likely interpretation of the directional terms.

[10] The spatial terminology used in vv. 4, 5, and 9 has all been horizontal, naming directions upon the earth. With v. 10, however, a vertical dimension is employed, as Antiochus literally storms heaven. Although in mundane terms Antiochus's actions took place in Jerusalem, for the author they are effectively events in the heavenly realm. The repetition of the root *gdl* in vv. 10–11 depicts this action as an extension of his previous aggrandizement (v. 9). Since the preposition ʿ*ad* can have both a spatial sense ("up to," "as far as") and a comparative sense ("as"), the little horn not only extends his power upward but also appears to be as great as the heavenly host themselves. The host of heaven is the divine entourage of God, often identified with the stars, though sometimes mentioned alongside the stars (Deut 4:19), as here. These heavenly beings function as God's divine council (1 Kgs 22:19), much as they do in Ugaritic mythology, and are also called upon to praise God (Pss 103:21; 148:2). In biblical tradition, worship of them was not permitted (Deut 4:19; 17:3; 2 Kgs 17:16; 21:3; Jer 8:2; Zeph 1:5), since they are merely creatures of God (Ps 33:6; Neh 9:6). In one text, Isa 24:21, which has similarities to later apocalyptic traditions (cf. *1 Enoch* 10; 17–19), the host is represented as punished for rebellion. More often, however, the host and the stars are represented as God's divine army, which is mustered for battle (Josh 5:13–15; Judg 5:20; Isa 40:26; 45:12), a theme extensively developed in the Qumran *War Scroll*. The notion of angels as leaders of angelic armies appears also in Dan 10:13, 20–21; 12:1.

The actions of the little horn echo the patterns of aggression exhibited by the he-goat in v. 7: both cast their opponents to the ground and trample them (cf. 7:7, 23). Thus he acts within the historical paradigm. But the fact that the little horn's aggression is directed against the heavenly host and stars also casts his actions in terms of the paradigm of the ancient myth of Athtar (the morning star Venus), known both from ancient Ugaritic sources (*CTU* 1.6 I 53–67) and from a summary of a similar myth in Isa 14:12–15. The relation between these two accounts remains contested (see Heiser), but many variants of the mythic pattern likely were in circulation. In Isa 14 the morning star Hêlēl ben-Shāḥar intends to ascend to heaven "above the stars of God" and to establish his throne there as a rival to the Most High. Instead, however, he is cast down to Sheol in ignominy. In Isaiah the myth is used to predict the downfall of a "king of Babylon" (v. 4). The version in Dan 8:10 contains a new detail, however: some stars of the host are hurled to earth and trampled (cf. Rev 12:4). Although this detail may be an invention of the author of Dan 8, it is also possible that he knows of that motif from a different version of the traditional myth (see A. Y. Collins 1976, 78). The connection of this myth with Antiochus may have been facilitated by the fact that some of Antiochus's coins depict his head as almost touching a star or with stars at the end of his diadem (Mørkholm 1970, 42). Similarly 2 Macc 9:10 similarly says of Antiochus that he "had thought that he could touch the stars of heaven."

[11] The pinnacle of Antiochus's aggression is recounted in v. 11. Described with the same verb and preposition as in v. 10, now the little horn makes himself as great as the prince of the host. Although some have attempted to identify this figure with Michael (so Willis 105n2; Smith-Christopher 113; Lacocque 162; cf. Dan 12:1; Josh 5:13–15), most agree that the reference is to none other than God (cf. v. 25). If indeed both of the verbs in v. 11b are passive (see trans. notes), what is the significance of this choice? The actual agent of these actions was Antiochus, but it seems unlikely that the author was simply being theologically squeamish, given what he has already said about Antiochus's deeds in vv. 10–11a. Perhaps the author points at a more mysterious reality. In ch. 7 the divine passive was used to suggest that the actions of the first three beasts were in fact authorized and controlled by God. Here too, the author may be suggesting that even these horrific events are mysteriously in the hand of God. A similar idea is expressed in the Two Spirits Treatise (1QS 3.13–4.26) of the Qumran *Community Rule*, where the power of the Angel of Darkness to corrupt and oppress the children of righteousness is "in accordance with the mysteries of God" and will prevail only for a set period of time (3.23). Inasmuch as the vision in Daniel is to have a predetermined length of time (vv. 13–14) and is shown to Daniel centuries before the events take place (v. 1), the divine determination of history is not in doubt. Thus even in describing the utmost horror of desecration of the temple, the author uses a verbal clue to hint at the difference between mundane appearances and divine reality.

Even though Antiochus's edict outlawed all traditional burnt offerings, sacrifices, and drink offerings (1 Macc 1:45), substituting instead offerings considered to be unfit abominations (1 Macc 1:59; 2 Macc 6:5), the author of Daniel focuses on the *tāmîd*, or daily whole offering, because it was the most frequent and the most important of the required sacrifices at the temple. The *tāmîd* is commanded in Exod 29:38–42 and Num 28:2–8 and consists of a lamb together with meal and wine offerings. Although Ezek 46:13–15 assumes it is offered once a day in the morning, the practice of offering two lambs, one in the morning and one in the evening, developed during the Second Temple period and is reflected in the pentateuchal laws (as in Sir 45:14). The use of the word *tāmîd* alone to designate the offering is unique to Daniel, though it later becomes the standard usage. In other biblical texts the offering is referred to as the ʿôlat *tāmîd*, the daily offering that "goes up" as smoke (e.g., Num 29:38; Neh 10:34).

The double term "place of his sanctuary" (*mĕkôn miqdāšô*) is unusual, though the words are used in poetic parallelism in Exod 15:17. *Miqdāš* is the common word for sanctuary in the priestly literature and in Ezekiel. *Mākôn* is less common but occurs in poetic contexts, where it is frequently used for the heavenly dwelling of God (1 Kgs 8:39, 43, 49; Isa 18.4; Ps 33:14), though it can also refer to the earthly habitation (Exod 15:17; 1 Kgs 8:13). Perhaps it is used here because the vision merges the events happening in Jerusalem with their effects also in heaven. That the sanctuary is said to be "thrown down" assimilates Antiochus's actions to the pattern established in v. 7, where the he-goat throws the ram to the ground. Although the word has a physical denotation, it can be used metaphorically as meaning to abandon or to treat with contempt (cf. Neh 9:26). It is historically unclear what actually happened to the sanctuary since 1 Macc 1:39 and 3:45 describe the sanctuary as "desolate like a desert" and "trampled down," though these passages are in poetic laments and may use stereotyped language. In the prose account of the recapture of the temple, a vivid scene is described: "There they saw the sanctuary desolate, the altar profaned, and the gates burned. In the courts they saw bushes sprung up as in a thicket, or as on one of the mountains. They saw also the chambers of the priests in ruins" (1 Macc 4:38). Yet the parallel account in 2 Macc 10 says nothing about destruction, only about pagan structures that had been built there (v. 2). It is likely that 1 Maccabees is a melodramatic exaggeration. Thus "thrown down" in Dan 8:11 is also probably used in the metaphorical sense.

[12] The first part of this verse is extremely obscure (see trans. notes) but seems to function as a summary of vv. 10–11. The expression "given over" (*tinnātēn*) is the equivalent of the Aramaic verbal expression *yityahăbûn*, used in a similar context in 7:25. Then 8:12b also summarizes the little horn's actions, but in a more general manner. Again invoking the formula of dominance from v. 7, the little horn is said to "cast truth to the ground." Many commentators assume that "truth" is a synonym for the Torah, the basis of the religious observances suppressed by Antiochus. But there is little evidence for this specific meaning

of *ʾĕmet* (Lacocque [163] alludes to Mal 2:6, but that phrase means something like "true instruction"). Bauer (171) suggests that *ʾĕmet* means something like "world-order," which he associates with the "times and seasons" of 2:21 and the "times set by decree" of 7:25. This seems more likely. Compare the use in 10:21, where Gabriel says he will reveal to Daniel "what is written in the book of truth," which is, in fact, the long historical account of the conflict between the king of the north and the king of the south in ch. 11. Thus *ʾĕmet* seems to refer to the course of history as determined by God and to the proper relation of divine to human sovereignty, which is the central topic of concern in both parts of the book of Daniel. Although the issue is framed more dualistically in some of the writings from Qumran, in the Two Spirits Treatise (1QS 3.13–4.26), the contrast between truth and deceit is the contrast between that which God loves and that which God abhors (1QS 3.18–19; 3.26–4.1), as it is manifested in the predetermined course of events in the world. The power of deceit is represented as acting aggressively against those associated with light and truth and righteousness. This is also what the little horn attempts to do in casting truth to the ground. In dramatic contrast to the preceding episodes, in which the sudden demise of the powerful king or kingdom was the final event, this account stops with the little horn fully ascendant. As Willis (106–7) suggests, the narrative seems to break the bounds of the myth of the rebellious subordinate, since rather than being cast down, he is the one who casts down.

[13–14] Although the first part of Daniel's vision is punctuated with references to his seeing (vv. 2, 3, 4, 5, 6, 7), vv. 8–12 have all been third-person description, drawing the reader's attention to the events themselves and away from Daniel as observer. Thus the abrupt reintroduction of first-person speech ("then I heard . . .") is somewhat startling. Yet Daniel does not see the holy ones but only hears them. Apparently, as v. 15 suggests, Daniel has been continuing to watch the vision. Certain features of the wording of v. 13 suggest an intentional deflection of attention from the holy ones themselves. They are referred to indefinitely as "a holy one" (*ʾeḥād-qādôš*), a phrase perhaps best rendered in English by "some holy one or other," and by the peculiar word *palmônî*, apparently an abbreviation of the more common phrase *pĕlōnî ʾalmōnî*, meaning "somebody or other," or "so and so." The effect is to suggest that Daniel's attention has been so focused on what he is seeing that he only gradually becomes aware of a conversation that has been going on between two angelic beings, who, like Daniel, have been witnessing the vision.

The influence of Zechariah on this short passage is evident, both in having the seer overhear an angelic conversation (cf. Zech 2:3–4 [7–8]) and in the outcry of the holy one, "How long?" (cf. 1:12). In Zech 1:12 the problem was the continuing desolation of Jerusalem, which had been under a curse for "seventy years," an allusion to the prophecy of Jer 25:11–12; 29:10, which will itself be the focus of Dan 9. Naturally, the attack on Jerusalem and the temple by Antiochus suggested the analogy with Nebuchadnezzar's earlier devastation of city and temple, though Daniel represents Antiochus as evil in a way that exceeds the characterization of Nebuchadnezzar in the writings from the sixth century. Correspondingly, the themes of the guilt of the Judeans and the anger of God, common to that literature, are largely absent from Daniel.

Verse 13 gives its own summary of vv. 10–12, mentioning first the *tāmîd* offering, but adding the phrase "and the transgression that desolates." Although this may simply refer to all of Antiochus's actions, as in v. 12, the term "desolating" is used in 9:27; 11:31; and 12:11 in connection with the noun "detestable thing" (*šiqqûṣ*); this apparently is a reference to something erected on the altar of burnt sacrifice in the temple, where the *tāmîd* was traditionally offered (cf. 1 Macc 1:54, 59). It is possible that such is also the reference here (so Goldingay 212). See the comments on 9:27 for further discussion. The angel then pairs "sanctuary" (cf. v. 11) and "host" (vv. 10, 12) with the image of their being trampled (vv. 7, 10), which figures in this chapter as an image of destructive rage (cf. 7:7).

The first angel replies to the question "How long?" with a precise answer: "2,300 evenings-mornings," though it is not clear how to interpret this phrase. In v. 26 a slight variant: "the evenings and the mornings" is used. The versions and many ancient commentators understood "evenings-mornings" to refer to days, much as Gen 1 does (as in 1:5: "And there was evening and there was morning, the first day"). This position is still defended by some modern commentators (Vogel 122–26; Seow 125; cf. Goldingay 213). Depending on whether a lunar or solar calendar was used, the time would be between 6⅓ and 6½ years. That is an odd amount of time, and attempts to correlate it with specific historical events have not been very persuasive (e.g., Seow 125; Burgmann 544–45).

Most modern scholars understand the phrase evenings-mornings as referring to the two daily sacrifices, although when those are discussed in the legal texts of Exodus and Numbers, the sequence is morning and evening, not evening and morning. But Daniel may simply be influenced by the normal reckoning of the day's beginning with the evening. Thus 2,300 *tāmîd* sacrifices would equal 1,150 days, or about 3¼ years. Although that is fairly close to the calculation in 1 Macc 4:52–54 concerning the time before the resumption of sacrifices (3 years), the calculation in Dan 8 does not appear to be a *vaticinium ex eventu* but an actual prediction. Presumably some connection exists with other symbolic predictions in Daniel, as in 7:25 ("a time, [two] times, and half a time") and in 9:27 ("half a week"), both of which are usually taken to mean 3½ years. The latter passage in particular is relevant since it, too, specifically has in view the cessation of the daily sacrifice. But if the author intends a period of 3½ years, it is not clear why he did not supply an exact calculation. It thus remains likely that 2,300 has its significance in relation to some symbolic calculation, but it is no longer possible to decipher the system. What is clear, however, is that the time permitted for the desecration of the sanctuary is strictly determined, and that at the end of the period it will be made right or, as Montgomery (343) prefers to translate, "vindicated," "restored to its rights."

[15–16] That a new section of the vision report opens with v. 15 is indicated by the similarity between v. 15 and v. 1. In both a form of the verb "to see" (*rā'â*) occurs, along with a reference to the vision (*ḥāzôn*) and the emphatic self-identification "I, Daniel" (*'ănî dānîyē'l*). Now, in addition to hearing the voices of the holy ones, Daniel suddenly sees one who appears in human form, the traditional way of envisioning divine messengers (Gen 18:2; 32:24 [25]; Josh 5:13–15; Judg 6:21–22; 13:6–21). The angelic dialogue continues, and the speakers are probably to be identified with the figures of vv. 13–14. One of the angels remains unidentified, with only his location in "the midst of the Ulai" specified. Why he should be associated with the river is unclear, but in 12:5–6 also the angels are associated with the river, perhaps reflecting the influence of Ezekiel's inaugural vision by the Chebar Canal. Given the preceding angelic dialogue in vv. 13–14, it is likely that the voice is that of the first angelic speaker in v. 13, not that of God (contra Plöger 128, followed by Goldingay 214). An early tradition cited by Jerome (on 10:10–14) identifies the speaking angel as Michael ("The Jews claim that this man who directed Gabriel to explain the vision to Daniel was Michael [himself]"; trans. Archer; cf. 10:13, 21; 12:1). Whoever gives the command, the angel who speaks to Daniel is identified as Gabriel, the archangel who will figure prominently in biblical tradition as a messenger (8:16; 9:20–27; Luke 1:11, 19, 26; cf. Luke 2:9; Acts 5:19; 8:26; 12:7). Here he is introduced via a wordplay. In 8:15 Daniel had seen one who had the appearance of a man (*kĕmar'ēh-gāber*), who is then identified as Gabriel, popularly understood to mean "man of God." Although Dan 8:16 is the first biblical reference to an angel's name, the somewhat earlier apocalyptic Book of the Watchers (*1 En.* 1–36) indicates that speculation about the angels, their names, and their functions was already developing in the third century B.C.E. In *1 En.* 9:1 the four archangels are named as Michael, Sariel, Raphael, and Gabriel. Each receives a specific commission from God, though in *1 Enoch* Sariel is the angel who delivers a message to Noah, whereas the other three punish and imprison the watchers and their giant children. Gabriel similarly has a military function in Dan 10:20–21. In the list of seven archangels in *1 En.* 20, Gabriel is said to be in charge of paradise, the serpents (perhaps meaning the seraphim), and the cherubim. In the Dead Sea Scrolls, Gabriel is also mentioned along with other archangels in the *Book of Noah* (1Q19 frg. 2 4) and in the *War Scroll* (1QM 9.16; 4Q285 frg. 1 3). Though the author of Daniel may have been familiar with a more developed speculation about the angels, he focuses on their revelatory and military functions.

[17–19] Much as the author tried to represent overlapping experiences of seeing the vision and hearing the angelic conversation in vv. 13–15 by juxtaposing verses reflecting one or another aspect of the experience, so vv. 17–19 intercut Daniel's emotional reaction to the presence of the angel (vv. 17a, 18) with the angel's words to him (vv. 17b, 19). The physical act of prostration was a typical social gesture communicating respect for someone of higher standing (Gen 33:7; 48:12; 1 Sam 20:41; 2 Sam 9:6; etc.) and was also used in cultic contexts in response to a display of divine power (Lev 9:24; 1 Kgs 18:39; 2 Chr 7:3). The sudden encounter with a divine being, however, is distinguished from these more conventionalized reactions by a genuine emotional fear (Josh 5:14; Judg 6:22; 13:6, 22). Ezekiel's reaction to the appearance of YHWH's Glory (prostration and requiring divine assistance to stand, Ezek 1:28–2:2; 3:23–24) becomes an influential model for later literature (e.g., Rev 1:17; *1 En.* 14:14, 24; *4 Ezra* [2 Esd] 10:29–30; *Apoc. Ab.* 10:2). Daniel renders the experience as a kind of trance state (*nirdamtî*). The deep sleep known as *tardēmâ* is generally regarded as divinely caused (Gen 2:21; 1 Sam 26:12; Isa 29:10) and is often associated with visionary experiences (Gen 15:12; Job 4:13; 33:15). Just as Ezekiel required a spirit to enter into him to allow him to stand before God (2:1–2), so the angel's touch allows Daniel to stand (cf. 1 Kgs 19:5, 7). Gabriel's address to him as "O mortal" (*ben-ʾādām*) is another indication of the influence of Ezekiel's vision (2:1) on Dan 8.

Gabriel's interpretation of the dream is preceded by two comments concerning the time to which it pertains (vv. 17b, 19). Two parallel phrases refer to "the time of the end" (*ʿet-qēṣ*) and "the time appointed for the end" (*môʿēd qēṣ*). Although the word *qēṣ* was developing the sense of "a period of time" (e.g., Sir 43:6; 1QS 4.25–26; 1QHa 7.16; 9.26 [line numbers follow DJD 40]), Daniel clearly uses it in the older sense of "end," "termination" (Amos 8:2; Ezek 7:2, 6; 21:25, 29 [30, 34]; etc.) The qualification of it as a fixed or "appointed" time is in keeping with the designation of a set number of days in v. 14 and is probably an allusion to Hab 2:3, which offered reassurance that the end of Babylonian rule was fixed, even if the time seemed to tarry. Less clear is the meaning of the more specific phrase "at the close of the wrath" (*bĕʾaḥărît hazzāʿam*). In contrast to Daniel's use of *qēṣ* to denote a fixed point in time, *ʾaḥărît* can be used either spatially or temporally to designate that which is remote from the speaker or the latter part of something or period of time (*HALOT* 36–37). The word *zāʿam* ("wrath") has to do with the act of cursing and the emotion of indignation that prompts it (*HALOT* 277). But against whom is the wrath directed? As noted in connection with v. 13, the allusion appears to be to Zech 1:12, which refers to God's wrath against Jerusalem itself. In general, the term "wrath" is used to describe God's emotion, which may be directed either to Israel (Ezek 21:31 [36]; Lam 2:6) or to the nations (Zeph 3:8; Hab 3:12; Mal 1:4). The reference to a period of time designated as a period of wrath, however, seems to refer to the period of Gentile rule (see v. 23), lasting from the Babylonian conquest until the expected eschaton. (In a similar usage in the *Damascus Document* [CD

1.5–12], the beginning of the end of the period of wrath is associated with the religious reform movement led by the Teacher of Righteousness.) The general assumption in Second Temple Judaism was that this period had been inaugurated because of the sins of Judah, though the book of Daniel is remarkable in its avoidance of this theology (cf. 1:1–2; 2:37–38; 7:2–7), employing it only in the Deuteronomistic prayer in 9:4–19. The excesses of the Gentile rulers, however, who exceed their commission or otherwise act on their own account, is sometimes cited as a reason for terminating this period (see 2:40; 7:8–11; *1 En.* 89:59–72a). Thus John Collins (338–39) is likely correct that "wrath" becomes a kind of technical term for this period of Gentile domination that can be used even when the theological context is not focused on the sins of the Judeans so much as the excesses of the Gentile rulers. Other texts from the same period continue the traditional motif of associating God's wrath with sin, as 1 Macc 1:64 characterizes the Antiochene persecutions as "great wrath [that] came upon Israel" because of the actions of the Jewish renegades.

[20–22] Gabriel quickly identifies the initial symbols of the vision in a terse "A is B" style that some have likened to the style of interpretation in the Qumran pesharim. But this style is also characteristic of dream interpretation, as in Joseph's interpretation of the dreams of his fellow prisoners in Gen 40 (e.g., v. 12: "This is its interpretation: the three branches are three days").

In contrast to Dan 2 and 7, which generally use vague language ("another kingdom," "a fourth kingdom"), Dan 8 explicitly identifies the kingdoms of Media/Persia and Greece. Thus later Jewish and Christian interpreters, who often tried to contemporize the visions to include references to Rome, were not able to reassign these symbols. Josephus (*Ant.* 10.276) correctly identifies the events with the actions of Antiochus Epiphanes, but he cannot resist adding "in the same manner Daniel also wrote about the empire of the Romans." Jerome skips over the passage altogether.

[23–25] Verse 23 confirms the interpretation given above that the author understands the present as coming at the end of a series of Gentile kingdoms characterized by "transgressions" or "rebellions" (see trans. notes)—that is, actions that exceed their mandate from God. The notion of transgressions being "completed" has a close parallel in Gen 15:16, which refers to the iniquity of the Amorites as having to be completed before Abram's descendants can return and take possession of the land. As a mode of thinking, this notion helps to reduce the cognitive dissonance between a belief in divine sovereignty and the continuing presence of evil. For other examples of this pattern of thought, see 2 Macc 6:14–15 (sins of the Gentiles); *4 Ezra* (2 Esd) 4:36–37 (souls of the righteous); Rev 6:10–11 (souls of the martyrs).

The appearance of Antiochus signals the beginning of the end of this period, its climactic moment. While some have suggested that the description of Antiochus is drawn from his actual reputation and actions, it is more likely that his depiction is based on a character type known from wisdom and early apocalyptic traditions (Lebram 1975, 738–42; Goldingay 217–18). But perhaps this is a false dichotomy. New experiences are necessarily comprehended by means of available templates. One should be cautious, therefore, about the extent to which this account can be used to reconstruct historical events.

There is no doubt that Antiochus is framed as a type of the arrogant king who opposes the God of Israel by oppressing his people, much as Isaiah casts the king of Assyria (Isa 10:5–14; 37:22–29). This stereotyped portrait has several recurring elements: (1) the king's initially near godlike domination of the situation; (2) his unbridled arrogance; (3) his ignorance of the fact that his success has actually been determined by God; (4) his downfall and humiliation. In Isa 10:13 the motif of the king's wisdom is included, an element that Ezekiel makes central to his portrait of the King of Tyre in Ezek 28:1–19. Thus in Dan 8:23–25, Antiochus is introduced as "hard-faced," an idiom for arrogant disregard or impudence (Deut 28:50; Prov 7:13) and "skilled in understanding riddles." Many interpreters take this second characterization in a decidedly negative fashion and translate "versed in intrigue" (NJPS) or the like (e.g., Plöger 121; J. Collins 327). But the quality is morally neutral in and of itself: it is often associated with the ways in which kings establish their preeminence, as when the Queen of Sheba tests Solomon's reputation for wisdom by propounding riddles to him (1 Kgs 10:1). Similarly, Josephus reports a riddle contest between Solomon and Hiram of Tyre (*Ant.* 8.143–49), and a similar contest between the Assyrian and Egyptian kings forms an important part of the plot in *Ahiqar.* Thus here the detail simply establishes the king's intellectual potency, though when coupled with his impudence, it suggests hubris.

Verse 24a focuses on the king's ability to accomplish his designs. The word *niplāʾôt* ("wonderful things") is frequently used of God's own miraculous deeds (e.g., Exod 3:20; Judg 6:13; Ps 78:11, 32; Neh 9:17), thus suggesting Antiochus's apparently godlike prowess and the blasphemous nature of his pretensions (cf. 7:8, 20; 11:36). The motif of his success echoes the similar climactic phrase from the vision account in v. 12. The second half of 8:24 identifies the objects of his destructive power, the "strong ones" and the "holy ones."

The perplexing text of the end of v. 24 and the beginning of v. 25 allows for different interpretations (see trans. notes). Following a suggestion of Charles (219), I take "strong ones" to be human antagonists of Antiochus and "holy ones" to be heavenly opponents (similarly J. Collins 327). It is not necessary to specify the "strong ones" as the other claimants to the Seleucid throne, as some do (Montgomery 350; J. Collins 341; Bauer 177). The parallelism simply makes the case that Antiochus is challenging, with apparent success, both earthly and heavenly powers.

Four poetic lines, v. 25a–d, construct an a-b-a'-b' pattern, alternating the motifs of deception and hubris. Unlike claims to wisdom, deceitful action is not clearly a part of the stereotypical figure of the arrogant king. This detail may be drawn more specifically from Antiochus's modus operandi. Contemporary Hellenistic historians also noted his use of deceit (see Lebram 1975, 742n23). So, too, the reference to his destroying many while they are unsuspecting might be taken as referring to the use of deceit by Antiochus's forces to take Jerusalem, as reported in 1 Macc 1:29–30. Lebram points out that it is possible that 1 Macc 1:20–30 is actually modeling its narrative on the obscure reference in Daniel. He suggests that Dan 8:25 might rather be comparing Antiochus to the mythic-eschatological figure of Gog, who in Ezek 38:8, 14 attacks a people living "securely." The vocabulary, however, is different, and so the notion of a typological model seems less likely than that this detail is drawn from the common perception of Antiochus as a king who used deception as a weapon of war.

The two lines having to do with the king's arrogance prepare the reader for the end of the account. Although the verb "to grow great" or "to do great things" has been used as an objective description several times (vv. 4, 8, 10), here the king grows great "in his own mind." Ironically, he is not only someone who deceives others; he also deceives himself. The outcome of this inflated self-perception is that he will stand against the Prince of princes, meaning God. To this point both in the vision and in the interpretation, Dan 8 has described Antiochus for verse upon verse almost wholly in terms of his strength and success against both earthly and heavenly opponents. In a stunning reversal, his demise is communicated in only three Hebrew words: *ûbĕ'epes yād yiššābēr*, "but he will be broken, and not by hands." The rhetorical economy of the text deflates Antiochus's massive pretensions.

[26–27] The final two verses of the chapter form a set of concluding remarks, first by Gabriel, concerning the vision, and then by Daniel, reporting on his reaction. Although the vision has largely concerned the role and fate of Antiochus as "the little horn," Gabriel picks up a phrase from the angelic conversation in vv. 13–14, referring to what was seen as "the vision of the evenings and the mornings." Thus the emphasis is shifted to the fate of the daily sacrifice itself. Gabriel's command to Daniel, "Seal up the vision" and so keep it a secret, is part of the pseudepigraphical rhetoric of the apocalypse, thus explaining how a revelation communicated centuries earlier would only now be known. The possibility that prophets could receive revelations that pertained to the distant future was already current in the exilic period, where this suggestion was allegedly used by Ezekiel's audience as a reason for paying little attention to his words (12:27). For apocalypses, the notion of prophecy for distant days becomes part of the authorizing strategy of the genre. The book of Daniel does not, however, explain who unseals Daniel's account and makes it available.

In 4:19 (16) Daniel reacted with distress and alarm to Nebuchadnezzar's dream report, not because it eluded him but precisely because he understood what it entailed. In 7:28 Daniel similarly reports being disturbed and even physically affected by the vision. In ch. 7, however, the dream vision is not for the king but for Daniel's knowledge, and so he does not share it with anyone. Yet there is no indication that he fails to grasp the import of what he has seen. The situation is different in ch. 8. The mental and physical distress Daniel experiences is even more pronounced and leads to his psychological isolation. His arising to do the king's business underscores the sharpening divide between the two contexts of Daniel's consciousness, one having to do with his role as adviser to the king, but a second and utterly incommunicable one having to do with his relation to a distant future at the end of the reign of Gentile kings. Daniel's distress is unrelieved because he does not understand what has been revealed. The reader of Dan 8, however, holds the key to what Daniel could not understand: the actual historical events of Antiochus's persecution and their predicted outcome. Once again, the reader is cast in the role of a skilled interpreter, the one for whom the revelation has been unsealed.

History of Reception, by Brennan W. Breed

The Little Horn: Supernatural Anti-Messiah

Daniel's descriptions of Antiochus IV Epiphanes's brutal persecution of the Jewish people (7:7–8, 11, 21–26; 8:9–14, 19–25; 9:24–27; 11:21–45) have been used throughout history as a lens through which to interpret opponents who seem to be stronger or more dangerous than one can imagine—including the force of evil itself (McGinn 2000, 27). For many readers of Daniel, and in particular Christians, this figure took the shape of a supernatural opponent. Early Christians were steeped in apocalyptic, and Dan 7–12 was vitally important to the development of their theological framework. The Little Apocalypse found in the Synoptic Gospels (e.g., Mark 13) is heavily influenced by Dan 2 and 7–12, as are the descriptions of the eschatological "lawless one" and "restraining one" in 2 Thess 2:1–12, and also the figures of the dragon and the beasts from the sea and land in Rev 12–13 (Hartman 195–205; Nicholl 225–49). Although the term "antichrist" used by the Johannine authors (1 John 2:18, 22; 4:3; 2 John 7) does not explicitly draw from Daniel, early Christians quickly conflated the resulting figure of the antichrist with the lawless one (2 Thess 2:3–12), the beasts from the sea and the land (Rev 13), and "the abomination of desolation" (KJV: Matt 24:15; Mark 13:14) to signify the final enemy of Christ who will perish during his second coming (Irenaeus, *Haer.* 5.25.1–2; Jerome, *Comm. Matt.* 4.24.15). Since the seven-headed depiction of the beast from the sea in Rev 13 clearly signifies Rome's famous seven hills, many early Christians associated this final eschatological opponent with Roman emperors, especially the self-styled savior Nero, as the cosmic opponent (Pattemore 166). Moreover, Rev 13:7–8 refers to Dan 8:10 and then adds an ironic inversion of the language extolling the humanlike one in Dan 7:14; this reveals that the apocalyptic Roman antichrist was understood in Danielic terms as a pseudo-humanlike one (Beale 234–37).

In the resulting Christian literature concerning the antichrist, one finds common elements from Dan 7–12: the immanent enemy will exceed human limitations, impiously blaspheme and deceive, alter religious rituals in the process, and finally herald a climactic turning point in history before decisive divine intervention destroys him. In the *Didache,* the final apocalyptic discourse includes the element of "the deceiver" who arrives before the messianic humanlike one (16.3–4); likewise, the author of the early second-century *Epistle of Barnabas* cites Dan 7:7–8 and 7:24 to discuss the imminent arrival of an oppressive cosmic tyrant (4:1–5). Yet *Barnabas*'s author seems to think that the two citations come from different prophets, suggesting an already well-worn tradition of using atomized segments of Dan 7–12 to interpret the coming cosmic opponent (Peerbolte 189). Justin Martyr's depiction of the final enemy in his *Dialogue with Trypho* draws heavily from Dan 7, but he uses different Danielic motifs than those used by the author of 2 Thess 2:1–12. As Justin argues, at Christ's resurrection "the times now run on to their consummation; and he whom Daniel foretells would have dominion for a time, and times, and an half, is even already at the door, about to speak blasphemous and daring things against the Most High" (*Dial.* 32.3–4; cf. 110.2).

This sense of the imminent arrival of the Danielic antichrist cooled significantly in the third century as theologians such as Hippolytus set the arrival of the opponent several centuries in the future. Yet interest in the details of this figure remained quite strong: Irenaeus and Hippolytus both wrote extensive treatments of the antichrist that used Dan 7–11 as primary sources (Irenaeus, *Haer.* 5.25–30; Hippolytus, *Antichr.* 25–28; *Comm. Dan.* 4.4–24). Irenaeus's theology of recapitulation led him to assert that the Messiah must be mirrored in the anti-Messiah, and thus the antichrist must be Jewish, in particular from the tribe of Dan (cf. Gen 49:17), and not a Roman emperor such as Nero (*Haer.* 5.26.2). Hippolytus's treatise on the antichrist and his commentary on Daniel follow Irenaeus's identification of the antichrist as Jewish due to his mirroring of Jesus: "Christ is a king, so Antichrist is a king" (*Antichr.* 6). In his reading of Dan 7 and 8, Hippolytus argues that the antichrist, "after gaining terrible power over all, being nevertheless a tyrant, shall stir up tribulation and persecution against men, exalting himself against them. For Daniel says . . ." (*Antichr.* 25).

By the time of Hippolytus, the basic scheme of the Christian narrative of the antichrist was set, and this narrative would hold sway until the seventeenth century (Dunbar). The antichrist would be of Jewish origin, he would rebuild the Jerusalem temple (cf. Dan 9:25–26), gather disciples and deceitfully spread a message of blasphemy (understood to refer to Dan 8:23–25), restore the Roman Empire (as in the traditional interpretation of the fourth beast in Dan 2 and 7 as

History of Reception 275

Rome), and persecute Christianity (understood as the "holy ones" in Dan 7:21) before being destroyed by a returning Christ, understood as the humanlike one (Dan 7:13–14). The dissonance between the Roman fourth beast and a Jewish little horn caused some Christian interpreters to fragment the antichrist into two parts, one Jewish and one Roman, as did the third-century poet Commodian, who wrote: "A man from Persia will be immortal; for us Nero is the Antichrist, for the Jews he is" (McGinn 2000, 66).

Origen's spiritualization of the antichrist tradition created a different trajectory in the Christian interpretation of the "little horn." Origen, who claimed that "anyone who likes may find the prophecy in Daniel respecting antichrist," shifted the debate by interpreting Dan 8:23–25 and 9:27 to refer primarily to the spiritual battle undergone by all Christians against the "lie," which is anything in the present that struggles against Christ (*Cels.* 2.50). For Origen, "the abomination of desolation" is the "word of the lie that is seen to stand in the place of Holy Scripture" (*Comm. Matt.* 24; McGinn 2000, 64). The Christian theologians Tyconius and Augustine, and later Gregory the Great, would follow Origen's path and interpret the spirit of the antichrist to be the lack of faith within the Christian community; these anti-apocalyptic antichrist traditions, however, rely more on 1–2 John than on Daniel, 2 Thessalonians, and Revelation (McGinn 2000, 81; cf. Augustine, *Tract. ep. Jo.* 3.4–10; 7.2).

The Little Horn: Historical Arch-Opponent

Many interpreters, such as the philosopher Porphyry, have understood the figures of the "little horn" (Dan 7:8; 8:9), the prince who is to destroy the sanctuary (9:26), and the "contemptible person" (11:21) to refer to Antiochus IV. A number of Eastern Christian interpreters, including Ephrem, Aphrahat, Polychronius, and Isho'dad of Merv, as well as the Western theologian Hippolytus, also understood at least some of these images to refer to Antiochus IV (Casey 1979, 53; Hippolytus, *Comm. Dan.* 4.54) as well as, typologically, the persecution of Christians in the last days (Casey 1979, 69). As Hippolytus of Rome writes: "Daniel predicted two Abominations, the first of destruction and the second of desolation. What is the one of destruction save that which Antiochus did at that time? What is that of desolation save the universal one when antichrist comes?" (*Comm. Dan.* 4.54). Aphrahat believed that these texts apply to any ruler who is not humble before God (Morrison 79). The Syriac identification of the little horn with Antiochus IV solidified by means of the inclusion of Antiochus's name in the manuscripts of Peshitta Daniel (Morrison 70).

Many readers reactualized the Danielic prophecies of the little horn, destroying prince, and contemptible person for their own day, interpreting these figures as their political oppressors or enemies. For many in the ancient world, this oppressor was Rome. The Jewish apocalypse *4 Ezra*, for example, interprets the final figures associated with the fourth beast as a cosmic enemy embodied by Vespasian, the Roman emperor responsible for the destruction of Jerusalem in 70 C.E.; his son and successor, Titus, who carried out the destruction of Jerusalem; and Titus's brother and successor, Domitian; this beast capitulates in an eschatological fight with the messianic lion (*4 Ezra* [2 Esd] 11:32–12:2; 12:30–33; Peerbolte 314). Likewise, the *War Scroll* from Qumran seems to interpret Dan 11:40–12:3 as a description of the downfall of Kittim (Rome) when invading Egypt (1QM 1.1–10; Vanonen 242). For early Christians, the terrors of Titus's destruction of Jerusalem were unimportant compared to the persecutions thought to have occurred at the behest of Nero; as Ambrosiaster (*Commentarius* 3.240) writes, the "mystery of lawlessness" was "initiated by Nero, who, in his zeal for idols and with the instigation of his father, the devil, killed the apostles," and it continues "up to Diocletian and most recently Julian." Thus he updates the little horn to reflect the latest oppressor, Julian the so-called Apostate, who planned to rebuild the Jewish temple in Jerusalem to spite the increasingly powerful Christians in the Roman Empire (Thiselton 234). Athanasius, likewise, saw the semi-Arian Emperor Constantius II as the "image of Antichrist" because of his patronage of nonorthodox theology (*H. Ar.* 67, 77).

Yet Tertullian influentially argued that the Roman Empire was not the antichrist but that instead the "restraining one" that held back the antichrist in 2 Thess 2:6–7 is Rome, which would herald the advent of the antichrist when it fragmented into ten pieces (Dan 7:7–8, "ten horns"). As Tertullian writes, "The great catastrophe threatening the whole world, the very end of the age with its promise of dreadful sufferings, is held back by the continuing existence of the Roman Empire" (*Apol. 32*). This interpretation may be related to the well-attested myth that, in the far East, Alexander the Great had built a giant wall secured by iron gates, which restrained the barbarian hordes, and thus that a break in the continuity of the Greek and Roman Empires' world dominance would unleash the catastrophic end (Bøe 219–30). After Constantine's official patronage of Christianity, this crucial role of Rome in preserving the world from cosmic oppression took on an even more important role; Eusebius, the court theologian of Constantine, understood the emperor's victory over Maxentius to be a victory over the antichrist (Bardill 363). During the fragmentation of the Roman Empire in the fifth century, apocalyptic expectations soared, with interpreters naming both Roman and Germanic invaders as antichrist; one redacted manuscript of the Donatist *Liber Genealogus* even names both the Vandal king Genseric and the Western Roman emperor Anthemius as antichrists (Dearn 133). Jerome, in a particularly anti-Semitic interpretation of Dan 7:25 in which the antichrist exists primarily to damn the Jews, urges people to recognize that the antichrist will be the eleventh king, or horn, that arises after the Roman Empire's disintegration (McGinn 2000, 75). Jerome (on 11:45) also advances an argument that 11:45 offers the place of the antichrist's demise, on the Mount of Olives. Although he admits that previous interpreters "assert that the antichrist will perish in the same place where Christ ascended to heaven," he is the earliest known author of this line of thought, which becomes an important element in the lore of antichrist.

After the fall of Rome, Augustine's influential spiritual interpretation of the antichrist, later adapted by Gregory the Great in his *Moralia in Job,* dampened Christian eagerness to associate the antichrist with particular individuals, but it did not stop all speculation. For example, as a part of the propaganda drive to promote the First Crusade at the close of the eleventh century, Guibert of Nogent claimed that Pope Urban II's speech that launched the Crusade included speculation that the reclamation of Jerusalem would hasten the end of the world: "The end of the world is already near.... According to the prophecies, before the coming of the Antichrist it is first necessary that the Christian Empire be renewed in those parts, either through you or those whom God pleases, so that the head of all evil who will have his imperial throne there may find some nourishment of faith against which he may fight" (McGinn 2000, 121).

In the Christian West, a major shift in discourse concerning the antichrist occurred in the wake of Gregory VII's reformist papacy in the eleventh century. Gregory increased the power of the papacy and pressured secular rulers to allow the pope to select bishops, which significantly diminished royal abilities to control the local church to their advantage. Many antireformist, pro-monarchy bishops began to use antichrist language to describe Gregory VII. Eberhard, thirteenth-century archbishop of Salzburg, for example, claimed that Gregory dealt with the ten kingdoms of the "Turks, Greeks, Egyptians, Africans, Spaniards, French, English, Germans, Sicilians, and Italians who now occupy the provinces of Rome," which proved that he was "a little horn [that] has grown up with eyes and mouth, speaking great things, which is reducing three of these kingdoms [Sicily, Italy, and Germany] to subservience, is persecuting the people of Christ and the saints of God with intolerable opposition, is confounding things human and divine, and is attempting things unutterable, execrable" (McClintock and Strong 258). The Vatican responded in kind. In 1245 Cardinal Rainer of Viterbo, among many others, declared Holy Roman Emperor Frederick II Hohenstaufen, who had flexed his imperial muscles against Rome from a stronghold of his in Sicily, to be the antichrist: "Since Frederick has in his forehead the horn of power and a mouth bringing forth monstrous things, he thinks himself able to transform the times and the laws and to lay truth in the dust" (McGinn 2000, 154).

Joachim of Fiore, the twelfth-century apocalypticist, fueled speculation with his list of seven forerunners of the antichrist: the fifth was Emperor Henry IV; the sixth was Saladin, who recaptured Jerusalem in 1187; and the seventh was to be a false Christian king who would usurp the papacy; after Joachim, both pro-papal and antipapal factions were worried about the role of the papacy in the rise of the antichrist (M. Reeves 305). Those calling for church reform, such as the Fraticelli, a fourteenth-century radical Franciscan group who advocated for absolute poverty, often used the trope of antichrist in the late Middle Ages. In a letter written to the citizens of Narni, the Fraticelli wrote: "These errors and heresies listed above [the condemnation of apostolic poverty], along with others invented, set forth, preached and defended by Pope John XXII, and confirmed and approved by his successors, are without doubt that Abomination of Desolation standing in the holy place that Daniel prophesied and Christ predicted" (McGinn 2000, 176). This reformist rhetoric was inherited by the Waldensians, John Hus, John Wycliffe, and others who precipitated the Reformation, including Martin Luther and John Calvin—all of whom declared the pope to be in some way the antichrist (Bostick; McGinn 2000, 206–13). The English monarchs who followed Henry VIII's break with Roman Catholicism in 1534 used the papal characterization to their own advantage, but during the seventeenth-century English Civil War, the Puritan forces used the image of the "little horn" to justify the shocking beheading of King Charles I in 1649; the Puritan William Aspinwall wrote that "the saints' act of slaying the Beast and taking away his dominion was no rash or seditious act, but an act of sound judgment, approved of God" (Hill 109). Yet the radical Protestants soon turned on Cromwell, too, naming him as a second little horn for his apparent desire to usurp the throne (Loewenstein 116).

Some Roman Catholic theologians rebutted the constant Protestant claims that the pope was the antichrist, such as the seventeenth-century Dutch scholar Willem Hessels van Est, who argued that the Protestant kings had inherited the antichrist status because of their persecution of the Roman Catholic Church, as the sanctuary mentioned in Daniel and 2 Thess 2 referred to the temple of Solomon, not the Roman church (Thiselton 227). But many more Counter-Reformation-era Roman Catholics, such as the sixteenth-century Jesuits Juan Maldonado and Francisco Ribera, as well as the seventeenth-century Jesuit Cardinal Roberto Bellarmino, preferred to follow Augustine's lead and imagine the little horn in Daniel to refer either to a general spirit of faithlessness or a distant future event; this refusal to attribute the status of antichrist to a known person became known as futurism (Newport 75–78).

Futurist apocalypticism, influenced by the early nineteenth-century English pastor John Nelson Darby, introduced a brand of apocalypticism now called dispensational premillennialism, which teaches that Jesus Christ will rapture the faithful before the "tribulation," a seven-year period of oppression; then Christ will return with those faithful at the second coming and institute a thousand-year reign before the last judgment. Darby taught that the little horn of Dan 7 will be distinct from that of Dan 8, since the former will appear through the resurgent Roman Empire, though not culminating in the pope, and the latter "is another power which will be found there, in special connection with the Jews, invading those eastern countries, but which is not the little horn of chapter vii" (Darby 38–39). C. I. Scofield, an American minister, made Darby's theological schema immensely popular through his *Reference Bible,* first published in 1909; Scofield's notes teach that Dan 8:19, for example, refers to two ends, the end of the Greek Empire, which climaxed with Antiochus IV, and also "the end of the times of the Gentiles when the 'little horn' of Dan 7:8, 24–26, the Beast, will arise—Daniel's final time of the end" (913). The *Scofield Reference Bible* finally shifted Protestant discussion of the antichrist away from the Roman pontiff, which had been an almost unquestioned assumption for hundreds of years.

The calamitous events of the twentieth century, including two world wars, the Holocaust, and the creation of a Jewish state in Israel, have offered much fodder to apocalyptists. The formation of the League of Nations led to speculation that a renewal of ancient Rome through a ten-nation group would activate the prophecy of Dan 7:7; Arno Gaebelein, a twentieth-century premillennialist preacher, argued that there were too many European countries for this association to make much sense, but I. M. Hadelman argued that the League paved the way for "the last kaiser" (McGinn 2000, 256). Mussolini's rise to power fueled fears of a new Roman Empire, and in 1927 Oswald J. Smith published a book titled *Is the Antichrist at Hand? What of Mussolini?* (Boyer 108). This Eurocentric speculation can also be seen in Hal Lindsey's wildly popular 1970 book *The Late Great Planet Earth,* which draws heavily from Scofield's apocalyptic teaching. Lindsey interprets Dan 7 and 8 to teach that a modern ten-nation United States of Europe will function as a revived Rome, and that this union will give power to a dictator who will become the antichrist (95, 105). This vein of apocalyptic speculation underlies the current obsession in some political circles on identifying President Barack Obama with the figure of the antichrist; one particular e-mail message forwarded countless times during the 2008 election season claimed that "The anti-Christ will be a man, in his 40s, of MUSLIM descent, who will deceive the nations with persuasive language, and have a MASSIVE Christ-like appeal. . . . The prophecy says that people will flock to him, and he will promise false hope and world peace, and when he is in power, will destroy everything. Is it OBAMA?" (Dittmer 73). Another popular figure for American speculation about the antichrist is Russia; during the breakup of the Soviet Union, the fragmentation reminded some readers of Dan 7:7–8, leading several conservative Christian authors to suggest that Vladimir Putin is the antichrist (Haddad and Smith 521; McKenzie 630).

Many Eastern Christian readers throughout history would puzzle at this modern speculation concerning Russia. Medieval Byzantine and later Russian Orthodox theologians took seriously their self-adopted identity as the inheritor of Rome's role as "the restrainer" of the antichrist, and they also lacked influential theologians such as Augustine, who dissuaded the faithful from apocalyptic speculation. Drawing from Eusebius's political theology, Byzantine apocalypticists such as the seventh-century Pseudo-Methodius read Daniel and Revelation in order to understand the role of the Byzantine Empire in world politics and history. Many of these apocalypses featured the character Daniel, were told in his name, and were popular enough to be translated into a wide variety of languages (P. J. Alexander 61–96). One contributing factor to the popularity of the medieval Daniel apocalypses was the stunning rise of Islam. At first, Christians understood Islam as a type of heresy, not a new religion, and thus Muhammad seemed to many Byzantines and Iberian Christians especially to be a candidate for the beguiling antichrist. During a sermon Sophronius, the patriarch of Jerusalem in the seventh century, argued that the invading Arabs were "the Abomination of Desolation predicted by the prophets," and Theophanes the Chronicler related that when Caliph ʿUmar first entered the city of Jerusalem after the siege of 637, Sophronius yelled, "Truly, this is the Abomination of Desolation established in the holy place, of which Daniel the prophet spoke" (Lamoreux 15). Likewise, the ninth-century Iberian Mozarab scholar Paulus Alvarus argued that Muhammad was the eleventh horn of the fourth beast in Dan 7:8, as he had uprooted the Franks, Greeks, and Goths, and thus was the last and most important of these figures that began with Antiochus IV (Wolf 98). After the fall of Constantinople in 1453 to Muslim Turkish armies, Western Christians outside of Iberia, as well, began to identify the little horn with the Turkish invaders; Luther had argued that the antichrist was the pope, but in later writings and sermons he clarified that one should also interpret Muhammad to be the little horn in Dan 7:8 (Francisco 81–83). Luther's *Army Sermon against the Turks,* written in the wake of the 1529 Ottoman siege of Vienna, expounded upon Dan 7; the printed editions include images that make an explicit connection between the four beasts and the invading Muslim army, imaged as a mass of weapons threatening Europe from Asia (see fig. 5 above).

The Little Horn: Jewish and Muslim Anti-Messiahs

Medieval Jewish and Muslim apocalypses borrowed and adapted many elements from Christian apocalyptic traditions, including the figure of the anti-Messiah; in one Jewish midrashic tradition, the anti-Messiah is even called "antichrist" (Patai 157). In Jewish eschatological speculation, the final opponent of the antichrist is generally named Armilus, understood to be the final ruler of Rome-Edom, the symbol for oppressive Christendom. The medieval *Midrash ʿAseret ha-Shevatim* recounts the legend: "Satan will descend and go to Rome to the stone statue and have connection with it in the manner of the sexual act, and the stone will become pregnant and give birth to Armilus. He will rule for forty days. And his hand will be heavier than forty measures. And he will issue evil decrees against Israel, and men of good deeds will cease while men of plunder will multiply" (Patai 157). This final king was expected to attack the Jews and kill the figure of the Messiah ben Joseph, a character derived from the anointed one who will restore the temple but nevertheless be "cut off" in Dan 9:26, before the king's defeat at the hands of the final Messiah ben David. As *Midrash Leqaḥ Tov* explains: "Israel will be gathered. . . . Messiah ben Joseph will look for them from the Galilee. And they will go up from there, and all Israel with him, to Jerusalem. . . . And he will go up and rebuild the Temple, and offer up sacrifices. . . . And after this, Gog and Magog [the armies of Armilus] will hear and go up against them . . . and will enter and kill him [the Messiah ben Jacob] in the streets of Jerusalem" (Patai 170).

A medieval Yemeni manuscript makes clear the connection between Armilus, Dan 7, and polemical versions of Jesus and Muhammad: A "false Messiah" will rise up,

> a speaker of lies and emptiness and deceit. And his name will grow great and his heart will become haughty, and many people will go astray after him and die. His feet will be like the feet of a bear, and his hands like the paws of a panther. . . . He will roar like a young lion and growl like a lion. He will make the dead come alive, and will set the prisoners free from the pit, and open the eyes of the blind. And he will bring manna down from heaven, . . . and all the Children of Kedar [Arabs] will go after him. And he will reign for forty days. (Patai 162)

After this forty-day reign, Armilus will be destroyed during a military campaign near Jerusalem, as in Dan 11:45: "Armilus will come and wage war against Egypt and capture it. . . . And then he will turn and put his face toward Jerusalem to destroy it a second time. . . . At that time Michael the great prince will rise and blow the shofar three times. . . . The Holy One, blessed be He, will fight for Israel" (Patai 157–59). Armilus also appears in Byzantine sources in stories of Jewish converts who attempt to convince other Jews that "Hermolaus Satan" is actually Muhammad, as in the seventh-century *Doctrine of Jacob Recently Baptized*, which presents Jacob as arguing that one can "truly see a diminution of the Roman Empire" in light of the Muslim invasions, but Muhammad is a "deceiving prophet among the Saracens," and this is clear because "prophets do not come with swords and chariots, do they?" (Lamoreux 16).

Rabbinic exegetical reflections on Dan 7:7–8 and 8:9–14 usually include a discussion of Vespasian and Titus, who showed arrogance by desecrating the temple; talmudic discussions begin here, as does Rashi, who also understands the anointed who was "cut off" in Dan 9:26 to refer to King Agrippa II, who was ruler of Judah at the time of Titus's victory (*b. Giṭ.* 56b; Gallé 96). But rabbinic interpreters usually conflate the Roman destruction in 70 C.E. with contemporary Christianity, figured as a continuation of the Roman Empire, and thus Titus flows seamlessly into the religious and political leaders of Christendom. For Abrabanel, the papacy is the little horn, because it was slow to grow, but eventually it challenged kings and God alike; it uprooted three horns, which either represents the three types of government used in Rome before papal rule (kings, republic, empire) or the fact that the Christian church began at the time of Tiberius, the third Roman emperor (Goldwurm 201). Malbim claims that the references to skill in "riddles" (Dan 8:23) refers to the Christian church, of whom the pope is the king, that creates incomprehensible theological teachings to confuse people; the "fantastic things" that the figure speaks (11:36) are taken to be the doctrines of the virgin birth and the incarnation (Goldwurm 234, 312). Likewise, Abraham ibn Ezra (d. 1164) argued that Dan 11:36 referred to Emperor Constantine, who "renounced the faith of his ancestors, who were in Rome serving Jupiter," when he made Christianity his preferred religion (Gallé 144), and Pseudo-Saadia understood Dan 11:40–41 as describing the Crusades (Goldwurm 314). Rashi thought that the phrase "distribute the land for a price" in 11:39 described unfair medieval land distribution by church and crown alike; each "will distribute land at a pittance to whomever he acknowledges" (Gallé 148). Some interpreters were keen to root some of these images in the Seleucid period, such as Ibn Ezra, who argued concerning Dan 8:23: "This is Antiochus and his general Gelinos. Yet there are some who say that this refers to the Arabs who left in the year 4345 (593 C.E.)" (Gallé 96). Ibn Ezra also understood some of the "little horn" texts, including 7:8, to refer to Muslims: "a people who will come from the East and adopt the law of the horns," that is, convert to Islam; similarly, Maimonides, in his *Epistle to Yemen*, says that Dan 7:8 "obviously alludes to the person who will found a new religion similar to the divine religion and make claim to a revelation and to prophecy. He will produce much talk and will endeavor to alter this Torah and abolish it," referring to the changing of the seasons and law in 7:25 (Maimonides 101).

Muslim apocalyptic thinkers, however, have had other ideas. While there is far more interest in the messianic figure of the Mahdi, a lively discussion of the anti-Messiah figure, called the al-Masih al-Dajjal, or "pseudo-Messiah," draws from Jewish and Christian traditions that themselves derive from Dan 7–12. According to various Muslim traditions, the Dajjal will appear near the end of time, and he will lead many to support his tyrannical and blasphemous forty-day rule before the Messiah ʿIsa (Jesus) returns to kill him (Saritoprak 291–92). A *Ḥadith* narrated by Nawas bin Saʿman relates that Muhammad "spoke at length about al-Dajjal," saying, "He is emerging from a place between Damascus and Iraq. He travels towards right and left" (Saritoprak 293). In a tenth-century Muslim apocalypse originating in Baghdad and written in the name of Daniel, probably reflecting the views of an anti-ʿAbbasid Sunni group, the Dajjal emerges and says, "I am the god who judges the people of the earth on behalf of the god of the heavens," persuading many people, including heretical Muslims, Christians, and Jews, to follow him (Cook 2002, 86). The Dajjal then corrupts the earth and rules with tyranny, tormenting the faithful by torturing them and feeding them poisoned food; next he tours the world and is only refused entrance to Medina when an angel slaps his face (Cook 2002, 88). Finally, in a passage interpreting Dan 7, the text claims that "the Messiah Jesus son of Mary will come down on a white cloud; all of the people of the earth will see him both in the east and the west, and a caller will call out: 'O people, this is the Messiah Jesus son of Mary, the intact virgin, whom God formed without a father, and God has caused him to come down [from heaven] to kill the lying Antichrist, and he will stay with you as an imam judging with the just judgment of God'" (Cook 2002, 89). And by means of the interpretive trajectory of Dan 11, many Muslim traditions claim that the Dajjal will emerge in the vicinity of Jerusalem and be killed there (Dan 11:45; Saritoprak 303). In the twentieth century, many Muslim apocalyptists have named Western culture as the Dajjal: some, like Austrian convert Muhammad Asad, because of its awe-inspiring technological advances that seem to dissuade belief in God; and others because of the West's support for Zionism and seeming to be in thrall to Jewish philosophers such as Karl Marx and Sigmund Freud (Saritoprak 302–3; Cook 2005, 187). In early twentieth-century Sudan, a revival of a religious and political revolt centered on the messianic Muslim figure of the Mahdi led to the repeated Sudanese claim that the British themselves were the Dajjal, strengthening the resolve of the Sudanese in their fight (Ibrahim 31). In more recent years, conspiracists who obsess over the state of Israel and believe in global Zionist conspiracies have taken to reading the book of Daniel to understand the nature of the Dajjal. As Muhammad ʿIsa Daʿud writes, "The Antichrist is from Yemen, and no wonder since they are the cleverest of the Jews. . . . A Jewish personality from England will adopt him and take him from the lands of the Arabs to the West to grow up there and study the latest sciences, to possess minds and build a fortress for himself" (Cook 2005, 186). Some, like Bashir Muhammad ʿAbdallah, conflate Israel and a global conspiracy: "As I watched, this horn (which is Israel on the outside and the secret world government on the inside) was waging war against the saints and defeating them . . . in Palestine, Afghanistan, India, Kashmir, Bosnia and Herzegovina, Azerbaijan . . ." (Cook 2005, 43). Others simply claim that the United States occupies the role of the little horn, especially after the American military presence in the Middle East throughout the late twentieth and early twenty-first centuries (Cook 2005, 45–46).

Daniel 9 Prophecy and the Deep Structures of History

1 In the first year of Darius son of Ahasuerus, of Median descent, who was made king over the kingdom of the Chaldeans— 2 in the first year of his reign, I, Daniel, perceived in the books the number of the years according to the word of YHWH to Jeremiah the prophet to be completed for the ruins of Jerusalem—seventy years. 3 And I turned my face to the Lord

God in order to make a prayer of supplication,[a] with fasting, sackcloth, and ashes.

4 I prayed to YHWH my God and confessed and said, "Oh, Lord, great and fearsome God, who keeps covenant faithfulness with those who love him and who observe his commandments, 5 we have sinned, and we have gone astray; we have done what is wrong, and we have rebelled; we have turned away from your commandments and your decrees. 6 We have not listened to your servants the prophets who spoke in your name to our kings, our princes, our fathers, and to all of the people of the land. 7 To you, Lord, belongs the right, and to us belongs the shame this very day, to the man of Judah and the inhabitants of Jerusalem and to all Israel, both near and far, in all the lands to which you have scattered them because of the unfaithfulness that they committed against you. 8 YHWH, to us belongs the shame—to our kings, our princes, and our ancestors who sinned against you. 9 To the Lord our God belongs compassion and forgiveness, although we rebelled against him.

10 "We did not listen to the voice of YHWH our God, following his teachings that he gave to us by the hand of his servants the prophets. 11 All Israel transgressed your teaching and turned away, not listening to your voice. And it gushed out upon us—the curse pronounced under oath,[b] which is written in the teaching of Moses, the servant of God, for we sinned against him. 12 He established his word, which he spoke against us and against our judges who judged us, in order to bring upon us a great calamity, the like of which has never happened under all the heavens as it happened in Jerusalem. 13 Just as it was written in the teaching of Moses, all this calamity came upon us, but we did not entreat YHWH our God, repenting of our iniquity and gaining insight into your constancy. 14 YHWH was intent upon this calamity and brought it upon us, for YHWH our God is justified in all his deeds that he has done; but we did not listen to his voice.

15 "And now, Lord our God, who brought your people out of the land of Egypt with a strong hand and made a name for yourself to this day—we have sinned, we have acted wickedly. 16 O Lord, according to all your righteousness, turn aside your anger and your wrath from your city Jerusalem, your holy mount, for through our sins and the iniquities of our ancestors, Jerusalem and your people have become a reproach to all our neighbors round about. 17 And now, listen, O our God, to the prayer of your servant and to his supplications. Let your face shine upon your desolate sanctuary for the sake of my Lord. 18 Incline your ear, O my God, and listen; open your eyes and see our desolations and the city that is called by your name, for it is not on account of our righteousness that we are casting our supplications before you but on account of your great

compassion. 19 O my Lord, hear! O my Lord, forgive! O my Lord, attend! Act without delay for your own sake, O my God, for your name is called over your city and over your people."

20 While I was still speaking and praying and confessing my sin and the sin of my people Israel and casting my supplication before YHWH my God concerning the holy mountain of my God— 21 while I was speaking in prayer, the man Gabriel, whom I had previously seen in a vision, was sent forth in flight,[c] reaching me at the time of the evening offering. 22 And he came[d] and spoke with me and said, "Daniel, now I have come to give you understanding. 23 At the beginning of your supplication a word went forth, and I have come to tell you,[e] because you are highly valued. Now pay attention to the word and understand the vision.

24 "Seventy weeks of years are determined concerning your people and your holy city, in order to finish transgression, to bring sins to completion,[f] and to expiate iniquity, to bring in eternal righteousness, to seal the prophetic vision, and to anoint the holy of holies. 25 And you should know and understand that from the going forth of the word to restore and rebuild Jerusalem until the time of an anointed ruler is seven weeks. For sixty-two weeks it will be rebuilt with plaza and fosse.[g] But in a stressful time,[h] 26 that is, after sixty-two weeks, an anointed one will be cut off and will be no more.[i] And the army[j] of a prince will destroy both city and sanctuary. The end will come[k] in a cataclysm, and until the end of the decreed war there will be desolations. 27 He will make a firm covenant with many[l] for one week, and for half a week he will make sacrifice and offering cease. In their place[m] will be a desolating abomination until the determined end is poured out upon the desolator."

a. The Hebrew expression "to seek prayer" does not make sense. The phrase should be construed as an Aramaism. See Zimmerman 263; cf. Dan 6:7 (8).

b. Following Lacocque's suggestion (176) that the phrase "the curse and the oath" is a hendiadys.

c. The OG renders this phrase as "being carried swiftly," Th as "flying." Most ancient and medieval interpreters understand the phrase in reference to flight. While $mu'āp$ can be interpreted as a Hophal of $'wp$ ("caused to fly"), the following word $yě'āp$ would represent an otherwise unattested nominal by-form of $'wp$. The root $y'p$ ordinarily signifies weariness, and Ibn Ezra interpreted the phrase as signifying that Gabriel was "weary from his long flight" (see Montgomery 372). Some commentators (e.g., Charles 235; Keil 335; Goldingay 228) take both words as forms of $y'p$, describing Daniel as "tired and weary," a reference to his condition in 8:27. It is also possible that $mu'āp/yě'āp$ is simply a double reading (so J. Collins 345).

d. MT: $wayyāben$, "and he instructed." Th apparently reads $wayyābennî$, "and he instructed me." Most interpreters follow the OG and Syriac and emend $wayyāben$ to $wayyābô'$, "and he came."

e. Supplying the pronoun, as do the OG and Th.

f. The Kethib reads *laḥtōm*, "to seal up"; the Qere reads *lĕhātēm*, "to complete." Either is plausible in context. If one reads with the Kethib, then a sequence of action results: complete, seal up, expiate (so Bentzen 66, Plöger 132, 134). But the fact that that infinitive also occurs in the second triad of verbs may indicate that *laḥtōm* here is the result of scribal error. The majority of commentators favor reading with the Qere, thus providing two synonyms for sin coming to an end.

g. The rare word *ḥārûṣ* refers to the ditch at the bottom of a rampart. Thus the phrase would refer to Jerusalem as a fortified city. Alternatively, the text may be an error for *ḥûṣ*, "street," a word that often pairs with *rĕḥôb* (cf. Prov 7:12; Jer 5:1).

h. The phrase is difficult. While it might be a gloss on the condition of Jerusalem during the sixty-two weeks, the phrase is better taken as introducing the dire events described in v. 26. The Syriac reads *lšwlm zbnʾ*, suggesting that the Hebrew read *ûbqēṣ hāʿittîm*, "at the end of the times." If so, then "at the end of the times" and "after sixty-two weeks" might be alternative readings, both preserved by the copyist. The Syriac translator, however, may have been assimilating a difficult Hebrew phrase to a more familiar expression.

i. MT: *wĕʾên lô*, "and he will have no one," makes little sense. Emend to *wĕʾênennû*, "and he will be no more," following the OG. Hartman and DiLella (240, 252) note that in a few MSS the following word is *hāʿîr* instead of *wĕhāʿîr* and so translates "when the city is no longer his."

j. The word *ʿam* ("people") can refer to a military body, as in 1 Sam 14:17; 2 Sam 2:26; 10:10; 2 Kgs 13:7; etc.

k. The latter part of v. 26 is obscure. The MT *nāgîd habbāʾ* ("a prince who is coming") is an odd way to refer to Antiochus IV. Moreover, *wĕqiṣṣô* ("and his end") would also be odd, since v. 27 devotes several clauses to the activity of Antiochus, only describing his fate in the very last words of the verse. Instead, follow the suggestion of *BHS*, emending slightly and redividing the phrases to read *ûbāʾ haqqēṣ*, "and the end will come."

l. Kooij (500–501) interprets the verb "make strong/firm" "in the negative sense of 'dominating'" the cult (i.e., the covenant) "with respect to the many who remain faithful to the law." It is difficult to find a convincing grammatical parallel, however. One might note the use of *higdîl* ("grow great"), though without an object, several times in ch. 8 (as in 8:4, 8) with the sense of domination and aggression.

m. Emending *kĕnap* ("wing") to *kannām* ("their place"; cf. 11:38). Similarly, Hartman and DiLella 240; J. Collins 357–58.

Overview

The book of Daniel returns again and again to the tropes of baffled understanding and the revelation of hidden meaning. Most often the teasing message is hidden in the ambiguous visual symbols of a dream or vision, as in Nebuchadnezzar's dreams in chs. 2 and 4 and Daniel's visions in chs. 7 and 8. However, here in ch. 9, as in ch. 5, the medium of revelation is a text. In Dan 5 the impenetrable mysteriousness of the writing is stressed, both in the startling way in which the text appears, written by a disembodied hand on the wall of the king's banquet hall, and also in the riddle-like quality of its surface meaning. By contrast, the text that Daniel considers in ch. 9 is familiar, with an apparently transparent meaning, and Daniel's actions indicate that he has no doubt that he has understood it. Though he does not yet realize it, the text has in fact baffled Daniel, for it contains a hidden meaning that can only be discerned by means of the esoteric exegesis that underlies Gabriel's interpretation of the passage.

Relation to Other Danielic Apocalypses

Daniel 9 differs from the other apocalypses in chs. 7–12 not only in its focus on a text as the medium of revealed knowledge but also in the different way it frames and analyzes the crisis that developed between 175 and 164 B.C.E. Chapters 7, 8, and 10–12 frame the situation in terms of legitimate and illegitimate exercise of sovereignty by human kings and kingdoms and their relationship to the sovereignty of the God of Israel, a topic also at issue in chs. 1–6. In this chapter, concern for the temple and its cult eclipses concern for rival sovereignties. Chapter 8 also highlights the fate of the temple but frames it within the mythos of the arrogant king who challenges YHWH. The most prominent difference between ch. 9 and the other apocalypses, however, is in the prominence given to Deuteronomic theology in the long prayer that Daniel prays (vv. 4–19). Although scholars have disagreed as to whether the prayer is original to the composition, in its final form the chapter focuses extensively on the relationship between YHWH and Israel—a topic absent from the other chapters. How the relation between the theology of the prayer and the theology assumed in the narrative frame relate to one another is discussed below.

The sharp differences between ch. 9 and the other apocalypses, as well as the striking similarities between chs. 8 and 10–12 (see comments on chs. 10–12) have led some scholars (e.g., Kratz 2001, 105–6; Berner 21–22) to posit that ch. 9 was secondarily added to the collection. Against this suggestion is the fact that ch. 9 also shares many similarities with ch. 8, both in terms of its focus on the fate of the sanctuary and also in terms of specific vocabulary (Willis 129). As 9:24 speaks of finishing transgression (*happeša'*) and completing sins (*lĕhātēm*, reading with the Qere), so 8:23 refers to completing transgression (*kĕtōm happĕšā'îm* or *piš'êhem*, reading with the Greek versions). In ch. 8 "the transgression that desolates" (*happeša' šōmēm*, 8:13) is what despoils the sanctuary, as in ch. 9 it is the "desolating abomination" (*šiqqûṣ'îm mĕšōmēm*, 9:27) and the "desolator" (*šōmēm*). Finally, the root "understand" (*byn*) plays an important role in linking the two chapters. Chapter 8 concludes with Daniel unable to understand (*wĕ'ên mēbîn*) the perplexing vision about the desolation of the sanctuary (8:27), whereas ch. 9 begins with Daniel perceiving (*bînōtî*) what he thinks is the announcement of the end of the desolation (9:2), though the angel Gabriel will come to give him true understanding (*bînâ*, 9:22).

The Relation of the Prayer to the Revelatory Account

Several considerations suggest that the prayer was not composed by the person who wrote the rest of the chapter, though that does not necessarily mean that the prayer was not original to the composition. First and most obviously, the prayer is composed in a simple and elegant Hebrew style. The rest of the chapter is composed far more awkwardly. Second, there appear to be literary "seams" in vv. 4a and 21a that mark the transition between narrative and prayer. Third, the theology of the prayer is not consistent with the theology of the conclusion of the chapter in vv. 24–27.

There are at least three ways to account for these observations. First, an earlier generation of scholars assumed a model in which a short narrative composition was expanded by a later editor, a position still held by some (e.g., Charles 226–27; Bentzen 75; Ginsberg 1948, 33; Hartman and DiLella 245–46). The strongest argument in favor of this position is the repetitiousness of vv. 4 and 21, suggesting a redactional insertion. The insertion of the Song of the Three Jews and the Prayer of Azariah in the Greek versions of Dan 3, as well as the insertion of prayers into Greek Esther, provide examples of just such a process of placing pious set pieces into the mouths of the main characters. The most important objections to this hypothesis are two: (1) without the prayer the chapter would be only a few verses long; (2) there are in fact several key words that appear both in the narrative frame and the prayer, suggesting intentional coordination between the two parts of the chapter (Jones 491; J. Collins 348). These include *lĕhaśkîl* ("to gain or give insight," vv. 13, 22; see also v. 25), *taḥănûnîm* ("supplication," vv. 3, 17, 18, 23), *ḥaṭṭāʾt* ("sin," vv. 20, 24), *tittak* ("poured out," vv. 11, 27), different grammatical forms of *šûb* ("return," vv. 13, 25) and *šāmam* ("to be desolate," vv. 17, 18, 27), and linked wordplays on *šĕbūʿâ* ("oath") and *šābūʿîm* ("weeks") in vv. 11 and 24.

A second approach assumes that the entire chapter was written by a single author. The contrasting theologies of the prayer and the angelic exegesis may be seen as intentionally contrasting, so that the angel's deterministic interpretation corrects the Deuteronomistic theology of the prayer (Jones 492). More plausibly, the contrasts might simply represent the plurality of modes used for understanding a complex religious and historical phenomena. As cultural anthropologists have demonstrated, persons regularly have multiple models by which they perceive situations, and when these have separate contexts (e.g., prayer and oracular interpretation), then they are usually experienced as complementary rather than contradictory (see Strauss and Quinn 215). More problematic is the difference between the smooth and elegant style of the prayer, and the rough and ragged Hebrew style of the narrative frame.

A third hypothesis, however, seems most likely, that the author who composed the narrative frame chose a well-known prayer as the centerpiece of the chapter, drawing on its vocabulary to unify the narrative and prayer sections of the composition (so Montgomery 362; Lacocque 180; J. Collins 348). This model accounts for the different linguistic registers, the differences in theology, the literary seams, and the presence of key words in both parts of the composition.

Structure and Outline

The chapter may be outlined as follows:

Introduction (9:1–3)
Prayer (9:4–19)
    Confession (9:4–14)
    Supplication (9:15–19)
Revelation (9:20–27)
    Angelophany (9:20–21)
    Gabriel Explains His Mission (9:22–23)
    Revelatory Discourse (9:24–27)

Comments

[1] The reference to the first year of Darius the Mede locates the narrative in Dan 9 as occurring after the death of Belshazzar in ch. 5 and the accession of Darius in 5:31 [6:1], but probably before the undated narrative in Daniel 6:1–28 [2–29]. Although Darius the Mede is a nonhistorical character (see comments on 5:31 [6:1]), he serves to open up an important narrative space in the book. Historically, it was Cyrus the Persian who defeated Babylon, and according to biblical tradition, issued an edict in his first year allowing the Judeans to return and rebuild the temple in Jerusalem, in order "that the word of YHWH by the mouth of Jeremiah might be fulfilled" (Ezra 1:1; cf. 2 Chr 36:22–23). By inserting the reign of the fictional Darius the Mede, the author locates Daniel at a moment when the defeat of Babylon has already occurred, confirming part of the prophecy of Jeremiah, but before any permission has been given to restore the temple in Jerusalem.

To provide a bit of narrative verisimilitude, Darius is given a short genealogy as the son of Ahasuerus. It is not clear why the author picks this name, which is the biblical rendering of the Old Persian *Khashayarsha*, represented in Greek as Xerxes (so the OG here). In the succession of *Persian* kings, Darius I was the father of Xerxes I, so the author may have borrowed the names and reversed the sequence to create the genealogy of Darius the Mede (see Ezra 4:4–6).

[2] The narrative proper opens with a scene of reading. Representation of the act of reading is quite rare in the Hebrew Bible and occurs most frequently

in a liturgical context (Deut 31:9–13; 2 Kgs 23:2; Neh 8:2–8) or where the contents of a document are read to a king or his officials (2 Kgs 22:10; Jer 36:4–10, 20–23). In contrast, Daniel is represented as reading in private, consulting a book in order to understand the intentions of God (Toorn 2007, 24). The only close parallel is the much later scene in Acts 8:26–40, where the Ethiopian eunuch is reading and pondering a passage from Isaiah. During the Second Temple period, the process of generating new revelatory disclosures through reading and interpreting prophetic texts largely displaced the activity of revelation through oral prophetic activity (see J. Barton 179–92). The *Community Rule* from Qumran provides for regular reading and study (*dôrēš bětôrâ*; *liqrō' běsēper*) in order to discern the hidden laws that could be revealed in these processes (1QS 6.6–8). In the depiction of the scribe Daniel reading and studying, we probably have a close description of the activities of the authors of Dan 7–12 themselves.

Daniel describes his activity as *bînōtî*, from the root *byn*. The word has a wide variety of nuances, including "perceive," "consider," and "understand," allowing the author to construct a mild irony at Daniel's expense. Although Daniel assumes he has understood what he has been considering, Gabriel will explain to him that he has in fact not understood. The object of Daniel's reading is described with a plural noun, *sěpārîm* ("books," "scrolls," "documents"). If one foregrounds the narrative setting of Dan 9 in exilic-era Babylon, then perhaps Daniel is consulting the two letters sent by Jeremiah to the exiles (cf. Jer 29:1, 31; so Wilson 93; Seow 139). But perhaps that is overly literalistic. Although we tend to think of prophetic books as single scrolls, a long book like Jeremiah might be divided up among more than one scroll. Less likely is that the plural "books" suggests that Daniel is doing "intertextual" interpretation, comparing Jeremiah's prophecies with passages from Leviticus (so Rigger 182–83; Berner 43). While such intertextual interpretation does underlie *Gabriel's* interpretation, this does not appear to be how Daniel initially reads the text. For an image of the book of Jeremiah as it was found at Qumran, see figure 20.

The reference to "seventy years" indicates that the passages Daniel is considering are Jer 25:11–12 and 29:10. His characterization of Jeremiah's oracle, however, does not entirely correspond to either passage. Daniel refers to "the completion [*mall'ōt*] of the ruin [*ḥorbôt*] of Jerusalem." Jeremiah 25:11 does refer to "all this land," Judah, becoming a "ruin" (*ḥorbâ*), but in that passage the seventy years refers to the time of the dominion of the king of Babylon, and the action that follows the completion of the seventy years is his overthrow. Jeremiah 29:10 recasts the seventy-year prophecy more explicitly as one of restoration, but it has in view the return of the exiles rather than the restoration of Jerusalem. Perhaps subconsciously, the author of Dan 9 assumes some of the extensive history of interpretation of these passages from Jeremiah that developed in the postexilic period. Already in the late sixth century, Zech 1:12–17

Prophecy and the Deep Structures of History

Figure 20. A manuscript of the book of Jeremiah from Qumran (4QJer^b), dating to the first half of the second century B.C.E. Courtesy Israel Antiquities Authority.

applied the seventy years to the time when YHWH was angry with Jerusalem, with its end as a time when the temple and Jerusalem would be rebuilt and restored. Even more pertinent is 2 Chr 36:21, which refers to the seventy years as a time when the land "lay desolate" (*hoššammâ*), using a different word than in Dan 9 but expressing a similar idea.

[3] As often in the book of Daniel, the author implicitly tests the interpretive skill of the reader. When Daniel finishes considering the passages in Jeremiah, he immediately prepares to seek (*baqqēš*) God by making a prayer (*tĕpillâ*) of supplication. Why? Many commentators have assumed that Daniel was perplexed by the passage in Jeremiah and sought for enlightenment (so, e.g., Hartman and DiLella 245–46). Yet the prayer that follows is not a prayer for illumination but a penitential prayer. The implied audience of Dan 9 is expected to be familiar with the context of the prophecies of Jeremiah, for these provide the key to Daniel's behavior. In Jer 29:10–14, just after the reference to the completion of the seventy years, YHWH assures the people of his plans for their welfare. But the people must perform an action: "Then when you call upon me and come and pray [*hitpallaltem*] to me, I will hear you. When you seek me [*biqqaštem 'ōtî*], you will find me, if you search for me with all your heart" (vv. 12–13 AT). Then God will bring the people back from exile. Thus Daniel's actions demonstrate that he has read the passage and understood that such a prayer is called for before the restoration can begin.

The physical actions of fasting, wearing sackcloth, and sprinkling oneself with ashes represent the individual's spiritual disposition of sorrow and self-abasement as he approaches God to make a request (cf. Jonah 3:6; Esth 4:1–4; Ezra 9:3–4; Neh 9:1). Daniel's action of turning his face toward God may suggest that he turns his face not only upward but also in the direction of Jerusalem and the now-destroyed temple, as in Dan 6:10 (11) (cf. 1 Kgs 8:35; 1 Esd 4:58). In the prayer, Daniel will primarily use first-person-plural speech, praying as an intercessor on behalf of the people, much like Moses and Jeremiah. In the summary verse after the prayer (v. 20), Daniel will also refer to "confessing my sin and the sin of my people," suggesting that he sees himself as their representative.

[4–19] Montgomery (361) describes the prayer in Dan 9 as "a liturgical gem." It is a classic example of a penitential prayer, a type of prayer developed in the postexilic period (see Ezra 9:5–15; Neh 1:4–11; 9:6–37; Bar 1:15–3:8; Prayer of Azariah; Tob 3:1–6; 3 Macc 2:1–10). In contrast to the communal laments of an earlier period, which characteristically contained complaints about the mistreatment by enemies and God's neglect of the people (e.g., Pss 44; 74; 79), the speaker(s) in penitential prayers consistently focus on the contrast between the sins of the people and God's righteous judgment of them. The people's repentance and the graciousness of God become the primary grounds for invoking God's aid in ending their suffering. The vocabulary and style of the various penitential prayers show a great deal of similarity, drawing extensively on words and phrases characteristic of Deuteronomistic theology. The vocabulary and set phrases form a dense intertextual web of allusions to other passages, particularly from Deuteronomy and Jeremiah (for a list of parallels, see Montgomery 363–38). It is difficult to say whether contemporary readers and hearers would have simply noticed the biblicizing style or whether they would have made the connections to specific intertexts. In antiquity, education included memorizing extensive repertoires of culturally important texts; thus it is possible that the better-educated members of the ancient audience would have heard the text in all of its allusive richness, a feat of understanding that modern readers can accomplish only with the laborious use of concordances.

Other literary features deserve notice. Frequently penitential prayers exhibit a repetitious style, employing strings of synonyms, but this device is particularly prominent in Dan 9. This repetitiousness has a variety of rhetorical functions. It slows down the prayer and gives it a sense of dignity and gravity, but it also allows the author to indicate elements of particular emphasis. The other dominant trope in the prayer is the contrast parallelism between the positive qualities and actions of God and the negative ones of the people, which serves both to explain the fate of Jerusalem and to ground hope for its restoration. Structurally, the prayer has two parts: vv. 4–14 are a confession, and vv. 15–19 are a supplication.

[4] Three words ("pray" [*pillēl*], "confess" [*hôdâ*], "say" [*'āmar*]) describe Daniel's action. "Pray" and "confess" also occur together in Ezra 10:1, but here they point to passages that are important intertexts for Dan 9. "Pray" is the action required by Jer 29:12. "Confess" describes the response expected of the people in Lev 26:40 when their land lies desolate. There are several echoes of Lev 26 in Dan 9 (e.g., Lev 26:13//Dan 9:15a; Lev 26:14–15//Dan 9:5; Lev 26:15, 42//Dan 9:4–11; Lev 26:31–33//Dan 9:17–18; see Willis 130). Since Lev 26 plays an important implicit role in the author's interpretation of the Jeremianic prophecy in Dan 9:24–27, perhaps the author is already foreshadowing the important conjunction of these two texts, Jer 29 and Lev 26, through his choice of words to describe the prayer.

The opening address to God is almost identical to that in the prayer of Neh 1:5, which in turn has appropriated the key phrases from Deut 7:9, 21. Theologically, the terms "great" and "fearsome" invoke God's transcendent power and authority (cf. Pss 47:2; 89:7), while the reference to keeping covenant and *ḥesed* ("faithfulness," "loyalty") refer to the special relationship between God and the people of Israel. That this relationship specifically requires devotion and obedience anticipates the contrast with the people's actual behavior, described in the following verses.

[5–6] The confession of sin receives emphasis through the piling up of five different verbs. The first three are elsewhere used as a set (1 Kgs 8:47; 2 Chr 6:37; Ps 106:6), and the last one is characteristic of Deuteronomistic style (Deut 17:11, 20). Through the use of so many near synonyms, the rhetoric of the prayer suggests the comprehensiveness of the people's wrongdoing. The end of v. 5 and v. 6 begin to give content to the wrongdoing, again worded in traditional phrases that highlight the covenant stipulations.

"Commandments" (*miṣwōt*) and "decrees" (*mišpāṭîm*) are a common word pair (cf. Lev 26:15, 43, 46; Deut 26:16–17; 30:16; Ps 147:19–20; Neh 1:7; 9:13; 2 Chr 33:8). In Deuteronomistic tradition, the prophets are presented as teachers of covenant law, to whom the Israelites and Judeans refuse to listen (e.g., 2 Kgs 17:13–14, 22; Jer 7:25–26; 25:4–5; 29:19; 44:4; cf. Ezra 9:11). The long list of those who refused to listen ("kings, princes, fathers, and all the people"), which is almost identical to the list in Jer 44:21, also serves the function of comprehensiveness. "Fathers" here is probably not a general term for ancestors but a reference to the heads of "fathers' houses," the extended family or lineage group. Notably, two groups sometimes criticized in other penitential prayers, priests and prophets (cf. Neh 9:32, 34), are absent here. Prophets are not mentioned because they are invoked in the positive role of covenant teachers, as in Jer 44. It is less clear why priests are exempted. Perhaps no significance should be attached to the omission, and the author is simply following the model of Jer 44:21. But the high priests Joshua and Onias III play an important role in Gabriel's account of history in Dan 9:24–27, and it may be that the chapter criticizes political leaders, while seeing in prophets and priests those whose leadership should have been heeded.

[7–9] These verses establish the contrast, common in penitential prayer, between the righteousness of God and the sinfulness and shame of the people; but they also begin to establish the grounds for a possible change in the people's desperate circumstances. The contrast is established through two syntactically balanced phrases, "to you" (*lĕkā*, v. 7) and "to us" (*lānû*, v. 8). The content of the contrast, however, is not expressed in semantically opposite terms. The "right" that is attributed to God has forensic connotations, though the term can also be broader, referring to moral right in general. Instead of the opposite term "guilt" or "wrong," however, what is attributed to the people is "shame of face" (*bōšet happānîm*; cf. Ezra 9:7). Shame is a powerful concept in biblical thought. It has an objective, social dimension: people who are dishonored through defeat and apparent abandonment by their God become objects of mockery and disgrace. The use of the term "face" in the idiom suggests the public aspect of such shame. But shame also has psychological dimensions. Although Lev 26:29–40 does not use the term *bōšet*, it describes the people's experience of shame and self-loathing when they belatedly recognize and confess their sins against God (cf. Ezek 36:31; Lapsley). Here, as also in Jer 3:25 and Ezra 9:6, shame at the recognition of sin is the emotion that both impels the confession and makes it difficult to approach God. The comprehensiveness of the guilt is suggested by two different groups of terms that encompass the entire people. They are first described geographically as those who are resident in Judah and Jerusalem and then those in exile ("all Israel, both near and far"; cf. 1 Kgs 8:46), concluding with a description of the people as "scattered" in many lands, a phrase characteristic of the Deuteronomistic prose in Jeremiah (16:15; 23:3; 32:37). (The reference to the exiles as "them" rather than "us" seems to put the speaker in Judah, perhaps another indication that the prayer was an already-existing composition appropriated by the author without adjusting it to the setting of the fictional Daniel in Babylon.) Verse 8 recapitulates v. 7 but uses the categories of political leadership ("kings, princes, and fathers/ancestors"; cf. v. 6) as those who have sinned. That the sin is understood in relational and even in political terms is suggested by the choice of the verbs "to be faithless, treacherous" (*māʿal*) and "to rebel" (*mārad*) in vv. 7 and 9.

Although the supplication will not begin until v. 15, here v. 9 begins to establish the grounds upon which it will be made. Using the same syntax that introduced v. 7, attributing to God the state of being in the right, the prayer now ascribes "to the Lord our God" the qualities of compassion and forgiveness (cf. Ps 130:4; Neh 9:17). Though the people have no claim of being in the right, they can still make an appeal based on the nature of God as a deity more disposed to gracious forgiveness and mercy than to prolonged punishment. This affirmation is at the heart of the liturgically very influential characterization of

God in Exod 34:6–7, which insists that while God will not remit all punishment, God's inclination to forgive is exponentially greater. (For the influence of this passage, see Fishbane 335–53.)

[10–14] In keeping with this logic, before the supplication is made, the history of sin and its consequent punishment is rehearsed. Recapitulating vv. 5–6, now vv. 10–11a use the characteristic Deuteronomistic language of "not listening" (Deut 4:30; Jer 26:4; 32:23; 44:23; etc.) to God or to the prophets (cf. v. 6; 2 Kgs 17:13; Ezra 9:11). Equally prominent are metaphors of physical movement. Instead of "walking" in the teachings (*tôrôt*) of God, the people have "crossed over, transgressed" (*'ābar*) and "turned aside" (*sûr*). The image is of a people who have a perverse disorientation.

Verses 11b–12 explain the consequences. Just as the teachings of Moses, the servant of God (cf. Deut 34:5; Josh 1:1; 8:31), contained instructions for proper living, so they also contained "a curse pronounced under oath." Using a similar phrase, Neh 10:29 (30) refers to entering into a covenant by swearing to "an oath with sanctions" (NJPS). Although that phraseology is not used in the pentateuchal covenant traditions, the solemn and ceremonial making of the covenant (Exod 24:6–8; Deut 29:1 [28:69]) was understood to bind the people to obedience and to require them to accept as legitimate the enforcement of the covenant curses in case of persistent disobedience. The reference here is to Deut 28:15–68, the harrowingly graphic description of the curses that will befall the disobedient people (cf. Lev 26:14–45).

While Dan 9 does not invoke the specific horrors of the covenant curses, it communicates their enormity in other ways. The verb used to describe the action of the oath is "gush" or "pour out" (*nātak*), a verb elsewhere used of God's anger and wrath (Jer 7:20; 42:18; 44:6; 2 Chr 12:7; 34:25). Using the verb here indicates that the imposition of the curses is not emotionally neutral but is an expression of divine rage (cf. Deut 29:21–27). The horror of these events is further underscored by the reference to their incomparable nature. In many texts Sodom and Gomorrah stood as the almost clichéd example of utter destruction (Gen 19:24–28; Deut 29:23; Isa 1:9; 13:19; Jer 49:18; 50:40; Amos 4:11; Zeph 2:9; Lam 4:6). Here, however, Jerusalem's fate, described as unique "under all the heavens" (cf. Deut 2:25; 4:19), suggests that it would replace Sodom and Gomorrah as the benchmark for the destruction of a sinful city.

The reference to something written in the "teaching of Moses" (*tôrat mōšeh*) in vv. 11, 13 is an indication of the increasingly authoritative role of written Scripture. Although the phrase is used occasionally in the Deuteronomistic History (Josh 8:31; 1 Kgs 2:3), it becomes more frequent in postexilic literature (Mal 4:4 [3:22]; Ezra 3:2; 7:6; Neh 8:1; 2 Chr 23:18; 30:16) and occurs several times in the Dead Sea Scrolls (e.g., CD 16.5; 1QS 5.8; 8.22). The Daniel passage assumes that the written warnings should have provoked a much earlier response from the people. Of the responses that the prayer suggests should have taken place, supplication (cf. Jer 26:19; Mal 1:9; 2 Chr 33:12) and repentance (cf. Deut 4:30; Jer 4:1–2) are actions one would expect. The mention of "gaining insight" (*lĕhaśkîl*), however, is unusual. The root *śkl* is something of a leitmotif in Daniel (1:4, 17; 9:13, 22, 25; 11:33, 35; 12:3, 10), and even if the prayer is an originally independent composition, the word stands out because of the role it plays more generally in the book. Appropriate religious dispositions are achieved through discernment, and the object of discernment in this case is God's *'ĕmet*. While this word can have connotations of "constancy, reliability," it can also mean "truth," and here probably refers back to the written teachings of Moses. In Dan 10:21 the term will be used to describe the heavenly "book of truth," an account of the divine plan for history and its eschatological culmination. The audience for which the book of Daniel is intended is presumed to have understanding of both types of writings.

[15–19] Verses 15–19 constitute the supplication, introduced by the transitional phrase "and now" (*wĕ'attâ*; cf. Ezra 9:8, 10; Neh 9:32). The first section (vv. 15–16) continues to include aspects of confession of sin (vv. 15b, 16b), an element that diminishes in the latter part of the supplication. While an appeal to the merciful character of God (cf. v. 9) appears twice (v.16a, 18b), the primary basis of the appeal is grounded on God's concern for reputation and honor. Both motives are developed through the frequent repetition of the second-person-singular possessive pronoun "your." The appeal refers to "your people" (3×: vv. 15, 16, 19), "your city Jerusalem," "your holy mountain," "your servant," "your desolate sanctuary," and "your city."

The supplication begins with a recollection of the deliverance from Egypt, the foundational event in the nation's life (cf. Deut 6:21; 9:26; Jer 32:20–21; Ps 106:8; Neh 9:10). That episode can be framed in a number of ways, depending on the rhetorical purposes of the author. Here it is not the relief of suffering or the benefit conferred on the people that is stressed, but the fact that through this event God established a reputation, literally, "making a name for yourself" (v. 15). Moreover, that action identified the Israelites as "your people." In other texts as well, this irrevocable relationship is used as a means of appeal to God to act for his own name's sake to rescue an undeserving people (cf. Deut 9:26–29; Ezek 20:22). Even though the people's sin is responsible for their devastation and thus the mockery to which they are subjected (Dan 9:16b), their own actions have also put at risk the honor of God, who might appear to be powerless to redeem them and to defeat the human enemies who have been the instruments of their punishment (cf. Ps 79:9–13). The appeal to God's honor is intensified in Dan 9:18–19, where twice it is emphasized that God's own name is attached to Jerusalem.

The centrality of Jerusalem and the sanctuary in the appeal is striking, mentioned six separate times in these five verses. Although the role of Jerusalem as the city that God had chosen and identified with his name (cf. Deut 12:5;

2 Sam 7:13; 1 Kgs 8:29, 43; Jer 7:10–11) had long been a major element in Judean political and religious identity, Jerusalem and the temple took on an even greater significance in the postmonarchical period as the focal point of national life. The resonant terms "desolate" and "desolation" (vv. 17–18) not only invoke the language of the covenant curses (Lev 26:22, 31–35; cf. Jer 4:27; Ezek 6:6) but also the phrases of grief and appeal for compassion in laments (Ps 79:9; Lam 5:18; 1 Macc 4:38). Various forms of the word occur in key places in the Danielic apocalypses (8:13; 9:26–27; 11:31; 12:11), referring to the profanation of the sanctuary.

In a prayer that has employed repetition in lush and sometimes sprawling sentences, the repetition of short imperative phrases in vv. 18–19 establishes a dramatic and effective conclusion. Verse 18 appeals to God's sensory attention: "incline your ear . . . and listen; open your eyes and see." Even more striking is v. 19 with its series of four short imperative phrases that not only repeat the call for attention ("hear," "attend") but also identify the needed response from God ("forgive," "act without delay"). Following the two sets of imperatives is a repetition of the two motives for the appeal: God's undeserved mercy (v. 18b) and God's honor (v. 19b). These verses are the entire prayer in nuce, though with the emphasis directed to the desired outcome rather than to the earlier emphasis on confession.

[20–21] Verses 20 and 21a are repetitious and awkward, which suggests to some critics that the prayer is a later insertion, since v. 21 would follow smoothly after v. 3. But that is not a necessary conclusion. Verse 20, which summarizes the content of the prayer, is such a long sentence that the author may have felt it useful in v. 21 to repeat the temporal phrase ("while I was [still] speaking") in order to indicate the synchronicity of the prayer and the arrival of the angel.

Given the context of Daniel's prayer in the time between the defeat of Babylon and the return of the exiles, and given his implicit interpretation of Jer 29:12–14 as anticipating an act of prayer to precede God's restoration of the exiles, the narrative sets up the expectation that Gabriel's message will be an announcement of return and restoration. The power of this narrative setting was so strong that this was how Daniel's prayer and its effect were remembered in one apocryphal writing, the *Testament of Moses*, which in its present form probably dates from the first century C.E. In a summary of the history of Israel, *Test. Mos.* 3 concludes with a reference to the exile. Its ch. 4 opens with the statement "Then one who is over them [i.e., Daniel] will come upon the scene, and he will stretch forth his hands, and bow his knees and pray for them, saying . . ." (trans. J. Priest). The prayer that is cited (vv. 2–4), however, is not really a summary of Dan 9 but simply a prayer for deliverance. But the prayer is seen as being efficacious, for vv. 5–6 read, "Then God will remember them . . . and openly show his compassion. And in those times he will inspire a king to have pity on them and send them home to their own land." Thus in the *Testament of Moses*, Daniel's prayer is remembered as the catalyst for Cyrus's decree allowing the exiles to return (Ezra 1:1–4; 2 Chr 36:22–23), not as the occasion for a revelation about a much later time, which is what happens in the rest of Dan 9.

Verse 21 may be evidence for developing speculation about the nature of angels. If the text indeed makes reference to Gabriel's flight (see trans. notes), then it is the first explicit mention of angelic flight and, by implication, their winged appearance. In earlier biblical texts (e.g., Gen 19:1; Judg 6:11; 1 Kgs 19:5, 7) no mode of angelic locomotion is specified, though in Judg 13:20 the angel who appears to Samson's parents ascends to heaven in the flames of the altar fire, and in 1 Chr 21:16 the angel stands between heaven and earth. It is possible that the winged nature of other semidivine beings—such as cherubim (Ezek 1), seraphim (Isa 6:2), the winged female figures in Zechariah's vision (Zech 5:9), and the winged genii of Mesopotamia—has been transferred to angels. Perhaps also the idea is derived exegetically from Ps 104:3–4. There God's chariot is said to move on the "wings of the wind" (*kanpê-rûaḥ*), followed by the comment that "[God] makes the winds [his] messengers" (*malʾākayw*). Since *rûaḥ* can refer not only to the wind but also to divine spirits, and as *malʾāk* can mean both "messenger" and "angel," the passage could have been read as referring to winged angelic spirits.

In the Second Temple period the "time of the evening sacrifice" (Exod 29:41; Lev 6:20 [13]; Num 28:4; 2 Kgs 16:15) came to be seen as a particularly appropriate and efficacious time to offer prayer (Ezra 9:4–5; Jdt 9:1; cf. Luke 1:10). While the practice of praying three times a day is already reflected in Dan 6:10 (11), the prayers explicitly associated with the evening sacrifice in Ezra, Daniel, and Judith are confessional and petitionary.

[22–23] Gabriel announces the purpose of his appearance to Daniel with words that are thematically important to the book: "to give you understanding" (*lĕhaśkîlĕkā bînâ*). Despite Gabriel's attempt (8:16) to interpret for Daniel the vision in ch. 8, that chapter ended with Daniel's statement that he did not understand (v. 27). Now Gabriel will again explain the preordained course of history to Daniel by means of an interpretation of the passage in Jeremiah. In Dan 11:33–34 the "wise" (*maśkîlîm*) will similarly bring understanding to the people. Thus the angel who is able to interpret the hidden meanings of visions and texts stands as the model for the authors of Dan 7–12 and their immediate circle.

The response to Daniel's prayer is said to occur "at the beginning" of his supplication. Thus it is a response to the fact of his praying and not specifically to the content. His action shows Daniel to be worthy of understanding. This evaluation of Daniel is reflected in the word used to describe him, *ḥămûdōt* ("highly valued," 9:23; also in 10:11, 19). Elsewhere it often refers to treasure

(11:38–43) or to something especially valuable and desirable (10:3). The "word" that goes forth is the hidden but true meaning of the prophecy of Jeremiah, which Gabriel will explain. The paired imperatives "pay attention" and "understand" are both forms of the thematically important root *byn*, which was used in a nominal form in v. 22. Although Berner (46–47) suggests that "vision" in v. 23 refers back to the vision of ch. 8 that Daniel did not understand, the angel's words do not actually explain the vision. Instead, it is more likely that the term for vision has taken on the broader sense of "revelation" (so Hartman and DiLella 244).

[24] As Daniel has been praying on behalf of his "people" and the "holy city" (vv. 15–19, passim), so the angel addresses his concerns for them. Yet the first words out of Gabriel's mouth undercut Daniel's understanding of the Jeremianic prophecy: Gabriel informs him that the prophecy refers not to "seventy years" (Jer 25:11–12; 29:10) but to "seventy sevens," that is, seventy weeks of years. Gabriel is not contradicting Jeremiah but disclosing a hidden meaning that rests on one or more accepted exegetical practices of the second century B.C.E. One possible hermeneutical key to Gabriel's interpretation is that of double reading. Since the Hebrew of the time was written only consonantally, the letters for the word "seventy" and the letters for "weeks" look the same, and the consonants of Jeremiah's prophecy, *šbʿym*, could be pronounced either *šibʿîm* ("seventy") or *šābūʿîm* ("sevens," "weeks"). The potential for double reading was undoubtedly activated by another hermeneutical practice, that of interpreting one text in light of another. Leviticus 26:18 (cf. v. 28) is one possible intertext. There, in the context of promised blessings and threats for covenant obedience or disobedience, God declares that he will punish the people "sevenfold" because they did not listen. Thus Jeremiah's seventy years can be multiplied by seven, and one might translate the rest of the line as "[they] are decreed *against* [*ʿal*] your people and your holy city" (so Montgomery 373). Thus Daniel's supplicatory prayer would in fact be premature. The following more detailed account of this period, however, is not one of punishment only but also includes important events of restoration. Indeed, the final words of v. 24 refer to the anointing of the holy of holies. Thus it is likely that more is informing the interpretation here than just an intertextual reading of Jeremiah's prophecy and Lev 26:18. One should probably think of Gabriel's interpretation as "overdetermined," that is, as motivated by various aspects of an already rich tradition of the interpretation of Jeremiah's prophecy that had been developed in the Second Temple period.

Daniel's concern for the city and sanctuary has an antecedent in Zechariah's interpretation of Jeremiah's prophecy in the late sixth century. In Zech 1:12 the angelic interpreter implicitly connects the prophecy with the time during which Jerusalem lies devastated, and marks the end of the period with the rebuilding of the temple, which occurred between 520 and 515 B.C.E. But for the author of

Daniel, the temple's travails do not end with its rebuilding. Thus there must be more to the prophecy than met the eye of Zechariah.

Another stream of interpretation that may have contributed to Dan 9 is found in 2 Chr 36. The Chronicler relates Jeremiah's prophecy to the duration of the exile, clearly relying on an interpretation of Lev 26—not vv. 18, 28, however, but vv. 32–35. The Chronicler interprets the seventy years to refer to the time during which the land was desolate and its people exiled to Babylon. In actual fact, although there was considerable devastation, population reduction, and diminished economic activity, the land of Judah remained occupied and engaged in agricultural production (see Lipschits). But the Chronicler envisions it as being an emptied, desolated land, and the cessation of agriculture as a form of keeping the sabbatical year. Here too, it is clear that the Chronicler is alluding to the covenant curses in Lev 26, which threaten desolation (26:32–33) and interpret the time of desolation as observance of sabbatical years that the people had failed to observe during the time they lived in the land (26:34–35). Thus only when the seventy sabbatical years had been paid back could the exile come to an end and the land again be occupied and farmed. Actually, the decree of Cyrus allowing a return and rebuilding of the temple occurred slightly less than fifty years after the destruction of Jerusalem (586–538 B.C.E.) or slightly less than sixty years after the first deportation (597 B.C.E.). The point, however, was not about a strict chronology but about constructing a meaning for the exile and a way of understanding the prophecy of Jeremiah as having been fulfilled. Perhaps the author of Daniel follows the Chronicler's lead in identifying the seventy years with sabbatical years but also used Lev 26:18, 28 to multiply them by seven. Not seventy sabbatical years but seventy times seven.

In the end, it is not possible to say which particular hermeneutical techniques were used by the author to generate Gabriel's interpretation of the Jeremianic prophecy, but that is less important than recognizing that readers might confirm the interpretation by a variety of recognized interpretive means. Indeed, the ambiguity of the text and the fact that it required readers to search for an appropriate hermeneutical key is part of the book's strategy of constructing the reader as an active interpreter of divine mysteries.

Although the traditions of interpreting Jeremiah's prophecy are the most important background for Dan 9, a broader tradition of speculation involving the numbers 70 and 490 was common in apocalyptic and eschatological texts of this era and would likely have been known to the early readers of Daniel. In *1 En.* 10:11–12 the duration of the imprisonment of the rebellious angels is 70 generations (cf. *Ages of Creation* [4Q181 frg. 2 3]). The people transgress for 70 weeks, according to *T. Levi* 16:1. Although the terminology of weeks is not used, in *1 En.* 89:59 Israel is subjected to the rule of the "70 shepherds" after the fall of Jerusalem and until the eschatological events that are expected at the time of the Antiochene persecution. The calculation of time according to Jubilee periods (Lev 25:8–10), which were often measured as 49-year periods (7 × 7) rather than 50-year periods, was also popular (see *Jubilees*, the *Apocryphon of Joshua*^{b} [4Q379 frg. 12], the *Apocryphon of Jeremiah*^{e} [4Q390 frg. 1]). In some texts significant periods were calculated as consisting of 10 Jubilee periods, that is, 490 years, the equivalent of 70 weeks of years (see the *Genesis Apocryphon* [1Q20 6.9–10], the *Apocryphon of Jeremiah*^{c} [4Q387 frg. 2 2], and especially *Melchizedek* [11Q13 2.18–21], which alludes to Daniel). Although Dan 9 makes a certain use of the Jubilee tradition (see comments on v. 25 below), it does not make any explicit connection between the 70 weeks of years by which it calculates time and the structure of 10 Jubilee periods that appear in these other texts and traditions.

Having announced that the seventy years of Jeremiah's prophecy are to be understood as seventy weeks of years, Gabriel goes on to characterize their nature and purpose. In Dan 9:24 the period of time is said to be "determined" (*neḥtak*), a word otherwise not attested in Biblical Hebrew (cf. *Commentary on Genesis*^{a} [4Q252 1.2]) but which becomes more common in Rabbinic Hebrew. It could be argued that a tension exists between the Deuteronomistic prayer that Daniel speaks, with its sense of a future dependent upon the decision of God to be merciful or not, and the deterministic theology implicit in a set period of time that has been decreed in advance. While this may be so in the narrowest sense, the two theologies are better understood as each expressing a truth about a situation that exceeds the capacity of a single explanatory mode. On the one hand, the predetermination of the period of time is a means of expressing the confidence that God alone is in control of history and that its events are meaningful and can be grasped as a coherent narrative. On the other hand, the Deuteronomistic prayer expresses the sense that the drama of which history is made is fundamentally motivated by the relationship between God and Israel. These are not the only two models of history in the apocalypses of Dan 7–12. In chs. 7–8, and again in ch. 11, the narrative structure provided by the myth of the rebellious subordinate and his challenge to the Most High God provides another means of grasping the unity of historical events. The redundancy created by the coordination of several alternative models of explanation serves to strengthen reassurance in a time of crisis. The reader need not choose among them.

In 9:24b the purpose of the seventy weeks of years is described in a list of six infinitival phrases: three have to do with sin, and three have to do with restorative transformation. Whose sin is in question is a matter of considerable dispute, with some arguing that the sin in question is Israel's (so Steck 69–70), and others arguing that the sin is that of Antiochus (so Seow 147), or at least that it includes that of the Jewish hellenizers as well as the Gentile oppressors (so J. Collins 354; Berner 50). From the perspective of the character Daniel, as he has been engaged in his prayer of confession, the three phrases "to finish transgression, to bring sins to completion, and to expiate iniquity" certainly seem to apply to Israel's sins. The phrase "to expiate iniquity" must refer to God's salvific forgiveness, as in Ps 78:38 (cf. Isa 22:14; Jer 18:23). In some cases this expiation is linked to the ending of sinful behavior (so Isa 27:9); hence, as the culminating infinitive phrase after two other references to sin, the whole sequence could be read as addressing Israel's relation with God. But the verbs "finish" and "bring to completion" are quite unusual expressions to use in connection with Israel's sin. The only close parallel to the phrase is to be found in 8:23, where the transgressions (or "transgressors"; see the translation note) that are brought to an end are clearly those of the Gentile kingdoms that are the successors to Alexander the Great. Even if Daniel professed not to have understood that vision (8:27), the reader is presumed to have understood and so will know what that phrase refers to: Gentile transgression. Similarly, in the nearly contemporary Animal Apocalypse in *1 En.* 83–90, the seventy shepherds exceed their authorization as to the number of Israelite "sheep" they are authorized to kill. Even though a record is kept, no intervention is made until the last of the shepherds complete their times (90:5). A more distant parallel is Gen 15:16, which refers to the delayed return of Abram's descendants to Canaan until the fourth generation because "the iniquity of the Amorites is not yet complete [*šallēm*]." The notion of evil that must run its course is primarily associated with Gentile sin and oppression. Thus the three infinitival phrases cryptically suggest a period of time that will see both an end to Gentile transgression and the expiation of those sins of Israel that Daniel has so poignantly confessed.

The three positive infinitives describe the restorative transformation that is to take place. The English term "righteousness" connotes only a part of what the Hebrew term *ṣedeq* conveys. Not only is it the opposite of "transgression," "sin," and "iniquity," but more comprehensively, it describes things rightly ordered, all as they should be. The phrase "eternal righteousness" is quite rare, though it does occur in the beautiful *Apostrophe to Zion* (11Q5 22.13) as part of the blessing of the city. It is an eschatological phrase, since it suggests that never again can anything disturb the proper and just order that will be established. A related term was used in Dan 8:14 to describe the setting right of the sanctuary.

The pair of terms "vision" and "prophet" are most likely to be taken as a hendiadys connoting "prophetic vision," that is, a revelatory message. The superscriptions (1:1) of Isaiah, Obadiah, and Nahum also use the term *ḥăzôn* as a general term for the entirety of the prophetic books, suggesting that by the Second Temple period the word no longer referred only to a visual revelation (cf. 2 Chr 32:32). Already in Hab 2:2 the *ḥăzôn* is something to be written down. While some have suggested that the referent is the vision that Daniel received in ch. 8 (so Seow 148), it more likely refers to the prophecy of Jeremiah that Gabriel is interpreting. It is also possible to take it as a general reference to eschatological prophecies as a whole, as seems to be the case in 11:14 (so J. Collins 354).

The term "to seal" has two different meanings. It can mean to "seal up" so that a document or other item is not accessible. That is the way the phrase is used in *Mysteries*[b] (4Q300), where the false interpreters are told that a vision has been sealed so that they cannot open it (frg. 1 2.1–6). The notion of concealing a revelation is present elsewhere in Daniel (8:26; 12:9), but it does not fit the present context. Here in Dan 9, "seal" has the meaning of "authenticate," as in 1 Kgs 21:8; Jer 32:10, 11, 44. More puzzling is the final phrase of Dan 9:24, "to anoint the holy of holies." Early Christian tradition saw a messianic reference in this phrase (cf. Peshitta, Vulgate), but in the Hebrew Bible the term "holy of holies" always refers to objects or locations. But there is no exact parallel for the phrase "to anoint the holy of holies." The tent of meeting, the tabernacle, and the ark of the covenant, however, are said to be anointed in Exod 30:26 and 40:9. Since the desecration of the temple is a major concern of both Dan 8 and 9, it makes sense that this resanctification is the climactic image of restoration. This resanctification is, in fact, what happens after the forces of Judah the Maccabee retake Jerusalem in 164 B.C.E., as described in the later works of 1 Macc 4:36–61 and 2 Macc 10:1–8.

Some have questioned whether the simple cleansing and rededication of the temple would have been sufficient for the author of Daniel. For the contemporary Animal Apocalypse of *1 En.* 83–90, the second temple built after the exile is taken away and a new eschatological temple is built in its place. While some suggest that the authors of Daniel similarly despaired of the desecrated temple (so Berner 56–58), there is nothing in Daniel explicitly suggesting that the old temple could not be restored. Indeed, the phraseology of 8:14 ("then the sanctuary will be made right") more clearly suggests that restoration of the old structure is what the authors of Daniel anticipate. The "anointing" of the holy of holies need not suggest a new structure but simply the resanctification of the old.

[25] Now Gabriel begins to communicate the structure of the seventy weeks and the events that are to happen in each portion of it. The beginning point is a matter of some interpretive controversy since Gabriel defines it as "from the going forth of the word to restore and rebuild Jerusalem." To what does that refer? The historicist tendencies of much interpretation have attempted to calculate dates literally and to use the 490 years of the 70 weeks as a precise figure. Thus, depending on how one sees the beginning or ending points of the calculus, several never quite satisfactory periods of time have been proposed (Hartman and DiLella 250–51). The remarkably diverse set of suggestions that all require some adjustment to match the time line suggests that the author was not intending to make a precise chronological calculation but simply to connect important events in history by means of a symbolic heptadonal system of time. Or as Grabbe (1979) puts it, the author was not interested so much in chronology as in chronography. Even if this is the case, the author does seem to

have something specific in mind as the starting point for the calculation. More historically inclined interpreters have tried to tie the starting point to actual decrees issued by Persian kings, for instance, the decree of Cyrus in 538 B.C.E. permitting the rebuilding of Jerusalem, or the later decrees of Darius (in 521) or Artaxerxes (in 458), or the permission given to Nehemiah to rebuild the walls (in 445) (see Doukhan 15). But none of this is warranted by any aspect of the text of Daniel, which seems quite oblivious with respect to these details of history.

As the text presents itself, the "going forth of the word" can refer only to one of two things. Either it refers to Jeremiah's own prophecies about the seventy years, or it refers to the decision in heaven in response to Daniel's prayer that Gabriel now announces to him. John Collins (354–55) notices the similarity between Gabriel's language in v. 23 ("at the beginning of your supplication a word went forth") and here ("from the going forth of the word to restore and rebuild Jerusalem"). That could suggest that it is Daniel's own prayer that triggers the start of the seventy weeks of years. Yet this would trivialize the prophetic word that Daniel had been pondering, which seems unlikely. The other alternative is to see Gabriel as indicating that the seventy weeks of years began when Jeremiah uttered the prophecy. Modern scholarship, of course, dates the two prophecies of Jeremiah to around 605 (Jer 25:11–12), and shortly after the first deportation, around 597–594 (29:10–12). Neither prophecy actually refers to a rebuilding of Jerusalem. Indeed, at the time of both prophecies, Jerusalem was still intact. From the perspective of someone writing in the second century B.C.E., however, these historical details may not have been known. More likely, Jeremiah's prophecy was more loosely interpreted as indicating the time between the destruction and restoration of Jerusalem, as it was already interpreted in Zech 1:12. If that is so, then Gabriel's account of history describes the time between the fall of Jerusalem and its anticipated restoration in the wake of the Antiochene desecrations.

The seventy weeks of years are divided into three unequal portions. Only the first and last are of interpretive significance. The middle section is simply what remains after the times of significance have been subtracted. The first period of time is measured as seven weeks, which is to say, the time of a Jubilee. Clearly this designation is important. It defines the time from the beginning of the exile to the return after the decree of Cyrus. In the priestly tradition the Jubilee was the time for release—the release of slaves indentured for debt and the time for the return of property that had been seized or sold for debt (Lev 25). Thus to name the period of exile as a Jubilee period was to bring it under the interpretive canopy of God's law. History was not determined by the independent wax and wane of imperial powers but was structured according to a divinely ordained sacral order.

The end of the Jubilee period in Dan 9, however, is not identified specifically as a return or restoration, but as "the time of an anointed ruler." Since "anointed" can refer either to political or priestly leaders, one could think either of Zerubbabel, the Davidide who was the Jewish governor of the early restoration period, or of Joshua, the high priest who returned with him from the Babylonian exile. Given Daniel's interest in the Jerusalem temple and cult, however, and particularly in light of subsequent references to a second anointed one who can only be a priest (v. 26), one should think here of Joshua. Thus the way of calculating time in relation to sabbatical and Jubilee periods, and the focus on high priests—both suggest that for the authors of Daniel, the temple and the priestly staff who serve it are the objects by which the well-being of the nation as a whole are to be measured.

The middle period, which is the longest (62 weeks), is described almost offhandedly as a time when the city is rebuilt with "plaza and fosse." This phrase identifies the reestablishment of Jerusalem as a proper city. The plazas were the broad open spaces located just within the city gates where public assemblies were held. This was the primary locus for civic life. The fosse was part of the defensive system of the city, a deep cut in the terrain located below the walls, so as to make them more formidable. Although walls are not explicitly referred to, the rebuilding of the walls of Jerusalem by Nehemiah was one of the landmarks in the restoration of the status of Jerusalem and would have been part of the normal state of Jerusalem for someone who lived in the second century B.C.E. Thus for the majority of the time that the prophecy refers to, Jerusalem is established as a well-built and well-defended city.

The Masoretic pointing and the later versification, along with most modern interpreters, take the following phrase "but in stressful times" (lit., "in tightness of times") as part of v. 25, qualifying the condition of the city with its plazas and fosse. If that is correct, then it suggests that the entire postexilic period, despite the well-built status of Jerusalem, is seen as a time of distress. A negative view of the entire period was indeed held by certain authors. The Enochic tradition considered the second temple to be unworthy and so envisioned it as being folded up and taken away so that an entirely new eschatological temple could be erected after the Antiochene persecutions were ended (*1 En.* 89:73–77; cf. 93:9). For some other writers, too, there was a sense that the exile never fully came to an end (Knibb). But one should be careful about importing those views into the book of Daniel without further warrant. Attitudes toward the temple were quite varied. The Chronicler makes the rebuilding of the temple the final act of his history and retrojects many of its arrangements to the activity of David and Solomon. Ben Sira also express great pride in the temple and the high priest (50:1–24). Daniel's evident distress over the desecration of the temple and concern that it be put right (8:14) may suggest that he held a more positive view of the state of things between the restoration in the late sixth century and its disturbance in the middle of the second than is reflected in the Enochic tradition. Given the difficulty of the Hebrew of this section, however, it is entirely possible that the phrase "in a stressful time" should be seen rather as introducing what follows (see trans. notes).

[26] This verse begins the narration of the events of the final week of years, though that terminology is not used until v. 27. While the contemporary readers would have known the complex series of events referred to, the schematic details provided by the author are almost unintelligible to the modern reader without historical background. The anointed one who is cut off is almost certainly to be identified as the high priest Onias III. Although the high priesthood was hereditary, according to Judean custom, the Seleucid king confirmed the high priest in his office. When Antiochus IV came to the throne in 175 B.C.E., however, Onias's brother Jason bribed the king to appoint him as high priest instead. Jason also introduced Hellenistic institutions to Jerusalem, a move that was apparently rather popular at the time, though later condemned in the strongest terms by the writers of 1 and 2 Maccabees (2 Macc 4:7–10). In 172 B.C.E., however, a rival from a prominent family, Menelaus, offered the king even more money to make *him* the high priest. Menelaus failed to pay the full sum, and in an attempt to bribe further Seleucid officials, stole golden vessels from the temple (2 Macc 4:23–32). Onias, who had taken sanctuary in a pagan temple near Antioch, the royal capital, exposed Menelaus's theft, whereupon Menelaus persuaded a Seleucid official to murder Onias (4:33–34). This murder, and the knowledge of the plunder of the temple by the very high priest who was supposed to protect it, led to riots in Jerusalem (4:39–42). Inconsistencies in the historical sources make the following events difficult to reconstruct, but the most likely reconstruction is that of Bickerman (1979, 104–11). It appears that after his first campaign against Egypt in 169, Antiochus, too, plundered the temple (1 Macc 1:20–23). Later, during Antiochus IV's campaign in Egypt in 168 a rumor reached Jason that Antiochus had died, prompting Jason to lead a small force against Menelaus in Jerusalem, though Jason ultimately failed to hold the city and fled again to Transjordan (2 Macc 5:5–7). Although Menelaus regained control, Antiochus treated the city as if it were in rebellion. It is entirely possible that a large segment of the population was supportive of the Oniad Jason rather than the discredited Menelaus. In any event, the assault on Jerusalem under Apollonius the Mysarch is what Dan 9:26 refers to as the destruction of the city and the sanctuary (see 1 Macc 1:33–40; yet 2 Macc 5:11–26 conflates Antiochus's earlier plundering of the temple with the attack by his official, Apollonius).

Although the gist of the first part of Dan 9:26 is fairly certain, the text itself is difficult and ambiguous (see trans. notes). The verb "cut off," used to describe the murder of Onias, may be an allusion to the promise in Jer 33:17–18 that neither the line of David nor the line of the Levitical priests will be "cut off" from before God (Berner 64). In fact, after Jason's ignominious death (2 Macc 5:8–10), no Oniad ever again reigned as high priest in Jerusalem, though subsequent high priests were also descendents of Levi. The murder of Onias, however, was a shock, and if the text does allude to the passage in Jeremiah, the tension between the promise and historical events expresses the acute anxiety of the times and the hope for an eschatological resolution.

Since Daniel elsewhere prefers the terminology of "king" (*melek*) for the Gentile rulers, it is somewhat surprising to see Antiochus referred to here as "prince" (*nāgîd*). A few commentators have suggested that the reference might be to Jason (so Bevan 158, followed by Goldingay 262) or Menelaus (so Seow 150). This suggestion, however, is unpersuasive. All of the Danielic apocalypses see the primary evil figure as the Gentile king, and it is most likely that this term also refers to Antiochus.

The last part of the verse is obscure and difficult. The MT text reads "his end will come in a cataclysm" or "flood." The oddity of this reading is that v. 27 continues to describe the activities and ultimate end of Antiochus IV. There are two ways of resolving this tension. Some (e.g., Berner 66–74) suggest that v. 27 may be an "actualizing update" that was added after Antiochus IV's end had in fact occurred. While that is possible, there is no independent evidence for such editorial activity. Alternatively, the text may not be properly preserved, and it may be that the text should be slightly emended to read "and *the* end will come," summarizing the general quality of the eschatological events, with v. 27 presenting the details of those still-anticipated events. This is the option chosen here. The terminology of v. 26 has echoes of Isa 10:22–23, which, however, describes a judgment on Israel.

[27] The first phrase of the verse is odd. The verb *higbîr* ("to make great or strong") is not otherwise used with the term for covenant (*běrît*). Moreover, the referent of "the many" is uncertain. In 11:33–34 the term appears to refer to the Judean populace in general. Since the second half of the verse appears to posit Antiochus as the subject of the verb, he is apparently also the subject here. Despite considerable obscurities, the phrase apparently refers to the agreement between Antiochus and the Jewish supporters of Jason and later Menelaus. Similarly 1 Macc 1:11 envisions the hellenizing Jews as saying, "Let us go and make a covenant with the Gentiles around us, for since we separated from them many disasters have come upon us." Perhaps, as Lacocque (198) and Berner (68) argue, the use of the term *běrît* is intended to suggest the false consciousness of the "many" and the hubris of Antiochus, who unknowingly parody the relationship between God and Israel.

The cessation of sacrifice and offering refers to Antiochus's deliberate interference with the cult of the Jerusalem temple as a form of punishment for the rebellious Judeans, and the establishment there of a cult to serve the religious needs of the Syrian troops of the military occupation forces in Jerusalem (cf. 1 Macc 1:44–50; 2 Macc 6:1–11). Although the other sources mention repression that also affected the people in the outlying regions of Judah, Daniel focuses solely on the sacrificial cult.

Unfortunately, the latter part of v. 27 is textually confused and deeply obscure. This part of the verse apparently describes some specific act by Antiochus IV. As preserved in the MT, the passage seems to read "and upon a wing of abominations is something that desolates, and [or 'even'] until the end that is decreed is poured out upon the one who desolates." In light of this very difficult text, exegetes should confess that any interpretation is largely guesswork. Given this situation, most commentators start from the clearer descriptions of Antiochus's activities in 1 and 2 Maccabees and other sources to see which of those actions might be the subject of this account. Attention focuses especially on 1 Macc 1:54, which describes how, on Chislev 15 (December 167 B.C.E.), Antiochus "erected a desolating sacrilege on the altar of burnt offering." Exactly what Antiochus put on top of the altar is a matter of dispute. Josephus suggested that it was a pagan altar placed atop the Judean altar (*Ant.* 12.253; cf. 2 Macc 6:5). Also, 1 Macc 4:43 makes reference to "defiled stones," different from the stones of the altar, which is consistent with the notion of a smaller pagan altar. Yet Bickerman (1979, 70) suggested that perhaps Antiochus placed a sacred stone or stones on the altar as a symbol of a pagan deity. While such customs are attested in the general cultural area, the notion of a superimposed altar seems much more likely. The key phrase from 1 Macc 1:54 literally translates as "an abomination that desolates" (*bdelygma erēmōseōs*), the Greek equivalent of a phrase that occurs in Dan 11:31 (*haššiqqûṣ mĕšômēm*). The phrase is a pun on the epithet of the Syrian God Baal Shamaim ("Lord of heaven"), with *šiqqûṣ* ("abomination") substituting for the epithet Baal/Lord, much as earlier Hebrew texts used the term "shame" (*bōšet*) to substitute for the name Baal, as in the traditions in which the names of Saul's descendants Ish-baal (1 Chr 8:33), Mephi-baal (conjectured), and Merib-baal (1 Chr 8:34; 9:40) are also identified by the names Ish-boshet (2 Sam 3:8), Mephi-boshet (2 Sam 21:8), and Meri-boshet (2 Sam 4:4). The word "heaven" (*šāmayim*) is similarly replaced with the word "desolates" (*šômēm* or *mĕšômēm*). Clearly, whatever action Antiochus took had the effect of rededicating the temple to this deity, who is identified with Zeus Olympios (2 Macc 6:2), the epithet by which Baal Shamem was designated in Greek (Nestle 248). Through that action he desolated the Jerusalem sanctuary with an object that was considered an abomination by many of the Jews.

What, though, is meant by "upon a wing" (MT)? Some commentators (e.g., Delcor 204; Lacocque 199) have attempted to take "wing" as a metaphorical description of some feature of the temple, perhaps an alternative term for the "horns" of the altar that marked its four corners (Ezek 43:15). But there is no other evidence for these elements being described as wings. More probably, the text is corrupt and should be emended to ʿal kannām, "in their place."

The seemingly grammatically awkward phrase kālâ wĕneḥĕrāṣâ is actually an intertextual allusion to Isa 10:23 ("a decreed destruction"). Daniel's prophecies draw on the authority of previous prophets to announce the actualization in his own time of a divine determination of history established long ago. Naming the object of this destruction as "the desolator," a clear reference to Antiochus, has the further effect of parodying his godlike pretensions, as it also echoes the previous pun on the divine name Baal Shamem.

In contrast to chs. 7 and 8, where a first-person account by Daniel concerning his emotional reaction to the revelation concludes the account, here there is no such conclusion. The effect is to remove the distancing that the historical framework places between the audience and the revelatory words. For the initial readers, who would have recognized their present as that which is described in the final sentences of the chapter, the effect would be rhetorically very powerful. The final half "week," the time of the decreed destruction, is in the process of unfolding. Moreover, they are in a position to grasp its place in the divine plan. Just as Dan 8 drew on mythic prototypes to organize the chaotic events of history into a pattern that was not only meaningful but also hopeful, so Dan 9 tries to exert conceptual control over the traumatic occurrences by relating them to ancient prophetic oracles. The events of history unfold according to a symbolic system that organizes time itself in units that are part of the cultic calendar, which is further evidence for the order and meaningfulness of history as God has determined it.

History of Reception, by Brennan W. Breed

The End

Five numerical references in the book of Daniel have dominated Jewish and Christian discussions concerning calculations of the eschaton: (1) two mentions of "time, times, and half a time," often taken to refer to 3½ years (7:25; 12:7); (2) 2,300 evenings and mornings, sometimes interpreted as 1,150 days, or as 2,300 days, or 2,300 years (8:14); (3) 70 weeks (of years), most often understood to be 490 years (9:24); (4) 1,290 days, often understood as either approximately 3½ years, but otherwise as 1,290 years (12:11); and (5) 1,335 days, also taken to be literal days or years (12:12). These numbers provide the basic matrix for almost all of the thousands of calculations and predictions of the end that have been given over the past two millennia. In general, the differences between calculations come from two sources: the different schemes used to manipulate the numbers, and the decision about where to begin the chronology. On top of eschatological prediction, Daniel has also produced an industry of prognostication manuals for individual and communal uses.

Daniel and Prognostication

Daniel's reputation for dream interpretation and prognostication led to the creation of diverse legends throughout the world about Daniel's acquisition of knowledge and his production of prophetic materials other than the book of Daniel itself. Two traditions of prediction manuals in particular, the *Somniale Danielis* and *Lunationes Danielis,* were incredibly popular examples of these texts. The *Somniale* and *Lunationes* are late antique works originally written in Greek but translated into many languages by the early Middle Ages (DiTommaso 231–83). Both often include prologues, sometimes identical to one another, that claim Danielic authorship under the rule of Nebuchadnezzar; the *Somniale* helps one decode prophetic dreams, while the *Lunationes* aids in astrological predictions. In Syriac Christian and Muslim communities, a similar prognosticatory manual titled *Malḥamat Dāniyāl* (Predictions of Daniel) circulated widely in Arabic, Persian, and Syriac versions (DiTommaso 283–307). The *Malḥamat Dāniyāl* begins with a prologue that, borrowing from the late antique *Cave of Treasures* tradition, explains how God instructed Adam in the skill of prediction; Adam then wrote his secret knowledge on clay tablets that could withstand the great flood to come and placed them in a magical cave that could be entered only once per year. Much later Daniel led an expedition that gained access to the cave and recorded the contents of the tablets, giving Daniel the ability to predict the future (DiTommaso 288). This idea of Daniel producing books with Adam's privileged knowledge also occurs in prologues to certain *Somniale* and *Lunationes* manuscripts from Western Europe (DiTommaso 288).

One encounters the idea of a secret Danielic book in various Christian, Jewish, and Muslim sources. Nu'aym bin Hammad's ninth-century eschatological book *Kitāb al-fitan*, for example, tells this story: On the authority of Muhhamah b. Yazid on Abu Khilda on Abu al-Aliya, who said, "When Tustar [modern Shushtar in Iran] was conquered, we discovered a manuscript next to the head of a dead person lying on the bed in the treasury of al-Humazan. . . . It was Daniel as we reckoned; . . . then we took it to [caliph] Umar. I was the first Arabic speaker to have read it. It was sent to Ka'b, who translated it into Arabic. It contained what was going to happen, meaning the *fitan* [the trials that accompany the end of time]" (Yücesoy 34).

From where did these prediction manuals come? A story from tenth-century Baghdad, found in an anonymous book dealing with "tricks and stratagems of all types," offers one explanation:

History of Reception 311

> A man in Bagdad who was known as al-Daniyali . . . would tell me that he produced books which he ascribed to [the prophet] Daniel in an ancient script, and put down in them the names of leaders of the state with disjoined letters, so that when they are connected, they are understood. . . . It occurred to me to ask him for a section in one of the books that he was writing and that he would divulge there what I asked him to. He agreed to this. . . . I gave the manuscript to al-Daniyali, and he perfected it in the work of a folio which mentioned these things in it, and made it a chapter in his compositions.

As a result, the author says that he had al-Daniyali add a prediction that a man fitting exactly his companion's description would assume a high position in the government, which then allowed the author to present his friend at court along with the pseudo-Danielic prophecy; his friend was then promoted to the position as described, thus proving the power ascribed to such texts (Cook 2002, 60–61). Pseudo-Danielic prophecies were effective in Christian contexts, as well: in his chronicle, thirteenth-century Italian scholar Salimbene de Adam describes how Byzantine soldiers were dismayed at the shocking invasion of Constantinople by Latin members of the Fourth Crusade in 1204, but when a supposed prediction from Daniel was read out loud that seemed to describe the situation and suggested Byzantine victory, the soldiers "sallied forth to engage the Latin invaders with renewed confidence and vigor" (DiTommaso 88).

Jewish Calculations of the End

From at least the first century C.E., Jewish thinkers were using numbers from the book of Daniel to structure the course of time and predict the Messiah's coming. Josephus, for example, seems to have derived his chronological framework for the high priesthood from the seventy-weeks schema (Dan 9:24; Adler 210–12), and he mentioned that Daniel "was not only wont to prophesy future things, as did other prophets, but he also fixed the time at which these would come to pass" (*Ant.* 10.268). In a conversation about "a time and times and the dividing of time," the talmudic sages suggest that Danielic calculations led to the timing of Bar Kochba's failed revolt in 132–135 C.E.; as Rabbi Akiba reportedly said, "Yet once, it is a little while and I will shake the heavens and the earth [Hag 2:6]: but the first dynasty shall last seventy years, the second, fifty-two, and the reign of Bar Koziba [= Kochba], two and a half years [Dan 7:25; 12:7]" (*b. Sanh.* 97b). This sense of disillusionment and concern about failed prophecies permeated the talmudic discussions about calculating the end: Rabbi Jonathan says, "Cursed be the bones of those who calculate the end," because disappointed believers "would say, since the predetermined time has arrived, and yet he has not come, he will never come," or as Rab says, "all the predestined dates have passed" (*b. Sanh.* 97b). And yet on that same page of the Talmud are multiple calculations of the final day, including Rabbi

Kattina's six-thousand-year schema and Rabbi Hanan ben Talifa's story about a Danielic book:

> I once met a man who possessed a scroll written in Hebrew in Assyrian characters. I said to him: "Whence has this come to thee?" He replied, "I hired myself as a mercenary in the Roman army, and found it amongst the Roman archives. In it is stated that four thousand, two hundred and thirty-one years after the creation the world will be orphaned [470–471 C.E.]. [As to the years following,] some of them will be spent in the war of the great sea monsters, and some in the war of Gog and Magog, and the remaining will be the Messianic era, whilst the Holy One, blessed be He, will renew his world only after seven thousand years." (*b. Sanh.* 97b)

The year 4231 on the Jewish calendar also appears in two more talmudic predictions of the final day, perhaps influencing the disastrous events surrounding mid-fifth-century Jewish messianic claimant Moses of Crete (*b. ʿAbod. Zar.* 9a).

The tenth-century Jewish exegete Saadia Gaon reckoned that the 70 weeks of years were 490 years that had already occurred in history, and that these years span "from the destruction of the first temple to the destruction of the second temple, and what would occur between these destructions, during 490 years" (Chazan 1996, 146). Saadia notes that the 7 infinitives in Dan 9:24–27 narrate in order the major events of this era, including the rebuilding of the temple and the reforms of Ezra, as well as the suspension of prophecy, elimination of the priesthood, and the destruction of the temple. Starting with the destruction of the first temple allows the first 7 weeks to cover the exile, and then the next 62 weeks, consisting of 434 years, approach the end of the second temple period; the last week covers the Roman destruction of Jerusalem under Titus (Chazan 1996, 147). Saadia also discusses the 1,335 days of Dan 12:12, which he interprets to be years; he does not, however, explicitly offer a starting point for the chronology, so there is no clear date of the end. Rashi, writing in eleventh-century France, expressly interpreted the days mentioned in Dan 12:11–12 in line with Saadia, but he also makes his end point explicit. Rashi reckoned that the "time, times, and half a time" from 7:25 referred to "the 1,335 years," calculating that the first "time" mentioned is the 480 years traditionally understood to have passed between the exodus from Egypt and the building of the first temple (Alshich 376). The second "time" is the 410 years that the first temple stood; these two "times" added together yield a total of 890 years. If one adds a half of this, namely 445, to the total, one then gets a sum of 1,335 for the "time, times, and half a time." If one starts counting from the discontinuation of daily sacrifice in the second temple—which occurred 6 years before its destruction due to the war—then one comes to the conclusion that the end will arrive in 1352 C.E.

Rashi claims independent confirmation for this number by looking at the 2,300 days from Dan 8:14. By converting the words "evening" and "morning" mentioned in 8:14 to their Hebrew numerical equivalents, a part of spiritual manipulation of letters and numbers known as "gematria," Rashi finds that these two words add up to 574. Adding this number to 2,300 yields 2,874; if one adds the number of years from the Egyptian captivity until the cessation of sacrifices in the temple, namely 1,584, to 1,290, the sum is 2,874 (Alshich 384). Concerning the discrepancy between the figures 1,290 and 1,335 in Dan 12:11–12, Rashi writes: "I found in *Midrash Ruth* that the king Messiah is destined to be hidden for forty-five years after he reveals himself" (Alshich 385). In light of the problematic nature of calculations, Rashi tells his readers, "But we shall hope for the promise of our King end after end," asking them to keep hoping even if the year 1352 C.E. comes and passes without the Messiah (Alshich 384). The tenth-century Persian scholar al-Biruni was aware of Jewish and Christian gematria that centered on the figure 1,335. He discusses Jewish calculations that the Hebrew word "conceal," found in Deut 31:18 ("I, God, shall conceal myself in that day"), converts to 1,335, as well as Syriac Christian attempts to find the number 1,335 in the Syriac phrase "Jesus the Messiah the greatest redeemer" (al-Biruni 19–21). Al-Biruni retorts that one could take the phrase "the deliverance of creation from infidelity by Muhammad" or "the plain of Faran shines with the illiterate Muhammad" and come to the same total of 1,335; he also criticizes the fact that Christian calculations of the 70 weeks often overshoot the birth of Jesus by several decades (al-Biruni 21–22). His assessment of both Christian and Jewish uses of Dan 9 is negative, but according to him the Christian attempts are even more shaky: "These are doubts and difficulties which beset the assertions of the Jews. Those, however, which attach to the schemes of the Christians are even more numerous and conspicuous" (al-Biruni 21). Muslims were not, however, immune to such speculations: the *Kitāb al-fitan* claims that "Al-Walid said, 'I have read in [the book of] Daniel that the conclusion of this community after its prophet Muhammad until [the coming of] Jesus is 274 years," and such Muslim Daniel-based calculations are not rare (Yücesoy 50; cf. Adang 27n24, 145–46, 157–58, 204–5, 236).

In the thirteenth century, Rabbi Naḥmanides was forced by the Christian authorities in Barcelona to defend the Jewish faith in a public debate; he was under tremendous pressure because both success and failure in the disputation could spark Christian outbursts against the Jewish minority population. His interlocutor, Dominican Friar Pablo Christiani, was a converted Jew who promised to prove Christianity from the Talmud. A large portion of the debate centered on the question of the Messiah's arrival, and the two scholars focused on Dan 9:24–27 (Chazan 1996, 153). Naḥmanides argued, as al-Biruni did before him, that 490 years from the destruction of the first temple would make the Messiah appear at the destruction of the second temple, not seventy years before it; thus Jesus is not the Messiah because "even according to your reckoning, he was more than ten weeks earlier [seventy years]" (Chazan 1996,

153). Instead, Naḥmanides claimed like Rashi that the first "time" in Dan 7:25 refers to the 440 years of Egyptian bondage, and that the dual "times" signifies double 440, or 880 years, and the half a time then adds 220, yielding 1,540 years. For Naḥmanides, this number signified Rome's domination, which began in 138 B.C.E. and will continue through the Christian Church for 1,540 years, or until 1403 C.E. In the Barcelona disputation, Naḥmanides said: "It is now 1,195 years since the destruction, or 95 years less than the Messianic figure of Daniel. We believe that the Messiah will come that year" (Silver 84). Though that calculation yields a date of 1358 C.E., Naḥmanides claimed that 45 years later, or 1403 C.E., the Messiah ben David will come, arriving after 40 years of war under the Messiah ben Joseph. Abraham bar Hiyya, a twelfth-century Spanish rabbi, and Gersonides, an early-fourteenth-century French rabbi, both used astronomical calculations stemming from the rare conjunction of Saturn and Jupiter along with calculations from Daniel to arrive at the same date for the coming of the Messiah, 1358 C.E. (Goldstein and Pingree 3–4). Abrabanel, the fifteenth-century Portuguese Jewish scholar and statesman, updated Abraham bar Hiyya's calculations to arrive at a window between 1503 and 1573 C.E. as the final date of redemption, beginning 12 years after the expulsion of Jews from Spain (Feldman 148).

In the wake of such predictive failures, Maimonides discouraged specific prophecies, but like Rashi he suggested that as long as one held such calculations loosely and did not build up expectation, predictions of the end could help especially those in oppressed communities to hold out hope that their situation might change. In this way, Maimonides defends Saadia and Naḥmanides, both of whom offered calculations of the end, but dissuades others from following in their footsteps (Goldwurm 212). Similarly Alshich, writing in the sixteenth century, explained why his commentary on Daniel does not include chs. 7–12: "The first part of the book was simple to understand—as straight as a plain—but the last part was difficult, like climbing down a steep cliff. Its message was hidden and elusive, its words sealed within another seal, for the vision describing the end of time is beyond humanity's grasp. . . . The Messiah will come and explain it to us" (Alshich xiii–xiv).

Christian Calculations of the End

Christian predictions differed from those of Jews for several reasons, the first of which was the textual divergences between the Jewish MT and Theodotion's version (Th), which was preferred by Christians. As Dan 9:25 MT and its interpretive tradition clearly divides between the first 7 weeks and then the following 62-week period, Dan 9:25 Th, as do the Vulgate and Syriac versions, conflates the 2 periods, allowing readers to assume a singular messianic interpretation for verses 25–26 instead of 2 separate anointed ones (Adler

223). Also, the Theodotionic version renders the Hebrew verb *neḥtak* in 9:24 as συνετμήθησαν, "been shortened," rather than "decided," which prompted some interpreters to question whether the last week had been severed from the preceding 69 and thus had not yet taken place. Second, Christians read Daniel through the lens of the New Testament, which itself had been deeply influenced by the apocalyptic portions of Daniel. The Synoptic Apocalypse refers to the "abomination of desolation" (Dan 9:27; 11:31; 12:11; Mark 13:14 KJV), which has been transposed to describe the destruction of the Jerusalem temple in 70 C.E. Apparently 2 Thess 2:3–4 draws from Dan 9:24–27 in its description of the "man of lawlessness," seen in a future event. And Revelation uses the 3½-year schema in various forms, all drawn from Daniel, to describe the ministry of the 2 witnesses (Rev 11:3), a period of relief for the woman clothed with the sun (12:6, 14), and the periods of suffering that will precede the final destruction of Rome (11:2; 12:6; 13:5).

Early Christians were eager to think in terms of such numerology. The second-century theologian Justin Martyr, for example, in thinking about the "time, times, and half a time," concluded that the "man of iniquity must reign at least 350 years" (*Dial.* 32.3). Clement of Alexandria, also from the second century, began his calculation of the eschaton with the rebuilding of the second temple, counting the end of the 62 weeks with Christ's incarnation and a last week that encompasses the Roman emperors Nero, Vespasian, and Titus, who were all involved in the war that led to the destruction of the Jerusalem temple in 70 (*Strom.* 1.125–26; cf. Tertullian, *Adv. Jud.* 8). Origen, bemused that he could not use the text allegorically (cf. Jerome on 9:24–27), took a more universal focus and interpreted the 70 weeks as 4,900 years, calculated from Adam to the end of the first century C.E., which constituted the close of the apostolic period (Origen, *Comm. Matt.* 24.14–18). Hippolytus of Rome, writing at the turn of the third century, seems to have introduced several important features of apocalyptic thought into Christian discourse, starting with his use of the Jewish model of a 6,000-year world history to situate the prophecy of the 70 weeks. According to Hippolytus, the 6 days of creation refer to 6,000 years of the world, followed by a 1,000-year period of rest, which represents the age to come (*Comm. Dan.* 2.4). Since Christ was born in the year 5500 after creation, Hippolytus argues, it stands to reason that 500 years remain. Hippolytus (*Comm. Dan.* 4.35) argues that Daniel confirms this: 62 weeks after Jesus' death, the abomination of desolation, referring to the antichrist, will arrive, and the free offering of salvation to the nations will be taken away. When Daniel "spoke of the one week, he was referring to the last week at the culmination of the whole cosmos," putting the final date of the eschaton sometime near the year 500, but with a final "week" of amorphous length (Hippolytus, *Antichr.* 43).

Yet Hippolytus also used the 70 weeks to trace the time between Cyrus's order to restore the Jerusalem temple and Jesus' birth; according to Jerome (on

9:24–27), "the dates do not agree at all," since from Cyrus's decree to Jesus' birth is 560 years. Hippolytus also argued that the distinction between the 1,290 days and the 1,335 days signified a 45-year period of respite and repentance for the faithful before the end; this idea, championed by Jerome (on 12:11–12), became a mainstay in medieval theology and gained the name "the refreshment of the saints" (Lerner 97–144). Sextus Julius Africanus, a contemporary of Hippolytus, argued that the 490 years began with Artaxerxes' order that Nehemiah rebuild the city and ends with Jesus' birth, but this is clearly about 15 years off, since it is 475 years from the twentieth year of Artaxerxes until the year 1 C.E. Julius claims that the 490 years are lunar years, not solar ones, and thus are of shorter duration; converted to solar years, the prophecy seems to align with Jesus' presumed birth date (Adler 221–22). Following Theodotion, Julius also proposes that the final week could be severed and enacted at a much later date, but he does not formalize this thought. Apollinarius, a fourth-century theologian, argued that the 490 years began with Jesus' birth and that the end would arrive near the year 500 without interruption; Jerome (on 9:24–27) responded that "by breaking away from the stream of the past and directing his longing toward the future, he very unsafely ventured an opinion concerning matters so obscure."

A major event occurred in the interpretation of Daniel when Augustine, following the exegetical arguments of Tyconius, dampened the millennial fervor of the early church through his polemics against calculating the eschaton; though some Christians continued to ponder the numbers in Daniel and Revelation, the decrease in speculation following Augustine is remarkable (*Civ.* 20).

In the twelfth century the Italian monk Joachim of Fiore re-ignited Christian apocalypticism with his commentary on Revelation, which posited a threefold division of cosmic time. From creation to the time of Christ was 1,260 years, called the "Age of the Father." Then the time from Christ's incarnation to roughly the year 1260 constituted the "Age of the Son," characterized by the church. In 1260, Joachim announced, there would begin the "Age of the Holy Spirit," in which humankind would be in direct communication with the divine; Joachim calculates these periods with reference to the 1,260 days in Revelation as well as the 42 months, which he figures as generations of somewhat flexible length (McGinn 2000, 135–42). After Joachim, prognostications about the end became commonplace, each trying to manipulate the numbers and their starting points to reach near to the interpreter's own time. For example, the fourteenth-century English apocalypticist Walter Brute claimed that the 1,290-year period began with the destruction of Jerusalem in 135 C.E. by Emperor Hadrian, which gave a final date of 1425 (Guinness 101). Some Reformation theologians continued to update predictions: Michael Stifel, a companion of Martin Luther, offered the precise time of 8:00 a.m. on October 19, 1533; David Chytreus argued that the 1,260 years began with Alaric's sack of Rome in 412 (Koetsier and Reich 293). In the virulently antipapal rhetoric of the Reformation era, suggestions for starting points of the chronological schema included the establishment of the Papal States in 727, the decree of the Byzantine emperor Phocas naming Rome as the "head of all churches" in 606, the similar decree of the Byzantine emperor Justinian I in 533, or the enactment of Justinian's decree when his general Belisarius conquered much of Italy in 538. But Martin Luther suggested caution even as he proposed new chronological schemes:

> I cannot well define or comprehend this prophecy: "A time, times, and half a time." I do not know whether it refers to the Turk, who began to rule when Constantinople was taken, in the year 1453, eighty-five years ago. If I calculate a time to be the age of Christ (thirty years), this expression would mean one hundred and five years, and the Turk would still have twenty-five years swing to come. Well, God knows how it stands. . . . Let us not vex ourselves with seeking over knowledge. (Luther 195)

In the wake of the Reformation, English millenarian exegesis produced reams of calculations concerning the end. Even Isaac Newton devoted the last decades of his life to biblical chronology; he determined that the 1,260 years corresponds to the supposed corruption of the church that began when Pope Leo III crowned Charlemagne emperor in 800 and the pope gained clear terrestrial political powers (Whitla 227–29). In response to Newton's calculations, Voltaire quipped: "Sir Isaac Newton wrote his comment upon the Revelation to console humankind for the great superiority that he had over them in other respects" (T. Newton 440).

Anglo-Irish theologian John Nelson Darby's "dispensationalism" offered an approach to apocalyptic calculations that became very popular among preachers of the nineteenth century; during the Second Great Awakening, the outpouring of apocalyptic fervor in the United States tended to use Darby's scheme. Dispensationalists, such as C. I. Scofield, who wrote the influential *Scofield Study Bible,* held that the 490 years began with Nehemiah's mission in 444 B.C.E.; 69 weeks of 360-day "prophetic years" later, Christ was crucified in 32 C.E. (Dorrien 29–31). The seventieth week, however, did not begin immediately after the crucifixion; rather, the chronology stops until the termination of the age of the church, which will begin the last week of terror (cf. Dan 9:27). William Miller, founder of the Adventist group (often called Millerites), argued that the 1,260 years of the little horn's authority began with the creation of papal authority in 538 C.E. and ended when Pope Pius VI died while imprisoned by Napoleon, which he connected to the events of the French Revolution (cf. Rev 13:3; Newport 182). But this only gave the date of the pope's wounding; Miller also interpreted the 2,300 evenings and mornings (Dan 8:13–14) as years, which he claimed began in 457 B.C.E., thereby leading to a final end date of 1843–44 C.E. When the expected date of March 21, 1844, brought nothing of note, Miller's follower Samuel Snow suggested that the "tarry" mentioned in Hab 2:3 meant that an extra seven months and ten days should be added, which yielded a date of October 22, 1844 (Land 21). When that day, named thereafter the Great Disappointment, did not bring the apocalypse, many of Miller's followers left the faith, but several reinterpreted the event and reorganized. One such group, led by Ellen White, called itself the Seventh-day Adventist Church; White taught that in 1844 God began a purge of the heavenly and spiritual sanctuary, not the terrestrial one; this "investigative judgment" is merely the beginning of the last judgment (Newport 172–96). The Jehovah's Witnesses are another group that formed from Adventist theology; they believe that Jesus returned invisibly in 1914, some 70 years after the investigative judgment in 1844 (Newport 166–67). The date 1844 is significant for another religious group, the Bahá'í, whose founder took inspiration from the overlapping values of 1844 in both Adventist interpretation of the book of Daniel and in Shiʿite prophecies concerning the appearance of the twelfth Imam, who is understood to be the messianic Mahdi (Stetzer 7–9). The Millerite traditions also developed particularly captivating graphic depictions of their chronologies; these images usually included the statue from Nebuchadnezzar's dream in Dan 2, the four beasts from Dan 7, and a series of overlapping prophetic calculations, including the numbers 490 and 1,260 and 1,290 and 1,335 and 2,300 (Rosenberg and Grafton 160–77). A former draftsman turned Baptist dispensationalist preacher named Clarence Larkin drew from this tradition in the creation of his massively popular charts depicting various prophetic schemas from the Bible; one can note his depiction of the dispensationalist views concerning the 70 weeks (see fig. 22) and the book of Daniel as a whole (see fig. 21), to which he often returned in his work (Larkin 67, 72).

In the late twentieth century, David Koresh's millennial readings of Daniel and Revelation sparked the Branch Davidian movement in Waco, Texas; Koresh "often told his followers that Daniel 11 was the most important prophecy in the Bible." Koresh saw linkages between the Persian Gulf War (1990–91) and the detailed political commentary of the ancient Levant (Tabor 414, 428). Likewise, contemporary Muslim apocalypticists saw that same war as the beginning of the 2,300 evenings and mornings that would initiate the apocalypse (Cook 2005, 89). Also in the late twentieth century, the radio preacher Harold Camping made highly publicized predictions, based on the Adventist interpretation of the 2,300 days of Dan 8, that the world would end in May 1994, or perhaps May 2011 (Camping 505). When the apocalypse failed to materialize on either date, Camping claimed that a spiritual event of judgment had occurred, much like the Adventists had in the nineteenth century; Camping also proposed a second date for the physical rapture, in October 2011. When that date also did not bring anything out of the ordinary, Camping responded by saying, "We humbly acknowledge we were wrong about the timing" (Burke).

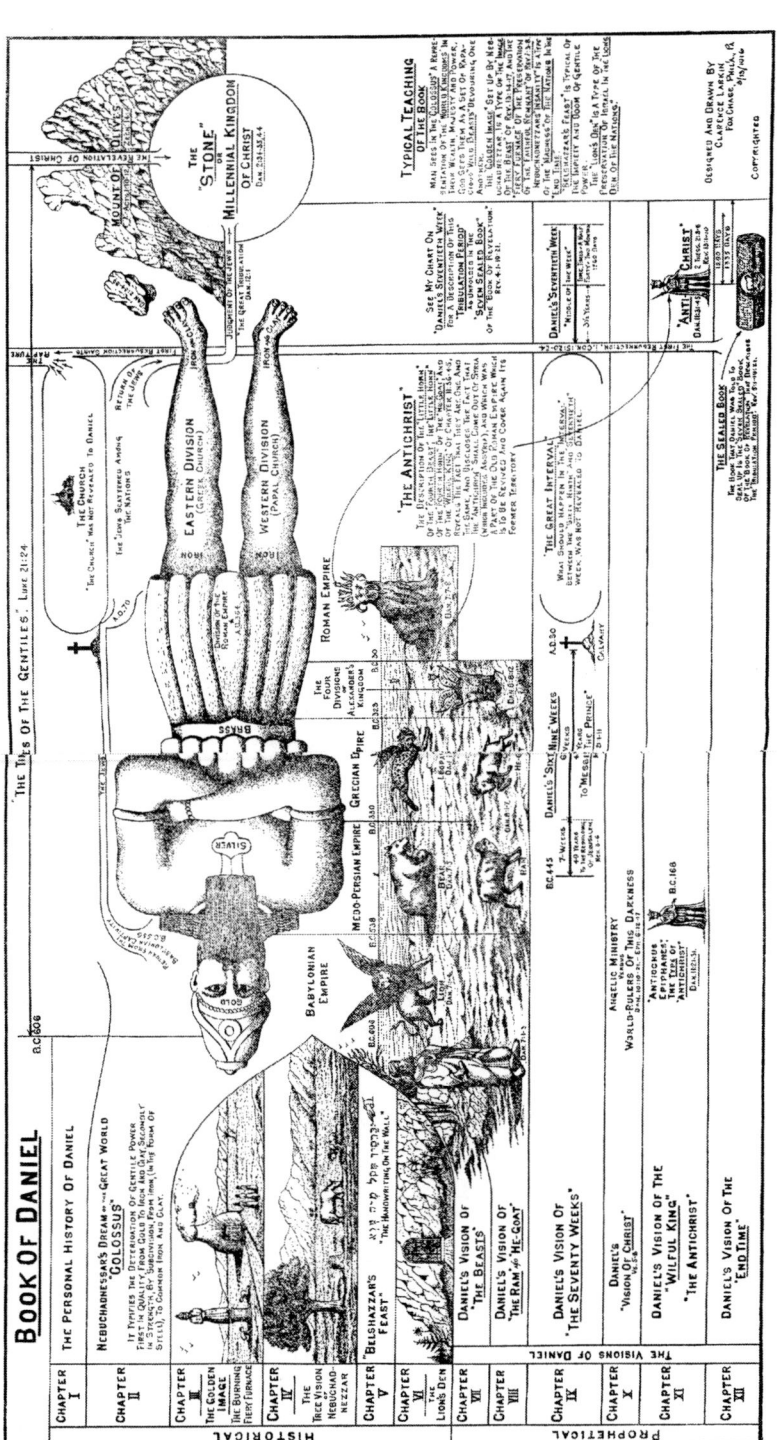

Figure 21. A chart designed by Clarence Larkin (1919) to depict the dispensationalist interpretation of the statue from Daniel 2, coordinated with the four beasts from Daniel 7 and other key prophecies, from his book *Dispensational Truth*. Public domain

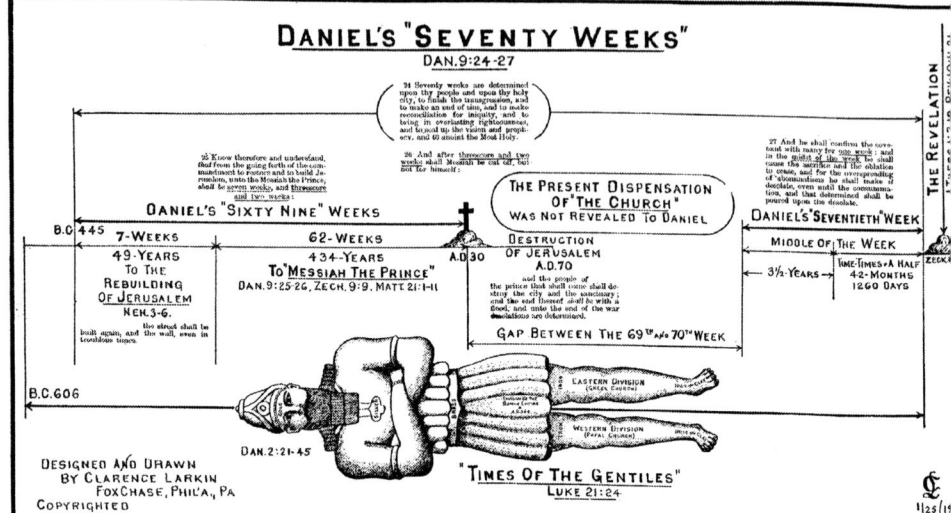

Figure 22. Larkin's chart (1919) coordinating the "seventy weeks of years" from Daniel 9 with the statue of the four kingdoms and other key biblical texts, from his book *Dispensational Truth*. Public domain

Daniel 10–12 Using History's Deep Structures to Predict the Future

10:1 In the third[a] year of Cyrus, king of Persia, a word was revealed to Daniel (who was also called Belteshazzar). The word was reliable, but it was a great struggle[b] to understand the word; yet understanding came to him in the vision.

2 In those days I, Daniel, was in mourning for three weeks. 3 I did not eat pleasant food, nor did wine enter my mouth, nor did I anoint myself with oil until the completion of three weeks. 4 On the twenty-fourth day of the first month, I was alongside the great river (that is, the Tigris). 5 I lifted up my eyes and looked, and suddenly there was this man, clothed in linen, his loins encircled with pure gold,[c] 6 and his body like topaz. His face was like the appearance of lightning, and his eyes like fiery torches. His arms and his legs were like the gleam of burnished bronze. The sound of his words was like the sound of a multitude. 7 I, Daniel, alone saw the vision, as the men who were with me did not see the vision; however, a great trembling fell upon them, and they fled in order to hide themselves. 8 So I remained alone and I saw this great vision, and there was no strength left in me. My energy was devastated,[d] and I retained no strength. 9 Then

I heard the sound of his words. And when I heard the sound of his words, I fell face-first into a trance, my face to the ground.

10 Then suddenly a hand touched me and set me shaking on my hands and knees. 11 And he said to me, "Daniel, you highly esteemed man, pay attention to the words that I am telling you. Stand up, because I have now been sent to you." And when he said this word to me, I stood trembling. 12 He said to me, "Do not be afraid, Daniel, for from the first day that you set your mind to understand and to humble yourself before your God, your words were heard, and I have come on account of your words. 13 The prince of the kingdom of Persia opposed me for twenty-one days, but suddenly Michael, one of the chief princes, came to aid me, when I was left there[e] with the prince of the kingdom of Persia.[f] 14 So I have come to make you understand what will happen to your people in the latter days, for there is still a vision for the future." 15 When he said these things to me, I bowed my face to the ground, dumbstruck. 16 Then suddenly someone who looked like a human was touching my lips, and I opened my mouth and spoke and said to the one who was standing before me, "My lord, because of the vision, anguish has come upon me and I have no strength left. 17 How can this servant of my lord speak with my lord, when I myself now have no strength remaining in me nor breath left in me?" 18 Then the one who looked like a human again touched me and gave me strength. 19 He said, "Do not be afraid, O highly esteemed man. It is well with you. Be strong! Be strong!" And when he spoke to me, I was strengthened, and I said, "May my lord speak, for you have strengthened me." 20 He said, "Do you understand why I have come to you? But now I must return to fight with the prince of Persia, and then when I go out, the prince of Greece will come. 21 But I will tell you what is recorded in the book of truth. There is no one who supports me against these except Michael, your prince. 11:1 And as for me, in the first year of Darius the Mede, I stood up[g] to strengthen and to be a refuge for him. 2 And now I will tell you what is true:

"Three further kings will arise for Persia, and a fourth will acquire greater wealth than all the rest. And when he has become strong through his wealth, he will stir up everything (namely, the kingdom of Greece). 3 A warrior king will arise, and he will rule a great dominion and do as he pleases. 4 But when he has arisen, his kingdom will be shattered and parceled out to the four winds of heaven, but not to his progeny nor with the authority with which he ruled, for his kingdom will be uprooted and left to others besides these.

5 "Then the king of the south will grow strong, but one of his princes will become stronger[h] than he and will rule a realm greater than[i] his own

dominion. 6 After some years, they will make an alliance, and the daughter of the king of the south will come to the king of the north to effect a treaty, but she will not retain power, and his offspring will not endure.ʲ She will be given over, she and those who brought her, and her childᵏ and the one who supported her in those times.

7 "And a shoot from her rootsˡ will emerge in his place,ᵐ and he will come against the army, and he will enter into the stronghold of the king of the north, and he will act against them and prevail. 8 And also their gods with their statues and their precious vessels of silver and gold he will take into captivity to Egypt. And for some years he will keep hisⁿ distance from the king of the north. 9 But then he will come into the kingdom of the king of the south, and he will return to his own country.

10 "But his sons will mobilize and assemble a massive horde and come, sweeping through like a flood, and again wage war as far as his fortress. 11 Then the king of the south will be enraged and go forth and fight with him, that is, with the king of the north, who will raise a great horde; but the horde will be given over into hisⁿ power. 12 When the horde is carried off, his heart will be exalted, and he will overthrow myriads, but he will not remain strong. 13 Again, the king of the north will raise a horde greater than the first one, and after a number of years he will come with a great army and with abundant equipment. 14 And in those times, many will arise against the king of the south, and the violent ones of your people will rise up in order to establish the vision; but they will stumble. 15 Then the king of the north will come and throw up a siege ramp and capture a fortified city, and the forces of the south will not be able to stand, not even his select troops, for there will be no strength to stand. 16 His attacker will do as he pleases, with no one able to stand before him, and he will stand in the beautiful land with destructionᵒ in his hand. 17 And he will set his face to penetrate the strength of his whole kingdom,ᵖ and he will make a treaty with him, and he will give him a daughterᵠ in order to destroy it,ʳ but it will not succeed or come to pass. 18 He will turnˢ his face to the coastlands, and he will capture many. But a commander will put an end to his insults, withoutᵗ his being able to return the insult. 19 And he will turn his face toward the strongholds of his own land, but he will stumble and fall and disappear.

20 "And in his place will arise one who will send out a tax collector of royal splendor. But in a short while he will be destroyed, but neither in anger nor in battle. 21 And there will arise in his place a contemptible man, one to whom has not been given the majesty of kingship. He will come in stealth, and he will lay hold of the kingdom through intrigue. 22 Armed forces will be utterly swept awayᵘ before him and shattered, and also a prince of the covenant. 23 After alliances are made with him,

he will act treacherously, and he will ascend to power with a small group. 24 In stealth he will enter the richest parts of the province, and he will do as his fathers and his fathers' fathers have never done—spoil and plunder and property he will distribute to them. And against fortresses he will devise plans, for a time.[v]

25 "He will arouse his power and his determination against the king of the south with a great army, and the king of the south will make preparations for battle with a great army, one that is even stronger. But he will not be able to stand firm, because plots will be devised against him. 26 Those who eat his provisions will destroy him, and his army will be overwhelmed,[w] and many will be slain. 27 And as for the two kings, their minds will be set on evil. At a single table they will lie to one another, but to no avail, for still to come is the end at the time appointed. 28 And he will return to his own land with great wealth, but his mind will be directed against the holy covenant, and he will do what he intends, and then return to his own land.

29 "At the appointed time he will again invade the south, but this latter occasion will not be like the first. 30 Ships of the Kittim will come against him, and he will be intimidated. He will again act out his fury against the holy covenant, and he will once more pay attention to those who abandon the holy covenant.[x] 31 Armed forces from him will arise and profane the sanctuary (the citadel),[y] and they will remove the daily offering, and they will put in its place the desolating abomination. 32 He will corrupt those who violate the covenant with slippery words, but the people who know their God will be strong and take action. 33 The wise among the people will cause the multitude to understand, though they will stumble by sword and flame and captivity and plunder for some time. 34 And when they stumble, they will find a little help, but many will join them deceitfully. 35 And some of the wise will stumble so that they may be refined among them and purified and made white until the time of the end, for the appointed time is still to come.

36 "And the king will do as he pleases, and he will exalt and magnify himself against every god. Against the God of gods he will speak shocking things, and he will succeed until wrath has come to an end, for what is determined will be done. 37 He will not pay attention to the gods of his ancestors or the beloved of women, nor will he pay attention to any god, for more than anything, he will magnify himself. 38 He will honor the god of strongholds instead. And a god whom his ancestors have not known he will honor with gold and silver and precious stones and treasures. 39 He will deal with fortified strongholds[z] with the help of an alien god,[aa] and whoever acknowledges (him)[bb] he will greatly honor, making them rule over the multitude. And he will distribute land for a price.

40 "And at the time of the end the king of the south will engage in battle with him, and the king of the north will storm against him with chariotry and with cavalry and with many ships. And he will invade the lands, sweeping through like a flood. 41 He will invade the beautiful land, and myriads^{cc} will stumble. But these will escape from his hands—Edom and Moab and the leaders of Ammon. 42 He will stretch forth his hand against the lands, and even the land of Egypt will not escape. 43 And he will gain control over the precious stores of silver and gold, and over all the treasures of Egypt. And the Libyans and Ethiopians will follow at his heel. 44 But rumors from the east and the north will disturb him, and he will go out in great anger to destroy and to slaughter many. 45 He will plant his palatial tents between the sea and the beautiful holy mountain, but so he will come to his end, with no one to help him.

12:1 "At that time Michael will arise, the great prince, the one who stands over your people. But it will be a time of distress, such as has not occurred from the time the nation came into being until that time. But at that time your people will be delivered, everyone who is found written in the book. 2 Many who sleep in the dusty earth will awaken, some to everlasting life, and some to reproaches and to everlasting abhorrence. 3 And the wise will shine brightly like the brightness of the firmament, and those who make the many righteous like the stars for ever and ever. 4 But you, Daniel, conceal the words and seal up the book until the time of the end. Many will run to and fro, and knowledge will increase."

5 Meanwhile I, Daniel, was looking, and suddenly there were two others standing, one on this side of the riverbank, and the other on the other side of the riverbank. 6 And one said to the man clothed in linen, who was further up the waters of the river, "How long until the end of the awesome events?" 7 And I listened to the man clothed in linen who was further up the waters of the river, and he raised his right hand and his left to the heavens, and he swore by the one who lives forever that it is for a time, and (two) times, and a half. And when the shattering of the power of the holy people has been completed,^{dd} then all these things will be completed.

8 I heard, but I did not understand, and so I said, "My lord, what is the outcome of these things?" 9 And he said to me, "Daniel, truly the matters are to be concealed and sealed up until the time of the end. 10 Many will be purified and made white and refined, and the wicked will commit evil. None of the wicked will understand, but as for the wise, they will understand. 11 From the time of the taking away of the daily offering and the placing of the desolating abomination is one thousand two hundred and ninety days. 12 Blessed is the one who waits and reaches one thousand three hundred and thirty-five days. 13 But as for you, go.^{ee} You will rest, and then you will rise for your destiny at the end of days."

a. The OG reads "first," perhaps harmonizing with 1:21.

b. The phrase ṣābāʾ gādôl could refer to the content of the revelation, "and [it concerned] a great war." Alternatively, ṣābāʾ could be a contrast term with the earlier ʾĕmet and refer to the difficulty of the revelation and the hard labor required to understand it. Plöger (145) suggests reading the infinitive lābîn ("to understand") for ûbîn ("and he understood"). Similarly NJPS.

c. ʾûpāz is perhaps a scribal error for ûpāz ("and fine gold"), but see Jer 10:9, or a by-form of pāz ("pure gold"). The two terms for gold, ketem and ʾûpāz, may be treated as a hendiadys.

d. The word hôd can refer to one's appearance or to one's vitality. The text literally says "my hôd turned upon me into corruption." If the idiom refers to appearance, then it may be the equivalent of the English expression "my complexion turned deathly pale." In the context of the other references to weakness, I take the phrase to refer to Daniel's vitality and vigor.

e. Many commentators follow the reading in OG and Th, "I left him there," which, however, may simply be the translators' attempt to smooth out the somewhat awkward Hebrew.

f. The MT reads "with the kings of Persia," but 6QDaniel reads mlwkt or śr mlkwt, a reading that appears to be variously reflected in the Greek versions.

g. Reading the perfect rather than the infinitive with suffix.

h. Deleting the waw.

i. The comparative particle mi- appears to have been accidentally omitted. Alternatively, one might translate "and he will rule his dominion as a great ruler."

j. Repointing zĕrōʿô ("his strength") to zarʿô ("his seed," "his offspring"). "His" refers to the king of the south. "His offspring" would be his grandson.

k. Reading yaldāh ("her child") instead of the MT hayyōlĕdāh, "the one who begot her," i.e., her father. Goldingay (277) argues that the MT seems to assume that v. 6 is concerned with those who established the marriage and so retains the MT reading. But would it be accurate to say that Ptolemy II was "given over"?

l. Reading nēṣer miššorāšêhā instead of minnēṣer šorāšêhā.

m. Heb. kannô. In vv. 20, 21, 38 the phrase is ʿal-kannô.

n. "he/his" = the king of the south.

o. The consonants klh could also be pointed to read "all of it," i.e., the glorious land, signifying Antiochus's complete control of Judea, as well as the rest of Coele-Syria.

p. The Hebrew is ambiguous and could also be rendered, "and he will come with the strength of his [i.e., the king of the north's] whole kingdom."

q. Lit., "a daughter of women." Here 4QDaniel^c reads "daughter of men." Both readings are attested in the versions.

r. The third-person feminine singular suffix can only meaningfully refer to the feminine noun malkûtô ("his kingdom"). 4QDaniel^c and Papyrus 967 have the third-person masc. sg. suffix, "to destroy him."

s. Reading with the Kethib, wĕyāšab.

t. Reading lĕbiltî instead of lô biltî, following a suggestion of Charles (294). This yields a rather complicated and repetitive sentence, however, and the verse may be corrupt.

u. Repointing haššeṭep as the infinitive absolute, hiššāṭōp.

v. The suggestion of *BHS* that *wĕʿad-ʿēt* is a dittography from the following *wĕyāʿēr* may well be correct.

w. Instead of *yištôp* read the Niphal *yiššāṭēp*. Cf. *4QDaniel^c*, which reads *yšṭp*.

x. I take the two occurrences of *wĕšāb* as adverbial, "again" (*IBHS* §39.3.1b). This usage does not imply a second visit of Antiochus to Jerusalem. See comments.

y. The word *hammāʿōz* is not grammatically coordinated with the preceding noun, *hammiqdāš*, and may represent an inserted gloss. The temple was fortified at this time (cf. 1 Macc 4:60; 6:7)

z. The first half of the verse is ambiguous and problematic, leading to a variety of interpretations. Montgomery (463), followed by many commentators, suggests repointing *mibṣĕrê* ("fortifications") as the Piel participle *mĕbaṣṣĕrê* ("defenders, fortifiers").

aa. Montgomery (463), following Hitzig (213), repoints *ʿim* ("with") as *ʿam* ("people"), "the people of an alien god," i.e., the foreign troops.

bb. In Kethib, *hikkîr* occurs without an object; also in 2 Sam 3:36.

cc. The feminine plural *rabbôt* does not make sense in context (*pace* Goldingay 280) and is better repointed *ribbôt* ("myriads").

dd. Since the focus of the end of ch. 11 is on the destruction of Antiochus, some revocalize *nappēṣ* as a participle (*nōpēṣ*) and transpose it with *yad*. So J. Collins (369), "At the end of the power of the shatterer of the holy people, all these things will be finished."

ee. Omitting *laqqēṣ*, which is likely a dittography from the end of the verse.

Overview

That the apocalypse in chs. 10–12 constitutes the climax of the book of Daniel is indicated in several ways. The length and elaborateness of the visionary encounter with the angel and Daniel's reaction to it, described in ch. 10, create an atmosphere of expectant awe and wonder that far exceeds the description of Daniel's encounter with angelic figures in previous chapters. Also, the extraordinary level of detail in the angel's revelatory discourse in ch. 11 indicates the significance of the content. And finally, ch. 12, after describing the eschatological events that bring history to an end, concludes with the angel sending Daniel on his way.

The final apocalypse resembles the previous ones in certain respects but also contrasts sharply with them. Daniel's fasting recalls his fast in ch. 9, though here it has a different function. As in that chapter, the medium of revelation is an angelophany and an angelic discourse. Also, the final apocalypse, like the preceding ones, is a meditation on the structure of history. But where the previous attempts to understand the nature of the historical process operate at a rough schematic level, the angelic discourse in ch. 11 is a deep investigation of the intrinsic structures of history as they are disclosed by the detection of patterns in a detailed chronicle of events. Through this intense study of the deep structures of history, apocalyptic historiography becomes a predictive tool. To be sure, the

Using History's Deep Structures to Predict the Future

discrepancy between the predicted events of 11:40–45 and the actual details of history allow historical criticism to identify the precise time at which the author composed the apocalypse, but one should not be dismissive about the project as a whole. In fact, a great deal of critical historiography has similar concerns. The contemporary philosopher of history Reinhart Koselleck (133) cites Kant's dictum that "recalling the past . . . occurs only with the intention of making it possible to foresee the future" (Kant, 77). The reason, as Koselleck explains, is that, in addition to unique events, history always contains discernible repetitions, recurrences of analogous phenomena. This "structural repeatability" allows one to study the past for clues to the likely course of future events.

Already in ch. 8, the author tries to discern such a basic pattern in history, observing that just when kingdoms and kings appear to be at the peak of their power, that is the moment when they will be destroyed. The author of ch. 11, however, attempts something much bolder. Without flinching from the untidy nature of historical events, he seeks to discern not only the unique details of history but also their embeddedness in a pattern of "structural repeatability." The structural pattern that the author discerns and depicts, with impressive control of historical detail, is what Clifford identifies as "containment." Despite alternating patterns of aggression, neither the king of the north nor the king of the south can "effect a permanent rule by reason of their containment of each other" (Clifford 24). So long as the king of the north cannot successfully sweep away the king of the south, that is, so long as the Syrian Seleucids cannot capture and hold Ptolemaic Egypt, history remains in balance. Only when Antiochus IV does conquer much of Egypt, and then seeks to challenge a heavenly rather than an earthly kingdom, will history break loose from its moorings and the determined vision of eschatological events unfold. One need not share the author's apocalyptic perspective to appreciate what an impressive intellectual and theological achievement this meditation on history is and why it deserves its role as the climax of the book.

The apocalypse in Dan 10–12 bears a particularly close relationship with ch. 8. Not only does it develop the interest in historical patterns of power, outlined there, but even at the level of narrative details and vocabulary, chs. 10–12 are modeled on ch. 8. The most extended comparison has been prepared by Willis (159n28, with Hebrew transliterated):

> Daniel on the bank of the river (10:4//8:2); Daniel's posture and trance (10:8–10//8:16–18); the shattering of Alexander's kingdom and the dispersion of his power (11:4//8:8); the inability to stand against the power of a king ($lō^{\cdot}$ $^{\cdot}āmad$) (11:15//8:4); the reference to the "beautiful land" (11:16, 41//8:9); the description of Antiochus as acting deceptively ($bĕšalwâ$) (11:24//8:25); the references to the end and the appointed time ($mô^{\cdot}ēd$ and $qēṣ$) (11:27, 35, 40//8:17, 19); the desolation of the $hammiqdāš$ and the disruption of the $tāmîd$ (11:31//8:11); Antiochus doing as he pleases ($wĕ^{\cdot}āśâ\ kirṣônô$) (11:36//8:11); Antiochus exalting

himself (*gādal*) even above the Most High (11:36–37//8:10, 11, 25); the reference to Antiochus's words and deeds as "wonders" (*niplāʾôt*) (11:36; 12:6//8:24); a reference to the completion of the wrath (*zaʿam*) (11:36//8:19); the command to keep the words secret and seal the book (12:4//8:26); the description of angelic figures (12:5//8:13–14); the question "How long?" (12:6//8:13–14); Daniel's failure to understand (12:8//8:27).

The apocalypse in chs. 10–12 is a revisiting and a deepening of the revelation in ch. 8, providing both a more finely grained historical account and the fully resolved ending that was absent from ch. 8.

Daniel 10:1–11:2a Revelation and Sublime Terror

Outline

The long introductory passage may be outlined as follows:

> Narrator's introduction (10:1)
> Daniel's first-person introduction (10:2–3)
> Angelophany (10:4–9)
>   The angel's appearance (10:4–6)
>   Daniel's initial reaction (10:7–9)
> The angelic revelation (10:10–11:2a)
>   Explanation of the mission and reason for delay (10:10–14)
>   Daniel's dialogue with the angel (10:15–19)
>   Further explanation of the mission and need to return (10:20–11:2a)

Comments

[10:1] The use of a third-person narration to introduce the following first-person account resembles the opening of ch. 7. In contrast, chs. 8 and 9 are entirely in the first person. For Daniel's court name Belteshazzar, see 1:7 and the discussion there (cf. 4:8 [5]; 5:12).

The date, the third year of Cyrus, is the latest one in the book. In 1:21 it was said that "Daniel was there until the first year of Cyrus the king." Since the decree of Cyrus (Ezra 1:1; 2 Chr 36:22–23) permitting the exiles to return and rebuild the temple of Jerusalem is dated to the first year of his reign, this notice suggests that Daniel was among the returnees. Yet according to 10:1 he is still in the Persian court in Cyrus's third year. While this discrepancy may simply reflect incomplete editing of the apocalyptic chapters in relation to a preexisting story collection, the claim that Daniel is not among the returnees may have to do with the relation between this apocalypse and the preceding one. In ch. 9, Daniel was shown in the act of reading and interpreting the imminent fulfillment of Jeremiah's prophecy of the restoration of the exiles after seventy years (Jer 29:10–14). But Gabriel revealed to him that there was another dimension to the prophecy that would not be fulfilled for seventy weeks of years. Thus having Daniel receive a further revelation after the initial group of exiles has returned to Jerusalem draws attention once again to the significance of the period between the end of exile and the events of the eschaton.

This first verse introduces the thematically important word *'ĕmet*, which will recur in 10:21 and 11:2 to characterize the revelation. In part the word continues its traditional meaning of "reliable," "trustworthy," but as employed in this chapter, it also suggests the notion of the deep reality of things, that is, truth as opposed to appearance. In that sense it is functionally similar to the use of *rāz* ("mystery") in ch. 2. In both contexts the referent is the revelation of the hidden course of history. This semantic development of *'ĕmet* is also evident in the slightly earlier text *4QInstruction* (4Q415–18, 423). There the "foundation of truth" (*sôd 'ĕmet*) is said to be laid out in the "mystery of existence" (*rāz nihyeh*), the body of esoteric knowledge concerning creation, history, ethics, and eschatological realities (4Q417 frg. 1 1.8–9).

More ambiguous is the phrase "great struggle," which could be taken to refer to the contents of the revelation with its conflicts between the king of the north and the king of the south. More likely, however, in light of the following affirmations that Daniel understood, the phrase should be taken to refer to the difficulty of understanding what was communicated. The aptness of this comment will be appreciated by any reader who tries to decipher the intricate details of the historical account, a task complicated by the author's intentional refusal to make explicit to whom various pronouns refer. As in other chapters, the style of the apocalypse forces the reader to become an interpreter as much as Daniel or the angelic mediators are. The trope of Daniel's not understanding the revelations he receives recurs, implicitly and explicitly, throughout the apocalypses. Even in this final revelation, Daniel will ask for clarification of an enigmatic detail (12:8), though the introductory verse (10:1) assures us that Daniel did understand the revelation, just as later the "wise" will understand it (12:10). Thus the series of revelations can end, because now Daniel has understood.

[2–3] As Daniel begins the narration of his account, he foregrounds the fact of his mourning, without making clear why he is engaged in this act. In ch. 9 Daniel's "fasting, sackcloth, and ashes" clearly signal an act of repentance on behalf of the people. Here, however, the purpose is not so evident. In usage elsewhere, persons may be said to mourn over the dead, the judgment of God, sin, or calamity of some sort. Even though the revelation of ch. 9 is dated more than three years earlier, the sequence of the chapters suggests that Daniel is in some way in mourning because of the calamitous but mysterious events that were revealed to him. Fasting was a regular feature of mourning (2 Sam 12:20; Neh 1:4), as was refraining from oiling the body (2 Sam 14:2). As v. 12

clarifies, Daniel's mourning was accompanied by a prayer for understanding, and it is possible that the fasting was also a means of preparation for receiving a revelation, as it was understood in later apocalyptic literature (*4 Ezra* [2 Esd] 5:13; *2 Bar.* 5:6–7; *Ascen. Isa.* 2:7–11).

[3–4] The duration of Daniel's fast, three weeks, is extraordinary (cf. the three-day fasts in Exod 19:10–16; Esth 4:16; though note the forty-day fast of Moses in Deut 9:9–10). Moreover, it continued, as v. 4 suggests, during the feasts of Passover (day 14 of the first month) and Unleavened Bread (days 15–21 of that month). Even the ascetic Judith broke her mourning fasts for the Sabbaths, New Moons, and prescribed festivals (Jdt 8:6). Apparently Daniel intended to fast until his prayer was answered. In v. 13 the angel will explain why the response has taken so long.

The location of Daniel's revelation by a river may be an indication that rivers were considered likely places for numinous encounters (cf. Gen 32:25–31). Ezekiel's vision, which influences the visionary imagination of this chapter (see below), also takes place by a watercourse, the Chebar Canal (Ezek 1:1). And even though Daniel may be physically in Babylon in ch. 8, his vision is also by the Ulai River (or Canal; 8:2). Later rabbinic tradition suggested that gazing into the waters of a river could reflect the heavens above as a means of incubating a visionary experience ("Visions of Ezekiel," in Halperin 265), though in the biblical examples the vision or encounter appears to come upon the person unexpectedly.

Exactly where Daniel is geographically is a bit unclear. The epithet "great river" normally refers to the Euphrates (Gen 15:18; Deut 1:7; Josh 1:4), which is the location of Babylon, the setting of the rest of the book of Daniel. Here, however, in what is probably an early gloss, it is identified with the Tigris (so Montgomery 407; Plöger 145; J. Collins 373; et al.). Whatever the original author's intentions, the glossator apparently considered that Daniel's service in the Persian court would have involved his relocation to a more easterly part of the empire.

[5–6] The figure that Daniel sees is never named. He is, however, almost certainly to be identified with Gabriel since he performs the same messenger function as in 9:21–22, where the angel is explicitly identified. There Daniel recognizes him as the angel he had previously seen in the vision (8:13–16), who interpreted the meaning of the vision for him. In 8:13–15 and later in this vision in 12:5–6, additional angelic figures appear, asking for clarification. Thus the authority of this messenger angel indicates special status. It is not so clear that the angel in 7:16 should be identified as Gabriel, since he is simply described as "one of those who stood in attendance."

The impact of Ezek 1–3 and 8–10 upon the way in which divine and angelic figures were envisioned in early Judaism and Christianity was profound. Although rabbinic tradition sometimes tried to restrict access to Ezek 1

Revelation and Sublime Terror

(*m. Ḥag.* 2:1; Halperin 25–31), it was evidently a closely studied text in antiquity. Although occasionally elements from Ezekiel's description of the divine throne chariot and angelic attendants might be cited directly, for the most part the various sensuous elements of his description were treated like mosaic tiles that could be recombined in various ways to depict a variety of heavenly realia. In this passage the numinous appearance of the angel creatively recontextualizes fragments of Ezekiel's langauge:

Daniel	Ezekiel
10:5, "a man clothed in linen"	9:2, "a man ... clothed in linen" (cf. 9:3, 11; 10:2, 6, 7
10:5, "loins encircled with pure gold"	1:27; 8:2, loins separate appearance of upper body from lower body
10:6, "body like topaz [cf. NJPS, NRSV: beryl]"	1:16; 10:9, the shining appearance of the wheels of the chariot throne are like topaz/beryl (cf. NJPS, NRSV)
10:6, "face like the appearance of lightning, . . . eyes like fiery torches"	1:13, fiery torches and lightning move around the living creatures
10:6, "arms and legs like the gleam of burnished bronze"	1:7, "gleam of burnished bronze" describes the legs of the living creatures
10:6, "sound of his words like the sound of a multitude" (*hāmôn*)	No precise parallel, but note the sound of the creatures in 1:24; 3:13; 10:5

Many of the details of the appearance of the angel in Dan 10 are also used by the author of Revelation to describe the Son of Man (1:13–16).

[7–11] The circumstances in which the angelophany occurs add to the numinous quality of the experience. In the previous vision accounts, Daniel appears to have been alone, either sleeping (7:1) or reading (9:2). No context is given for the vision in 8:1–2. Here Daniel mentions companions, suggesting that he is on official business with his retinue. Nevertheless, only Daniel sees the vision, and the flight of his companions again leaves him alone. What frightens the others is not specified. Perhaps it was simply a sense of numinous dread. Or perhaps, though they did not see anything, the companions heard the inarticulate but terrifying roaring of the angel's voice. This scene is most similar to the Acts account of Paul's vision, where his companions hear the voice but do not see the light (Acts 9:7; but cf. 22:9, where they see the light but do not hear the words). The account in Acts may have been influenced by Dan 10. In any event, fear is often a response to the presence of the divine (cf. Exod 19:15–16; Josh 5:14; Judg 6:22; 13:6, 22).

The passage describing Daniel's reaction is an elaboration of his previous encounter with Gabriel in 8:18 (see comments on 8:17–19), both of which are influenced by details from Ezek 1:28b–2:2. There Ezekiel falls on his face in response to the divine vision, hears a voice, and is commanded to stand, a movement enabled by a spirit that enters into him. Although Daniel experiences weakness in response to the vision, it is the sound of the angel's voice that induces the trancelike sleep (cf. 8:18a), and the angel's touch that empowers him (cf. 8:18b). Here, however, the angelic touch suffices only to get Daniel to his hands and knees, indicating the greater gravity of this encounter. Even when Daniel stands in response to the angel's command, his weakness and distraught emotional state is emphasized, heightening the drama. Two further angelic touches (vv. 16, 18) are required to enable Daniel to speak and endure the angelophany.

[12–14] In contrast to God's rather peremptory address to Ezekiel (Ezek 2:3), the angel not only calls Daniel "highly esteemed" (v. 11) but also addresses him with an oracle of assurance, as often occurs in a theophany (e.g., Gen 15:1; 26:24; 46:3; Jer 1:8). The angel explains that, as in the previous occurrence of Daniel's fasting and praying, a response was immediately dispatched (cf. 9:23). The contrast between the two situations, however, suggests the heightened importance of this situation. Whereas Gabriel's appearance was almost instantaneous in 9:23, here he has been delayed for twenty-one days by the opposition of the prince of Persia.

The prince of Persia is apparently not a human figure but an angel who is in charge of the nation of Persia. The background for this concept is Deut 32:8–9, the Song of Moses. The poem describes how the Most High divided the peoples according to the number of the "sons of God," retaining Israel as his own portion (cf. Sir 17:17). (Although the MT reflects a demythologizing change of the phrase to "sons of Israel," texts from Qumran [$4QDeuteronomy^j$ = 4Q37, "sons of God"] and the LXX ["angels of God"] preserve the original meaning.) This theory explained why other nations worshiped different gods. In the Second Temple period, with the development of a more monotheistic perspective, the heads of the other nations were understood to be angels. Daniel does differ from the classic understanding, however, in maintaining that Israel also had its patron angel, Michael (10:13, 21; 12:1), who is described here as intervening to allow Gabriel to continue his mission.

Excursus 5: Michael

The earliest reference to Michael, whose name means "Who is like God?" occurs in the third-century-B.C.E. Book of the Watchers (*1 En.* 1–36), where he is mentioned as one of the four archangels (9:1) and as the angel responsible for Israel (20:5). In Daniel also, he is designated as "one of the chief princes" (10:13). In *1 Enoch*, he is the angel charged with imprisoning the rebellious angels known as the watchers and destroying their vicious giant offspring (10:11–15). His military functions are explicit in the Qumran *War Scroll* (1QM 17.6–7) and in certain later apocalyptic writings (e.g., *2 En.* 22:6–9; 33:10; *3 Bar.* 11:4), as well as in the New Testament book of Revelation (12:7–9), where he and his angelic host fight against Satan in the form of a dragon, together with his angels (cf. Jude 9). Among the Dead Sea Scrolls, in *Rule of the Community*, Michael is probably to be identified with the Prince of Light who opposes the Angel of Darkness (1QS 3.20) and also with the angelic Melchizedek (*Melchizedek* = 11Q13). In some traditions Michael also has priestly functions in the heavenly temple, receiving the prayers of the pious and offering them on the altar (*3 Bar.* 11–16). Michael is designated as the angel in charge of paradise in *1 En.* 24–25, and he leads the angels who bury Abraham's body and conducts his soul to paradise in the *Testament of Abraham* 20. Most of these traditions continue into later Judaism and Christianity.

Daniel 10–12 provides important evidence for the development of an increasingly dualistic conception of reality understood in terms of a military conflict between cosmic forces of good and evil. The title "prince of Persia" may itself indicate the military function of the angel, as the figure who encounters Joshua in Josh 5:14 similarly identifies himself as "prince of the host [i.e., army] of YHWH" (AT). This role fits the military-political interests of Dan 10–12 in the conflicts of different kingdoms. Here, however, the motives of the prince of Persia are not immediately clear. Why does he try to detain Gabriel, and what does he hope to accomplish by doing so? As Gabriel's message will make clear, the duration of Persian sovereignty has already been determined (11:2). The prince of Persia cannot change that by his actions. All he can do is to try to prevent Gabriel from communicating the future course of history to Daniel and thereby prevent that knowledge from reaching its ultimate recipients during the persecutions suffered under Antiochus IV. For the authors of Dan 7–12, insight into "the truth" was vital; it was the basis not only for courage and confidence but also for knowing the proper actions to take in response to the persecution (see 11:33–35). Thus the actions of the prince of Persia appear to be part of a general Gentile hostility toward God and Israel.

Throughout the book of Daniel, a variety of evaluations of Gentile power have been expressed. The narratives of chs. 1–6 could envision Gentile kings confessing the power of the Most High, though the dream in ch. 2 made clear that Gentile sovereignty would eventually be destroyed when the Most High's own sovereignty is manifested. Although both chs. 2 and 7 appear to treat only the fourth kingdom (i.e., the Hellenistic powers) as truly evil, the apocalypse in chs. 10–12 has a somewhat more negative view, treating the angelic patrons of both Persia and Greece as actively hostile to the divine will (10:13, 20). The Qumran *War Scroll* (1QM), which is influenced by the book of Daniel, more directly depicts the eschatological conflict as a two-storied affair, occurring not only between Israel and the Gentiles, but also between Michael with his angelic armies versus Belial, the leader of the hostile angelic armies.

The angel's announcement of the purpose of his mission includes again the key word "understand" (*bîn*) and a temporal reference to "the latter days" (Dan 10:14; cf. 2:28). These two words point toward an important intellectual tension that existed in the second century B.C.E., namely, the sense that God's public exercise of sovereign rule was mysteriously delayed. Although "the latter days" was originally simply an expression that referred to the future, it comes to designate a decisive turning point (cf. KJV: Deut 4:30; 31:29; Hos 3:5; Jer 48:47; etc.). Eventually, it came to have a specialized meaning referring to eschatological or messianic time (e.g., Isa 2:2//Mic 4:1; Ezek 38:16), a usage particularly common in the Dead Sea Scrolls (CD 6.11; 1QS^a 1.1; 1QpHab 2.5–6; 4QpIsa^a [4Q161] frgs. 8–10 3.18; 4QpNah [4Q169] frgs. 3–4 2.2; etc.). The final phrase of Dan 10:14, "for there is still a vision for the future" (*kî-'ôd ḥāzôn layyāmîm*), is an intertextual allusion to Hab 2:2–3, which explains the necessity of writing down the prophetic vision, since its fulfillment will be at an appointed time (*lammô'ēd*) in the future. Daniel 11:14, 27, 35 also allude to the verse from Habakkuk to identify the temporal gap between the present time and the time of fulfillment. Similarly, the Qumran community's pesher *Commentary on Habakkuk* interprets the verse as follows: "Its interpretation: The last times will be extended and last longer than all that the prophets said, because the mysteries of God are a cause of wonder" (1QpHab 7.7–8).

[15–19] These verses describe the final preparation and strengthening of Daniel for the communication of the vision, as the effect of the angel's words is to leave him once again limp and speechless. Although the passage draws on previous prophetic models, it apparently wishes to elevate the sense of awe in Daniel's encounter beyond its prophetic predecessors. In 10:16 it appears that Daniel distinguishes between a second angelic figure, one "who looked like a human" and who touches his lips, and the angelic figure "who was standing before me," that is, the angelic figure of vv. 5–6, though it is possible that both phrases refer to the same being. In prophetic texts the touching of the lips prepares the prophet (cf. Isa 6:5–7; Jer 1:9). Here, however, a second touch is required to strengthen Daniel. The angel repeats a version of his reassuring words (cf. vv. 11–12). As Montgomery (414–15) observes, the salutation "Peace!" is conventional, but here it restores Daniel's sense of well-being (cf. Tob 12:15–17). Similarly, the double imperative ("Be strong! Be strong!") addresses Daniel's literal lack of strength, restoring it to him, as Daniel notes in his reply.

[10:20–11:2a] These verses are the despair of commentators since they seem to be a jumble of ideas. Some, like Goldingay (292–93), attempt to make sense of the verses as they stand, seeing statements about the purpose and intent of the angelic message interwoven with comments about the angelic conflict in an a-b-a-b-a pattern, as Montgomery (416) also noted. While one can make sense of the verses in this way, the result is a depiction of Gabriel as a highly distracted angel. Others like Plöger (146) delete portions of the passage (10:21a; 11:1) as later glosses, though why the glosses would have been added is not clear. Montgomery's suggestion (416) of an ancient doublet is perhaps the most appealing. One version (10:20a, 21a) would consist of a rhetorical question and the angel's statement of intent to disclose what is in the book of truth. The other (10:20b, 21b; 11:1b, 2a) would have the angel begin by explaining why his time is limited (i.e., the angelic conflict), and then announce his intent to "tell you what is true." (Montgomery also treats 11:1a as a gloss, though if it is, it is early since it occurs in 4QDan^c.) It is still unexplained why these two accounts would have been garbled together when they could be read intelligibly as a sequence. In sum, there is no fully persuasive way to account for what seems to be a disturbed text.

As the text now stands, Gabriel follows the rhetorical question about his purpose in coming with the news that he must quickly return to continue the struggle with the prince of Persia. What is unclear is what he means by saying, "And then when I go out, the prince of Greece will come." One would assume that it would be the defeated prince of Persia who goes out, only to be followed by the prince of Greece, and indeed some commentators (e.g., Ginsberg 1948, 90–91; Hartman and DiLella 265) emend to "and when he goes out." But the presence of the independent first-person pronoun (*waʾănî*) makes that emendation difficult. Moreover, Gabriel refers to the Gentile angelic princes in the plural in v. 21b ("these"). The author does not make his ideas concerning angelic combat explicit, but it appears that just as Michael came forward to assist Gabriel, so the angelic prince of Greece will come forward to support the prince of Persia rather than see him overwhelmed by Michael and Gabriel. Moreover, the reference in 11:1 to an earlier joint effort "in the first year of Darius the Mede" suggests a previous period of struggle. In any event, a dualistic vision of angelic conflict is presented in this apocalypse.

Apart from references to the angelic conflict, Gabriel's words concern his intent to tell Daniel "what is written in the book of truth." Although books and records were part of Israelite political and religious culture since the beginning of the monarchy, the frequency of references to books and written documents increases in the Persian and Hellenistic periods, with the increasing bureaucratization of state administration. Since the heavenly world was often envisioned in ways borrowed from that of earthly monarchies, it is not surprising that reference to heavenly books becomes more frequent in the literature of this time. Some of these heavenly books contain the names of the righteous or of sinners (e.g., Exod 32:32; Mal 3:16; *1 En.* 47:3; CD 20.19) and their deeds (*1 En.* 98:7–8; *4 Ezra* [2 Esd] 6:20), which are opened for judgment. Similarly, such records may be kept for the nations and their angelic rulers (e.g., Dan 7:10; *1 En.* 89:61–64; 90:17, 20). Other types of heavenly books contained laws that were the source of torah, as often in *Jubilees*. The "mystery of existence" (*rāz nihyeh*), referred to often in *1QInstruction* (1Q26) and *4QInstruction* (e.g., 4Q416 frg. 2 3.18), is a more comprehensive transcendent account of cosmological, ethical, historical, and eschatological knowledge, though it is not explicitly said to be a written document. Closest to the reference in Dan 10:21, however, are those references to heavenly writings that contain the course of world events written before their unfolding and revealed to the apocalyptic seer (cf. *1 En.* 81:1–4; 93:2). As in *1 Enoch*, these accounts are couched in allusive terminology, requiring the reader's attention to understand and interpret them.

Daniel 11:2b–45 History as Revelation

Overview and Outline

Chapter 11 contains one of the most unusual compositions in any apocalyptic writing. It is a minutely detailed history of political and military events, narrated in a slightly coded fashion, as it consolidates the various Seleucid and Ptolemaic monarchs as "the king of the north" and "the king of the south," respectively. The historical details are so precise and so generally accurate that scholars have cogently argued that the author must have had access to a chronicle of the history of Seleucid and Ptolemaic political and military interactions, probably one written in Greek (Rappaport 223–24). The account is largely focused on Seleucid activity, though the bias of the narration is anti-Seleucid. Since the authors of the Daniel apocalypses are clearly educated scribes, it is not implausible that some of them might have actually been in the employ of the Seleucid bureaucracy or the high priest's administrative staff (Redditt 472–73).

Even if the authors of Dan 11 had access to Greek chronicles of political and military events, their model for shaping and articulating these events is not that of a historiographical chronicle so much as it is like the Mesopotamian genre of pseudoprophecy of political events. These texts purport to be prophecies but are clearly written after the occurrence of most of the events they prophesy. But they use an account of history to attempt to make real predictions. The most pertinent to Daniel is the *Dynastic Prophecy* (Neujahr 58–62), which records a period from the reigns of Neo-Assyrian kings to the reigns of Alexander's successors. Though the purpose of this text has been debated, the most persuasive interpretation is that it was originally composed soon after Alexander's initial defeat of Darius III in 334 or 333 B.C.E. (Neujahr 70). It contains a prediction that Darius would repel the Greeks, carry off spoil, and bring well-being to his land. This prediction failed, however, but the text was later updated to cover the reigns of Alexander's successors in Babylon, though whether it then served as anti-Seleucid propaganda (Ringgren) or as a text supporting Seleucus I against his rival Antigonus (Sherwin-White 11, 14) is uncertain. In either case the similarities to Dan 11 are striking and may suggest knowledge of this type of literature, though no evidence exists for direct dependence.

What distinguishes Daniel, however, is the attempt to identify an intrinsic pattern in history, the "pattern of containment," as well as the use of scriptural patterns to facilitate the work of prediction and lend persuasiveness to the account. In particular, key texts from Isaiah are alluded to, so that passages originally referring to the Neo-Assyrian kings in Isaiah are seen either as models for understanding the Seleucid monarchs or even as prophecies concerning them, which have now been deciphered by the wise authors of Daniel (cf. Isa 8:7–8; 10:22–23). Also critical is the servant passage in Isa 52:13–53:12, which provides a model for the wise teachers themselves (see below on vv. 33–35). In addition to Isaiah, other prophecies are also alluded to, including Num 24:24; Hab 2:3; and Ezek 38–39. The capacity to see in contemporary events the realization of scriptural promises and predictions served as a warrant for the authority of the claims made in Dan 11.

The rich detail of ch. 11 makes it difficult to discern a clear outline, but a sense of its flow can be represented as follows:

Transition from Persian to Greek Rule (11:2b–4)
The failed alliance between the Seleucids and the Ptolemies (11:5–6)
Reciprocal invasions (11:7–9)
The career of Antiochus III (11:10–19)
Seleucus IV and the early career of Antiochus IV (11:20–24)
Antiochus IV's first invasion of Egypt (11:25–28)
The second invasion and attack on the "holy covenant" (11:29–35)
The impiety and injustice of Antiochus IV (11:36–39)
The final battle and death of Antiochus IV (11:40–45)

The author of this chapter assumes a sophisticated knowledge of history on the part of the implied reader. Whether the actual audience in 164 B.C.E. possessed such knowledge is not known, but very few modern readers do. Therefore the notes that follow will supply much more detailed historical information than has been necessary for most of the chapters of the book. For an overview, see the skeleton key to Dan 11 (Excursus 6).

Excursus 6: Skeleton Key to Daniel 11

11:2	Four Persian kings: not a reference to specific individuals but a symbol of totality.
11:3–4	Alexander's empire, his sudden death (323 B.C.E.), division of his kingdom among four generals.
11:5	King of the south, Ptolemy I (305–283), rules in Egypt. One of his officers, Seleucus I (315/312–281), rules the (northern) Seleucid kingdom (Syria/Mesopotamia).
11:6	Berenice, daughter of Ptolemy II (283–246), married to Antiochus II (261–246) in 250. Unsuccessful alliance.
11:7–8	Berenice's brother becomes Ptolemy III (246–221). Invades Seleucid kingdom with initial success but returns to Egypt without completing conquest.
11:9	Seleucus II briefly invades Ptolemaic territory (242).
11:10	Seleucus II's sons: Seleucus III (226–223) and Antiochus III (223–187). Antiochus III was a militant and largely successful king.
11:11–12	Battle of Raphia (217) between Ptolemy IV (221–204) and Antiochus III. Victory for Ptolemy IV, but not such a victory as to break the power of Antiochus III.
11:13–14	Further military activity by Antiochus III in Syria and Palestine. Internal rebellions in Egypt. The upheaval in Judea alluded to remains obscure.
11:15–16	Antiochus III takes Sidon on the Phoenician coast (199), effectively taking Palestine back from Ptolemaic control.
11:17	Antiochus III marries his daughter Cleopatra to Ptolemy V (204–181) in 194/193.
11:18	Antiochus III tries to expand into Asia Minor and Greece. Rome confronts him, defeats him in battle of Magnesia (189), imposes heavy tribute.
11:19	Antiochus III dies in attack on temple of Bel (187) in Elemaïs.
11:20	Seleucus IV (187–175) sends Heliodorus to take money from Jerusalem temple (2 Macc 3). Assassinated in 175.
11:21	Antiochus IV (175–164) becomes king though not in the line of succession. Displaces the son of Seleucus IV.
11:22	A prince of the covenant: Onias III. Replaced as high priest by brother Jason and eventually murdered in 172.
11:23–24	Antiochus IV makes common cause with the radical hellenizers in Jerusalem under Menelaus, the high priest who replaces Jason.
11:25–26	Antiochus IV invades Egypt (170–169); defeats Ptolemy VI (180–164, 163–145).

History as Revelation

11:27	An alliance formed between Antiochus IV and Ptolemy VI to oust Ptolemy VIII (170–163, 145–116), brother of Ptolemy VI, who shared the Egyptian throne.
11:28	Antiochus IV visits Jerusalem on return from Egyptian campaign. Seizes money from the temple.
11:29–30	Antiochus IV invades Egypt again (168). Rome intervenes to halt his invasion.
11:30–31	Antiochus IV institutes persecution: desecration of sanctuary, establishment of garrison in the Acra (167 B.C.E.).
11:32	Response to the persecution: some collaborate, some resist (see 1 Maccabees).
11:33–35	The wise: the group associated with Danielic traditions. The many: the population at large.
11:36–39	Summary of Antiochus IV's relation to deities. God of gods: YHWH (desecration of temple); god of his father: Apollo; the one whom women worship: Dionysius, a Greek god popular in Egypt; god of fortresses: Zeus Olympios = Baal Shamem.
11:40–45	Eschatological predictions of Antiochus IV's final overwhelming invasion and victory over Egypt, followed by his death in Judea.

Comments

[11:2–3] The reference to four Persian kings is simply the use of a round number, since there were many more than four kings who followed Cyrus. Four are specifically mentioned in the Hebrew Bible, however: Cyrus, Darius, Xerxes (= Ahasuerus in Esther), and Artaxerxes. The popular image of the Persian kings in Greek sources, as here, was of fabulously wealthy monarchs who hoarded precious metals. Thus the last monarch, Darius III Codomannus, would have been the richest of all (cf. Briant 695, 800–804, who demonstrates that the popular image was not correct). The "warrior king" is Alexander the Great, whose astonishing military conquests across the eastern Mediterranean and the Near East from 333 to 323 B.C.E. made a profound impression on the ancient imagination. The phrase "do as he pleases" echoes the description of the powerful kings in 8:4. It will be further used in this chapter to describe Antiochus III (v. 16) and Antiochus IV (v. 36). From the author's point of view, these three were the most important of the kings who are collectively designated as the king of the north.

Alexander died suddenly in Babylon in 323, perhaps from a fever. The brevity of his reign over a unified empire and its disintegration into several successor stages is described in v. 4 (cf. 8:8, 21–22). The reality was far messier than this verse suggests. Following Alexander's death, his ranking generals initially represented themselves as the regents and protectors of his heirs, his half-brother Philip Arrhidaios and his posthumously born son, Alexander IV. In fact, they were intent either on usurping control of the entire empire or carving out their own kingdoms from it. By 310 both Philip and Alexander IV had been executed, and between 306 and 304 the dominant generals proclaimed themselves kings. Although the details of shifting power during these years are complex, Cassander ruled in Macedonia, Lysimachus in Thrace, and Ptolemy in Egypt. Seleucus had been assigned the satrapy of Babylon, but Antigonus ("the One-Eyed"), who controlled most of Alexander's Asian empire, ousted Seleucus in 315, who then fled to Ptolemy in Egypt. With Ptolemy's help Seleucus regained Babylon in 312. Recognizing that Antigonus wished to reconstitute Alexander's empire under his own direct rule, the other four generals allied against him, forcing Antigonus to a decisive battle at Ipsus in Phrygia in 301. Ptolemy, though he conquered Palestine and Syria on his march north, did not actually participate in the battle itself. Thus when the generals met to divide Antigonus's territory, they awarded the Syria-Palestine area (known in Greek sources as Coele-Syria) to Seleucus. Ptolemy, however, refused to vacate his troops from the territory and treated it as "spear-won land," his by right of conquest. This conflict set the stage for the animosity between the Ptolemies and the Seleucids that concerns most of Dan 11. All in all, a total of six "Syrian wars" were fought between these two powers between 274 and 163 B.C.E.

[5] The detailed history of Seleucid-Ptolemaic relations begins here. The identities of the individual kings are assimilated into the symbolic figures of the king of the south (Ptolemies) and the king of the north (Seleucids). While the basic structure is one of containment, the Seleucid kingdom is depicted as the more powerful and the one that will ultimately upset history's natural balance. Thus the events of 315–312 as represented in v. 5 are clearly identifiable but assimilated to the author's view of the historical process.

Since the aggression of the Seleucid kings is at the heart of the story that the author wishes to tell, this topic shapes his characterization of Seleucus. It is somewhat misleading to refer to Seleucus as "one of his [i.e., Ptolemy's] princes," since he was initially assigned an independent satrapy. When Seleucus fled to Egypt, however, he did accompany Ptolemy on a military campaign against Antigonus's son Demetrius in Palestine, near Gaza in 312. It was at the conclusion of that campaign that Ptolemy gave him a small contingent of soldiers, whom he led back to Babylon, where he ousted Antigonus's troops and retook control of his satrapy. As the notes to the translation indicate, it is uncertain whether the verse maintains that Seleucus's dominion was greater than Ptolemy's. For most of the third century, the Ptolemaic kingdom was more powerful. But from the perspective of someone writing in the mid-160s B.C.E., the dominance of the Seleucid kingdom would be the accurate perception.

History as Revelation

[6] The author passes over the First (274–71) and Second (260–53) Syrian Wars, focusing on the dynastic marriage in 250 B.C.E. by which this period of conflict was temporarily ended. Antiochus II married Berenice, daughter of Ptolemy II, who brought with her a large dowry. Antiochus, however, was already married to the powerful Laodice, whom he divorced in order to marry Berenice. Antiochus died in 246, probably of illness, though Jerome (on 11:6) claims that he was poisoned by Laodice. Both women were the mothers of sons who had claims to succeed Antiochus II, but Berenice and her son were murdered at the behest of Laodice and her son Seleucus II. The text of v. 6 is extremely difficult. Although it clearly refers to these events, the identities of "those who brought her" and "the one who supported her" are uncertain.

[7–9] The "shoot from her roots" is Berenice's brother, Ptolemy III, who had become king in January 246 and who instigated the Third Syrian War (246–241) in retaliation for her murder and that of her child. The text of Daniel may overstate his victories in the interests of developing a pattern of alternating dominance. Although Ptolemy's initial victories were impressive, extending into the heart of Seleucid Mesopotamia, they were mostly ephemeral. His victories had their symbolic aspects also. The "gods," "statues," and "precious vessels" referred to in v. 8 were the statues of Egyptian deities taken away by the Persian king Cambyses after the conquest of Egypt in 525. "Godnapping," as it has been called, was a regular practice of war in the ancient Near East, a way of symbolizing that the defeated nation's deities were powerless against the victor and his gods. The restoration of these images to their respective Egyptian temples was a highly significant event and earned Ptolemy the epithet of "Benefactor," in Greek, *Euergetes*.

Further evidence for how the author gently shapes history to fit his pattern is contained in vv. 8–9. The observation in v. 8 that Ptolemy III desisted from further engagement with the Seleucid kingdom is historically correct. Despite the internal troubles that the Seleucid kingdom was having in Anatolia and the eastern provinces after 241, Ptolemy did not try to take advantage of the situation. Verse 9, however, massages the historical evidence to fit the pattern of alternating aggression and dominance. The verse appears to suggest that Seleucus II invaded the territory of Ptolemy III. The historical reality is rather that Seleucus II quickly took back most of the land temporarily conquered by Ptolemy in the Third Syrian War. In 242 Seleucus briefly tried to press toward the south and for a short time took parts of southern Syria and Phoenicia, but then was driven out. Thus v. 9 somewhat exaggerates the significance of Seleucus's movement and, chronologically, would be better placed before v. 8.

[10–12] To serve his patterning of history, the author of Daniel uses the collective term "his sons" to merge the reign of Seleucus III Soter (226–223) with that of his much more impressive brother Antiochus III the Great (223–187). Seleucus III's nickname, "Thunderbolt" (*Keraunos* in Greek), was given in irony: he was an impetuous and ineffectual commander who was soon assassinated by his own troops. This period was actually a low point in Seleucid history. After dealing with a rebellion in the East, the militarily and politically astute Antiochus III soon turned his attention to the reconquest of Coele-Syria, initiating the Fourth Syrian War (219–217). Verse 10 refers to the opening movements of this war, in which Antiochus III captured the port city of Seleucia-in-Pieria. Moreover, the governor of Syria defected, turning over Tyre and Ptolemais-Acco to Antiochus III. In the campaign of 218 the Ptolemaic defenses between Sidon and Damascus meant that Antiochus's army could not be supplied from the north. He therefore turned his troops eastward, securing northern Palestine both east and west of the Jordan, including Galilee and the productive Jezreel valley. Although the military campaign did not reach Jerusalem, Samaria was occupied.

The language and imagery of v. 10, comparing his forces to a floodwater that sweeps over the land, are not inappropriate, but more than mere description is involved here. The terms "to flood and cross over" (*wĕšāṭap wĕʿābār*) are an intertextual allusion to Isa 8:8 (*šāṭap wĕʿābar*), where the prophet describes the anticipated invasion by the king of Assyria in the eighth century. The language lends an epic quality to the description, enhanced by the historical allusion, though it may also subtly indicate that these events are not, finally, the outcome of the autonomous will of the kings but are part of the divine plan. The author of Daniel also begins to employ various psychological and emotional terms for the kings in this section, describing Ptolemy IV in v. 11 as "enraged." The effect is to make the clashes of these kings appear to be the conflicts of larger-than-life forces.

The final words of v. 10, "as far as his fortress," are not entirely clear but probably refer to Egypt itself (so Montgomery 437; J. Collins 379). The following verses describe the Battle of Raphia (June 22, 217 B.C.E.), at the gateway to Egypt, some 19 miles south of Gaza. Although Ptolemy IV Philopator is usually judged to have been an ineffective king, his Greek adviser, Sosibius, took control of the situation. Sosibius had trained a large army of 25,000 Greek and Macedonian soldiers, as well as hiring mercenaries from various locations (Grainger 202–6). For the first time, he also enrolled about 20,000 native Egyptians as infantry. Thus the characterization in vv. 10–11 of the armies as "a massive horde" and "a great horde" is not inaccurate. Against Ptolemy's 50,000 troops, Antiochus III led approximately 65,000 troops. Both armies had cavalry and war elephants, as well as heavy infantry. This was the largest engagement since the Battle of Ipsus in 301 B.C.E. Although the fight initially went in favor of Antiochus, Ptolemy's forces, which he personally led, counterattacked and prevailed. A legendary account of the Battle of Raphia, highlighting the battlefield role of Ptolemy's sister Arisinoe III, can be found in 3 Macc 1.

[12] In his characteristic idiom, the author refers to Ptolemy's heart as being "exalted," and the pattern of his behavior following his victory at Raphia does suggest an unwise overconfidence and even grandiosity. Ptolemy lavished 300,000 gold pieces on his soldiers, built an absurdly large but impractical ship, and also made large bequests to Egyptian temples. These and other public expenditures were part of his embrace of an ideology of *tryphē*, "magnificence" (Grainger 230), though, as Dan 11 suggests, it might be characterized as hubris. One of the results of the war and Ptolemy's subsequent policies was inflation, which effectively increased the already substantial tax burden on the peasantry. By 207 B.C.E. the agricultural hinterland, known as the *chōra*, was in revolt. The 20,000 demobilized Egyptian peasant soldiers undoubtedly provided leadership for the rebellion, which lasted over a decade. The pattern described by v. 12 is thus apt: the overconfidence and complacency resulting from the victory at Raphia was soon followed by a near collapse of the Ptolemaic state. Ptolemy's successor, Ptolemy V Epiphanes, was a child of six, and his accession to the throne was the occasion for political murders and coups.

[13–14] Following the pattern that he sees in history, the author of Dan 11 describes the subsequent aggression of Antiochus III. In fact, the peace treaty following the Battle of Raphia had ensured that the two states would not attack one another while both kings lived. With Ptolemy's death in 204, however, Antiochus III was no longer bound to peace. The author of Dan 11 acknowledges this lapse of time with the phrase "after a number of years." Antiochus III made a pact in 203/202 with Philip V, king of Macedonia, for a coordinated attack on Egypt in what is known as the Fifth Syrian War. In 202 Antiochus invaded Syria and Palestine, apparently meeting little resistance except for the strategically vital city of Gaza, which was captured in 201 after a lengthy siege. The statement in v. 14 that "many will arise against the king of the south" could be a compressed allusion both to the native rebellion in Egypt and to the involvement of Philip of Macedon in the Fifth Syrian War (so Jerome [on 11:14] understands it). But it might also be a reference to support for Antiochus III in Syria and Palestine. The Ptolemaic governor of Coele-Syria, Ptolemy son of Thraseas, did defect to Antiochus, and it is possible that this Ptolemy used his influence as governor to encourage various cities in the region to switch their allegiance to Antiochus.

In order to understand the reference to "the violent ones of your people" in v. 14, additional historical background is required. Ptolemaic forces led by the general Scopas counterattacked in a winter campaign in 201/200, when Antiochus had sent most of his troops to winter quarters. Scopus quickly recaptured Palestine, including Jerusalem. Josephus (*Ant.* 12.136) quotes the Greek historian Polybius as saying "Scopas . . . during the winter subdued the Jewish nation." This phrasing suggests that the Jews, too, had switched sides and freely supported Antiochus. Certainly, when Antiochus counterattacked in 200, defeating Scopas at the Battle of Panion in northern Palestine, the Jews supported him with provisions and helped expel the Ptolemaic garrison in Jerusalem. At the conclusion of the war, they were thanked by Antiochus for these actions, given substantial support to restore the city and temple damaged by war, and granted a variety of tax remissions. They were also given permission to enforce purity regulations in Jerusalem. The documents authorizing these provisions are quoted by Josephus (*Ant.* 12.138–46).

Given the comment in v. 14 about more general uprisings against Ptolemy, one might assume that the further reference to "the violent ones of your people" refers to the Jews who supported Antiochus. Jerome (on 11:14) seems to understand the passage this way: he refers to Judeans as divided into pro-Ptolemaic and pro-Seleucid factions (though note his confusion in associating the flight of Onias IV to Egypt, which occurred several decades later, with these events). Verse 14, however, describes the persons in question as "stumbling," failing. While it is true that there was a temporary setback when Scopas recaptured Jerusalem, the pro-Seleucid Jews were, on the whole, quite successful. Also, this interpretation does not clearly make sense of the phrase "in order to establish the vision" or the fact that "the violent ones" is a traditionally negative expression (cf. Jer 7:11; Ezek 7:22; 18:10). An alternative explanation, suggested by Täubler (16–30), is that the verse refers to an otherwise unknown messianic movement. It does seem plausible that some Jews may have interpreted the upheavals of the Fifth Syrian War in eschatological terms, much as the author of Dan 11 is interpreting the events of the Antiochene crisis as the fulfillment of an eschatological vision. From the perspective of the author of Daniel, however, this earlier movement failed because the appointed time had not in fact arrived. Thus, whether or not these persons were actually "violent" or whether this is just a pejorative label, they did not, in the eyes of the author of Dan 11, understand the divine plan. Consequently they failed.

[15–16] These verses continue the description of Antiochus III's aggression. The "siege ramp" and "fortified city" refer to Sidon, where Scopas retreated with the remains of his army after the Battle of Panion, specifically his "select troops," the Aetolian mercenaries he had hired for the campaign. Antiochus blockaded the city and besieged it. Although Ptolemy sent additional forces, they were not able to break the siege, leading Scopas to surrender in 199 B.C.E. Jerome (on 11:15–16) mentions the siege of Sidon, but he thinks that the verse also refers to the siege of the Ptolemaic garrison in Jerusalem. Most scholars disagree since the verse appears to focus on a single event.

Verse 16 depicts Antiochus III at the pinnacle of his might. The phrases "he will do as he pleases" and "no one able to stand before him" recall the description of the ram at the peak of its power in 8:4, signaling that his demise will soon follow (cf. 11:3, 36). The climactic moment is also signaled by locating Antiochus III in "the beautiful land," that is, Judea (see 11:41; cf. Jer 3:19; *1 En.*

89:40; 90:20). Whether one reads "with destruction in his hand" or "all of it in his hand" (see trans. notes), the image is of someone all-powerful. Though the author does not explicitly depict this as a challenge to God, there may be an implication of divine pretensions (cf. v. 36).

[17–19] Once again, the author's interest in the pattern of historical events seems to lead him to attribute intentions to Antiochus III that he did not possess (Grainger 189). Antiochus had no plan to invade Egypt itself at this time, having secured his dynasty's historic claim to Coele-Syria, though he did capture Ptolemaic possessions on the coast of Asia Minor in 197/196. Since Antiochus IV will be the one who invades Egypt in vv. 25–28 and 40–43, the author may here be foreshadowing those events by attributing such an intention to Antiochus III, as also seems to be the case in the following part of the verse.

Although negotiations were begun as early as 197, the peace treaty was not finalized until late 196 or 195. It entailed Ptolemy V's recognition of Antiochus III's territorial claims and the betrothal of Antiochus's daughter Cleopatra to Ptolemy V. The marriage took place, fittingly, at Raphia in 194/193. Although the Ptolemies later claimed that Cleopatra's dowry included the revenues or even the territory of Coele-Syria, Judea, and perhaps other lands (Jerome, on 11:17; Josephus, *Ant.* 12.154), modern historians agree that it was "an invented detail" of Ptolemaic propaganda (Grainger 270; cf. Gera 80). The claim indicated, however, that the Ptolemaic kingdom was not reconciled to its losses.

The second half of v. 17 describes Antiochus III's intent in marrying Cleopatra to Ptolemy V as the destruction of his kingdom, and yet, in keeping with the pattern of containment, "it will not succeed or come to pass" (*wĕlōʾ taʿămōd wĕlōʾ-lô tihyeh*). This phrase is an intertextual echo of Isa 7:7 (*lōʾ tāqûm wĕlōʾ tihyeh*), in which the prophet declared that the aggressive intentions of Aram against Judah would not succeed. Historically, too, Cleopatra appears to have embraced Ptolemaic ambitions. As Jerome (on 11:17) reports, she "inclined more to her husband's side than to her father's." Following Ptolemy's death in 180, Cleopatra I became regent for her underage son and remained a powerful figure.

Antiochus III's wars had largely been motivated by his desire to reconquer lands possessed by his ancestor Seleucus I and subsequently lost. Now, following the end of the Fifth Syrian War, he turned his attention to Thrace and Greek territories, referred to in v. 18 as "the coastlands." This action brought him into conflict with Rome. Although Antiochus was initially successful, the Roman army defeated him initially at Thermopylae in central Greece in 191 and then decisively at Magnesia in Asia Minor in early 189.

Although v. 18 is difficult and possibly corrupt, it clearly alludes to these events. The "commander" would be P. Cornelius Scipio, who presented the conditions for peace to Antiochus III at Apamea in 188. Although stringent (loss of territory in Europe and Asia Minor, 15,000 talents in war indemnities to be paid in installments, loss of much of the elephant corps and naval power, and the holding of hostages in Rome for the fulfillment of the treaty), Antiochus had no choice but to accept the terms, even though they were intended to weaken the Seleucid Empire. This is what the text refers to as the "insult" that he was not able to return.

Verse 19 describes the aftermath of the Treaty of Apamea. Not surprisingly, rebellions broke out in the eastern parts of the empire after Antiochus's defeat by the Romans. Antiochus was killed in 187 in Elemaïs, a Persian city, after sacking the temple of Bel and clashing with local forces. The attack on the temple may have been motivated not only as reprisal for rebellion but also as a way of securing funds to pay the war indemnities to Rome.

[20] Antiochus III was succeeded by his son Seleucus IV (reigned 187–175). Of the events of his reign, the author of Daniel alludes to an episode narrated more fully, though in legendary form, in 2 Macc 3. According to that account, Simon, a jealous rival of the high priest Onias III, reported to Seleucid officials that the Jerusalem temple was filled with treasure. At that time temples functioned as quasi-banking institutions as well as places of worship. Seleucus sent his chief minister Heliodorus to confiscate these funds, but he was foiled in the attempt. According to 2 Maccabees, the temple was defended by angelic figures, who beat Heliodorus senseless. Presumably, early readers of Dan 11 would have been aware of these events and legends, though the author does not elaborate.

Seleucus IV was assassinated by this same Heliodorus in 175, hence v. 20's characterization of his death as "neither in anger nor in battle." Heliodorus's motives are not explained by the ancient sources, and modern historians can only speculate. His action, however, set in motion a complex and messy struggle for succession, to which v. 21 alludes.

[21–23] These verses serve to introduce and characterize Antiochus IV as lacking honor and legitimacy. The reference to his not being given the "majesty of kingship" alludes to the fact that he was not the heir to the throne, since he was the younger brother of Seleucus IV. After Seleucus's assassination, the crown should have gone to his eldest son, Demetrius. He, however, was a hostage in Rome, fulfilling the terms of the Treaty of Apamea. Demetrius's younger brother, also named Antiochus, was proclaimed king, with his mother Laodice as regent, since he was only a small child. Thus only by "stealth" and "intrigue" did Antiochus IV became king. He was in Athens, having recently been released from his own status as a treaty hostage in Rome. With the help of Eumenes II, the king of Pergamon, who gave him a small military force, Antiochus IV returned to Syria. Eumenes may also have been instrumental in removing Heliodorus, who quickly disappeared from the scene (so Gera 112; but cf. Grainger 286). Although the reference in v. 22 to "armed forces" being swept away suggests military action, there is no other evidence to suggest that

Antiochus fought his way to the kingship. It may rather be that this phrase is a general characterization of his kingship as a whole (so J. Collins 382). Little is known of conditions at the Seleucid court, but presumably there were various factions, some supporting and some opposing Heliodorus. Both the support of Eumenes and, presumably, some of the factions at court appear to be what v. 23 refers to as "alliances" and "a small group." The key to the situation was Laodice, whom Antiochus IV promptly married. Although Antiochus IV initially ruled as coregent with his nephew and stepson, the boy was murdered five years later, after Antiochus and Laodice had produced a son of their own. Antiochus IV had no intention of being displaced by the boy or of sharing real power with him. Thus he well deserves his designation as treacherous.

The reference in v. 22 to the "prince of the covenant" being swept away is somewhat intrusive and chronologically out of place. It clearly refers to the death of the high priest Onias III in 172. (See comments on 9:26 for the circumstances of his death.)

[24] The description of Antiochus IV as engaging in behavior that exceeds what "his fathers and his fathers' fathers have never done" is a leitmotif of the author's characterization of him (cf. vv. 37, 38) and indicates that he is the one who will break the pattern of containment and thus trigger the eschatological intervention of God. While extravagant spending and lavish gift giving were ways in which ancient monarchs demonstrated their power and secured gratitude from followers (cf. comments on v. 12), Antiochus IV impressed ancient writers as being excessive even by these standards (see Polybius 26.10; Livy 41.20; Josephus, *Ant.* 12.294). When their spending exceeded regular revenues, kings were tempted to engage in predatory and risky behavior. So 1 Macc 3:27–31 describes the situation of Antiochus IV in the midst of the Maccabean uprising. Having paid the army a year's pay in advance in order to motivate them, "he feared that, as had happened once or twice, he would not have enough for his expenses and for the gifts that he was accustomed to give with a lavish hand—more so than all previous kings. Greatly perplexed, he decided to go to Persia and levy tribute on those provinces, and so raise a large sum of money" (1 Macc 3:30–31 NABRE).

[25–26] The pattern of history that the author of Daniel perceives requires casting Antiochus IV as the aggressor. But who actually began the Sixth Syrian War (170–168), to which this verse refers, is less clear than Daniel makes it out to be. Both sides had been building armies and reinforcing defenses for several years. There is no indication, however, that the Ptolemaic army was "greater" than the Seleucid, as v. 25 suggests. Each side blamed the other for starting the war. Other Jewish sources agree with Daniel that Antiochus was the aggressor (1 Macc 1:16; Josephus, *Ant.* 12.242). It was the Ptolemaic army, however, that first initiated hostilities, though it was swiftly met and defeated by the Seleucid army while it was still in the Sinai desert, not far from Pelusium.

Antiochus restrained his army from massacring the defeated Ptolemaic forces, which retreated (Grainger 296). Then Antiochus brought his forces into the Delta, gaining control of the Nile. This was the first successful invasion of Egypt since Alexander the Great.

The Ptolemaic kingship was in disarray. Although Dan 11 schematizes the monarchy simply as "the king of the south," the situation was much more complex. From 180 to 176, the widowed queen Cleopatra had been regent for her son, Ptolemy VI Philometor. After her death, the regency of the still-underaged child passed to two members of the court, Eulaios, a eunuch and former tutor of Ptolemy VI, and Lenaios, a slave of Cleopatra's household, who oversaw the kingdom's finances. They also made Ptolemy VI's sister, Cleopatra II, his queen and consort, and in 170 added their younger brother Ptolemy VIII Physcon as the third coregent. Rivalry between the two brothers encouraged factions at court. Following the initial victories of Antiochus IV, two members of the Alexandrian aristocracy, Comanos and Cineas, staged a coup and replaced Eulaios and Lenaios as regents. The book of Daniel blames these various courtiers ("those who eat his provisions") for the Ptolemaic failure and the deaths resulting from the war, a judgment also made by other ancient sources (see Polybius 28.20).

[27] A face-to-face negotiation was arranged between Antiochus and Ptolemy VI and a settlement agreed upon. The terms of the treaty are unknown, but they certainly involved some kind of political subordination of Ptolemy VI to Antiochus and apparently Antiochus's support of Ptolemy VI in regaining sole kingship in Egypt. Ptolemy VI established a court at Memphis, and thus it is hardly surprising that both he and the treaty were repudiated by the regents and their supporters in Alexandria, who ousted him from the co-kingship. Antiochus besieged Alexandria, though he did not have the troops or the time to take the city. Probably because of the coming of winter, Antiochus removed his troops from Egypt in autumn, 169, retaining Pelusium, however, so that a return to Egypt would be a simple matter.

It remains unclear what specifically v. 27 refers to as the "lies" that the two kings spoke to one another. Though they saw each other as mutually useful, each was playing his own game. Porphyry (summarized in Jerome, on 11:25–26) also refers to Antiochus feigning friendship and then subjugating Egypt, though modern historians do not think Antiochus had serious territorial ambitions on Egypt. In his second invasion in 168, however, there is evidence that he issued at least one decree as the Egyptian king (Grainger 306n37), so he may have kept his options open. As for Ptolemy, though Jerome (on 11:27) dismisses the notion that a mere child could scheme against a monarch like Antiochus, the fact that Ptolemy VI was quickly reconciled with his siblings and reinstated as coregent after Antiochus's departure from Egypt suggests that it is not impossible that his dealings with Antiochus were part of a more

History as Revelation 349

elaborate strategy that also provided him with alternative options to his political subordination to Antiochus (cf. Morgan 61, 65; Grainger 300–301).

[28] The reference to his determination against "the holy covenant" alludes to Antiochus's assault on Jerusalem, the massive violence against the citizens, and the plundering of the temple as he returned to Syria, but if Daniel were our only source, we would be utterly in the dark as to what the words allude to. The primary sources for these events are 1 Macc 1:20–21; 2 Macc 5:11–21; and Josephus (*Ant.* 12.246–47), though the badly broken Qumran *Historical Text A* (4Q248) also refers to these matters. See the comments above on Dan 9:26 for a discussion of the context and events.

[29–31] The author's temporal phrase, "at the appointed time" (*lammôʿēd*), points to the divine determination of events behind history (cf. vv. 14, 27). A similar idea is reflected in various texts from the Dead Sea Scrolls (e.g., 1QS 3.13–16; 9.12–14; 1QH^a 9.17–22; 1QpHab 7.5–14). The notice that "this latter occasion will not be like the first" prepares the reader that what follows will describe the climactic period of history. From the critical historian's perspective, the restoration of the coregency between Ptolemy VI and his siblings, together with their attempts to reinforce their army, made it clear that Antiochus's war aims (the definitive protection of Coele-Syria from invasion) had not been fully secured. Thus he again invaded Egypt in 168. Once again, he tried to negotiate terms with the Egyptian government that would have given him effective overlordship of Egypt, though not direct control. When these overtures were rejected, he advanced on Alexandria, though it would have been difficult for him to take the city. The new element in the equation is the intervention of Rome. For a long time, Rome had been concerned with the balance of power in the eastern Mediterranean. During the time that Rome was engaged in its own war with Macedon, it largely tried to affect Seleucid-Ptolemaic relations through diplomacy. Only when it appeared that Antiochus might indeed achieve overlordship over Egypt was Rome moved to act. Neither Rome nor the Seleucid kingdom, however, wished to stumble into war with one another.

Here Dan 11:30 interprets the events in light of a passage from Num 24:24, "Ships come from the quarter of Kittim; They subject Asshur, subject Eber" (NJPS). Daniel uses the phrase "ships of the Kittim" to refer to the delegation from Rome under the leadership of C. Popillius Laenas. "Kittim," which originally referred to the town of Kition (now Larnaca) on the southern coast of Cyprus, came to be used first as a term for Greeks, as in Gen 10:4; 1 Chr 1:7, and later for a variety of places in the Mediterranean, including both mainland Greece (1 Macc 1:1; 8:5) and Italy (1QpHab 2.12, 14; 3.4, 9; 4.5, 10; 4QpIsa^a [4Q161] frgs. 8–10 3.5–8; 4QpNah [4Q169] 1.3). Here as elsewhere, Asshur is taken as an allusion to the Seleucid kingdom.

Because Dan 11:30b–31 appears to connect what happened to Antiochus in Egypt with his violent actions in Jerusalem, it is important to see once again how complex the reality actually was. Popillius confronted Antiochus in Eleusis, a suburb of Alexandria, in a dramatic meeting known in antiquity as the "Day of Eleusis." Although many ancient writers gave an account of this meeting (see Gera 172n171 for a comprehensive list), the influential Polybius set the tone for much interpretation by describing it as a personal humiliation for Antiochus. According to Polybius (29.27.1–8), Popillius handed Antiochus the Roman terms, and when Antiochus said he wished to consult with his counselors, Popillius drew a circle around Antiochus in the sand and demanded that he decide before he stepped out of the circle (29.27.7). While Polybius suggests that the incident humiliated Antiochus, modern historians have a more nuanced view and have even suggested that Antiochus might have been relieved that the Romans provided a solution to the intractable situation in which he had landed himself (Morgan 67; Gera 215; Grainger 308). Antiochus lacked the strength to take Alexandria, and even if he had succeeded, he would have risked war with Rome, which could not tolerate Seleucid domination of Egypt. Although Antiochus had to return Pelusium to Ptolemaic control, Rome reaffirmed Seleucid claims to Coele-Syria. That security, plus the enormous loot taken during the campaign, which Antiochus was allowed to keep, both refreshed his treasury and left the Ptolemaic kingdom impoverished and militarily impotent.

Daniel seems to suggest that Antiochus's actions against "the holy covenant" were both sequentially and perhaps causally related to his experiences in Egypt (e.g., J. Collins 2001, 49). Indeed, some historians have even used these verses to suggest a second violent attack by Antiochus himself on Jerusalem in 168, besides the looting of the temple in 169, obliquely alluded to in v. 28 (Tcherikover 186, 473–74n20; Mørkholm 1966, 142–43). More recent analysis, however, makes a strong case that there was only one assault by Antiochus on Jerusalem (Gera 153–57). Since it is clear that v. 31 refers to events that occurred in 167, it appears that the author of Daniel has telescoped events somewhat and tried to tie them narratively to Antiochus's forced withdrawal from Egypt. Thus it is likely that the expression "to act in fury" ($zā'am$, v. 30) here does give the author's characterization of Antiochus's state of mind and motivation (though cf. Portier-Young 135–36).

If the violence of v. 31 is not to be connected with Antiochus's return from Egypt, to what does it refer? The context has to do with the continuing struggles in Jerusalem over the office of the high priest. While Antiochus was campaigning in Egypt, a rumor circulated in Jerusalem that he had been killed. This prompted the ousted high priest Jason to return to Jerusalem and try to overthrow the current high priest Menelaus in late 169 or early 168. The result was a civil war. Although Jason seems initially to have had considerable popular support, his violence against the citizens of Jerusalem turned them against him, and he again fled (2 Macc 5:6–10), leaving Menelaus once again in charge. The events to which v. 31 refer appear to be the mission of the Seleucid official

Apollonius the Mysarch (1 Macc 1:29; 2 Macc 5:24), who arrived in Jerusalem with a substantial body of troops, likely in the summer of 167 (so Gera 224). Why Seleucid troops were sent to Jerusalem at this time remains a matter of dispute. There is no direct evidence of continuing revolt (as Tcherikover 187 and Schwartz 251, 255 suggest), but this remains a possibility. Whatever the specific events, the reprisals of 167 appear be Antiochus's response to what he judged to be conditions of revolt. Antiochus's favorable attention to "those who abandon the holy covenant" (v. 30) refers presumably to Menelaus and his supporters. The placement of this phrase just after an account of Antiochus's state of mind and just before the description of the persecution lends some support to Bickerman's thesis that the strategy of the persecution was guided by this faction of the Jews (1979, 83).

Although Apollonius entered Jerusalem peacefully, which 1 and 2 Maccabees take as a ruse, his troops soon attacked the city, slaughtering the men, capturing women and children for sale as slaves, and plundering and burning the city (1 Macc 1:30–32; 2 Macc 5:25–26). Portier-Young (140–75) aptly describes these actions as "state terror." The book of Daniel, however, does not mention the violence against citizens but focuses on what it considers the primary horror, the defilement of the temple. The reference to "the citadel" in v. 31 is syntactically awkward and may be a gloss indicating one source of the pollution. The citadel was the fortified high area (Acra/*akra*), somewhere near the temple, where the foreign troops were stationed. Similarly 1 Macc 1:36 refers to the citadel as "an ambush against the sanctuary" (NRSV), and 2 Macc 6:3–6 says that Gentiles used the temple precincts for their own forms of worship and sacrifice (so Tcherikover 194–96), though the 2 Maccabees account likely exaggerates the lurid aspects of the activity. The "desolating abomination" (Dan 11:31) refers to a pagan altar that was apparently erected on top of the altar of burnt offerings (1 Macc 1:54), thus making it impossible to conduct the daily burnt offerings according to the law (see comments on 8:11; 9:27).

[32] If one follows the MT (see trans. notes), then the king's action in using verbal inducements ("slippery words") to persuade persons to violate the covenant can be illustrated by the scene dramatized in 1 Macc 2:18, where the king's officials try to persuade Mattathias, father of Judah the Maccabee, to offer an improper sacrifice. They describe him as an honored leader and promise that if he sets such an example, "then you and your sons will be numbered among the Friends of the king, and . . . will be honored with silver and gold and many gifts" (NRSV). The Greek and Latin versions of v. 32 suggest that it was apostate Jews (cf. 11:30, "those who abandon the holy covenant") who were the ones attempting the persuasion. Either scenario is historically plausible.

While one often thinks of conflictual situations as involving two sides, more often than not each side involves many different groups, who do not necessarily share a common understanding of the situation. So here, "the people who know their God" (v. 32) probably refers to the cross-section of those Jews who resisted, including the followers of Mattathias (1 Macc 2:19–26), the group known as the Hasidim (1 Macc 2:29–38, 42, "Hasideans"), the circles of resistance behind the Enochic literature (*1 En.* 90:6–12), and behind the figures of Taxo and his sons in *Testament of Moses* (= *As. Mos.* 9:1–7), as well as the "wise" (*maśkîlîm*) in Danielic literature. One should also include the many individual resisters represented by the idealized figures of Eleazar and the seven brothers and their mother in 2 Macc 6–7. The modes of "taking action" varied among these resisters, from the militancy of the Hasidim, the Maccabees, and their Enochic supporters; to the voluntary martyrdom of Taxo and the martyrs of 2 Maccabees; to the teaching by the wise in Daniel (see below).

[33–35] The use of the term "wise" (*maśkîlîm*) by Daniel sets up a variety of significant resonances. While this is a term at home in the Wisdom literature and has already been used to designate Daniel and his friends (1:4, 17), the combination of this word with the reference to the Jewish public as "the many" (*rabbîm*) and the further reference to the *maśkîlîm* as "making the many righteous" in 12:2–3 strongly suggest an intentional intertextual allusion to the so-called Suffering Servant song in Isa 52:12–53:13, especially 52:13 and 53:11–12 (Ginsberg 1953, 402–3). But the Danielic "wise" have a distinct function. What they cause "the many" to understand is the divinely ordained pattern in history that governs the sequence of the four kingdoms (ch. 7), the mystery of the increasing power and sudden downfall of mighty kings (ch. 8), the hidden prophecy in Jeremiah's words and the nature of its fulfillment (ch. 9), and the very detailed pattern of history that will culminate in the events of the "appointed time" (ch. 11; cf. 8:19; 11:27, 29, 35). Not only is such knowledge a form of agency in itself; it also enables persons to know when action would be premature (cf. 11:14) and when it is timely. Knowledge of the divine plan strengthens the people's resolve to adhere to the requirements of the covenant, even if that fidelity results in death.

The stance of the Danielic *maśkîlîm* is often described as "quietistic" or even "pacifistic," but such terms may be misleading. There is no evidence whether the *maśkîlîm* opposed or supported violent resistance. It is simply not the topic of the chapter. What concerns ch. 11 is the teaching of the *maśkîlîm* and their apparent defeat at the hand of the state terror practiced by Antiochus. The verb *kāšal* (lit., "to stumble") occurs six times in this chapter (vv. 14, 19, 33, 34, 35, 41) with various subjects, but it always implies defeat. One purpose of the vision in Dan 10–12 is to set the apparent defeat of the wise in a context that explains the reasons for eschatological hope. Such a primary focus on the fate of the *maśkîlîm*, however, need not imply disapproval of the Maccabean militancy. Likewise 2 Maccabees endorses the actions by Judah and his brothers, even while insisting that the key factor in "turning away the wrath" of God (7:38 AT) is the death of the martyrs. In Daniel the critical element appears to be the teaching rather than death in martyrdom, though the willingness to die may itself be a testimony that will "make the many righteous" (see comments on 12:3).

Many commentators understand the expression "little help" in v. 34 as an allusion to the efforts of Mattathias and Judah. So Porphyry, according to Jerome (on 11:34), suggests that the efforts of Mattathias and Judah are described as "little" because of their early deaths. The immediate context does not favor this interpretation, however (J. Collins 386; Goldingay 303). The emphasis of this verse is on the misfortunes of the *maśkîlîm*. More likely the phrase "little help" is a comment on the inability of this group to develop a stable following. This is suggested by the following complaint that many who join them act "deceitfully" or "insincerely" (an expression derived from Isa 30:10 and related to the "slippery words" of Antiochus in Dan 11:32). No evidence exists to suggest what group or individuals might have been characterized this way by the author of Daniel.

The concern to interpret the apparent failure of the wise continues in v. 35. The ambiguous syntax allows for a variety of interpretations. The "stumbling" of the wise has the effect of "refining," "purifying," and "cleansing"—but whom or what? The verb *ṣārap* refers concretely to the process of removing impurities from metal and can be used metaphorically both of purifying persons of their sins (e.g., Isa 48:10; Zech 13:9; Mal 3:2–3) and of sorting or making a selection of the good from the bad (e.g., Jer 6:27–30; cf. Judg 7:4). Similarly, although *bārēr* occurs in the Piel only here, the Qal can mean to purge transgressors out of the community (Ezek 20:38; cf. Neh 5:18; 1 Chr 7:40; 9:22), while the Niphal refers to ritual or moral purity of individuals (Isa 52:11; Ps 18:26 [27]). The verb *labbēn* ("to whiten") is used metaphorically to refer to the results of moral purification (Isa 1:18; Ps 51:7 [9]). Thus the issue is to whom the pronoun in the prepositional phrase *bāhem* ("to them," Dan 11:35) refers. Although it is possible that it could refer to a purging of the ranks, identified by who was willing to suffer martyrdom and who was not (Goldingay 303), this does not seem like a text that is most concerned to settle scores. Others (Montgomery 459; Portier-Young 256–58) interpret the deaths of the wise as having an atoning function for the many. But it may simply refer either to the people at large (so Bevan 195), or to the wise themselves (so J. Collins 386) who are made worthy through their suffering for the eschatological reward they are promised in 12:3. These three verbs are used again in 12:10 (in passive forms: "purified, made white, refined") to establish a contrast between the righteous and the wicked.

[36–39] These verses interrupt the historical narration in order to focus on the person of Antiochus and in particular his relationship with deity. They come at a strategic place, since the final section, vv. 40–45, contains the actual historical prediction, based on the understanding of the dynamics of divinely determined history developed throughout the chapter. What these verses serve to explain is why the pattern of containment will be ruptured. Previous kings had challenged one another, but now this king even challenges heavenly powers. Key words in v. 36 hark back to the vision of ch. 8, which similarly described Antiochus's assault on heaven via his desolation of the Jerusalem temple. The phrase "will do as he pleases" is an expression for unchecked power (cf. 8:4; 11:3, 16). Also echoing 8:10, 11 is the verb "to become great," although here in a reflexive form, "make himself great" or "magnify himself," paired with another reflexive verb, "exalt himself." These actions, which properly belong to the sovereign deity (cf. Isa 33:10; Ezek 38:23), amount to blasphemous arrogance for a human king. Curiously, Antiochus's arrogance is not only directed against the God of Israel but also against "every god," perhaps the author's allusion to the fact that Antiochus plundered the temples of various gods. More significantly, although the title "god" (Greek: *theos*) had been previously used to honor Seleucid monarchs, Antiochus IV was the first to exploit this designation as part of his popular image. Some of his coins used the title *BASILEŌS ANTIOCHOU THEOU EPIPHANOUS* ("Antiochus the King, God Manifest"). Since coins were a major means by which imperial self-representation was propagated, it would be likely that the author of Daniel was aware of these claims, and considered them blasphemous.

The extent to which Antiochus actually thought of himself as a god has been debated. In 1900, Bevan argued that some of the coins of Antiochus actually depicted him *as* Zeus Olympios, a position that was widely held for many years. More recent study of the coinage by Mørkholm (1966, 131), however, has disproved this claim, and it cannot be maintained that Antiochus had any systematic plan to use a cult of the ruler as a unifying feature of the empire.

The author's primary concern is not Antiochus's arrogance against "every god" but against "the God of gods," that is, the God of Israel. As in 7:8, 11, 20, and 25, the focus is on Antiochus's blasphemous speech. While this might be an allusion to the decrees against Jewish religious practices, it more likely is the use of a stock motif that goes back at least to Isaiah's parody of Assyrian imperial rhetoric in Isa 10:8–11, 13–14; 37:23–25. Notably, in Israelite and Judean rhetoric, it is not the gods of other nations who are depicted as the opponents of YHWH but the Gentile kings. Their power and success creates a cognitive dissonance that must in some way be resolved (see Newsom 2011). Already in the narratives in Dan 1–6, the fictionalized Gentile monarchs are led to recognize the supreme sovereignty of the God of Israel (Nebuchadnezzar, Darius) or are destroyed for their blasphemous arrogance (Belshazzar). As a king of this type, Antiochus will also be destroyed at the moment of his apparent unstoppable power.

The entire tension of the drama between Antiochus IV and the God of Israel is modeled in this verse. The first part of v. 36 exhibits an *a-b-b'-a'* chiastic structure that emphasizes Antiochus's overweening behavior. The *b* and *b'* elements refer to Antiochus's arrogance against deities, while the *a* and *a'* elements describe his dominance ("[he] will do as he pleases") and success ("he will succeed"), phrases that echo 8:4 and 24. His ascendency will only last, however, "until wrath has come to an end," which also echoes 8:19 ("at the close of the wrath"; cf. Isa 26:20). As noted in the comments on 8:19, "wrath" (*zaʿam*) appears to have become a technical term denoting the period of Gentile domination. Just as 8:19 ends with a reference to "the appointed time of the end," so here an even stronger reference to the divine determination concludes the verse in the alliterative phrase *kî neḥĕrāṣâ neʿĕśātâ*, "for what is determined will be done" (cf. Isa 10:23; 28:22). Since the entire history of the Hellenistic kingdoms in vv. 2–36 has been presented as determined by God and revealed to Daniel before it occurred, these words offer confidence that the final events will also occur as described.

[37–39] Whereas v. 36 gives a general characterization of Antiochus's self-aggrandizement, the following verses provide specific details, though they are difficult to interpret. The general gist of the accusation is that Antiochus abandoned the worship of other gods, including the ancestral god of the Seleucid dynasty, Apollo. This is simply not the case. In 166 Antiochus staged a spectacular festival and procession at the sanctuary of Apollo at Daphne, near Antioch. A special coin was issued honoring Apollo, and the procession featured the statues of many deities (Mørkholm 1966, 98–99; Polybius 30.25–26). It is the case, however, that the mint at Antioch, as early as 173/172, had replaced the figure of Apollo on the reverse of Antiochus's coins with the figure of a seated Zeus Olympios (though other mints retained the traditional images), and perhaps this was sufficient for the author of Daniel to have derived the impression that Antiochus's veneration of Zeus Olympios amounted to a rejection of Apollo, since within Judaism one could not honor a second god without betraying one's ancestral deity. That Antiochus is accused of not honoring "the beloved of women," that is, Tammuz-Adonis (Ezek 8:14), is even more odd, since there is no evidence that this deity ever had any standing with the Seleucid dynasty.

In place of these deities, Daniel argues, Antiochus magnifies himself and honors "the god of strongholds." This phrase is not a stock epithet for any known deity, and early translators (i.e., LXX Th; Jerome, Vg) took it as a proper name, "Maozin." But the noun occurs several times in Dan 11 (vv. 7, 10, 19, 31), clearly representing the center of military power. Perhaps the author refers to the occupation of the fortress in Jerusalem, the Acra (citadel), by troops of Antiochus IV. According to 2 Macc 6:2, the temple in Jerusalem was rededicated to Zeus Olympios. Although the Jewish sources generally interpret this action as a hostile and punitive act that was part of the general aggression against Jewish religious practices (cf. v. 31; 1 Macc 1:44–61; 2 Macc 6:1–11), modern historians have suggested that the changes introduced into the temple were to accommodate the worship practices of the largely Syrian troops of Antiochus IV. The Syrian deity Baal Shamaim ("lord of heaven") was commonly identified with the Greek deity Zeus Olympios. To describe Baal Shamaim as "a god whom his ancestors have not known" is not true in the strict sense. The Seleucid dynasty supported the temples and cults of various important deities in their empire. The phraseology here, however, echoes Deut 13:13 (14), where an Israelite town that worships alien gods "whom you have not known" is subjected to annihilation (cf. also Deut 32:16–17). Thus Antiochus's veneration of other gods besides the ancestral god of the Seleucid dynasty is framed within the Jewish prohibition of promiscuous worship and cast as a religious horror.

Verse 39 continues to frame the issues in religious terms, attributing Antiochus's prowess to the "alien god." The subject and object of "acknowledge" could be understood in various ways. It might refer to those whom Antiochus chooses to acknowledge. More likely, however, it refers to Jews who acknowledge either Antiochus himself or, more probably, the "alien god" he favors. Thus in the view of the author, the hellenizing Jews around Menelaus imitate Antiochus's own religious apostasy. These persons he honors and rewards. Antiochus not only gives them political authority ("making them rule over the multitude," meaning the Jewish people; see v. 33; 12:3) but also land. The land in question would be property expropriated from those who resisted, and following Seleucid practice, was resold for a token price to the hellenizing Jews (Bar-Kochva 441). A similar interpretation of events is reflected in 1 Macc 1:43; 2:17–18, 23.

Verse 39 is difficult and has been the basis for some far-reaching theories about the legal status of Jerusalem at this time. Many scholars follow the suggestions of Hitzig (215) and Montgomery (463) and emend v. 39 so that it refers to the Syrian troops who were garrisoned in the Acra. So John Collins (368), "He will act for those who fortify strongholds, the people of a strange god. He will greatly honor [them] and make them rule over the common people and divide the land as their wages." The difficulty with this interpretation, however, is that the second half of the verse does not fit well with the garrison as subject. "Ruling" is more properly a political rather than military authority. Moreover the phrase *bimḥir* does not mean "as wages" but is regularly used to describe the act of buying for money (BDB 564; contra *HALOT* 569). This interpretation, however, underlies the influential theory of Tcherikover (189–91) that the garrison had the status of a military colony, or *katoikia*, and that the verse refers to the confiscation of land from the resisters and its reallocation to the soldiers for their support. It now seems clear, however, that the legal status of the city was not changed: it remained a *polis* (so Mørkholm 1966, 164; Bar-Kochva 438–44).

[**40–45**] The events of the end are framed according to the author's sense of patterns and predetermined times for events. In v. 27, the relations between the king of the north and the king of the south could not be definitively concluded, because the predetermined time had not yet arrived. Similarly, in v. 35 the suffering of the wise must continue "until the time of the end" (ʿad-ʿēt qēṣ). Now v. 40 announces that "the time of the end" has arrived (ûbʿēt qēṣ) and the final movement of history is to unfold. Here the author tries to use the structural repeatability of historical patterns to predict coming events, though these are events that will explode the pattern of history itself. As the previous act of aggression was initiated by the king of the north (v. 29), so now it will be the king of the south who attacks, provoking a massive response by his opponent. The description of the counterattack is modeled most closely on v. 10, which describes the beginning of the Fourth Syrian War by Antiochus III. Corresponding to the "massive horde" that is assembled in v. 10, here the forces are detailed as "chariotry and cavalry and many ships." As in v. 10, so here Antiochus IV's army is said to "sweep through like a flood," another intertextual echo of Isa 8:8, which describes the assault of the king of Assyria.

Other deep patterns structure the unfolding events. Verse 41 parallels v. 16 above, where Antiochus III is said to "stand in the beautiful land [i.e., Judea] with destruction in his hand." The assault on Judea and the destruction of myriads (cf. v. 12) suggests that the author invokes the paradigm of the eschatological battle against Judah and Jerusalem as described in the postexilic prophets, especially the invasion by Gog in Ezek 38:8–13 and the gathering of "all the nations" against Jerusalem in Zech 14:2. These late prophetic texts in turn depend on the mythic pattern of the assault of the "kings of the earth" on Jerusalem in Pss 2 and 48, which will be repulsed not by human armies but by the overwhelming majesty of the God of Israel. The blending of this motif with the historical pattern allows the author to construct a persuasive scenario for the end.

Why Edom, Moab, and Ammon are mentioned is unclear, as they do not figure by name in the earlier prophetic eschatological scenarios. In Israelite tradition they are related to Israel, Edom deriving from the line of Esau (Gen 36:40–43), and Moab and Ammon from the line of Lot (Gen 19:30–38). These nations were often at war with Israel and Judah and so were often seen as enemies (e.g., 2 Sam 11–12, David's war with Ammon; 2 Kgs 3, Jehoram's war against Moab), though Edom was regarded with particular hatred, perhaps because of opportunistic aggression after the fall of Judah to the Babylonians (cf. Lam 4:21–22; Obadiah). Since these three countries are said to escape from the power of Antiochus in Daniel's eschatological scenario, whereas Judah is attacked, they are in some sense Judah's symbolic opposites. The Qumran *War Scroll*, composed later than the book of Daniel and influenced by it, lists Edom, Moab, and the Ammonites, along with Philistia, as allied with the army of Belial (1QM 1.1–2; cf. Ezek 25).

In contrast to the prophetic eschatological scenarios of the final war against Jerusalem, however, the historical pattern sketched in Dan 11 is framed in terms of a recurrent conflict between the Seleucid powers of Syria and the Ptolemaic powers of Egypt. That the decisive moment in this relationship has arrived is signaled by the fact that, in contrast to v. 30, where the king's aggression was checked by the ships of the Kittim (i.e., Romans), now Egypt does not escape. The reference to the looting of silver, gold, and treasures of Egypt in v. 43 echoes and intensifies the outcome of the previous invasion of Egypt in v. 28.

The mention of Libya and Ethiopia is also curious, since the author generally avoids actual geographical designations (with the exception of v. 8). Because Libya and Ethiopia were the only two nations that shared borders with Egypt, the author may be adapting the notion of the gathering of the nations for the final battle, especially the nations that follow Gog in Ezek 38:5–7.

That earlier prophecies concerning Gentile kings form part of the template for the construction of this prediction is evident from v. 44, which is modeled on Isa 37:5–7//2 Kgs 19:5–7. There Isaiah reassures Hezekiah that God will cause the blasphemous king of Assyria, who has been besieging Jerusalem, to hear a rumor and return to his land, where he will be killed. So here also, the king of the north will hear a rumor from the direction of his homeland and will leave off the destruction of Egypt to return and annihilate the rebels. In this case, however, the king does not make it back to his homeland. The death of Antiochus IV is predicted enigmatically in v. 45. The term *'appadnô* is derived from Persian (*apadāna*) and means "his palace." In conjunction with the word for tent, it would apparently refer to the king's royal pavilion, appropriate for an account of a king on military campaign. The location of the event is specified as between "seas," apparently a term for the Mediterranean (so Charles 322) and "the beautiful holy mountain," clearly a designation of Mount Zion. The main coastal highway from Egypt toward Syria and the East would, indeed, lead in this direction. Moreover, the location would fit, at least in a general sense, the place of Gog's demise on "the mountains of Israel" (cf. Ezek 38:14–39:20). Given the author's invocation of various mythic and prophetic-eschatological templates for envisioning the events of the final period of history, a reader might anticipate a graphic description of Antiochus's end. Instead, his death is described in utterly understated terms, similar to the account of his demise in 8:25. This reticence about eschatological events is characteristic of the author of Daniel, in contrast to the more fulsomely described end-time events in the roughly contemporary *1 Enoch* 83–90.

The relationship between prediction and actual events has intrigued interpreters from ancient times until the present. Porphyry, persuaded that the entirety of ch. 11 was based on historical events from the life of Antiochus, understood the assault on Egypt to refer to the events of 168, Antiochus's second invasion of Egypt, and his subsequent death in the eastern part of his empire in 164. But that would merge the description of 11:40–43 with the previously described events of vv. 29–30. Jerome (on 11:44–45) rightly points out the difficulties of reconciling the account here with the actual events of Antiochus's death. Jerome argued that the account has not been describing historical events since v. 21 but is giving a prophecy of the antichrist. His argument, however, overlooks the extent to which the details of the historical record can be identified up until v. 40.

Modern scholarship recognizes that, in order to construct a sketch of what must come next, at v. 40 the author begins trying to build upon his account of the patterns of history and the normative patterns bequeathed to him from cultic and prophetic accounts of mythic and eschatological confrontations between the God of Israel and Gentile kings. Since the author of Dan 11 does not seem to know about Antiochus's actual campaign in the East in late 165, the rededication of the temple by Judah the Maccabee in December of 164, or the death of Antiochus in Elam at about that same time, it seems that the author of Daniel wrote this prophecy sometime before those events.

So how well did the author of Dan 11 do with his predictions? Although the details of the historical events do not match, the author was a sufficiently good student of history to recognize the basic pattern of royal overreaching that made Hellenistic kingship rather fragile and prone to sudden reversals. Moreover, the author's association of Antiochus's tragic flaw as self-aggrandizement and blasphemy is consistent with one of his last acts as king, the attempted robbing of a temple of Nanaia in Elymaïs. Unfortunately, there is no objective account of the death of Antiochus. The earliest accounts are those of Polybius and 1 and 2 Maccabees. Polybius, who was ill-disposed toward Antiochus IV, reports that after the abortive attempt to plunder the temple, he went mad as a result of divine displeasure and died at Tabae in Persia (Polybius 31.9). Although 2 Macc 1:14–16 indicates that Antiochus died in the very act of robbing the temple, 2 Macc 9:1–20 has him driven back from an attempt to rob temples in Persepolis and subsequently receiving word that his forces in Judea were defeated by Judah the Maccabee. Then the God of Israel sends a deadly disease upon Antiochus, who attempts to repent, giving up his claim to be equal to God, and to convert to Judaism, only to be rebuffed by God. A similar but less lurid account appears in 1 Macc 6:1–13: Antiochus, turned back from the temple at Elymaïs and hearing news of the reverses in Judea, falls into depression and realizes that his impending death is due to his desecration of the temple in Jerusalem.

Thus, whether predicted in advance or interpreted in retrospect, the death of Antiochus was a historical datum that interested parties struggled to interpret as supporting their own way of construing the broader meaning of events. In many ways, the author of Daniel's analysis of the dynamics of power comes closest to modern understandings of the factors that led to Antiochus's death. Where the author failed, however, is in the assumption that Antiochus represented a climax of blasphemous arrogance that would provoke the end of history itself.

Daniel 12:1–13 Revelation of the End

Overview and Outline

Although ch. 12 continues and concludes the angel's revelation, it marks the transition from the historical prediction to the prediction of eschatological deliverance. It is likely that this conclusion originally consisted only of vv. 1–4, 13. Verses 5–12 interrupt the flow of the text and introduce new angelic characters who initiate a dialogue with the angel who has been talking to Daniel concerning the time until the end. Daniel, too, questions the angel about this issue, leading to a final prediction of the time until the completion of the eschatological events.

The chapter may be outlined as follows:

Prediction of deliverance and resurrection (12:1–3)
Command to Daniel to seal up the book (12:4)
Daniel sees two angels (12:5)
Dialogue among the angels about the time until the end (12:6–7)
Dialogue between Daniel and the angel about time until the end (12:8–10)
Number of days remaining until the end (12:11–12)
Daniel's dismissal by the angel (12:13)

Comments

[1] With the opening verses of ch. 12, the scene shifts from its focus on Antiochus to consider the fate of the Jews whose situation under Antiochus was described in 11:32–35. The opening phrase "at that time" coordinates what follows with what is described in vv. 40–45, a section also introduced by the temporal phrase "at the time of the end." The scene also shifts from an earthly perspective to a heavenly one, featuring the role of the archangel Michael. Referred to here as "the great prince," his role is presumably military, recalling the confrontation with the princes of Persia and Greece in 10:20–21. What appears to be alluded to is Michael's defeat of the angelic prince of Greece, which would be the action in heaven that correspondingly results in the demise of Antiochus on earth "with no one to help him" (11:45).

The narrative arc of apocalyptic eschatology is similar in many ways to that of the modern thriller. Tension and conflict build over a long period of time, culminating in an almost unendurable scene of violent conflict, which is suddenly resolved in favor of the heroes. So also here, the situation is described as an incomparable "time of distress," a phrase that alludes in all probability to Jer 30:7. Indeed, depending on whether the word *gôy* refers to the nation of Israel (so most commentators) or to people in general (so Plöger 170), this time of distress is unparalleled either since the days of the formation of the nation in the oppression in Egypt or since creation itself. Although a few commentators think that the time of distress follows after the death of Antiochus IV Epiphanes (so Lebram 122), it is more likely, given the coordinating temporal phrases in 11:40 and 12:1, that the final period of Antiochus's presence in "the beautiful land" is the time of the "great distress" (11:41).

That something beyond a simple military victory is envisioned, however, is implied by the description of the rescue as involving "everyone who is found written in the book" (v. 1f). Since apocalyptic literature was the product of scribes who were very self-conscious about their craft and its significance, heavenly books of various sorts play an important role (see Baynes). Indeed, the account of these events is a report from Gabriel based on the heavenly "book of truth," that is, the book that records the events of history even before they unfold (10:21). The book alluded to here, however, is elsewhere referred to as a "book of life" (Ps 69:28 [29] NJPS; cf. Exod 32:32–33; Isa 4:3; Mal 3:16–18). The closest parallel is found in the roughly contemporary text known as *Words of the Heavenly Luminaries* from Qumran: "Rescue Your people Isr[ael from all] the lands, near and far, to wh[ich You have banished them—] each one who is written in the Book of Life" (4Q504 19.13–15; trans. *DSSR*). These references assume that God is the keeper of the book, and those who are listed in it are members of the covenant community. To be "blotted out" or "erased" (Exod 32:32) would presumably mean separation from the community by death. The mundane background to this notion is the phenomenon of the citizenship or census lists that recorded the persons enrolled in the community of Israel (Exod 30:11–16; Ezek 13:9) or as members of the priesthood in the postexilic period (Neh 7:5, 61–65). Participation in the community or priesthood depended on one's name being on the list. With the popularization of the idea of resurrection, however, "the book of life" came to refer to those who were to be granted eternal life and citizenship in heaven (*Jub.* 30:22; *Jos. Asen.* 15:4; *Apoc. Zeph.* 9:1–3; Phil 4:3; Rev 3:5; 13:8; 17:8; 20:12; 21:27; 22:19; see Baynes 36, 204).

But how is the book to be consulted, and by whom? The passive construction, "everyone who is found written in the book," leaves this unclear. In the earlier biblical references, the book is associated directly with God. In apocalyptic literature, however, angels are mostly the ones who are in charge of the books (Baynes 205). If one assumes that is the case here, then perhaps the archangel Michael also has a juridical role to play in presenting the list to God (cf. Nickelsburg 2006, 24–26). In contrast to several other texts, however, nothing explicit is said in Daniel about an intercessory or juridical role for Michael or any other angel (cf. *Jub.* 18:9; *T. Levi* 5:6–7; *T. Dan* 6:1–5; 11QMelchizedek).

[2] Older scholarship was inclined to see this verse, describing a resurrection of some of the people, as a sharp break with previous views about the finality of death. It was thought that the change was prompted by the intolerable suffering and theological dissonance caused by the Antiochene persecutions. More recent

scholarship, however, has shown that ideas about death and afterlife were much more complex and varied, even in the First Temple period, than was generally thought (see Hays 2011, 133–201; Levenson 23–34). The prevailing notion was that the dead continued a shadowy existence in Sheol, though even in Sheol the dead experienced different conditions depending on the nature of their death and burial or lack of burial (Isa 14:15–20; Ezek 31:18). Offerings left at tombs and expressions such as "to sleep with one's ancestors" (e.g., 1 Kgs 11:43) suggest that some form of continuity and community existed between the living and the dead (Hays 2011, 147–53). Although the claim is still contested, some scholars have argued that kings were thought to enter into a beatific afterlife, divinized and associated with the stars (e.g., Spronk). While this belief is well attested in Egypt and Ugarit, and may have been known in ancient Israel, there is little evidence that it was a widely accepted part of the Israelite belief system (J. Collins 2000, 125–27). More directly relevant is the fact that ancient Israelites did not distinguish as sharply as moderns do between life and death. The frequent use of the language of "sleep" to describe death (e.g., with *yāšēn*, Jer 51:39, 57; Job 3:13; 14:12; with *šākab*, Ps 88:5 [6]; Job 7:21; 1 Kgs 2:10; 11:21, 43) is not simply a euphemism. As Levenson (186) argues, in the Hebrew Bible "sleep . . . is a mini-death," or "a death that is—or one devoutly hopes will be—temporary." A person suffering from severe illness or misfortune might also speak of oneself as already in Sheol and beseech God to bring him up to life again (e.g., Ps 88; cf. Ps 40:2 [3]; 1 Sam 2:6). There was a stage, of course, at which the entry into death was ordinarily irreversible, though occasionally even the fully dead were said to be miraculously revived (1 Kgs 17:17–24; 2 Kgs 4:32–37; 13:21).

The origins of a specific notion of the resurrection of the dead are difficult to trace and, like most cultural ideas, emerge gradually and unevenly. Ezekiel's vivid depiction of the restoration of the dry bones into refleshed and breathing persons (37:1–10) is a visionary metaphor for the restoration of the nation (37:11–14), though in the *Pseudo-Ezekiel* text from Qumran (4Q385), roughly contemporary with Dan 12, the vision is interpreted as a description of the actual resurrection of the righteous. Scholarly opinion is divided as to whether the probably postexilic Isa 26:19 is also to be interpreted as a metaphorical use of resurrection to refer to national revivication (so Segal 2004, 260; contrast Levenson 198). The language is quite explicit: "Let your dead live, (their) corpses arise! Awake and sing, you who dwell in the dust, . . . and the earth will give birth to the spirits of the dead" (AT). Not only is there no contextual indication that this is a figure of speech, as there is in Ezekiel, but there also is an explicit contrast with the fate of the overlords who are described as the "dead who cannot live, spirits of the dead who cannot rise" (v. 14 AT). Thus there is good reason for taking this verse as expressing a hope for an actual resurrection in the context of God's judgment of the oppressors and deliverance of the people. If so, it is a very close parallel to Dan 12:2.

Not all ideas of an afterlife involved resurrection of the body. Thus *1 Enoch* 22 (probably late fourth or early third century B.C.E.) depicts four hollow chambers inside a mountain in the far west, where the souls of the dead are stored until the day of judgment. The four chambers are for (1) the righteous, (2) the sinners who died unpunished for their sins, (3) the murdered whose murders were not avenged, and (4) another class of sinners, apparently those who were punished during life. The righteous and the unpunished sinners receive reward and punishment in their chambers and will be raised at the time of judgment for further reward and punishment (Nickelsburg 2001, 306). The fate of the third group is not further specified, while it is explicitly said that the already-punished sinners will not be raised. The book of *Jubilees* (mid-second century B.C.E.) envisions the bones of the righteous as resting in the earth while their spirits rejoice at the time of eschatological deliverance (23:31). Nothing is said about the fate of the spirits of the wicked. Indeed, what is striking about the early texts that refer to the raising of either bodies or souls is that there is no reference to a general resurrection. The primary concern is with the fate of the righteous, the people of God (Isa 26:19; *Pseudo-Ezekiel*; *Jubilees*). They are to be raised. The wicked may either be left in Sheol/the earth and not raised (Isa 26:14; implicitly *Pseudo-Ezekiel*; *Jubilees*) or may be selectively raised for further punishment (*1 En.* 22).

Some of the emerging ideas about the fate of the dead may well reflect Egyptian, Mesopotamian, Canaanite, Persian, and Greek notions. Such cultural ideas are never simply "borrowed" but are selectively adapted to the needs of the society that appropriates them. The variety of ways in which the nature and purpose of an afterlife was envisioned suggests that a great deal of ideological experimentation was going on. Yet even though ideas about resurrection of the body or raising of souls were current by the fourth and third centuries B.C.E., they were still contested. Both Ecclesiastes (3:16–22; 9:3–6) and Ben Sira (Sir 14:16–17; 41:4) reject any notion of an afterlife and reassert the idea of Sheol as the common fate. Even in the first century C.E., opinion remained divided with the Pharisees affirming resurrection and the Sadducees rejecting it (Mark 12:18–23; Acts 23:6–8; Josephus, *J.W.* 2.154, 163, 165; *Ant.* 14, 16, 18).

The author of Daniel is thus not so much innovating as making use of ideas already in circulation for his own purposes. As in other early texts, what is envisioned is not a general resurrection but a resurrection of those with unfinished business. The language of the first phrase in Dan 12:2 is evocative of Isa 26:19 and may be an allusion to it. The construct phrase "earth of dust" (*'admat-'āpār*, "dusty earth") is odd, though perhaps an allusion to Gen 3:19, where both terms appear in the description of death.

Those who will be resurrected are not explicitly identified. Although some have argued that v. 2 refers only to the resurrection of the righteous (Alfrink; Hartman-DiLella 308; Kellerman 69–70), the language clearly speaks of two contrasting groups. For the first, in the context of 11:33–35, one might think specifically of the fallen *maśkîlîm*, though it is clear that a broader group of the righteous is intended, since Daniel is told in 12:13 that he too will be raised. Although the phrase "everlasting life" (*ḥayyê ʿôlām*) has no exact biblical parallel (but cf. 1QS 4.7), it is similar to God's grant to the king in Ps 21:4 (5) of "life" (*ḥayyîm*) and "length of days forever and ever" (*ʾōrek yāmîm ʿôlām wāʿed*). Everlasting life is a characteristic of deity (Dan 4:34 [31]; 12:7; cf. Gen 3:22). The fate of the second group is described through an allusion to the final verse of Isaiah (66:24), which refers to the exposed corpses of those who rebelled against God as subjected to undying worms and unquenchable fire. Although Daniel does not cite those details, he employs the rare word *dērāʾôn*, "abhorrence," which occurs elsewhere in MT only in Isa 66:24. Indeed, the more common word, "reproaches," may well be a gloss explaining that obscure word. The earlier part of Isa 66 specifically accuses the rebels of cultic abominations (vv. 3–4, 17), a fitting parallel for the hellenizing Jews who collaborated with Antiochus in the desecration of the sanctuary.

Daniel's notion of resurrection thus seems to be developed in part from a combined reading of Isa 26:19 and 66:24, though in both of the Isaiah passages the wicked are not raised. Given the physically graphic nature of those verses, it seems likely that Daniel envisions a bodily resurrection, though v. 2 does not specify that. The only details that are given concern the wise (*maśkîlîm*), who are given a special reward.

[3] One more critical passage from Isaiah plays an important role in the author's development of his ideas about resurrection. In v. 3 the wise are also described as "those who make the many righteous," an allusion to the suffering servant in Isa 53:11, whose death had an atoning effect for the many. While it is possible that the death of the wise is thought to have similar effects (so Lacocque 243; Portier-Young 258), it seems more likely that their teaching (Dan 11:33) is what makes the many righteous. The context here is on the fate of the wise themselves, which is read by analogy with that of the servant. The servant's exaltation ("exalted and lifted up and made very high," Isa 52:13 AT) can also be understood as a resurrection from death. The imagery of lofty height in Isaiah is rendered in Daniel in terms of the firmament and the stars and their brightness. It is debated whether the verse envisions the fate of the wise to be a form of astral immortality (so J. Collins 393), since it is difficult to judge the force of the preposition "like" (*kĕ*). The roughly contemporary *Testament of Moses* 10:9 is more explicit in describing the fate of the martyred Taxo and his sons: "And God will exalt you, and set you in heaven above the stars" (trans. Charles; cf. *1 En.* 104:2–6). In any event, some kind of transformation of the wise that distinguishes them from the other resurrected righteous is clearly in view.

[4] The angel's words to Daniel in v. 4 are also important for the role that they implicitly provide for the reader of the book. The angel commands him to conceal the words by sealing the book until the time of the end (cf. Isa 8:16;

Revelation of the End 365

29:11–12). Up to this point there has been no explicit reference to Daniel's writing down the words of the angel nor to the angel as giving Daniel a copy of the book of truth (10:21). The first-person style of the apocalypses, however, gives the impression that Daniel wrote down his visionary experiences (cf. 7:1). Thus the angel's command probably refers to the entire book of Daniel. In antiquity, documents were sealed with wax or wet clay, onto which the owner's stamp seal or signet ring was pressed (e.g., 1 Kgs 21:8; Esth 8:8, 10; Dan 6:17 [18]). The seal both authenticated the document by indicating the owner or author and protected it from tampering. Only an appropriately authorized person was to open the document. For sealed prophecies, the time of the fulfillment of the prophecy is the time when it may be opened (cf. Rev 5:1–5).

Thus whoever reads the book of Daniel has the sense of standing in the time of the end, since the book is now unsealed. As Hendel (272) aptly puts it, "The act of reading and understanding the book [is] an apocalyptic initiation, a rite of passage into a higher identity." The reader is one of the "many" who has become wise through the knowledge disclosed in this book. Such an idea is not unique to Daniel. The trope of secret knowledge passed down through time and reserved for those capable of understanding becomes common in apocalyptic literature (e.g., *1 En.* 1:2; *4 Ezra* [2 Esd] 14:45–46).

The second half of v. 4 is obscure. Does it describe the time during which the book is sealed and the words hidden? Or does it refer to the time of the end? The unusual verb (*yĕšōṭĕṭû*) marks the words as an allusion to Amos 8:12, "People will wander from sea to sea and from north to east. They will run to and fro [*yĕšōṭĕṭû*] to seek the word of YHWH, but they will not find it" (AT). In contrast to the situation described in Amos, here it is said that "knowledge will increase." Thus the words would seem to refer to the time of the end and the unsealing of the book, such that the dire situation Amos described will be reversed (cf. Montgomery 473–74; Plöger 172; Seow 189–90). Yet it seems more natural to expect a reference to the conditions of the time during which the book is sealed. Thus some emend *daʿat* ("knowledge") to *rāʿâ* ("evil"), words that look quite similar in Hebrew. Moreover, the reading has some support in the OG (see Bevan 203–4; J. Collins 399). Others suggest that the word is to be derived from a different root and means "humiliation, suffering" (Goldingay 281).

[5–12] It is widely thought that vv. 5–12 are a later supplement and that in the earliest version v. 4 was followed by v. 13, in which Daniel is promised resurrection at the time of the end (Hartman and DiLella 277; and with more nuance, J. Collins 371). The inserted material in vv. 5–10 differs in small but significant ways from the core vision. The verses are incorporated into the existing material by resuming the encounter with the angels described in ch. 10. The scene is modeled after the angelic dialogue in 8:13–14, which was concerned with the length of time that the sacrifices would be suspended and the temple desolated. Although many scholars consider vv. 11 and 12 to be two further supplements (e.g., Gunkel 350n110; Charles 144; Montgomery 477; Hartman and DiLella 311; J. Collins 401), this is not necessarily the case (see below).

[5–6] In 10:4–6 Daniel saw a single angel. Now he reports seeing two other angels, standing on opposite banks of the river, which is for unknown reasons referred to with the word that ordinarily designates the Nile (*yĕʾōr*; but see Isa 33:21). As in 8:13, an angelic dialogue ensues, introduced in each case with the words "How long . . . ?" The words are addressed to Gabriel ("the man dressed in linen"; see comments on 10:5–6), who is described either as being "upstream" or "above" (*mimmaʿal l-*, v. 6) the waters of the river. Since he was described in 10:10, 16, 18 as touching Daniel, the angel is not likely hovering over the waters (contra Seow 192). The question addressed to him concerns the end of the "awesome" things (*happĕlāʾōt*), a term used in 8:24 and 11:36 to describe Antiochus's arrogant words and deeds. Here, however, it may refer generally to the events of the end time.

[7] The angel's gesture in swearing, raising both hands, has long perplexed commentators since ordinarily only the right hand was raised (cf. Gen 14:22–24; Deut 32:40). The claim often made, that raising both hands makes the oath more emphatic or solemn, is without support. More likely is the explanation of McGarry, that a variant of Deut 32:40, upon which this passage is based, and which is attested in many Septuagint manuscripts, contained a tricolon in which YHWH says, "For I raise my hand to heaven, and I swear by my right hand, and I say: 'As I live forever . . .'" As sometimes happens when poetry is interpreted in prose, the prose writer misunderstands the poetic parallelism and assumes that two actions, not one, are involved. The most notorious case is Matt 21:1–7, which misinterprets the poetic parallelism of Zech 9:9 and has Jesus straddling both a donkey and a colt on his entry into Jerusalem. So in Dan 12:7 this version of Deut 32:40 was misunderstood to mean that both hands were to be raised. Although the usual oath formula is "as YHWH lives . . ." (e.g., Judg 8:19; 1 Sam 14:39, 45), Deut 32:40 also appears to be the source of the angel's reference to "the one who lives forever." The oath may also explain why two, not one, additional angels appear, since oaths required at least two witnesses (Deut 19:15).

Throughout the Danielic apocalypses, symbolic numbers have expressed the divine determination of times. Now in this final communication with the angel, the issue of symbolic times is addressed once again. The angel's promise that the duration of the awesome events will last "a time, (two) times, and half a time" (*lĕmôʿēd môʿădîm wāḥēṣî*) picks up the similar expression from 7:25 (*ʿiddān wĕʿiddānîn ûplag ʿiddān*). Although the second term, "times," is plural rather than dual, the symbolic calculation is based on half a week of years: 3½ years. Each of the apocalypses has dealt with the duration of this period or some aspect of it in slightly different ways. In 8:14, the desolation of the sanctuary is to last 2,300 mornings and evenings, or just short of 3½ years. In 9:27, Antiochus's activity takes place during the last of the 70 weeks of years, with the cessation of sacrifice and the desecration of the temple lasting half a week. A further gloss on the time until the end occurs in 12:11–12 and is discussed below.

The last part of the verse contains a phrase that has puzzled commentators. Literally, it reads "at the completion of the shattering of the hand [i.e., power] of the holy people these things will be completed." Presumably, it describes the three and a half years as a period of violence similar to how Antiochus "will wear out the holy ones" in 7:25. Recently, Tawil has noted that the Hebrew phrase *nappēṣ yad* ("shatter the hand") has an equivalent in the Akkadian idiom for repudiation of treaty relations, *qāta napāṣu*, "to push back the hand." Thus he suggests the passage in Daniel can be rendered "at the time of the termination of thrusting the hand [i.e., of the covenantal rejection] of the holy people all these things will come to an end" (82). In general, however, Daniel does not construe the suffering of the people as a divine repudiation of the covenant, though it is not impossible that, as with the term "wrath" in 8:19, this is also a conventionalized term for the time of trouble.

[8–10] In contrast to 10:1, which claims that understanding came to Daniel, here he protests that he does not understand. The angel's reply picks up terminology from v. 4, now describing the message itself as mysterious and difficult (Ginsberg 1948, 31). Paul (2004) has identified the phrase as the equivalent of a Mesopotamian scribal technical term, *kakku sakku*, with *kakku* meaning "sealed up" and *sakku* meaning "obscure." In v. 10 the angel gives no additional information, but paraphrases 11:35, though he applies the description to the "many" rather than to the wise. But it is the wise who will understand—presumably the numerical calculation that follows.

[11–12] For the last time the book offers a calculation of the time until the end. Both of the figures offered, 1,290 days and 1,335 days, slightly exceed 3½ years, whether calculated on a lunar or solar calendar. The dates thus appear to be an updating added to the original book of Daniel, added when the expected events did not take place at the end of 3½ years. In fact, the temple was retaken by Judah the Maccabee and purified just three years after the desecration, in December 164 B.C.E. Although Antiochus IV also died in December of 164, it is not known when word of his death reached Jerusalem. Even so, the entire eschatological scenario, with the decisive breaking of the Gentile kingdoms, the deliverance of the people, and the resurrection of the righteous and the wicked had not taken place. Thus the reference to "the one who waits," an allusion to Hab 2:3 ("if it [the vision] seems to tarry, wait for it"; cf. 1QpHab 7.9–12).

But what is the significance of the numbers given? They are not transparently symbolic, and yet numbers in apocalyptic literature are almost always based on some symbolic principle that demonstrates the divine rationality manifest in time (A. Y. Collins 1996, 83). Also, are they successive prophecies, the 1,335 being suggested after 1,290 days had expired without the eschaton? This suggestion, made by Gunkel (350n101), has been widely accepted, though it is not clear why the failed prophecy would be retained. Alternatively, the two numbers could represent two parts of the period corresponding to the final week of years in 9:27, which is divided into two half-week periods (cf. Lebram 137). Although Hartman and DiLella (314) shrug their shoulders and say that the symbolism, "undoubtedly obvious to the biblical writers and their original audiences, eludes today's readers completely," they are on the right track in noting that 1,290 days equals 43 months of 30 days, and 1,335 days equals 44½ such months. What they fail to see is the pattern of what is left over from the original prediction of "a time, (two) times, and half a time," which amounts to 42 months (cf. Rev 11:2–3). What remains is 1 extra month in the first part, and 2½ months in the second part. The length of the delay would have the same numerical pattern as the original prediction—a time, two times, and half a time. This pattern would also account for why the 2 parts of the final period are not presented as of equal duration. The total number of days also lends itself to other symbolic numerical play, which, whether intentional or not, would lend authority to the calculation. The total of the 2 numbers is 2,625. If one calculates by weeks rather than by months, 7 years of 52 weeks of 7 days equals 2,548 days. Subtracting that from 2,625 leaves 77 days, a number of symbolic significance. Truly, one cannot say definitively what the author had in mind. That matters less, however, than the fact that the numbers lend themselves to symbolic patterns that feature prominently in other parts of the book of Daniel. The "outcome of these things" (v. 8) is, as the angel said, "concealed and sealed" (v. 9), but "the wise will understand" (v. 10). The book entrusts the reader with this one last puzzle.

[13] The final verse is the angel's dismissal of Daniel. The "rest" is a euphemism for death, though it may also be an allusion to Isa 57:2, which refers to the reward of the righteous. The term *gôrāl* originally refers to the lot that is cast for making decisions. Here it takes on the nuance of destiny, as in Jer 13:25. In the Dead Sea Scrolls it also comes to refer to those who are "allotted" to God or to Belial (e.g., 1QS 2.2, 5). Daniel's destiny is to be resurrected with the righteous at the end of days.

History of Reception, by Brennan W. Breed

After the End

The final vision in the book of Daniel offers an enigmatic series of images to describe the events that follow the decisive divine intervention that will crush the evil kingdom (12:1–3, 13). Some interpreters have argued that these verses are an allegorical description of the aftermath of the Maccabean revolt. According to Jerome's report, while explaining 12:1–3 Porphyry argues that after

History of Reception

the generals of Antiochus had been slain and Antiochus himself had died in Persia, the people of Israel experienced salvation, even all who had been written down in the book of God, that is, those who defend the law with great bravery. Contrasted with them were those who proved to be transgressors of the law and sided with the party of Antiochus. Then it was . . . that these guardians of the law, who had been, as it were, slumbering in the dust of the earth and were cumbered with a load of afflictions and even hidden away in the tomb of wretchedness, rose up once more from the dust of the earth to a victory unhoped for, and lifted up their heads, rising up to everlasting life. . . . [Porphyry] also adduces the historical account concerning the Maccabees, in which it is said that many Jews under the leadership of Mattathias and Judas Maccabeus fled to the desert and hid in caves and holes in the rocks and came forth again after victory. (Jerome, on 12.1–3)

Several prominent Syriac Christian interpreters, including the ninth-century Syriac Christian exegete Isho'dad of Merv, also followed this allegorical reading, as did medieval Spanish Rabbis Hayyim Galipapa and Joseph Albo (Albo 418). Theodoret of Cyrus, however, along with many Christian interpreters throughout history, argued that Dan 12:1–3 cannot refer to the Maccabean revolt:

Let those who try to apply these things to Antiochus tell us who was resurrected in his day—with some obtaining eternal life and others reaping the fruit of reproach and eternal shame. And if someone should say that the Maccabees are referred to by these words, inasmuch as they went out from the caves, he would incur rather much laughter, for . . . they will say that the Maccabees were themselves both evil and good or that some of them were good and others evil. (Theodoret 317)

The vast majority of interpreters have understood Dan 12:2–3 as a description of the resurrection of the dead. As Rashi tersely comments on Dan 12:2, "the dead will be resurrected" (Gallé 150). And to Raba's question, "From where is resurrection derived?" the fifth-century sage Rabina replied, "From this verse: 'And many of them that sleep in the dust of the earth shall awake'" (*b. Sanh.* 92a). This interpretive trajectory arose early: the first-century C.E. *Testament of Moses*, a Jewish apocalyptic response to Roman authority over Judah, includes an exhortation given by the Levite Taxo to his seven sons during the reign of an evil king that relies upon Danielic imagery: "The Heavenly One will arise from his kingly throne... And God will raise you to the heights; yea, he will fix you firmly in the heaven of the stars, in the place of their habitations, and you will behold from on high" (*T. Mos.* 10:3, 9–10). Daniel 12:2–3 informed New Testament descriptions of resurrection and the final judgment, as well; in Matt 13:43, for example, Jesus finishes a metaphorical depiction of the final judgment with this image: "Then the righteous will shine like the sun in the kingdom of their Father." Daniel's status as a witness to the resurrection may help explain the near ubiquity of images from the book of Daniel, including the stories of Susanna and Bel and the Dragon, in Christian funerary liturgy and art (Spier 9–10; cf. Irenaeus, *Haer.* 5.5.2). And in various Muslim traditions, as well, the description of resurrection in Dan 12:2–3 has left an impact: the Ismaʿilis, a revolutionary Shiʿite sect that emerged in the ninth century, believed that Muhammad bin Ismaʿil bin Jaʿafar, a descendent of Muhammad's cousin ʿAli, would return as the messianic Mahdi "and then preside over the end of the world and the last judgment as the 'Riser of the Resurrection,'" likely drawing from Dan 12:1–3 (Arjomand 390).

Despite widespread agreement over the general referent of Dan 12:1–3, controversy arises, however, over the precise details of the resurrection depicted. In Christian and Jewish circles, the corporeality of Daniel's resurrection became a topic of particular concern because of the astral imagery in v. 3. As Hippolytus, an early commentator on Daniel, argued, "Who are the ones sleeping in 'the tombs of the earth' but the bodies of those people who will receive . . . pure, transparent, and radiant bodies 'like the brilliance of the firmament?' Others will arise 'to the resurrection of judgment,' receiving bodies suitable to everlasting punishment" (*Comm. Dan.* 4.56.2). For fourth-century Christian theologian Cyril of Jerusalem, the resurrected body "will become spiritual, a marvelous thing, beggaring description. 'Then shall the just,' it is said, 'shine forth like the sun'" (*Catech.* 18.18.19). John of Damascus, an eighth-century Syrian theologian, argued against the notion that one's soul entered into sleep at the moment of death and then was revived at the resurrection by using Dan 12: "'Many shall awake' means the resurrection of their bodies, for I do not suppose that anyone would speak of souls sleeping in the dust of the earth. . . . No person of right mind would say that it was the souls that were in the graves" (*Orthodox Faith* 4.27).

Perhaps the most controversial comments on resurrection in the medieval Jewish rabbinic tradition came from Maimonides, who argued that Dan 12:2 was evidence of a thoroughly corporeal resurrection—and that those resurrected bodies, being corporeal, would eventually perish a second time. Many influential medieval rabbinic interpreters, such as Naḥmanides, thoroughly rejected Maimonides' arguments in his *Treatise on Resurrection,* especially the following: "Those people whose souls will return into their bodies [in Dan 12:2] will eat and drink and copulate and give birth and die after a very long life, just like those who will be found [alive] in the days of the Messiah. However, the life after which there is no death is the life of the world to come, in which there is no body, . . . [but] souls without bodies, like the angels" (Patai 206).

Another debate centered on the extent of the resurrection described in Dan 12:1–3. Abraham ibn Ezra (d. 1164), for example, stressed that the word "many" actually means "few," and then suggested a two-stage resurrection not unlike Maimonides' interpretation: "In my opinion the righteous who died in exile will be resurrected when the Redeemer comes. . . . They will then delight in the Leviathan, the Ziz, and the Behemoth and die a second time, to live at the resurrection of the dead when they will be in the world-to-come [in which] they will not eat or drink, but enjoy the radiance of the *Shekhinah*" (Gallé 149–50). The trio Leviathan, Ziz, and Behemoth appear in a rabbinic tradition concerning the primordial chaos monsters who will be served to the righteous during an eschatological feast (cf. *b. B. Bat.* 74b–75a). Saadia Gaon, as well, emphasized the limited nature of the resurrection:

> He does not say *all . . . who sleep . . .* because *all . . .* would include all of humankind, and He made this promise only to Israel. Therefore he says, *many.* . . . Those who awaken will have everlasting life, and those who will not awaken will be for *shame and* for *everlasting abhorrence.* For all the righteous, those who repented, will live; only the unbelieving and those who died without repentance will remain. (Goldwurm 320)

Abrabanel, however, argued that all of humankind will be raised, as that is the only way to fulfill the eschatological predictions involving the nations (cf. Zeph 3:9; Goldwurm 320). Rabbi Hasdai Crescas, a fourteenth-century Jewish leader in Aragon, Spain, suggested that both the righteous and the wicked are resurrected, the former for a beatific afterlife and the latter for their torturous punishment, but the many individuals who are neither righteous nor wicked remain dead (Sarachek 202–3). This notion affected medieval Christian and Jewish pastoral care, as illustrated in the early eleventh-century response of Rabbi Hai Gaon concerning redemption:

> Who will be resurrected? All those in Israel who were completely righteous and those who even though they committed sin made repentance, but those whose iniquities are more numerous than their merits and did not make repentance will not arise during the time of the Messiah, for Scripture states: "many of those who sleep in the dust . . ." This is why our sages have taught: "If someone is ill and approaching death, they say to him: Make confession!" . . . Tell them: "Say—I have sinned, I have erred, and I have transgressed! May death serve as an atonement for my wickedness!" This ensures that all Israel will merit resurrection from the dead. (J. Reeves 140)

In general, Christians argued for the resurrection of all humankind in the end in spite of Dan 12:2 by developing apologetic exegesis. As Augustine wrote, "Nor is there any real contradiction between John's 'all who are in the tomb' [John 5:28] and Daniel's 'many' in place of 'all.' As an illustration of this, notice how, in one place, God said to Abraham, 'I have made you the father of many nations' [Gen 17:5] and in another, 'In your descendants all the nations of the earth shall be blessed' [22:18]" (*Civ.* 20.23).

The precise identity of "those who are wise" and "those who lead many to righteousness" became another point of disagreement. Rashi argued that "the wise" are "those who have occupied themselves with Torah and *mitzvot,*" while the talmudic sages declared that "these are the judges who adjudicate their cases with absolute truth, [while those who make the many righteous] are the collectors of charity and teachers of children" (*b. B. Bat.* 8b). *Lamentations Rabbah* simply claims that "these are the rabbis" (23), while *Leviticus Rabbah* includes all the righteous (30.2). Christians likewise offered a wide variety of potential identifications: Pachomius, the fourth-century Egyptian monastic, argued that "the face of ascetics will shine like the sun" (Pachomius 27), while Jerome (on Dan 12:1–3) focused on teachers, who "shall resemble the very heavens.... For it is not enough to know wisdom unless one also instructs others; and the tongue of instruction that remains silent and edifies no one else can receive no reward for labor accomplished."

The esotericism of Dan 12 has attracted the attention of mystics throughout history. The *Zohar,* a medieval Jewish text that heavily influenced Kabbalah and other traditions of Jewish mysticism, draws its title from Dan 12:3, which uses the root *zhr* twice to describe the luminescence of the wise. Light is an important metaphor for mystics because of its liminal materiality: it does not have many of the properties of ordinary matter such as weight, smell, or the ability to be transported, and it is often used as a visual image to represent learning, spiritual perception, and the insight of wisdom. As the *Zohar* says in its interpretation of Dan 12:3: "'The enlightened will shine'—Who is enlightened? The wise one who contemplates by himself, from himself, words that human beings cannot mouth. 'Will shine like the *zohar* of the sky'—Which sky? The sky of Moses which stands in the center; this *zohar* of his is concealed and not revealed" (Matt 108). For the *Zohar,* the wise are those who learn from the *Zohar* (Horowitz 146).

Daniel 12 has also enchanted many adherents of new religious movements in the twentieth century. For example, the Raëlian Movement, founded in 1974 by Claude Vorilhon in the wake of his alleged encounter with an extraterrestrial being, returns to Dan 12:3 often in their teachings because of its astral and wisdom imagery. Vorilhon, who changed his name to Raël, claims that the extraterrestrial being was named Yahweh and was a representative of the Elohim, who also call themselves "the scientists." Humans, Yahweh told Raël, are cloned from the Elohim—and thus literally made in their image—but humans have developed immoral behaviors in spite of the Elohim's constant assistance (Shuck 246–50). Raël claims that he is the fortieth and last prophet sent by the Elohim to teach humanity about the truth of science and the importance of attaining ever increasing levels of technological sophistication. According to Raël, the Hebrew Bible records many botched attempts by the Elohim to jump-start human technological and scientific achievements; the ark of the covenant, for instance, was actually a nuclear-powered radio that communicated with the Elohim's spacecraft that orbited the earth. Satan, in this understanding, was a skeptic who doubted that humans could ever attain true enlightenment. Among other things, Raël believes in advancing science and technology at all costs: he even proposes political rule by geniuses, or a "Geniocracy." In his book *Intelligent Design: Message from the Designers,* Raël exegetes Dan 12:2–3 as follows:

> The "Last Judgment" will enable great individuals to live again. Those people who have acted positively for humanity and who have truly believed their creators and followed their commandments will be welcomed. . . . On the other hand, all the wicked people will feel shame before their judges. . . . The geniuses will be the most highly esteemed and the most highly rewarded. Those just individuals, who allowed the geniuses to blossom, or the truth to triumph, will also be rewarded. . . . These words will only be understood when humanity has reached a sufficient level of scientific understanding—that is to say, now. (Raël 54)

INDEX OF SOURCES UP TO REFORMATION TIMES

This index follows versification of most English Bibles, with books in NRSV sequence.

ANCIENT NEAR EAST IN GENERAL

Inscriptions, Artifacts 104
Achaemenid 142
ANEP 225
Babylonian 146
Behistun Inscr. 69, 192
Cyrus Cylinder 17, 163
Darius cylinder 199
Esagila (temple, Marduk) 146
"the great tree" 137
Harran Inscr. 128–32, 134, 141
horned crown 225
iconography 104, 137, 225
Ishtar Gate, Babylon 147
Nabonidus Inscr. 9, 66–67, 129
Naqš-i Rustam 192
Neo-Assyrian 44, 43, 137–38
Neo-Babylonian 138
Panamuwa Inscr. 176
Persian 17, 104–5, 134, 146, 261
reliefs, paintings, seals 165
Sefire Stela 234–35
Standard of Ur 167
statue, Darius 17
statues 75–76
Syrian seals 137
weights, Babylon 176

Texts, Various 217–18
Baal myth 221, 234.
  See also Ugaritic

Babylonian Chronicle 39, 163–64
Babylonian school text 106
Canaanite mythology 258.
  See also Baal myth; Ugaritic
Ctesias 80
Dynastic Prophecy 81, 216, 336–37
Egyptian texts 42–43, 362
Enuma Elish 217–18, 221–22
Esarhaddon 170
Gilgamesh Epic 141
I Will Praise. *See Ludlul*
incantation/exorcistic 22
Laws of Hammurabi 106
Ludlul, I Will Praise 12, 193, 195
Mari, King of, letter 42
Marriage of the God Martu 141
Mesopotamian 13, 45, 128, 145, 148, 177, 226
mukallimtu (commentary) on omens 171
Neo-Assyrian 177, 193
Persian 76
Ugaritic 217–18, 226, 229, 264, 362
Urad-Gula to Ashurbanipal 195
Weidner tablets 21

Texts, Collections

ANET
265–67 80
311–12 172
312–15 144
313 101
315 17, 74, 78, 129
315–16 163
317 78
436 (IIIr 68) 195
475 43
560 166
562 134

COS
2:158–60 176
2:315 17, 74, 78, 129, 163

CTU
1.1 III 24 229
1.2. I 24–29 229
1.2 IV 8 219
1.2 IV 9–10 217
1.2 IV 29 219
1.4 IV 24 229
1.6 I 36 229
1.6 I 53–67 264
1.17 VI 49 229

TAD
1.A 4.3, 7–9 71

OLD TESTAMENT

Genesis
1 141, 267
1–2 78
1–3 156
1:2 221
1:3 106
1:5 267
1:21 222
1:26 78
1:28 156
2–3 137, 141

Genesis (*continued*)		41	64, 67, 70, 135, 242	40:9	303
2:7	136	41:1–7	67		
2:9	138	41:8	37, 64, 67–68, 143,	**Leviticus**	
2:19–20	78		171, 236		290
2:21	269	41:10–12	62	6:12	298
3:19	363	41:22	64	9:24	269
3:22	364	41:24	37, 67	18:5	205
6:1–4	139	41:25	64	20:14	232
6:3	136	41:33–36	84	21:9	106, 232
6–8	203	41:37–45	85	25	304
10:4	349	41:38	136	25:8–10	301
10:10	36	41:40–43	193	26	293
11:2	36	41:42	171	26:13–15	293
11:4	139	41:45	47	26:14–45	295
14:1	36, 62	43:34	45	26:15	293
14:9	36	46:3	332	26:18	299–300
14:18–20	135	48:12	269	26:22	297
14:19	112	49:1	73	26:28	299–300
14:22	135	49:17	274	26:29–40	294
14:22–24	366			26:31–33	293
15:1	332	**Exodus**		26:31–35	297
15:7–21	93–94		57, 267	26:32–35	300
15:12	269	1:8	172	26:40	293
15:16	270, 302	3:1–3	112	26:42	293
15:18	330	3:2	230	26:43	293
16:7	112	3:20	271	26:46	293
17:5	371	6:22	46		
18:2	268	7:3	134	**Numbers**	
19:1	298	7:11	37		267
19:24–28	295	7:13	174	14:14	230
19:30–38	357	7:22	37, 174	16:27–33	200
21:33	148, 229	8:7	37	23:19	235, 246
22:18	371	8:18–19	37	24:14	73
24:3	71	9:11	37	24:16	112
24:7	71	13:21–22	230	24:24	337, 349
26:24	332	14:19	112	27:18	136
32:24	268	14:21	221	28:2–8	265
32:25–31	330	14:24	230	28:4	298
33:7	269	15	6, 238	29:38	265
35	14, 39	15:8	221		
36–50	14	15:15	260	**Deuteronomy**	
37	12	15:17	265		288, 293, 301
37–50	39	19:10–16	330	1:7	330
38–50	12	19:15–16	332	2:25	295
38:24	106, 232	19:18	230	4:15–20	229
39	14	24:6–8	295	4:19	263, 295
39:1	62	29:38–42	265	4:27–28	108
39:21	48	29:41	298	4:28	168, 175
40	270	30:11–16	361	4:30	73–74, 295–96, 334
40:1–3	69	30:26	303	6:21	296
40:3–4	62	32:32	336, 361	6:22	134
40:6	143	32:32–33	231, 361	7:9	293
40:12	270	33:18–23	229	7:19	134
40:13	69	34:6–7	295	7:21	293
40:18–19	143	36:4–10	290	8:14	174
40:19	69	36:20–23	290	9:9–10	330

9:26	296	10:10	201	8	197
9:26–29	296	13:6	269, 332	8:13	265
10:17	84, 209	13:6–21	268	8:29	297
12:5	296	13:20	298	8:30	197
13:13	356	13:22	269, 332	8:35	197, 292
17:3	263			8:38	197
17:11	293	**1 Samuel**		8:39	265
17:20	174, 293	1	298	8:42	197
19:15	366	2	6	8:43	265, 297
24:16	201	2:2	77	8:44	197
26:8	134	2:6	362	8:46	294
26:16–17	293	2:6–7	174	8:46–50	206
28:15–68	295	2:27–36	164	8:47	293
28:50	271	2:36	269	8:48	197
29:1	295	8:14	63	8:49	265
29:2–3	134	14:17	286	8:54	197
29:21–27	295	14:39	366	10:1	173, 271
29:23	295	14:45	366	10:4–5	165
30:16	293	15:13–26	164	10:8	43
31:9–13	290	17:26	199	11:3	167
31:18	313	17:34–37	224	11:21	362
31:29	74, 334	20:30–34	45	11:43	362
32:4	77	26:12	269	12:1–20	164
32:8–9	135, 332			12:8	43
32:16–17	356	**2 Samuel**		15:13	172
32:22	232	2:26	286	17:17–24	362
32:39	109, 174, 261	3:8	308	18:39	269
32:40	366	3:20–21	165	19:5	269, 298
33:2	237	3:36	326	19:5–8	112
33:26	219	4:4	308	19:7	269, 298
33:27	229	7:13	297	21:8	303, 365
34:5	295	9:6	269	21:20–24	164, 173
34:11	134	9:9–13	45	22:9	37
		10:10	286	22:19	43, 226, 229, 263
Joshua		11–12	357	22:19–20	229
1:1	295	12:7–12	164	22:19–22	230
1:4	221, 330	12:20	329	22:19–23	142, 164
3:10	199	14:2	329		
5:13–15	263–64, 268	17:8	224	**2 Kings**	
5:14	269, 332–33	19:8	228		39, 231
7:1	232	21:5–9	200	2:24	224
7:6	197	21:8	308	3	357
7:10–26	200	22:14	135	4:32–37	362
8:31	295	22:32	77	5:17–19	108
24:19	127, 136			7:2	171
		1 Kings		7:17	171
Judges			39, 231	7:19	171
5:20	263	1	107, 172	8:31	37
5:20–21	238	1:2	43	9:25	171
6:11	298	1:31	68	10:27	62, 69
6:13	271	2:3	295	11:1–3	172
6:21–22	268	2:10	362	13:7	286
6:22	269, 332	4:3	231	13:21	362
7:4	353	5:2–3	165	14:6	201
8:19	366	6:1	169	15:25	171
8:31	37	6:37	169	16:15	298

2 Kings (continued)		33:10–16	149	10:28	46
17:13	295	33:12	296	**Nehemiah**	
17:13–14	293	34:25	295		71
17:16	263	36	300	1	304, 317
17:22	293	36:6–7	40	1:4	329
17:34	37	36:7	40, 167	1:4–11	292
18:17	37	36:10	40	1:5	293
18:28–35	109	36:18	40, 167	1:7	293
19:4	199	36:22–23	52, 74, 176, 219,	1:11	48
19:5–7	358		289, 298, 328	2:1	48, 107
19:16	199	36:21	291	2:1–2	69, 143
19:35	112	36:23	16, 78	2:1–8	223
21:3	263			2:3	68
22:10	290	**Ezra**		3–5	320
23:11	37		16, 18, 72, 312	3:8	46
23:34	47	1:1	260, 289, 328	3:23	46
24:1	40	1:1–4	52, 176, 219,	5:18	353
24:12	172		223, 298	7:5	361
24:13	40, 167	1:2	71	7:61–65	361
24:15	260	1:2–4	78	7:64	47
24:17	47	1:7–10	40	8:1	295
25	39	1:7–11	167	8:2–8	290
25:4	44	1:8	47	8:4	46
25:8–20	62	2:62	47	9:1	292
25:13–17	40, 167	3:2	47, 295	9:3	197
25:27–29	179	4:4–6	289	9:6	263
25:27–30	48	4:11	134	9:6–37	292
25:29	166	4:13–15	188	9:7	37
25:29–30	45	4:15	231	9:10	134, 296
		4:17	134	9:12	230
1 Chronicles		4:22	188	9:13	293
	39, 71	5:7–8	134	9:17	271, 294
1:7	349	5:12	71	9:19	230
3:10–24	245	5:14	40	9:26	265
7:40	353	5:16	214	9:32	293, 296
8:33–34	308	5:17–6:5	231	9:34	293
9:22	353	6:1–2	196	10:6	46
9:40	308	6:1–12	74, 223	10:29	295
12:38–40	165	6:8–10	72	10:34	265
16:8–36	6	6:10	197		
21:16	298	7:1	46	**Esther**	
23:30	197	7:6	295		4, 12–14, 22, 47, 100,
		7:11–26	74		107, 109, 339
2 Chronicles		7:12	134, 188	1:1	192
	16–17, 39, 71	7:14	193	1:2	260
6:13	197	8:2	46	1:3	260
6:34	197	9:3–4	292	1:8	166
6:37	293	9:4–5	298	1:9	167
6:41–42	6	9:5	197	1:10	37, 166
7:3	269	9:5–15	292	1:12	69, 109
12:7	295	9:6	294	1:14	193
18:1–3	165	9:7	294	1:14–19	260
23:18	295	9:8	296	1:19	196
30:16	295	9:10	296	1:22	134
32:32	302	9:11	293, 295	2:7	47
33:8	293	10:1	293		

2:9	48	8:4	235	105:27	134	
2:15	48	10	201	106:1	6	
2:17	48	16:3	237	106:6	293	
2:19	63	17:3	199	106:8	296	
2:21	63	17:15	199	106:47–48	6	
2:23	231	18:8	230	113:2	72	
3:1–11	107	18:10–12	236	113–18	116	
3:2	63, 85	18:26	353	115:4–7	168, 175	
3:10–14	196	18:31	77	119:160	220	
3:12	134	21:4	364	121:1–5	140	
4–5	14	22:13	195	122:5	228	
4:1–4	292	25:6	71	130:4	294	
4:5	150	33:6	263	132:8–10	6	
4:11	69, 71	33:14	265	132:17	225	
4:16	330	34:9	237	135:9	134	
5:4–8	48	37:35	135	136:2–3	84	
6:1–2	231	40:2	362	139:16	231	
6:1–11	69	44	292	144:3	235	
7:1–2	48	45:9	167	145:13	135	
7:5–10	69	47:2	293	147:16	230	
8:2	85	48	357	147:19–20	293	
8:8	196, 365	50:5	119	148:2	263	
8:8–14	196	51:7	353			
8:9	134, 192	52:8	135	**Proverbs**		
8:10	365	55:17	197	3:18	137	
8:15	171	57:4	195	6:17	226	
9:13–14	200	68:17	231	7:12	286	
10:2	260	68:33	219	7:13	271	
10:2–3	85	69:28	361	10:6	226	
14:17	48	72	139	10:11	226	
		74	292	10:32	226	
Job		74:13–14	222	11:11	226	
	14, 203	75:7	174	15:28	226	
1–2	190	77:3	136	16:9	175	
1:21	72	77:6	136	18:6	226	
3:13	362	78:11	271	19:28	226	
4:13	269	78:32	271	21:4	226	
5:1	237	78:38	302	26:16	62	
7:21	362	79	292	28:15	224	
12:10	175	79:9	297	30:3	237	
12:13	63	79:9–13	296			
14:7	140	88	362	**Ecclesiastes**		
14:12	362	88:5	237, 362	3:16–22	363	
14:20	170	89:7	293	9:3–6	363	
15:15	237	89:9–10	218	10:19	161	
25:6	235	89:10	222			
33	149	92:14	135	**Song of Solomon**		
33:15	269	93	142	6:8	167	
40:11–12	139	95–98	142			
41	222	96:1–13	6	**Isaiah**		
42	190	97:9	135	1	251	
		103:21	263	1:1	302	
Psalms		104:3	219, 236	1:4–6	249	
	18	104:3–4	298	1:9	295	
2	142, 219, 357	104:26	222	1:18	230, 353	
7:17	135	105:1–15	6	2:2	74, 77, 334	

Isaiah (continued)		37:21–29	74, 238	**Jeremiah**	
2:2–6	233	37:22–29	271		22, 39, 41, 106
2:11	226	37:23	226	1:8	332
2:12–17	139	37:23–25	354	1:9	334
4:3	231, 361	39:7	42, 57	1:11	75
5:15	226	40–55	79, 108, 129	1:11–12	177
6	226	40–66	22	1:13	75
6:1–2	229	40:18–20	108	3:19	344
6:2	229, 298	40:1–5	140	3:25	294
6:3	77	40:2	255	4:1–2	296
6:5–7	334	40:3	146	4:7	223
7:7	345	40:6	146	4:27	297
8:7–8	337	40:14	229	5:1	181, 286
8:8	342, 357	40:17	148	5:6	224
8:16	220, 364	40:26	106, 263	6:27–30	353
9:7	146	40:28	229	7:10–11	297
10:5–6	74	41:3	262	7:11	344
10:5–14	271	41:6–7	108	7:20	295
10:7–14	74	41:14–15	77	7:25–26	293
10:8–11	354	41:21–24	108	8:2	263
10:13–14	354	44	6	9:2	20
10:22–23	307, 337	44:6–20	108	10:3–5	164, 168, 175
10:23	309, 355	44:8	77	10:10	199
11:1	138, 140, 246	44:9–20	164, 168, 175	10:23	175
11:6	224	44:24–45:8	223	13:18	172
11:11	36	44:24–45:13	130	13:25	368
13:17	81, 192, 223	44:25–26	45, 70	16:15	294
13:19	295	45	142–43	17:8	135, 260
14	258, 264	45:1–8	18, 52, 79, 176	18:23	302
14:4	264	45:1–9	219	21:4	44
14:4–20	152	45:3	143	22:10–12	40
14:9	260	45:3–5	74	23:3	294
14:12–15	264	45:6	143	23:21–22	142
14:14	112	45:9	148	25:1	39
14:15–20	362	45:12	263	25:1–11	40
14:16–17	152	47:1	44	25:4–5	293
18:4	265	48:10	353	25:9	77
19:1	219	49:22–23	233	25:9–11	18
20:22	296	51:1	77	25:11–12	20, 180, 266,
22:14	302	51:9–10	222		290–91, 299,
24:21	263	51:9–11	221		302, 304
26:14	362–63	52:11	167, 353	25:12	18
26:19	362–64	52:12–53:13	337, 352	25:26	181
26:20	355	52:13	364	26:4	295
27:1	222	53:7–8	290	26:19	296
27:9	302	53:11	364	27	142–43
28:22	355	56:3	37	27–28	77
29:7	72	56:4–5	58	27:5	143
29:10	269	57:2	368	27:5–7	18, 78, 219
29:11–12	365	59:3	47	27:5–8	74, 77
30:8	220	65:6	231	27:6	41
30:10	353–54	66:3–4	364	27:6–7	149
33:11–12	232	66:15–16	232	27:7	18
33:21	366	66:17	364	27:16–22	40
34:12	148	66:24	232, 364	28:1–9	40
37:5–7	358			28:1–11	66

28:14	66, 77–78	**Ezekiel**		21:31	269
29	293	1	4, 22, 258, 265	25	357
29:1	290	1	20, 227, 231	26:7	78
29:10	20, 266, 290–91,	1–3	330	28:1–19	271
	299, 302	1:1	260, 330	28:3	18
29:10–12	304	1:3	44	28:11–19	78
29:10–14	291, 329	1:4	230	29:21	225
29:12	293	1:6–7	331	31	138, 174
29:12–14	297	1:7	229, 331	31:3–5	138
29:19	293	1:13	331	31:4	137
29:21–23	106	1:13–14	230	31:6	139
29:31	290	1:15–21	230	31:10	174
30:2	220	1:16	331	31:11	260
30:6	170	1:24	331	31:11–12	140
30:7	360	1:27	331	31:18	362
32:1	66	1:28–2:2	269, 332	34:17	260
32:10–11	303	2:1	235, 269	36:31	294
32:20–21	134, 296	2:1–2	269	37:1	220
32:23	295	2:3	332	37:1–14	362
32:37	294	3:13	331	37:9–10	115
32:44	303	3:23–24	269	38–39	337
33:17–18	306	6:6	297	38:5–7	358
39:1	39	7:2	269	38:8	272
39:3	228	7:6	269	38:8–13	357
39:9–14	62	7:19	117	38:14	272
42:18	295	7:22	344	38:14–39:20	358
44	293	8–10	330	38:16	334
44:4	293	8–11	239	38:22	232
44:6	295	8:1–3	260	38:23	354
44:15–25	108	8:2	331	39:6	232
44:21	293	8:3	220	40:1–2	220
44:23	295	8:14	355	43:15	309
48:47	334	9:2	230	45:12	176
49:18	235, 295	9:2–3	331	46:13–15	265
49:36	221	9:11	331	47:1	230
49:38	228	10	227		
50:8	260	10:1–8	232	**Daniel**	
50:17	223	10:2	230, 331		2–12, 27, 29–30, 32, 57,
50:40	295	10:5	331		85, 107, 275, 280,
51:11	81, 192, 223	10:9	331		316, 318–19
51:28	81, 223	11:24	220	1	4, 10, 21, 33, 35–58, 66,
51:39	362	12:27	272		107, 109, 149, 151,
51:41	181	13:9	361		165, 194
51:57	362	14:14	18	1–2	101
51:59–64	66	14:20	18	1–4	10, 38–39, 127
52:12–30	62	16:40–41	69	1–6	1, 5–6, 8, 10, 12, 14–16,
52:17–23	167	17:1–8	138		17, 22, 33, 39–41, 52,
52:29	99	17:2	173		63, 74, 78–79, 84, 86,
52:33	166	17:3	223		119, 127, 132, 152, 176,
		17:11–21	74		183, 189, 195, 211, 215,
Lamentations		17:24	139, 143		219, 234, 240, 261, 287,
2:6	269	18:10	344		333, 354
3:10	224	19:2–9	195	1:1–2	106, 270
4:6	295	20:38	353	1:1–7	57
4:21–22	357	21:25	269	1:1–2:4	8
5:18	297	21:29	269	1:1–4:37	33

Index of Sources Up to Reformation Times

Daniel (*continued*)
1:2   36, 78, 152, 166, 173
1:3–5   106
1:4   20–21, 57–58, 296
1:5   21
1:6–10   126
1:7   136, 328
1:8   14
1:8–16   55
1:9   57
1:10   201
1:10–17   3
1:16   54
1:16–20   3
1:17   20, 173, 296, 352
1:17–20   133
1:18–19   66
1:19   57
1:21   8, 38, 79, 179, 201, 325, 328
2   8–11, 13, 17–18, 20, 27, 34, 38–40, 46, 51, 53, 59–97, 102, 107, 112–13, 127, 133, 135–36, 138, 142, 153, 164, 169, 173, 176, 202, 211, 215–16, 218–20, 223–24, 233–34, 236, 242–45, 248, 251–52, 255, 260–61, 270, 273–74, 286, 318–19, 329, 333
2–3   133, 149
2–4   16, 21, 75, 201
2–6   8–9, 30, 38, 148, 215–16
2–7   8
2:1   168
2:2   37, 136, 171
2:2–6   3
2:2–12   171–72
2:3   143, 236
2:4   4, 171–72, 236
2:5   201
2:8–12   145
2:9–11   3
2:12   109, 172, 201
2:16–23   174
2:19–49   3
2:21   174, 240–41, 266
2:21–45   320
2:25–28   172
2:26   46, 134
2:27–30   173
2:28   220, 243, 334
2:30   136
2:31   138
2:31–32   103
2:31–35   135
2:34   139
2:34–35   235, 243, 249, 319
2:35   233, 244
2:37   174, 234
2:37–38   144, 176, 223, 270
2:37–39   177
2:37–40   233, 262
2:38   103, 219
2:39   224
2:40   223, 225, 270
2:44   135, 234, 319
2:44–45   233, 235, 241, 243, 249, 251
2:45   243
2:46–49   52
2:47   113, 132–33, 136
2:48   193
2:48–49   21, 178
3   2, 6, 9–10, 13–15, 33–34, 38–39, 46, 49–50, 54, 97–124, 132, 174, 190, 194, 196, 200, 203–4, 208, 288
3–4   85, 174, 192
3–5   8
3:1–2   3
3:4   134, 174, 234
3:6   232
3:7   174, 234
3:8   200
3:8–10   3
3:8–12   197
3:9   172
3:11   232
3:12   21
3:13   198, 201
3:15   174, 190, 198, 232
3:19   201
3:20–23   232
3:22–30   3
3:23–24   4
3:23–25   3
3:24–27 LXX   121
3:25   168, 200
3:26   135
3:27   232
3:27–28   200
3:28–29   133, 190
3:29   134, 174, 201, 234
3:30   52, 178
4   5, 9, 12–13, 34–35, 38, 46, 51, 64, 124–58, 163, 168, 173–74, 176, 179–80, 208, 223, 242, 286
4–5   39, 215
4–6   2, 4–5, 10, 38, 127
4:1   234
4:1–3   10, 190, 201, 223
4:2   174
4:3   83, 201, 234
4:5   168, 236
4:5–9   3
4:6   4
4:6–7   171
4:7   75, 171
4:8   161, 328
4:8–9   172
4:9   193
4:10   75
4:12   78
4:12–16   3
4:13   237
4:14   78, 247
4:15   238
4:16   174
4:16–17   241
4:17   16, 174, 237
4:18–19   173
4:19   272
4:22   78
4:23   237, 241
4:25   41, 174–75, 241
4:29   78
4:29–30   3
4:29–34   219
4:30   174
4:31   168, 364
4:31–32   241
4:32   174–75, 240
4:32–33   174–75
4:33   175
4:33–34   223
4:34   83, 234, 240–41
4:34–37   161
4:37   174
5   13, 21, 38, 127, 159–86, 259, 286–87
5–6   158, 189
5:2–3   173
5:5–7   3
5:7   193
5:10–12   3
5:10–16   259
5:11   171
5:11–12   9, 127
5:12   46, 134, 136, 328
5:12–14   3
5:14–16   3
5:16   193
5:16–19   3

Index of Sources Up to Reformation Times

5:18	135, 234	7:7–8	273–74, 276, 279, 281	8:20–21	3, 80
5:18–21	127, 176			8:21–22	339
5:18–22	223	7:8	271, 275, 280, 282, 354	8:23	287, 302
5:19–22	3			8:24	237, 355, 366
5:21	135	7:8–11	270	8:25	358
5:23	149	7:9–10	20	8:26	21, 303
5:27	95	7:10	21–22, 336	8:27	19, 143, 285, 287, 298, 302
5:29	193	7:11	3, 273, 354		
5:30	44	7:11–12	262	9	11, 20, 36, 53, 202, 212, 266, 283–320, 326, 328–29, 352
5:30–31	79	7:13–14	275		
5:31	289	7:14	274		
5:31–6:1	189, 191–92	7:15	19, 143	9:1	44, 283–320
6	5–6, 10, 13–16, 21, 38–39, 49–50, 54, 100, 121, 127, 154, 171, 176, 179, 186–210, 215, 223, 289	7:15–23	3	9:2	22, 331
		7:16	229–30	9:4–19	270
		7:18	87	9:12–17	3
		7:20	271, 354	9:13	296
		7:21	275	9:20–27	268
6:3	136	7:21–26	273	9:21	236
6:5	53	7:23	264	9:21–22	330
6:6	172	7:24	274	9:22	296
6:7	285	7:24–26	279	9:23	332
6:8–22	3	7:25	135, 265–67, 309, 311–12, 314, 354, 366–67	9:24–27	273, 320
6:10	292			9:25	296
6:11	298			9:25–26	274
6:11–12	106	7:25–28	3	9:26	275, 281, 347, 349
6:12	260	7:26	262	9:27	20, 267, 275, 351, 367–68
6:17	365	7:26–28	3		
6:21	172	7:27	20, 83, 255	10	20, 260, 365
6:25	134, 234	7:28	4, 19, 169, 272	10–12	11–12, 202, 212, 287, 320–28, 333, 352
6:26	83, 86, 234	8	11–12, 212, 252–83, 299, 302, 318, 327–28, 330, 352, 354		
6:26–27	10, 132			10:1	38, 79, 367
6:27–29	3			10:1–11:2a	328–36
6:28	8, 38, 79	8–9	38, 303	10:3	299
7	8, 10–11, 18–20, 21, 27, 83, 86, 92–93, 211–52, 256, 258–61, 264, 270, 273–74, 278, 280–81, 283, 318–19, 333, 352	8–12	8, 10–12, 19, 22, 38, 200, 216	10:4	28
				10:4–6	366
		8:1	4, 160, 214, 252–83	10:5	230
		8:1–2	331	10:5–6	219, 236, 366
		8:1–5	3	10:5–9	3
		8:1–8	3	10:7–19	19
7–8	20, 202, 279, 286–87, 309	8:2	28, 330	10:8–16	3
		8:4	286, 339, 344, 354–55	10:10	366
7–12	1, 7–8, 18–19, 28–30, 38, 52, 87, 211, 282, 287, 290	8:8	221, 286, 339	10:10–11	319
		8:9–12	239	10:10–14	268
		8:10	231, 238	10:11	53, 298
7:1	19, 21–22, 160, 212–52, 259, 328, 331, 365	8:10–11	354	10:11–16	3
		8:11	351	10:13	231, 236, 263, 268
7:1–6	3	8:13	287, 297, 366	10:14	74
7:2	254, 262	8:13–14	317, 365	10:16	366
7:2–7	270	8:13–16	3, 330	10:16–20	3
7:2–13	75	8:14	302–3, 305, 309, 312–13, 366	10:18	366
7:3–7	262			10:19	298
7:4	155	8:16	236, 298	10:20–21	236, 263, 268, 360
7:4–6	262	8:16–17	3	10:21	3, 21–22, 231, 238, 266, 268, 296, 361, 365
7:5–6	177, 261	8:17–18	19		
7:5–7	3	8:17–19	332	11	6, 20, 26, 266, 283, 318
7:7	82, 264, 267	8:19	74, 352, 355, 367	11:1–2	3

Daniel (continued)		Hosea		Haggai	
11:2b–45	336–59	3:5	334	1:1	192
11:3	261	5:14	261	2:1	192
11:4	221	13:7	224	2:6	311
11:6	83	13:7–8	223		
11:13–16	3	13:8	224	**Zechariah**	
11:13–17	3	22:19	228		258
11:14	302, 334			1–8	217
11:16	254–55, 261	**Joel**		1:8	220
11:17	83	2:3	232	1:8–10	236
11:21	226, 275	3:2	228	1:12	266, 269, 299–300, 304
11:21–31	319	3:12	228	1:12–17	290
11:21–45	273			1:18	75, 225
11:25–29	3	**Amos**		2:1	75, 220
11:27	334	4:11	295	2:1–4	236
11:30–31	26	5:19	224	2:5	220
11:31	267, 297, 308, 315	7:7–9	171	2:6	221
11:32	3	7:8	75	2:7–8	266
11:32–35	360	8:1–2	171, 177	4:1–7	236
11:33	296, 364	8:2	75, 269	4:2	75
11:33–34	298, 307	8:12	365	5:1	75, 220
11:33–35	23, 333, 363	9:11	246	5:9	75, 298
11:33–36	3			5:11	36
11:35	296, 334, 367	**Obadiah**		6:1–8	236
11:36	175, 226, 261,		357	6:1	75, 220
	271, 282, 366	1	302	6:5	221
11:38	3, 286	12	226	9:9	320, 366
11:38–43	299			9:25–26	320
11:39–41	282	**Jonah**		10:3	260
11:40–41	361		203	13:9	353
11:40–45	27, 327–28,	3:6	292	14:2	357
	360			14:5	237
11:40–12:3	276	**Micah**		14:16	233
11:41	254–55	2:6	167		
11:45	281, 283, 360	4:1	74, 334	**Malachi**	
12	4, 27, 360–73	4:1–3	233	1:4	269
12:1	21–22, 231, 236,	4:2	77	1:7	47
	238, 255, 263–64,			1:9	296
	268, 319, 332	**Nahum**		1:12	47
12:2–3	352	1	302	2:6	266
12:3	23, 296, 353, 356	2:10	170	3:2–3	353
12:4	19, 21–22, 220			3:16	231, 336
12:5–6	268, 330	**Habakkuk**		3:16–18	361
12:5–12	20, 27	1:6–8	262	4:4	295
12:6–7	230, 255	1:8	223–24		
12:7	23, 309, 311, 354	1:12	77	**OT APOCRYPHA**	
12:7–12	23	2:2	220, 302		
12:8	74	2:2–3	334	**Tobit**	
12:8–12	23	2:3	269, 318, 337, 367		12, 14
12:9	220, 303	3:12	269	1–2	100
12:10	3, 23, 296,			1:10–11	48
	329, 353	**Zephaniah**		1:17–18	14
12:11	23, 267, 297,	1:5	263	3:1–6	292
	309, 315	2:9	295	3:11	197
12:11–12	312–13	3:8	269	4:5–10	145
12:12	309, 312	3:9	371	12:6–10	145

Index of Sources Up to Reformation Times

12:15–17	334	1:1	349	3:22–30	239
14:4	80	1:1–4	240	4	25
		1:2–4	262	4:7	47
Judith		1:11	109, 307	4:7–10	306
	12	1:16	347	4:18–20	25, 109
1:6	62	1:16–40	257	4:23–24	26
8:6	330	1:20–21	349	4:23–32	306
9:1	197, 298	1:20–23	306	4:25–32	26
12:1–4	48	1:20–24	239	4:33–34	306
		1:20–30	272	4:39–42	26, 306
Additions to Esther		1:24	226	4:43–50	26
	6, 228	1:29	351	5	257
		1:29–30	272	5:5	26
Sirach		1:30–32	351	5:5–7	306
3:30	145	1:33–40	306	5:6–10	350
8:18	71	1:36	351	5:8–10	307
13:2–3	75	1:39	265	5:11	26
14:16–17	363	1:41–64	257	5:11–21	349
17:17	332	1:43	356	5:11–26	306
18:1	148	1:44–50	308	5:24	351
40:29	177	1:44–61	355	5:25–26	351
41:4	363	1:45	240, 265	6	257
42:17	237	1:45–46	255	6–7	15, 194, 352
43:6	269	1:54	267, 308, 351	6:1–11	308, 355
44–50	52	1:54–59	11	6:2	308, 355
45:2	237	1:59	265, 267	6:3–6	351
45:14	265	1:62–63	48	6:4–5	255
50:1–24	305	1:64	270	6:5	265, 308
		2:17–18	356	6:6	240
Baruch		2:18	351	6:14–15	270
1:15–3:8	292	2:23	356	7	109
		2:42	352	7:11	144
Epistle of Jeremiah		2:59	106	7:18	119
	6, 164, 168, 175	2:19–26	352	7:38	352
		2:29–38	352	9	149
Prayer of Azariah		2:59–60	14, 52	9:1–20	359
	4, 6, 100, 114,	3:18–19	144	9:10	264
	121, 288, 292	3:27–31	347	9:17	84
9	114	3:45	265	10	265
17	114	4:36–61	303	10:1–8	303
23–27	115	4:38	265, 297	10:2	265
66	114	4:43	308		
		4:46–61	11	**1 Esdras**	
Song of the Three		4:52–54	267	2:3	112
	4, 6, 100, 114, 288	4:60	326	3	12
		6	149	3:2	192
Susanna		6:1–13	359	3:6–7	171
	2, 4–6, 54, 203–4, 369	6:7	326	3:9	192–93
		8:5	349	3:17–24	50, 166
Bel and the Dragon				4:29–31	167
	2, 4–6, 10, 14, 168,	**2 Maccabees**		4:42	48
	170, 200, 207–8, 369		25–26, 239, 352	4:58	197, 292
		1:14–16	359		
1 Maccabees		1:16	69	**Prayer of Manasseh**	
	26	3	25–26, 346		149
1	27				

3 Maccabees

	190
1	342
2:1–10	292

2 Esdras
See OT Pseudepigrapha, 4 Ezra

4 Maccabees

8–13	109
13:9	119, 202
16:3	119, 202
16:19	119
16:21	202
18:12–14	202

OT PSEUDEPIGRAPHA

Ahiqar

	12–14, 64, 100, 148, 190, 271
2:28–3:39	109
3:32–33	69
7:97	63

Apocalypse of Abraham

10:2	269

Apocalypse of Moses

	18

Apocalypse of Zephaniah

9:1–3	361

Ascension of Isaiah

2:7–11	330

Assumption of Moses
See Testament of Moses

2 Baruch

5:6–7	330
13:1	147
22:1	147
39	86

3 Baruch

11–16	333
11:4	333

1 Enoch

	1, 18, 22
1–36	18–19, 22, 45, 258, 268, 332–33
1:2	365
9:1	268, 333
10	263
10–16	139
10:9	139
10:11–12	300
10:11–15	333
12:2	237
12:3	139
13:10	139
14	227
14:8	220
14:14	269
14:18–23	218–19, 227
14:19	230
14:20	230
14:22	229
14:23	229, 237
14:24	269
17–19	263
18:11	233
20	268
20:1	140
20:5	333
21:7	233
22	363
22:6	139
24–25	333
27–71	245
38:4–5	237
39:12–13	140
45:3	229
47:3	336
60:1–2	227
62:3	229
62:5	229
71:2	248
71:7	140
72–82	22, 45, 258
81:1–4	336
81:6	220
82:1	220
83–90	19, 302–3, 358
89	231
89:40	344–45
89:59	300
89:59–72	270
89:61–64	336
89:73–77	305
90	232
90:5	302
90:6–12	352
90:17	336
90:20	219, 227–28, 231, 336, 344–45
90:24–27	233
90:30	233
90:37–38	233
91:9	232
91:11–17	225
93:1–3	231
93:1–10	225
93:2	139, 336
93:9	305
98:7–8	336
100:5	237
100:9	232
102:1	232
103:2	231
104:2–6	364

2 Enoch

22:6–9	333
33:10	333

3 Enoch

	230

4 Ezra

	18, 245
4:36–37	270
5:13	330
6:20	336
10:29–30	269
11–12	86
11:32–12:2	275–76
12:11–12	86
12:30–33	275–76
13	80
13:6–7	83
14:42	220
14:45–46	365

Joseph and Aseneth

7:1	48
15:4	361

Jubilees

	301, 336, 363
4:15	139
4:22	139
5:12–19	231
7:21	139
10:5	139
16:29	231
17:11	237
18:9	361
22:16	48
23:31	363
23:32	231
30:22	361

Letter of Aristeas

180–86	48

Liber antiquitatum biblicarum			12:18–23	363	Hebrews	
			13	273	11:33–38	121
6		190	13:14	273, 315		
			13:26	245	1 John	
Pseudo-Ezekiel			14:62	245	2:18	273
		362–63			2:22	273
			Luke		4:3	273
Sibylline Oracles			1:10	298		
2:15		225	1:11	268	2 John	
4		81	1:19	268		275
4:49–101		80	1:26	268	7	273
			2:9	268		
Testament of Abraham			3:22	147	3 John	
20		333	10:20	231		275
			15:18	144		
Testament of Dan			18:11	197	Jude	
6:1–5		361	18:13	197	9	333
			20:18	83		
Testament of Joseph			21:24	319–20	Revelation	
2:3		48	22:41	197		275, 280, 316, 318
					1:7	245, 249
			John		1:13–16	331
Testament of Levi			3:27	144	1:17	269
3:3		237	5:28	371	3:5	361
5:6–7		361			4	227
16:1		300	Acts		4–10	319
Testament of Moses			5:19	268	4:2–4	228
1:16		220	8:26	268	4:4	229
3		297	8:26–40	290	5	231
4:2–6		297–98	9:7	331	5:1–5	365
9:1–7		352	9:40	197	6:10–11	270
10:3		369	12:7	268	7:3–8	319
10:9		364	16:17	112	10:4	319
10:9–10		369	22:9	331	10:10–11	319
			23:6–8	363	11:2	315
NEW TESTAMENT					11:2–3	368
			1 Corinthians		11:3	315
Matthew			12:12–27	244	12–13	273
3:12		232	14:33	237	12:1	96
3:17		147			12:4	264
6:5		197	Ephesians		12:6	315
13:42		232	6:12–17	319	12:7–9	333
13:43		369			12:14	315
19:28		229	Philippians		13:1–10	86
21:1–7		366	1:1	237	13:3	317
21:1–11		320	4:3	361	13:5	315
21:25		144			13:7–8	116
24:15		53, 273	1 Thessalonians		13:8	361
26:39		197	1:7–10	320	13:14–15	116
28:3		230			13:14–17	319
			2 Thessalonians		17:8	361
Mark				275	19:11–21	320
1:11		147	2	278	20:12	361
9:2		230	2:1–12	273–74	21:5	220
9:43		232	2:3–4	315	21:27	361
9:47–48		232	2:3–12	273	22:19	361
11:25		197	2:6–7	276		

DEAD SEA SCROLLS

Qumran pesharim 270

Ages of Creation (4Q181)
frg. 1 2.4 237
frg. 2 3 300

Amram (4Q546)
22.1 139

Apocryphon of Jeremiah
4Q387[b] frg. 2 2 301
4Q390 frg. 1 301

Apocryphon of Joshua (4Q379)
frg. 12 301

Apostrophe to Zion (11Q5)
22.13 302

Aramaic Levi Document
4Q213–14 22

Book of Noah (1Q19)
frg. 2 4 268

Book of Giants
4Q203, 532 139
4Q530 219, 227–30
4Q530 2.16 227

Damascus Document (CD)
1.5–12 269–70
2.18 139
6.11 334
13.8 63
16.5 295
20.19 336

Daniel
1Q71–72 3–4
4Q112 3, 37–38, 63, 82, 99, 254
4Q112–13 4
4Q113 3, 189, 254
4Q114 3, 325–26, 335
4Q115 3–4
4Q116 3
pap6Q7 3, 325

Deuteronomy[j]
4Q37 332

Florilegium
4Q174 3

Four Kingdoms
4Q552–53 3

1QGenesis Apocryphon (1Q20)
2.1 139, 237
2.10 214
2.16 139
6.9–10 301
6.13 139
7.2 139
21.2 229
21.13 235
22.2 214

Genesis Commentary (4Q252)
1.2 301

Habakkuk Pesher (1QpHab)
2.5–6 334
2.12 349
2.14 349
3.4 349
3.9 349
4.5 349
4.10 349
7.5–14 349
7.7–8 334
7.9–12 367

Historical Text A
4Q248 349

Hymnic Compositions (1Q36)
1 237

Instruction
1Q26 336
4Q415–18, 423 329
4Q416 frg. 2 3.18 336
4Q417 frg. 1 1.8–9 329
4Q423 329

Isaiah Pesher[d] **(4Q161)**
frgs. 8–10 3.18 334
frgs. 8–10 3.5–8 349

Jeremiah (4Q71)
4QJer[b] 291

Melchizedek (11Q13)
219, 333, 361
1.9 237
2.7 225
2.18–21 301

Mysteries (4Q300)
frg. 1 2.1–6 303

Nahum (4Q169)
1.3 349
frgs. 3–4 2.2 334

Prayer of Nabonidus
4Q242 3, 9, 12, 128, 130, 132, 164, 168

Proto-Esther
4Q550 12

Pseudo-Daniel[a–c]
4Q243–44 3
4Q245 3

Pseudo-Ezekiel
4Q385 362

Reworked Pentateuch
4Q365 6

Rule of the Community (1QS)
1.1 (1QS[a]) 334
1.5 (1QS[b]) 237
2.2 368
2.5 368
3.13–16 349
3.13–4.26 264, 266
3.18–19 266
3.20 333
3.23 264
3.26–4.1 266
4.7 364
4.25–26 269
5.8 295
5.26 (1QS[b]) 238
6.6–8 290
8.22 295
9.1 63
9.12–14 349
11.7–8 237

Songs of the Sabbath Sacrifice
4Q400–407 219, 247

Index of Sources Up to Reformation Times

4Q405 frg. 15 2	230
4Q405 frg. 16 2–3	230
4Q405 frg. 20 2	227
4Q405 frg. 22 10	230
11Q17	219
Mas1k	219

Targum of Job (11Q10)
9.9	235
26.2–3	235

Thanksgiving Hymns (1QH)
3.21–22	237
7.16	269
9.17–22	349
9.26	269
10.35	237
11.22–23	242
16.8	260
16.11	260
26.14–15	84

War Scroll (1QM)
	263, 333–34
1.1–2	357
1.1–10	276
1.10–13	239
1.16	237
9.8	47
9.16	268
10.11–12	237
12.1	237
12.4	237
12.7	237
12.8	242
15.14	237
17.6–7	333
17.7–8	236, 242
4Q285 frg. 1 3	268
4Q491 frg. 11 1.12	229

Words of the Heavenly Luminaries (4Q504)
19.13–15	361

RABBINIC WORKS

Mishnah

ʿAbodah Zarah
2.3	48
4.8–12	48
5.1–12	48

ʾAbot
1.3	144
2.12	144

Berakot
5.1	197

ʿEduyyot
3.3	176

Ḥagigah
2.1	330–31

Babylonian Talmud

ʿAbodah Zarah
2b	93
9a	312
36a	54

Baba Batra
4a	150
8b	371
10a	154
14b	53
60b	54
74b–75a	371

Berakot
31a	206–7
34b	206

Giṭṭin
56b	281

Ḥagigah 14a | 247 |

Megillah
3a	53
11a	93
11b	180

Pesaḥim
6b	180
118a	116

Qidduŝin
72a	93

Sanhedrin
22a	181
38a	247
92a	369
93a	114
93a–b	53, 58
93b	42, 57–58
96b	246
97b	311–12
98a	245
110b	119

Šebiʿit
20	93

Taʿanit
18b	115
21b	176

Yoma
10a	93
69d	209–10
77a	93

Jerusalem Talmud

Šabbat
1.3d	54
1.4	54

Tosefta

Soṭah
13.3	147

Targumic Texts

Targum Onqelos | 174, 178 |

See also Dead Sea Scrolls, *Targum of Job* (11Q10)

Other Rabbinic Works

ʾAggadat Bereŝit
23.1	245

Genesis Rabbah
34.9	119
65.21	229
85.2	179–80

Exodus Rabbah
35.5	93

Lamentations Rabbah
1.16	119
23	371

Index of Sources Up to Reformation Times

Leviticus Rabbah
13.5   93, 155
30.2   371
33.6   116

Mekilta
    152

Mekilta de-Rabbi Ishmael
    152
Bahodesh 5, Shirta 4   247

Mekilta R. Simeon b. Yohai
Bashalah 15   247

Midrash Ruth
    313

Midrash Psalms
21.5   243
114.5   120

Numbers Rabbah
13.14   245

Pesiqta de Rab Kahana
Piska 21.100b   247

Pesiqta Rabbati
4   53
35   120

Pirqe Rabbi Eliezer
28   93–94

Qohelet Rabbah
2.2   53

Seder 'Olam Rabbah
28   180

Semahot
8.15   115

Sipra
9.5   115

Song Rabbah
4   58
5.1   114
7.13   120
7.14   115

Tanhuma
Mishpatim 4   150

Toledot 20   245–46
Vayera 17   154

RABBIS CITED
Akiba   154, 247, 311
Eleazar   155
Hanan ben Talifa   312
Jonathan   311
Kattina   311–12
Maharsha   150
Meir   154
Nahman   155, 180, 246
Rab   311
Raba   369
rabbis on Dan 4   149
Rabina   369
Rav   93, 181
Rava   180
Shmuel the Small   181
Yosi the Galilean   247

LATER JEWISH SOURCES

AUTHORS, TRADITIONS, ARTIFACTS
Abbahu   246
Abraham bar Hiyya   314
Abraham ibn Ezra   182, 247, 282, 370–71
Alshich   182, 205, 246, 312, 314
Aramaic incantation bowl   123
Benjamin of Tuleda   28–30
Blois execution accounts   120–21
Daniel al-Qumisi   94
Elephantine papyri   108, 176
frescoes at Rome   203
Hai Gaon   371
Hasdai Crescas   371
Hayyim Galipapa   244, 369
iconography,   202
Isaac bar Shalom,
    piyyut   121
Joseph Albo   244, 369
Judah HaLevi, poem   95
Kimchi   256
magic spells   54
Malbim   113–14, 247, 282
medieval apocalypses   280
mosaic, Susiya   203
Na'aran mosaic   202–3
Pseudo-Saadia   247, 282
rabbis, later   281
Rashi   93, 182, 189, 207–8, 246, 256, 281–82, 312, 369, 371
Saadia(h) Gaon   116–17, 224, 312, 314, 371
Sambari   95
synagogue floor   116
tomb of Daniel in Susa   260
Torah shrine,
    En Samsam   203
Zohar commentaries   371

AUTHORS WITH TITLES

ABRABANEL, ISAAC BEN JUDAH
Commentaries on the Prophets
    154, 281–82, 314, 371

ANONYMOUS
Vision of Daniel
    117

GERSONIDES
    314
Commentary on Daniel
1.5   54

IBN EZRA
    189, 246–47, 282, 285
Commentary on Daniel
1.5   54

JOSEPHUS
    178, 180
Against Apion
1.134–41   146
1.151–53   163

Jewish Antiquities
4.137   54
8.143   173
8.143–49   271
10.186   57
10.188   42
10.195   68
10.202   71
10.206–10   80
10.210   86
10.237   172
10.242   155
10.243–44   161, 175
10.248–49   191–92

Index of Sources Up to Reformation Times

10.257–58	202, 208	**Naḥmanides**		**Diodorus Siculus**	
10.264	260		313–14, 370	*Historical Library*	
10.266	119	*Commentary on Genesis*		2.1–34	80
10.266–68	53	18.1	53	2.29.2–3	44
10.268	311			17.30	196
10.269–72	28	**Rambam**		17.112–14	45
10.276	86, 270	*Hilchot Tefillah*		frg. 21	45
11.326–39	23	1.5	206–7		
11.329–39	84	5.6	206	**Dionysius of**	
12.136	343–44			**Halicarnassus**	
12.138–44	24	**Tobia ben Elieser**		*Roman Antiquities*	
12.138–46	344	*Midrash Leqah Tov*		1.2.2–4	80
12.154	345		281		
12.160–85	24			**Herodotus**	
12.196–219	24	**Wiszniewitz, David**			13
12.239	47	**Aharon, Elijah ben**		*Histories*	
12.242	347	**Solomon, and Rabbah bar**		1.86	106
12.246–47	349	**Bar Ḥana**		1.95	80
12.253	308	*Midrash ʿAseret*		1.107–8	67, 135
12.294	347	*ha-Shevatim*		1.120	70
13.282	147		280–81	1.128	70
14	363			1.178–82	99
14.429–30	109	**GRECO-ROMAN**		1.178–86	146
16	363	**SOURCES**		1.183	103
18	363			1.185–87	172
18.55–59	115	**Authors, Traditions,**		1.185–88	181
18.263–67	115	**Artifacts**		1.190–91	163
		Abydenus	146	1.191	164
Jewish War		Amelius Sura	80	3.20	171
1.312–13	109	Antiochus, coins	240, 264,	3.89	192
2.154	363		354	3.120	85
2.163	363	Babylonian Diadochi		5.18	166–67
2.165	363	Chronicle	216		
		Berossus	146, 163–64, 180	**Hesiod**	
The Life		coin for Apollo	355	*Works and Days*	
3.14	48	coin for Zeus Olympios	355	1.109–201	76
13–14	54	Greco-Roman art	52		
		Greek historians	67	**Livy**	
Maimonides		Megasthenes	146	*History of Rome*	
	314	Quintus Curtius 5.1	166	41.20	347
Epistle to Yemen		Teucer of Babylon	261		
	246, 282			**Macrobius**	
		Authors with Titles		*Saturnalia*	
Guide for the Perplexed		**Aelian**		7	167
2.45	53	*Varia historia*			
		12.1	166	**Plutarch**	
Treatise on Resurrection 370				*Convivial Questions*	
		Appian			167
Mayenei HaYeshua		*Roman History*			
Commentary on Daniel		Pref. 9	80	**Polybius**	
6.4	154				343–44
		Athenaeus		*Histories, The*	
Menasseh ben Israel		*Deipnosophistae*		26.10	347
De termino vitae		4.144a	166	28.20	348
	181–83	4.145b–c	166	29.27.1–8	350

Histories, The (continued)
30.25–26 355
31.9 359
38.22 80

PORPHYRY
Against the Christians
6–7, 85, 180, 226, 243,
275, 348, 353, 358,
368–69

TACITUS
Histories
5.8–9 80

XENOPHON
180

Anabasis
1.2.27 171
1.5.8 171
8.29 171

Cyropaedia
2.4.6 171
5.1–36 163
5.2.28 167
7.5.15 164
7.5.24–30 178
7.5.25 164
7.5.29–30 164
8.1.6 85
8.5.15 171

POSTBIBLICAL CHRISTIAN SOURCES

AUTHORS, TRADITIONS, ARTIFACTS
Adso of Montier-en-Der 89
African-American
 spiritual 209
Alvarus, Paulus 280
Amalarius of Metz 249
amulet, Constantinople 204–6
Apollinarius 316
art and artifacts 203
Aspinwall, William 278
Beatus tradition, illuminated.
 See below, Authors with
 Titles, Beatus of Liébana
Bellarmino, Roberto 278
bowl, Montenegro 204
Brute, Walter 316
Bullinger, Heinrich 155
Carion, Johannes 89
cathedral in Laon 204

Celtis/Celtes, Conrad 89
Charles VI, king,
 France 152–53
Chrétien de Troyes 89
church, Abbey, Beaulieu-
 sur-Dordogne 248
church decorations,
 Nubia 122–23
church, St. Gabriel,
 Provence 204
Chytreus, David 316
Commendatio
 Animae 122, 204
Commodian 275
Cornelius à Lapide 244
Cosmas Indicopluestes 251
Cromwell speech 245
Eberhard, Archbishop 277
English millenarians 317
Fraticelli 278
frescoes 121–23, 203, 248
Froissart, Jean 153
George III, king, UK 153
Giovanni Diodati 155
Gonçalo Anes Bandarra 90
Gregory the Illuminator 151
Gregory VII,
 Pope 151, 244, 277
Guibert of Nogent 277
Henry IV's penitence 151
Hooker, Thomas 91
Hugh of St. Victor 249
Hugo Grotius 90
Huguenot nonviolence 208–9
Hus, John 278
iconography 122, 202–4,
 208, 248–49
illuminated MSS 31, 58, 96,
 183, 186, 204,
 248–50, 291
Isho'dad of Merv 275, 369
Jean de Roquetaillade 89
Joachim de Fiore 277, 316
John Chrysostom 58, 154
Justinian laws 202, 317
Leander of Seville 55
Leo III, Pope 88
liturgical poetry,
 Byzantine 248
magic spells/texts 54, 123
Maldonado, Juan 278
Mark the Deacon 54
martyr legends 15
Mayer, John 154–55
Milescu, Nicolae 93
Missal, Stammheim 204

mosaics 203, 122
Newton, Isaac 317
Otto von Freising 244
Pablo Christiani, Friar 313
Pachomius 371
Pannonia casket 203
Paul of Tella 4
Peshitta of Daniel 71, 85,
 110, 161, 243,
 255, 275, 303
Peter Chrysologus 207
Peter of Blois 249
Philothetus of Pskov 92
Phocas's decree 317
Polychronius 275
Puritans 245, 278
Rainer of Viterbo,
 Cardinal 277
Ribera, Francisco 278
Richard of Bury 89
Salimbene de Adam 311
Sanchez, Miguel 96–97
sarcophagi 203
Sextus Julius Africanus 316
shrine, three youths,
 Theophilus 122
Sleidanus, Johannes 89
Sophronius 280
Stifel, Michael 316
Symeon Metaphrastes 58
Syriac Christians 85
Theodore bar Koni 244
Theophanes the
 Chronicler 280
Theophylatikos of Ohrid 58
Tyconius 275, 316
Urban II, Pope 118, 277
Vieira, António 90–91
Voltaire 317
Waldensians 278
Willem Hessels van Est 278
Wycliffe, John 278

APOSTOLIC FATHERS
1 Clement
45.6–7 121

Didache
16.3–4 274
16.8 248

Epistle of Barnabas
4.1–5 274

Martyrdom of Polycarp
14.1–2 121

Index of Sources Up to Reformation Times

AUTHORS WITH TITLES

ADAM OF BREMEN
Deeds of Bishops 88

AMALARIUS OF METZ
Liber ordine
8.7 251

AMBROSIASTER
Commentary on Paul's Epistles
3.240 276

ANONYMOUS, ARMENIAN
History of the Armenians 151

ANONYMOUS, BELGIAN MS
"Typological Scenes from the Life of Jesus" 186

ANONYMOUS, BYZANTINE
Visions of Daniel 92

ANONYMOUS, COPTIC
Fourteenth Vision of Daniel 249

ANONYMOUS, DONATIST
Liber Genealogus 276

ANONYMOUS, GREEK
Lunationes Danielis 310

Somniale Danielis 310

ANONYMOUS, MIDDLE ENGLISH
"Cleanness" (poem) 156, 186

ANONYMOUS, PTOLEMAIC
"Daniel's Dream Map" 90–91

ANONYMOUS, SYRIAC
Cave of Treasures 310

Gospel of the Twelve Apostles 93

Letter to the Mountaineers 156

Malḥamat Dāniyāl 53–54, 310

Pseudo-Methodius 92, 280

Vita Danielis 156

ANTIONE DE CHANDIEU
Tragi-comedie 117

APHRAHAT 152, 275
Demonstrations
5.20–21 243
21.18 204

ATHANASIUS
History of the Arians
67 276
77 276

AUGUSTINE 277–80
City of God
18.34 53
20 316
20.23 87–88, 371

Ennarations on the Psalms
42.4 244
98.14 244

Epistles
93 116
93.3.9 150–51

Nature and Grace
42 53

Tractates on 1 John
3.4–10 275
7.2 275

Tractates on the Gospel of John
1.12 249

BEATUS OF LIÉBANA
Commentary on Daniel 183

Commentary on Revelation 248–50

Las Huelgas Beatus
Morgan Library 248–50

BOULAESE, JEAN
history chart 90

BROUSSON
Apology for the Project of the French Reformed 209

CALVIN, JOHN 89
Commentary on Daniel
118, 152, 208, 278

Institutes
3.3 207

CHAUCER
Canterbury Tales
Monk's Tale 58

CLEMENT OF ALEXANDRIA
Paedagogus
3.16.4 247–48

Stromata
1.122.4 53
1.125–26 315

CYPRIAN
Testimonies against the Jews
2.26 249

Works and Almsgiving
5 154

CYRIL OF CONSTANTINOPLE
"Cyrillic Prophecy" 89

CYRIL OF JERUSALEM
Cateches
1.8 249
2.17–19 155
10.4 248
15.12 87
18.18.19 370

EPHREM THE SYRIAN
155, 243–44, 275
Hymns against Julian
1.18–20   87

Hymns on Paradise
155–56

EUSEBIUS
276, 280
Demonstration of the Gospel
25   87

Life of Constantine
75   87

Preparation for the Gospel
9.41.6   146

FAUST, LORENZ
Anatomia statue Danielis
90, 95–96

GREGORY OF NAZIANZUS
Oration in Praise of Basil the Great
1.5   122

GREGORY THE GREAT
275
Moralia in Job
277

GUIARD DES MOULINS
Bible Historiale
58

HANDEL
Belshazzar
181

HIPPOLYTUS
Against the Heresy of Noetus
4   251

Christ and Antichrist
6   274
25   274
25–28   274
43   315–16

Commentary on Daniel
1.28.5   53
2.4   315
2.15   103
3.4.1–4   150
3.7   143–44
4.3–4   86
4.4–24   274
4.8   86
4.10   86
4.35   315–16
4.54   275
4.56.2   370

Refutation of all Heresies
5.26.2   274

HONORIUS OF AUTUN
Speculum ecclesiae
204

IRENAEUS
Against Heresies
3.19.2   248
4.33.1   248
5.5.2   122, 371
5.25.1–2   273
5.25–30   274
5.26   83
5.26.1   86
5.26.2   249

JEROME
4, 6, 58, 68, 80, 83–84, 87–88, 141, 143, 155, 161, 172, 175, 180, 191–92, 205–7, 243, 248, 268, 270, 273, 276, 315, 316, 341, 343–45, 348, 353, 355, 358–59, 368–69, 372
Against Jovian
1.25   58

Commentary on Daniel
illuminated copy   248
1:13, on   58
2:3   68
2:40   83
2:31–40   80, 87
4:15   141
4:19   143
5:1   180
5:10   180
5:26–28   161, 175–76
6:1   191–92
6:10   206–7
6:11   205
7:4–8   87
7:17   243
7:25   276
9:24–27   315–16
11:6   341
11:14   343
11:15–16   344
11:17   345
11:25–26   348
11:27   348
11:34   353
11:44–45   358–59
11:45   276–77
12:1–3   368–69, 371
12:11–12   316

Commentary on Matthew
4.24.15   273

GOWER, JOHN
"Confessio Amantis"   156

JOHN OF DAMASCUS
Orthodox Faith
4.27   370

JUSTIN MARTYR
First Apology
51.9   248

Dialogue with Trypho
14.8   248
31.1   248
32.3   315
32.3–4   274
76   249
110.2   274

KONRAD VON MEGENBERG
Lament
89

LACTANTIUS
The Divine Institutes
7.16   87

Epitome of the Divine Institutes
4.21   249

LUTHER, MARTIN
89–90, 152, 251, 278, 280, 317
Army Sermon against the Turks
280

Index of Sources Up to Reformation Times   395

MICHELANGELO
Last Judgment
fresco, Sistine Chapel   248

MONOPHYSITES
Doctrine of Jacob Recently Baptized
    93, 281

ISKANDER, NESTOR
Tale of the Taking of Tsargrad
    92

MÜNTZER, THOMAS
Letter to Frederick the Wise
    244

"Sermon to Princes"
    244–45

NOTKER BALBULUS
Deeds of Charlemagne
    88

ORIGEN
    180
Against Celsus
2.50   275

Commentary on Matthew
24   275
24.14–18   315

Commentary on Romans
4.10   122
6.9   53

OTTO OF FREISING
Chronica
    88

REMBRANDT
Belshazzar's Feast
    169, 181–82

RUBENS, PETER PAUL
Daniel in the Lions' Den
    200

SWIFT, JONATHAN
"The Run upon the Bankers"
    184–85

TERTULLIAN
Against Marcion
3.7.4   248
4.10.9   249

Against the Jews
8   315

Apology
32   276

Fasting, against the Psychics
9   54

Idolatry
15   116

Repentance
12.7–8   155

THEODORET OF CYRUS
Commentary on Daniel
    53, 180, 208, 369

THOMAS AQUINAS
Summa theologiae
    151

VICTORINUS OF PETTAU
Commentary on the Apocalypse
17.9   87

MUSLIM SOURCES

AUTHORS, TRADITIONS, ARTIFACTS
ʾAbu Allah ibn ʾAbbas   251
Abu Nasr Mutahhar
   ibn Tahir   252
al-Biruni   313
al-Tabarī   208
apocalyptists   53–54, 280, 282–83, 310

chroniclers   30–31
Great Mosque, Cordoba   183
Ibn Hazm   251
Ibn Qutayba   251
interpreters   252
Islamic formula   183
magic spells   54
miniature, Jamasp
   and Gabriel   31–32
Muhammad Abūʾl-Qāsim
   Ibn Ḥawqal   30–31
Muhammad ibn Jarir
   al-Tabarī   151–52
Najm al-Dīn al-Ṭūfī   251
Nawas bin Saʿman   282
Qurʾan   53, 251
scholars   251–52
Yemeni MS on
   Armilus   280–81

AUTHORS WITH TITLES

ANONYMOUS
One Thousand and One Nights
"Queen of the Serpents"   31

Baghdad book on "tricks and stratagems"
    310–11

Malḥamat Dāniyāl
    53–54, 310

Tafsir
10.115   251

ISMAIL IBN KATHĪR
Stories of the Prophets
    208

MUSA (OTTOMAN POET)
Book of Jamasp
    31

NUʾAYM BIN HAMMAD
Kitāb al-fitan
    310, 313

INDEX OF SUBJECTS AND AUTHORS

Page references in italics indicate images.

Aaron ha-Cohen, 119
Aaronson, Joshua, 117
Abbahu, 246
Abednego, 10, 46, 118
Abiesdri, 37
abomination
    abomination of desolation, 273, 275, 278, 280, 315
    terminology: abomination (*šiqqûṣ*), 308
    desolating abomination (*šiqqûṣʾim měšōmēm*), 287
Abrabanel, Isaac ben Judah, 154, 281, 314
Abraham, 116, 333, 371
Abraham bar Hiyya, 314
Abu al-Aliva, 310
Abu Khilda, 310
Abydenus, 146
Achaemenids, 107, 165–66
Ackroyd, Peter R., 167
Acra (citadel), 351, 355, 356
Adad-guppi, 128, 172
Adam, 310, 315
Adam/Michael, 249
Adang, Camila, 251, 252, 313
Adonijah, 172
Adventist theology, 318
Afonso V, 154
afterlife, 362, 363, 371
Against the Christians (Porphyry), 243
aggression, 238, 239, 240
Agrippa II, 281
Ahab, 106
Ahasueres, 48, 109, 180, 289
Ahiqar, 12, 13, 64, 271
Ahura Mazda, 17, 72, 76,134, 135, 142, 146
Akiba, 154, 247, 311
Akītu Festival, 129, 162, 164
akra, (citadel), see Acra
al-Ashʾari, Abu Musa, 30, 31
Albertz, Rainer, 5, 8, 10, 11, 127, 143, 216
al-Biruni, 313
Albo, Joseph, 244, 369

al-Daijal, al-Masih, 282
al-Daniyali, 311
Aleijadinho, 56, *57*
Alexander, Paul Julius, 92, 280
Alexander IV, 340
Alexander the Great
    and Chaldean astrological experts, 45
    death of, 18, 92, 339–340, 262
    emergence of, 1–2
    as the fourth kingdom, 240
    as the he-goat, 262
    and high priest, 84
    imagined defeat of, 11
    in ominous dream, 9
    surrender of Jerusalem to, 23
    as the "warrior king," 339
    and wars of successors, 211
Alexandria, 4, 24, 348, 350
Alfrink, Bernardus, 363
al-Hawli, Saudi Safari, 252
Allen, Richard, 123–24
all-powerfulness, 261
    See also power
al-Maqdisi, 252
almsgiving, 145, 154
al-Qumisi, Daniel, 94
Alshich, Moshe ben Shayim, 117, 182, 205, 246, 312, 313, 314
Alt, Albrecht, 171
al-Tabarī, Muhammed ibn Jarir, 151, 152, 208
Alvarus, Paulus, 280
Al-Walid, 313
Amalarius of Metz, 249
Amel-Marduk, 79
Amen, Daniel, 55
American temperance movement and Daniel 1, 55
Ammon, 357
Amorites, 141
Amsterdam, Netherlands, 181
amulets, 204, *205, 206*
Anani, 246, 245

Index of Subjects and Authors

anarchism, 185
Anatomia statue Danielis, 95, 96
Ancient of Days
  as archangel Michael, 247
  and Christ, 249
  as mythic-realistic figure, 233
  taking his seat, 229
Anderson, Gary A., 145, 154
angel, of YHWH, 112
Angel of Darkness, 264
angelic dialogue, 268
angelophanies, 1, 328, 331, 332
angels
  and Daniel's prostration, 269
  at divine court judgment, 227, 228
  elohization of, 219
  as heralds and messengers, 139, 140, 330
  high numbers of, 230–31
  as "holy ones," 215, 237, 241
  as leaders of angelic armies, 263
  linen garments for, 230
  and the lions' den, 204, 207
  and Nebuchadnezzar, 152
  as part of the divine council, 142
  predictions by, 360
  temple protection by, 239
  touch by, 332
  winged nature of, 298
  and worship of God, 229
  See also Gabriel (archangel); Michael (archangel)
animalized humans, 141, 144
Anna of Constantinople, 93
Anthemius, 276
anthromorphism, 252
antichrist
  as the abomination of desolation, 315
  Barack Obama as, 279
  as Jewish, 274, 275, 283
  as the lawless one, 273
  the pope as, 277, 278, 280
  predicted location of demise, 277
  Rome as, 276
  Russia as, 279
Antigonus, 216, 337, 340
Antigonus Monophthalmus, 262
anti-Messiahs, 280–83
Antiochene crisis, 19, 21, 24
Antiochene persecutions, 7, 215, 225–26
Antiochus I, 225
Antiochus II, 341
Antiochus III, 11, 216, 339, 341–45, 346, 357
Antiochus IV, 6, 7, 11, 225, 226, 339
  and apocalyptic historiography, 327
  arrogance of, 240, 271, 354–55, 359
  and Belshazzar, 259

  coins of, 264
  and conflict with Judean Jews, 2, 23
  death of, 11, 27, 358–59
  depiction of, 269–72
  Egyptian invasions of, 348, 349, 350
  honor and legitimacy of, 25, 346, 347
  Jewish cultic prohibition decree of, 240, 241, 307, 308
  and Laodice, 347
  as the little horn, 225–26, 231, 239, 263, 273
  and Nebuchadnezzar, 266–67
  temple violation by, 239, 348, 354
anti-Semitism, 120, 121
apadāna (hypostyle hall), 358
Apamea, Treaty of, 345, 346
Aphrahat, 152, 243, 275
Aphroditopolis, 4
apocalypse definition, 19
Apocalypse Group of the SBL Genres Project, 19
apocalypses
  Aramaic and Hebrew, 7
  Danielic, 92, 93
  and Danielic narratives, 18, 201–2
  Daniel's influence on development of, 1
  knowledge conveyed by, 20
  medieval, 280
  prophecy in, 272
  symbolism in, 2
  template of basic features for, 19
apocalyptic dream visions, 18–21
Apollinarius, 316
Apollo, 355
Apollonius, 257, 306, 351
Apology for the Project of the French Reformed (Brousson), 209
Arabs, 281, 282
Aramaic apocalypses, 7
Aramaic language, 2, 4, 7, 8
Aramaic Levi Document, 22
archangels. *See* Gabriel (archangel); Michael (archangel)
Arioch, 62, 70, 71, 72; *see also* head of Nebuchadnezzar's staff
Arisinoe III, 342
Arjomand, Said Amir, 251, 370
ark of the covenant, 372
Armenia, 151
Armilus, 280–81
Army Sermon against the Turks (Luther), 280
Arnold, Bill, 161, 169
arrogance
  of Antiochus IV, 240, 271, 354, 359
  of Belshazzar, 175, 220
  of the little horn, 226, 231
  of Nebuchadnezzar, 174

Artaxerxes, 48, 304, 339
Artaxias of Armenia, 226
ascension, 249
Ashkenazic Jews, 121
Ashtar, 264
Ashurbanipal, 69, 166, 195
Aspinwall, William, 278
Asshur, 349
Aster, Shawn Zelig, 111
astral imagery, 370
astrology, 44, 136
Astyges, 67, 70, 135, 191
"at the appointed time," 349
Athanasius, 276
Augustine, 116, 150, 151, 244, 275, 277, 278, 279–80, 316, 371
Austin, Daniel, 245
Azariah, 14, 46, 99–100, 121

Baal myths, 217, 219, 220, 234
Baal Shamaim/Baal Shamayin, 257, 308, 356
Baal-Hadad, 218
Babylon, 9, 340
   astrological and divinatory learning, 45
   and Euphrates River, 330
   fall of, 65, 163, 164
   and the god Marduk, 17
   Ishtar Gate of, *147*
   Jewish settlement in, 21
   as lion with eagles' wings, 223
   magnificence of, 146
   Nabonidus's absence from, 128, 129
   Saddam Hussein's rebuilding of, 153
Babylonian Chronicle, 163, 164
Babylonian Diadochi Chronicle, 216
Babylonian Diaspora, 6, 19, 21
   status of Jews in, 21–23
Bagasro, 12
Baghdad, 310, 311
Bahá'í, 318
banquets. *See* royal banquets
baptism, 203
Bar Kochba, 247, 317
Bar Nafle, 246
Barcelona disputation, 313, 314
Barclay, John M. G., 109
Bardill, Jonathan, 276
Barton, John, 290
The Basement Tapes (album), 186
Bashir Muhammad ʿAbdallah, 252, 283
Basil I, 117
Basil II, 93
Bathsheba, 172
Battle of Ipsus, 342
Battle of Magnesia, 25, 345
Battle of Panion, 344
Battle of Raphia, 342, 343

Bauer, Dieter, 40, 70, 221, 225, 240, 255, 263, 266, 271
Baynes, Leslie, 20, 21, 361
Beatrice, P. F., 243
Beatus of Liébana, 183, 248
Beaulieu, Paul-Alain, 9, 67, 106, 129, 164
"the beautiful land," 344, 361
"the beautiful holy mountain," 358
Beckwith, Carl, 152, 155, 251
Behemoth, 370, 371
Behistun Inscription, 69, 105, 192
Bekkum, Wout van Jac., 94
Bel, statue of, 103
Bel and the Dragon
   canonicity of, 30
   cartoonish effects in, 170
   as court tale, 5, 14
   Daniel's cleverness in, 6
   lions' den scene, 196, 198
   narrative summary of, 207
   on pagan idolatry emptiness, 2, 168
Belial, 334, 357
Belisarius, 317
Bell, Catherine M., 104
Bellarmino, Roberto, 278
Belshazzar, 9, 10, 46, 79
   and Antiochus, 259
   arrogance of, 175, 220
   authority of, 163–64
   banquet of feast of, 162, 165–67
   and Darius, 189
   etymology of name, 46
   as feckless king, 158
   historical fate of, 178–79
   idolatry of, 161, 162
   in Napoleon caricature painting, *184*
   and Nebuchadnezzar contrasted, 127, 128, 162, 163, 166, 172
   in Rembrandt painting, 169
   as the sheqel, 176
   as son of Nabonides, 128
   See also Belshazzar's Feast; royal banquet
Belshazzar (oratorio), 181
Belshazzar (song), 186
Belshazzar's Feast
   inscription interpretations, 179, 181, 182, 183
   political uses of, 183–86
   as reference to last judgment, 186
   Rembrandt's depiction of, *169,* 182
Belteshazzar, 46, 134, 136, 328
bēl'šaṣṣ'ar, bēlša'ṣṣar, 214
Ben Sira, 52, 305
"Benefactor" epithet, 341
Benjamin of Tuleda, 28, 29, 30
Benton, Tim, 56
Bentzen, Aage, 46, 101, 286, 288

Berenice, 341
Berner, Christoph, 12, 287, 301, 302, 307
Berossus, 163
Berquist, Jon L., 72
Bevan, Edwin R., 173, 307, 353, 354
Beyer, Klaus, 241
Bhabha, Homi, 16
Bible, 29
Bickerman, Elias, 27, 226, 306, 308, 351
Bildungsroman (novel of education), 33
bilingualism, 7–8
bin Hammad, Nu'aym, 310
Black, Jeremy, 141
Blaine, James G., 185
Blake, William, 153, 157
Blasius, Andreas, 225, 226
Blenkinsopp, Joseph, 17
Blois, France, execution of Jews, 120–21
Bobover Hasidic community, Brooklyn, New York, 117
body parts, in Israelite tradition, 226
Bøe, Sverre, 276
book, books, 290
    book of deeds, 21, 231
    book of fate, 21
    book of life, 21, 231, 248, 250, 361
    book of truth, 28, 266, 296, 335
Book of Jamasp, 31
Book of the Watchers (*1 Enoch 1–36*), 18, 22, 332
Born Jesus de Matosinhos sanctuary, Minas Gerais, Brazil, 56, *57*
Bostick, Curtis V., 278
Bowen, Nancy R., 56, 172
Boyce, Mary, 76, 78
Boyd, Arthur, 156
Boyer, Paul S., 279
Brading, David A., 97
Braght, Thieleman J. van, 55
Branch Davidian movement, 318
Brazil, 56, 57
Brekelmans, Christianus H., 237
Briant, Pierre, 72, 104, 105, 107, 129, 134, 138, 165, 166, 339
bridge
    Daniel and Gabriel on, 31, *32*
    holding Daniel's bones, 29–30
British Empire, 184
Brockington, Leonard H., 254
Broida, Marian, 171
Brooks, Joanna, 124
Brousson, Claude, 208, 209
Brute, Walter, 316
Bullinger Heinrich, 155
Bungey, Darleen, 157
Burke, Garance, 318
Burnier-Genton, Jean, 221

Byzantine Empire, 58, 92, 93, 280
Byzas, 92

Caliph ʿUmar, 280
Calvin, John, 118, 152, 208, 278
Cambyses, 78, 171
Camping, Harold, 318
canon, 2
Canterbury Tales (Chaucer), 58
Caquot, André, 222
Caragounis, Chrys, 245, 246
Casey, Maurice, 235, 243
Cash, Johnny, 186
Cassandar, 340
Cassian, John, 207
Catholic canon, 2
Chaldeans, 43–45, 106, 107–9, 197
    as mantic experts (*kaśdim*), 44, 65, 67–68
Chandieu, Antione de, 117
changing times and seasons, 69
chariot throne, 230
Charlemagne, 317
Charles, Robert H., 7, 8, 38, 173, 255, 285, 288, 358, 366
Charles I, 278
Charles VI, 152, 153
Charles VII, 95
Chaucer, Geoffrey, 58
Chazan, Robert, 312, 313
Chebar Canal, 260, 268, 330
cherubim, 298
chiasm, 354–55
chōra (agricultural hinterland), 343
Christ
    Adam delivering stewardship to, 249
    and the Ancient of Days, 249
    as the humanlike one, 275
    as rock cut without human hands, 244
    thousand year reign of, 278
Christian (Protestant) canon, 2
Christiani, Pablo, 313
Christianity, 87, 91, 116, 151, 275, 282, 313
Chrysologus, Peter, 207
Chrysostom, John, 58
Chytreus, David, 316
"the citadel," 351, 355; *see also* Acra
City of God (Augustine), 87
"Cleanness" (poem), 156, 186
Clement of Alexandria, 247, 315
Cleopatra, 226, 345, 348
Clermont-Ganneau, C., 176
Cleyre, Voltairine de, 185
Clifford, Richard J., 327
clothing and ornaments, 171
clouds, 219, 236, 246, 248
Codex Chisianus manuscript, 4
Coele-Syria, 23, 24, 340, 342–45, 349, 350

coins, 264, 354, 355
Collins, Adela Yarbro, 264, 368
Collins, Anthony, 7
Collins, John, 5, 8, 9, 63, 68, 70, 72, 76, 110, 111, 128, 176, 177, 179, 214, 215, 221, 223, 226, 232, 235, 237, 240, 242, 255, 270, 271, 286, 288, 289, 301, 303, 326, 330, 342, 350, 353, 356, 362, 364, 365
Colpe, Carsten, 234
combat myth, 221
command and execution sequences, 105, 106, 109
commandments and decrees, 293
Commendatio Animae ("commendation of the soul"), 122, 204
Commentary on Daniel (Jerome), 248
Commodian, 273
communism, 185
Community Rule (Qumran), 264, 290
composite animals, 222
concubines, 167
"confess," 293
Confessio Amantis (poem), 156
confession of sins, 294, 296
confessor legends/tales, 15, 100, 190
conflict
  with authorities, 14
  court, 14
  and earthly sovereignty to Gentile kings, 27
  between God and Gentile king, 34
Constantine I, 54, 92, 116, 122, 150, 151, 276, 282
Constantine V, 248
Constantinople, 92, 311
Constantinople amulet, 204
Constantius II, 276
Containment as trope, 327, 337, 340, 345, 354
conversion, 151
Conybeare, Frederick C., 148
Cook, John, 244, 282, 283, 311
Coptic Egypt, 122
Cordoba, 183
Corrodi, Heinrich, 7
cosmic conflict/imagery, 221, 222, 234
Counter-Reformation, 152, 154, 278
court tales
  cultural negotiation in, 16
  in Danielic narratives, 1–6, 5, 6
  moral conflict in, 13
  popularity of, 12
  ruled ethnic perspective, 13
  setting and social function, 12–15
  tales of conflict and contest, 13
courtiers, 12, 13, 197, 348
covenant curses, 295, 297, 300
covenant keeping, 293
Cowley, Arthur E., 176

Cowper, William, 55
Coxon, Peter, 110
Craon, Pierre de, 152–53
Crescas, Hasdai (rabbi), 371
Cromwell, Oliver, 245, 278
Cross, Frank M., 84
Crusades, 55, 56, 277, 282, 311
crypto-observance, 117
Ctesias, 80
cultic calendar, 241
Cumont, Franz, 261
cuneiform scribes, 22, *44*, 45
Cyprian, 154
Cyril of Jerusalem, 370
Cyrus, 10, 143, 167, 176, 339
  authenticity of decrees of, 16, 17
  Babylon conquest by, 164
  Daniel in first year of, 8, 179, 201
  and Darius the Mede, 191–92, 289
  decree of allowing Jerusalem rebuilding, 298, 300, 303, 315, 328
  God's authorization of, 223
  God's intentions expressed through, 52
  and Jewish exile community, 129, 130
  as king in statue, 79
  and Marduk, 74, 78, 129
  as rock in Nebuchadnezzar's dream, 79
Cyrus Cylinder, 17, 163
Cyrus the Great, 128, 262, 289

the Daijal, 282, 283
daily whole offering (*'ōlat tāmid*), 265, 267, 327
Daniel
  alleged burial spot locations, 28, 32
  anxiety about four beasts dream, 241–43
  appearance of, 52–53
  as dreams interpreter, 1, 8
  and food, 164
  and gender identity, 57, 58
  and head of staff, 47–49
  legacy of, 36, 260
  as a prophet, 53–54, 56–58, 173
  the Prophet sculpture of, 56, *57*
  sepulcher of, 28–31
  and three friends, renaming of, 46, 47
  wisdom of, 172–73
Daniel, book of
  "Additions" to, 4
  bilingualism in, 7–8
  composition date of, 7, 8, 10, 11
  as court tale, 164
  Daniel 4–6 as booklet in, 10
  Dispensationalist chart on, *319*
  effect of on religious imagination, 1
  eschatological predictions/calculations in, 309–19

Index of Subjects and Authors

Greek versions, 4–5
historical influence of, 2
and knowledge, 42
literary features, 133, 135, 137, 138–40
patterns in, 20, 217–18, 341, 345, 352, 356–57, 359
and revelation of hidden meaning, 286–87
social location of authors, 21–23
spiritualization of themes in, 116
status as resurrection witness, 369–70
structure, 132–33
two versions of, 207
various evaluations of Gentile power in, 333–34
Daniel 1
 as fictitious, 42
 genre of, 39
 naming of Daniel and friends in, 46, 47
 outline, 38–39
Daniel 2
 and Joseph story, 64–65
 narrative and reader in, 65
 outline, 65
 resistance to imperial power in, 64
Daniel 3
 and martyrdom, 119–22
 outline, 102
 retellings of, 115–18
Daniel 4
 Belteshazzar and Daniel names in, 134
 and Harran inscriptions, 130–32, 134
 narrative of, 133, 134, 135
 outline, 132–33
 Vorlage, 128, 130, 131
Daniel 5
 and Daniel 6, 189
 outline, 165
 varying translations of, 162–63
 wordplay in, 178
Daniel 6
 and Daniel 5, 189
 relation to Daniel 3, 190–91
 outline, 191
Daniel 7
 literary/historical features, 217–20
 overview, 215
 outline, 216–17
 as two-stage composition, 216
Daniel 7–12
 difficulty of, 314
 historical context of, 23–28
Daniel 8
 and Aniochene Crisis, 256–58
 composition date, 256–57
 and historical structures of events, 256
 literary features, 259
 outline, 258–59
Daniel 9
 and other Danielic apocalypses, 287–89
 outline, 289
Daniel 10–12
 and Daniel 8, 327–28
 outline, 328, 337, 360
 overview, 326–28
Daniel 11
 as political and military history, 336
 skeleton key to, 338–39
Daniel in lions' den
 depictions/icons of, *200*, 202–4, *205*
 as judgment, 199
Daniel in the Lions' Den (painting), 200
Daniel Variations (musical composition), 158
"Daniel's Band" (poem), 55
Danker, Frederick, 171
Darby, John Nelson, 278, 279, 317
Darius I, 10, 12, 17, 46, 142, 192, 199, 289, 339
 in Behistun Inscription, 69
 and Belshazzar, 189
 confession of, 190
 decree allowing Jerusalem temple rebuilding, 304
 doxology of, 16
 as feckless, 158
 fondness of for Daniel, 198–99
Darius III, 196, 262, 337, 339
Darius the Great. *See* Darius I
Darius the Mede
 as amiable, 223
 and Belshazzar, 158
 and Cyrus, 270
 historicity of, 10, 289
 identity of, 179, 191–92, 199
 as a half-minas, 176
Darkness, forces of, 239
Davidic kingship ideology, 219, 220
Davidic Messiah, 247
Davies, Philip R., 23, 79, 241
Day, John, 217, 235
"Day of Eleusis," 350
De termino vitae (Manasseh ben Israel), 181
De Wet, Chris L., 203
Dead Sea Scrolls
 on angels, 237
 Danielic manuscripts in, 3, 12, 30
 and *Prayer of Nabonidus*, 128
 and theological anthropology, 175
Dearn, Alan, 276
death
 and the afterlife, 362, 363
 and burial, 362
 in furnace motif, 106
 in martyrdom, 352–53
deception, 271, 272, 274

decrees
   Antiochus IV Jewish cultic prohibition, 240, 241, 307, 308
   and commandments, 293
   Cyrus's allowing temple rebuilding, 298, 300, 303, 315, 328
   of Darius, 158, 201, 303
deities, 230, 355, 356
   See also gods; specific deities by name
Delcor, Matthias, 162, 235, 255, 308
deliverance, 209, 296
Delmonico's (restaurant), 185
Demetrius, 226, 340, 346
demons, 148, 151, 155
Denkard, 76
desolation, 297, 300
Deuteronomic theology, 287
Diadochi, wars of, 11, 18, 216, 262
Diadorus Siculus, 44
Diaspora, 6, 11, 19, 21, 29, 51, 64, 65, 102
   food laws in, 48
   lifestyle for, 15
   under the Babylonians, 21–22
   under the Persians, 107
Dickey, Laurence, 92
Dickinson, Emily, 186
Didache, 248, 274
diet restrictions, 42, 45, 47–48, 54–55
   vegetable/fruit diet, 49, 50, 54–55
   American temperance movement, 55
   "Daniel fasting" in evangelical Christianity, 55
DiLella, Alexander A., 4, 70, 84, 103, 111, 137, 189, 214, 221, 226, 228, 235, 237, 260, 286, 288, 291, 299, 303, 363, 365, 366, 368
Diocletian, 276
Diodati, Giovanni, 155
Diodorus, 196
Diogesis Danielis, 92
Disful Karun, 260
Dispensational Truth (Larkin), *319, 320*
dispensationalism, 278, 317, 318, *319*
DiTommaso, Lorenzo, 92, 310
Dittmer, Jason, 279
divination, 67, 136
   See also manticism
divine council, 226, 263
divine judgment, 179, 232, 233
divine sovereignty, 135, 142, 232
divine throne, 227
divine voices, 146–47
Doctrine and Covenants (Mormon document), 55, 249
Doctrine of Jacob recently Baptized, 93, 281
Dodds, Jerrilynn, 183
dominion, 224, 234, 235, 262

Domitian, 276
Doob, Penelope, 156
Dorrien, Gary J., 317
Dossin, Georges, 42
double names, 46, 47
doxologies, 16, 135, 148, 234
Drawnel, Henryk, 22
Dreams
   ḥēlem (dream), 220
   interpretation of, 270
   portentous, 9
   and visions, 220
Driver, Samuel R., 74, 101, 110, 235
Droy, Alf, 153
dualism
   in apocalyptic literature, 83
   of cosmic forces of good and evil, 333
   of sovereign God and Gentile monarchs, 130
Duhm, Bernhard, 149
Dunbar, David, 274
Dura, plain of, 103, 115
Durbridge, Nicola, 56
Dylan, Bob, 186
Dynastic Prophecy, 11, 81, 216

Eanon, Franz, 15
Eberhard (archbishop), 277
Edom, 94, 357
education, 43
Egypt, 2, 4, 122, 296, 348
Eidels, Shmuel, 150
Eincke, 69
Eissfeldt, Otto, 161
El, 217, 229
Eleazar, 155, 180
Elephantine Jewish colony, 108
Elephantine papyri, 176
Eliakim, 47
Elisha, 108
Elohim, 372
elohization, 219
Elymaïs, 359
Emerson, Ralph Waldo, 156
Emerton, John A., 217
Encyclical to nations, 5, 134, 142
Engelke, Matthias, 156
English millenarian exegesis, 317
Enkidu, 141
Enuma Elish, 217, 218, 222
Ephrem, 155, 243, 244, 275
Ephʿal, Israel, 22
epiphanic rhetoric, 19
Epistle of Barnabas, 274
Epistle to Yemen (Maimonides), 246, 282
Epstein, Shifra, 117
Erdman, David, 153

Index of Subjects and Authors

Esarhaddon, 12, 170
Esau, 357
eschatological opponents, 279, 315
Esther, 12, 14, 48, 109
Eumenes II, 346, 347
eunuchs, 57, 58
Euphrates River, 164, 330
Eusebius, 276, 280
"evenings-mornings," 267
evil, 221, 270, 273, 302, 365
Evil-merodach, 45, 179, 180
executions, 106, 120, 190, 232
exorcism, 22, 67
Ezekiel, 120, 260, 330, 331, 332
Ezra, 40–41, 207, 312

faith, 120, 121, 122, 275
Faras, Nubia, 122, 123
fasting, 326, 329, 330
Faust, Lorenz, 95, 96
fear, 172, 208, 269, 330
Feldman, Seymour, 314
Fewell, Danna Nolan, 46
fiery furnace
  as Christian visual art, 112, 122, 123
  possible derivation of, 106
  See also three youths
Fifth Syrian War, 23, 343, 344, 345
final judgment, 186, 369
Finet, Andre, 42
fire, 230, 232, 233
First Crusade, 55, 277
first person speech, 19, 266, 328
fitan (the trials that accompany the end of time), 310
Fitzmyer, Joseph A., 134, 235
Flusser, David, 76
food provisions/choices, 42, 45, 47–48, 54–55
  See also diet restrictions
forgiveness, 294, 295, 302
four, the number, 20, 76, 221
four beasts, 221–22, 232–34, 238, *250, 319*
490 years, 309, 312, 313, 316
four kingdoms, 17, 262, *320*
four kingdoms schema
  anti-imperial use of, 93–97
  in Daniel 7, 218
  imperial use of, 86–93
  Median dominion in, 192
  northern European Jewish construals of, 95, *97*
  as resistance literature, 81
  as time-structuring device, 85, 86
Fourteenth Vision of Daniel of the eighth–twelfth century, 249
fourth beast
  autonomous actions of, 222
  execution of, 232
  and the first three beasts, 233, 234
Fourth Crusade, 311
fourth figure, in furnace, 112
fourth kingdom
  associated with iron, 82
  destructiveness of, 34, 82
  as Islam, 94–95
  as Rome, 80, 85–86, 93
  as Moscow, 92
  as the Seleucid kingdom, 224
Fourth Syrian War, 342, 357
the four archangels, 268
the four horns, 262
Frahm, Eckart, 171
Fraticelli, 278
Frederick II Hohenstaufen, 277
Frederick the Wise, 244
Free African Society, 123
French Revolution, 153, 317
Freud, Sigmund, 182, 283
Freyre, Gilberto, 56
Fried, Lisbeth, 17
Friedenberg, Daniel B., 203
Friesing, Otto von, 244
Fröhlich, Ida, 79
Froissart, Jean, 153
Futurist apocalypticism, 278
  See also Darby, John Nelson

Gabra Manfras Qeddus, 208
Gabriel
  and angelic conflict, 236, 335
  and Daniel on bridge, 31, *32*
  explanation of prophecy to Daniel, 290, 299
  history account of, 293, 304
  and the prince of Persia, 333
  vision explanations of to Daniel, 268, 269, 272, 297, 366
  and youths in fiery furnace, 120
Gadatus, 178
Gadd, Cyril J., 128, 131
Gaebelein, Anna, 279
Galipapa, Hayyim, 244, 369
Gallé, A. F., 208, 246, 247, 282, 369, 371
Gandhi, Mahatma, 196, 209
Gaon, Hai, 371
Gaon, Saadia, 312, 371
Gardom, Simcha, 117
Gaugamela, 262
Gaza, 340, 343
Geissen, Angelo, 4
gematria, 313
gender identity, 57, 58
genres, 2, 12–15
Genseric, 276

Gentile kingdoms sequence, 80
  See also four kingdoms; four kingdoms schema
Gentile sovereignty
  delegated, 219
  dispossession of, 10–11
  and divine sovereignty, 33, 150, 258
  and oppression, 204–5
  See also God: sovereignty of in relation to Gentile rule
Gentiles, 233, 302
George III, 153
Gera, Dov, 345, 346, 350, 351
Gersonides, 314
Gibb, E .J. W., 31
gift giving, 343, 347
Gilgamesh Epic, 141
Gillray, James, 183, 184, 185
Ginsberg, Harold L., 49, 233, 288, 352, 367
Gobryas, 178
God
  and the book of life, 361
  epithets for: $\,^{\prime}\bar{e}l\bar{a}h\bar{a}^{\prime}\ hayy\bar{a}^{\prime}$ (living God), 191; $\,^{\prime}\bar{e}l\bar{a}h\ ^{\prime}\bar{e}l\bar{a}h\hat{i}n$ (God of gods), 84; $\,^{\prime}\bar{e}l/^{\prime}\bar{e}l\bar{o}h\hat{e}\ ^{\varsigma}\acute{o}l\bar{a}m$ (God of Ages), 229; $\,^{\prime}\bar{e}l\bar{a}h\ \check{s}\check{e}mayy\bar{a}^{\prime}$ (God of Heaven), 33, 71, 72, 78, 83; $\,^{\prime}\bar{e}l\bar{a}h\bar{a}^{\prime}\ ^{\varsigma}ill\bar{a}y\bar{a}^{\prime}/^{\varsigma}ill\bar{a}^{\prime}\hat{a}$ (God Most High), 112,135, 215; $m\bar{a}r\bar{e}^{\prime}\ malkin$ (Lord of kings), 84.
  forgiveness of, 302
  graciousness of, 292, 294
  honor of, 296, 297
  and idols, 175
  judgment of, 199, 200
  and pagan deities, 6
  physical descriptions of, 229, 230
  relationship with Israel, 301, 302, 354
  resistance to, 209–10
  silence of, 120, 121
  sovereignty of, 1, 34, 191
  sovereignty of in relation to Gentile rule, 10, 14, 16, 27
  times and seasons control by, 240
  wrath of, 269, 270, 295
  See also El, Elohim
Godfrey, Richard, 184
"Godnapping," 341
gods
  Antiochus IV's assaults on, 354
  materials for images of, 168
  See also specific gods by name
Gog, 272, 281, 312, 357, 358
golden image, 34, 103, 111
Goldingay, John, 63, 68, 69, 83, 110, 137, 161, 164, 171, 176, 214, 215, 221, 223, 224, 225, 226, 228, 229, 230, 232, 241, 267, 268, 285, 307, 325, 326, 334, 353, 365

Goldman, Harry Merton, 186
Goldwurm, Hersh, 94, 114, 117, 119, 150, 179, 182, 207, 247, 282, 314, 371
Golstein, Bernard, 314
Gower, John, 156
Grabbe, Lester L., 11, 17, 163, 192, 303
Grafton, Anthony, 318
Grainger, John D., 342, 343, 345, 346, 348, 350
Granicus, 262
Grayson, Albert Kirk, 39, 192, 216
Great Mosque of Cordoba, 183
great tree image, 137, 138
  See also tree
"the Great Disappointment," 318
"the great sea," 221
Greece, 17, 80, 223, 261, 270
Greek versions, of Daniel, 4–5
Green, Rosalie B., 203
Gregory the Great, 275, 277
Gregory the Illuminator, 151
Gregory VII, 151, 244, 277
Grelot, Pierre, 5, 127
Guibert of Nogent, 277
Gunkel, Hermann, 217, 221, 366, 368

Haag, Ernst, 15, 149, 162, 222
Habakkuk, 198, 207, 208, 248
$habb\bar{e}l$ (harm), 191, 193
Hachlili, Rachel, 203
Hadassah, 47
Hadelman, J. M., 279
Hadrian, 316
Hagen, Rainer, 182
Hagen, Rose-Marie, 182
Haggai, 53
Halevi, Judah Hal, 95
half-minas ($pars\hat{i}n$), 176, 182
Hallett, Mark, 184
Halperin, David J., 229
Haman, 48
Hamm, Winfried, 4
Hanan ben Talifa, 312
Hananiah, 14, 46, 121
hand-writing on the wall, 168, 169, 170, 171
Harran Inscriptions, 9, 128, 129, 130
Hartman, Lars, 4, 70, 84, 103, 111, 189, 214, 221, 226, 228, 235, 254, 260, 273, 286, 288, 291, 299, 303, 335, 363, 365, 366, 368
Hasib (son of Greek sage Daniel), 3131
Hasidim, 352
Hasmoneans, 244
Hasslberger, Bernhard, 11
Hayes, John H., 24
Hays, Christopher B., 362
head of gold, 103

head of Nebuchadnezzar's staff, 47–49, 51
  see also Arioch
heavenly books, 21, 231, 335, 336, 361
Hebrew apocalypses, 7
Hebrew Bible
  act of reading in, 289–90
  descriptions of God, 229
  and judgment, 226
  reading of, 114
  tree symbol in, 138
Hebrew language, 2, 4, 7, 8, 256–58
Heiser, Michael S., 264
Hêlēl ben-Shāchar, 264
Heliodorus, 25, 26, 226, 239, 346, 347
Hellenistic period
  political events, 1–2
  royal overreaching in, 359
  and taxation, 24–25
Heller, Roy L., 110
Henri II, 118
Henry IV, 151, 244
Henry VIII, 278
Henze, Matthias, 128, 141, 152, 155
Heraclius, 93
"Hermolaus Satan," 281
Herodotus, 13, 70, 80, 135, 146, 163, 164, 167, 181
heroes, 14, 15
Hezekiah (king), 358
hidden meaning, revelation of, 286–87
high priests
  buying office of, 25, 26
  as religious and political leaders, 23–24
Hill, Christopher, 278
Hillers, Delbert, 170
Himmelfarb, Martha, 92
Hippolytus, 274, 275, 315, 316, 370
Hiram of Tyre, 271
historiography, 39, 40, 326
history
  of Bible's reception, 29, 32, 33
  coded, 20
  Daniel's patterning of, 341, 345, 352, 356–57, 359
  interpreting, 179–81
  as revealed through prophecy, 19
  structural repeatability in, 326, 327
  symbolic/numerical systems for, 309–19
History of the Armenians, 151
Hitler, Adolf, 118
Hitzig, Ferdinand, 326, 356
Holocaust, 114, 117
Hölscher, Gustav, 7, 215
holy of holies, 303
"holy ones," 237, 238, 242, 243
Hommel, Fritz, 128
horns, 225, 226, 260

host, host of heaven, 255, 263
Howell, Thomas Bailey, 153
Howell, Thomas Jones, 153
hubris, 271, 272
Huegenot nonviolent resistance, 208–9
Hugh of St. Victor, 249
humanlike one, 234–35, 237–38, 243, 245–52, 275; see also Son of Man
Humphreys, Lee, 13, 15, 16
Hungarian freedom fighters, 118
Hus, John, 278
Hussein, Saddam, 153
hybridity, 16
Hyman, Mark, 55
hymns, in narrative, 6
Hymns on Paradise, 156
Hyrcanus, 26
Hystaspes, 192, 194

ibn Abbas, Abu Allah, 251
ibn Ezra, Abraham, 94, 95, 182, 246, 247, 282, 285, 370
Ibn Hawqal, Muhammad Abū'l-Qāsiml, 30, 31
Ibn Hazm, Andalausian, 251
Ibn Qutayba, 251
ibn Tahir, Abu Nasr Mutahhar, 252
identity
  culture negotiation of, 47, 48
  of Daniel, 52–53
  of Darius the Mede, 179, 191–92, 199
  gender, 57, 58
  and resistance, 55–57
idolatry/idol worship, 2, 6, 108, 109, 161–64, 175
  and Caesar effigies, 115
image of gold. See golden image
imperial ideology, 142
incarnation, 249, 251, 282
Indicopluestes, Cosmas, 251
inscriptions
  Behistun, 69, 105, 192
  Belshazzar's Feast, 162, 163, 183
  "Darius the Great King," 199
  Harran, 128, 129, 130–32, 134
interpretation
  of dreams, 270
  dynamics of, 182
  punning, 177, 178
  by the reader, 272, 273, 329
  terminology (*pĕšar*), 65, 236
Ipsus, Battle of, 340, 342
Iraq, 153
Irenaeus, 274
Is the Antichrist at Hand? What of Mussolini? (Smith), 279
Isaac bar Shelom, 121
Isaac ben Eleazar, 120

Index of Subjects and Authors

Isaiah, 358
Isakhan, Benjamin, 153
Ishmael/Ishmaelites, 94
Isho'dad of Merv, 275, 369
Ishtar, 47, *129*
Ishtar Gate of Babylon, *147*
Islam
  anti-Messiahs in, 280–83
  conversion to, 282
  Daniel as prophet in, 53
  Daniel and lions' den in, 208
  and Daniel apocalypses, 280
  and Daniel-based calculations, 313
  as fourth kingdom, 95
  interpretation of stone cut without hands in, 251, 252
  the little horn as, 282
  and Nebuchadnezzar's story, 151
  rise of, 183
  See also Muslim apocalypticists
Ismaʿilis, 370
Israel
  and Armilus, 280–81
  and global conspiracy, 283
  God's relationship with, 301, 302
  Michael patron angel for, 333
  as representing humanlike figure, 235
  and resurrection, 371
  as threshing sledge, 77
  transfer of sovereignty to, 237

Jamasp, 31
Jason, 25, 26, 257, 306, 307, 350
Jehoiachin, 21, 45, 48, 179
Jehoiakim, 39, 40, 41, 47
Jehovah's Witnesses, 318
Jellicoe, Sidney, 4
Jepsen, Alfred, 82
Jeremiah
  influence on Daniel 1–6, 41, 66
  in Islamic story, 208
  Qumran manuscript of, *291*
  relation of Daniel's prayer to, 290, 293
  on the seventy years, 229, 300
Jerome, 6, 58, 68, 141, 155, 180, 205–6, 248, 276, 315, 316
Jerusalem
  and Antiochus IV visit, 25
  Armilus's actions in, 281
  Babylonian siege of, 39
  centrality of, 297
  destruction of, 180, 312
  eschatological final battle against, 357
  in Fifth Syrian war, 23
  high priest office struggle in, 350
  prayer orientation to, 196, 197, 202, 206
  rebuilding/restoration of, 289, 290, 291, 303
  and rival aristocratic family conflict, 24, 26
  temple vessels, 162, 166, 167, 173
  walls of, 305
Jesus
  and the Dajjal, 282
  as the Son of God, 252
  as type of descending rock cut without human hands, 244
Jewish Diaspora, 21, 64, 65, 102
Jews
  in court of Gentile king, 12
  Daniel 3 and medieval, 116–17, 120
  European persecution of, 27
  execution of, 120
  first century revolt of, 2
  medieval and modern attempts to eradicate, 117
  Worms Massacre of, 56
Joachim of Fiore, 277, 316
Job, 14
John Chrysostom, 154
John of Damascus, 370
Jonathan, 311
Jones, Abraham, 123–24, 288
Joseph, 12, 14, 47, 64, 84
Joseph the Tobiad, 24
Josephine, Empress, 183
Josephus, 23, 24, 28, 47, 68, 84, 86, 115, 119, 178, 180, 270, 308
Joshua (high priest), 293, 305
Jubilee periods, 301, 304, 305
Judah bar Aaron, 120
Judah the Maccabee, 11, 23, 27, 303, 351, 352, 353, 359, 367, 369
Judah the Priest, 120
Judea, 11, 24, 344, 345
judgment
  from divine council, 226
  earth as scene of, 228
  the final, 186, 369
  fire of, 232
  of God, 199, 200
  scene in Daniel, 248
Judith, 12, 330
Julian the Apostate, 276
Julius Africanus, Sextus, 316
Jung, Carl G., 155
Junius Bassus sarcophagus, 203
Justinian, 202
Justinian I, 317

Kabbalah, 372
Kairos Document, 57
Kant, Immanuel, 327
Karaites, 94
Kattina, 311–12
Keel, Othmar, 78, 137, 222, 235, 237

Kellermann, Ulrich, 15
Kelsey, Neal, 123
Kierkegaard, Søren, 156
Kimchi, 256
King, Martin Luther, Jr., 118
king of the north (Seleucids), 266, 336, 340, 357
king of the south (Ptolemies), 266, 336, 340, 343, 348, 357
kings
  burlesquing of, 13, 109
  conversions of, 151
  divine and exalted status of, 141
  empowerment of by deities, 78
  furious anger of, 109
  and kingdoms, 236
  power of, 111
  praise of God by, 201
  and sages, 72–73
  and sovereignty of God of Daniel, 1, 14, 16, 191
  spending by, 343, 347
  and universal kingship, 134
Kirchmayr, Karl P., 171
Kirkpatrick, Shane, 15
Kishon River, 238
Kittim, 349, 358
Knibb, Michael, 305
Knowledge and understanding
  Babyloninian astrological and divinatory, 45
  differential access to, 41
  of the divine plan, 74, 352
  and intellectual capacity, 42–43,
  and power, 38, 49–51, 65, 101–2
  and scribes, 20, 42
  terminology, *bîn* (understand), 287, 290, 334; *bînâ* (understanding), 37; *haśkîl* (to gain or give insight), 288, 296, 298; *hokmâ* (wisdom), 37, 65, 72.
  understanding of, 365
Koch, Klaus, 8, 9, 38, 40, 45, 46, 48, 63, 64, 71, 76, 82, 83, 85, 99, 104, 110, 134, 135, 140, 142, 192, 216, 221
Koetsier, T., 316
Kohlberg, Etan, 31
Konin, Poland, 117
Kooij, Arie van der, 286
Koresh, David, 318
Koselleck, Reinhart, 327
Kothar-wa-Hasis, 217
Kratz, Reinhard G., 12, 63, 79, 287
Kuhl, Curt, 15
Kuhrt, Amélie, 16, 47, 105, 192, 216
Kvanvig, Helge S., 140

Labashi-Marduk, 79

Lacan, Jacques, 182–83
Lacocque, André, 85, 172, 266, 283, 289, 307, 308, 364
Lactantius, 249
Ladd, William, 208
Lambert, Wilfred G., 217
Lamoreux, John, 280, 281
language
  Aramaic, 2, 4, 7, 8
  Hebrew, 2, 4, 7, 8, 256–58
  of narratives, 8
  symbolic, 2, 11, 217, 221, 366
  of Torah, 258–59
Laodice, 341, 346, 347
Lapide, Cornelius, 244
Lapsley, Jacqueline, 294
Larkin, Clarence, 318, 319, 320
Las Hueglas Beatus manuscript, 249, *250*
Lash, Archemandrite Ephrem, 248
Lasine, Stuart, 68
The Late Great Planet Earth (Lindsey), 279
the latter days, 334
law, custom (*dāt*), 188, 194, 241
  "law of the Medes and the Persians," 260
League of Nations, 279
Leander of Seville, 55
Lebram, Jürgen-Christian, 11, 171, 194, 201, 216, 240, 241, 255, 361
Lengerke, Cäsar von., 140
Lenglet, A., 10
Leningrad Codex, 3
Leo III, 317
leopards, 221
Levant, 318
Levene, Dan, 123
Levenson, Jon D., 362
Leviathan, 222, 370, 371
Lévinas, Emmanuel, 110
Levison, John R., 136
Liber Genealogus, 276
liberation theology, 97
Lindsey, Hal, 279
lions, 195, 196, 208, 221, 222, 224
Lipchits, Oded, 300
Lipiński, Edward, 46
Lisboa, Antônio Francisco, 56
lists
  in Belshazzar's feast, 168
  as stylistic and ideological device, 104
Little Apocalypse, 273
little horn
  aggression of, 264, 266
  as Antiochus IV, 225, 275
  arrogance of, 226, 231
  Muhammed/Turkish Empire as, *91*, 280, 282
  as the papacy, 281–82

little horn (*continued*)
    as Pope Gregory VII, 277
    as the United States, 283
    See also Antiochus IV Epiphanes
"living God," 199, 201
"Lord of kings," 34, 84, 113
Louis XIV, 209
Ludlul bēl nēmeqi (Babylonian literary composition), 193, 195
Lullianus, 115
Lunationes Danielis, 310
Luther, Martin, 152, 251, 278, 280, 316, 317
Lysimachus, 340

Maccabean revolt, 14, 243, 244, 352, 368, 369
Macedonian army, 262
madness, 152, 153, 155, 156
    lycanthropy, 155
    See also mental illness
Magnesia, battle of, 25, 345
Magog, 281, 312
Maharsha, 150
the Mahdi, 252, 282, 283, 318, 370
Mailloux, Steven, 186
Maimonides, Moses, 246, 282, 314, 370
Malamat Dāniyāl (Predictions of Daniel), 310
Malbim, 113, 247
Malbon, Elizabeth Struthers, 203
Maldonado, Juan, 278
Manasseh ben Israel, 181, 183
Mandell, Sara, 24
mantic experts
    and Belshazzar, 170–71
    and Nebuchadnezzar, 69, 145
    terms used for, 62, 67–68, 136; *'aššāpîm* (exorcists), 22, 38, 67; *gāzĕrîn* (fate determiners), 63; *ḥarṭummîm* (magicians), 37, 67 (*kaśdîm*), 44, 65, 67–68; *mĕkaššĕpîm* (diviners), 67, 136
manticism, 51
"the many" (*rabbîm*), 352
Marduk
    and Cyrus, 78
    epithet of, 136
    priests of, 101, 128, 129, 163
    sea battle of, 217, 221
    temple restoration of, 146
Margoliouth, David S., 178
Mark the Deacon, 54
Marriage of Heaven and Hell (Blake), 153
Martyr, Justin, 249, 274, 315
martyr legends, 15, 100, 109
martyrdom
    in antiquity and early midrash, 119
    Christian, 121–22, 208
    death in, 352–53
    three youths medieval reading of, 120

Martyrdom of Polycarp, 121
Marx, Karl, 283
Masoretic text
    Daniel, composition of, 6–12
    of Daniel in literary context, 2–3
    and Danielic Qumran fragments, 4–5
    and Greek versions, 5, 162–63, 196
    and Theodotion's version, 314–15
Massachusetts Total Abstinence Society, 55
Mastin, Brian A., 127
Mattathias, 14, 244, 351, 352, 353, 368
Maxentius, 276
Mayer, John, 154
McCarthy, James III, 57
McClintock, John, 277
McDougall, Walt, 185
McGinn, Bernard, 275, 276, 277, 278, 279, 316
McLay, Timothy, 4
McNamara, Martin, 9
Media, Medes, 17, 223
Media and Persia, 177–78, 260, 261, 270
medieval period
    apocalypses, 280
    and Daniel 3, 116–17, 120
    factions in appealing to Daniel, 2
    fiery furnace frescoes, 112, 122
    theology, 316
    three youths story reading, 120
    wall mosaics, 122
Medina, 283
Mediterranean Sea, 221
Megasthenes, 146
Meinhold, Johannes, 7
Meir, 154
Mekilta de-Rabbi Ishmael, 152
Melchizedek, 333
Memmi, Albert, 15
Menas, 208
Menasseh ben Israel, 181, 182
Mene, Mene, Tekel, u-Parsin inscription, 163, 183
    In OG, 162
    See also Belshazzar's Feast; Inscription interpretations
Menelaus, 26, 257, 306, 307, 350, 351, 356
mental illness, 152, 153
    See also madness
Meshach, 10, 46, 118
Messiah
    date for coming of, 314
    the humanlike one as, 245–52
    Messiah ben David, 314
    Messiah ben Joseph, 281, 314
    messianic pretenders, 246, 247
    the Messiah Jesus Son of Mary, 283
Metaphrastes, Symeon, 58

Metzger, Martin, 137, 138
Meyer, Marvin, 123
Mezoughi, Nouradine, 204
'*Mi sheana le-Daniel begot haarayot,* 210
Michael (archangel), 204, 235, 236, 238, 247, 268, 332–33, 335, 360
Michel Wisser ben Jehiel (Malbim), 113
Michelangelo, 248
Midrash Leqah Tov, 281
Midrash Ruth, 313
Midrash Tanhuma, 154
Midrash ʿAseret ha-Shevatim, 280
Mikhailovich, Aleksei (Romanov tsar), 93
millennialism, 318
Miller, William, 317, 318
Millerite chronology depictions, 318, *319*
Millerites, 317, 318
mina, (*měnēʾ*), 161, 176, 177, 182
Minas Geras, Brazil, 56, *57*
miraculous survival, 202, 203
Mishael, 46. 14, 121
Mithra, 46
Moab, 357
monasticism, 122
Monophysites, 93
monotheism, 109, 247
monstrous beasts, 219, 220
Montgomery, James A., 4, 8, 45, 50, 62, 63, 103, 110, 111, 112, 127, 135, 137, 140, 161, 166, 173, 175, 177, 189, 214, 215, 221, 229, 232, 237, 254, 256, 268, 271, 285, 289, 292, 299, 326, 330, 334, 335, 342, 353, 365, 366
Moore, Sean D., 185
Moralia in Job (Gregory the Great), 277
Mordecai, 47
Morenz, Siegfried, 225
Morgan, M. Gwynn, 350
Mørkholm, Otto, 264, 350, 354, 355
Morrison, Craig E., 275
Moses, 292, 295, 296
Moses of Crete, 312
Moss, Candida, 122, 208
Most High/Most High God. *See* God, epithets for
Mother Hubur, 222
Mount of Olives, 277
Mount Zion, 358
mourning, 329
Muhammad (Prophet), 251, 252, 280, 281, 313
Muhammad Asad, 283
Muhammad bin Ismaʿil bin Jaʿafar, 370
Muhammad ʿIsa Daʿud, 283
Muhammah b. Yazid, 310
Müller, Hans-Peter, 14, 173
Müntzer, Thomas, 152, 244–45

Murray, Robert P. R., 140
Musa (Ottoman poet), 31
Muslim apocalypticists, 318
  See also Islam
Mussolini, Benito, 279
mystery
  in four beasts dream, 242
  God as revealer of, 136
  of hidden course of history, 329
  of horrific events, 264
  rhetoric of, 28
  as strategic term, 71, 73
  terminology, (*rāz*), 20, 63, 65, 71, 73, 329
"mystery of existence" (*rāz nihyeh*), 329, 336
mysticism and Daniel 12, 372
mythic patterns, 217–18

Naaman, 108
Nabonidus, 9, 51, 101, 146
  and Belshazzar, 163–64
  basalt stele, 129
  dream of, 66–67
  encyclical of, 168
  and the great tree, 140
  healing of, 12, 128
  as Nebuchadnezzar in Daniel 4, 130
  and status as king, 79
  supporters of, 129
  traditions, 144, 192
  and worship of Sin (moon-god), 101, 128, *129*
Nabonidus Chronicle, 192
Nabopolasar, 43, 146
Nabû-kudduriusur (Nabu has protected the son who will inherit), 36
Nahman, 155, 246
Nahmanides, 313, 314, 370
Najm al-Dīn al-ūfī, 251
names/renaming, 8, 46, 47
Nanaia, temple of, 359
Napoleon Bonaparte, 183, 184, 317
Naram-Sin, 225
A Narrative of the Black People, during the Late Calamity in Philadelphia, in the Year 1793, 123
narratives
  as cycle of stories, 9
  and Daniel's apocalypses, 18, 201–2
  for ethnic dignity, 13
  heroes of, 21
  languages of, 8
  and the reader, 65
  of resistance to assimilation, 15
  wisdom-didactic, 14, 100, 190
Nathan, 172
National Movement for the Restoration of Pakistani Sovereignty, 158

Near Eastern mythicism, 219, 221
Nebuchadnezzar
  and Antiochus IV Epiphanes, 266–67
  arrogance of, 17
  and Belshazzar contrasted, 127, 128, 161, 163, 166, 172
  characterization of, 41–42
  contrasted to Darius, 198
  Daniel's concern for, 143–44
  Daniel's dreams interpretation for, 1
  Dispensationist statue depiction of, *319*
  doxology of as fantasies, 16
  dream response of, 84–85
  education of, 33–35, 113, 133, 142, 148
  eschatology in dream of, 18
  etymology of name, 36
  as Gentile monarchs figure, 64
  madness of, 152, 153, 155, 156
  and mantic experts, 67–69
  as the mina, 176
  as Nabonidus in Daniel 4, 128, 130
  and Pharaoh, 134
  punishment of, 141, 144–48
  redemption of, 75, 223
  restoration of, 148–49, 155–56
  sovereignty of descriptions, 78–79
  stories transferred to, 9, 10
  as story protagonist, 100–101, 109
  symbolism and acknowledgment in dream of, 17, 18
  tree dream of, 137–44
  and understanding of status change, 34–35
  See also tree in Nebuchadnezzars's dream
Nebuchadnezzar in a Fire (painting), 157
Nebuchadnezzar on Fire Falling over a Waterfall (painting), 157
Nebuchadnezzar with Blue Flowers and White Dog (painting), 157–58
Nebuchadnezzar's Dream of the Tree (painting), 157
Neco, 47
Nehemiah, 107
Neher, André, 120
Neo-Assyrian scribes, *44*
Neo-Babylonina dynasty, 146
Neriglissar, 79
Nero, 273, 274, 275, 276, 315
Nestle, Eberhard, 308
Netanyahu, Benzion, 154
Neujahr, Matthew, 81, 336, 337
New York World (newspaper), 185
Newport, Kenneth, 317, 318
Newsom, Carol A., 9, 19, 128
Newton, Isaac, 317
Nicholl, Colin, 273
Nichols, Joel, 57
Nickelsburg, George W. E., 18, 361, 363

Niditch, Susan, 30
Niewisch, 216
Nikkarchus, 47
Nile River, 366
Nissinen, Martti, 177
Nitocris, 172, 181
Noegel, Scott B., 177, 178
non-Masoretic Danielic compositions, 5–6
nonviolent resistance, 208–9
Noth, Martin, 215, 237, 238
Nubia fiery furnace frescoes, 122, *123*
numerical patterns, 20
numerology, 315
Nuremberg, Germany, 103
Nyman, Monte, 249

oaths, 366
Ohm, Juliane, 203
Old Greek (OG) version
  and Masoretic text, 162–63, 196
  and Theodotian version, 5
omens, 170–71
One Thousand and One Nights, 31
1,335 days, 309
Oniads, 24
Onias II, 24
Onias III, 25, 257, 293, 306, 346, 347
  "cut off," 306–7
Opis, battle of, 164
Oppenheim, A. Leo, 45, 67, 68, 69, 70, 78, 145, 220
orans prayer position, 202, 203
Origen, 53, 180, 275, 315
Otto, Bishop of Freising, 244
Ovadiah, Asher, 202
Oxus River, 31, *32*

Pace, Sharon, 148
Pachomius, 372
paintings, 168, *169,* 181, *200*
Panion, Battle of, 344
papacy, 281–82
Papal States, 317
Papos, 115
parallelisms, 137, 145, 226, 233, 259, 292, 366
Parpola, Simon, 12, 138, 141, 193
Patai, Raphael, 280, 370
Pattemore, Stephen, 273
Paul (apostle), 331
Paul, Shalom, 170, 367
Paul of Tella, 4
Pearce, Laurie E., 22
Pearl, Daniel, 158
Peerbolte, L. J. Lietaert, 274, 276
Pelagianism, 53
penance, 156

Index of Subjects and Authors

penitential prayer, 292, 294
penitential ruler motif, 150
peoples, nations and languages, 234
persecution
  under Antiochus IV, 23, 333
  apocalypses originating from, 7
  during the Crusades, 56
  of Jewish religious observances, 26
Persepolis reliefs, 104, *105*, 106
Persia, 10, 17, 332
Persia and Media, 260
Persian court life, 45, 107
Persian Empire
  Alexander's destruction of, 262
  ethnic diversity, 103–4, 134
  ideological self-presentation, 15, 17
  immense size of, 81
  Jewish roles in, 107
  public spectacles, 104
Persian Gulf, 31
Persian Gulf War (1990–91), 318
Persian imperial ideology, 17, 142
Persian kings, 17, 339
Pesenson, Michael, 93
Peshitta Daniel, 275
Peter of Blois, 249
Petros Cathedral, Nubia three youths fresco, *123*
Petuchowski, Jacob J., 121
Pfau, Aleksandra Nicole, 153
Pharaoh, 69, 134
Pharisees, 363
Philadelphia, Pennsylvania, 123
Philip Aridaeus, 262
Philip Arrhidaios, 340
Philip V, 343
Phocas, 317
Pilate. *See* Pontius Pilate
Pingree, David, 314
Pinhas the Priest, 94
Pins and Needles (musical), 185–86
pit of lions
  in Bel and the Dragon, 196, 198
  description of, 198
  as judicial ordeal, 199
  as punishment, 195, 200–201
Pitarakis, Brigitte, 204
Pius VI, 317
plain of Dura, 103, 115
Plöger, Otto, 77, 83, 135, 149, 176, 215, 223, 226, 254, 268, 286, 325, 330, 360, 365
polis (Greek city), 25, 356
political historiography, 222
political theology, 77, 78
Polybius, 350, 359
Polycarp, 121
Polychronius, 275

Pontius Pilate, 115
Popillius, 350
Porphyry, 6, 7, 85, 180, 226, 243, 275, 348, 358, 368, 369
Porter, Paul A., 222
Portier-Young, Anathea, 25, 241, 350, 351, 353, 364
Postgate, J. Nicholas, 139
Powell, Marvin A., 176
power
  dynamics of, 110–11, 261
  Gentile imperial, 111, 195
  of God, 293
  and the king's food, 50
  and knowledge, 38, 49–51, 65, 101–2
  and wisdom, 72
  and written text, 168
prayer
  customs/postures, 197
  by Daniel before interpreting dream, 72, 73
  of Daniel for the temple, 288–98
  to illustrate characters' piety, 6
  literary features of, 292–93
  orans position in, 202, *203*
  regular, 206–7
  resistance through, 207–10
  Second Temple daily, 197
  for the sick, 123
  and survival, 204–6
  at time of evening sacrifice, 298
Prayer of Azariah, 4, 6, 100, 114, 288
Prayer of Nabonidus, 130, 132
Prayer of the Three Youths, 114
prediction manuals, 310
premillennialism, 278, 279
priests, 293, 294
prince of Greece, 335
prince of Persia, 332, 333, 335
prisoners of war, 43
prognostication, 310
Progress of Error (Cowper), 55
prophecy, 19, 171, 311–19, 336
prophets, 293, 294
Protestant canon, 2
Protestant Reformation, 2, 244
pseudepigraphy, 7, 258
pseudo-Messiah, 282
Pseudo-Methodius, 92, 280
Pseudo-Saadia, 247, 282
psychoanalysis, 182
Ptolemies, Egyptian
  emergence of, 2
  Jewish experience under, 23–24
  and Syrian Seleucids, 327, 358
  system of taxation, 24
Ptolemy I, 23, 262

Ptolemy II, 341
Ptolemy III, 341
Ptolemy IV, 342, 343
Ptolemy V, 343, 345
Ptolemy VI, 226, 348, 349
Ptolemy VII, 226
punishment, 199, 200, 294, 295, 296, 363, 371
purification, 353
Puritan English Fifth Monarchy Men, 245
Pusey, Edward H., 7
Putin, Vladimir, 279

queen mothers, 172, 180
Queen of Sheba, 165
Queen of the Serpents, 31
Qumran
   Community Rule, 264, 290
   Danielic fragments, 3–5
   Jeremiah manuscript, *291*
   War Scroll, 236, 239, 263, 276

Rabina, 369
Raëlian Movement, 372–3
Rahab (sea monster), 222
Rainer of Viterbo (cardinal), 277
Raphael, 268
Raphia, Battle of, 342, 343
Rappaport, Uriel, 11, 23, 336
the rapture, 318
Rashi, 117, 177, 179, 182, 207, 208, 246, 256, 282, 312, 313, 314, 369, 371
Rava, 180
rebellions, 17, 270, 343
Redditt, Paul L., 23
redemption, 156, 371
Reeves, Marjorie, 278
Reformation, 152, 154, 316, 317. *See also* Counter-Reformation; Protestant Reformation
Rehoboam, 164
Reich, K., 317
Reich, Steve, 158
Reinhold, Meyer, 171
relief
   of gift-bearing emissaries, 105
   of tribute presentation, *105*
Rembrandt. *See* van Rijn, Rembrandt
renaming, 8, 46, 47
repentance, 155, 329, 371
repetition, 190–91, 259, 292, 297
resistance
   to assimilation, 15
   to God, 209–10
   and identity, 55–57
   to imperialism, 15
   in liberation theology, 97
   literature, 81
   by the marginalized, 56–57
   narratives as stories of, 16. 15
   new form of, 2
   nonviolent, 196, 208–9
   three youths as model for, 115–18
   through prayer, 207–10
resurrection
   and the book of life, 361
   corporeal, 370
   Daniel's description of impact, 370
   of the dead, 362, 363, 364, 369
   and Israel, 371
Revelation (book of)
   and the 3½-year schema, 315
   beast signifying Rome in, 116
   commentaries, 183, 316
   and new beast from the sea, 86
rhetoric, Danielic apocalypses, 19, 28
Ribera, Francisco, 278
Richard, Pablo, 97
riddles, 271, 282
Rider of the Clouds, 217
Riefenstahl, Leni, 103
Riessler, Paul, 128
Rigger, Hansjörg, 290
righteousness, 302, 364, 371
the righteous, 363, 364, 368, 371
Rimmon (god), 108
Ringgren, Helmer, 337
Ringrose, Kathryn, 58
rivers, 330, 366
rivers of fire, 230, 232, 248
Rizal, José, 185
Roca-Puig, Ramón., 4
Rochberg, Francesca, 171
rock. *See* stone cut without hands
Rome
   and Antiochus's Egypt invasion, 26, 349, 350
   in battle of Magnesia, 25
   as fourth kingdom, 80, 85–86, 93
   legitimization of empire by, 80
   as the little horn, 275, 276
   as United States of Europe, 279
Rome, Harold, 186
Root, Margaret Kool, 146
Rosenberg, Daniel, 318
Rosenmüller, Ernst, 31
Rosenthal, Ludwig A., 99
Rowley, Harold H., 192
royal banquets
   cups used at, 166
   political significance, 165
   Sumerian depiction, *167*
royal decrees, 196
Rubens, Peter Paul, 200
"The Run upon the Bankers" (poem), 184

Index of Subjects and Authors 413

Rush, Benjamin, 123
Russia, 92, 93, 279
Rustow, Marina, 94

Saadiah, 116, 312, 314
sacrilege, 162, 175
Sadducees, 363
sages, 72, 73
Sa'id Ayyub, 252
Salaphtha, 54
Salimbene, Adam de, 311
Sambari, 95
Samḫarû, 36
Samuel bar Nahman, 180
the Sanballats, 24
Sanchez, Miguel, 96
sanctuary, 265
    terminology: place (*mākôn*), 265;
    sanctuary (*miqdāš*), 265, 326, 32;
    holy place (*qōdeš*), 255
Šanḫara, 36
Sarachek, 371
Sariel, 268
Saritoprak, Zeki, 282, 283
Satan, 280, 333, 372
Satran, David, 5, 54, 127, 150, 151
satraps, 104
sayagraha (nonviolent resistance), 196
Schaudig, Hanpeter, 67
Scheindlin, Raymond P., 95
Schmidt, Nataniel, 235
Schwartz, Daniel R., 11, 351
Scofield, Cyrus I., 279, 317
Scofield Reference Bible (Scofield), 279, 317
Scopas (general), 343, 344
scribes
    alphabet, 22
    as authors of Daniel narratives, 21, 22
    cultural power of, 23
    and editing/updating of Bible, 29
    and knowledge, 20
    Neo-Assyrian scribes recording war booty, *44*
    and *tupšarrūtu* (Babylonian scribal culture), 22
sea, 217, 221
sea monsters, 222, 371
seals, 303, 365
seating, 229, 231
Second Great Awakening, 317
Second Isaiah, 129, 130
Second Temple period
    and almsgiving, 145, 154
    and angelic descriptions, 236
    and concern for temple vessels, 40
    Daniel in variety of forms in, 30
    literature, 18
    prayer, 197
    reading and interpreting of texts, 290
    secrecy and mystery, 20, 21
Sefire Stela, 234
Segal, Alan F., 362
Seleucid kings, 45, 82–83, 225, 340
Seleucid war elephants, 225
Seleucid kingdom, 1–2, 327, 358
Seleucus I, 23, 225, 262, 337, 340, 345
Seleucus II, 341
Seleucus III, 341–42
Seleucus IV, 25, 226, 346
Sellin, Ernst, 215
Sennacharib, 226
Sennacharib Palace prisoners of war, *43*
Seow, Choon-Leong, 48,166, 267, 290, 301, 302, 307, 365
seraphim, 298
Sermon to Princes, 245
Serpent (Bel and the Dragon). *See* Bel and the Dragon
Sevcenko, Nancy Patterson, 248
seven, the number, 20, 141, 142
Seven-Hilled Daniel, 92
Seventh-day Adventist Church, 318
seventy times seven, 300, 301
seventy weeks, 303, 304, 309, 311, 312, *320*, 367
seventy years, 290, 291, 299, 300, 313, 315
Shadrach, 10, 118
    Etymology, 46
Shalev, Eran, 153
Shamash, sun disk of, *129*
shame, 294, 308
Shea, William H., 163
Shekhinah, 371
Sheol, 264, 362, 363
Shepkaru, Shmuel, 117, 118, 119, 121
sheqel (*tĕqēl*), 162, 176, 177
Sherwin-White, Susan M., 47, 216, 337
Sheshbazzar, 47
Shibtu, 42
Shmuel the Small, 181
shrines, 202, 293
Sibylline Oracles, 81
Sidon, siege of, 344
"signs and wonders," 134, 135
silence, 120, 121
Silver, Hillel, 314
Simeon bar Yochai, 94
Simon (opponent of Onias III), 25, 26, 346
Simplicissimus (publication), 209
Sin (moon-god)
    Nabonidus's championing of, 9, 101, 128
    symbols of, *129*
    temple restoration of, 130

Sinjar, 29, 30
sins
 confession of, 294
 and God's righteous judgment, 292
 and God's wrath, 270
 of Israel, 301, 302
Šinʿār, 36
Sippar, 164
Sistine Chapel Last Judgment fresco, 248
Sixth Syrian War, 347
Skemer, Don C., 204
sleep, 362, 370
Smith, Joseph, 249
Smith, Oswald J., 279
Smith, R. Payne, 177
Smith-Christopher, Daniel, 15, 16, 75, 196, 223
Snow, Samuel, 318
Soden, Wolfram von, 128
Sodom and Gomorrah, 295
Sokoloff, Michael, 214
Solomon, 164, 165, 172, 271
Somniale Danielis, 310
Son of Man
 and messianic pretensions, 246
 as seated, 229
 termiology, *bar ʾĕnāš*, 234; *ben-ʾādām*, 235, 269; *ben-ʾĕnôš*, 235
 see also humanlike one
Song of Hannah, 6
Song of Miriam, 6
Song of Moses, 332
Song of the Three Jews, 4, 6, 100, 288
Sons of Light, forces of, 239
soothsaying, 44
Sophronius, 280
Sosibius, 342
South Africa, 123, 209
sovereignty, 1, 2, 8, 237
 See also Gentile sovereignty; God: sovereignty of
Spafarii, Nicolae Milescu, 93
Speculum ecclesiae (Honorius of Autun), 204
Spier, Jeffrey, 370
Spock, Jennifer, 93
Spronk, Klaas, 362
Stages on Life's Way (Kierkegaard), 156
Standard of Ur (Sumerian work), *167*
stars, 263, 264, 362
statue, in Nebuchadnezzar's dream
 in chronology depictions, *319, 320*
 description of, 75, 76
 four parts of interpretations, 79, 85–89
 gold at base of, 117
 rock and, 76–77
Staub, Urs, 225

Steck, Odil Hannes, 301
Sternberg, Meir, 41
Stifel, Michael, 316
stone cut without hands, 76–77, 83, 95
 and the humanlike one, 243
 Lorenz Faust depiction of, 95
 and political uprisings, 244–45
 as type of Christ, 244
Stories of the Prophets (ibn Kathīr), 208
stories. *See* narratives
Strauss, Claudia, 288
Strayer, Eugene, 209
Strong, James, 277
structural repeatability, 326, 327
"stumbling" of the wise, 353
Suffering Servant song, 352
Summa theologiae (Thomas Aquinas), 151
Summers, Mark Wahlgren, 185
survival, 114, 202, 203, 204–6
Susa, 28–31, 260
Susanna, 2, 4, 5, 6, 30, 203, 369
Swain, Joseph, 64, 80
Swift, Jonathan, 184
Sylvester I (pope), 150
symbolic numbers, 366, 367, 368
symbolism/symbolic language, 2, 111, 217, 221, 366
Synoptic Apocalypse, 315
Syriac Christian community, 243
Syriac Peshitta, 71
Syrian wars
 Fifth, 23, 343, 344, 345
 Fourth, 342, 357
 Sixth, 347
 Third, 341
Syro-Hexapla manuscript, 4

Tabae, Persia, 11
Tabor, James, 318
Tale of the Taking of Tsargrad, 92
Tammuz-Adonis, 355
Targum Onqelos, 178
Täubler, Eugene, 344
Tawil, Hayim, 367
Taxo, 352, 364, 369
Tcherikover, Victor, 27, 350, 351, 356
Teima, Arabia, 9, 128, 130, 163
temperance movement, 55
temple
 Antiochus's violation of, 239, 257, 351
 centrality of, 296, 297
 concern for, 287
 and its sacrifices, 11
 rebuilding/restoration of, 289, 290, 291
 resanctification, 303
 Roman destruction of, 2
temple plundering/robbing, 359

Index of Subjects and Authors

temple vessels, 8, 38, 40, 162, 166, 167, 173, 180
ten, the number, 225
ten horns, 276
Tepeyac, Mexico, 96
Tertullian, 54, 155, 276
Testament of Moses, 297, 298, 369
Teucer of Babylon, 261
The Gospel of the Twelve Apostles, 93
Thecla, 208
Theodore bar Koni, 244
Theodoret, 53, 180
Theodoret of Cyrus, 208
Theodotian (Th) version, 4–5, 71, 221
    and Masoretic text, 314–15
    and Old Greek version, 5
theology
    Adventist, 318
    Deuteronomic, 287
    liberation, 97
    medieval period, 316
    political, 77, 78
Theophanes the Chronicler, 280
theophanies and angelophanies, 269, 332
    fiery phenomena and, 230
Theophilus, 122
Thermopylae, 345
Thiselton, Anthony, 276, 278
Thomas, Samuel I., 71
Thomas Aquinas, 151
thousand year reign, 278
three youths
    in African American community, 118
    and bodily/social restoration, 123–24
    frescoes of, 121, 122, *123*
    marginalized/oppressed people and, 117
    as models of faith, 121, 122
    symbolic counterpart to golden image, 111
    use of by African American community, 118
    use of by those in power, 118
3½ years, 267, 309, 367
threefold division of cosmic time, 316
the three horns, 226
thrones, 228–31, 247
    and debates over monotheism, 247
Tiamat, 217, 221, 222
Tiberius, 282
Tigris River, 28, 164, 260, 330
time, terminology
    set time (*ʿiddānāʾ*), 69
    appointed time (*môʿēd*), 327, 334, 349; the time appointed for the end, (*môʿēd qēṣ*), 269
    end (*qēṣ*), 269, 327; time of the end (*ʿēt-ēṣ*), 269, 357; end of the times, (*ûbqēṣ hāʿitîm*), 286

time of distress (*ʿēt ṣārâ*), 360, 361
"a time, times, and half a time," 241, 309, 312, 315, 366, 368; (*ʿiddān wĕʿiddānîn ûplag ʿiddān*), 312, 366; (*môʿēd môʿādîm wāḥēṣî*), 366, 368
"times and law" (*zimnîn wĕdāt*) 240
Titus (emperor), 276, 281, 312, 315
Tkacz, Catherine Brown, 204
Tobiad family, 24, 26
Tobit, 12, 14, 18, 48
Toorn, Karel van der, 168, 193, 195, 290
Torah
    and chronological sequence, 180
    language of, 258–59
    on life, 205
    shrines, 202, 293
    studying as act of defiance, 117
totality, 20, 221, 225, 262
touch, 332, 334
Tower of Babel, 139
Tragi-comedie (play), 117
transformation, 156, 301, 302
transgressions, 270, 287, 302
    See also sins
Travis, William J., 203
Treaty of Apamea, 345, 346
tree in Nebuchadnezzar's dream
    Daniel's interpretation of, 144
    destruction of, 140
    imperial power symbol, 137–38
    source of well-being, 139
    stock motifs concerning, 138
    as tree of life, 137
tribute presentation, Persian king, *105*
the tribulation, 278
tricola, 137, 138, 139
Triumph of the Will (documentary), 103–4
Trotter, Jonathan, 228
truth, (*ʾĕmet*), 265–66, 296, 325, 329
Turbach, 216
Tustar, 310
the twelfth Imam, 318
Twelve Prophets (sculptures), 56
Two-Spirits Treatise (Qumran), 266
Tyconius, 275
Tyre, king of, 271

Ugaritic myths, 218
Ugbarui/Gubaru, 192
Ulai, 260, 268
Ulrich, Eugene, 4
Umar (caliph), 310
Ummayad dynasty, 95, 183
understanding, 298, 329, 365, 367
United States, 92, 185, 245
United States of Europe, 279
universal kingship, 134, 135

Urad-Gula, 195
Urban II (pope), 118, 277
Utt, Walter, 209

Valeta, David, 15
van Est, Willem Hessels, 278
van Peursen, Wido, 85
van Rijn, Rembrandt, 168, *169*, 181, 182
Vander Kam, James C., 64, 241
Vanonen, Hanna, 276
Venus, 264
Vespasian, 276, 281, 315
Vienna, Ottoman siege of, 280
Vietnam War protest, 157
violence, 223, 232
virgin birth, 204, 251, 282
Virgin of Guadalupe, 96, 97
Vision of Daniel (Hebrew manuscript), 117
Visions (*ḥāzôn*), 255, 268, 302
　apocalyptic dream, 18–21
　"of the head," (*hezwê rēʾšēh*) (visions of his head), 220
　Paul and, 331
　and prophets, 302
　as revelation, 299
　and waters of a river, 330
Visions of Daniel, 92
Vladimir (monarch of Kiev), 93
Vogel, Winfried, 267
Voltaire, 317
Vorilhon, Claude, 372
Vulgate, 224

Waco, Texas, 318
War Scroll (Qumran), 236, 239, 263, 276
Warad-ilišu, 42
Warren, Rick, 55
watchers (*ʿîr*), 139, 140, 142, 146
week heptad (*šābūʿîm*), 20, 288, 299
Weidner tablets, 21
Wernberg-Moller, Preben, 72
White, Ellen, 318
whiteness, 229, 230, 248, 353
Whitla, William, 317
Whittier, John Greenleaf, 118
Wiesel, Elie, 209–210
Williamson, Hugh G. M., 17
Willis, Amy C. Merrill, 240, 255, 266, 287, 327
Wills, Lawrence M., 5, 13, 16, 69, 127, 137, 141, 162

Wilson, Gerald, 290
wine, 48, 50, 166, 167
wisdom-didactic narratives, 14, 100, 190
wise, the wise (*maśkîl, maśkîlîm*), 22, 23, 216, 298, 352, 353, 357, 364, 371
Wiseman, Donald J., 146
Wixom, William, 204
Wolf, Kenneth Baxter, 280
Wolters, Albert M., 164, 170, 176, 177, 178
Woolever, Frank, 209
world tree, 138
Worms Massacre, 56
wrath, 269, 270, 295, 355
Wright, Jacob L., 165
writing, 196, 231
writing on the wall, 168–71, 187
"Written—in—Red" (poem), 185
Wycliffe, John, 278

Xenophon, 163, 164
Xerxes, 142, 167, 289, 339
Xerxes I, 289

Yahweh (extraterrestrial being), 372
Yam (the Sea), 217
Yefet ben Ali, 94
YHWH
　angel of, 112
　descriptions of, 229
　intentionality of, 143–44, 223
　king opponents of, 109, 238–39
　and relationship with Israel, 287
　as seated, 229
　temple vessels representing, 166–67, 180
　and worship of other deities, 108
Yosi the Galilean (rabbi), 247
Yücesov, Hayrettin, 310, 313

Zadok, Ran, 22
Zarathrusta, 76
Zechariah (prophet), 53, 106, 236
Zedekiah (king), 42, 47, 66, 77
Zell, Michael, 182
Zerubbabel, 47, 305
Zeus Olympios, 257, 308, 354, 355
Zimri-Lim (King of Mari), 42
Zion, Mount, 358
Zionism, 283
Ziz, 370, 371
the *Zohar*, 372
Zululand, South Africa, 123

CPSIA information can be obtained
at www.ICGtesting.com
Printed in the USA
FFOW04n0324221114
8892FF

9 780664 2601